A Volume in
Managing the Complex

Volume One
Managing Organizational Complexity:
Philosophy, Theory, and Application

D0980498

Dedicated to Caroline, Alexander, and Albert

... and to Mumsie for staying that extra week!

Managing the Complex: Volume One

Managing Organizational Complexity: Philosophy, Theory, and Application

Edited by
Kurt A. Richardson
ISCE Research

Series Editors
Kurt A. Richardson & Michael R. Lissack
ISCE Research

INFORMATION AGE
PUBLISHING

80, Mason Street
Greenwich, Connecticut 06830

Library of Congress Cataloging-in-Publication Data

Managing organizational complexity : philosophy, theory and application /
editor, Kurt Richardson.
 p. cm. - (I.S.C.E. book series - managing the complex)
Includes bibliographical references and index.
 ISBN 1-59311-318-8 (pbk.) - ISBN 1-59311-319-6 (hardcover)
 1. Organizational effectiveness. 2. Complex organizations--Management. 3.
System theory. I. Richardson, Kurt. II. Series.
 HD58.9.M36 2005
 658'.001--dc22
        2005000079

Printed in the United States of America

The primary aim of the ISCE Group is to facilitate the conversation between academics and practitioners regarding the implications of complexity thinking for the management of organizations. To support this aim ISCE (which stands for the *Institute for the Study of Coherence and Emergence*) organizes a variety of events and also publishes the international interdisciplinary journal, *Emergence: Complexity and Organizations* (or, *E:CO*; formerly known as *Emergence*) now in its seventh year. The ISCE Group comprises three divisions, namely: ISCE Research, ISCE Publishing and ISCE Events.

ISCE Research is primarily concerned with coordinating the research activities of the ISCE fellows to ensure that each fellow is aware of each other fellow's research to facilitate cross-disciplinary collaboration and synthesis. We also maintain a list of the research publications that emerge from this group of complexity researchers. ISCE Research also provides a legitimate academic home for freelance researchers who would like to apply for government research grants concerning the application of complexity thinking. ISCE Research also maintains a small inhouse research capability which is concerned with a range of different research issues including: the philosophical implications of complexity, the role of language in understanding organizations, coherence in organizations, the simplification of the irreducible, complexity-based tools for policy analysis.

ISCE Events endeavours to bring together complexity researchers from all over the world to discuss the profound implications of assuming complexity for our understanding of such systems. Each event has a particular mode of interaction - either *conference*, *workshop* or *seminar*, as well as a particular thematic focus such as policy analysis, management, philosophy, etc. ISCE Events provide an environment for both furthering the field and diffusing the concepts and tools that emerge from the complexity community.

ISCE Publishing is where much of the content from ISCE Research and ISCE Events is published for wider consumption. The heart of our publishing activities is the international journal *E:CO* which is read by both academics and scholars worldwide. ISCE Publishing also publishes in collaboration with *Information Age Publishing* the *Managing the Complex*, the first volume you are holding in your hands! In January 2005 ISCE Publishing also developed the capacity to publish complexity related books inhouse. We now provide the necessary support for authors of complexity-related literature to get published in a professional and timely manner.

For further information please visit: http://isce.edu, or contact Kurt A. Richardson directly at kurt@isce.edu.

CONTENTS

Section 1
Philosophy

Section 2
Theory

Series Introduction

*M*anaging the Complex is an ambitious title - and it would be an audacious one if we were not to begin the series with a frank admission: to date few to none of us have a skill set which includes managing the complex. We try various things, we write about others, and we wonder about still others. When a tool, perspective, or technique comes along which seems to evoke success, we emulate it probe it and recoil at the all too often admission that it was situation and context which afforded success its opportunity, and not some quality intrinsic to the tool perspective or technique.

Indeed, if the study of complexity has done anything for managers, and for those who espouse managerial theory, it is in providing a 'scientific foundation' for the notion that *context matters*. Those who preach abstract ideas have then to reconcile themselves to the notion that situation and embodiment matters. Those who believe in strong causality and determinism are left to wrestle with the role of chance, uncertainty, and chaos. Those who prefer to argue that men move history are confronted with the role of environment and affordances, while those who argue the reverse are left to contend with charisma, irrationality of crowds, and the strange qualities we know as emotions.

A series on complex systems has less ambitious goals to contend with than this. Such a series can deal with classifications, and categories, and speak of 'noise' as if it were not the central focus of the problem. *Managing the complex* is about managing noise or perhaps we should say it is about 'dealing with' 'accepting' 'making room for' and 'learning from' noise. The articles in this volume and in the series as a whole will each be considered as noise by some and as gems by others. Situation and affordance will dictate how each is perceived at any given time by any given reader.

The value of the effort lies in the web of ideas it spawns in its readers. If true knowledge is to be found in these pages it lies in the ideas and concepts which the words evoke in you the reader. Our task as authors is to jar your neurons into summoning into being the very adjacent possible which you regard as a 'keeper'. Thus, the series and each of its volumes is like a conference - if you walk away with one or two good ideas and a sense of new opportunities we have done our jobs.

Our authors have accepted this challenge, but theirs is in some ways the easier task. They put pen to paper (okay fingers to keyboard) and left you an artifact to deal with. Whether that artifact will afford you good ideas is your task - much harder than the authors'… but potentially much more rewarding.

We urge you to seek the rewards herein. Set aside the personal complexity you face moment to moment and create enough space for intellectual emergence. Oh dear, we've suggested that perhaps you can manage the complex at least long enough to get something from your reading. Silly of us. Or is it?

Michael R. Lissack
Kurt A. Richardson
March 26th, 2005

Volume introduction

Systemic thinking has been given a well needed injection of enthusiasm in the last 20 years with the growing recognition of the need to acknowledge the complexity of the systems (organizations) we attempt to interact with. Of course, systems thinking itself is not new, tracing back to the days of Aristotle. As a formal science we must give due credit to the likes of Ludwig von Bertalanffy (1969) who set out to develop a full-blown science of systems, but it is really with the development of the computer that widespread interest in complex systems has grown. The systems theorists of 50 years ago did not have the computational resources to rigorously explore the intricate dynamics of complex systems. It is a credit to the systems pioneers that they achieved as much as they did without the use of computers, given what we now know about nonlinearity and intractability. In my opinion, however, (general) systems theory faltered because of the inability to 'test' many of the theories that were put forward. Many of these theories were based on astute observation and reasoning, which, although powerful tools in themselves, severely limit our ability to rigorously explore complex systems' behavior. Computers allow us to build complex representations and perform experiments in a scientific way (it is perhaps ironic, yet fortunate, that the technology that has contributed to so much of modern life's complexities, also offers new means to help understand that same complexity). The exponential growth in available processing capacity has facilitated the development of a 'science' of complexity. The tools developed in the process of doing science become available to a broader community and are available to solve real world problems. However, we must be wary of becoming overly tied to scientific-only discourses. Seeing complexity as just another problem that can be solved through the rigorous application of scientific method(s) misses the point in my view. Undoubtedly, we can learn an awful lot about complexity through science, but there are other avenues open to us in our attempts to understand and manipulate complexity.

I have already mentioned that scarce computational resources would have restricted early systems theorists to speculation rather than science (except in the analytical solution of relatively trivial problems - which by the standards of linear mathematics certainly were not 'trivial'). Another limitation was the focus on scientific discourses. This bias changed in the early 1970s with research from the likes of Peter Checkland and his "systems-based methodology for real-world problem solving" (Checkland, 1972). More recently analytical frameworks such as: the *soft systems methodology* (Checkland, 1981), *system of systems methodologies* (Jackson & Keys, 1984), *total systems intervention* (Flood, 1995), and *systemic intervention* (Midgley, 2000), have been developed

Managing Organizational Complexity: Philosophy, Theory and Applications
A Volume in: Managing the Complex, pages iii-viii.
Copyright © 2005 by Information Age Publishing, Inc.
All rights of reproduction in any form reserved.
ISBN: 1-59311-319-6 (cloth), 1-59311-318-8 (paper)

that explicitly acknowledge the subjectivity and uniqueness of experiencing complexity. These systems-based approaches embrace critique (which is certainly not absent in classical science) and pluralism in which a multitude of discourses are given a hearing, not just mathematical (some might say, rational) approaches. We might classify this move from a discourse monism to a discourse pluralism as a shift from a focus on objectivity to an awareness that subjectivity cannot be removed simply through the application of method, and therefore must be addressed explicitly. Often the distinction quantitative / qualitative is applied (inappropriately in my opinion).

Ken Wilbur (1996), in his excellent *A Brief History of Everything* (if you are still struggling to understand the difference between 'modern' and 'post-modern' then read this book), distinguishes between *exterior* and *interior* understanding (p. 71). An example of exterior understanding is quantitative reductionist science in which we pretend to view the world from the outside - understanding complexity becomes an issue of making really good maps. Interior understanding, on the other hand, relates to our experience of complexity, what it feels like to be embedded in a complex system. Exterior is the natural sciences, interior is the social sciences (when they're not pretending to be natural sciences). In a sense, we can suggest that the recent development in systems thinking is a move from the exterior to the interior, or at least, a more balanced approach to real world systems.

In his recent comparison of complexity and systems theory, Phelan (1999) suggested that "[s]ystems theory is predominantly focused on confirmatory analysis" by which he meant there is a focus on problem-solving and an effort to "improve" the systems of interest - applied science, if you like. Of course, if Phelan was assessing the systems theory of the 1950s and 1960s then he would find that the focus was more on how he characterized complexity theory in 1999 - that complexity theory is exploratory in nature, more akin to a 'blue-sky' research programme rather than applied science. It seems clear that from the 1950s to the 1970s the systems community shifted its focus from 'exterior' to 'interior' in an effort to be able to work with and 'solve' (in a sub-optimal manner) real world problems. It is quite possible that having started out as exploratory in nature, the complexity community is itself expanding and becoming more confirmatory in style. This by no means suggests that 'blue-sky' approaches to complexity will diminish (as it hasn't in systems theory). However, the rapid growth in the literature that attempts to apply complexity principles and ideas to real-world organizations demonstrates that 'complexity' as a body of knowledge has matured sufficiently to allow direct application to real-world problems. Indeed, if this wasn't the case then this particular volume would not have been possible! There is a lot more about complexity that we do not know, and there is a whole lot that we will never know (complexity is as much to do with the limits to our understanding and how we manage those limits, as it is about what we can and do know). Both exploratory research programmes and confirmatory problem solving are needed to allow continued development of complexity as a body of knowledge. The collection of papers that form this volume contributes to both these different, but by no means independent, endeavors.

The papers in this volume, as the subtitle suggests, have been divided into three sections, namely: philosophy, theory and application. The logic behind this classification is that papers in the philosophical section approach complexity in a very general way. These papers do not necessarily focus on human organizations or networks, but on complex systems in whatever form they are found (although each author was asked to make an effort at drawing some conclusions for organizational management). The theory section contains papers in which the concepts and ideas of complexity have been applied specifically to human organizations. Rather then being specific applications of complexity thinking in real life organizations, they are more concerned with the question: if human organizations are complex systems, then so what? Again, contributors were asked to offer specific advice to the practicing manager. The chapters comprising the last section offer case studies and application of complexity thinking to *real* organizations, not hypothetical ones.

As with all classifications, the three categories are not independent of each other. In a perfect world (from a Platonic perspective at least) everything we see, do, hear, achieve, etc. would be unambiguously labeled and shelved in the correct taxonomic cubby hole. It would also be an easy exercise to take something seemingly new and place it correctly in such a grand scheme. The imperfect real world is not like this - thankfully! Every thing has to be man-handled into our taxonomic cubby hole desk[1], even if it doesn't quite fit. Even though any classification we could ever conceive of would be incapable of providing convenient 'storage' for every 'thing', we do have a tendency to forget that the real world is not so readily classifiable, and that by classifying we simultaneously bastardize reality. The process of classification, with all its shortcomings, does provide a handle on which to grip onto. Such a grip is necessary to initiate the process of thinking. The three categories chosen to divide the chapters in this volume are no different. Some chapters fit rather snuggly in their taxonomic home, whereas others are struggling to co-occupy other cubbies. The point is that the reader should not take these divisions too seriously. If you don't rate yourself as much of a philosopher don't use that as an excuse to skip the philosophy section.

Much of what we do as humans is the result of simplistically representing complexity. One such activity is having one name on the cover of an entity as complex as an edited book. I will discuss the complexity of such a project shortly, but here I'd like to mention the people who freely offered their time and expertise to ensure that the chapters published herein were of a high standard - some of them even contributed a chapter as well! I do, of course, mean the review board. It is very much down to these individuals that it is unlikely that anyone with an interest in complexity and organization will find reading this book a waste of his or her time. The majority of the reviewers also agreed that the review process would be open and not the usual double-blind process familiar in journal publishing. In some cases this led to an ongoing constructive dialogue between reviewer and contributor that was undoubtedly more useful than the anonymous criticism that results from one-way double-blind reviewing. I am therefore very much indebted to:

Alicia Juarrero	Prince George's Community College, US
Andreas Kemper	International University Schloß Reichartshausen, GER
Andrew Tait	Idea Sciences, US
Bill Frederick	University of Pittsburgh, US
Bill McKelvey	UCLA, US
Bill Young	USAF, US
Colin Crook	Citicorp (retired)
David Boje	New Mexico State University, US
David Byrne	University of Durham, UK
Dick Knowles	Independent Consultant, US
Edoardo Mollona	Bocconi University, Italy
Eleodoro Ventocilla	DKV Group, Venezuela
Glenda Eoyang	Chaos Limited, US
Heather Wood Ion	Independent Consultant, US
Hugh Gunz	University of Toronto, CA
Jeffrey Goldstein	Adelphi University, US
Jerry Chandler	Washington Evolutionary Systems Society, US
Jerry Zhu	Virginia Commonwealth University, US
Ken Baskin	The ISCE Group, US
Mary Evans	Office of the Secretary of Defense, US
Max Boisot	ESADE, SP
Michael Lissack	The ISCE Group, US
Paul Cilliers	University of Stellenbosch, South Africa
Rex Draman	St. Edward's University, US
Stan Salthe	City College of New York, US
Steve Maguire	McGill University, CA
Willard Uncapher	Network Emergence, US
William Fulkerson	Deere & Company, US

Of course, the quality of the manuscripts submitted ensured that the review board members did not waste their time reviewing poorly written essays. I am thrilled at the overwhelming enthusiasm with which all the contributors approached this project.

Before moving onto the results of the reviewer / contributor system - the book itself - I'd like to spend a moment to offer some of my experiences in 'managing' my first edited book project.

What could be easier than an edited book? The 'editor' (which should really be called a 'manager' - or even better, a 'facilitator') puts together a calling notice for abstracts providing some topical guidelines and some indication of abstract length. A subset of those contributors are invited to submit a full paper, again some formatting guidelines are offered. The contributions are then reviewed by members of a review board which is specifically convened solely for the edited book project. The reviewer feedback is fed back to the contributors who then resubmit their manuscripts after some time to allow for revisions. These 'final' submissions are then typeset, the typeset pages are checked through by the contributors, final corrections are made, a few introductory words are written by the 'manager' / editor, and "hey presto!" you have an edited book.

If it is so simple then why is this particular volume nearly five months late compared to my original schedule?

What I found at every stage in 'facilitating the emergence' of this volume was that my simplistic view of how the process would unfold did not adequately reflect the true complexity of the project. Even something as simple as having all submissions clocked-in by a certain date is not a straightforward exercise. In a linear view of management this of course is a trivial undertaking. You set a deadline and everyone should meet it. If someone does not meet the deadline then they are cast aside in order to ensure that project Gantt chart does not have to be rewritten. In practice, just about everyone has his or her own excuse as to why they did not meet the deadline. What is important to acknowledge is that every excuse from "my dog ate it" (no, I didn't actually receive this one) to "I am snowed under at work" is perfectly valid. It is up to the 'manager' to provide the 'space' in which accomplishments can happen. In a linear view of management, we would be looking for someone to blame. In a nonlinear view of management, diversity is an inherent characteristic that needs to be understood and embraced (unless you want to drive yourself insane ☺).

A diversity in formatting, especially references, was equally present, despite the rather strict guidelines provided. Again, this is to be expected and can in no way be regarded as a negative reflection on the contributor. In his "Sources of Complexity in Human Systems," Biggiero (2001) lists *gnosiological* complexity and *semiotic* complexity as important sources. Gnosiological complexity refers "to the idea that a system or an environment contains all the information an observer is able to distinguish in it, [but] it depends on the observer's capacity to perceive this information" (p. 9). Semiotic complexity refers to the different meanings we all draw when presented with the same information (although gnosiological complexity suggests we all extract different information in the first place). These sources of complexity are readily apparent in all human organizations (even virtual ones) and so it is no surprise that the same formatting guidelines can result in different formats. This is a feature of a system that has incredible creative capacities, not a flaw (however frustrating it can be at times).

There are many other sources of complexity that I did not foresee when embarking on this project - even I did not follow my own guidelines accurately! Are there general lessons to be learnt? One thing I am sure of, failing to deliver on time does not constitute a project failure (in this case at least). If something was 'wrong' it was my overly simplistic vision, or plan, of how this volume would come together. If the original plan had been executed to the letter then a book of some kind would have certainly resulted. However, its quality would have been comprised for the sake of following a poorly designed plan. This volume really is the result of an emergent process.

A clear lesson, which follows directly from complex versions of management theory, is that project boundaries (if one chooses to organize around the notion of a 'project') must not be reified, they must not be taken too seriously; they need to be allowed to flow. At the same time, they must not be taken too lightly. This is the key challenge for a manager trying to facilitate the fulfilment of certain goals and aims in a complex uncertain system: following guidelines, but at the same time ignoring them. The traditional boy scout motto quickly comes to mind: "be prepared!"

References

Bertalanffy, L. von (1969). *General System Theory: Foundations, Development, Applications*, NY: George Braziller.

Biggiero, L. (2001). "Sources of Complexity in Human Systems," *Nonlinear Dynamics, Psychology, and Life Sciences*, 5(1): 3-19.

Checkland, P. B. (1972). "Towards a Systems-Based Methodology for Real-World Problem Solving," *Journal of Systems Engineering*, 3(2): 87-116.

Checkland, P. B. (1981). *Systems Thinking, Systems Practice*, Chichester, UK: John Wiley & Sons.

Flood, R. L. (1995). "Total Systems Intervention (TSI): A Reconstitution," *Journal of the Operational Research Society*, 46: 174-191.

Jackson, M. C. and Keys, P. (1984). "Towards a System of Systems Methodologies," *Journal of the Operational Research Society*, 35: 473-486.

Midgley, G. (2000). *Systemic Intervention: Philosophy, Methodology, and Practice*, NY: Kluwer Academic.

Phelan, S. E. (1999). "A Note on the Correspondence Between Complexity and Systems Theory," *Systemic Practice and Action Research*, 12(3): 237-246.

Wilber, K. (1996). *A Brief History of Everything*, Dublin, Ireland: Newleaf.

Notes

[1] For readers unfamiliar with what a 'cubby hold desk' is, a picture of one is available at: http://kurtrichardson.com/cubbyholedesk.jpg.

SECTION ONE

PHILOSOPHY

Section introduction
Why philosophy?

Managers seem reluctant to study philosophy. Thus, it seems appropriate to begin this volume with an explanation of why philosophy is so important to both management scientists and practitioners. Philosophy is a study of what underlies choice. In both management and research choices abound. Researchers have to choose which methodology they are to employ in understanding a particular aspect (which of course also has to be chosen) of management; the boundaries of the research study need to be chosen (which is strongly dependent upon research methodology), etc. Managers have to continually decide which information is required to make a particular decision; how to interpret that information for the purposes at hand, and even choose what the actual purpose might be, as well as what the issue is that needs to be decided upon (although, often this is done very much unconsciously without much attention to the actual framework within which they have been 'taught' to operate).

From the perspective of the researcher Hughes (1990: 11) suggests that philosophy underpins the whole selection process because:

"... *every research tool or procedure is inextricably embedded in commitments to particular versions of the world and to knowing the world. To use an attitude scale, to take the role of a participant observer, to select a random sample, to measure rate of population growth, and so on, is to be involved in conceptions of the world which allow these instruments to be used for the purposes conceived. No technique or method of investigation (and this is true of the natural sciences as it is of the social) is self-validating: its effectiveness, that is its very status as a research instrument making the world tractable to investigation, is, from a philosophical point of view, ultimately dependent on epistemological justifications. Whether they may be treated as such or not, research instruments and methods cannot be divorced from theory; as research tools they operate only within a given set of assumptions about the nature of society, the nature of human beings, the relationship between the two and how they may be known.*"

When managers choose to adopt a particular perspective, or set of procedures, or what issue to focus upon, these choices are philosophically equivalent to the researcher's selection of a particular methodology. Both sets of choices are underpinned by particular views of how the world we observe is constructed, and how it should respond to our actions upon it. More often than not we are unaware of the commitments that our choices imply. It is not a question we are often taught to ask. It is not a question we have evolved to be too concerned with either. Of course, researchers often spend some time on these concerns, because many of them have been taught to. However, many managers, as well as most of us at large, are very rarely concerned with the underlying assumptions upon which our choices made. If we were, we would be rather surprised as to the absurdity of some of our most cherished beliefs.

Philosophers often refer to the dominant worldview (or philosophy) of the average layperson as *naïve realism*. The 'naïve' part is possibly a poorly chosen label as it would seem to indicate that all of us who are not philosophers are a little daft, in that we have been so poorly misguided into ever believing that realism could possibly be a sensible way to view our surroundings. I think, given that much of our sensory and decision making equipment has evolved in a way that naturally leads to a kind of realism, perhaps we can be forgiven for not knowing any better. Maybe common sense realism is a more positive way of distinguishing a layperson's realism from a philosopher's realism.

Realism is based on a what-you-see-is-what-you-get (or WYSIWYG for those fluent in computer jargon) worldview, i.e., that our senses tell us accurately what the world is comprised of and how those parts interact - what-you-sense-is-what-there-is (WYSIWTI), if you like. The first implication of realism is that the way in which we 'see' the world is quite independent of what our senses, and our beliefs, guide us to 'see'. This is quite contrary to the quote given above which suggests that our senses and beliefs profoundly affect what we 'see'. If our senses are truly unbiased (as naïve realism suggests) then understanding the world around us simply becomes a process of map making. For this reason realism is often referred to as *representationalism*.

A second implication of realism is to regard causality as a first order process, i.e., if a change in object A results in a change in object B we have a tendency to assume that such a correlation refers to some causal mechanism - 'A caused B to ...' So not only do the objects A and B exist as such, they also affect each other directly. The 'existence' of A and B would be seem to be a trivial matter especially when considering objects such as cars and computers, though as we shall see later in this section even the notion of existence cannot be taken for granted. Furthermore, given WYSIWTI, the possibility that it is an unseen object C that affected A and B (or mediated the affect), or that two unrelated objects C and D affected A and B directly, or that the change in B resulting from a change in A was no more than a coincidence (and therefore not causal even if there was some correlation) are all scenarios that are omitted from a simplistically realist perspective. The natural sciences have developed tools to allow us to 'see' objects that remain 'unseen' with the naked eye, but even here any explanations offered must necessarily be based on what has been detected.

Quite often realism is associated with 'linearity', but this would be a mistake. The advent of the computer has allowed us to 'model' scenarios in which rather complicated loops of interaction can be represented and explored, a trick which the human mind seems woefully inept at doing. The main consequence of realism that concerns me here is that it leads to an overconfidence in what we have represented and analyzed as being exactly how the real world works. Quite clearly this is not a view devoid of merit. If it was then our ability to successfully achieve anything would be very much lower than it actually is. Clearly, to a useful degree, realism produces rather good results.

Given the successes of modern science, it is not surprising that realist viewpoints dominate Western thought - it is a natural way to view things, and such impressive machines as computers have been built that surely prove the power of realist thinking. Relating this back to philosophy, the success of modern science is arguably the reason that philosophy has fallen by the wayside. If science leads to correct knowledge all the time, then what is the point of questioning its underlying assumptions; surely the way in which modern science and the realists view the world is how the world *is*?

Two of the big questions for philosophers are what objects *exist* and how can we *know* about those objects. Jargon-wise, the study of what exists is referred to as *ontology* and the study of how we come to know these objects of existence (the study of knowledge) is referred to as *epistemology*. These two areas of interest have been enthusiastically investigated for at least 2500 years, until very recently that is. The Newtonian view of the Universe leads to an 'exquisitely intricate timepiece' model, i.e., the Universe is a really big machine. As a big machine it can be taken apart, its parts can be studied in isolation, and knowledge of the whole can be accurately gleaned by summing together the knowledge of its component parts. In popular views of modern science, there is something referred to as the scientific method which guides us in the study of these parts. So ontologically the Universe is a big machine, and epistemologically we have the scientific method to give us knowledge of the Universe's parts and eventually the Universe as a whole.

What is often missed from popular views of modern science is that science does not always work very well, and that there is no such well-defined process called the scientific method. This may come as a surprise to the many opponents and critics of modern science, but most decent scientists are well aware of their chosen occupation's shortcomings. Questions of ontology and epistemology really haven't been answered to complete satisfaction, thus there is still very much a role for philosophy.

The famous physicist Louis de Broglie once said "May it not be universally true that the concepts produced by the human mind, when formulated in a slightly vague form, are roughly valid for reality, but that, when extreme precision is aimed at, they become ideal forms whose real content tends to vanish away?"[1]. This suggests that we should use scientific understanding (not knowledge) to guide our decisions, not determine them. This is true of all understanding once we accept the limitations of the realist worldview. Rather than regarding our knowledge as faithful maps of reality we must see it as a potentially useful, but not necessarily so, caricature of reality, or as a metaphor[2].

A recent emerging field of study in modern science is complexity theory, which includes topics such as chaos theory, fractals, catastrophe theory, non-linear dynamics, cellular automata, etc. What is different about 'the complexity revolution' (or more accurately 'the complexity evolution') is that some of the results from complexity research suggest that all is *not* how it *appears*. The boundaries that mark the edges of objects are emergent, temporary, fluid, critically organized, provisional, etc. Causality is complex, intricate, multi-ordered, and intractable. All this suggests a renewed concern with ontology and epistemology and therefore with philosophy. What is ironic is that, though it has taken a revolution in science (spurred by a technological revolution which resulted from the dogmatic application of realist thinking for the past 400 years) to bring complexity to the fore, philosophers[3] have been concerned with complexity for hundreds if not thousands of years.

References

Cory, D. (1942). "The Transition from Naïve to Critical Realism," *The Journal of Philosophy*, 39(10): 261-268.
Hughes, J. (1990). *The Philosophy of Science*, Longhand.

Notes

1. Quoted in Cory (1942: p. 268).
2. Metaphor is the description of certain aspects of one thing in terms of certain aspects of another. If we consider the Universe to be one 'thing' then human knowledge is the partial representation of the Universe in terms of the 'things' that constitute human language. Language itself determines to a great extent what aspects of reality are promoted to the 'foreground' and what apects are demoted to the 'background' in the same way that the fox metaphor - 'He is as cunning as a fox' - highlights a particular trait of an individual and compares it to the cunningness of the fox. At the same time traits like the fox's shyness are ignored. By describing knowledge as metaphor, the bias and limited nature of knowledge is explicitly acknowledged.
3. I would like to point out that there have been plenty of philosophers through the ages that have had very limited notions of what philosophy should be. For the logical positivists, as an example, philosophy was more about the rigorous application of logic. When I use the term philosophy, I am meaning critical thinking, or contextual thinking, i.e., a process of ongoing review and revision of what we think we know, in light of 'evidence' or concepts derived from a broad range of perspectives, not necessarily only scientific discourses.

CHAPTER 1

KNOWING COMPLEX SYSTEMS

Paul Cilliers

In this article a general description of complex systems is provided. This is used to analyze to what extent we can understand complex things. It is argued that understanding is an attribute of a subject, and that our knowledge of complex things will therefore always be limited. If this is the case, then we can never avoid normative elements when working with complexity, i.e. our knowledge of complex systems can never be the result of calculation only. We have to choose. This is not an argument against calculation, or against formal models, but it does underscore that such models are inevitably limited. Some implications for our understanding of organizations are also spelled out.

Managing Organizational Complexity: Philosophy, Theory, and Application
A Volume in: Managing the Complex, pages 7-19.
Copyright © 2005 by Information Age Publishing, Inc.
All rights of reproduction in any form reserved.
ISBN: 1-59311-319-6 (cloth), 1-59311-318-8 (paper)

Introduction[1]

The aim here is to the introduce a general theory of complexity and to investigate its implications for social institutions and organizations. Complexity theory has implications for the way we conceive of the structure of an organization, as well as for the way in which complex organizations should be managed. However, a preliminary warning is necessary: The lessons to be learned from the study of complexity are somewhat oblique. Any hope that a study of complex systems will uncover *the* way of running an organization is in vain. However, while we will not come up with a quick fix, the lessons are most certainly important.

To start off I will investigate what we can learn from a theory of complexity. Most of these insights are widely accepted, but it is useful to revisit them briefly. This general understanding of complex systems provides the background for the rest of the paper in which I investigate what we cannot learn from complexity theory, specifically with reference to the problems of knowledge and understanding. The 'negative' part of the paper is at least as important as the 'positive' part. There I will investigate the unavoidability of an ethical dimension to all decisions made in a complex environment.

Complexity in a nutshell

I will not provide a detailed description of complexity here, but only summarize the general characteristics of complex systems[2].

1. Complex systems consist of a large number of elements which in themselves can be simple.

2. The elements interact dynamically by exchanging energy or information. These interactions are rich. Even if specific elements only interact with a few others, the effects of these interaction are propagated throughout the system.

3. The interactions are nonlinear.

4. There are many direct and indirect feedback loops.

5. Complex systems are open systems - they exchange energy or information with their environment - and operate at conditions far from equilibrium.

6. Complex systems have memory, not located at a specific place, but distributed throughout the system. Any complex system thus has a history, and the history is of cardinal importance to the behavior of the system.

7. The behavior of the system is determined by the nature of the interactions, not by what is contained within the components. Since the interactions are rich, dynamic, fed back, and above all, nonlinear, the behavior of the system as a whole cannot be predicted from an inspection of its components.

The notion of 'emergence' is used to describe this aspect. The presence of emergent properties does not provide an argument against causality, only against purely deterministic forms of prediction.

8. Complex systems are adaptive. They can (re)organize their internal structure without the intervention of an external agent.

Certain systems may display some of these characteristics more prominently than others. These characteristics are not offered as a *definition* of complexity, but rather as a general, low-level, qualitative *description*. If we accept this description (which, judging from the literature on complexity theory, appears to be reasonable), we can investigate the implications it would have for social or organizational systems.

Complexity and organizations

The notion of complexity has been applied to organizations in a number of different ways, and with varying degrees of rigor. I would like to emphasize two things here. In the first place, the principles discussed here are of a very general nature. The contingent conditions at stake when investigating a specific case will be vital, and may affect the importance of some of the implications radically. Despite this remark, I wish to stress, secondly, that this does not mean that the acknowledgement of the complexity of a situation allows us to be vague, nor does it imply a chaotic state of affairs. Complexity theory has important implications for the general framework we use to understand complex organizations, but within that (new) framework we must still be clear, as well as decisive. I will return to these issues below.

1. Since the nature of a complex organization is determined by the interaction between its members, relationships are vital. This does not mean that everybody must be nice to each other, on the contrary. For example, for self-organization to take place, some form of competition is a requirement (Cilliers, 1998: 94-95). The point is merely that things happen during interaction, not in isolation.

2. Complex organizations are open systems. This means that a lot of energy and information flow through them, and that an invariable state is not desirable. More importantly, it means that the boundaries of the organization are not clearly defined. Statements of 'mission' and 'vision' are often attempts to define the borders, and may work to the detriment of the organization if taken too literally. A vital organization interacts with the environment, and other organizations. This may (or may not) lead to big changes in the way the organization understands itself. In short, no organization can be understood independently from its context.

3. Along with the context, the history of an organization co-determines its

nature. Two similar looking organizations with different histories are not the same. Such histories do not consist of the recounting of a number of specific, major events. The history of an organization is contained in all the individual little interactions that take place all the time, distributed throughout the whole system.

4. Unpredictable and novel characteristics may emerge from an organization. These may or may not be desirable, but they are not per definition an indication of malfunctioning. For example, a totally unexpected loss of interest in a well-established product may emerge. Management may not understand what caused it, but they should not be surprised that such things are possible. Novel features can, on the other hand, be extremely beneficial. They should not be suppressed because they were not anticipated.

5. Because of the nonlinearity of the interactions, small causes can have large effects. The reverse is, of course, also true. The point is that the magnitude of the outcome is not only determined by the size of the cause, but also by the context and by the history of the system[3]. This is another way of saying that we should be prepared for the unexpected. It also implies that we have to be very careful. Something we may think to be insignificant (a casual remark, a joke, a tone of voice) may change everything. Conversely, the grand five-year plan, the result of huge effort, may retrospectively turn out to be meaningless. This is not an argument against proper planning. We have to plan. The point is just that we cannot predict the outcome of a certain cause with absolute clarity.

6. We know that organizations can self-organize, but it appears that complex systems also organize themselves towards a critical state[4]. This not only means that at any given point we can expect the system to respond to external events on all possible scales of magnitude, but also that the system will organize itself to be maximally sensitive to events that are critical to the system's survival. Think of language as a complex system. If there is a desperate need for new terms to describe important events, the system will organize itself to be critically sensitive to those terms specifically, and not necessarily to other novel terms. The 'need' is determined by the context and the history of the system, not by a specific 'decision' by some component of the system. Similarly, an organization will self-organize to be critically sensitive to specific issues in the environment that may affect its well-being. The implications of self-organized criticality for organizational systems seems to be a subject that demands further investigation.

7. Complex organizations cannot thrive when there is too much central control. This certainly does not imply that there should be *no* control, but rather that control should be distributed throughout the system. One should not go overboard with the notions of self-organization and distributed control. This can be an excuse not to accept the responsibility for decisions when firm decisions are demanded by the context. A good example here is the fact that managers are often keen to 'distribute' the

responsibility when there are unpopular decisions to be made - like retrenchments - but keen to centralize decisions when they are popular. I will return to the problem of responsibility below. This point is also related to the next one.

8. Complex organizations work best with shallow structures. This does not mean that they should have no structure. This point needs a little elaboration. Complexity and chaos - whether in the technical or the colloquial sense - have little to do with each other. A complex system is not chaotic, it has a rich structure. One would certainly not describe the brain or language, prime examples of complex systems as 'chaotic'[5]. I certainly would not put my trust in a chaotic organization.

A complex system does have structure, but not a strictly hierarchical structure. Perhaps not even a shallow structure. Structure can be shallow, but still extremely hierarchical. Perhaps the best way to think of this would be to say that there should be structure on all scales, and lots of interaction between different structural components. This is another aspect of complex organizations that could be fleshed out with insights from self-organized criticality.

These few implications of complexity theory for organizations are important, and can affect our understanding of complex organizations dramatically. They can be spelled out in much more detail, but as I insisted above, this will have to be done in the context of specific organizations and their contingent conditions. In order to do that we should also be clear about what we can not learn from a theory of complexity.

What we cannot learn from a theory of complexity

I hope to show that the implications of this negative part of the paper are at least as important as those following from the positive part. The acknowledgement of the limitations of our knowledge lies at the root of the whole Western tradition of Socratic philosophical reflection, but I am sure that the mere *acknowledgement* of limitations is not enough. On the one hand it suppresses the challenge to shift the boundaries of our knowledge. On the other hand it stops short of investigating the ramifications of such limitations. I want to argue that one important consequence is that we are forced to take up an ethical position.

What are the limits of a theory of complexity? Looking at the positive aspects we discussed above, you will notice that none of them are specific. They are all heuristic in the sense that they provide a general set of guidelines or constraints. Perhaps the best way of putting it is to say that a theory of complexity cannot help us to take in specific positions, to make accurate predictions. This conclusion follows inevitably from the basic characteristics discussed above.

In order to predict the behavior of a system accurately, we need a detailed understanding of that system, i.e., a model. Since the nature of a complex system is the result of the relationships distributed all over the system, such a model will have to reflect all these relationships. Since they are nonlinear, no set of interactions can be represented by a set smaller than the set itself - superposition does not hold. This is one way of saying that complexity is not compressible. Moreover, we cannot accurately determine the boundaries of the system, because the system is open. In order to model a system precisely, we therefore have to model each and every interaction in the system, each and every interaction with the environment - which is of course also complex - as well as each and every interaction in the history of the system. In short, we will have to model life, the universe and everything. There is no practical way of doing this.

Before I continue, two qualifications are required in order to prevent mis-understanding. The first is to re-emphasize that this is not the same as saying that complex systems are chaotic. Emergence is not a random or statistical phenomenon. Complex systems have structure, and moreover, this structure is robust. Secondly, this does not imply that there is no point in developing formal models of complex systems. We can develop models on the basis of certain assumptions and limitations, just as with any scientific model. I will return to this below.

Let me put the matter in slightly different terms. The prediction of complex behavior is only possible as a form of generalization. However, when we deal with a complex system, we can never escape the necessity of facing the *particular* nature of the system at any given moment. Since we do not know what the boundaries of the system are, we never know if we have taken enough into consideration. We have to make a selection of all the possible factors involved, but under nonlinear conditions we will never know if something that had been left out because it appeared to be insignificant was indeed so.

What does this amount to in practice? It means that we have to make decisions without having a model or a method which can predict the exact outcome of those decisions. A theory of complexity cannot provide us with a method to predict the effects of our decisions, nor with a way to predict the future behavior of the system under consideration. Does this mean we should avoid decisions, and hope that they will make themselves? Most definitely not. We cannot avoid them. Without activity in the system, without the energy provided by engaging with the system, it would probably wither away into a state of equilibrium, another word for death. Not to make a decision is of course also a decision. What then are the nature of our decisions? Because we cannot base them on calculation only - calculation would eliminate the need for choice - we have to acknowledge that our decisions have an ethical nature.

Complexity and understanding

If we understand 'knowledge' as something constituted within a complex system of interactions, that is as something complex, our understanding of the 'nature' of knowledge is affected. It would, on the one hand, deny that knowledge can be seen as atomized 'facts' that have objective meaning. Knowledge comes to be in a dynamic network of interactions, a network that does not have distinctive borders. On the other hand, this perspective would also deny that knowledge is something purely subjective, mainly because one cannot conceive of the subject as something *prior* to the 'network of knowledge', but rather as something constituted *within* that network. The argument from complexity thus wants to move beyond the objective / subjective dichotomy. The dialectical relationship between knowledge and the system within which it is constituted has to be acknowledged. The two do not exist independently, thus making it impossible to first sort out the system (or context), and then to identify the knowledge within the system. This co-determination also means that knowledge and the system within which it is constituted is in constant transformation. What appears to be uncontroversial at one point may not remain so for long.

The points made above are just a restatement of the claim that complex systems have a history, and that they cannot be conceived of without taking their context into account. The burning question at this stage is whether it is possible to do that formally or computationally. Can we incorporate the context and the history of a system into its description, thereby making it possible to extract knowledge from it? This is certainly possible (and very useful) in the case of relatively simple systems, but with complex systems there are a number of problems. These problems are, at least to my mind, not of a metaphysical, but of a practical nature: the incompressibility of complex systems. We have seen that there is no accurate (or rather, perfect) representation of the system which is simpler than the system itself. In building representations of open systems, we are forced to leave things out, and since the effects of these omissions are nonlinear, we cannot predict their magnitude. This is not an argument claiming that reasonable representations should not be constructed, but rather an argument that the unavoidable limitations of the representations should be acknowledged.

This problem - which is related to the problem of boundaries[6] - is compounded by the dynamic nature of the interactions in a complex system. The system is constituted by rich interaction, but since there are an abundance of direct and indirect feedback paths, the interactions are constantly changing. Any activity in the system reverberates throughout the system, and can have effects that are very difficult to predict - once again as a result of the large amount of nonlinear interactions. I do not claim that these dynamics cannot be modelled. It could be possible that richly connected network models can be constructed. However, as soon as these networks become sizeable, they become extremely difficult to train. It also becomes rather hard to figure out what is actually happening in them. This is no surprise if one grants the argument that a model of a complex system will have to be as complex as the system itself. Reduction of complexity always leads to distortion.

What are the implications of the arguments from complexity for our understanding of the distinction between data and knowledge? In the first place it problematizes any notion that data can be transformed into knowledge through a pure, mechanical and objective process. It however also problematizes any notion that would see the two as totally different things. There are facts that exist independently of the observer of those facts, but the facts do not have their meaning written on their faces. Meaning only comes to be in the process of interaction. Knowledge is interpreted data. This leads us to the next big question: what is involved in interpretation, and who (or what) can do it?

Knowledge and the subject

The function of knowledge management seems to be either to supplement the efforts of a human subject who has to deal with more data than is humanly possible, or to free the subject up for other activities (perhaps to do some thinking for a change). Both these functions presuppose that human subject can manipulate knowledge. This realization leads to two distinct questions. Firstly, one could question the efficiency of human strategies to deal with knowledge and then attempt to develop them in new directions. This important issue will not be pursued further here. Secondly, there is another, perhaps philosophically more basic question, and that has to do with how the human subject deals with knowledge at all. Given the complexities of the issue, how does the subject come to forms of understanding, and what is the status of knowledge as understood by a specific subject? This issue has been pursued by many philosophers, especially in the discipline known as hermeneutics. However, I am not aware that this has been done in any depth in the context of complexity theory[7]. How does one perceive of the subject as something that is not atomistically self-contained, but is constituted through dynamic interaction? Moreover, what is the relationship between such a subject and its understanding of the world. A deeper understanding of what knowledge is, and how to 'manage' it, will depend heavily on a better understanding of the subject. This is a field of study with lots of opportunities.

Apart from calling for renewed effort in this field, I only want to make one important remark. It seems that the development of the subject from something totally incapable of dealing with the world on its own into something that can begin to interpret - and change - its environment is a rather lengthy process. Childhood and adolescence are necessary phases (sometimes the only phases) in human development. In dealing with the complexities of the world there seems to be no substitute for experience (and education). This would lead one to conclude that when we attempt to automate understanding, a learning process will also be inevitable. This argument leads one to support computing techniques which incorporate learning (like neural networks) rather than techniques which attempt to abstract the essence of certain facts and manipulate them in terms of purely logical principles. Attempts to develop a better understanding of the subject will not only be helpful in building machines that can manage knowledge, it will also help humans to better understand what they do themselves. We should not allow the importance of machines (read computers) in our world to lead to a machine-like understanding of what it is to be human.

In Nicholas Roeg's remarkably visionary film *The Man Who Fell to Earth* (1976), an alien using the name Thomas Jerome Newton (superbly played by David Bowie), tries to understand human culture by watching television - usually a whole bunch of screens at the same time. Despite the immense amount of data available to him, he is not able to understand what is going on directly. It is only through the actual *experience* of political complexities, as they unfold in time, that he begins to understand. By then he is doomed to remain earthbound.

I am convinced that something similar is at stake with all of us. Having access to untold amounts of information does not increase our understanding of what this information *means* one bit. Understanding, and therefore knowledge, follows only after interpretation. Since we hardly understand how humans do it, we should not oversimplify the problems involved in doing knowledge management computationally. This does not imply that we should not attempt what we can - and certain spectacular advances have been made already - but that we should be careful in the claims we make about our (often still to be finalized) achievements. The perspective from complexity urges that, amongst other things, the following should be kept in mind:

- Although systems which filter data enable us to deal better with large amounts of data, it should be remembered that filtering is a form of compression. We should never trust a filter too much.

- Consequently, when we talk of mechanized knowledge management systems, we can (at present?) only use the word 'knowledge' in a very lean sense. There may be wonderful things to come, but at present I do not know of existing computational systems that can in any way be seen to be producing 'knowledge'. Real breakthroughs are still required before we will have systems that can be distinguished in a fundamental way from mere database management. Good data management is tremendously valuable, but cannot be a substitute for the interpretation of data.

- Since human capabilities in dealing with complex issues are also far from perfect, interpretation is never a merely mechanical process, but one that involves decisions and values. This implies a normative dimension to the 'management' of knowledge. Computational systems which assist in knowledge management will not let us escape from this normativity. Interpretation implies a reduction in complexity. The responsibility for the effects of this reduction cannot be shifted away onto a machine.

- The importance of context and history means that there is no substitute for experience. Although young and old will probably have different opinions, the tension between innovation and experience will remain important.

These considerations should assist in developing an understanding of knowledge management which could be called 'organic', but perhaps also 'ethical'.

Ethics and complexity

Before I continue, I want to make clear how the notion of ethics is used here. I do not take it to mean being nice or being altruistic. It has nothing to do with middle class values, nor can it be reduced to some interpretation of current social norms. I use the word in a rather lean sense: it refers to the inevitability of choices that cannot be backed up scientifically or objectively.

Why call it ethics? Firstly, because the *nature* of the system or organization in question is determined by the collection of choices made in it. There are, of course, choices being made, on all scales, major ones, as well as all the seemingly insignificant small ones, all the time - and remember that the scale of the effect is not related to the scale of the cause. In a way, the history of the organization is nothing else but the collection of all such decisions. Secondly, since there is no final objective or calculable ground for our decisions, we cannot shift the responsibility for the decision onto something else - 'don't blame me, the genetic algorithm said we should sell!' We *know* that all our choices to some extent, even if only in a small way, incorporate a step in the dark. Therefore we cannot but be responsible for them. This may have a pessimistic ring to it, but that need not be the case. An awareness of the contingency and provisionality of things is far better than a false sense of security. Such an awareness is also an integral part of the notion 'adaptive'.

Of course this does ultimately translate into a value system, but this system is not a given, something that is governed by *a priori* notions of good and bad. The system of values is itself a matter of choice. Our decisions are guided by some notion of what we think the organization should be - and it is in this 'should' that the ethical dimension is contained. If an organization decides 'the bottom line is our first priority', then that is the kind of organization it will be: nothing comes in the way of making money. The central issue here is that a system of values is exactly that. Values are not natural things that we can read off the face of nature, we *choose* them. It is not written in the stars that the bottom line is vital to the survival of a company, it comes with accepting a certain understanding of what a company should be under, say, capitalist conditions. Of course it is not only the nature of the organization that is determined by choices, but also our nature as individuals. We are also the result of our choices. A thief is not a thief when she is caught out, or found guilty under some legal system. A thief is a thief when she steals.

A further implication of this 'ethical' position needs to be spelled out. 'Ethics' is part of all the different levels of activities in an organization. These ethical components, related to the values and preferences of the members of the organization, are often referred to as only 'politics', something separate to the real operation and goals of the organization. The argument here is that the political aspects of the interactions in an organization are not something extraneous to the workings of that organization. It is not something that has to be 'dealt with' in order to guarantee the proper working of the organization, it is integral to the proper working of the organization. The individual and collective values of members of the system cannot be separated from their functional roles. This point is probably instinctively accepted by most good managers. The fact of the matter is that this is the case, whether it is accepted by management as such, or not.

To summarize the argument: The ethical stance is not something imposed on an organization, or something that is expected of it. It is an inevitable result of the inability of a theory of complexity to provide a complete description of all aspects of the system[8].

Modelling and calculation

It may appear at this stage as if I am arguing against any kind of calculation, that I am dismissing the importance of modelling complex systems. Nothing is further from the truth. The point I want to make is that calculation will never be *sufficient*. The last thing this could mean is that calculation is *unnecessary*. To the contrary, we have to do all the calculation we possibly can. That is the first part of our responsibility as scientists and managers. Calculation and modelling will provide us with lots of vital information. It will just not provide us with all the information. Perhaps it may become possible in the future for some sophisticated model to provide *all* the information about a specific system. The problem would remain, however, that this information has to be interpreted

When talking about the problem of interpretation, we have to keep the problematic nature of models of complex systems in mind. All the models we construct, whether they are formal, mathematical models, or qualitative, descriptive models, have to reduce the complexity, and thus they are limited. We cannot model life, the universe and everything. There may not be any explicit ethical component contained within the model itself, but ethics (in the sense in which I use the notion) has already played its part when the limits of the model were determined, when the selection was made of what will be included in the frame of the investigation. The results produced by the model can never be interpreted independently from that frame. This is no revelation, it is something every scientist knows, or at least should know. Unfortunately less scrupulous people, often the popularizers of some scientific idea or technique, extend the field of applicability of that idea way beyond the framework that gives it sense and meaning.

The position argued for here could be interpreted as an argument that contains some mystical or metaphysical component, slipped in under the name 'ethics'. In order to forestall such an interpretation, I will make a brief digression. It is often useful to distinguish between the notions 'complex' and 'complicated'. One could say that a jumbo jet is complicated, and that mayonnaise is complex (it has emergent properties). A complicated system is something we can model accurately (at least in principle). Following this line of thought, one may argue that the notion 'complex' is merely a term we use for something we cannot model yet. I have a lot of sympathy for this argument. If one maintains that there is nothing metaphysical about a complex system, and that the notion of causality has to be retained, then perhaps a complex system is ultimately nothing more than extremely complicated. It should therefore be possible to model complex systems in principle, even though it may not be practical.

Would the advent of adequate models of complex systems relieve us from our ethical responsibility? My contention is that it would not. Here is why: We cannot make simple models of complex systems which capture all their complexity. Their nonlinear nature, or, in other words, their incompressibility, demands that a perfect model of a system must be as complex as the system itself. If it is in the nature of the system to behave, at least sometimes, in novel and unpredictable ways, the model must also do so. In any case, how would we be able to determine if the model is indeed an adequate model of the system if we are already in trouble when trying to decide what the system itself comprises of? It will be as difficult to interpret the model as it is to interpret the system itself. I repeat, good models of complex systems can be extremely useful. I just do not believe that they will allow us to escape the moment of interpretation and decision.

Complexity and the humanities

I want to close with a remark that one would hope is not really necessary to make, but that can now be made with a new urgency. Whatever we take the notion of ethics to mean, our analysis of what we can and cannot learn from a theory of complexity has shown that a proper reflection on complex organizations will have to involve the humanities. Perhaps we can describe the humanities exactly as those disciplines that realize that their subject matter cannot be studied only by formal means.

There are of course a number of disciplines that immediately come to mind: political science, sociology, psychology and of course, philosophy. Allow me the opinion that philosophy, the mother of all the sciences - but in an instrumental and outcomes-based world often seen as redundant - may yet prove to be one of our greatest resources. The need to reflect critically on the nature and the limits of our knowledge and understanding is indispensable to a study of complexity.

I do, however, not want to end with that cheer for the home team. I also want to stress the importance of the arts. Artists through the ages have attempted to find new ways of portraying and understanding the complexities of our world. Under certain conditions, a good novel may teach us more about human nature than mathematical models of the brain, or the theories of cognitive psychology. This is not an argument *against* formal models. We should do all the formal work we can, but remember that it should always be supplemented with other forms of meaning. Following from this it should be clear that an engagement with the arts should not be a luxury we indulge in after 'work', it should be intertwined with our work. In order to deal with complexity, and to create better futures, we need a healthy imagination, we all have to be artists in some sense of the word. This will hopefully not only help us to a better understanding of our world, it will also make us better human beings.

References

Bak, P. (1997). *How Nature Works: The Science of Self-Organized Criticality*, Oxford: Oxford University Press

Caputo, J. D. (1997). *Deconstruction in a Nutshell*, New York: Fordham University Press.

Cilliers, P. (1998). *Complexity and Postmodernism: Understanding Complex Systems*. London: Routledge.

Cilliers, P. (2000). "Boundaries, Hierarchies and Networks in Complex Systems," *International Journal of Innovation Management*, 5(2): 135-147.

Cilliers, P. and De Villiers, T. (2000). "The Complex 'I'," in W. Wheeler (ed.), *The Political subject*, London: Lawrence & Wishart, pp. 226-245.

Juarrero, A. (1999). *Dynamics in Action: Intentional Behavior as a Complex System*, Cambridge, MA: MIT Press.

Notes

1. This essay is based on two articles previously published in *Emergence*.

2. This summary is based on an extended analysis of complex systems in Cilliers (1998).

3. In this regard I have to stress that the butterfly-metaphor borrowed from deterministic chaos is very misleading. There is no way in which the statement "a butterfly flapping its wings in Borneo could 'cause' a hurricane in Florida" can have any sense. The notion of causality loses all its meaning. There are many better ways of talking about the hurricane in Florida, despite the fact that we cannot be sure about exactly what caused it. Causes can be investigated, even if at best retrospectively.

4. For an introduction to self-organized criticality, see Bak (1997). For a discussion of some implications, see Cilliers (1998: 96-98).

5. I am not implying that there are no lessons to be learnt from chaos theory, but that they are more limited than is often believed. The notion of the 'edge of chaos' is often useful, but even here I think we are better served by using the idea of critical organization.

6. The problem of boundaries is discussed in more detail in Cilliers (2000).

7. An important contribution was made by reinterpreting action theory from the perspective of complexity (Juarrero, 1999). Some preliminary remarks, more specifically on complexity and the subject, are made in Cilliers and De Villiers (2000).

8. This argument can also be made from a strictly philosophical position, particularly from the perspective of deconstruction. Despite the resistance to Derrida's post-structural insistence on undecidability, it is a strongly argued position that does not imply indecision or relativism. For a good philosophical introduction to this perspective, see Caputo (1997).

CHAPTER 2

"TO BE OR NOT TO BE? THAT IS [NOT] THE QUESTION": COMPLEXITY THEORY AND THE NEED FOR CRITICAL THINKING

Kurt A. Richardson

If we assume that much of what we see around us is the result of underlying nonlinear processes then it follows that much of what we think we see is no more than a filtered version of a temporary pattern that will inevitably change both quantitatively and qualitatively. The aim of this chapter is to explore what it means to exist, or not, in terms of complexity theory. It is argued that the nature of object boundaries are quite different in complexity thinking than they are in conventional linear approaches which essentially assume that what-you-see-is-what-there-is. The investigation of boundaries presented herein is based upon the assumption that the Universe itself is a complex system. It is argued that the notion of existence cannot be adequately represented by the binary opposition exist/not exist, but is a continuum. This conclusion leads to a complexity-inspired philosophy that highlights the important role of critical thinking and pluralism (theoretical, methodological, and paradigmatic) in making sense of life within a complex system.

Managing Organizational Complexity: Philosophy, Theory, and Application
A Volume in: Managing the Complex, pages 21-46.
Copyright © 2005 by Information Age Publishing, Inc.
ISBN: 1-59311-319-6 (cloth), 1-59311-318-8 (paper)

Introduction
Realism versus constructivism

There are at least two broad perspectives from which the status of our scientific knowledge claims can be understood. The first is a purely realist view of scientific knowledge, referred to as scientific realism. According to this view the "theoretical entities that are characterized by a true theory actually exist even though they cannot be directly observed. Alternatively, that the evidence that confirms a theory also serves to confirm the existence of any theoretical or 'hypothetical' entities characterized by that theory." (Fetzer and Almeder, 1993: 118). What this definition suggests is that our scientific knowledge gives us direct knowledge of entities that exist independent of any observer, i.e., rigorous application of scientific methods yields theories of certain entities that exist mind-independently (independently of what we believe or feel about those entities). In this view an objective reality does exist, and through the application of method we can have objective scientific knowledge of 'reality'. In complete opposition to the realist position is constructivism. This position argues that, though there does exist an objective reality, we can never have direct objective knowledge concerning that reality. According to this view, knowledge is manufactured rather than discovered. The manufacturing process is inherently biased by our methods of production and is incapable of delivering objective knowledge of some external reality: objectivity becomes no more than a myth. Social constructivism, which is a form of idealism, in its extreme form regards scientific knowledge as merely a socially-constructed story that is inherently subjective in nature. As there can be no objective knowledge then there can be no dominant discourse, because there can be no test or argument that could conclusively support the dominance of one discourse over another. Accordingly, science is just another approach 'out there' to making sense and should be treated with no more reverence than any other approach. As Masani (2001) laments, "constructivism is anti-scientific to the bone."

The relationship between language and objective reality

An alternative way to distinguish between realism and constructivism is to consider the relationship between the language we use to describe reality and reality itself. Realists argue that there is a one-to-one correspondence between our language and 'reality'. This leads to a number of interesting consequences like, for example, the belief that there is a best, or universal, language for describing reality and that, that language happens to be the language of science, namely mathematics. Constructivists, or relativists, on the other hand argue that there is no relationship whatsoever between our language and reality. The terms or labels we use are no more than useful sense-making tools that, though convenient, have no intrinsic basis in some notional objective reality. Though I do not believe that anyone who supports either of these positions is naïve enough to believe in them wholeheartedly, this is generally how the debate between realism and constructivism is set up. Physical scientists are criticized for their intellectual arrogance / imperialism, which is justified through strongly realist beliefs, and constructivist critics are ridiculed for their apparently wild and poorly argued descriptions of what they think science actually is as well as their omission of 'reality' in their theories.

This concern with what's the right way to see things might seem irrelevant to the practicing manager who assumes that because they are higher up the organization, and can therefore 'see' more of the organization, their view of organizational matters must be more accurate than their supposed sub-ordinates. In the same way science is often privileged over all other approaches, the manager's views are often privileged over their sub-ordinates' views. Fortunately, not all managers are so naive.

The dominance of the physical sciences

Primarily because of the success of science-driven technology there is an enormous wealth of evidence that supports the privileging of scientific discourse over every other. This success has perhaps blinded us to the shortcomings of the scientific process and has lead to an unquestioned belief that because science has successfully explained so much it can probably explain everything. Every facet of human life can supposedly be productively examined through the eyes of science. This position is commonly referred to as scientism (although practical science - as opposed to some popularized caricature of science - is not synonymous with scientism). Despite the growing evidence of science's (or at least that of reductionist science) shortcomings, putting the brakes on the train of scientism is no trivial undertaking. Often the failures of science, which are considerable when we consider social planning or environmental policy (management science, particularly, has a very checkered history), are put down to the bad application of scientific methods rather than seeing these failures as the result of applying scientific methods to inappropriate subject matter.

Contrary to popular belief science is not capable of considering all phenomena. In fact, it is quite inflexible in its requirements. The principle requirement that will be considered herein is that scientific methods require that the object of interest is stable, i.e., the boundaries (or, patterns) that delimit the object from the 'background' (the object's complement) must be stable and assumed to be real. This stability allows repetitive examinations to be undertaken that allow the knowledge concerning that object to be refined and tested, so much so that our confidence in our knowledge of that object becomes so great that we might begin to unquestionably assume that we have an accurate description to hand. In a more generic way, what I am saying is that scientific knowledge can only be obtained for contexts which are incredibly stable. This approach yields a tremendous amount of understanding that can be turned to the development of cars, computers, building methods, etc. - just about anything that can be constructed from parts that behave qualitatively in much the same way whatever context they are placed within.

What about objects of interest that have far less rigid boundaries? Social systems for example change and evolve. The boundaries, or patterns, that describe such systems continuously change and emerge such that the extraction of uniformities is far from a trivial matter. By their very nature the context changes and repetitive examinations are at worse impossible, and at best highly problematic. To apply science to such systems we have to fake stability; we are forced to reduce the system of interest to an idealized caricature that remains steady over time. Of course this is what we really do when we look at any system, be it an atom or an ecology, but for some reason our reductions seem to be more harmful when considering complex systems, as the relationship between the description that would allow a scientific analysis, and a notional 'real' description, is gaping. In such contexts it is questionable as to how useful a role traditional science can play. If we assume that organizations are complex, for example, is a *science of management* meaningful at all?

These cracks in the scientific façade have been made more apparent with our ability, supported through incredible growth in computer power (and, ironically, through the dogmatic application of science) to construct models of simple[1] complex systems. The emerging science of complexity forces us to revisit the nature of scientific knowledge and at the same time presents us with an alternative approach to understanding the limits of scientific methods. The interest for me personally is that, though many criticisms of science have been made by those whom the scientific community has regarded as outsiders and non-scientists, complexity science leads to a critique of science couched in the language of science itself. In a sense, the scientific language contains within it compelling evidence of its own limitations.

The aims and scope of this chapter

The aim of this chapter is to consider the limits of the physical sciences from a complex systems point of view, and develop a philosophy that is more sensitive to complexity. The discussion assumes that the Universe itself is a complex system, more specifically, a *cellular automata experiment*. By considering simple cellular automata systems, as well as utilizing some of the techniques of *computational mechanics*, the nature of object boundaries, i.e., what allows us to recognize an object as an object, within a complex Universe will be explored. This will lead to a philosophical middle-path that shows that realism and constructivism are really two ends of the same philosophical chain. The resulting philosophy may be called quasi-'critical pluralism'. This position, despite its realist foundations, neither denies the potential of any particular perspective to yield useful understanding nor unquestionably privileges one select perspective over all others for all contexts. In some ways the resulting philosophy is quite empty. My hope is that quasi-'critical pluralism' will be seen as a natural conclusion from the realist assumptions of complexity. If, for example, postmodernist type arguments might be 'derived' scientifically then perhaps the current stalemate in the philosophy of science, fuelled by a stubborn polarization between extremes, might be alleviated allowing an honest and humble exchange of ideas to occur.

Cellular automata and quasi-particle dynamics

Before exploring the implications of assuming a cellular automaton (CA) Universe this section will present some of the findings derived from the development of computational mechanics. This exploration will provide the key elements necessary in supporting a broader knowledge paradigm than currently prevails. It may seem that we're taking on rather too much by considering the Universe as a whole. The reason for this is simply to show what follows from assuming that complexity is the general case, not the limiting case. Everything we observe around us is the result of underlying nonlinear processes.

Cellular automata explained

It is not my intention here to provide the mathematical details of cellular automata. For the interested reader there are a wealth of online websites that discuss the construction of such systems. Richardson (2004), which is an alternative version of this chapter, there is a more detailed introduction to CAS. Here I will simply comment on some of their more interesting characteristics.

In a cellular automata world every 'atom' is described and accounted for. No shortcuts are taken to approximate the CA's overall behavior; everything is described and modelled in exact detail. Figure 1 depicts the evolution of a selection of simple 1-dimensional CA worlds. The first line in each image depicts the starting configuration $S_{t=0}$ for the CA world; every point, atom, or pixel in that world is described completely (the state of each atom being restricted to only two possibilities). Each subsequent line shows how each world evolves as the particular *theory of everything* for that world (which simply states how an individual atom will evolve depending on the current state of its neighbors) is applied. What is represented in each image is a history of each world (up to an arbitrary point). We might refer to these images as 'bitmap' (BMP) images of these worlds, as they contain all there is to know about each world; they are complete descriptions. Whereas a JPEG description would employ an algorithm to compress the images (i.e., extract trends or dominant patterns) via some mathematical shorthand, a BMP image contains complete and perfect information for each and every member of the CA world[2].

It is clear from Figure 1 that, despite the elementary underlying mechanics, such systems "support a whole hierarchy of structures, phenomena, and properties" (Toffoli, 1984: 119).

There are two very important points to be noted concerning such CA worlds. The first is that almost all initial configurations evolve to configurations with the same statistical properties, i.e., they are qualitatively equivalent (Wolfram,

1985). The rule of interaction determines the structure that emerges, not the initial conditions. Even if the initial conditions were random, the overall qualitative evolution would be unaffected, i.e., the evolution of these CA worlds is independent of their starting conditions[3] - there is no (deterministic) chaos present.

Secondly, and possibly more importantly, the reader may notice that for a particular world different groupings, or entities, emerge; entities that comprise, say, 3 black on-pixels in a row for example. Not that it is easily appreciated from the examples given, but it is possible to extract some sketchy properties for these 'entities' allowing a rough appreciation of how they might interact. The recognition and ontological status of these entities will be the focus of the second half of this paper.

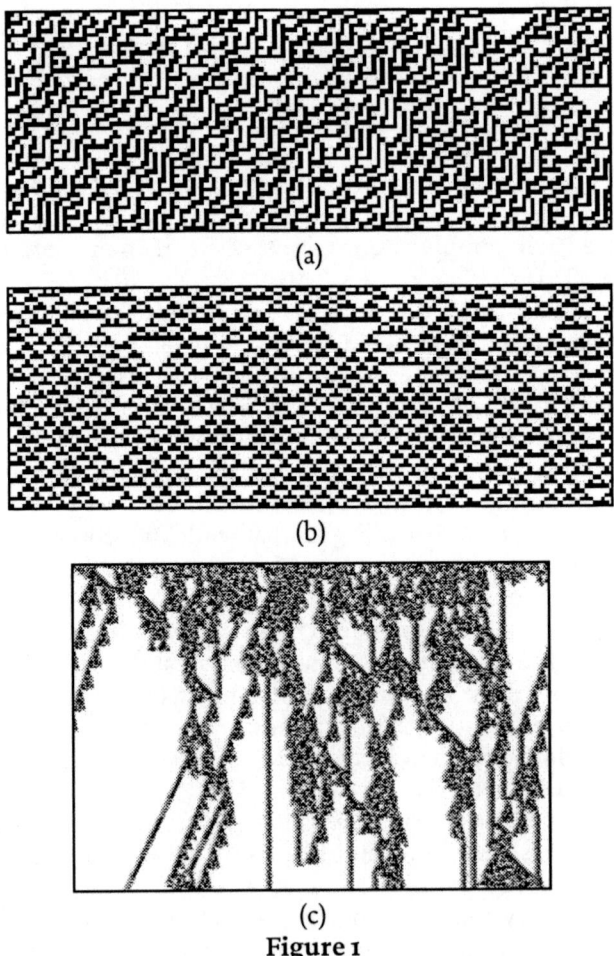

(a)

(b)

(c)

Figure 1
Examples of Cellular Automata Worlds.

Domain filtering and computational mechanics

Although the existence of some kind of emergent particle dynamics is perhaps apparent in Figure 1c, it is not so obvious from the other examples in Figure 1. A distinction between a stable 'background' and a changeable 'foreground' are apparent but their details are difficult to extract by eye alone. In this section we will briefly a way in which the 'background' might be filtered to reveal an emergent level of dynamics not obviously apparent from the BMP level and certainly not apparent from the elementary rule-based description, i.e., the 'Law of Physics'.

Computational mechanics and domain / bases filtering

"Computational mechanics is a synthesis of nonlinear dynamics and computation theory, which characterizes patterns and structure occurring in natural processes by means of formal models of computation… computational mechanics attempts to discover and characterize the typical patterns occurring in a given CA" (Hanson & Crutchfield, 1997: 169-170). Though computational mechanics is useful in understanding how computations are performed in CAS, we will be more interested in the characterization of the particle dynamics revealed by filtering as an analogy for physical reality.

The first step in distinguishing the 'background' canvas from the 'foreground' particle dynamics is to identify the dominant patterns that define the overall organization of a particular CA. "[A] pattern is considered to be a set or ensemble of configurations sharing some common spatial structure" (Hanson & Crutchfield, 1997: 170). In many CAS it is found that there are a few important patterns that dominate any system's organization. The set of these dominant patterns is referred to as the system's pattern basis (Hanson & Crutchfield, 1992).

As an example, in Figure 1b the dominant pattern is ▙ ▪. Once the pattern basis has been identified[4] a mathematical transducer is constructed that parses the space-time data into data that pinpoints domain 'defects' or 'walls'. Figure 2 shows the result of filtering the 'background' pattern basis for a CA similar to Figure 1b. For this particular system, Hanson and Crutchfield (1997) identify the four fundamental particles that emerge from the filtering process, and also detail the particle reactions that take place a this level of description (refer to Figure 2).

Where the initial transducer uncovered 'defects' in the pattern basis to reveal particles, Hanson and Crutchfield (1997) then go on to develop a transducer that uncovers 'defects' at the particle level. This additional step is useful in determining how complete the particle-based description is compared to the CA level (BMP) description. Unfortunately, the persistence of defects in the particle description indicates that this level of description is incomplete. This probably shouldn't be a surprise given that the particle level description (or JPEG level) is a reduction of the BMP level description. However, though the particle description is incomplete, it is far simpler and very stable over different system sizes. This greater stability is illustrated by considering the number of qualitatively different attractors (at the BMP level) for increasing network size. Figure 3 plots the number of attractors and the number of qualitatively different attractors against increasing network size. The detail of how these attractors are identified and constructed is given in Wuensche and Lesser (1992) and Wuensche (1999). The logarithm of the number of qualitatively different attractors scales roughly to network size, whereas the particle level description is found to be quite independent of the network size. It would seem that completeness is traded for simplicity and stability.

Hanson and Crutchfield (1997) also present evidence for higher level patterns supporting a hierarchy of particles and particle aggregates. It is easy to see how researchers of CAS find them so compelling. Given the apparent analogy to the hierarchy of physical matter, it becomes easy to understand how authors such as Wolfram (2002) and his grandiose claims of a *New Kind of Science* come about.

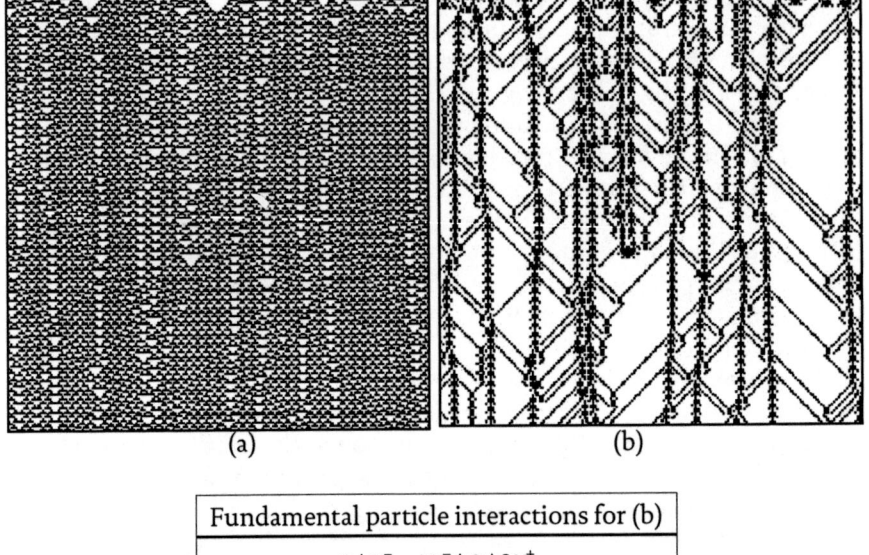

(a)   (b)

Fundamental particle interactions for (b)
$\alpha+\gamma^{-}\longrightarrow\gamma^{-}+\alpha+2\gamma^{+}$
$\gamma^{+}+\alpha\longrightarrow2\gamma^{-}+\alpha+\gamma^{+}$
$\beta+\gamma^{-}\longrightarrow\gamma^{+}$
$\gamma^{+}+\beta\longrightarrow\gamma$
$\gamma^{+}+\gamma^{-}\longrightarrow\beta$
$\gamma^{+}+\alpha+\gamma^{-}\longrightarrow\gamma^{-}+\alpha+\gamma^{+}$
$\gamma^{+}+\beta+\gamma^{-}\longrightarrow\emptyset$

Figure 2
Taken from Hanson (1999).

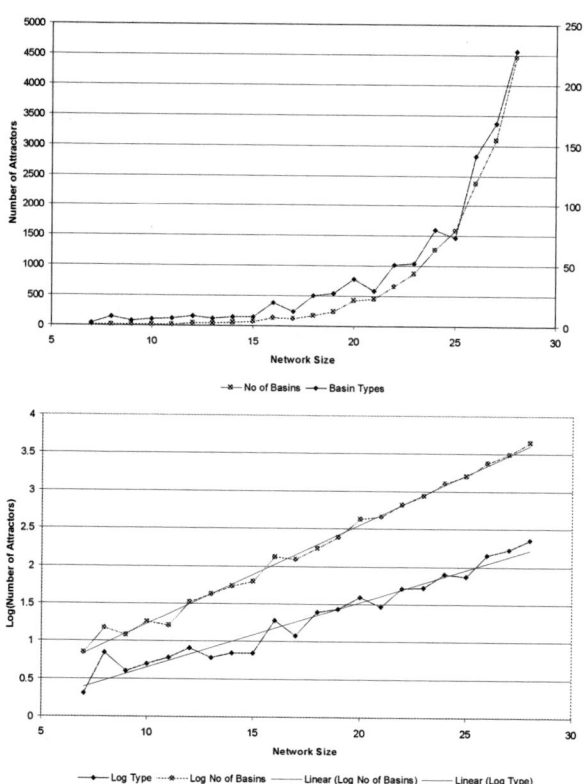

Figure 3
The Relationship Between Number of Attractors and Network Size for a
Particular Cellular Automaton

Two-Dimensional CAs and Conway's game-of-life

In this section we will briefly look at an example of two-dimensional CA, namely
Conway's *Game-of-Life*, from which objects-in-themselves seemingly emerge
in a way more amenable to direct observation. As with the one-dimensional
CA already discussed, a full description of the Game-of-Life, or *Life*, is not
necessary here. The interested reader is strongly encouraged to refer to William Poundstone's excellent text, *The Recursive Universe* (1985) and to explore
Paul Callahan's (2001) interactive website[5] (though other examples are easily
found[6]).

What one finds in exploring the Life world, as in the simpler CA worlds
discussed in the previous section, is that some seemingly coherent structures
emerge that appear to be entities unto themselves. Despite Life being a simple
recursive system, in which a seemingly trivial rule is applied over and over,
these entities seem to maintain themselves and move around the 'checkerboard
space' in quasi-determinable ways, as well as 'interact' with other entities (see

for example Poundstone, 1985: Ch. 2). Figure 4 illustrates this to a very limited degree. Along the top of the figure, from left to right, are four such entities that have been named 'loaf', 'boat', 'beehive', and 'ship' respectively. There are many others such as 'blinkers', 'period-2 oscillators', 'gliders', etc. (Evans, 2001; Eppstein, 2002)[7].

Figure 4
'Objects' in the Life Universe

"To be or not to be? That is [NOT] the question"

Thus far, the emergence of comparatively complex (when compared with the basic building blocks of CAS) entities have been discussed. The 'existence' of these entities indicate another level of existence somehow separate from the basic BMP definition. The remainder of the paper is devoted to the status of these emergent entities and how, assuming them to be analogous to real world objects, we might generate knowledge of them. In this move from the scientific to the philosophic we begin with the words of Dennett's (1991: 39):

"... should we really say that there is real motion in the [CA] world, or only apparent motion? The flashing pixels on the computer screen are a paradigm case, after all, of what a psychologist would call apparent motion. Are there really gliders that move, or are there just patterns of cell state that move? And if we opt for the latter, should we say at least that these moving patterns are real?"

The success of computational mechanics in uncovering and analyzing patterns and particle hierarchies implies that "their salience as real things is considerable, but not guaranteed" (Dennett, 1991: 40). So even though we can be sure that these 'entities' do not really exist in the BMP description, the fact that they can be treated as having *some level of existence* is a staggering discovery as it allows us to work with a higher-level (JPEG), albeit approximate, version (this is synonymous with the relationship theory has with reality). These quasi-entities, or parts, can be used to construct a high-level system that would be nigh on impossible to do if we were restricted to the BMP domain. In short, Life[8] shows that we can legitimately invoke alternative higher-level quasi-ontologies that are reasonable approximations of the absolutely correct BMP ontology, in which only two-state cells exist. Complex systems are, it seems, tractable or compressible to a degree.

Again in Dennett's (1991: 39) words, what is so incredible with Life is "that there has been a distinct ontological shift as we move between levels; whereas at the physical [BMP] level there is no motion, and only individuals, cells are defined by their fixed spatial location, at this design level we have the motion of persisting objects..." I believe that this observation alone will have a deeply profound impact upon the philosophy of science.

Before we move on let's briefly summarize the discussion thus far presented concerning the ontological status of object boundaries from a Life perspective. In Life there are no absolutely real boundaries at all except those that define the individual cells; there are no other real objects in Life. However, the emergence of persisting entities in Life, which can be described in a rough and sketchy manner, suggests that there may be another level of reality in Life that can, to some degree be treated, as such. For example, cellular automaton structures can be identified that can interact in such a way so as to mimic the components of a conventional digital computer (Wolfram, 1985). So, in some instances these rough and sketchy rules may be sufficient to even model a computer system that will perform sophisticated calculations[9]. Hordijk, *et al.* (1996); Mitchell, *et al.* (1993); and Das, *et al.* (1994) all demonstrate the use of elementary CAS in solving simple computational problems.

These quasi-real or substantially real entities can interact with each other to produce super-quasi-entities that also persist and have associated with themselves rough and sketchy rules of interaction; the possible emergence of another level of existence[10]. In fact, Hanson and Crutchfield (1997) have already demonstrated this phenomenon even in a simple 1-d automaton[11]. Within CAS there seems to be the potential for hierarchical quasi-existence in which increasingly sophisticated entities emerge which, though not real in an absolute sense, can in a limited way be treated as having existence, and can be (incompletely, though profitably) described without resorting to the detail of Life cell-states. Ontological shifts can legitimately and profitably be taken in Life - albeit to a limited degree (and the fact that it is to a limited degree only is very important to note, as this affects the way(s) in which we approach and use such representations).

One other point to remember is that Life is perfectly 100% deterministic; if the game is rerun with the same rules and initial configuration, exactly the same history will be produced; "[e]verything that happens in Life is predestined" (Poundstone, 1985: 25). To be exact, what we should say is that Life is forward-deterministic but not backward-deterministic as "a [particular] configuration has only one future but (usually) many possible pasts" (Poundstone, 1985: 48). Life (being Class 4)[12] is irreversible.

Exploring the Universe as a cellular automaton

In this section I will explore the implications of assuming that there is only one True system and that is the Universe itself - an indivisible whole. Though it is impossible to prove in any scientific sense, I begin by making the assumption that the Universe is a CA, in that it comprises an unimaginably large number of nonlinearly interacting elements. Why would we want to consider this as the case? To realize the dream of having absolutely Truthful knowledge then "[t]he state of everything - everywhere - at every time - must be defined. The most economical way to specify such information is through a complexity-generating recursion of physical law" (Poundstone, 1985: 231) like in Life.

According to the latest physical theories the interacting elements of the real Universe might be incredibly minute superstrings that oscillate in eleven-dimensional 'space', where the oscillation frequency of a string corresponds to a particular fundamental particle (this needn't be the case - but an atomist view of some sort is necessary). This view of the Universe is incredibly simple yet it has the capacity (because of the recursive application of a simple nonlinear rule) to account for everything we observe in our view of reality and a lot more besides[13]. It is the capacity of nonlinearity to create an infinitude of potentially different structures (and sub-structures) and behaviors that lead to this possibility. Conway, the inventor of Life, "showed that the Life universe ... is not fundamentally less rich than our own" (Poundstone, 1985: 24).

A cellular automata universe and the status of scientific knowledge

Imagine if you will a eleven-dimensional (a little hard to imagine I know) CA model comprising a vast number of 'superstring' cells whose evolution is determined by a single simple rule; the fundamental *Law of Physics* which would look something like $S_{t+1}=O(S_t)$[14]. Each step in the Universe's evolution is simply the result of this rule being applied to each cell. This view is impossible to prove of course - like other *Theories-of-Everything* (TOEs) endeavours it is more ironic science (Horgan, 1996: 3), or pseudo-science, than science - but its explanatory powers are surprisingly impressive indeed[15].

A view from without

The first observation is that such a Universe would be completely 100% deterministic. The entire evolution of the Universe would be totally predetermined by the characteristics of the comprising 'superstrings' and the one (nonlinear) rule of interaction. This would please our scientific forefathers' view of a Universe as a perfectly tuned machine. For such a construction there isn't even any need for a specific set of initial conditions necessarily[16]; the initial conditions might be completely random and the consequent Universe would still be qualitatively the same. (The initial conditions of the Universe have been a hot topic of discussion for sometime. It is only recently that it has been suggested that maybe there are models of the Universe that do not require a specific set of starting conditions, Chown, 1998; and Tegmark, 1998). This suggested model of the Universe is based upon a strongly realist ontology; what truly exist are '11-d superstrings' (or, whatever turns out to be the viable candidate, though scientists may never know - and it does not really matter), no more, no less. All other 'objects', 'entities', 'particles', 'boundaries', are no more than different 'cell state' combinations that manifest themselves as the 'loaves', 'ships' and 'beehives' of Life. In this Universe a fermion is a type of 'boat', say, having no absolute existence, but having a *substantial realism* (Emmeche, *et al.*, 2000), so substantial in fact as to often allow its absolute existence to be taken for granted. An atom is no more than a 'fleet of ships' in this Life Universe. In physics the term used is quasiparticles[17] (the discoverers of quasiparticles received the 1998 Nobel Prize in Physics - Seife, 1998). According to the CA model all the physical particles that have been discovered will eventually be found to be quasiparticles. Even we humans are not as we appear to ourselves. We are not sentient beings with free will and learning capacities. A human is just a collection of interacting 'boats', 'ships', 'beehives', 'super-beehives', i.e., a very intricate 'cell state', the occurrence and behavior of which was always inevitable in a CA Universe. It has been recently shown that it is in fact quite easy to construct a cellular automaton system that more often than not yields self-reproducing quasi-entities (Chou & Reggia, 1997).

Another fascinating outcome of assuming a CA Universe is that there is no adaptation in any absolute sense of the term. At the BMP level, the ultimate objective reality, 'superstrings' do not learn new tricks; they do not become 'superduperstrings' (unless it is through an ontological shift on our part). Adaptation is a feature of an ontology that some scientists have chosen to take for granted; it is a way of usefully understanding the changes in the Life 'cell states' without having to deal directly with those real 'cell states'. Adaptation is an illusion created by taking an ontological shift away from absolute reality, as is Life[18]. So when complexologists are heard speaking of complex adaptive systems (CASS) they are taking some enormous strides away from what absolutely exists. A great deal of assumptions (which are often perfectly reasonable from our limited human perspective) have to be made before one can even infer the (quasi-) existence of CASS. Even the ontology that complexologists hail as the best lens to view parts of the Universe is reductionist to some extent - the CAS ontology is a poor to reasonable JPEG approximation of an absolute BMP reality.

And what of causality? Causation as a necessary connection between two events in a CA Universe cannot be inferred from correlation or association in any absolute sense. Causality, like Life's 'boats' and 'ships' is an emergent 'cell state' pattern that can only be recognized as such by making an ontological shift away from the BMP view that assumes it's existence. Causality, therefore, is an abstraction rather than a real operating process. The psychotherapist Carl Jung wrote (with the cooperation of the eminent physicist Wolfgang Pauli) an interesting treatise on this exact point: what "if the connection between cause and effect turns out to be only statistically valid and only relatively true..."? (Jung, 1973: 5). Though as Hume has already noted "causation is a notion fundamental to human cognition, so fundamental that it is unlikely to ever be eradicated" (Wagner, 1999: 83), and so it shouldn't. Whether causation is real or not, it has proven to be a very productive concept, but that is no excuse to take it for granted.

This is the view from the outside however; a view that we will never be privy to[19].

A view from within

Though it is interesting that such a complex systems view does lead to differences in knowing dependent upon a theistic (without) and atheistic (within) position, it is not of much help to us as members (however unreal) of the Universe. Though I must admit to finding it extremely interesting that such a vision of the Universe provides a common context that allows the Universe to be both deterministic and non-deterministic depending upon the position of an observer. Such a vision has the capacity to allow for the co-existence of apparently opposing positions depending upon where one is standing. However, though it may seem to provide little value when considering the Universe as a whole, what if we could approximate parts of the Universe that appear to be real systems in their own right as complex systems, or even CASS? Again, it is the ability to associate substantial realism to the various Life 'entities' that facilitate (or even allow) this activity. Our own existence as such can only be realized by making a shift from The Universal (physical BMP) Ontology of Life to an irrealist (albeit substantially real) ontology; human existence is an arbitrary paradigm, a shared illusion, rather than a given.

As already mentioned, the complex systems view does differentiate between the knowledge one can obtain when we regard ourselves as outside a (particular) system (of 'loaves') and that knowledge we can obtain when we regard ourselves as a member of the system. This illustrates that the subject-object distinction often made does limit the knowledge we can have in some way. How much can an outside consultant know about a particular organization and how valuable is his / her knowledge? What is more important, the opinions of members of society, or the view of politicians often seen as disengaged from society? How much can an earthbound science know about the Universe in which it is supported? I will not investigate this aspect of complexity much further, but it is interesting to note that complexity thinking does legitimate subjective knowledge (often excluded from the scientific domain) as well as quasi-objective knowledge. We need to ask ourselves: if science claims to extract real patterns (which, from the discussion on Life, has shown not to be the case - science considers 'loaves' and 'blinkers' which do not ultimately exist) to what extent are those patterns more real than those patterns we each extract from our surroundings in the process of sense making. Are our personal opinions based upon patterns less real than those found in science? Why should science be allowed to claim that the 'objects' it considers are more real than the 'objects' we each 'see' in our daily lives? In what sense are the boundaries of an 'electron' more real than my own personal boundary that defines 'friend' given that neither is absolutely real?

From within the Universe it is impossible to have a complete representation of anything. There is only one true system; all other systems are temporary and contingent structures whose boundaries are, in a strict sense, illusory. In the sense that boundaries are hard resilient objects that demarcate the part from the whole, no boundaries actually exist (except those that define the Universal Cellular Automaton). Despite this *no-boundary* hypothesis, which when taken too literally demands an unachievable, radically holist, approach to knowledge creation (if one demands) True knowledge, models that do indeed assume boundaries do have considerable practical use.

Boundary (or, pattern) distributions

At his point we can say that there are no real boundaries in the Universe except those that define its fundamental components (superstrings?). All objects of human experience, including organizations, are no more than quasi-entities. Our conception of these quasi-entities, which result from changes in the fundamental cell-state configurations of Life, is an approximate and subjective experience that results from an unavoidable shift from the BMP expression of reality to a (sometimes arbitrary) JPEG ontology. How are we to do derive knowledge of particular systems then (particularly if no systems really exist)? As mentioned above the situation is not as dire as it might immediately seem. There is no need to follow the radical holists to model the world, the Universe and everything (which we could not do even if we wanted to). The discussion thus far suggests that there is strong (theoretical) evidence that, though there may be no *absolutely real boundaries*, there are resilient and relatively stable emergent structures or patterns that can be treated with a reasonable degree of accuracy as having existence. It is this very ability to profit from an ontological shift away from reality that allows science to provide knowledge that is incomplete, indirect, approximate, yet useful.

The existence of stable quasi-entities can be seen as one end of a continuous spectrum of quasi-existence. At the other end there are one-off unique patterns, or structures, whose fleeting appearance makes the very question of their existence impossible to answer. So there exists a distribution of levels of existence. No evidence is given herein for what this distribution may actually be; it is simply argued that there is a distribution.

At one end of the stability spectrum there are boundaries / structures that are so persistent and stable that, for most intents and purposes, it can safely be assumed that they are in fact real and absolute. Boundaries that traditionally describe the objects of science-based technology exist toward this end of the spectrum. Such long-term stability allows a 'community of enquirers', e.g., the scientific community, to inter-subjectively converge on some agreed principles that might actually be tested and confirmed through experiment. Under such conditions it is quite possible to develop quasi-objective knowledge, which for most intents and purposes (but not ultimately) is absolute. The existence of such persistent boundaries, or patterns, allows for a something other than a radically holistic analysis - this may account for why the scientific program has been so successful when it comes to technological matters - it has hit upon a very powerful quasi-ontology that reflects rather well the real and absolute state-of-affairs. In many circumstances reductionism (the assumption that 'beehives' actual do exist, and everything is made up from them) is a perfectly valid, though still approximate, route to understanding, contrary to the popular complexity literature. In short, what is suggested here is that scientific study depends upon the assumption that object boundaries are static in a sense, and that if one can demonstrate that the boundaries of interest are in fact stable and persistent, then the methods of reductionist science are more than adequate[20].

It is exactly this stability, this apparent 'movement' of persistently stable 'quasi-entities' (as is observed in Life) that can be attributed some substantial level of realism, that allows us as modellers / scientists / observers to "proceed to predict - sketchily and riskily - the behavior of larger configurations or systems of configurations, without bothering to compute the physical [BMP] level" (Dennett, 1991: 40); an enormous computational saving indeed. It is exactly this substantial realism of levels (Emmeche, *et al.*, 2000), or entities that supports the efficacy of the hierarchy of sciences without having to know everything there is to know about each ascending level away from the fundamental physical BMP reality.

At the other end of the stability spectrum we have essentially 'noise' in which the lifetime of apparent boundaries / patterns / entities might be so fleeting as to render them unrecognizable as such and therefore unanalyzable. Under such circumstances attempts to develop knowledge are strongly determined by the whims of the individual (as a result of their subjective skills in extracting patterns from what is essentially randomness), with observed boundaries being more a function of our thirst to make sense, rather than an actual feature of 'reality'. To maintain a purely positivistic position, one would have to accept radical holism and consider the entire Universe - a practical absurdity and a theoretical impossibility, as has already been stated. This is the only method by which truly absolute and infallible knowledge could possibly be derived.

Fortunately the vast majority of the perceived Universe isn't quite so nebulous. This doesn't mean however that boundary recognition and allocation is a trivial exercise. In fact without the ability to not only determine the stability distribution, but also recognize where the objects of interest might occur on the continuum of quasi-existence it is not clear how to approach them. Radical positivists might argue that a rigorous implementation of the scientific method is appropriate across the board. I have already suggested that the application of scientific method(s) makes clear assumptions about the ontological status of objects that I believe cannot be supported. This position sympathizes with Shweder's (2001) argument that, as science was designed to study observable material entities that can easily be located in time and space, there are subjects beyond the proper realm of science. Relating this back to Life: the ontological leap from the physical (BMP) reality to the "design [JPEG] level" (Dennett, 1991: 39) of 'loaves', 'boats', 'ships' etc. is imperfect, therefore some, what is generally referred to as, 'noise' is removed to allow the leap to occur. Science does not, and cannot, deal with the 'noise' (which is really the detail of reality). I would argue that the social sciences with their willingness to work with a plurality of (possibly incommensurable) methods and perspectives, to view the patterns from different angles, and therefore at different 'noise' levels, is more suited to deal with a state of affairs in which both boundary recognition and allocation are deeply problematic. This position reflects Cilliers (2001: 142) concern that "[i]n accepting the complexity of the boundaries of complex systems, we are committed to be critical about how we use the notion since it affects our understanding of such systems, and influences the way in which we deal with them."

Towards an evolutionary philosophy

The first step in making an argument for an evolutionary philosophy is to justify ontological (or metaphysical) pluralism. In a way, this step has already been justified by the observation that a leap from the physical ontology of Life's 'cell states' to a design ontology in which the apparent 'objects' of the physical ontology are treated as such, i.e., rather than regarding them as useful 'non-real' approximations they are accepted as having substantial realism that often masquerades as full blown realism. The hierarchy of the sciences takes advantage this feature of Life's 'cell states' creation of a hierarchy of ontologies from superstrings to galactic clusters. Each science is justified to a limited degree with the assumption that its objects of study are real. Complexologists do not quite support this view. They argue that each subsequent layer of the hierarchy of entities is an emergent property of the (quasi-real) layer below. So, rather than seeing cells (as in biology) as real, they are regarded as the emergent products of the molecular (as in chemistry) layer. The problems of bootstrapping from one layer to another is problematic (the intractability of the emergent process basically prevents bootstrapping from ever happening in a complete way), and though each of the distinct branches of science probably except that its particular objects of interest are not real in an absolute sense, the assumption that these objects have substantial realism is sufficient to not undermine their efforts much at all. The fact that each science has indeed made great contributions to human understanding is a testament to the accuracy of these various ontological assumptions for certain purposes. In the absence of a bootstrapping method from the physical BMP model, quasi-'ontological pluralism' has been rather successful. It is quite astounding that science has progressed so far based on poor to good ontological assumptions, but this possibility could only be achieved if the Universe was indeed reasonably well behaved, and again is a demonstration of the power of ontological shifts.

Even though there is a strong argument that suggests that there is only one absolutely real level of existence (the BMP level), we are forced on practical grounds (and justified on theoretical grounds) to at least adopt a scientific pluralism which works rather well indeed. Above I refer to this as quasi-'ontological pluralism' in recognition that each of the scientific ontologies are only approximate ontologies (in the same way that the particle-based description discussed earlier is approximate) and also that there are only a limited number of these approximate ontologies in science meaning that it is not totally pluralistic - pluralism with unknown limits.

Horizontal and vertical pluralism

Even though the above view has the capacity to allow the exploration of the same phenomena from different ontologies, all the ontologies are scientific in nature. This view is exemplified by W. V. Quine's brand of ontological relativism. "Here the plurality consists in the possible existence of a range of alternative scientific worldviews, each empirically adequate to more or less the same degree, and none, even in principle, have privileged claim to provide a 'truer' description of the world" (Price, 1992: 389). Even "incompatible theories can explain the same facts equally well and make equally good predictions" (Masani, 2001: 279). Price (1992: 389) goes on to argue that,

"[t]here may be equally valid possible scientific worldviews, but all of them are scientific worldviews, and in that sense are on the same level of linguistic activity. In other words, this is what might appropriately be called horizontal pluralism."

But why should ontological pluralism be restricted to the horizontal? Why should ontological pluralism be associated only with what we might call 'discourse monism'? The answer to these questions again depend on *how substantially real an entity must be for it to be temporarily assumed to be real.* Scientists would undoubtedly argue that the patterns they develop Natural Laws for are more real than the patterns that society, or even individuals, deem real (is a proton more real than an idea?). Given the (stable-ish) objects of scientific investigation, then I would generally support the scientific community in this assertion. However, like some social scientists I believe that the subject matter of the social sciences, as an example, puts them outside the proper realm of the physical sciences (see also Shweder, 2001). The CA view of the Universe also supports this position. Note that this belief certainly does not deny the possibility that more traditional scientific approaches have a lot to offer the social sciences (or the analysis of any complex system). However, the physical sciences are quite intolerant to 'noise'; they require a high 'signal-to-noise' ratio that may not be present in social systems. Scientific methods generally seek to extract clear patterns from the 'noise' of reality. Sometimes this process is straightforward, sometimes it isn't. My point is simply that the pattern extraction (filtering) process / method is generally problematic, depending upon the relationship between an observer and the 'noise' of reality. Substantially "real but (potentially) noisy patterns abound in ... the Life world, there for the picking up if only we are lucky or clever enough to hit on the right perspective" (Dennett, 1991: 41). Traditional science has a knack of extracting the more apparent patterns and expressing their form in an implementable way (generally through mathematics). What about everything else? Returning to Price (1992: 390):

"If these [scientific discourses] are cases of horizontal pluralism, what would be a vertical pluralism? It would be the view that philosophy should recognize an irreducible plurality of kinds of discourse - the moral as well as the scientific, for example. This is the species of pluralism with which we ... [should] be most concerned."

Price refers to this type of vertical pluralism as *discourse pluralism*. Here we have arrived at a description of what is meant by ontological pluralism in an evolutionary philosophy. This type of pluralism is not irrealist at all. It simply accepts that in the absence of a completely realist position, we may profit from the examination of a variety of other worldviews and discourses whose scale-of-compression (i.e., the way in which patterns are extracted) varies. Different scientific worldviews maybe as useful as different moral worldviews or different artistic worldviews (such as cubism or abstract expressionism), all of which are metaphors, or caricatures, of reality. This does not lead to an 'anything goes' relativism (except as a starting point perhaps). But how, if we are to make a decision one way or another, are we to untangle the pluralist web and agree upon, albeit temporarily and locally, a dominant perspective?

Critical dialogue as conceptual investigation

It would be very convenient indeed to be able to answer the question above by simply offering a systematic framework that we could employ that would associate each discourse and comprising worldview with a context in which we could be confident that we had selected the best position to base our decisions upon. The problem with any such approach is the risk of idolatry or reification, so I won't attempt to provide a coherent framework except as to suggest that there are an enormous number of ways to exploit pluralism each with their own idiosyncrasies (see as examples Jackson & Keys, 1984; Flood, 1995; or Midgley, 2000).

Here I simply argue that it is through critical dialogue that we may temporarily reshape the default position of ontological pluralism to a local (in space and time) monism, i.e., it is through critical dialogue that the general position of including everything is tailored to the perceived specific. Critical dialogue here is regarded in much the same way that Socrates and Plato regarded criticism, i.e., "no more baffling an enterprise than investigating a concept" (Gottlieb, 2000: 174). The process is one of an ongoing three-way exchange between a decision-making body (which may be the one or the many), the perceived context (which will undoubtedly evolve[21]), and the pluralist realm of ideas and theories. The relationship between these three elements is certainly non-trivial and would require extensive investigation to understand fully. But the essence of this process is that the default position is 'nothingness', i.e., to the extent that we can, no perspective is privileged over all other perspectives, and that through a critical process a context-specific perspective is negotiated that will inform our actions; it is a *group decision process* (on which there is a wealth of literature already in existence, see for example, Vennix, 1996 and selected chapters in Mingers & Gill, 1997 on multi-methodology). The process is imperfect and explicitly acknowledges the potential of all perspectives, and is ultimately determined on changing pragmatic rather than rigid ideological grounds. I have referred to this evolutionary philosophy elsewhere (Richardson, *et al.*, 2000 and Richardson, 2001) as quasi-'critical pluralism' (Q-CP). The 'quasi' is included to explicitly acknowledge the impossibility of being truly critical or pluralistic.

This view undoubtedly denies the sort of (naïve) realism that perfectly maps our conceptual boundaries (that are implied by our explanations) to real objects (despite being 'constructed' from a purely realist ontology). There is no one-to-one mapping of our ideas, scientific or otherwise, to objective reality. However, this denial of realism (as a default position) does not recoil into an argument for constructivism or extreme relativism. Constructivists, as I have already said, argue that all boundaries are created in our minds and as such do not correlate with objective reality at all[22]. Q-CP is based upon the distribution of quasi-existence (derived from a purely physical foundation), and falls between these two extreme. Rather than having a fixed relationship with quasi-objects, or having no relationship at all, our conceptual boundaries do have a complex and changing relationship to quasi-reality. Sometimes this link might be so tenuous as to be unusable. Sometimes this link is so strong as to give us the impression that we might actually have absolute Truth to hand. The key difference between this position and (naïve) realism is that it explicitly acknowledges the problematization of object / context recognition which is trivialized in most realist philosophies. The key difference between Q-CP and constructivism is that Q-CP acknowledges that the world of substantially real patterns does play an integral part in the evolutionary relationship between reality 'out there' and our ideas. Figure 5 attempts to illustrate the changing relationship(s) between our conceptual boundaries and quasi-real boundaries for these different philosophies.

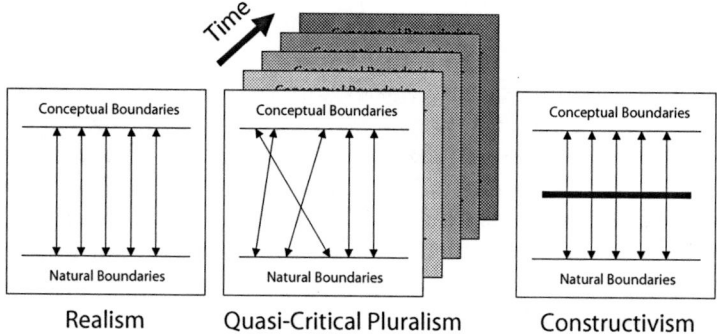

Realism   Quasi-Critical Pluralism   Constructivism

Figure 5
The Relationship Between Conceptual / Mental Boundaries and Natural /
Physical Boundaries

Summary and conclusions

Traditionally the notion of existence has been based upon a very simplistic binary opposition that suggests that 'objects' either do exist or do not exist. This rather naïve (from a complexity perspective) dichotomy paints the Universe in a black and white fashion which is quite inappropriate given the inherent complexity and ambiguity of our surroundings. One of the major risks with viewing the Universe in such simple terms is that the efficacy of our models (whether they be formal mathematical models of less formal world views) of parts of that Universe is often overestimated.

In this chapter I have presented a complex systems based argument that places the notion of existence along a continuum of possibilities. As a starting point the assumption that, at some arbitrary level, the Universe can be well-described as a cellular automaton was made. From this radically realist ontology it was shown (through the application of computational mechanical methods) that 'objects' 'emerge' that, though they are not recognized as 'real' in the CA substrate, they can be treated as real objects in a limited way and modelled with a useful degree of accuracy. The existence of such quasi-entities permits alternative (incomplete) quasi-ontologies to be assumed and employed successfully (meaning that they yield practical understanding), without having to deal directly with the absolutely complete BMP ontology. Such ontological shifts allow us to make limited sense of the Universe through astonishing computational savings of many orders of magnitude. The emergent quasi-objects that are the basis of these alternative quasi-ontologies are said to be substantially real rather than simply real or nonreal.

The recognition of quasi-entities, or patterns, is not a trivial exercise. Followers of scientism would argue that the methods of science are the only legitimate means by which such 'objects' should be recognized and analyzed. Following Price (1992) such a position is referred to as horizontal pluralism.

It is patently obvious that scientific thinking has been incredibly successful in yielding practical understanding about simple systems in the material world, and it is nothing new to suggest that we are beginning to see the limits of traditional reductionist science. Assuming we are currently experiencing a paradigm shift in thought (in reaction to the increased complexity of the social world) we needn't assume that the result will simply be a slight revision / addition to the scientific paradigm. In his book *Against Method* Paul Feyerabend asks "Should we transfer to [the scientific tradition] the sole rights for dealing in knowledge, so that any result that has been obtained by other methods is at once ruled out of court?" Feyerabend, 1975: 20). Like Feyerabend my answer to this question is a resounding "No".

The position developed herein, which is referred to as critical pluralism, is an evolutionary philosophy that privileges no theory over any other in the general sense, but allows for the dominance of any theory in the particular sense. If the argument that the Universe is a complex system holds then "We must ... keep our options open and we must not restrict ourselves in advance" (Feyerabend, 1975: 20). Critical pluralism holds "that there is only one principle that can be defended under all circumstances and in all stages of human development. It is the principle: anything goes." (p. 28). This means that at a general level "anything goes" but not necessarily in particular contexts. Through critical examination of the perceived context, ourselves and our ideas we develop arguments / proofs / narratives that permit us to temporarily and provisionally privilege certain positions above others - to 'fake positivism' if you like. It may be that in many instances scientific-like theories emerge as the dominant perspective, but this should never be prescribed up-front. Critical pluralism is a democratic philosophy that observes the 'rights' of all positions, but at the same time acknowledges the need for selection in order to legitimately justify action in specific circumstances. In some ways we need to learn to be schizophrenic in that we must both acknowledge boundaries but resist the temptation to reify them (given that they are nonreal).

Many of the conclusions contained herein are not unique; indeed there is a strong hint of Greek skepticism. However, the fact that they can be 'derived' from a strongly realist approach, even the more postmodern conclusions, is most certainly of interest and not an interpretation of complexity theory that has received much attention. There are very few philosophies, particularly those that have a scientific basis, that manage to bring together notions of subjectivity / objectivity, internal / external, individual / collective, etc. under the same roof. Complexity thinking and critical pluralism achieves this by problematizing the fundamental concept of existence.

References

Callahan, P., *Wonder's of Maths: Conway's Game of Life*, http://www.math.com/students/wonders/life/life.html

Chou, H.-H. and Reggia, J. A. (1997). "Emergence of Self-Replicating Structures in a

Cellular Autotmata Space," *Physica D*, 110: 252-276.

Chown, M. (1998), "Anything Goes," *New Scientist magazine*, 158(2137): 26.

Cilliers, P. (2001). "Boundaries, Hierarchies and Networks in Complex Systems," *International Journal of Innovation Management*, 5(2): 135-148.

Das, R., Mitchell, M. and Crutchfield, J. P. (1994). "A Genetic Algorithm Discovers Particle-Based Computation in Cellular Automata," in Y. Davidor, H. -P. Schwefel and R. Männer (eds.), *Parallel Problem Solving from Nature III*, Springer-Verlag, pp. 344-353.

Dennett, D. C. (1991). "Real Patterns," *The Journal of Philosophy*, 88(1): 27-51.

Emmeche, C., Köppe, S. and Stjernfelt, F. (2000). "Levels, Emergence, and Three Versions of Downward Causation," in P. B. Andersen, C. Emmeche, N. O. Finnemann, and P. V. Christiansen (eds.), *Downward Causation*, Aarhus: Aarhus University Press.

Eppstein, D. (2002). "Searching for Spaceships," in *More Games of No Chance*, (ed.) Richard J. Nowakoski, Cambridge University Press.

Evans, K. M. (2001). "Larger than Life: Digital Creatures in a Family of Two-Dimensional Cellular Automata," *Discrete Mathematics and Theoretical Computer Science Proceedings*, Vol. A A (Discrete Models: Combinatorics, Computation, and Geometry), pp. 177-192.

Fetzer, J. H. and Almeder, R. F. (1993). *Glossary of Epistemology/Philosophy of Science*, New York: Paragon House.

Feyerabend, P. (1975). *Against Method*, London, UK: NLB.

Flood, R. L. (1995). "Total Systems Intervention (TSI): A Reconstruction," *Journal of the Operational Research Society*, 46: 174-191.

Gottlieb, A. (2000). *The Dream of Reason: A History of Western Philosophy from the Greeks to the Renaissance*, New York, NY: W. W. Norton & Co.

Hanson, J. E. (1999). *The Computational Mechanics of Cellular Automata*, Revised and updated PhD thesis.

Hanson, J. E. and Crutchfield, J. P. (1992). "The Attractor-Basin Portrait of a Cellular Automaton," *J. Stat. Phys.*, 66: 1415-1462.

Hanson, J. E. and Crutchfield, J. P. (1997). "Computational Mechanics of Cellular Automata: An Example," *Physica D*, 103(1-4): 169-189.

Hordijk, W., Crutchfield, J. P. and Mitchell, M. (1996). "Embedded-Particle Computation in Evolved Cellular Automata," in T. Toffoli, M. Biafore, and J. Leão (eds.), *Physics and Computation 96* (Pre-Proceedings), New England Complex Systems Institute, pp. 153-158.

Horgan, J. (1996). *The End of Science - Facing the Limits of Knowledge in the Twilight of the Scientific Age*, London: Little, Brown and Company.

Jackson, M. C. and Keys, P. (1984). "Towards a System of Systems Methodologies," *Journal of Operational Research Society*, 35: 473-486.

Jung, C. G. (1973). *Synchronicity: An Acausal Connecting Principle*, Princeton, NJ: Princeton University Press.

Masani, P. R. (2001). "Three Modern Enemies of Science: Materialism, Existentialism, Constructivism," *Kybernetes*, 30(3): 278-294.

Midgley, G. (2000). *Systemic Intervention: Philosophy, Methodology, and Practice*, New York, NY: Kluwer Academic / Plenum Publishers.

Mingers, J. and Gill, A. (1997). *Multimethodology: The Theory and Practice of Combining Management Science Methodologies*, Chichester, UK: John Wiley & Sons.

Mitchell, M., Hraber, P. T., and Crutchfield, J. P. (1993). "Revisiting the Edge of Chaos: Evolving Cellular Automata to Perform Computations," *Complex Systems*, 7:

89-130.

Oreskes, N., Shrader-Frechette, K., and Belitz, K. (1994). "Verification, Validation, and Confirmation of Numerical Models in the Earth Sciences," *Science*, 263(4 February): 641-646.

Poundstone, W. (1985). *The Recursive Universe: Cosmic Complexity and the Limits of Scientific Knowledge*, New York, NY: William Morrow & Company.

Price, H. (1992). "Metaphysical Pluralism," *The Journal of Philosophy*, 89(8): 387-409.

Richardson, K. A. (2001). "On the Status of Natural Boundaries: A Complex Systems Perspective," *Proceedings of the Systems in Management 7th Annual ANZSYS Conference 2001*, pp. 229-238.

Richardson, K. A. (2004). "The Problematization of Existence: Towards a Philosophy of Complexity," Nonlinear Dynamics, Psychology, and Life Sciences, 8(1): 17-40.

Richardson, K. A. , Mathieson, G., and Cilliers, P. (2000). "The Theory and Practice of Complexity Science: Epistemological Considerations for Military Operational Analysis," *SysteMexico*, 1(1): 25-66.

Samuel, E. (2002). "What Lies Beneath?" *New Scientist magazine*, 173(2329): 24.

Seife, C. (1998). "Into the Vortex," *New Scientist magazine*, 160(2157): 7.

Shalizi, C. R. and Crutchfield, J. P. (2001). "Computational Mechanics: Pattern and Prediction, Structure and Simplicity," *Journal of Statistical Physics*, 104: 817-879.

Shweder, R. A. (2001). "A Polytheistic Conception of the Sciences and the Virtues of Deep Variety," in A. R. Damasio, A. Harrington, J. Kagan, B. S. McEewn, H. Moss, and R. Shaikh (eds.), *Unity of Knowledge: The Convergence of Natural and Human Sciences*, Annals of the New York Academy of Sciences, Vol. 935.

Tegmark, M. (1998). "Is 'the Theory of Everything' Merely the Ultimate Ensemble Theory?" *Annals of Physics*, 270: 1-51. http://www.hep.upenn.edu/~max/toe.pdf

Toffoli, T. (1984). "Cellular Automata as an Alternative to (Rather than an Approximation of) Differential Equations in Modeling Physics," *Physica D*, 10: 117-127.

Vennix, J. A. M. (1996). *Group Model Building: Facilitating Team Learning Using System Dynamics*, Chichester, UK: John Wiley & Sons.

Wagner, A. (1999). "Causality in Complex Systems," *Biology and Philosophy*, 14: 83-101.

Wolfram, S. (1984). "Universality and Complexity in Cellular Automata," *Physica D*, 10: 1-35.

Wolfram, S. (1985). "Twenty Problems in the Theory of Cellular Automata," *Physica Scripta*, T9: 170-183.

Wolfram, S. (2002). *A New Kind of Science*, Champaign, IL: Wolfram Media, Inc.

Wuensche, A. (1999). "Classifying Cellular Automata Automatically: Finding Gliders, Filtering, and Relating Space-Time Patterns, Attractor Basins, and the Z Parameter," *Complexity*, 4(3): 47-66.

Wuensche, A. and Lesser, M. J. (1992). *The Global Dynamics of Cellular Automata*, Santa Fe Studies in the Sciences of Complexity, Reading, MA: Addison-Wesley.

Notes

1. "Simple complex systems" may seem oxymoronic, but what I am trying to emphasise is that the models we create of complex systems are still very much simplifications of what actually is. We are capable of modelling only the simplest of complex systems.

2. Note that as a BMP image becomes more complex, or random, the size of the corresponding JPEG file would converge to that of the BMP file, i.e., the image would

become incompressible.

3. "It remains conceivable, however, that there exists cellular automata in which two sets of initial states that occur with nonzero probabilities could lead to two qualitatively different forms of behavior." (Wolfram, 1985).

4. The pattern of the top row, and every second row following, is built up from sequences of (1000). The second row and every alternate row are examples of sequences of (1101).

5. In fact it is very difficult indeed to appreciate the full significance of the *Game of Life* without interacting with it dynamically which of course is greatly limited by traditional publishing methods. In Dennett's (1991: 37) opinion "every philosophy student should be held responsible for an intimate acquaintance with the Game of Life. It should be considered an essential tool in every thought-experimenter's kit, a prodigiously versatile generator of philosophically important examples and thought experiments of admirable clarity and vividness." Try: http://psoup.math.wisc.edu/mcell/download.html

6. I have found MCell particularly useful and easy to use: http://psoup.math.wisc.edu/mcell/

7. For an up-to-date summary of *Life* discoveries go to Jason Summers's Game-of-Life status page at: http://entropymine.com/jason/life/status.html

8. For the remainder of the paper the term Life refers not only to Conway's Game-of-Life but all ca systems that display the emergence of complex quasi-entities (often referred to as complex (class 4) systems after Wuensche, 1999).

9. The simulation of a conventional serial processor though would seem to be a rather limited way to utilize the parallel processing capabilities of cellular automata.

10. The notion of another 'level of existence' is of course problematic. Are the successive quasi-ontologies really at higher levels? Or are they simply alternative descriptions/models of the bmp reality which include no notion of level? What is certainly clear is that different ontologies privilege different quasi-entities of varying (descriptive) complexity. Often this is how the hierarchy of sciences is constructed with less complex entities at the lower levels and the more complex entities at the higher levels. It would, however, be inappropriate to assume that the hierarchy of sciences is based upon a natural hierarchy.

11. Refer to Shalizi and Crutchfield (2001) for the underlying theory.

12. In his influential paper "University and Complexity in Cellular Automata" Wolfram (1984) proposed a classification of cellular automaton rules into four types, according to the results of evolving the system from a "disordered" initial state: (1) evolution leads to a homogeneous state; (2) evolution leads to a set of separated simple stable or periodic structures; (3) evolution leads to a chaotic pattern, and; (4) evolution leads to complex localized structures, sometimes long-lived.

13. This statement is of course pure speculation. However, the rich and complex behaviors that some (complex) CAS exhibit is incredibly compelling.

14 .Of course such a definition of the Universe would also have to include all the paraphernalia that supports the 'checkerboard' and provides the 'energy' to apply the rule at each timestep. Some might wonder about how this paraphernalia came into being. However, such questioning has no end in sight, requiring a stake to be put in the ground. The Greeks had their First Cause, this paper has its First CA.

15. I prefer to think of it as a *Gedanken* experiment rather than non-science.

16 .Except the existence of the CA in the First place. Initial conditions here refers to the initial configuration of the Universal CA.

17. "Many other kinds of emergent creature live inside matter, including vibrational waves called phonons, electrical excitations called excitons in semiconductors, and

waves of charge called plasmons. These are called variously 'collective excitations' and 'quasiparticles'. From inside the material, these bizarre objects would seem as real as any other particle.

"But if quasiparticles are indistinguishable from real particles, could it be that things we think of as real-electrons and so on-are themselves quasiparticles, emerging out of some ubiquitous but undetectable cosmic stuff?" (Samuel, 2002).

18. This by no means suggests that the theory of evolution is wrong. It simply means that, like all theories, it is a reduction of what actually is the case - it results from the fact that scientists are part of the Universe and therefore do not have access to the complete picture. If by some miracle, and that is exactly what would be required, scientists had access to the complete picture then there would be no need for an evolutionary explanation as they would be privy to the exquisite determinism of the Universe.

19. Though I think it is interesting that a CA description of the Universe does distinguish between the 'internal' and the 'external', and co-supports seemingly completely opposing views.

20. Often such 'proof' is based as much upon faith and wishful thinking than on empirical evidence. Oreskes, et al. (1994) suggest that proof (or more accurately, verifiability) is no more than "forced empirical adequacy".

21. Both the real world context and our perception of the real world context will evolve.

22. Though we often learn to unconsciously accept, through reification, such sociological boundaries as natural boundaries.

CHAPTER 3

HOW CAN WE THINK COMPLEX?

Carlos Gershenson and Francis Heylighen

This chapter does not deal with specific tools and techniques for managing complex systems, but proposes some basic concepts that help us to think and speak about complexity. We review classical thinking and its intrinsic drawbacks when dealing with complexity. We then show how complexity forces us to build models with indeterminacy and unpredictability. However, we can still deal with the problems created in this way by being adaptive, and profiting from a complex system's capability for self-organization, and the distributed intelligence this may produce.

Managing Organizational Complexity: Philosophy, Theory, and Application
A Volume in: Managing the Complex, pages 47-61.
Copyright © 2005 by Information Age Publishing, Inc.
All rights of reproduction in any form reserved.
ISBN: 1-59311-319-6 (cloth), 1-59311-318-8 (paper)

Classical thinking

The majority of scientific models - as well as much of our intuitive understanding - implicitly rely on a 'classical' or Cartesian mode of thinking, which is expressed most explicitly in the classical or Newtonian mechanics that dominated the scientific worldview until the beginning of the 20th century. It is based on the following assumptions (Heylighen, 1990a, 1990b):

- *reductionism or analysis*: to fully understand a system you should decompose it into its constituent elements and their fundamental properties.

- *determinism*: every change can be represented as a trajectory of the system through (state) space, i.e., a linear sequence of states, following fixed laws of nature. These laws completely determine the trajectory towards the future (predictability) as well as towards the past (reversibility).

- *dualism*: the ultimate constituents of any system are particles, i.e., structureless pieces of matter (materialism). Since matter is already completely determined by mechanistic laws, leaving no freedom for intervention or interpretation, the only way we can include human agency in the theory is by introducing the independent category of mind

- *correspondence theory of knowledge*: through observation, an agent can in principle gather complete knowledge about any system, creating an internal representation whose components correspond to the components of the external system. This establishes a single, true, objective mapping from the realm of matter (the system) to the realm of mind (the representation).

- *rationality*: given such complete knowledge, in its interaction with the system, an agent will always choose the option that maximizes its utility function. Thus, the actions of mind become as determined or predictable as the movements of matter.

These different assumptions are summarized by the *principle of distinction conservation* (Heylighen, 1989, 1990a, 1990b): classical science begins by making as precise as possible distinctions between the different components, properties and states of the system under observation. These distinctions are assumed to be absolute and objective, i.e., the same for all observers. They follow the principles of Aristotelian logic: a phenomenon belongs either to category A, or to not A. It cannot be both, neither, in between, or 'it depends'. The evolution of the system conserves all these distinctions, as distinct initial states are necessarily mapped onto distinct subsequent states, and vice-versa (causality, see Heylighen, 1989). Knowledge is nothing more than another such distinction-conserving mapping from object to subject, while action is a mapping back from subject to object.

Of course, we know that these assumptions represent ideal cases that are never realized in practice. Yet, most educated people still tend to assume that a complete and deterministic theory is an ideal worth striving for, and that the scientific method will lead us inexorably to an ever closer approximation of such objective knowledge. The lessons from complexity research point in a different direction, however.

Complexity

What is complexity? Let us go back to the Latin root *complexus*, which means 'entwined' or 'embraced'. This can be interpreted in the following way: in order to have a complex you need: 1) two or more distinct parts, 2) that are joined in such a way that it is difficult to separate them. Here we find the basic duality between parts which are at the same time distinct and connected. Therefore, the analytical method alone won't allow us to understand a complex, as by taking apart the components it will destroy their connections.

This means that using classical methods the behavior of a complex system will be hard to describe, explaining the connotation of 'difficult' that the word 'complex' has later acquired. The components are mutually entangled, so that a change in one component will propagate through a tissue of interactions to other components, which in turn will affect even further components, including the one that initially started the process. This makes the global behavior of the system very hard to track in terms of its elements. Unlike the simple 'billiard-ball-like' systems studied by classical mechanics, complex systems are the rule rather than the exception. Typical examples are a living cell, a society, an economy, an ecosystem, the Internet, the weather, a brain, and a city. These all consist of numerous elements whose interactions produce a global behavior that cannot be reduced to the behavior of the separate component.

Complexity is itself a complex concept, as we cannot make a unambiguous distinction between simple and complex systems. Many measures of complexity have been proposed for different contexts, such as computational, social, economic, biological, etc. (Edmonds, 2000). However, there is no universal measure that would allow us to establish the degree of complexity of an arbitrary system. Yet, within an agreed frame of reference, we can sometimes compare two systems, noting that the one is more complex than the other, from a certain perspective. Thus, complexity at best determines a partial ordering, not a quantitative measure. Overall, we can say that the complexity of a system increases with the number of distinct components, the number of connections between them, the complexities of the components, and the complexities of the connections. This is a recursive definition that is general enough to be applied in different contexts. For example, everything else being equal, a firm will be more complex than another one if it has more divisions, if its divisions have more employees, if the divisions have more channels of interaction, and/or if its channel of interactions involve more person-to-person interactions.

While we do not really need an absolute measure of complexity, using such relative comparison may be useful to indicate when it becomes necessary to abandon our simple, classical assumptions and try to develop a more sophisticated model. Shifting from classical to 'complex' thinking brings both gains and losses. Let us start with the expectations we have to abandon, and then point out some of the novel insights we gain.

Indeterminacy

Relinquishing classical thinking means giving up the principle of distinction conservation. This implies, first, that we can no longer assume given, invariant distinctions: a distinction made by one observer in one context may no longer be meaningful - or even possible - for another observer or in another context.

This point was made most forcefully in quantum mechanics (Heylighen, 1990a, 1990b): in some circumstances, an electron appears like a particle, in others like a wave. Yet, according to classical thinking, particle and wave are mutually exclusive categories. In quantum mechanics, on the other hand, the 'particle' and 'wave' aspects are complementary: they are jointly necessary to characterize the electron, but they can never be seen together, since the observation set-up necessary to distinguish 'particle-like' properties is incompatible with the one for 'wave-like' properties. This was formulated by Heisenberg as the *principle of indeterminacy*: the more precisely we distinguish the particle-like properties, the more uncertain or indeterminate the wave-like properties become.

A more intuitive example of indeterminacy is the well-known ambiguous figure that sometimes looks like a rabbit, sometimes like a duck. While both 'gestalts' are equally recognizable in the drawing, our perception - like a quantum observation set-up - is incapable to see them simultaneously, and thus tends to switch back and forth between the two interpretations. Complementary properties, like the rabbit and duck gestalts, are distinct yet joined together. But while we see the one, we cannot see the other!

Because of the correspondence assumption, classical thinking tends to confuse what things are and how we see or know them to be. Thus, observers have engaged in controversies on 'what things are', while actually disagreeing on how to model or represent these phenomena. When we speak about a phenomenon it is hard to specify whether we refer to the representation or to the represented, because our language does not make such a distinction, using the verb 'to be' for both. To avoid such confusion we have proposed an ontological distinction between 'absolute being' and 'relative being' (Gershenson, 2002). The absolute being (abs-being) refers to what the thing actually is, independently of the observer (Kant's *Ding-an-sich*). The relative being (rel-being) refers to the properties of the thing as distinguished by an observer within a context. Since the observer is finite and cannot gather complete information, rel-beings are limited, whereas abs-beings have an unlimited number of features. Therefore, there exists an infinity of potential rel-beings for any abs-being.

We can illustrate this abstract notion by imagining a sphere which is black on one hemisphere and white on the other, as depicted in Fig. 1. Suppose we can observe the sphere only from one perspective. For some, the sphere will (rel)be white, for others it will (rel)be black, for others it will (rel)be half black and half white, and so on. How can we decide which color the sphere (abs) is? Taking an average does not suffice, since it could be the case that more than ninety percent of people see the sphere white, and we would conclude that it is mostly white, while it actually (abs)is half white and half black. The best we can do is to indicate the perspective (context) for which the sphere (rel)is of a particular color. With real systems, we will never reach their abs-being, because there are always more properties (dimensions) than we are aware of. This task would be like determining the color of an infinite-dimensional sphere when you can only see one two-dimensional projection at a time.

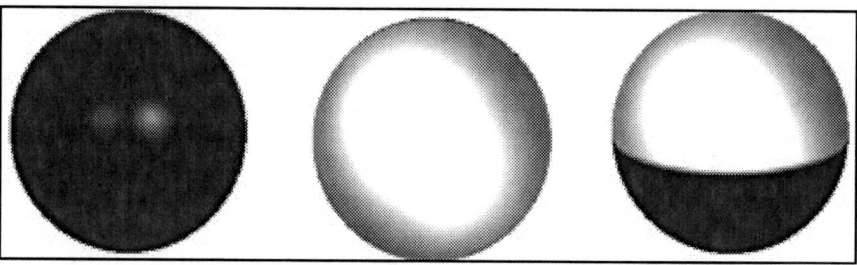

Figure 1
The same black-and-white sphere seen from three different angles

With simple systems such as the 3-dimensional sphere, the number of rel-beings is limited. However, complex systems have so many types of component and connection that observers can have rel-beings that are so different that it may appear impossible to recognize them as aspects of the same thing. For example, organizations have been described using metaphors such as an organism, a machine, a brain, a community, a market, and a political power game, and models such as a hierarchy, a network, and a linear input-output system. For a classically thinking executive, this constant shift in models and concomitant management styles is bewildering, as it seems that only one (or none) of these approaches can be correct. Yet, an organization has both mechanistic and organic aspects, is simultaneously a cooperative community and a competitive arena, a rule-bound system and an open, creative environment, a hierarchy and a network.

There is no 'best' model, as different rel-beings are appropriate for different contexts, and different purposes (Beer, 1966; Heylighen, 1990a, 1990b). With a classical way of thinking, we can spend all our efforts in trying to decide what is the system. Complex thinking, on the other hand, allows us to contemplate different representations at the same time (e.g., by proposing a metarepresentation - Heylighen, 1990a, 1990b), in order to have a less-incomplete understanding of the system. To tackle concrete problems, we can then choose the representation that is most appropriate for that specific context, being well aware that a different problem may require a radical shift in representation. For example, when tackling internal conflicts it may be useful to see a firm as a network of interdependent communities; when optimizing production, as a matter- and information-processing mechanism.

Nonlinearity and chaos

According to classical thinking, distinctions are invariant not only over observers, but over time. The principle of causality can be formulated as 'equal causes have equal effects', or equivalently as 'effects co-vary with their causes'. This is nothing more than a statement that the distinctions between causes or initial states must necessarily carry through to their effects, and vice-versa. While we may hold this principle to be true at the level of absolute being, i.e., the complete things-in-themselves (microscopic causality, Heylighen, 1989), it is in general not true at the level of relative being, i.e., the coarse, finite distinctions made by an observer. Thus, microscopic causality (i.e., determinism) does not in itself produce macroscopic causality (i.e., predictability). This can be inferred most directly from the existence of (deterministic) chaos, which follows from the nonlinearity that characterizes complex systems.

A system is linear if effects (outputs) are proportional to their causes (inputs). For example, if you put twice as much ore in your furnaces, the plant will produce roughly twice as much steel. This can be understood through the principle of conservation of energy and matter: the amount that comes out depends directly on the amount you put in (though there will of course be a few losses here and there). But what happens if (part of) the output is redirected and added back to the input? In principle, the next output will be larger, since it uses both the input and the previous output, and therefore no longer proportional to the input alone. The next output will be even larger, as it uses not only the new input but the two previous outputs. For example, a firm can reinvest some of the money it gets for its products to increase production. Increasing production brings in more money and thus further increases production, leading to an exponential growth in output.

Thus, nonlinearity can be understood as the effect of a causal loop, where effects or outputs are fed back into the causes or inputs of the process. Complex systems are characterized by networks of such causal loops. In a complex, the interdependencies are such that a component A will affect a component B, but B will in general also affect A, directly or indirectly. A single feedback loop can be positive or negative. A positive feedback will amplify any variation in A, making it grow exponentially. The result is that the tiniest, microscopic difference between initial states can grow into macroscopically observable distinction.

This is called *sensitive dependence on initial conditions*, and is a defining feature of *chaos*. Because the initial difference is too small to perceive, the principle of causality cannot help us in predicting the final outcome. A well-known example of such a difficult-to-predict, chaotic system is the weather, as the fluttering of a butterfly in Tokyo can grow into a hurricane devastating New York. The observation that small causes can have large effects is obvious in social systems as well. For example, during a tense negotiation the tiniest hint of a smile on the lips of a CEO may create the impression with the other party that this guy is not to be trusted, thus leading them to harden their stance, and finally reject a billion-dollar merger operation. Such a system in a sense creates distinctions, as an indistinguishably small difference in initial state leads to macroscopically distinct outcomes.

The inverse of the amplifying effect of positive feedback is the dampening effect of negative feedback. Here any variation is counteracted or resisted, bringing the system back to its equilibrium state. As a result large causes (variations) may have little or no effect. For example, an entrenched culture in an organization can be very difficult to change, as new measures are actively or passively resisted, ignored or deflected. Such a system destroys distinctions, as distinct causes lead to the same outcome.

Complex systems will typically exhibit a tangle of interconnected positive and negative feedback loops, where the effects of any change in a component cascade through an increasing number of connected components, in part feeding back, positively and/or negatively, into the initial component. If there is a variable time delay between these effects, it becomes in principle impossible to make predictions, because we do not know who will affect who first and thus whether an effect will be dampened before it has had the chance to get amplified or not (cf. Gershenson, et al., 2003). An example can be found in the stock exchange where stocks are bought and sold depending on their price, while the price is determined by how much is bought and sold. This intrinsic feedback loop has both negative and positive aspects. The law of supply and demand implies a negative feedback, since an increase in price normally reduces the demand, and this - after a variable delay - will reduce the price again. However, the parallel mechanism of speculation entails a positive feedback, as an increasing price makes buyers anticipate an even higher price in the future, thus enticing them to buy more of the stock now. The interaction between both nonlinear effects produces the chaotic movement of stock prices that we know so well.

In the simpler situation where the delays are known (or can be neglected), it is sometimes possible to get at least a qualitative estimate of what can happen by identifying the signs (positive or negative) and the strengths of the different feedback loops in the network of influences. This method, which is often used to build computer simulations, is developed in the discipline of system dynamics (Sterman, 2000).

Adapting to complexity

Given the intrinsic unpredictability of complex systems, how can we design, build or generally deal with them? First we have to accept that we will never be able to control or predict their behavior completely. It is only natural that there will be surprises, errors and problems, as there have always been. However, we can always try to cope with unexpected events by adapting our actions to the new situation; if necessary, reconfiguring the system without destroying it. Different principles and methods for adaptation have been investigated in cybernetics (Heylighen & Joslyn, 2001), artificial intelligence (Russell & Norvig, 1995), neural networks (Rumelhart, *et al.*, 1986), multi-agent systems (Wooldridge, 2002; Schweitzer, 2003), genetic algorithms (Mitchell, 1998), chaos control (Chen & Yu, 2003), and many other disciplines. Research is going on still, trying to design and build systems that are even more adaptive.

To adapt to any change, whether anticipated or not, it suffices to compensate for any perceived deviation of the actual situation from the desired course. This is the basic method of feedback control: correcting errors after the fact (Heylighen & Joslyn, 2001). If the reaction comes quickly enough, before the problem has had the chance to grow, feedback-based regulation can be extremely effective. The core innovation that engendered the field of cybernetics was the observation that it does not matter how complicated the system of factors and interactions that affect a variable that we wish to keep under control: as long as we have some means of counteracting the deviation, the underlying causality is irrelevant (Kelly, 1994). For example, it does not matter which complicated combination of social, political or technological changes causes an economy to overheat: in general, the central bank can regulate the rate of growth simply by increasing its interest rates.

Feedback control, however, still requires that we have a sufficiently broad repertoire of counteractions at our disposal (requisite variety), and that we know which action to execute in which circumstances (requisite knowledge) (Heylighen & Joslyn, 2001). The cybernetic *law of requisite variety* notes that the greater the variety of perturbations that the system may be subjected to, the larger the variety of actions it needs to remain in control. Since the number of perturbations that a present-day organization may encounter is in practice unlimited, the recommendation is for that organization to maximize the diversity of its possibilities for intervention, as you can never predict what will be necessary when.

However, in order to react quickly and appropriately, it is good to have at least an expectation of what may happen and which reaction would be appropriate. Expectations are subjective probabilities that we learn from experience: the more often circumstance B appears after circumstance A, or the more successful action B is in solving problem A, the stronger the association A $\longrightarrow$ B becomes. The next time we encounter A (or a circumstance similar to A), we will be prepared, and more likely to react adequately. The simple ordering of options according to the probability that they would be relevant immensely decreases the complexity of decision-making (Heylighen, 1994). Thus, we do not need deterministic models or predictions: having realistic default expectations with the possibility to correct for errors or exceptions after they have appeared works pretty well in practice. Moreover, we can tackle as yet unencountered combinations of circumstances by aggregating the recommendations made by different learned associations in proportion to their strength, using the method of spreading activation (Heylighen, 1999).

That is how our brains deal everyday with other complex systems: colleagues, children, pets, computers, etc. However, much to our dismay and frustration, most designed systems still lack this characteristic. For example, computers programmed according to rigid rules cannot recover on their own when something goes wrong (Heylighen & Gershenson, 2003). Organizations rarely have procedures to learn from experience, and those that do usually try to store acquired knowledge as formal data rather than as a constantly evolving network of associations between circumstances and actions. The only working paradigm to do this outside the brain are neural network simulations, but these are usually limited to very specialized applications such as handwriting recognition, rather than broad issues of management and procedure. They are also extremely difficult to analyze. Yet, our research suggests that these 'brain-like' mechanisms are easily extended to the organizational level, thus supporting an adaptive, collective intelligence (Heylighen, 1999).

Self-organization

While adaptation tells us how we may cope with complexity, we can also have the complex systems working for us. Indeed, any dynamical system is in principle capable of self-organization (Ashby, 1962; Heylighen, 2002; Heylighen & Gershenson, 2003), and the more complex the system, the more 'interesting' the results. We can define organization as structure with function. Our definition of complexity already implies structure, which we see as the combination of distinction (differentiation) and connection (integration). Function means that the structure is developed to achieve some goal or purpose. The basic mechanism of self-organization is that sooner or later dynamic systems evolve to an attractor of the dynamics, i.e.,. a stable configuration of states, which the system can enter but not leave. We can say that the components in this configuration have mutually adapted (Ashby, 1962), limiting their interactions to those that allow this collective configuration to endure.

Thus, the 'function' of this configuration is to survive, and the further behavior of the system can be understood as supporting that function. For example, a firm will sooner or later evolve its own culture consisting of a range of unwritten rules and preferences that constrain the employees' behavior. While 'officially' the purpose of any rules may be to maximize the productivity of the firm, in reality the function of this culture will be basically to maintain itself. While self-maintenance implies a minimal level of productivity so that the firm does not go bankrupt, attempts to further increase the workload may be resisted because they endanger the social culture itself.

The advantage of self-organizing systems is that they search by themselves for solutions, without the need for a manager or engineer intervening. Moreover, they are intrinsically open and flexible: when unexpected changes come about, they can adapt seamlessly, without the need for centralized control. The organization is distributed over all the participating components and their connections. This means that the system is robust: it can survive destruction of part of its components without too much damage, as the other components make up for the lost functions.

Self-organization contradicts the classical way of thinking in several respects. To start with, self-organization by definition cannot be reduced to independent components, as it emerges wholly out of their interactions. Then, self-organization not only allows, but thrives on, randomness or indeterminacy: the more perturbations or fluctuations the system undergoes, the quicker it will reach an attractor, and the more stable the eventual attractor will be. This is the *order from noise principle* (von Foerster, 1960; Heylighen, 2002). Of course, too strong perturbations will destroy any organization, and therefore natural systems will typically evolve to the *edge of chaos* where there is sufficient variation to make the system creative and flexible, but not enough to make it wholly chaotic. Self-organization is a nonlinear process, since tiny perturbations can decide which out of two completely different attractors the system enters, while once the attractor is reached, major perturbations will have little or no effect. Most fundamentally, self-organization does not conserve distinctions: it not only destroys the distinction between two initial states that end up in the same attractor, while creating a distinction when the same initial state can end up in two different attractors; it moreover creates and destroys distinctions at a higher level by integrating components in a new coherent, organizationally 'closed' system (Heylighen, 1991b, 2002) that has novel properties.

This is the phenomenon of emergence. Emergent properties characterize a system that cannot be reduced to the sum of its parts. For example, the mass of a gas is the sum of the masses of all the molecules in that gas. But the temperature and pressure of the gas simply do not exist for a single molecule, as they measure the intensity of interactions between the molecules. Gold is yellow, shiny, and malleable, but we cannot deduce these properties by observing the atoms of gold (Anderson, 1972). We say that a cell is alive, but it is made of non-living elements.

We cannot fit emergence within a classical framework since it presupposes that things can only be one thing at a time. If a cell is a collection of molecules and molecules are not alive, then how could a cell be alive? We cannot speak about different levels of abstraction, since classical thinking assumes that there is only one 'true' representation. But in complex thinking we can characterize the same abs-being at different levels using different rel-beings. Then the mystery disappears, and we can speak comfortably about emergence. We can understand it as a process that requires us to change our model of a system (Rosen, 1985; Heylighen, 1991b) in order to better understand and predict the system's behavior (Shalizi, 2001).

Distributed intelligence

Self-organization even deals a blow to the dualism of classical thinking, as it blurs the distinction between matter and mind. Organization clearly cannot be reduced to the matter of its elements, as the same organization can be implemented in different material substrates (e.g., brains and computers), whereas an isolated particle of matter lacks any organization. But is organization a form of mind?

Our definition as structure with function does include the apparently 'mental' property of goal-directedness. However, the fundamental insight of cybernetics is that goal-directedness can be understood as a type of negative feedback loop which can be implemented just as easily in mechanical systems, such as a thermostat or an automatic pilot, and in living and cognitive systems, such as the brain. What allows us to model all of these in a similar way is the concept of information, which has been defined by Bateson (1972) as 'the difference that makes a difference'. Whether this difference is carried by material objects, spoken language or electrical impulses in the brain is irrelevant: what counts is in how far it helps the system to understand its actual situation and take appropriate action so as to reach its goal - in spite of constantly changing circumstances. Information is what reduces the uncertainty as to the next thing that is going to happen or next action to take.

Self-organization can be seen as a spontaneous coordination of the interactions between the components of the system, so as to maximize their synergy. This requires the propagation and processing of information, as different components perceive different aspects of the situation, while their shared goal requires this information to be integrated. The resulting process is characterized by distributed cognition (Hutchins, 1995): different components participate in different ways to the overall gathering and processing of information, thus collectively solving the problems posed by any perceived deviation between the present situation and the desired situation. For example, the navigation of a large ship, as investigated in detail by Hutchins (1995), requires the activity of several people in different roles, coordinated by means of formal and informal procedures, instruments, maps, ship navigation manuals and a variety of communication channels.

Some of these 'distributed' components are intelligent, cognitive agents, such as human beings, but others are mere physical supports, such as notebooks, flip charts, or telephones, that store and transmit information between the agents. From the cybernetic perspective, there is no strict boundary between the 'material' and the 'mental' components: the information stored in my notebook is as much a part of my memory as is the information stored in my brain, and my email connection is as much part of my communication equipment as are the nerves that control my speech. What counts is in how far the information carried by each medium is under control, i.e., can be registered and transmitted as easily and reliably as desired. Thus, for remembering appointments I may trust my notebook more than my brain, and for explaining a complex task to a colleague I may rely more on an email message than on a spoken explanation. Clark (1997) has called this perspective *the philosophy of the extended mind*.

In the context of complexity, what counts is not whether we classify an information medium as 'mind' or as 'matter', but how we can ensure that this channel will pass on the right information at the right time. Classical thinking is completely unhelpful in this respect, since it assumes that in order to make rational decisions we simply need all information about the system under consideration, since otherwise there is indeterminacy. The complexity perspective notes not only that indeterminacy is unavoidable, but that having too much information is as bad as having too little. Indeed, we only need the difference that makes a difference with respect to our goals: what happens in the rest of the world is irrelevant, and trying to include it in our models will only burden the very limited capacities we have for information processing. In complex thinking, knowledge is a subjective model constructed to make problem-solving as easy as possible, not an objective reflection of outside reality, and decision-making aims for the solution that is good enough while using any opportunity to improve it later, rather than for the optimal one that classical thinking presupposes. The crux therefore is to be selective, and distill the essential difference from the infinite supply of data.

Happily, self-organization again comes to the rescue. An organization formed by a collection of agents connected by a variety of communication channels will spontaneously improve itself by learning from experience: communications that are effective will be used more often, while those that are ineffective will be increasingly ignored. In that way, information will be propagated ever more efficiently, filtering out the noise, while making sure the right messages reach the right places. This learning happens simultaneously on the two levels: 'mentally' - when a person experiences that another person reacts either appropriately or inappropriately to a particular type of message, and thus becomes more discriminative about whom to communicate with about what, and 'materially' - when more useful supports, such as a handbook or Internet connection, are made more accessible, while inefficient ones, such as phone directory or fax machine, are relegated to the dust heap. However, this distributed learning is still pretty slow and unreliable in typical organizations. Applying the principles of self-organization and cybernetics (Heylighen, 1992, 2002; Heylighen & Joslyn, 2001) may help us to design a much more effective organization.

Most concretely, we can build this self-organized learning into the very media rather than have it be imposed on them by the users. For example, when employees are bombarded every day with email messages from colleagues and departments, it would be helpful to prioritize these automatically, so that the most important messages - such as a request for an urgent meeting with the CEO - are attended to immediately, while the less important ones - such as the latest offerings at the company canteen - are classified at the bottom of the heap, where they can be attended to if there is time, but otherwise safely ignored. This ordering by priority is something that the communication system could learn from experience, by observing which kinds of messages tend to be attended to most actively by which employees. A slightly more sophisticated version of the system would also learn the typical workflow and division of labor in an organization, making sure that the right task is sent to the right person at the right moment. Our research group is presently investigating through computer simulation how a group of agents using various communication media can self-organize so as to achieve such coordination (Crowston, 2003) between their activities.

Conclusions

We still do not understand complexity very well, and there is much to be done and explored in this direction. Our culture now is immersed and surrounded by complexity. But facing this complexity forces us to change our ways of thinking (Heylighen, 1991a). We argued how classical thinking, with its emphasis on analysis, predictability and objectivity, breaks down when confronted with complex systems. The core problem is that classical philosophy assumes invariant, conserved distinctions, whereas complex systems are entangled in such a way that their components and properties can no longer be separated or distinguished absolutely. Moreover, because of the inherent nonlinearity or 'loopiness' of the system, they tend to change in a chaotic, unpredictable way. At best, we can make context-dependent distinctions and use them to build a partial model, useful for a particular purpose. But such model will never be able to capture all essential properties of the system, and a novel context will in general require a different model.

This chapter did not so much propose specific tools and techniques for managing complex systems, as this would require a much more extensive discussion. Moreover, introductions to and reviews of existing concepts are available elsewhere (e.g., Kelly, 1994; Heylighen, 1997, 2002; Battram, 2002). Instead we have brought forth a number of ideas that allow us to better understand and speak about complex systems. First, we must be aware that complex systems are never completely predictable, even if we know how they function. We should be prepared to deal with the unexpected events that complexity most certainly will bring forth, by as quickly as possible correcting any deviation from our planned course of action. To achieve this kind of error-based regulation we should not try to predict or determine the behavior of a complex system, but to expect the most probable possibilities. This will make it easier for us to adapt when things go off-course. Because then we are ready to expect the unexpected.

Yet, complexity does not just make our life harder. By better understanding the mechanism of self-organization, we may make a complex system work for us. This we could do by preparing the conditions so that self-organization is stimulated in a way that fits with our desires. We may even make use of, and stimulate, the inherent intelligence that characterizes a self-organizing system. By stimulating people as well as media to interact and learn from their interactions we may foster a distributed form of information-processing that coordinates the different activities in the system.

References

Anderson, P. W. (1972). "More is different," *Science*, 177 (4047):393-396.

Ashby, W. R. (1962). "Principles of the Self-organizing System," in von Foerster, H. and G. W. Zopf, Jr. (Eds.), *Principles of Self-organization*, Pergamon Press, pp. 255-278.

Bateson, G. (1972). *Steps to an Ecology of Mind*, New York: Ballantine.

Battram A. (2002). *Navigating Complexity: The Essential Guide to Complexity Theory in Business and Management*, Spiro Press.

Beer, S. (1966). *Decision and Control: The Meaning of Operational Research and Management Cybernetics*, John Wiley & Sons, Inc.

Chen, G., and Yu, X. H. (eds.). (2003). *Chaos Control: Theory and Applications: Lecture Notes in Control and Information Sciences*, 292. Springer Verlag.

Clark, A. (1997). *Being There: putting brain, body, and world together again*, Cambridge, MA: MIT Press.

Crowston, K. (2003). "A taxonomy of organizational dependencies and coordination mechanisms," in T. W. Malone, K. Crowston G. and Herman (eds.), *Tools for Organizing Business Knowledge: The MIT Process Handbook*. Cambridge, MA: MIT Press.

Edmonds, B. (2000). "Complexity and Scientific Modelling," *Foundations of Science*, 5: 379-390.

Gershenson, C. (2002). "Complex Philosophy," *Proceedings of the 1st Biennial Seminar on Philosophical, Methodological and Epistemological Implications of Complexity Theory*, La Habana, Cuba. Also in *InterJournal of Complex Systems*, 544. http://arXiv.org/abs/nlin.AO/0109001.

Gershenson, C., Broekaert, J. and Aerts, D. (2003). "Contextual Random Boolean Networks," in Banzhaf, W, T. Christaller, P. Dittrich, J. T. Kim, and J. Ziegler, *Advances in Artificial Life*, 7th European Conference, ECAL 2003, Dortmund, Germany, pp. 615-624. LNAI 2801. Springer. http://arxiv.org/abs/nlin.AO/0303021

Heylighen, F. (1989). "Causality as Distinction Conservation: a theory of predictability, reversibility and time order," *Cybernetics and Systems*, 20: 361-384.

Heylighen, F. (1990a). "Classical and Non-classical Representations in Physics I", *Cybernetics and Systems*, 21: 423-444.

Heylighen, F. (1990b). *Representation and Change. A Metarepresentational Framework for the Foundations of Physical and Cognitive Science*, Gent: Communication and Cognition.

Heylighen, F. (1991a). "Coping with Complexity. Concepts and principles for a support system," *Systemica*, 8(1): 39-55.

Heylighen, F. (1991b). "Modelling Emergence," *World Futures: the Journal of General Evolution*, 31: 89-104.

Heylighen, F. (1992). "Principles of Systems and Cybernetics: an evolutionary perspective," in *Cybernetics and Systems '92*, R. Trappl (ed.), World Science: Singapore, pp. 3-10.

Heylighen, F. (1994). "Fitness as Default: the evolutionary basis for cognitive complexity reduction," in *Cybernetics and Systems '94*, R. Trappl (ed.), World Science: Singapore, pp .1595-1602.

Heylighen, F. (1997). "Publications on Complex, Evolving Systems: A Citation-Based Survey," *Complexity*, 2 (5): 31-36.

Heylighen, F. (1999). "Collective Intelligence and its Implementation on the Web: Algorithms to Develop a Collective Mental Map," *Computational and Mathematical Theory of Organizations*, 5(3): 253-280.

Heylighen, F. (2002). "The Science of Self-organization and Adaptivity," in L. D. Kiel, (ed.) *Knowledge Management, Organizational Intelligence and Learning, and Complexity*, in The Encyclopedia of Life Support Systems (EOLSS), Eolss Publishers: Oxford, http://www.eolss.net

Heylighen, F. and Gershenson, C. (2003). "The Meaning of Self-organization in Computing," *IEEE Intelligent Systems*, 18(4): 72-75.

Heylighen, F. and Joslyn, C. (2001). "Cybernetics and Second Order Cybernetics," in R.A. Meyers (ed.), *Encyclopedia of Physical Science and Technology* (3rd ed.), Vol. 4, (Academic Press, New York), pp. 155-170.

Hutchins, E (1995). *Cognition in the Wild*, MIT Press.

Kelly, K. (1994). *Out of Control*, New York: Addison-Wesley.

Mitchell, M. (1998). *An Introduction to Genetic Algorithms*, MIT Press.

Rosen, R. (1985). *Anticipatory Systems*, Pergamon.

Rumelhart, D. E., McClelland, J. L. and the PDP Research Group (eds.) (1986). *Parallel Distributed Processing: Explorations in the Microstructure of Cognition*, MIT Press.

Russell, S. J. and Norvig, P. (1995). *Artificial Intelligence: A Modern Approach*, Prentice Hall.

Schweitzer, F. (2003). *Brownian Agents and Active Particles, Collective Dynamics in the Natural and Social Sciences*, Springer.

Shalizi, C. R. (2001). *Causal Architecture, Complexity and Self-Organization in Time Series and Cellular Automata*, Doctoral Dissertation, University of Wisconsin at Madison.

Sterman, J. D. (2000). *Business Dynamics: Systems Thinking and Modeling for a Complex World*, McGraw-Hill/Irwin.

von Foerster, H. (1960). "On Self-Organizing Systems and Their Environments," in *Self-Organizing Systems*, M.C. Yovits and S. Cameron (eds.), Pergamon Press: London, pp. 30-50.

Wooldridge, M. (2002). *An Introduction to MultiAgent Systems*, John Wiley and Sons.

CHAPTER 4

EMERGENCE, CREATIVE PROCESS, AND SELF-TRANSCENDING CONSTRUCTIONS

Jeffrey Goldstein

I am proposing a new formalism to cover the varied processes involved in emergence in complex systems: self-transcending constructions (STC) offered as a replacement for the idea of self-organization. I show how an overcommitment to the latter has served to mislead rather than enlighten what actually goes on in emergence. Self-transcending constructions are many and varied, but the prototype I am using is derived from the anti-diagonal construction that was critical to the set theoretical investigations of Georg Cantor as well as the limitative theorems in mathematical logic achieved by Gödel and Turing. In fact, the anti-diagonal construction is implicated in several important approaches in the study of emergence, namely, Ian Stewart's and Jack Cohen's so-called Existence Theorem for Emergence, Charles Bennet's construct of logical depth, John Holland's call for a new mathematics for emergence, Walter Fontana's and Leo Buss's work on artificial life by way of proof theory and others. Self-transcending constructions will be interpreted along the lines of the special "logic" of creative processes. This logic follows a scheme of following and negating. Several examples of this creative logic are offered. Finally, a few suggestions are presented on the application of the idea of self-transcending constructions for workplace innovation.

Managing Organizational Complexity: Philosophy, Theory, and Application
A Volume in: Managing the Complex, pages 63–78.
Copyright © 2005 by Information Age Publishing, Inc.
All rights of reproduction in any form reserved.
ISBN: 1-59311-319-6 (cloth), 1-59311-318-8 (paper)

The construction of emergent order

In the diverse fields making-up the study of complex systems, one of the most exciting areas of research has to do with the emergence of new patterns and structures with new properties, phenomena identified according to the following characteristics (Goldstein, 1999): radically novel, i.e., neither predictable nor deducible from lower level components or antecedent conditions; dynamical, i.e., arising over time; coherent, i.e., possessing relatively enduring wholeness; and ostensive, i.e., exhibiting themselves only as the system evolves. These same characteristics, though, have rendered the concept of emergence enigmatic from within classical perspectives on causal and deterministic processes, a dilemma exacerbated by the general lack in the sciences of not only suitable constructs for investigating structure and pattern but for processes capable of generating new structures and patterns.

One construct has achieved pre-eminence in accounts of emergence, namely, *self-organization*, an idea connoting inner-driven and spontaneous processes. The 'self' of 'self-organization' alludes to such descriptors as 'innate,' 'inherent,' 'automatic,' 'unplanned,' and 'natural.' Perhaps nowhere have these self- undertones of self-organization been more enthusiastically received as an apotheosis of scientific and philosophical import than by Kauffman's (1993) notion of 'order for free', a phrase specifically crafted for the purpose of drawing biological and metaphysical implications far beyond the electronic networks where he first observed 'self-organizing' emergence. To be sure, there's no doubt that the inner-directed connotations of 'self-organization' have supplied a much needed corrective to the hoary, but still lingering, presumption that the onset of novel order in a system requires an imposition from outside. Hence, an important theoretical advantage stemming from appeals to self-organization has been a call of attention to whatever internal dynamics may be involved in the emergence of new order instead of the stubborn insistence it must have a source external to the system.

In my opinion, however, the setting-up of this close alliance between emergence and self-organization has led to a misunderstanding of how emergent order actually comes about in each instance when it does. I argue instead that a careful inspection of research into emergence reveals that the emergence of new order is more appropriately conceived as *constructed* and not self-organized *per se*, albeit according to a special type of construction which I have termed *self-transcending construction* (STC) (see Goldstein, 2001, 2002, 2003). It needs to be pointed out that the way 'construction' is being used here does not entail there being a 'constructor' as such (see below for more on the specific sense of 'construction' I will be using). Understanding emergent order as constructed in this special sense results in several very different implications than those currently emanating from the association of emergence with self-organization.

In this chapter I hope to demonstrate why approaching emergence from a constructional, and not self-organizational, point of view is more in line with the facts of emergence. Next, I will lay-out the unique 'logic' of the self-transcending constructional activity involved with emergence, a 'logic' closely related to the way creative processes in general are able to generate radically original patterns and properties. Then, I will offer a few suggestions on how this new approach to emergence can be appropriated in conceiving and practicing organizational innovation.

Beyond self-organization and 'order for free'

To support my contention that emergence in complex systems is more accurately thought of as constructed rather than self-organized, I offer two representatives from contemporary research into the emergence of new order: first, the coherent order observed in putatively self-organizing physical systems; and, second, the order emerging in that species of artificial life to which Kauffman (1993) has devoted his attention. The first instance of emergent order to be examined concerns the laser, a phenomenon of coherent order which the Synergetics School founded by the German physicist Hermann Haken has put forward as an exemplar, emblem even, of self-organization. A closer scrutiny, however, of how lasers are actually constructed in the laboratory reveals that the coherence characterizing laser light is expedited only through the most strenuous of non-internal and non-spontaneous laboratory constraints including, among others (see Haken, 1981; Nicolis & Prigogine, 1989; and, Strogatz, 2003):

- Because atoms generate light only when they fall to their lowest energy or ground state, laser light requires a large investment of energy from outside the system in order to keep lifting them up, or as Strogatz (2003: 12) puts it, "[an]...injection of energy inverts the population, in the sense that it hoists a large fraction of the atoms up to a higher energy level than their preferred spot in the ground";

- In order to intensify and channel the light beams so as to make them coherent, a 'resonant cavity' must be constructed, e.g., a long glass tube filled by an appropriate gas or a solid such as a ruby rod;

- In order to further focus the light rays in the laser, mirrors are constructed at both ends of the resonant cavity, with one mirror being slightly less than 100 % reflective so that light can escape at this end.

The extent of these constraining factors (and this is only a partial list) makes it puzzling to me why laser light was ever thought in the first place as self-organized as such, rather than constructed through stringent laboratory-induced constraints. Here, it might be argued that lasers are simply not a good example of self-organization precisely because of the many constraining operations required to bring them about. Yet, similar utilizations of numerous constraints and other external shaping factors can be found throughout the literature on what are spoken of as self-organizing systems. To point to just two salient examples: Haken (1981) has achieved notoriety for describing the coherent order of self-organizing systems as an 'enslavement' of system variables to an order parameter driving the system; and, Prigogine (Lissack, 2000) once qualified what he meant by the 'self-' of 'self-organization' through the caveat of 'constrained situated dependentness' - a far cry indeed from the usual associations of self-organization!

To be sure, the idea of constraints as such need not entail a strictly external imposition of order and thus preclude the possibility that self-organizing processes are indeed at work in the systems studied by Haken and Prigogine. In this context, Juarrero (1999) has pointed out that one meaning of a constraint has to do with the relational properties parts acquire by virtue of being unified into coherent wholes; that is, an orderly context that embeds and thereby constrains the components of a system. She gives the example of how the tibia's connection to the knee constrains the movement possibilities of the lower leg. Moreover, constraints need not only serve to reduce a system's degrees of freedom since, as Juarrero suggests, constraints can also open up a system to new possibilities by moving it away from pure chance, e.g., the fixed alphabet of English simultaneously constrains and opens up possibilities for what words can be meaningfully constructed.

Consequently, the issue stemming from over-emphasizing self-organization as the key to emergence is not the presence of constraints as such, but rather the driving of a conceptual wedge between spontaneous, inner-directed processes and those otherwise constructional in nature. In effect, this conceptual wedge has served to associate self-organization with what is natural while construction has become, by contrast, allied with what is unnatural, i.e., artifice, design, intentionality, purpose, and similar ideas. In point of fact, though, construction can be as natural as self-organization is supposed to be, a fact attested by such natural phenomena, to mention just a few, as bone growth, turtle shells, beaver dams, bird nests, hurricanes, ant hills, termite cones, protein assemblies, and so forth. Indeed, in evolutionary biological literature more and more references can be found to naturally occurring constructional activities.

Furthermore, the notion of construction was tied directly to emergence right at the beginning of contemporary neo-emergentist research when the Nobel Prize winning solid state physicist Philip Anderson (1972) offered his *Constructionist Hypothesis* as a response to the arch reductionism rampant among particle physicists. This hypothesis proposed that although it might be possible to reduce nature to certain simple, fundamental laws, this did not then entail a similar ability for re-constructing the universe from these simple laws since each new level of complexity involved the emergence of entirely new properties and laws not appearing at the lower levels. Each new level of complexity accordingly can be said to exhibit the construction of new structures with new properties that transcend lower level constructional characteristics and dynamics. Moreover, the construction of each new level does not necessarily imply a intentional designer or constructor behind the constructional activities, since construction as such can arise in countless ways as lower level parts are constrained by each other and their environments and interact in relation to each other to generate even more constructional constraints.

The second example I offer to support my point about the limited applicability of self-organization for understanding emergence concerns Kauffman's above mentioned 'order for free,' his appellation for the patterns emerging in his electronic Boolean networks. Kauffman coined this phrase to indicate that the emergent order exhibited in his networks rules had to arise in a self-organizing fashion from their inner dynamics since the rules governing the operation of the networks were assigned randomly. That is, it was the random nature of this assignation of rules that guaranteed that the resulting order was the outcome of self-organization, since randomness entailed there was no pre-set design as one would find, for example, in an intentional construction.

However, as Kauffman himself has admitted, "...if the network has more than $K = 2$ inputs per light bulb, then certain *biases* in the Boolean rules, captured by the P parameter, can be adjusted to ensure order" (p. 103, my emphases). 'Biases' here refer to just those 'canalyzing' rules, i.e., the 'or' and the 'and' rules, which serve to generate and propagate redundant order through the networks, in other words, the operation of constraining factors in the sense described above. It is important to emphasize that it was only the biased rules which channeled the electric current to generate redundant order. To be sure, the identification of this bias as a bias had to wait until afterwards because the rules were assigned randomly. The important point to note, however, is that whether the biases were known beforehand or only afterwards, the emergent order only ensued when the biased rules were operative. This means it was the built-in bias of the rules that constructed the ensuing order, not some 'free', supposedly spontaneous self-organizing activity of the network.

An analogy can push my point home. Consider an unexpectedly long run of sevens during initial 'come-out' dice rolls in the game of craps. A pit boss in a casino who observed such a redundant (and hence orderly) pattern would not surmise it was the result of some sort of mysterious 'order for free' or a spontaneous, self-organizing phenomenon. Instead, the redundancy had to be due to loaded dice, even though ahead of the event the pit boss didn't know the dice were so biased. To load dice means to construct a bias in them towards exhibiting specific orderly patterns when tossed. Such a construction might involve building a die with different weights on each side. Such a constructed difference in weights would bias a roll of loaded dice. Similarly, in Kauffman's networks, the order which emerged was constructed to emerge, even though Kauffman might not have known until afterwards which specific biases in the rules were instrumental in constructing the propagating order. The emergence of order was not due to what a self-organizational picture would have it. Kauffman's 'order for free' was not actually 'free' but came with the high cost of having been constructed to be so ordered by the built-in constraint of a biased Boolean rule. To be sure, the random assignation of such biased constraints would mean that each time the network was run, new patterns of emergent order would ensue at different times and show different patterns. This corresponds to how in the highly constrained constructed emergent order of

Bénard cells, the exact directionality of each hexagonal convection cell cannot be predicted (see Nicolis & Prigogine, 1989).

Constructing emergent order

In being truer to the facts of what actually happens in the case of emergence, a constructional perspective comes with the benefit of calling attention to all of the varied resources for the emergence of new order, previously occluded by conceiving emergence purely in terms of self-organization. Since emergent order does not just emerge spontaneously 'for free' but comes from somewhere and by means of constructional operations, explanatory attention can now be directed at these sources of order and how seminal order is transmuted during processes of emergence. An analogy is the construction of a dam by a beaver where the sources of the construction may include the topography of the creek bed and bank, the available sticks, twigs, and leaves, the beaver's ability to manipulate the former, and so forth. Another example is how the internal organization of a cell is constructed out of a complex interaction of self-regulatory feedback loops, protein folding, multimolecular modularization, and other spatial and temporal constraining operations in tandem with genetic information (see Moss, 2003). It is also critical to note that construction in this sense doesn't necessarily entail an external constructor, but rather can arise out of the interaction of elements which are already ordered to some nascent extent. Self-organization as such may still play an important role but it is no longer over-emphasized as the key to emergence.

Conceiving emergent phenomena as constructed implies the presence of requisite constructional resources and constructional 'costs' including such factors as (see Goldstein, 2004):

- Already present, nascent order as well as ordering generating operations, e.g., the ordering action of those canalyzing Boolean rules which establish and then propagate order in Kauffman networks;
- Ordering constraints, e.g., the stringent laboratory conditions and manipulations discerned in the production of lasers recounted above;
- 'Containers', e.g., in Bénard convection, the actual physical container of the liquid plays a critical role in shaping the emerging cells - the distance separating two neighboring currents is on the order of the vertical height of the container (Berge, *et.al.*,1984) and instabilities in the thermal boundaries of liquid systems, similar to the Bénard system, lead to more complicated kinds of convection (Weiss, 1987);
- Amplification and recombination strategies which serve to expand and complexify the nascent order, e.g., the presence of strong nonlinearities, the incorporation of random events, or recombination processes along the line of Holland's (1994) genetic operators.

Furthermore, if emergence is to amount to something more than ordinary change, it must come to terms with how the production of radically novel outcomes can be brought about since, whether of the computational, physical, or organizational variety, emergence refers to a radical, not ordinary novelty - a property of innovation I have tried to capture with the phrase self-transcending to indicate a transcending of the antecedent framework (or self), out of which emergent phenomenon emerge (see Goldstein, 2002, 2003). Furthermore, by adding a constructional perspective to this necessity for self-transcendence, the result is the expression 'self-transcending constructions' (STC), a construct which puts the focus on the special potency that processes of emergence must possess in order to effectuate in self-transcending novelty.

Self-transcending constructions

In arriving at the idea of self-transcending constructions as a replacement for self-organization in order to understand emergence, I have been guided by several clues which demand some adumbration in order to give a fuller sense of the richness of this new construct. The first clue came from the proto-emergentist thinker Oliver Reiser (1935), who had made the unusual suggestion of conceiving emergent phenomena as similar to transfinite sets: "Just as assertions about the properties of finite classes cannot be made to apply to transfinite aggregates, so in a similar way, the peculiar non-additive properties of an emergent whole (*gestalt*) cannot be predicated of the constituent parts' (p. 63). Reiser was here appealing to the German mathematician Georg Cantor's theorems on transfinite sets ('aggregates' was Reiser's translation of the German 'Menge' which today is usually translated as 'set'), as an analogy to how emergent phenomena similarly transcended any piecemeal addition of the properties of the components from which they are generated. Cantor had proved his transfinite sets possessed this unique non-piecemeal property through the utilization of a particular mathematical construction called *diagonalization* (or more precisely *anti-diagonalization* as we shall soon go over). As there is not space here to detail how Cantor's argument proceeded (see Goldstein, 2002, and Simmons, 1990, for a logical formalism for anti-diagonalization), it must suffice to say that his anti-diagonal construction was constructed out of antecedent elements while at the same time transcending each element at every point. It was precisely this simultaneous operation which lent transfinite sets their unique, radically novel quality.

Investigating further, I came across a derogatory evaluation of Cantor's anti-diagonal construction as being a type of 'self-transcending construction' by the Austrian philosopher of mathematics Felix Kaufmann (1978) who asserted, "... no construction can ever lead beyond the domain determined by the principle underlying it" (p. 36). Although Kaufmann clearly meant this expression in a derisory sense, it struck me that it was exactly such 'self-transcending constructions' which were representative of processes capable of the emergence of the radically novel since they self-transcend the antecedent domains on which they operate. To be sure, I'm not claiming that emergence consists in the type of mathematical operation in which Cantor's construction consisted but, rather, the latter provides a transparent way to conceive how radically novel outcomes can be constructed.

Reiser's was not the end of allusions to Cantor's anti-diagonal construction as I also discovered the latter was implicated in the physicist Charles Bennet's (1986) idea of *logical depth*, devised as an improvement to *algorithmic complexity* as a metric for complex systems. It turns out that logical depth uses a version of the same Cantorian anti-diagonal argument used in the proof of transfinite sets. Whereas deterministic programs cannot quickly transform 'shallow' objects into 'deep' ones, and probabilistic computations can only do so with low probability, Bennet's 'deep' metric comes about by first generating a complete list of all 'shallow' N-Bit strings and then outputting the first N-bit string not on the list. For Bennet, the Cantorian-like computational construction of logical depth serves to introduce a richness of structure, possessing a greater capacity for doing justice to the real complexity of complex systems, including the complexity exhibited in emergence.

The Cantorian anti-diagonal, self-transcending construction showed up yet again, but this time more indirectly in Jack Cohen's and Ian Stewart's (1994) so-called *Existence 'Theorem' for Emergence* which applies a Turing-like conjecture on the non-computability of emergent phenomena in terms of their 'lower' level or antecedent conditions. Turing's non-computability theorem was itself inspired by Gödel's *limitation theorems*, and the proofs of both Gödel's and Turing's theorems employed a variant of the same Cantorian anti-diagonal method we have been discussing. Hence, Cohen and Stewart were proving the existence of emergence by indirect appeal to Cantor's self-transcending construction.

Furthermore, Gödel's and Turing's theorems, and therefore by implication their Cantorian self-transcending constructional core, were also seminal to yet another hint in the direction of emergence of de Lorenzana's (1993) and Rosen's (1996) respective appeals to limitative theorems in order to argue that emergence was essentially nonformalizable. Thus, according to Rosen (p. 212), "(M, R)-systems [his term for emergent biological systems] are inherently unformalizable as mathematical systems. That means: not only do they have noncomputable models, but any model of them that is computable is not itself an (M, R)-system, and hence misses all of its biology." Although Rosen was here using the term 'model' in its mathematical logical sense, what he was saying here can be interpreted as the claim that emergent systems would always transcend any particular formal coding scheme adopted to represent them. Rosen's appeal, however, to Turing noncomputability in the case of emergence could be said to rest on the fact that emergent phenomena self-transcend that from which they emerge - in other words, emergent phenomena are not reducible in a formal manner to their antecedent or lower level components.

Yet, in contrast to Rosen's recourse to a Turing (or Gödelian) based claim for the purported nonformalizability of emergence, I contend this same appeal to the arguments of Gödel and Turing can be turned inside-out, so to speak, in order to yield the opposite conclusion. But to see how, it is first necessary to say a few words about what Gödel's and Turing's limitative theorems actually demonstrated concerning formalizability. Relevant in this regard is Webb's (1980) compelling argument that the work of Gödel and Turing demonstrated how Cantorian anti-diagonalization was itself formalizable by the very codings, including self-referential schemes, that were used in their respective proofs. Hofstadter (1979, 1985) has offered an understanding of Gödel's and Turing's theorems along the same lines, a paradoxical sounding 'mechanization' of creativity, but with 'mechanization' here referring to the sort of formalism found in Turing's idea of computation. The upshot of both Webb's and Hofstadter's interpretations is that the limitative theorems of Gödel and Turing can be understood as actual formalizations of Cantor's anti-diagonal construction. But, since Cantor's anti-diagonal constructional method can be considered an example of a 'self-transcending construction', I can draw the implication that what I mean by a STC is a generalized formalization of the self-transcending generation of radically novel outcomes, that is, a generalization of what's involved with processes of emergence. In other words, rather than suggesting that emergence is not formalizable, what an appeal to the work of Gödel and Turing instead reveals is that emergence is precisely formalizable through the use of self-transcending constructions like those at the Cantorian core of Gödel's and Turing's limitative theorems.

Such an interpretation of Cantor's anti-diagonal construction as a possible framework for formalizing emergence is further supported from several additional sources. Thus, Holland (1994) has called for a new mathematics for emergence that involves a change in cardinality which is exactly what Cantor's construction accomplished, since his anti-diagonalization can generate transfinite sets of higher and higher cardinality. There is also the 'object construction' thesis of Fontana and Buss (1994) for the emergent phenomena observed in artificial life. In their scheme for understanding emergence they rely on proof theory in mathematical logic which itself emanates out of the work of Gödel and Turing. Similarly, Crutchfield's (1993) 'calculi of emergence' for artificial life involves a cognate transcendental leap in innovation classes or sets. Finally, there is Piaget's (1971) suggestion for a Cantorian-like constructional process in the development of novel insights. At the heart of all these seemingly disparate indications is Cantor's anti-diagonal construction, a construction serving as a prototype for what I'm calling a self-transcending construction (see Figure 1).

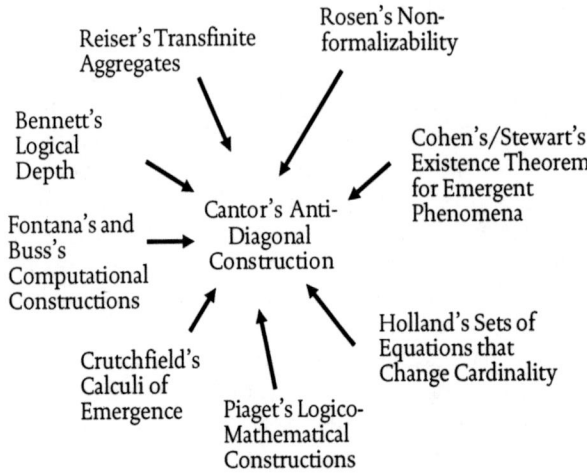

Figure 1
Clues Towards Anti-diagonalization (and Self-transcending Constructions)

The creative process of following and negating

Following-up on these hints, I made a closer inspection of Cantor's anti-diagonal method and found in it a surprisingly transparent way for not only how to
conceptualize how radically novel outcomes can be generated but also how this
generation can be formalized. Moreover, I discovered an added advantage in
the fact that self-transcending constructions, as Cantor demonstrated with his
anti-diagonal construction, can be applied repeatedly in order to produce ever
more radically novel outcomes. However, Cantor's proof method as well as both
the various elaborations of it and the later use of it by mathematicians in the
twentieth century remain enshrouded in the obscure language of mathematical logic which does not easily offer itself as a way to provide insight outside of
its own arcana. Hence, I found it was still necessary to try to get a less obscure
handle on what precisely is going on with the 'logic' of the processes operative
in STCs which enable them to generate radical novelty.

A way to address this issue came from an entirely different quarter (albeit
close to Piaget's suggestion mentioned above), namely, the study of creative
process since creativity is, by definition, that set of processes, methods, procedures, and inspirations that have to do with the coming about of the radically original, or, what in the workplace is usually referred to under the term
'innovation'. The 'logic' of creativity consequently presents itself as a way to
probe even deeper into how self-transcending constructions can bring about
radically novel emergent phenomena. Indeed, it has not been an uncommon
terminological move among those interested in emergence to characterize the
processes involved in it through appeal to the term 'creative'. This is evident
in such expressions for emergence (see Goldstein, 1999, 2004) as 'creative

evolution' (Bergson), 'creative synthesis' (C. L. Morgan), a general theory of creativity (Whitehead), even Prigogine's and his followers' description of the self-organizing emergence of new order as a creative process.

Yet, it seems odd to me that not one of these appeals to the term 'creative' went so far as to actually consider creative process itself whereas that is precisely what the study of creativity has been all about whether scientifically, mathematically, philosophically, culturally, or artistically. Spanning across many disciplines including cognitive science, psychology, linguistics, sociology, anthropology, philosophical aesthetics, education, art, communication, even marketing and advertising, creativity studies have even begun to employ the term 'emergent' as a description for the way creative ideas, images, and insights can arise unexpectedly and radically distinct from whatever inputs that may have served as a groundwork for the created product (see the use of 'emergent cognition' in Fauconnier & Turner (2002); and in Finke, *et al.* (1996).

Of course, it is neither the case that creative processes require sudden leaps, nor are they confined to the creation of art. Rather, creativity is a pervasive element of everyday life, showing up in decision-making, problem-solving, cooking, setting up a home, decorating a room, coordinating a wardrobe, getting a job done efficiently and effectively, as well as music appreciation and music making, creating a television show, directing a movie, coming up with an advertising campaign, devising a new product and its packaging and marketing, designing a business, and innumerable other manifestations of bringing about something that wasn't there before. Moreover, creativity is a phenomenon that can be nurtured and encouraged so as to demonstrate a blend of intentional construction and spontaneous inspiration.

An important aspect of the unique 'logic' of creative process can be thought of as a simultaneous following and negating, a logic that is connoted in the very phrase 'self-transcending constructions' through its suggestion that emergent novelty both comes out of, while simultaneously transcends, antecedent conditions. This is in line with the creativity researcher Albert Rothenberg's (1990) point that every creation must have familiar aspects or it would not be recognized as departing from the familiar. Thus, while it is necessary that radical newness implies some kind of discontinuity with the past, the novelty that is generated in the creative process must be at the same time inextricably tied-up with the past. This indeed was critical to Cantor's proof of transfinite sets mentioned above since the anti-diagonal construction both followed and negated at each step that from which it was constructed. Likewise, Baughman and Mumford (1995) have emphasized that it is extant and not new knowledge which is then used to generate new knowledge by being combined in uniquely novel ways. They cite research which demonstrates how such recombination operations contrast with mechanically-run, inductive searches for rote associations between static features. Thus, when subjects were asked to discern common features among different elements, a typical inductive / abstractive procedure, creativity diminished whereas it increased when searching for atypical features or when mundane features were eliminated as a basis for constructing a new category. Similarly, Weisberg (1998) has pointed out that the degree of originality and quality of an art product is correlated to how much the created product departs from a simple rearrangement of what already has been done by radically modifying it. Thus, whereas Picasso's notorious painting *Guernica* could be interpreted as a rearrangement of an earlier work *Minotauromachy*, his *Les Demoiselles d'Avignon* of 1907 expressed an even more radical restructuring by uprooting all the conventional presumptions at work in representing a typical scene in a brothel. The resulting creative potency of this painting is at the basis of the literary critic George Steiner's (2002) proposal that while the *Demoiselles d'Avignon* used the same, long established brush strokes of tradition, Picasso subverted this very tradition in the very process of painting the picture.

The logic behind recombinatory creative strategies is to take antecedent arrangements, follow, at least initially, this extant arrangement, and then change or negate aspects of it as the creative process proceeds. It is important to note that 'negation' here does not denote a change to an exact opposite, e.g., white becoming black. Instead, negating white can be a change to any color not-white, i.e., red, blue, yellow, tan, and all colors in between as well, of course, black. Unless there is a both a following of the past pattern and then a negation of that very pattern, the creative product will either seem to appear like magic out of the blue or will not suggest enough of a transgression to allow for radically novel outcomes. This can be seen in another example of the creative logic of following and negating, namely the film *Bound* written and directed by the same Wachowski brothers of *The Matrix* fame. In *Bound*, it's as if every conventional plot device were followed and then simultaneously negated. Thus, instead of such a conventional plot as a 'made man' working for the mob who gets involved in a nefarious criminal enterprise accompanied, of course, by the appropriate, sizzling gun molls, the main characters in *Bound* are two women who fall for each other and attempt to rob the mob itself! Moreover, rather than an expected protagonist in the form of a recently released male convict, one of the women herself is an ex-con! This creative logic of following and negating continues on up to the film's 'happy ending' when the two women ride off into the sunset together.

It is important to note that the following side of the logic of following and negating need not unfold sequentially, as in a movie narrative, but may instead consist of a holding operation whereby negation is continually applied to what it is held against. For example, in Rothenberg's (1990) research into creative process, art work rated as the highest quality was demonstrated to result from the projection onto a screen of two slides of quite disparate imagery onto the same physical space of the screen like a lamination of the two slides on top of the other. The following side of following and negating here consisted in the holding together of the oppositions, that is, a continuity of tension between the oppositions whereby one group of images continues to 'negate' the imagery in the other. Similarly, the following aspect of the creative logic may be constituted by an ongoing, tacit background against which the foreground supplies the negation, e.g., in musical compositions where themes, once they have been introduced, recede into the background, yet allusions to them in the form of variations, as well as smaller scale versions, of the original may consistently remind the listener of the original theme(s). Indeed, if this sort of following wasn't taking place there wouldn't be a sense of the musical piece having coherence. The famous conductor Daniel Barenboim (Said & Barenboim, 2002) bears this out in remarks to the effect that music-making partakes of paradox by somehow keeping extremes essentially linked. As Finke, *et al.* (1996) have emphasized in their studies of emergent cognition, creativity reflects a balance between novelty and connectivity to previous ideas. This fits with Atlan's (1974) interpretation of self-organizing physical systems as needing to be redundant enough in order to sustain themselves under the constant bombardment of that 'noise' which adds novelty into the system.

Self-transcending construction, innovation, and the 'transformational imperative'

In earlier days of applying the idea of self-organization to organizations, there was a general sense that innovation would inevitably result from the mere dismantling of command and control managerial hierarchies (I myself was inclined in this direction, see Goldstein, 1994). As stated above, however, although such a dismantling may be one of the important ingredients involved in the facilitation of innovation, self-organization by itself is not sufficient for accounting for the emergence of radically new patterns, structures, and properties. Instead, other constructional resources and 'constraints' along the lines of self-transcending constructional resources are also necessary, processes in concordance with the above described logic of following and negating. The point being made here corresponds to a similar one made by the creativity researcher David Feldman (1994) concerning Piaget's ultimately unsuccessful struggle to develop an adequate theory of creativity, because of the limitations of his two epistemological presumptions, viz., assimilation and accommodation within a stable world; assumptions stemming from a Chomskian, neo-nativist view that qualitative change in thinking simply did not occur. By contrast, Feldman has called for a 'transformational imperative' in which creative processes resulting from a complex interaction between persons, the social milieu, and the environment, produce what Feldman has called the 'crafted world' of innovative constructions. The obviousness of the novelty in the created, constructed, and crafted world in which we live undermines that failure of the imagination on the part of arch reductionists which disables them from conceiving the very possibility of something radically novel coming along at all.

Understanding the emergence of new order in terms of self-transcending constructions can also supplant those earlier metaphysics of emergence offered by such philosophers as Whitehead (1978) which, founded on an experientialist basis, failed to take into consideration the actual creative construction of created objects and instead focused on structures common to mundane experience (see Goldstein, 2004). Since self-transcending constructions are essentially about the coming into being of the radically novel, they can consequently formalize how what is radically original can originate through creative process, thereby indicating what's involved in that which transcends mundane, repetitive experience.

Furthermore, self-transcending constructions are 'free' acts of construction - not free in the sense of Kauffman's 'order-for-free' mentioned above - but rather 'free' in the sense of not being opposed by some countervailing force, such as entropy has often been understood to be (misunderstood in my opinion). Of course, STCs must operate under constraints just as the construction of a skyscraper must contend with the force of gravity, the durability of building materials, and so forth. But what indeed is free about them is the impetus to construct and create even if there is no constructor behind them. It is only when emergence is conceived as operating against a force opposed to the building-up of order, e.g., the classical understanding of the Second Law, that it is then necessary to posit an impetus or motive force behind it pushing for the building-up of new order.

Emergence, according to the construct of self-transcending constructions, is always a local event occurring in a great variety of circumstances, an event neither rare nor everywhere. Moreover, understood as employing self-transcending constructions, emergence can include the whole panoply of constructional resources, constructional operations, seminal order and structure and form, the constructional principles of self- / cross-referential mechanisms, and so forth; all the things that entail that the actual construction of emergent order is not free but costly. Similarly, although innovation is a 'free' act, it must utilize what is present but do so in such a manner that the order that is currently present is transformed in ways not previously conceivable.

References

Atlan, H. (1974). "On a Formal Definition of Organization," *Journal of Theoretical Biology*, 45: 295-304.

Anderson, P. (1972). "More Is Different: Broken Symmetry and the Nature Of the Hierarchical Structure Of Science," *Science*, 177(4047): 393-396.

Baughman, W. A. and Mumford, M. D. (1995). "Process Analytic of Creative Capacities," *Creativity Research Journal*, 8: 37-62.

Bennet, C. (1986). "On the Nature and Origin of Complexity in Discrete, Homogeneous, Locally-Interacting Systems," *Foundations of Physics*, 16(6): 585-592.

Berge, P., Pomeau, V. and Vidal, C. (1984). *Order within Chaos: Towards a Deterministic Approach to Turbulence*, (L. Tuckerman, trans.), NY: John Wiley and Sons.

Cohen, J. and Stewart, I. (1994). *The Collapse Of Chaos: Discovering Simplicity In A Complex World*, NY: Penguin.

Crutchfield, J. (1993). "The Calculi of Emergence: Computation, Dynamics, and Induction, Santa Fe Institute Working Paper # 94-03-016, (Electronically published).

de Lorenzana, A. (1993). "The Constructive Universe And The Evolutionary Systems

Framework," appendix in S. Salthe, *Development and Evolution: Complexity and Change in Biology*, Cambridge, Mass: MIT Press.

Fauconnier, G. and Turner, M. (2002). *The Way We Think: Conceptual Blending and the Mind's Hidden Complexities*, NY: Perseus.

Feldman, D. (1994). "Creativity: Dreams, Insights, Transformations," in D. H. Feldman, M. Csikszentmihalyi, and H. Gardner (eds.), *Changing the World: A Framework for the Study of Creativity*, Westport, CT: Praeger.

Finke, R., Ward, T. and Smith, S. (1996). *Creative Cognition: Theory Research and Applications*, Cambridge, MA: MIT Press.

Fontana, W. and Buss, L. (1996). "The Barrier of objects: From Dynamical systems to Bounded Organizations," in J. Casti and A. Karlqvist (eds.) *Boundaries and Barriers: On The Limits To Scientific Knowledge*, Reading, MA: Perseus Books.

Goldstein, J. (1994). *The Unshackled Organization*, Portland, Oregon: Productivity Press.

Goldstein, J. (1999). "Emergence as a Construct: History and Issues," *Emergence: Complexity Issues in Organization And Management*, 1(1): 49-62.

Goldstein, J. (2001). "Emergence Radical Novelty, and the Philosophy of Mathematics," in W. Sulis and I. Trofimova (eds.) *Nonlinear Dynamics in the Life and Social Sciences*, Amsterdam: IOS Press. (NATO Science Series, Vol. 320).

Goldstein, J. (2002). "The Singular Nature of Emergent Levels: Suggestions for a Theory of Emergence," *Nonlinear Dynamics, Psychology, and Life Sciences*, 6(4): 293-309.

Goldstein, J. (2003). "The Construction of Emergence Order, Or How to Resist the Temptation of Hylozoism," *Nonlinear Dynamics, Psychology, and Life Sciences*, 7(4): 295-314.

Goldstein, J. (2004). "How Emergence Flirts with Paradox," *Capital Science 2004: Proceedings*, Washington, D.C.: Washington Academy of Sciences.

Haken, H. (1981). *The Science of Structure: Synergetics*, NY: Van Nostrand Reinhold.

Holland, J. (1994). *Hidden Order: How Adaptation Builds Complexity*, Reading, MA: Addison-Wesley.

Hofstadter, D. (1979). *Gödel, Escher, Bach: an Eternal Golden Braid*, NY: Basic Books.

Hofstadter, D. (1985). *Metamagical Themes: Questing for the Essence of Mind and Pattern*, NY: Basic Books.

Juarrero, A. (1999). *Dynamics in Action*. Cambridge, MA: MIT Press.

Kauffman, S. (1993). *The Origins of Order: Self-organization and Selection in Evolution*, NY: Oxford University Press.

Kaufmann, F. (1978). *The Infinite in Mathematics: Logico-mathematical Writing*, Dordrecht: Reidel.

Lissack, M. (2000). Personal communication.

Moss, L. (2003). *What Genes Can't Do*, Cambridge, MA: MIT Press.

Nicolis, G. and Prigogine, I. (1989). *Exploring Complexity: An Introduction*, NY: W. H. Freeman and Company.

Piaget, J. (1971). *Biology and Knowledge: An Essay on the Relations Between Organic Regulations and Cognitive Processes*, Edinburgh, Scotland: Edinburgh University Press.

Reiser, O. (1935). *Philosophy and the Concepts of Modern Science*, NY: Macmillan.

Rosen, R. (1996). "On the Limitations of Scientific Knowledge," in J. Casti and A. Karlqvist (eds.) *Boundaries and Barriers: On The Limits To Scientific Knowledge*, Reading, MA: Perseus Books.

Rothenberg, A. (1990). *The Emerging Goddess: The Creative Process in Art, Science, and*

Other Fields, Chicago: University of Chicago Press.

Said, E. and Barenboim, D. (2002). *Parallels and Paradoxes: Explorations of Music and Society*, NY: Pantheon Books.

Simmons, K. (1990). "The Diagonal Argument and the Liar," *Journal of Philosophical Logic*, 19: 277-303.

Steiner, G. (2002). *Grammars of Creation*, New Haven: Yale University Press.

Strogatz, S. (2003). *Sync: The emerging Science of Spontaneous Order*, NY: Hyperion.

Webb, J. (1980). *Mechanism, Mentalism, and Metamathematics: an Essay on Finitism*, Dordrecht: Reidel.

Weisberg, D. (1998). "Creativity and Knowledge: A Challenge to Theories," in R. Sternberg (ed.) *Handbook of Creativity*, Cambridge, England: Cambridge University Press.

Weiss, N. (1987). "Dynamics of Convection," in M. Berry, I. Percival, and N. Weiss (eds.), *Dynamical Chaos: Proceedings of the Royal Society of London*, Princeton: Princeton University Press.

Whitehead, A. N. (1978). *Process and Reality: An Essay in Cosmology*, D. Ray Griffin and D.W. Sherburne (eds.), NY: The Free Press.

CHAPTER 5

AN APPROACH TO CAUSALITY IN ORGANIZED COMPLEXITY: THE ROLE OF MANAGEMENT

Stanley N. Salthe

Organization and self-organization are defined in the context of complexity. The scale hierarchy is used to locate workplaces in firms, firms in industries and these in economies. The specification hierarchy is used to organize a discussion of information. Using the Aristotelian complex causal analysis (material / formal and efficient / final), management is found to be the efficient manipulation of material causes so as to appropriate a firm's formal causes and anticipate an industry's final causes in the service of the overall final cause of firm profitability.

Managing Organizational Complexity: Philosophy, Theory, and Application
A Volume in: Managing the Complex, pages 79–92.
ISBN: 1-59311-319-6 (cloth), 1-59311-318-8 (paper)

Introduction

This chapter takes an *ecological* perspective on organization, utilizing two forms of *hierarchy theory* as frameworks for the discussion, as well as the full range of the Aristotelian *causal categories*. The umbrella concept is complexity. Ecology deals only with complex systems. As well, any form of hierarchy theory is an approach to complexity. And the Aristotelian analysis of causality is the only one so far in Western discourse that is, in my view, capable of dealing fully with complex causality.

I view organization as a viewpoint, which necessarily places it in a system of organizations - an ecology - because a viewpoint is always just one among many. I take viewpoints to be the results of self-organization, hence an organization is a self with a developing viewpoint, its information preserved in its habits, routines and traditions.

Hierarchy theory is usually employed to model synchronic aspects of the world. So, the scale hierarchy is a spatio-temporal construct, [large scale / higher level [small scale / lower level]], showing that any process or form discerned at a level in focus results from lower scalar level possibilities, mediated by larger scale arrangements, as in: [[focal level phenomenon [lower level generativity]] higher level constraints]. Less well known is what I call the *specification hierarchy*, which models the fact that any complex system could be viewed from more than one perspective. Thus, an organism could be viewed as just a physical system of energy dissipation and diffusion. Or it could be taken to be a chemical system, focusing on its metabolism. Alternatively, it could be viewed as a biological system, considering, say, circulation or reproduction. This can be displayed using the logic of sets, as: {physical realm {chemical realm {biological realm}}}, showing that each realm to the right arises out of the one to its left by the addition of further specification, at the same time preserving all the more general constraints of the enveloping class and subclasses. So, in this case we have {lower level {higher level}}. Furthermore, each higher level integrates the properties of the more general levels under its rules, as when biology integrates diffusion by way of circulatory systems.

I have found that the specification hierarchy can be used as well to model certain aspects of development, as in: {immature system → {mature system → {senescence}}}. In a sense this structure, which I refer to as a developmental trajectory, is synchronic in spirit because development (as opposed to evolution / individuation) can be expected to produce known changes, as in {stage 1 → {stage 2 → {stage 3}}}. Self-organization would be just the combination of development and individuation.

The Aristotelian causal categories include the synchronic material cause and formal cause, as well as the diachronic efficient cause and final cause. Referring back to the levels in the scale hierarchy, we can display these as: [[focal level phenomenon [material causes]] formal causes], showing that formality mediates materiality into some phenomenon. Referring to the specification hierarchy as used to model change, we would have: efficient cause → {stage

Specification hierarchy

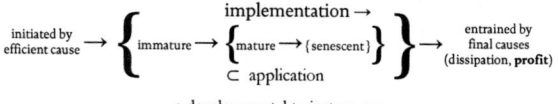

a developmental trajectory, or
self-organized self with an accumulating tradition

Scale hierarchy

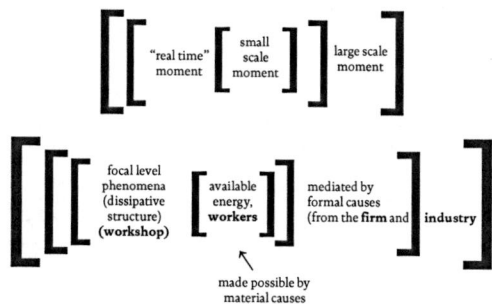

Figure 1

General aspects of the two hierarchies used in this paper, showing as
well labels referring to their application herein. Relationships with the
Aristotelian causal categories are also indicated.

1 → {stage 2 → {stage 3}}} → final cause. *Efficient cause* (a "push") perturbs a
system, starting or triggering some change, while *final cause* (a "pull") entrains
that change in a direction made possible by *material causes* and allowed by
bearing *formal causes*.

Organized complexity

Organized complexity (Collier & Hooker, 1999.) characterizes configurations
of more than a few components or relations that, in the absence of a key to
understand them, appear disorderly. Nevertheless, they cannot be fully ap-
prehended statistically. That is , they do not exemplify Collier and Hooker's
'unorganized complexity', which could be understood adequately as being
randomly configured. If a system's internal relations were mostly known,
and taken into account, it would not appear disorderly, however complicated
it might be.

Disorder (Salthe, 2002) reflects the absence of an observer's, or potential
user's, information about a locale or system. Whether a configuration actually is
orderly according to unknown principles, or completely unconstrained, one can
model it as random. After all, that is formally the most likely configuration in
the absence of bearing informational constraints (Boltzmann, 1886). However,

if it actually is organized by unknown principles, the random model will not deliver functional enlightenment, even if it is predictive. Yet, not knowing the governing constraints is often taken as equivalent to there being none. Indeed, observing even a well-understood system by using statistical means will fit it to a random model (Salthe, 1975)! Pure caprice (Lewontin, 1967) cannot be distinguished from intentional arbitrariness (Salthe, 1993b). Yet in conflating them we would be ignoring most of the causal relations involved in a system, reducing them to just the material cause of unconstrained fluctuations in a maze of contingencies.

Organization

What then, generally, is an organization? I advance the idea that it is an historically emergent viewpoint within some discourse or tradition, configured out of informational constraints within the substance of the world. We may note first that this substance itself appears organized. As elucidated by Western science, this substance is itself intensionally complex (Salthe, 1993a), as in the specification hierarchy:

{physical world {material world {biological world {sociocultural /socioeconomic world}}}}.

This is a formal refinement of Rosen's (1985) general definition of complexity as being present to the degree that different approaches need to be taken in trying to understand a complex system. This kind of hierarchy serves as a science-based, intelligible model of the world in the style of natural philosophy. It is one way to partially "tame" complexity - by frameworking it.

A specification hierarchy is a set theoretical-style model, parsing in an orderly manner (as: more general ↔ more particular) the many ways (in the above example) that science has contrived to apprehend the world. The classes, in whichever direction they are read, are referred to as integrative levels (Salthe, 2002). Taken analytically from right to left, we would have {generality ← {particulars}}, while developmentally, the other way round, we would see {vaguer → {more definite}}. As read from left to right, this ordering reflects either temporal precedence, logical priority, or both. This left to right interpretation traces out a developmental trajectory (Salthe, 1993a). This is a larger scale system immediately entraining any changing material organization, which, at any point in its existence, would be one of its trajectory's consecutive constituents - say, an organism as one stage in its ontogeny, or a workplace as a momentary embodiment of a firm. With respect to such constituents, a trajectory is larger in scale, and so changes at a slower rate than the homeostatic dynamics of the organization it entrains (Salthe, 1985). Note that we need to distinguish this diachronic larger scale entity from synchronic ones that a system might also be nested within - like a population and species for an organism, an industry and an economy for a firm (Dosi, 1982). I refer to a developmental trajectory as an entraining discourse in respect to a material organization in momentary focus, which would be a self, organization, or any system of interest, viewed spatio-temporally over just the few moments necessary to display its routine functioning.

A more dynamic example from the world of human economic organizations using the developmental structure of the specification hierarchy can be found in the distinction between application and implementation (Alan Cotterell, personal communication; see upper row of Figure 1). The direction of implementing specifications for some job would be to consult first the most generally applicable level - international standards. Next, national standards would be taken into account, then industry codes of practice, and finally company internal procedures - this process of refinement making up a developmental trajectory increasingly focused upon a job. On the other hand, in the material process of applying a design / strategy, while actually doing a job, the company's internal procedures are the first in use, and are always the most prominent. After all, one works locally. Local constraints are kinds of up front, strong influences compared with more generally applicable ones, which, nevertheless, are simultaneously present as "weaker" (because more general) influences backing up a procedure by way of prior influence through implementation. Formally, the inner (higher) levels of a specification hierarchy imply (in the sense of conceptual subordination) the more outer (lower) levels. So, in designing an airplane, for example, the talk might be about seat design but not about seating capacity, and certainly not about gravitation. Seating capacity would be negotiable only over a much longer period of time, involving trans-state negotiations already accomplished. Note that, since we have in implementation a canonical sequence of tasks, we are considering there a style of change - constitutive change - that I have assigned to development (Salthe, 1993a), defined (in contrast to evolution / individuation) as 'predictable directional change'. A developmental trajectory would have substance only insofar as its sequence of stages is largely predictable.

We turn now to another factor of any developmental process: the scattering process of history. Via the results of impinging fluctuations and contingencies, historicity records individuation (i.e., evolution - Salthe, 1993a - the 'irreversible accumulation of historical information'), a process of continually increasing specificity that drives instances and examples ever away from the central tendency of their common generic inheritance. Much effort is expended in manufacture to contain this scattering process within some standard, but note that we, as individual selves, *are* our integrated history, and so would be any entity stable enough to form an internal record. (Of course, it would not currently be convenient for us if our fabrications took on a life of their own!)

The most general result of historicity is information. Pattee (e.g., 1977) distinguished between dynamics and the information controlling them. Dynamics are processes realizing local tendencies elicited by natural and material laws, while information is embodied in the particular constraints that locally squeeze these processes in given directions - sometimes according to the interests of particular systems. So, history is the source of the idiographic constraints that fit natural laws to a given locale, and which we call information. Formally, in an equation, for example, these constraints would be represented in the values of constants. So an organization is a momentary informational embodiment of a history that includes most recently its own adventures. Yet, much of the information included in an organization's internal records has been acquired prior to its own existence. This is clearly seen in genetic information in organisms, with some genes antedating even the species an organism is part of. For a workplace, its information could be represented as the developmental trajectory: {information from an economy → {ditto from an industry → {ditto from a firm → {a workplace's own routines}}}}. This is isomorphic to: {physico-chemical information → {biological information → {socioeconomic information → {personally acquired information}}}} for a human being.

So we see again that the specification hierarchy has a developmental interpretation, as in: {stage 1 → {stage 2 }}, with the different 'worlds' (in the first specification hierarchy in the text above) then being viewed as stages in the development of the world, while that whole hierarchy would represent the world's developmental trajectory (Salthe, 1993a). In this reading, the biological realm is being viewed as necessarily having emerged out of the chemical (material) realm (and, a firm out of an industry). This continues to be, more proximately, the case in each particular example of a kind of trajectory, as when an embryo develops - from just a material gradient in an egg cell to an organism at a later stage. So, pairs of brackets in this kind of hierarchy, { }, each record emergences. Since the emergences shown, moving from left to right in the above hierarchies would have been in a necessary sequence, we are justified in taking the modeled process to be developmental. Insofar as the process of implementation described above would also have to be canonical, it too would be developmental, in this case a development of regulatory intensity.

Then, why is it interesting to characterize an organization as a viewpoint? - especially since even abiotic organizations exist, like tornadoes. A viewpoint is necessarily just one frame of reference among many. Viewpoints are always poised with reference to others, and so are necessarily parts of systems. What history produces out of natural tendencies is material diversity, including a diversity of perspectives. In a given region or arena these make up an ecology of needs and desires that must take into consideration (must actually be configured with respect to) others. Darwinians stress competitive relations among similar viewpoints, while ecologists emphasize the mutual dependence of different perspectives. The former might be taken to be a microscopic model with respect to the latter, which stresses the overall regulation of systems.

Finally for this section, then, a tradition is an accumulating record associated with a continuing, or replicated kind of, dissipative structure (an actual energy consuming system - see below) in the material world. As a record of the individuation of a developmental trajectory, a tradition is a comparatively large scale concept, and functions as the genealogical setting for smaller scale systems, like the organisms or workplaces in the above examples. The entraining tradition of the former would be an evolving lineage, which (as that which continually maintains it and passes it on) should be viewed as "owning" the genetic information consulted during organismic ontogeny. For business sites, company internal procedures, or routines - the continuing presence of a firm - serve the same function. And so species and firms evolve in their respective developmental trajectories, as their guiding information changes, often in response to changes in their ecological settings (which might for some purposes, be viewed as themselves yet larger scale developmental trajectories).

A tradition, given its continuing accumulation of information, can also be parsed as a specification hierarchy. For example:

{material → {living → {animal → {mammal → {primate → {human → {person}}}}}}.

Again, in this interpretation of this kind of hierarchy, the integrative levels are implicitly taken to model the stages of development of a developmental trajectory. What this example invites us to realize further is that (although not shown in this representation) a specification hierarchy formally branches into its subclasses, so that all traditions must be taken to have emerged from a single ancestral matrix, and each subclass is one of increasingly many coordinate ones as we move toward the right, higher up into the hierarchy. As well, the innermost subclasses always (if implicitly) remain open to further refinement as a result of continuing self-organization, as well as to further mutations.

Here it can be useful to sum up the relations among the various entities described above (see also Figure 1). So, with [X [Y]] brackets meaning: [larger in scale [smaller in scale]], we have:[discourse [developmental trajectory - a developing organization (organized system or self) with a viewpoint informed by its evolving / individuating tradition [dissipative structure - a material organization or system of energy flows]]]. This scans also as: [informational constraints [informed executive processes]]. Again, do not confuse these brackets with those used in the specification hierarchy - { } - which represent classes denoting integrative levels in a specification hierarchy. This comes up here particularly inasmuch as all, except the innermost scalar level here, are actually developmental trajectories, some nested within others. It is important to keep in mind that specification and scalar hierarchies are analytical frameworks, either or both of which can be employed to understand any material system. Note as well that in a scale hierarchy (Salthe, 2002) the level in focus can be shifted up or down, so that, say, an organism (or workplace) could take, relative to one of its cells (or workers), the place its species (or industry) occupies with respect to itself, thus becoming the constraining developmental trajectory for that cell's (or worker's) behavior (or productivity).

Self-organization and causal complexity

Self-organization is the progressive organization of a self, or viewpoint. It begins relatively vague, becoming progressively more definite. A self is just *an historically accumulated, increasingly unique organization or system steering a dissipative structure.* A dissipative structure (Prigogine, 1980) is a local material configuration capable of dissipating some kind(s) of energy gradient(s), assimilating some of the energy, and using some of that (via free energy, as *exergy*) for work, including in that work its own self-organization. As it dissipates external energy gradients, it produces entropy while working. So, a dissipative structure is the material basis or carrier of any organization (or system), that which actually advances an organization into a future and mediates its informational changes along the way. For a biological population, (as well as for a human self) this would be an organism; for a firm, it is a site (say, a manufactory) of the deployment of its routines. The activities of the material entity (the dissipative structure) result in further individuation of its entraining trajectories at all levels.

A viewpoint develops (Matsuno & Salthe, 2002). Any material locale, if not disrupted, will accumulate a record of its encounters. In an organized configuration this record will function as a formal cause in guiding / limiting an organization's advances and reactions. In generating habits, its record also leads a system to project a future (I am doing → I have been doing → I will have been doing), accompanied by the construction of finality (goals, values). The Aristotelian causal categories - the synchronic pair: material cause / formal cause, and the diachronic pair: efficient cause / final cause - are all required in order to understand causality in complex locales (see Figure 1). Material cause generates possibilities (it proposes); formal cause mediates change (it disposes); efficient cause initiates change (pushes, triggers), while final cause calls for it ("pulls"). Because of the current unfamiliarity of this system, I apply it here to a manufactory. Material causes of production would be the structured presence of workers, utilities and raw materials. Formal causes are the routines of the firm. Efficient causes are the arrival of orders, the onset of work hours, encouragements. Final causes are the planned profits, enlargements and modernizations, as well as (this site being necessarily a dissipative structure in a nonequilibrium world) the production of entropy. Below I will attempt to evaluate the significance of these causal distinctions in respect to the allocation of accountability within a managerial hierarchy.

Energy relations and thermodynamics

The most general finality impinges upon all change, confronting any energy consumption used for self-organization and action. This is the Second Law of Thermodynamics, imposed by the continuingly accelerated Universal expansion of the Big Bang. The Second Law increases the cost of all activities beyond that required for exergy derivation, taking a physical entropy tax, via heat and waste products, by generating somewhat disordered relations between consumer and energy gradient (Salthe, 2003) to the extent that work is done rapidly. It can be moderated somewhat by increasing energy efficiency (via evolution or design), but is always increased by working as fast as possible, which in turn tends to be encouraged in the context of competition (Matsuno

& Swenson, 1999).

The continuing acceleration of its expansion during the Big Bang (Kirshner, 2003; Seife, 2003) necessarily generates a radically disequilibrated Universe. The sequence: energy → matter → mass → form → organization (e.g., Chaisson, 2001, or Morowitz, 2002) registers the developmental effects of the Universe's increasing disequilibrium (and could also be parsed as stages of development in a specification hierarchy). The cooling of Universal expansion generates the force of gravitation, whose strength reflects the magnitude of the acceleration, and at the same time generates the Universe's opposite reaction in its tendency to equilibrate, which we call the Second Law of Thermodynamics. (I do not cite anyone on these last points; I have checked with several physicists, who did not object.) Gravitation, as the most fundamental source of structure, is built upon by selection and further by intentional fabrication to give the full sweep of the above developmental sequence.

The result of impingement by the Second Law on a system's trajectory is to deflect it in uncertain directions, increasing its informational entropy, as well as that of the higher scale discourse supporting that organization (Brooks & Wiley, 1988). Informational entropy measures a system's uncertainty of behavior. All things being equal, the more power (rate of energy flow thru) supporting an organization's activities, the more possibilities would tend to be generated, tending to increase produced uncertainty. For example, the faster we manufacture something, the greater the variety of waste products that would ensue, as well as more unwanted variant products, forcing us toward increasing energy efficiency even in the face of competition for energy. The faster we drive, the more likely some unforeseen contingency may change the course of our history! Such deflection of inertia, habits and intentionality is the irreducible basis of the branching in the interpretive specification hierarchy, materially causing, for example, speciation in biology, and accidental discoveries of all kinds during cultural evolution. Haste makes waste, but in a changing context, waste may be the material basis for insight. Here the Second Law is working, through a generalized friction (Salthe, 1993a) as a material cause of change, generating mutations and excursions willy-nilly.

As important is the Second Law's function as a final cause of all construction. Inasmuch as, at typical workloads, about 50% of dissipated energy gets deducted from free energy during work (Odum, 1986), one could with justification say that all work is directed (at a low integrative level, of course) toward producing entropy. The more slowly any task is done (above the point of evolved or designed maximum efficiency), the more efficient it can be - but also the less effective. Overall speed might be increased through combining the results of parallel tasks, each being done separately as efficiently as possible, but that is not the thermodynamic issue here. And so we have to manage a trade-off between speed and effectiveness versus haste and waste (which, however, might be parlayed into creativity!).

In competition for finite resources, effectiveness counts, and the fastest consumer, generating the most power, gets most of it (Matsuno & Swenson,

1999), throwing much of it away as - or (in gradients of lesser quality) in the direction of - entropy. So, sharks tearing apart a tuna create all kinds of scraps as well as frictional heat from their muscle activity. Then competition can be understood as a more highly specified embodiment of the Second Law, as in: {universal equilibration {competition}}. It is worth noting that, if instead of having a consumer driven situation like this (based on finite energy endowments), we would have an energy supply dominated one, the average rate of energy consumption would tend to drop toward the average level at which the renewable energy is supplied (this based on the Prigoginian view of nonequilibrium thermodynamics - e.g., Prigogine, 1955). This de-emphasis on competition, because of the guaranteed supply, would tend to support (by deflecting it less) a tradition's own generated final goals, as well as making energy utilization less wasteful from an organization's point of view, by decreasing the need for scrambling competition. This could be an important factor in the issue of economic sustainability versus productivity.

We see here, then, a universal law of nature (the Second Law) acting as a steady, pervasive weak force at a low integrative level. Its import, and even its effective strength, increases, however, as we ascend the specification hierarchy into higher integrative levels, where the law's vicars increasingly focus it. In the framework: {physics {biology {sociology}}}, we would have, for example, {the Second Law {competition {contradiction}}}, or the coordinate {Second Law {cooperation {alliances}}}. We must note here as well, however, that physical conflict is perhaps the most whole-hearted way that human organizations serve the Second Law of thermodynamics - and that wars have been the frame for much human creativity as well.

What, in these contexts, is the role of management?

The first thing to notice is that management and managers are only parts of larger systems. As such, they can 'control' or 'regulate' only limited aspects of the systems they are part of. In terms of the scale hierarchy approach (Salthe, 1985), large scale systems control smaller scale ones, and so industries (and, we are discovering, investment networks) control firms, which in turn control workplaces, which control workers. So the management of firms can be involved in regulating workplaces, while that of the latter can be involved in regulating workers. Having said this, we must note that some individuals do have virtual larger scale roles. CEOs are concerned with entire firms, and so must exercise some influence over a larger actual geographic range than, say, an office manager, who is concerned with activities in his own workplace. Chains of command move downscale in both space and time. Yet it must be said that effective managers assess the views of workers, which, in the scale hierarchy perspective, gain import insofar as they are aggregated into larger than individual opinions (one example would be unionization). A worker consensus can be the equal of a manager in scale, while a single worker cannot. It is therefore the role of wise management to seek (and even to catalyze into existence) 'consulting partners of equal scale'.

We can assess management's role further in the framework of the Aristotelian causal categories. As just pointed out, human organizations work within larger scale discourses. These discourses are the source of finality (values and goals), which must be embraced in order to stay in the game. A major goal of a firm is to turn a profit, and management at all levels must serve this interest, as well as, in capitalist systems, growth of operations. Nonprofit organizations interpret profit as the avoidance of net loss. Profit must be maximized (or 'nonprofit' minimized), while other functions are optimized under this constraint. In practice this latter can get tricky, inasmuch as it is difficult in a complex system to judge just how much some function has contributed to what is being maximized. The logic here is displayed in genetic algorithms (e.g., Mitchell, 2001), where it is impossible to tell just how a simulation will manage to hone some function, and surprises frequently ensue. For example, if we wish to design a car with faster speed at the most energy efficient power, we could be quite surprised as to how the simulation effects this in respect to, e.g., wheel base, streamlining, tire pressure, type of oil, etc., all of which will be simultaneously optimized under the speed increase constraint. Management would need to deploy the functions that may be susceptible to optimizing, thus manipulating the material causes of a hoped-for maximization.

Formal causality too is linked throughout the tradition in question (to be changed, if at all, only by intermittent revolutionary change). Management's input to formality comes through managing records, as well as images like logos and sponsorships. In some industries, like banks and law firms, records could be said to be the only material products of the work done. In a firm of this kind with multiple work sites, management needs to be alert to mutations in procedures that may occur at the individual sites, perhaps slowly diverging from the firm's routines. Oversight needs to be done to make sure that practices at the different sites each fairly represent a firm's routines. Changes accruing in such records could at some point signal altered, or altering, work routines. In any case, records management is a matter of space constraints, involving guiding record collection, collation and condensing, and even contriving the kinds or means of storage required. Again, this is manipulating material causes - in this case of the maintenance and deployment of formality.

Customer persuasion, via the management of advertising, is the soliciting of finality - digging a channel for demand, as it were, toward company production from the great outside. That channel, as such, would be a material cause of profit and growth.

Turning our attention from space to time, managing inventory is a major rates problem in industries producing and moving material goods. For maximum effectiveness, production must be tailored to delivery, supply to demand. This problem involves keeping close track of an important final cause of industrial activity - fluctuations of demand, which vary at the beck and call of many higher scale boundary conditions in an economy. This would involve deploying efficient triggers of activity here and there. Functions like market research would entail the examination of the current status of the wider discourse's affordances for a system's output, with the aim of constructing a guide to manipulating material causality in the service of maximum efficiency (output / input = 1.00). Demand calls for a certain level of throughput of goods, to be fulfilled by our company, or by its competitors. When space-time inertias put producing firms in key bottleneck / profit roles, management needs to assume a pseudo-large scale status, thinking as though it were large enough to control an industry.

A given large scale scenario implies the deployment of particular commands. This involves modeling, and simulations that relate industry time scales to real time activities at the plant. The results imply the deployments of various company material causes in particular configurations, so, once again, managers are manipulators of material causes - in this case directed at anticipating finality. Of course, thermodynamics has implications here too. An economic situation calling for slower and slower production is one that not only implies a possible failure of the firm, but is as well an insult to the Second Law of Thermodynamics. From the Universe's point of view, production must be pushed as fast as limitations allow. In this, management will necessarily always serve the Second Law as well as may be. This necessity promotes growth (a time of increased dissipation) as well. Here, of course, management needs to keep in mind the trade-off between haste and waste. For example, if a sudden change in market configuration invites increased rate of production, this needs to be assessed with respect to the possibility of increasing waste.

Then, as mentioned above, management of staff is the construction of motivation and facilitation. These particular personnel activities might have effects on finality as well, inasmuch as some workers will be involved in sales. Here managers are once again manipulators of material causes.

It seems clear that management is occupied with manipulating material causality - and so, with generating possibilities. That is, steering is done (keeping the finalities in view, and relying on the formal arrangements of the firm) by directing material causes into and within the system.

What about efficient cause? It is clear that this often arrives as perturbations from the discourse (new technology, new players), or even from the wider context (hurricanes, droughts, diseases). But we know, for example, from simulations that, say, perturbing a Boolean automaton in different ways gives rise to slightly different results of the same general form (in this case, a limit cycle), achieved by different detailed routes (Atlan, et al., 1986). Perhaps management could arrange for impacts to be received and fielded in different ways, always keeping in view the satisfaction of finalities. This again, however, would just be manipulating material causation. Doing anything is, of course, efficient causation, and so the actual actions of managers (suggesting, persuading, directing) are just that.

So, summing up: management is efficient action at the personnel level, deployed so as to arrange material causes at the workplace in order to mediate input into growth and profit, by harnessing a firm's formal procedures at the workplaces to the final goals of growth and profit at the level of the firm (and, today, it seems necessary to acknowledge, profit at the still larger scale level of the securities exchange as well).

Acknowledgements

I have had useful input to this paper from David Byrne, Aleks Jakulin, Gary G. Nelson and Eric P. Salthe.

References

Atlan, H., E. Ben-Ezra, F. Fogelman-Soulie, D. Pellegrin and Weisbuch, G. (1985). "Emergence of Classification Procedures in Automata Networks as a Model for Functional Self-organization," *Journal of Theoretical Biology*, 120: 371-380.

Boltzmann, L. (1886). "The Second Law of Thermodynamics," *Populare Schriften*, Essay 3, address to a formal meeting of the Imperial Academy of Science, 29 May, 1886, reprinted in Ludwig Boltzmann, *Theoretical Physics and Philosophical Problems*, 1974, B. McGuinness (ed.), S. G. Brush (transl.), Boston: D. Reidel Publishing.

Brooks, D. R. and Wiley, E. O. (1988). *Evolution As Entropy: Toward a Unified Theory of Biology*, Chicago: University of Chicago Press.

Chaisson, E. J. (2001). *Cosmic Evolution: The Rise of Complexity in Nature*, Cambridge, MA: Harvard University Press.

Collier, J. and Hooker, C. A. (1999). "Complexly Organized Dynamical Systems," *Open Systems and Information Dynamics*, 6: 241-302.

Dosi, G. (1982). "Technological Paradigms and Technological Trajectories: A Suggested Interpretation of the Determinants and Directions of Technological Change," *Research Policy*, 11: 147-162.

Kirshner, R. P. (2003). *The Extravagant Universe: Exploding Stars, Dark Energy, and the Accelerating Universe*, Princeton: Princeton University Press.

Lewontin, R. C. (1967), "The Principle of Historicity in Evolution," in *Mathematical Challenges to the Neo-Darwinian Interpretation of Evolution*, P. S. Moorhead and M. M. Kaplan (eds.), Philadelphia: Wistar Institute Press.

Matsuno, K. and Salthe, S. N. (2002). "The Origin and Development of Time," *International Journal of General Systems*, 31: 377-393.

Matsuno, K. and Swenson, R. (1999). "Thermodynamics in the Present Progressive Mode and its Role in the Context of the Origin of Life," *BioSystems*, 51: 53-61.

Mitchell, M. (2001). *An Introduction to Genetic Algorithms*, Cambridge, MA: MIT Press.

Morowitz, H. J. (2002). *The Emergence of Everything: How the World Became Complex*, New York: Oxford University Press.

Odum, H. T. (1986). *Systems Ecology: An Introduction*, New York: Wiley Interscience.

Pattee, H.H. (1977). "Dynamic and Linguistic Modes of Complex Systems," *International Journal of General Systems*, 3: 259-266.

Prigogine, I. (1955). *Introduction to Thermodynamics of Irreversible Processes*, New York: Interscience.

Prigogine, I. (1980). *From Being to Becoming*, San Francisco: Freeman.

Rosen, R. (1985). *Anticipatory Systems: Philosophical, Mathematical and Methodological Foundations*, Oxford: Pergamon Press.

Salthe, S. N. (1975). "Problems of Macroevolution (Molecular Evolution, Phenotype Definition, and Canalization) as Seen From a Hierarchical Viewpoint," *American Zoologist*, 15: 295-314.

Salthe, S. N. (1985). *Evolving Hierarchical Systems: Their Structure and Representation*, New York: Columbia University Press.

Salthe, S. N. (1993a). *Development and Evolution: Complexity and Change in Biology*, Cambridge, MA: MIT Press.

Salthe, S. N. (1993b). "Creativity in Natural Science," *WESS Comm*, 3: 30-33.

Salthe, S. N. (2002). "Summary of the Principles of Hierarchy Theory," *General Systems Bulletin*, 31: 13-17.

Salthe, S. N. (2003). "Entropy: What Does it Really Mean?" *General Systems Bulletin*, 32: 5-12.

Seife, C. (2003). "Galaxy Maps Support Theory that the Universe is Flying to Pieces," *Science*, 302: 762-763.

CHAPTER 6

ADVANCING COMPLEXITY THEORY INTO THE HUMAN DOMAIN

Barbara Simpson

This chapter argues that complexity theory is currently struggling to find relevance in the domain of human activity because it is trapped within the dualistic distinction between two quite different worldviews. On one hand, adherents of the Platonic way of thinking, see complexity as the myriad different ways that reality may be constructed from basic building blocks of concrete substance. On the other hand, followers of the Heraclitean doctrine that 'all things flow' see complexity as the unpredictable outcome of myriad, time-dependent, relational processes. Although this dualism is pervasive in contemporary Western thinking, there are significant examples of radical new theory development that transcend this fundamental distinction between substance and process. Specifically, Einstein's special theory of relativity, Bergson's theory of duration, and Kelly's theory of personality are presented as illustrations of theories that have emerged from the unsticking of dualistic assumptions. Suggestions for the advancement of complexity theory are then derived from these illustrations.

Managing Organizational Complexity: Philosophy, Theory, and Application
A Volume in: Managing the Complex, pages 93-106.
Copyright © 2005 by Information Age Publishing, Inc.
All rights of reproduction in any form reserved.
ISBN: 1-59311-319-6 (cloth), 1-59311-318-8 (paper)

Introduction

If, as Maguire and McKelvey (1999) argue, human organizations epitomise complex adaptive systems, then it should be possible for complexity theory to directly inform organization theory and vice versa (Van Uden, et al., 2001). Indeed, complexity does offer tantalizing prospects for extending existing theories of organization, which, despite their success in explaining forms, structures, functions, and behaviors, nevertheless struggle to grapple with the dynamic nature of organizational processes. Nowhere is this more evident than in theories of organizational change and innovation. The notion of emergence as the unpredictable consequence of multiple, complex interactions is particularly relevant in this context; it draws attention to the historicity and temporality that is inherent in any time-dependent process while also maintaining a focus on the interacting entities themselves. There is, therefore, rich potential here for new insights into the ways that creative novelty and change may arise in organizations (see, for example, Goldstein, this volume).

As yet, however, this potential is far from realized. This is, at least in part, because complexity theory is still very much a work-in-progress. From its relatively recent beginnings in theoretical biology (e.g., Kauffman, 1995; Goodwin, 1994), complexity theory has grown rapidly, extending its reach into an ever-increasing range of disciplines and areas of inquiry. Thus the theory is itself emergent, evolving and transforming according to its own predictions. Within organization studies, complexity has so far been used mainly as a metaphor, but any more comprehensive application of the theory to human systems will inevitably require a fundamental shift in the way we approach theorizing (see for instance chapters in this volume by Gilpin, Connor & Napolitano, Horn, Richardson, J.). But how might such a transformation be achieved? My aim in this chapter is to explore what such fundamental, paradigmatic change might entail, and then to suggest a way forward in the ongoing evolution of complexity theory.

Changing paradigms

A paradigm is a way of viewing the world; it classifies what is known and knowable, and erects barriers to exclude knowledge that is deemed irrelevant or unusable. Because they are inherently bounded, paradigms tend to pigeonhole knowledge and ideas while at the same time breeding intolerance of alternative perspectives. 'Paradigm wars' have provided a combat arena for intellectual warriors for at least two millennia. Even today, the classical debate between Platonic and Heraclitean worldviews is frequently referenced. On one hand, followers of Plato argue that Nature is comprised of stable, unchanging units of substance that constitute the essential building blocks of existence. On the other hand, Heraclitus maintained that the fundamental 'stuff' of the world is not material substance but volatile flux, process, passage, and change (Rescher, 2000). Clearly these two worldviews are built on profoundly different and conflicting assumptions, so changing from one to the other would involve radically overhauling adherents' most cherished beliefs and deeply held convictions - a difficult task by any reckoning.

In the context of complexity theory, this same debate has been eloquently laid out by Robert Chia (1998), who distinguished two different types of complexity. Firstly, *taxonomic complexity* refers to the almost infinite, 'new' permutations and combinations that can be formed out of a set of finite and immutable elements. For example, the letters of an alphabet may be combined in a multitude of ways to create "syllables, words, sentences, paragraphs, books, genres and so on" (Chia, 1998: 48). There seems to be no limit to the possibilities that an alphabet permits, but importantly, the letters themselves never change. Chia, therefore, aligned taxonomic complexity with the classical Platonic view of the world as composed of 'essences' or substances that may be categorized into various fixed types. He further asserted that this view of complexity is consistent with the paradigm of classical science, with its particular metaphysical assumptions, objectives and methods of inquiry, and, of course, prejudices.

The second type that Chia discussed is *dynamic complexity*, which he described as a radically different mode of thinking that accentuates movement and change in an evolving world.

"Dynamic complexity is ... associated with a living reality that is perpetually becoming, renewing itself and perishing. It recognizes that the primary units of analyses are not discrete, isolatable and stabilized entities, but perpetually changing configurations of relations which are continuously transforming themselves." (Chia, 1998: 350)

In proposing this perspective, Chia was explicitly informed by the process philosophers Henri Bergson and Alfred North Whitehead, who ultimately aligned their thinking with the Heraclitean doctrine that 'all things flow' (Rescher 2000). Chia defined dynamic complexity as the antithesis of science, drawing parallels instead with the arts, humanities, and literature, where the subjectivity of meanings and the limitations of language confound the taxonomic definition of virtually everything. In Chia's view, science is unable to access this sort of complex thinking.

Thus the stage is set for yet another bout in the paradigm wars. In the blue corner we have complexity science with its imputation of systematic and deliberate simplification of Nature, and in the red corner we have complex thinking, a uniquely human activity where the exercise of freewill results in unpredictable outcomes. With the contest defined in these terms, the combatants have little option but to slug it out between them, the strongest / loudest / most persuasive invariably emerging as the victor. It is this same dynamic that underpins calls for paradigm shifts, whereby the assumptions of one worldview are ousted by its opposite. However, this achieves little more than to, once again, rehearse the arguments originally posed by the Greek philosophers more than 2500 years ago. Certainly this combative approach falls far short of the promise that lies at the heart of every dialectic opposition, namely a new synthesis.

Much of Western philosophy is characterized by this practice of separating the world into Cartesian dualisms, or paired categories that are defined in opposition to each other. These dualisms operate as simplifying mechanisms, imposing a bipolar sense of order onto an otherwise chaotic and incomprehensible world. But they also impose boundaries that cut across the natural ebb and flow between poles, eliminating the possibilities of 'shades of grey', and inevitably concentrating power in one pole at the expense of its opposite. The American pragmatists (e.g., William James, John Dewey, and George Herbert Mead) were implacably opposed to this practice of dualistic separation. Dewey (1916) was particularly incensed by the separation of knowing and doing in the educational sphere, arguing that this is the source of numerous evils in educational and learning theories. Although these grand dualistic debates are undeniably fascinating, they tend to obscure opportunities for genuine theoretical advancement. The pragmatists maintained that rather than choosing one pole or the other, it is more productive to open a dialogue between poles in order to explore the continuities within these intellectual tensions. They sought new theoretical syntheses by focussing on specific, limited problems, such as the functioning of consciousness in human actions, or the role of self-reflexivity in social situations (Joas, 1993). Thus they were able to advance theory for specific issues rather than aiming for broadly generalizable, grand theories of everything.

In a different way, the contemporary philosopher, Ian Hacking (1999) has also endeavoured to break through the bonds of Cartesian dualisms. He noted that since the poles of a dualism are defined in opposition to each other, then they are necessarily incommensurable. That is, they are like oil and water, and no amount of mixing will ever create an homogeneous blend. He referred to these incommensurable differences as 'sticking points', and suggested that a necessary first step towards advancing debate is to tease out the sticking points so as to better understand exactly where the obstacles lie. For instance in the philosophical debate between realism and constructionism, Hacking identified three specific sticking points, which he elaborated in detail in an attempt to unmask the underlying ideologies. Ultimately the theorist's aim is to then unstick these sticking points.

So, drawing together the threads of my argument so far, it seems that the problems of advancing complexity theory, especially into the human domain, may be construed as paradigmatic and ideological. Paradigmatic problems cannot be overcome simply by switching from one pole of a dualism to the other, or by somehow papering over the differences to produce a bland, seemingly unified position from which to advance theory. Following Hacking and the pragmatists, it seems to me that there is a two-stage process that might usefully be pursued in the face of seemingly insurmountable obstacles to theory development. Firstly, the real sticking points must be identified and then teased out to discover the source of their deep differences. Secondly, a limited problem scenario should be identified with a view to uncovering a genuine, emergent synthesis that accommodates these differences. This all sounds straightforward enough, but of course, revolution is never easy. In the next section, I will outline three historical examples of sticking points that have been unstuck. The first of these is Albert Einstein's special theory of relativity, the second is Henri Bergson's theory of duration, and the third is George Kelly's theory of personality. In each case, my intention is to examine the nature of the 'unsticking' that occurred. Readers who seek a deeper understanding of any of these theories should refer to the original sources.

Three sticking points unstuck
Illustration #1: Special theory of relativity

Some readers may be surprised by my choice of such an icon of science as my first illustration of unsticking and theory advancement. My reasoning is that the special theory of relativity launched an intellectual revolution not only in Western science, but also across the broader spectrum of Western philosophical thinking, to the extent that Einstein's name has now entered the popular lexicon. The theory makes a significant break from those absolutes and universals that had so characterized the classicism of Descartes and Newton, and have been so widely reviled and denounced by philosophers and scholars of the arts and humanities. Instead, Einstein recast the universe as a multiplicity of reference frames each of which provides a different perception of reality.

To really appreciate the magnitude of this change, it is salutary to reflect for a moment on the context of science at the beginning of the 20th century when Einstein was formulating his radical views. At that time absolute space was conceived as a vast geometrical container filled with a passive medium, 'the ether'. Much scientific effort was focussed on the detection of this all-pervasive medium. Perhaps the most famous example was the Michelson-Morley experiment, which set out to measure the difference in travel distances and times of two light beams, one running parallel to the absolute motion of the Earth through the ether, and the other running perpendicular to this. Without going into all the mathematics, the hypothesis was that the ether would affect the travel distance and time of each beam differently, and that by measuring this difference, the physical existence and nature of the ether would be revealed. However, although the experiment was repeated using many different configurations, the anticipated difference in travel distance and time was never found.

These unexpected negative findings were explained by an ingenious suggestion that distances and times are transformed by the speed of motion of any given frame of reference[1]. So, for example, consider two trains that are moving relative to each other; suppose that you are a passenger sitting on one train watching the other train passing by; a passenger on the other train will also note that you are passing by in the opposite direction. According to the proposed transformation, each passenger observes the slowing down of time and the distortion of space in the other train. But paradoxically, this then means that the clocks on both trains are slower than each other, so the notion of absolute time, or indeed any other absolute, ceases to have any meaning. The simple, yet enormously significant step that Einstein took in formulating the special theory of relativity was to recognize that in all moving systems, these contractions of length and the dilation of time are both reciprocal and referential. Einstein himself was very clear it is not merely that we cannot observe these absolutes, but that the assumption of their existence adds nothing to our understanding.

The particular sticking point that Einstein had to overcome was the way that classical science had separated space and time, conceiving them as absolute, objective, all-encompassing dimensions that exist independently of each other. In a sense this objectification of space and time may be seen as an expression of the ancient Platonic / Heraclitean dualism that separates stable substances (which occupy space) and dynamic flows (which occupy time). The specific problem area that Einstein invoked in developing this new theory was that of high-speed physics, and out of this he synthesized an entirely new, relativistic science. This science of relativity redefines the dimensions of space and time in terms of the relative motion of observer and observed. Put simply, perceived distances become a function of time, and perceived times, a function of distance. It is meaningless then, to speak of either timeless space or spaceless time hence Einstein's adoption of the term *spacetime* to reflect the inextricably interwoven nature of relativistic time and space.

Illustration #2: Theory of duration

During his lifetime (1859-1941), Henri Bergson was arguably the most famous philosopher in Europe. His accolades included election to the Academie Française in 1914, and the award of a Nobel Prize for literature in 1927. The scope of his scholarship was vast, encompassing metaphysics, ethics, methodology, and philosophies of mind and biology. Throughout this body of work, Bergson consistently rejected the absolutism of classical science, espousing instead a philosophy that is 'close to real life'. Interestingly, a number of commentators have noted parallels between these aspects of Bergson's philosophy and that of the American pragmatists (Linstead & Mullarkey, 2003). Although his often-controversial ideas and his association with the discredited philosophy of Vitalism resulted in his post-war slump into obscurity, Bergson's ideas have recently enjoyed something of a renaissance (for instance in the area of organization studies see Chia, 1998, 1999, 2002; Letiche, 2000; Linstead, 2002; Tsoukas & Chia, 2002).

The nature of time was a recurring theme throughout Bergson's work. He maintained

"No question has been more neglected by philosophers than that of time." (Bergson, 1923 / 1999: xxviii)

In fact, time has always been problematic for philosophers. For instance, Ricoeur (1984) described Saint Augustine's struggle with this issue - if the future is not yet, the past is no longer, and the present does not endure, then how is one to grasp such an ephemeral concept as time? And yet, time-reckoning is the very essence of human existence. In his extended essay on this subject, Elias (1992) argued that time is a social datum by means of which we humans orient ourselves to the social world. From earliest civilization, people have situated themselves socially in terms of naturally occurring cycles (e.g., seasons and tides) or events (Clark, 1985, 2000). With the rise of modern, industrialized society however, this primitive, sociocentric means of time-reckoning has been usurped by its dualistic opposite, machine-centred clock-time, to the extent that

"this all-pervasive sense of [clock-]time, is so compelling that most members of these [industrialized] societies find it extremely difficult, if not impossible to imagine that their own time experience is not shared by human beings everywhere" (Elias, 1992: 135).

It was precisely this 'universalization' of the human experience of time that Bergson saw as a major obstacle to understanding the dynamic nature of processes. He argued that both event-time and clock-time are examples of 'spatialized time'. That is, they express time by projecting our own temporal experience onto an external, spatial proxy (like the moving hands of a clock, or the revolving Earth). By spatializing time, we are disassociating it from the experiential realm while rendering it quantifiable and measurable. Processes can then be conceptualized as successions of instants, resulting in what Bergson (1919) called a cinematographical mechanism of thought.

Perhaps the most famous illustration of the problems inherent in this approach to process is *Zeno's Paradox of the Arrow* (Rescher, 2001), which may be simply stated as:

At any given instant an arrow does not move; a span of time consists of nothing other than instants; therefore the arrow is immobile; but of course we know that arrows can, and do, move.

Essentially Zeno's problem is how to construct motion out of immobility. Even by reducing the time separation between instants to ever more fine-grained scales, process is nevertheless reduced to a stop-start lurch from one (static) moment to the next. Neither classical science nor philosophy bothered unduly about this problem, although Descartes did invoke a *deus ex machina* solution whereby the necessary dynamic connections between instants were provided by continuous divine creation.

Bergson recognized that, in order to capture the dynamic nature of process, it is necessary to admit some expression of continuity, or enduring spatio-temporality, into theory (Čapek, 1971). This in turn implies a form of consciousness that bridges between the present and the past, providing the continuity that is denied when time is spatialized into a succession of instants. By focussing on the uniquely human experience of temporality, Bergson developed a new theory of duration that transcends the limitations of spatialized time, whether it be event-time or clock-time.

"[Duration] is the continuity of our inner life ... It is memory, but not personal memory, external to what it retains, distinct from a past whose preservation it assures; it is a memory within change itself, a memory that prolongs the before into the after, keeping them from being mere snapshots and appearing and disappearing in a present ceaselessly reborn." (Bergson, 1923 / 1999: 30)

This theory of duration evolved throughout Bergson's career. He not only laid out the philosophical foundations of his argument (Bergson, 1910, 1919), but he also specified a method of inquiry, the *Method of Intuition* (Bergson, 1903 / 1913), to be used in the exploration of duration. The theory achieved its most comprehensive elaboration through his analysis and extension of Einstein's special theory of relativity (Bergson, 1923 / 1999). This analysis lead him to differentiate the meanings of the terms *simultaneity* and *contemporaneity*, which in turn allowed him to theorize the relationship between temporality and spatialized time. Ultimately he argued, in contradiction to Einstein's unconstrained relativism, that in fact there does exist a "unity of real time" (Bergson, 1923 / 1999: 53), which is the personal or psychological time that is immanent in the frame of reference of the observer, regardless of that frame's rate of motion.

When Bergson published these conclusions in his book *Duration and Simultaneity*, the scientific establishment adopted a defensive stance, assuming that he was directly criticizing the hallowed special theory of relativity. Bergson ruefully commented about this in a letter written to Čapek in 1938:

"This particular point [i.e., his philosophy of physics] has hardly been noticed for one very simple reason: since my views about this question were formulated at the time when it was regarded as self-evident that the ultimate material elements should be conceived in the image of the [macroscopic] whole, they confused readers and were most frequently set aside as an unintelligible part of my work. It was probably assumed that this was an accessory part. Nobody, with the possible exception of the profound mathematician and philosopher Whitehead, noticed ... that this was for me something essential which was closely related to my theory of duration and which lay in the direction in which physics would move sooner or later." (Čapek, 1971: xi)

These words proved to be prophetic as subsequent developments in physics have indeed proceeded along the general direction anticipated by Bergson.

Illustration #3: Theory of personality

My third illustration of unsticking and advancing new theory draws on the work of George Kelly, whose major theoretical contribution, *Personal Construct Psychology* (PCP), was published in two volumes in 1955. Kelly identified himself primarily as a clinical psychologist, but his thinking was shaped by diverse influences, ranging from debates that were current in the field of psychology, to his earlier education in mathematics and physics, as well as his broader philosophical interests in humanity (Fransella & Neimeyer, 2003). He particularly acknowledged his intellectual debt to the pragmatist, John Dewey, but more generally, Shotter (1970: 224) located Kelly as a "spiritual brother" to Mead, Vygotsky and Wittgenstein. His very significant scholarly achievements were ultimately recognized in 1965 through the American Psychological Association's Award for Distinguished Contribution to the Science and Profession of Clinical Psychology.

Kelly's theorizing was motivated by his frustration with the divisions within psychology, and the obstacles that these divisions present to the working psychologist whose task it is to assist clients to better understandings of themselves. In particular, the classical Cartesian dualism separating mind and body, or thought and feeling, is manifest as two quite distinct psychologies. On one hand, *cognitive psychology* is concerned with aspects of perception, reason and memory, while on the other hand, *affective psychology* deals with the emotions involved in motivation, drive, and libido. But the clinician's client is a whole person who both thinks and feels. It is hardly surprising then, that these psychologies have contributed little to understanding aspects of human existence such as humour, creativity, art, ethics and love, that cannot be conceived as either purely cognitive or purely affective (Bannister, 1977). In developing his theory of personality then, Kelly took great pains to emphasize his concern with the whole person: passions, actions, thoughts, warts and all.

Secondly, the academic distinction between psychology and sociology as different levels of analysis, separates thinking about the individual from thinking about the social context within which individuals interact. This separation leads to the person being conceived as a behaving organism, passively reacting to stimuli in its environment rather than actively co-constructing its reality. Kelly turned the spotlight onto the issue of human agency in a socially constructed world, emphasizing that the construction of a social reality implies the existence of interacting agents of construction. PCP explains how this agency is exercised in a social context, resulting in both social stability and the creative generation of novelty and innovation.

Recognizing that these dualisms are deeply embedded in the language of psychology, Kelly endeavoured to find an alternative way of talking about the whole person. He seized upon the fact that, far from being inert entities responding to external or internal stimuli, people are alive and by definition, constantly moving and changing. Accordingly, Kelly located human action at the centre of his theory development, especially the actions that arise out of the psychological process of anticipation. He argued that anticipation allows us to progressively elaborate our capacity for meaning-making, better preparing us for an unknown, emergent future. Indeed, he described PCP as

"a theory of man's personal inquiry - a psychology of the human quest. It does not say what has or will be found, but proposes rather how we might go about looking for it" (Kelly, 1970: 1).

The philosophical foundation for PCP is what Kelly called *constructive alternativism*, by which he meant to imply that "all of our present interpretations of the universe are subject to revision or replacement" (1955 / 1991: 11). While some constructions may serve us well at present, others may need to be changed in order to improve our anticipatory processes. Kelly encouraged a playful, 'as if' approach to even our most everyday constructions of events so that we might explore how they would appear if construed differently. A second important philosophical plank in PCP is Kelly's insistence that since the theory is itself a product of psychological processes, then it must be capable of reflexively explaining its own construction. It is this characteristic of reflexivity that most strongly distinguishes PCP from other, more traditional psychological viewpoints that tend to have one theory for the client (subject) and another for the clinical specialist (Bannister, 2003).

PCP is a comprehensive, coherent, practical, and generative theory of personality, that is still being elaborated by contemporary theorists and practitioners. However, the critical commentary on the theory continues to reflect significant misunderstandings of Kelly's intentions. He was particularly perplexed by the repeated misrepresentation of PCP as a cognitive theory and consequent criticisms that the theory fails to address emotions. In his own words:

"The reader may have noticed that in talking about experience I have been careful not to use either of the terms, 'emotional' or 'affective'. I have been equally careful not to invoke the notion of 'cognition'. The classic distinction which separates these two constructs has, in the manner of most classic distinctions that once were useful, become a barrier to sensitive psychological inquiry. When one so divides the experience of man, it becomes difficult to make the most of the holistic aspirations that may infuse the science of psychology with new life" (Kelly, 1969: 140).

Discussion

The three illustrations that I have provided here demonstrate that new theoretical syntheses can, and do, emerge from the apparently insoluble differences between dualistic opposites: the special theory of relativity arose from the classical separation of space and time as independent absolutes; the theory of duration generated a non-spatialized view of temporality out of the clock-time / event-time dualism; and the theory of personality emerged from differences between cognitive and affective psychologies as well as the separation of psychological and sociological levels of analysis. All three theories were quite radical at the time of their publication, and were widely criticized by their contemporary academic audiences, but in the intervening years, each has opened up entirely new ways of thinking and new questions to be explored by successive generations of scholars. Thus although, Einstein, Bergson and Kelly are all long dead, their ideas continue to invigorate new thinking that challenges the current assumptions of 'normal science'.

Complexity theory also has considerable potential to provide just such a challenge, but Chia (1998) has suggested the theory is trapped within a dualism that separates substance and process, and science and art. As a consequence, the theory is currently developing along two parallel paths located at the opposing poles of this dualism. The essential sticking point that Chia identified is the difference between unconscious, reactive (nonhuman) behavior as exemplified by taxonomic complexity, and the conscious, responsive (human) behavior that characterizes dynamic complexity. The primary assertion of complexity theory is that variations arising out of the interactions between entities, whether human or nonhuman, are the source of new, self-organized order in complex systems. But the differences between human and nonhuman behaviors imply differences in the ways that variations are generated in interactions. If complexity is to fulfil its promise, especially as it applies to the human domain, it is imperative that this dualism is unstuck, and a new synthesis is found that in some way transcends these differences.

My choice of illustrations for this chapter was by no means random. The three theories I have presented may in fact provide a useful springboard for the further development of complexity theory. Like complexity, the theories of relativity, duration and personality are all concerned with bodies in motion. That is, they all transcend the classical Platonic / Heraclitean dualism that separates bodies from their processes. So, rather than getting caught up in debates about whether reality is better conceived in terms of essential substance or dynamic process, these theories explicitly acknowledge the interdependence of substance and process in their formulations. Thus one way of advancing complexity theory would be to maintain a central focus on entities and their interactions, rather than on either states of emergent order or the dynamics of self-organizing.

In addition, Bergson and Kelly were both concerned with the whole person. Bergson emphasized the role of consciousness in providing continuity in human processes, while Kelly focussed on anticipation as a way of understanding human action. This approach is consistent with the notion of the person as a complex system. It recognizes that all aspects of a person may potentially be involved in interactions, and should therefore be included in any attempt to theorize the occurrence of variations and the emergence of new order in human systems. Furthermore, Kelly's theory of personality explicitly recognizes interpersonal engagement as a source of learning, and hence variation. Thus this theory provides direct insights into the relational nature of those very human interactions that lie at the heart of complexity theory.

Each of these three theories demonstrates the importance of language and new terminologies in theory building. But even meticulous attention to redefinitions of key terms may not deflect critics from more familiar interpretations. Čapek suggested that the most interesting and most significant implications of radical revisions in thinking are almost invariably obscured by the limitations of language. In fact radical conceptual revisions demand a radical transformation of language

"otherwise we are pouring a new wine into the old vessels with the familiar result ... nothing is more stubbornly resistant than 'ordinary language', whose resistance measures the inertia of the mental habits of which it is a depository" (Čapek, 1971: 226).

An obvious example of terminological confusion in complexity theory relates to the word 'emergence'. Those scholars who adhere to a Platonic worldview tend to see emergence as a reference to fixed properties appearing at one level of a system that could not have been predicted from properties at lower systemic levels (Checkland, 1981). Conversely, a Heraclitean perspective sees emergence as the unpredictable outcome of complex, time dependent, relational processes (Emmeche, *et al.*, 1997). It is difficult to see how the theory can advance whilst ambiguity as to the meaning of such a central concept as emergence remains unresolved.

As I suggested in the introduction to this chapter, complexity theory is a work-in-progress that is actively evolving through cross-disciplinary conversations amongst scholars and practitioners. We can all participate in these formative conversations, but in order to advance the theory, we need to do this with an awareness of the assumptions and language that we each bring to the table. In particular, the examples I have presented here of radical new theory development suggest we must take care that our underlying assumptions do not fall into one or other of the Platonic or Heraclitean worldviews, but rather, that they acknowledge the essential interdependence of interacting entities and their relational processes. Secondly, we should be vigilant about the language that we use and the meanings that we intend to convey, and where necessary the community of complexity theorists should seek to develop new shared understandings of commonly used terms. If we, the members of this community, consciously modify our assumptions and language, the nature and quality of our interactions will necessarily change, and this in turn will shape the ongoing evolution of complexity theory, exactly as the theory itself would predict.

Acknowledgements

I gratefully acknowledge the patient guidance and support of the editor and two reviewers who all contributed significantly to the final form of this chapter, as well as the willingness of my colleague, Paul Hibbert, to read and comment on emergent drafts and to maintain essential chocolate supplies.

References

Bannister, D. (1977). "The Logic of Passion," in D. Bannister (Ed.), *New Perspectives in Personal Construct Theory*, London: Academic Press, pp. 21-37.

Bannister, D. (2003). "Kelly Versus Clockwork Psychology," in F. Fransella (ed.), *International Handbook of Personal Construct Psychology*, Chichester: John Wiley & Sons.

Bergson, H. (1903/1913). *An Introduction to Metaphysics*, T. E. Hulme (trans.), London: Macmillan and Co.

Bergson, H. (1910). *Time and Free Will: An Essay on the Immediate Data of Consciousness*, New York: Macmillan.

Bergson, H. (1919). *Creative Evolution*, A. Mitchell (trans.), London: Macmillan & Co.

Bergson, H. (1923/1999). *Duration and Simultaneity: Bergson and the Einsteinian Universe*, L. Jacobson (trans.), 2nd edition including additional material supplied by Mark Lewis (ed.), Manchester: Clinamen Press Ltd.

Čapek, M. (1971). *Bergson and Modern Physics*, Dordrecht-Holland: D. Reidel Publishing Company.

Checkland, P. (1981). *Systems Thinking, Systems Practice*, Chichester: Wiley.

Chia, R. (1998). "From Complexity Science to Complex Thinking: Organization as Simple Location," *Organization*, 5(3): 341-369.

Chia, R. (1999). "A 'Rhizomic' Model of Organizational Change and Transformation: Perspective from a Metaphysics of Change," *British Journal of Management*, 10: 209-227.

Chia, R. (2002). "Essai: Time, Duration and Simultaneity: Rethinking Process and Change in Organizational Analysis." *Organization Studies*, 23(6): 863-868.

Clark, P. (1985). "A Review of the Theories of Time and Structure for Organizational Sociology," in S. B. Bacharach and S. M. Mitchell (eds.), *Research in the Sociology of Organizations: A Research Annual*, Greenwich, CT: JAI Press Inc., pp. 35-80.

Clark, P. (2000). *Organizations in Action: Competition Between Contexts*, London: Routledge.

Dewey, J. (1916). *Democracy and Education*, New York: Macmillan.

Elias, N. (1992). *Time: An Essay*, Oxford, UK: Blackwell.

Emmeche, C., Køppe, S., and Stjernfelt, F. (1997). "Explaining Emergence: Towards an Ontology of Levels," *Journal for General Philosophy of Science*, 28: 83-119.

Fransella, F. and Neimeyer, R. (2003). "George Alexander Kelly: The Man and His Theory," in F. Fransella (ed.), *International Handbook of Personal Construct Psychology*, Chichester, UK: John Wiley & Sons.

Goodwin, B. (1994). *How the Leopard Changed Its Spots: The Evolution of Complexity*, London: Phoenix.

Hacking, I. (1999). *The Social Construction of What?* Cambridge, MA: Harvard University Press.

Joas, H. (1993). *Pragmatism and Social Theory*, Chicago: University of Chicago Press.

Kauffman, S. (1995). *At Home in the Universe: The Search for the Laws of Self-Organization and Complexity*, Oxford; New York: Oxford University Press.

Kelly, G. (1955/1991). *The Psychology of Personal Constructs*, reprint of the original published by Norton (ed.), London: Routledge.

Kelly, G. (1969). "Humanistic Methodology in Psychological Research," in B. Maher (ed.), *Clinical Psychology and Personality: The Selected Papers of George Kelly*, New York: John Wiley & Sons.

Kelly, G. (1970). "A Brief Introduction to Personal Construct Psychology," in D. Bannister (ed.), *Perspectives in Personal Construct Theory*, London: Academic Press, pp. 1-30.

Letiche, H. (2000). "Phenomenal Complexity Theory as Informed by Bergson," *Journal of Organizational Change Management*, 13(6): 545-557.

Linstead, S. (2002). "Organization as Reply: Henri Bergson and Casual Organization Theory," *Organization*, 9(1): 95-111.

Linstead, S. and Mullarkey, J. (2003). "Time, creativity and culture: Introducing Bergson." *Culture and Organization*, 9(1), 3-13.

Maguire, S. and McKelvey, B. (1999). "Complexity and Management: Moving from Fad to Firm Foundations," *Emergence*, 1(2): 19-61.

Rescher, N. (2000). *Process Philosophy: A Survey of Basic Issues*, University of Pittsburgh Press.

Rescher, N. (2001). *Paradoxes: Their Roots, Range, and Resolution*, Chicago: Open Court.

Ricouer, P. (1984). *Time and Narrative*, K. McLaughlin and D. Pellauer (trans.), Chicago: University of Chicago Press.

Shotter, J. (1970). "Men, the Man-Makers: George Kelly and the Psychology of Personal Constructs," in D. Bannister (ed.), *Perspectives in Personal Construct Theory*, London: Academic Press, pp. 223-253.

Tsoukas, H. and Chia, R. (2002). "On Organizational Becoming: Rethinking Organizational Change," *Organization Science*, 13(5): 567-582.

van Uden, J., Richardson, K., and Cilliers, P. (2001). "Postmodernism Revisited? Complexity Science and the Study of Organizations," *Tamara: Journal of Critical Postmodern Organization Science*, 1(3): 53-67.

Notes

1. For a more comprehensive explanation of relativity see Bergson (1923/1999) or Čapek (1971)

SECTION TWO

THEORY

Section introduction
Pluralism in management science

What if organizations were merely complicated?

What if human organizations were *complicated* rather than *complex*? The simple answer to this question is that the possibility of an all-embracing Theory of Management would almost certainly exist. Why is this? What is the difference between complicated and complex that leads to *theoretical monism* from the former and *theoretical pluralism* from the latter?

A very common (but not particularly useful) description of a complex system is that such systems comprise a large number of nonlinearly interacting parts. By this definition the modern computer would be a complex system. A modern computer is crammed full of transistors which all respond nonlinearly to their input(s). Despite this 'complexity' the average PC does not show signs of emergence or self-organization; it simply follows the instructions given to it by its programmer. Even the language in which it is programmed is rather uninteresting. Although there are many programming languages, they can all be translated into each other with relative ease, i.e., computer languages are *commensurable* with each other. There also exists a universal language into which all such languages can be translated without loss - we call it 'logic'. More often though, if a programmer wants to use a language very close to the universal language of computing, *assembler* is used as this at least contains concepts that are more readily used in writing programs. This is then translated into machine code (which is based on Boolean logic) - writing directly in Boolean logic would be nigh on impossible for any human programmer. The computer cannot choose the way it interprets the program, it cannot rewrite the program (unless it is programmed to in a prescribed manner), and it cannot get fed up with running programmes and go to the pub. So, what is it about the modern computer that prevents it from being a complex system, but rather a complicated system?

The critical element is *feedback*. It is the existence of nonlinear feedback in complex systems that allows for *emergence, self-organization, adaptation, learning* and many other key concepts that have become synonymous with complexity thinking. It is not just the existence of feedbacks loops that leads to complex behavior. These loops must themselves interact with each other. Once we have three or more *interacting* feedback loops (which may be made up from the interactions of many parts) predicting the resulting behavior via standard

Managing Organizational Complexity: Philosophy, Theory, and Application
A Volume in: Managing the Complex, pages 109-114.
ISBN: 1-59311-319-6 (cloth), 1-59311-318-8 (paper)

mathematical analysis becomes impossible for most intents and purposes. In a relatively simple complex system containing, say, fifteen parts / components there can be hundreds of interacting feedback loops. In such instances the only way to get a feel for the resulting dynamics is through simulation, which is why the computer (despite its rather uninteresting dynamics) has become so important in the development of complexity thinking. We say that the prediction of overall system dynamics from knowledge of its parts is *intractable*. Basically, absolute knowledge about the parts that make up a system and their interactions provides us with very little understanding indeed regarding how that system will behave overall. Often the only recourse we have is to sit back and watch. In a sense the term complex system refers to systems which, although we may have a deep appreciation of how it is put together (at the *microscopic* level), we may be completely ignorant of how the resulting *macroscopic* behavior comes about. In the computer (which we will now class as a complicated system) causality is simple, i.e., low dimensional - few (interacting) feedback loops. In complex systems causality is networked, making it very difficult indeed, if not impossible, to untangle the contribution each causal route makes.

Another unexpected property of complex systems is there exist stable abstractions, not expressible in terms of the constituent parts, that themselves bring about properties different from those displayed by the parts. I have here described the process of emergence, but in a rather awkward way. This is deliberate. More often than not emergence is portrayed as a process from which macroscopic properties 'emerge' from microscopic properties, i.e., the properties of the whole emerge from the properties of its parts. But this in an overly simplistic view of emergence. When recognizing the products of emergence, e.g., novel wholes, what is really happening is that we are abstracting (which includes a filtering process) away from the description in terms of parts and interactions, and proposing a new description in terms of entities quite different from the constituent parts we started with. These new entities have novel properties in relation to the properties the constituent parts have. What is even more interesting is that these supposed abstractions can interact with the parts from which they emerged - a process known as *downward causation*. I won't go into the problematic nature of the concept of emergence any further here - please refer to Richardson (2004) - suffice to say a belief that the process of emergence is captured by the expression "the whole is greater than the sum of its parts" (even if we include their interactions) is too simplistic. For further analysis of the concept of emergence, please refer to chapters 2 and 4 of this volume and Sulis (2004), in which the notions of *vertical* and *horizontal* emergence are explored.

In complex systems such as in (Boolean) cellular automata the parts are very simple indeed, and yet they still display a great deal of emergent phenomena and dynamical diversity. Complex systems which contain more intricate parts are often referred to as *complex adaptive systems* or CASs. The parts of CASs contain local memories and have a series of detailed responses to the same, as well as different, contexts / scenarios. They often have the ability to learn from their mistakes and generate new responses to familiar and novel contexts. Because of this localized decision-making / learning ability such parts are often referred to as agents. There is a profound relationship between simple complex systems (SCSs), i.e., complex systems comprised of simple parts, and CASs, i.e., complex systems comprised of intricate agents. The Game-of-Life, which is discussed in chapter 2, shows how a CAS can be abstracted, or emerges, from a SCS! Intuition would tell us that a CAS is simply a more intricate SCS. The Game-of-Life demonstrates that our intuition is, again, too simplistic.

Complexity and incompressibility

Paul Cilliers (Chapter 1, this volume) introduces the idea of incompressibility:

"We have seen that there is no accurate (or rather, perfect) representation of the system which is simpler than the system itself. In building representations of open systems, we are forced to leave things out, and since the effects of these omissions are nonlinear, we cannot predict their magnitude." (p. 13).

In my view, it is this concept of incompressibility that leads us away from a managerial monism to a managerial pluralism (assuming organizations are complex rather than merely complicated). Restating Cilliers, the best representation of a complex system is the system itself, and any representation of the system will be incomplete and, therefore, can lead to inappropriate understanding. One must be careful in interpreting the importance of incompressibility. Just because a complex system is incompressible it does not follow that there are (incomplete) representations of the system that cannot be useful - incompressibility is not an excuse for not bothering. For example, building on the work of Bilke and Sjunnesson (2001) I recently showed (Richardson, 2005) how Boolean networks (which are a type of SCS) could be reduced / compressed in such a way as to not change the qualitative character of the uncompressed system's phase space, i.e., the compressed system had the same functionality as the uncompressed system. If nothing was lost in the compression process, then Cilliers's claim of incompressibility would be incorrect. However, what is lost is a great deal of detail of how the different attractor basins (qualitatively different regimes of dynamical behavior) are reached. Furthermore, the reduced systems are not as tolerant to external perturbations as their unreduced parents. This evidence would suggest that stable and accurate representations of complex systems do indeed exist. However, in reducing / compressing / abstracting a complex system certain properties are lost. Different representations capture different aspects of the original system's behavior. We might say that, in the absence of a complete representation, the overall behavior of a system is *at least* the sum of the behaviors of all our reduced models of that system. In Richardson (2005), I concluded that:

"Complex systems may well be incompressible in an absolute sense, but many of them are at least quasi-reducible in a variety of ways. This fact indicates that the many commentators suggesting that reductionist methods are in some way anti-complexity - some even go so far as to suggest that traditional scientific methods have no role in facilitating the understanding complexity - are overstating their position. Often linear methods are assessed in much the same way. The more modest middle ground is that though complex systems may indeed be incompressible, most, if not all, methods are capable of shedding some light on certain aspects of their behavior. It is not that the incompressibility of complex systems prevents understanding, and that all methods that do not capture complexity to a complete extent are useless, but that we need to develop an awareness of how our methods limit our potential understanding of such systems."

The suggestion that there are multiple valid representations of the same complex system is not new. The complementary law (Weinberg, 1975) from general systems theory suggests that any two different perspectives (or models) about a system will reveal truths regarding that system that are neither entirely independent nor entirely compatible. More recently, this has been stated as: a complex system is a system that has two or more non-overlapping descriptions (Cohen, 2002). I would go as far as to include "potentially contradictory" suggesting that for complex systems (by which I really mean any part of reality I care to examine) *there exists an infinitude of equally valid, non-overlapping, potentially contradictory descriptions.* Maxwell in his analysis of a new conception of science asserts that:

"Any scientific theory, however well it has been verified empirically, will always have infinitely many rival theories that fit the available evidence just as well but that make different predictions, in an arbitrary way, for yet unobserved phenomena." (Maxwell, 2000).

The result of these observations is that to fully understand complex systems we must approach them from many directions - we must take a pluralistic stance.

Complexity and pluralism

The pluralism inherent in complexity thinking undermines the whole notion of a unified theory of complexity, i.e., theoretical monism. A simplistic view of unification would be similar to the example above of computer languages. Unification of this sort would suggest that if we work very hard indeed, eventually we will not only have at hand all the relevant laws of complexity, but that these different laws could be derived from *one* underlying principle. This is very much the basis of Theories of Everything (TOEs) in the physical sciences. Although there will exist a plurality of theories, they will all be coherent in that they can be expressed in terms of a more fundamental / general language (a form of mathematics, say) without any loss of detail. We might refer to this as *commensurable pluralism*. However, if we assume that a complex systems perspective provides a more appropriate basis from which to understand our surroundings, then we come up against incompressibility. Incompressibility leads to a different sort of pluralism altogether; a pluralism in which the different theories / representations are not all reducible to a fundamental language without loss of detail. In such a pluralism the different representations are generally incommensurable with each other, and rather than leading to a coherent TOE, a patchwork of theories results. Within such *incommensurable pluralism* there will be opportunities for translation, reduction and simplification, but a TOE will never result. In this situation the importance of context also becomes apparent. Each approach in the patchwork will be valid only for a certain range of contexts, and so matching theory to context becomes ever so important. However, a feature of complex systems is that context recognition is not a trivial exercise. Contexts which appear similar may actually be quite different, and so the process of matching theory to context is problematic at best. Furthermore, complex systems evolve (in a qualitative sense) and so fundamentally novel contexts emerge requiring new theoretical syntheses. If we assume that human organizations are best described as complex systems then this has quite profound implications for management science; implications that are at odds with traditionalist views in management science.

The main criticism traditionalists have of the 'others' is that by refusing to focus management studies on a single perspective / theory, the potential political and influential clout of management academics has been vastly reduced. According to Pfeffer (1993):

"Without a recommitment to a set of fundamental *questions and without working through a set of* rules *to resolve theoretical disputes, the field of organization studies will remain ripe for a hostile takeover."* (emphasis added)

Donaldson (1995) built an entire book around this idea: *American Anti-Management Theories of Organization: A Critique of Paradigm Proliferation.* Donaldson's book is an indictment of existing management science which, he claims, has fragmented into competing paradigms. Donaldson argues that this profusion of perspectives is driven not by a genuine need to further the body of knowledge, but by a "push for novelty fuelled by individual career interests" typical of the academic environment. He asserts that the resulting fragmentation of the field into mutually incompatible ideas has significantly weakened management science as an intellectual enterprise worthy of attention and support. Donaldson's book calls for building a unified theory of organizations. Clearly this is at odds with what has been discussed above. In my view, paradigm proliferation is healthy for management science - not a disease that needs to be eradicated.

In the chapters that follow the reader is unlikely to be able to parse them into a neatly packaged theory of management (without losing substantial detail, that is). However, they will certainly add to the theoretical patchwork that is essential if we are to have any genuine appreciation of organizational life.

References

Bilke, S. and Sjunnesson, F. (2002). "Stability of the Kauffman model," *Physical Review E*, 65: 016129.

Cohen, J. (2002). Posting to the Complex-M listserv, 2nd September.

Donaldson, L. (1995). *American Anti-Management Theories of Organization: A Critique of Paradigm Proliferation*, Cambridge Studies in Management, No. 25, Cambridge, UK: Cambridge University Press.

Maxwell, N. (2000). "A New Conception of Science," *Physics World*, August: 17-18.

Pfeffer, J. (1993) "Barriers to the Advance of Organizational Science: Paradigm Development as a Dependent Variable," *The Academy of Management Review*, 18: 599-620.

Richardson, K. A. (2004). "On the Relativity of Recognizing the Products of Emergence and the Nature of Physical Hierarchy," *proceedings of the 2nd Biennial International Seminar on the Philosophical, Epistemological and Methodological Implications of Complexity Theory*, January 7th-10th, Havana International Conference Center, Cuba.

Richardson, K. A. (2005). "Simplifying Boolean Networks," submitted to *Advances in Complex Systems*.

Sulis, W. (2004). "Archetypal Dynamical Systems and Semantic Frames in Vertical and Horizontal Emergence," *Emergence: Complexity and Organization*, 6(3): 52-64.

Weinberg, G. (1975). *An Introduction to General Systems Thinking*, NY: John Wiley.

CHAPTER 7

FROM EXCELLENCE TO EMERGENCE: THE EVOLUTION OF MANAGEMENT THINKING AND THE INFLUENCE OF COMPLEXITY

Buck Lawrimore

This chapter analyzes the evolution of management thinking as revealed in the most popular and thoroughly-researched management books of the past 23 years, beginning with Tom Peters and Robert Waterman's In Search of Excellence, *and continuing into the present, illustrating ways in which Complexity thinking is becoming more widely used, both with and without the Complexity rubric. The paper focuses especially on the 'critical success factors' identified by numerous authors and clusters them into five main categories with widespread application. A brief analysis of key complexity 'success factors' is provided as a basis of comparison, then a pre- and post-Complexity synthesis is offered, with illustrations of the author's real-world applications, followed by a prognosis of future management thinking evolution.*

Managing Organizational Complexity: Philosophy, Theory, and Application
A Volume in: Managing the Complex, pages 115-132.
Copyright © 2005 by Information Age Publishing, Inc.
All rights of reproduction in any form reserved.
ISBN: 1-59311-319-6 (cloth), 1-59311-318-8 (paper)

Introduction

Take two businesses with similar initial characteristics. Why does one succeed and grow, while the other one become stagnant, decline or die? As a consultant to business, government and nonprofit organizations since 1979, that question has long intrigued me. Discovering Complexity, which deals among other things with how living systems adapt and evolve, was one of the most interesting intellectual experiences of my life. But learning how to make it practical (income generating) in my consulting work has been a continuing challenge.

This article recounts one man's ongoing journey to discover both the most intellectually rigorous and the most universally practical approaches to guiding business and organization managers toward dependably greater success, including Complexity applications in recent years. In the process I recount key points on the path which others have traveled since the publication in the early 1980s of Tom Peters and Robert Waterman's (1982) now legendary book, *In Search of Excellence: Lessons from America's Best-Run Companies,* and Phil Crosby's (1980) *Quality Is Free,* which kicked off America's interest in total quality. I am not aware of any linear tracking study of the evolution of management thinking in the U.S. and other advanced countries, but I believe my own 23-year tracking study of the management literature as revealed in the steady march of top-selling business books will be a functional and interesting substitute.

It is important for the reader to understand that, of the thousands of management-thinking books published in the period 1980-2003, the ones I focused on and have reported in this chapter were either:

a. based on objective studies of many different companies, looking for patterns of differences which could explain outstanding success; or

b. very popular business books, among the top 10 best-sellers in that category at the time; or both.

I do not attempt to include the works of seminal thinkers like Peter Drucker, which are too diverse and evolving to adequately capture in this brief paper. To avoid a lengthy and perhaps boring history of the management literature, I will summarize the dominant themes and developments below, then turn to the influence of Complexity and some predictions as to what might come next.

To serve as a guide-map as well as to reveal how it evolved, I will use the framework of a system I developed in the late 1990s which I call the Strategic Alignment System™ (SAS). This system is a synthesis of the dominant 'critical success factors' of the leading management books of the previous two decades, which I used in my consulting work quite happily until I began discovering some deficiencies which only Complexity could address. So this will be sort of like a movie that begins with the ending, then goes back to reveal how that ending evolved as a series of events. To extend the metaphor, the Complexity 'movie' will then function as a sequel - 'Management Thinking II: The Rise of the Complex System' or something, as well as hints of a third in the series.

One caveat should be clearly stated: I believe the vast majority of managers, untrained in disciplined management thinking, simply learn from experience what works best for them. They are not interested in theory - just practical stuff. All who enjoy the insights of Complexity must keep in mind that it is still highly conceptual and not yet ready for the theory-averse majority. But progress is being made, as will be revealed below and in other chapters in this volume.

The Strategic Alignment System™

The Strategic Alignment System™ which I developed was a combination of my wrestling with the limitations of traditional strategic planning (TSP) and my studies of the business-management literature of the time, especially two books published in the late '90s: *The Balanced Scorecard* by Robert Kaplan and David Norton (1996), and *The Power of Alignment* by George Labovitz and Victor Rosansky (1997).

The Balanced Scorecard, currently being used by many organizations worldwide (see www.balancedscorecard.org), has several very appealing components:

- It reduces all management variables to four sets: Finances, Customer, Internal Business Processes, and Learning & Growth. This is by no means all-inclusive, but the authors claim that if an organization focuses on managing and measuring these four key factors, it will cover the most important contributors to corporate success.

- It strongly advocates the measurement of all four variable sets as a 'balance' to the lop-sided dominance of finances being the only business management yardstick in widespread use. Finances they call a 'lagging indicator' of success because once the numbers are in, they are history. The other variables are 'leading indicators' of success because they come before financial success and allow control of an organization's future.

- It shows how these four variable sets are interrelated and interdependent:

  - To achieve financial success, customers must be satisfied
  - To satisfy customers, internal business processes must be improved
  - To improve internal processes, personnel must continually learn and grow

While this sounds obvious to any reader who has also tackled Complexity, it was at the time an enormous breakthrough in management thinking, simplifying the dizzying array of variables which managers must attempt to control and showing how these four are interconnected. In other words, the

Balanced Scorecard is a true system, which the authors consider appropriate for the Information Age, but others familiar with Complexity would likely consider too linear and mechanical to function effectively in a rapidly changing environment.

The Power of Alignment, developed after extensive research by Organizational Dynamics, Inc., is a system for measuring the alignment of four somewhat different variable sets: Strategy, Operations, Customers and People. They developed a simple diagram as shown in Figure 1 which shows the interrelationships of the variable sets.

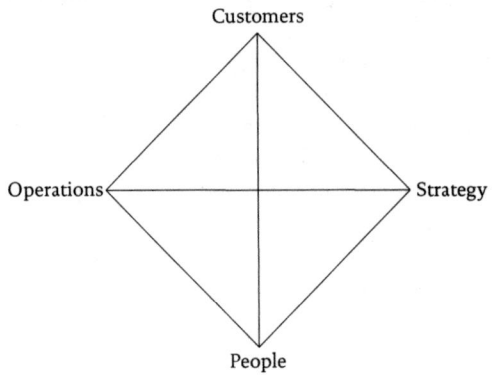

Figure 1
The Power of Alignment

And they were able to use this diagram to measure the degree of alignment or misalignment of an organization based on a survey of its people. For example, 'vertical alignment' indicates that the people in the company are aligned with what customers value most. 'Horizontal alignment' indicates that operations and strategy are aligned - that the company is doing what it says it intends to do. A skewed alignment chart, showing any of the points reduced or pulled toward the center, shows organizational deficiencies that need to be addressed. Again, like the Balanced Scorecard, this approach is somewhat simplistic. But most manager-types in my experience like things to be simple, especially systems which claim to be all-encompassing or at least sufficient. What I found most intriguing was the similarity between the key variables identified by Organizational Dynamics following extensive original research, and the key measures used in the Balanced Scorecard, both being developed independently of the other.

Since I had earlier faulted the Balanced Scorecard for taking strategy for granted (it is an implementation system, not a strategy development system), the Power of Alignment provided just the shift I felt was needed. But one thing is missing from it - finances, the oldest form of business measurement in existence. Also, because of my marketing background, I felt that the 'customers' variable was dangerously limiting. As much as companies need to focus on customer needs and satisfaction, the real growth potential is in the market, which includes noncustomers, who can only become customers through an effective marketing program, enabling the organization to increase its sales. The market also includes competitors who will try to take and keep customers for themselves, and market forces such as the economy, technology, demographics and cultural change, which an organization - especially a business - ignores at its peril.

And so my Strategic Alignment System consisted of these five variable sets (see Figure 2):

- *Strategy*: Focus on a distinctive way to be a market leader; this variable includes values, purpose, vision and other 'organizing-directional' principles;
- *People*: Personnel, structure, learning;
- *Operations*: The work people do inside the firm;
- *Markets*: Relationships with customers, noncustomers and the various forces in the market environment;
- *Finances*: The bottom line, including facilities and equipment.

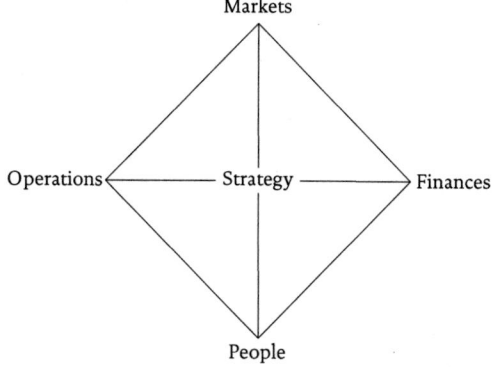

Figure 2
Strategic Alignment System

The logic of these five variable sets reflects actual business practices in many organizations. It is common for evolved companies to have departments broken out as sales and marketing, operations, finances, and personnel, with upper management responsible for the guiding strategy. These departmental terms in fact are so common it is easy to take them for granted without appreciating how they are just about essential. That is, every human organization is composed of people who engage in some type of activity (operations), usually providing products or services for customers (markets). They receive money (finances) in return, and that money is used to pay the people as well as cover operating expenses and overhead. Managing all the people and providing overall direction (strategy) are the top officers of the company - who are also people, but who have a different role, a higher level of responsibility, for guiding and directing the enterprise with some kind of strategy.

So that's the ending of the first movie. Now let's go back to the beginning and very quickly illustrate how each of these five variable sets can logically contain the primary critical success factors of leading management books of the previous 23 years. In fact I have found them to be very useful in analyzing any complex set of issues faced by an organization or community into five groups that include every issue mentioned (although some issues of course impact multiple variable sets). In the following outline I will present each book's 'critical success factors' and mark them with an M for Markets / Marketing, F for Finances, P for People, O for operations or S for Strategy, to indicate which of the five variable sets they best fit into. And then we will see how this variable set needs to change with the insights of Complexity.

In Search of Excellence begins our search

In *Search of Excellence: Lessons from America's Best-Run Companies* was based on an in-depth study of 75 leading businesses. Tom Peters and Bob Waterman identified eight critical success factors of these top companies, which I have summarized as follows:

- A bias for action - "Do it, fix it, try it." (O)
- Close to the customer - Learn from the people you serve. (M)
- Autonomy and entrepreneurship - Foster many leaders and innovators throughout the organization. (P)
- Productivity through people - Treat the rank and file as the root source of productivity and quality gains. (P+O)
- Hands-on, value driven - Emphasis on core values, leaders walking the floor. (S+P)
- Stick to the knitting - Do what you know best; don't conglomerate. (S)
- Simple form, lean staff - Few hierarchies, no complex structure. (P)
- Simultaneous loose-tight properties - Hold core values centrally, give production people autonomy, allow chaos. (S+P)

The Total Quality Management movement

Around the same time as the publication of *Search*, a very different movement emerged with enormous impact on management thinking worldwide, in part because it appealed to the fact-based preference of many managers. Total Quality Management became popular primarily as a tool for American manufacturers who were losing market share to Japanese companies like Toyota, Sony and Panasonic because American-made products were found to be of embarrassingly inferior quality. Philip Crosby's now-famous paperback, *Quality Is Free*, was the first to popularize the idea that a company could improve product quality without incurring additional production costs - indeed, the right quality controls could actually save money. (TQM is largely a combination of O, F and P.)

Many other books were written about TQM, but one of the best at summarizing its key insights was *Total Quality Management* produced in 1993 by Stephen George and Arnold Weimerskirch (1993). Their study was based on the practices of 53 leading companies with these key TQM principles:

- Focus on the customer. (M)
- Align internal processes with customer satisfaction. (O+M)
- Everybody in the company works on shared goals. (P+S)
- Long-term approach to continuous improvement. (S+O+P)
- Management by fact (measure everything). (O)
- Prevention rather than reaction. (O)
- Seek ways to be faster and more flexible at all levels. (O)
- Look for opportunities to partner with customer, suppliers, and other companies; benchmark; be a corporate citizen. (M)
- Value results. (S+F)

The importance of quality was strongly reinforced by the work of Bradley Gale, who with his partner Robert Buzzell conducted a confidential 'blind' study of over 3,000 business units for more than 12 years. Their study and subsequent book (1987) was entitled *The PIMS Principles - The Profit Impact of Market Strategy*. Gale and Buzzell analyzed how these thousands of SBUs did or did not achieve profits based on their market strategy - a term meant to be broader than marketing, rather encompassing a business's overall strategy in dealing with the marketplace. They determined that the most important single factor affecting a business unit's performance is the quality of its products and services relative to competitors (O + M).

Competitive strategy and its benefits

Harvard Professor Michael Porter in 1985 brought the importance of competitive strategy to the forefront with his very influential book, *Competitive Advantage: Creating and Sustaining Superior Performance*. He later published *Competitive Advantage Of Nations* and others extending his initial ideas. Porter said a sustainable competitive advantage can be achieved with basically one of three strategies (all S variables by definition):

- Offering lower prices than competitors (always aiming to be the lowest)
- Differentiating products or services (being superior is a widely valued attribute - image, speed etc.)
- Focusing on a narrow target with low price or differentiation - e.g., being

the lowest-cost public school architect.
- Firms which do not excel in 1 of these 3 are 'stuck in the middle' and can't win long-term, Porter claimed.

A similar approach was taken by Michael Treacy and Fred Wiersema in their 1995 publication of the No. 1-selling business book that year, *The Discipline of Market Leaders: Choose Your Customers, Narrow Your Focus, Dominate Your Market.*
Based on a study of 80 leading corporations over three years, Treacy and Wiersema urged managers to provide the best offering in the marketplace by excelling in a specific dimension of value (all S variables again):

- Operational excellence: Wal-Mart, FedEx, McDonald's
- Product leadership: Nike, Intel
- Customer intimacy: Airborne Express, Johnson Controls.

While excelling in one dimension, it is also important to maintain threshold standards on other dimensions of value, they noted. In this way companies can dominate their market by improving value year after year. They urged readers to "build a well-tuned operating model dedicated to delivering unmatched value."

The importance of managing customer value

The Discipline of Market Leaders emphasized strategic focus but also highlighted a success-factor theme which grew increasingly significant in the mid-1990s: the concept of value as the total package of benefits which customers want in exchange for their money. Bradley Gale, co-author of the earlier *Profit Impact of Market Strategy*, had become a sought-after quality consultant and was distressed to see that many companies were becoming too focused on physical products, losing sight of the importance of customer perceptions as the key to business success. In 1994 he published a highly influential book seeking to correct that management-thinking error, *Managing Customer Value: Creating Quality & Service That Customers Can See*, with these highlights:

- Understanding customer needs allows a business to produce a Customer Value Map, portraying on x and y axes the things that customers value most compared with their levels of satisfaction on each dimension of value (M).
- By adding effective design and quality control, a company can produce superior quality in areas that matter most to customers. (O)
- If these customer-value benefits are then promoted through focused advertising and other marketing communications, the result will be what he called Market-Perceived Quality. (M)

- When this is combined with the cost-saving benefits of consistent quality management, the result is Exceptional Customer Value, leading to superior profits, growth and shareholder value. (F)
- Gale developed seven graphical metrics to illustrate different aspects of the process of managing customer value in his attempt to make this approach just as 'hard' as the data-oriented TQM methodology.

Chaos, systems and change: Precursors to complexity

Two books published about the same time mark a turning point in the management literature from linear thinking models of previous years to chaos and systems thinking models that were precursors of complexity thinking.

In 1987 the ever-advanced Tom Peters published *Thriving On Chaos: Handbook for a Management Revolution*. Like others at the time, Peters picked up on new books and articles about chaos theory, which revealed patterns of order in nature underlying seemingly chaotic forms such as currents in rivers and weather fronts. Peters identified a highly structured set of success factors which one might summarize as follows:

- *Creating total customer responsiveness* - creating niches, providing top quality as perceived by customers, becoming obsessed with listening, creating uniqueness etc. (a holistic approach including M+S+P)
- *Pursuing fast-paced innovation* - investing in applications-oriented small starts, pursue product / service development with teams, support fast failures, etc. (O+P)
- *Achieving flexibility by empowering people* - involve everyone in everything, use self-managing teams, spend time lavishly on recruiting, train and retrain, etc. (P)
- *Learning to love change: A new vision of leadership at all levels* - master paradox, develop an inspiring vision, manage by example, defer to the front line. (S)
- *Building systems for a world turned upside down* - Measure what's important, revamp the chief control tools, decentralize (everything), demand total integrity. (S+O).

Then in 1990 Peter Senge sought to make sense of the changing management-thinking landscape through his highly influential book, *The Fifth Discipline: The Art and Practice of the Learning Organization*. The five critical success factors or 'disciplines' he identified were:

- Systems thinking (actually the 'fifth' discipline the title refers to) (P)
- Personal mastery (P)

- Mental models (P)
- Building shared vision (S)
- Team learning (P)

Reengineering the Corporation: A Manifesto for Business Revolution by Michael Hammer and James Champy, published in 1993, encouraged managers to embrace change. Although often later blamed for brutal downsizing and other impersonal change traumas, Hammer and Champy were actually citing how change needs to occur for companies to be more successful. They identified:

- Jobs change - from simple tasks to multidimensional work. (O)
- People's roles change - from controlled to empowered. (P)
- Job preparation changes - from training to education. (P)
- Performance measures change - from activity to results. (O)
- Advancement criteria change - from performance to ability. (P)
- Values change - working for customers, not bosses. (S)
- Managers change - from supervisors to coaches. (S+P)
- Organizational structures change - from hierarchical to flat. (P)
- Executives change - from scorekeepers to leaders. (S+P)

An increasing focus on people

Recent years have seen the publication of very popular books which emphasize the importance of people (including learning and growth). At the top of the business best-sellers list for many months in 1999 and 2000 was *First, Break All The Rules: What the World's Greatest Managers Do Differently*, by Marcus Buckingham and Curt Coffman of the Gallup Organization. They coordinated probably the most massive study of critical success factors of all time, interviewing over 80,000 managers in 400 companies over several years as part of Gallup's ongoing research and development. The biggest insight of their study was this: "People don't change that much. Don't waste time trying to put in what was left out. Try to draw out what was left in. That is hard enough." What that translates into is these practices (all P variables by definition):

- "Select people for talent, not just experience or intelligence."
- "Set expectations by defining the right outcomes, not the right steps."
- "Motivate people by focusing on strengths, not weaknesses."
- "Develop people by helping them find the right fit, not just the next rung on the ladder."

One of the most popular books of 2003 was *Good To Great: Why Some Companies Make the Leap and Others Don't* by Jim Collins, who also authored the popular *Built To Last* in 1994. Collins did yet another comparative study of successful ('great') vs. mediocre ('good') companies and determined that the major difference was the quality of people "on the bus." As he put it, "First Who

... Then What." He also found that brutal honesty, simplicity and discipline were valuable attributes of companies who "made the leap" from good to great. Great companies have "Level 5 Leadership" that "builds enduring greatness through a paradoxical blend of personal humility and professional will."

What's wrong with this picture?

So, if these many forms of late 20th-Century management thinking can be adequately captured as some combination of the five variable sets of the Strategic Alignment System, what could possibly be missing? I began sensing some deficiencies as I used this framework to guide the strategic planning processes of 15 public libraries over a two-year period. In each case we gathered input from people inside the library and the community, conveniently clustered the initiatives into the five variable sets, developed vision, mission and goals, and set the strategic plan down in a few short pages to make it easy to understand and follow. When I checked back with these libraries a few months later, some were following the plans enthusiastically, some with little emotion, and some not at all. No movement - just excuses.

After all the time, effort and money (mostly federal grants) that had been spent, this was a disappointment, and something of an epiphany. My elegant, much researched and carefully developed Strategic Alignment System did not work reliably as a strategic planning system for these organizations. Not that failure of implementation was my fault, but it weighed on me heavily. And so I began searching for insights, a better way, actively encouraged by a couple of newer clients who had done strategic planning with other consultants and become totally disappointed with and skeptical of anything named 'strategic planning'. A footnote, a mere footnote, in one of Peter Senge's Fieldbook chapters, referred to a new field known as Complexity. I went to Google, typed in Complexity, and fell right down the rabbit hole. This was Wonderland.

Stages in the evolution of complexity thinking and management

Since that first encounter, I have learned that Complexity has many roots, including systems thinking and cybernetics going back several decades. After extensive study, I have seen Complexity evolve through three different phases. Since we may assume that any reader of this chapter is already familiar with basic Complexity concepts, I will not present them here in as much detail as the evolution of previous management thinking - just hit the high spots to provide a quick frame of comparative reference.

Apparently the term Complexity was first used in its present meaning by the leading scientists working at the Santa Fe Institute in the mid-90s. They pooled their diverse disciplines in an effort to better understand what they called complex adaptive systems (CAS), which by definition possess the capacity to learn new behaviors. So the first phase of Complexity can be defined as the scientists doing their work, based on computer modeling and other research.

The second phase involved authors like Roger Lewin and Mitchell Waldrop writing their books entitled *Complexity*, describing the work that the scientists were doing and the discoveries they were making, intended for popular audiences. Some of the scientists themselves like Stuart Kauffman, John Holland and Murray Gell-Mann also wrote their own books intended for lay audiences.

Phase 3: Organizations using complexity

The third phase in the evolution of Complexity as a management tool focused on businesses and organizations using Complexity in various forms to guide, structure or operate their enterprise. These included Roger Lewin and Birute Regine's *The Soul At Work*, Michael McMaster's *The Intelligence Advantage: Organizing for Complexity*, Susanne Kelly and Mary Ann Allison's *The Complexity Advantage*, and others. Paralleling that was the evolution of other books intended to serve as guides for using Complexity in management and organization development, such as Edwin Olson and Glenda Eoyang's *Facilitating Organization Change* and Arthur Battram's *Navigating Complexity*.

Each of these books takes a different tack, and no one has yet developed a widely accepted set of Complexity 'success variables'. After her own exhaustive study of the Complexity literature and related fields, Eoyang developed a set of three *metavariables*, as she calls them, which many people have found to be appealing:

- *Container* - that which enables a complex system to cohere, including external boundaries ('fences') and internal pulls ('magnets'), plus affiliative connections
- *Differences* - different people, different values, different elements, and the differences between them enhancing adaptability as well as energy flow
- *Exchanges* - the interactions and 'transforming exchanges' between the people inside the organization, outside the organization, and other systems.

Fritjof Capra in *The Web of Life* provides another, somewhat similar set of three:

- "Pattern of organization - the configuration of relationships that determines the system's essential characteristics"
- "Structure - the physical embodiment of the system's pattern of organization"
- "Life process - the activity involved in the continual embodiment of the system's pattern of organization."

Other Complexity variables or concepts frequently mentioned in Complexity-related books include:

- Complex adaptive systems composed of diverse interacting agents, guided by a few simple rules
- Environmental interdependence (success is fitting with the environment)
- Feedback, information flow, experimentation, learning and adaptation
- Emergence, self-organization, small changes can lead to large effects
- Leaders creating and nurturing favorable conditions (as opposed to top-down management control)

A comparison of Complexity and previous management thinking

It is very important to realize that Complexity offers a framework for understanding complex living systems, especially their processes and structures, which is not intended to be a substitute for fundamental business practices such as accounting and production. In other words, Complexity is inadequate as a framework for understanding and managing all the critical factors of organizational success.

A number of consultants who use Complexity apparently follow the Organization Development tradition of intervention. They enter the organization, they use their Complexity tools and processes, the clients have new insights, and the consultants leave. For example, in a recent address to members of the Plexus Institute and the Mayo Clinic, Glenda Eoyang referred to her version of Complexity, *human systems dynamics*, as giving her and her clients "better options for action." Richard Knowles has traveled around the world helping companies deal with safety and other organizational issues with a nine-point enneagram inspired by Complexity and overtly process-oriented.

Every Complexity book I have encountered so far uses this new field of thought for insights into human organization dynamics, but I have yet to find one which attempts to use Complexity to understand and manage all the key variables and challenges which confront a typical business or organizational manager in a 'normal' hectic workweek. This realization of the limitations of Complexity as a management consulting tool was a huge disappointment for me. At first I thought it would prove to be a whole different point of view, comprehensive enough to deal with virtually all organizational management issues in a new and dynamic way. Since then I have learned that Complexity is indeed a useful tool for gaining organizational insights, but not a tool for understanding and managing all aspects of a dynamic human organization in the real world every day. No wonder some companies which tried Complexity as an 'operating system,' like Citibank under John Reed, cast it aside when

Reed left the CEO position.

In the months, going on years now, since I came to terms with the limitations of Complexity as a management consulting tool, I have continued to struggle with the cognitive dissonance resulting from the powerful appeal of Complexity concepts and the real-world necessity of broader management systems which I attempted to capture in the Strategic Alignment System. In the process, I fell back on my personal metaphysics developed about 15 years ago based on the primal importance of order and energy, which led to my personal discovery of chaos theory, the works of Ilya Prigogine, von Bertalanffy's *General Systems Theory*, and other precursors to Complexity. Rather than recount that evolution in detail, let me cut to the chase and share with you where I am in my systems thinking in late-2004 and the tools I use as a consultant in the real world.

A Complexity-influenced hybrid management system

I have modified the five major management-thinking categories I developed through my Strategic Alignment System in light of Complexity thinking, as follows:

- *Strategy / Structure* is a complex variable (metavariable) which includes all the decisions and their consequences of providing the enterprise with organization and direction, including vision, mission, strategic advantage, and the organization of people into flexible teams, able to adapt rapidly to the constantly changing environment, requiring more attention to monitoring trends and changes in the broad marketplace than most organizations are accustomed to.

- *Operations / Processes* is a metavariable that includes all the decisions and their consequences of what the organization does, how it creates value for customers, with increased emphasis on internal communication, making better use of intranets and email to keep everyone informed of the latest developments, as well as linking internal activities more closely to continuous feedback from the market environment.

- *People / Learning* acknowledges that not only do we need to care about people as individuals, respect them and give them more autonomy, but also the organization needs to provide for continuous learning (the very essence of complex adaptive systems), not just on the part of individuals, but the organization itself, constantly refining its own self-concept, or as Senge calls them, mental models.

- *Market / Environment* refers to everything that goes on outside of the organization which does or might impact its success, including not only customers and prospects but also competitors, suppliers, market forces and trends, which need to be addressed more interactively, shifting from over-reliance on outbound messages such as advertising and PR to a two-way emphasis, monitoring and responding to changing needs and perceptions.

- *Finances / Facilities* are always very important, a topic rarely covered by Complexity, but absolutely essential to sustain the life, growth and evolution of any organization. Cash flow is like water - you can take it for granted until you have to do without it.

Now this is not radically different from my pre-Complexity approach, but one of my greatest insights from using Complexity as an approach to organizational problems is the importance of structure and processes as opposed to any kind of planning. Strategic planning can be beneficial for objects like buildings and roads, but it is of little use for forecasting or predetermining the behaviors of complex human systems such as organizations, communities and the market environment. If an enterprise focuses its efforts instead on flexible structures and processes which allow rapid adaptation to change, the likelihood of success are greatly increased - and the people involved will be much happier and more enthusiastic about this realism as opposed to the idealism (fantasy?) of strategic planning.

A Complexity-influenced approach in the real world

In working with client organizations who are experiencing difficulties, I have found that abstract concepts such as those abounding in the Complexity literature get in the way of useful work. They create barriers to building trust early in the client-consultant relationship. So usually I leave the concepts behind and just deal with more inclusive structures and processes which seem to work remarkably well (without any jargon), thanks to what Complexity has taught me.

Instead of traditional strategic planning, when a broad-scale approach is needed, I have found it highly effective to begin with a large-group discussion of what the participants want to accomplish, their purposes or intentions (what Complexity might consider *attractors*). Then we discuss the critical issues which the organization must deal with or manage to achieve those intentions or purposes. From a Complexity perspective, these might be viewed as adaptational challenges. Then I cluster those discussion points into broad categories, sometimes the five variable sets of my expanded conceptual system outlined above, and sometimes others - it must be authentic to each organization's situation.

Next we form teams of people (agents) interested in working on each issue category, help them focus with a team mission statement, and after a little training in team processes, cut them loose to get the job done. People are very excited with this approach, and a higher level of energy and innovation results.

Key to its ongoing effectiveness is continuous communication. Each team is required (with "a few simple rules") to share notes of its meetings with all others in the process, and an executive team representing all groups works to further ensure good communications, avoid overlaps, and keep everything on track. An intranet or online portal greatly facilitates this communication flow.

Again, this is a structure and process orientation, intended to replace traditional strategic planning with a more realistic, adaptive approach to preparing for the future and managing change. To more effectively ensure the enduring success of the enterprise, professional practices are still needed for day-to-day operations, marketing and financial accounting.

A metaphysics of organizations and Complexity

Why is one system of management thinking and practice superior to another? Although many in the field of Complexity prefer relativism or subjectivism to such judgments, it still falls to each individual to make choices in his or her thinking and decisions. In the 1980s I developed my own system of metaphysics which I have found to be an adequate framework to provide meaning and coherence for all my life experiences including Complexity. Although this brief chapter does not allow much explication, this system which I call *Ordergy* helps me keep Complexity in perspective and provides insights into what may happen next in the evolution of management thinking.

In brief, everything that exists is composed of order and energy. All forms of energy, matter, living beings, systems, so-called Laws of physics and other sciences, and the entire universe, are composed of ordered energy. Energy is the very stuff of life, and our survival instincts compel us to maintain our energy through eating, drinking, sleeping, staying warm, a wide variety of defensive behaviors, interacting with others, and when appropriate, procreating. Just as individual people are living energy systems, so also are organizations and communities. The work of Ilya Prigogine concerning dissipative structures, Ludwig von Bertalanffy's General Systems Theory, and others of the pre-Complexity era noted that increasing and sustaining the order of a dynamic system requires a higher flow of energy.

Traditional management thinking greatly constrains human energy by relating to the organization, often unconsciously, as a machine. Putting people in boxes or 'silos', top-down control, departmentalization, standardization and other practices which can actually facilitate manufacturing also serve to constrain human energy, innovation, the organization's potential, and its capacity to adapt to rapid change.

Complexity is a valuable corrective to that, unleashing human energy and creativity. Organizations which are 'on the edge of chaos' and able to shift structure and activities very quickly, facilitated by a high flow of information, are much more likely to survive and thrive in the fast-changing 21st Century than those limited by 'mechanical' thinking. Adaptive organizations monitor the changing environment and seek to maximize new opportunities while avoiding new threats before they become overwhelming.

As we all struggle to cope with the increasing demands of constant change and technology, I predict we will see an increasing emphasis on the importance of optimizing human energy. In confirmation of that, I recently encountered an outstanding new book, *The Power of Full Engagement: Managing Energy, Not Time, Is the Key to High Performance and Personal Renewal* by Jim Loehr and Tony Schwartz. I could not agree more with that statement. Of course it is not raw energy per se that makes surviving and thriving more likely, but intelligently ordered energy, focused on the greatest opportunities and emphasizing a high degree of information flow. The very popular *First, Break All The Rules* is also much about getting peak performance from people by recognizing and encouraging their natural talents, which are inborn tendencies to use our energy in certain ways.

As long as we don't expect too much from Complexity, as long as we use it as a tool for fresh insights and a process for unleashing energy and creativity, it can provide a valuable and hopefully enduring contribution to the management and success of organizations. What is needed are more syntheses of proven management principles and new Complexity-based insights, using language which average people can understand and relate to. Some books like that are starting to emerge, such as *It's Alive: The Coming Convergence of Information, Biology, and Business* by Christopher Meyer and Stan Davis (2003). But none have inspired the excitement of managers as some of the 'fad' books of earlier years. Personally I believe the concept of managing human energy has such potential, but time will tell whether Complexity-inspired concepts become enduring components of enlightened management thinking and practice, or just a footnote, some interesting ideas that a relatively small group of people found very interesting, sometime around the early 21st Century. What do you think?

References

Battram, A. (1998). *Navigating Complexity: The Essential Guide to Complexity Theory in Business and Management*, London: The Industrial Society.

Buckingham, M. and Coffman, C. (1999). *First, Break All The Rules: What the World's Greatest Managers Do Differently*, New York: Simon & Schuster.

Capra, F. (1996). *The Web of Life: A New Scientific Understanding of Living Systems*, New York: Anchor Books.

Collins, J. and Porras, J. (1994-97). *Built To Last: Successful Habits of Visionary Companies*, New York: HarperBusiness.

Collins, J. (2003). *Good to Great: Why Some Companies Make the Leap... And Others Don't*, New York: HarperBusiness.

Crosby, P. (1980). *Quality Is Free: The Art of Making Quality Certain*, New York: Mentor.

Gale, B. and Buzzell, R. (1987). *The PIMS (Profit Impact of Market Strategy) Principles: Linking Strategy to Performance*, New York: Free Press.

Gale, B. (1994). *Managing Customer Value: Creating Quality & Service That Customers*

Can See, New York: Free Press.

George, S. and Weimerskirch, A. (1993). *Total Quality Management: Strategy and Techniques Proven at Today's Most Successful Companies*, New York: John Wiley & Sons.

Hammer, M. and Champy, J. (1993). *Reengineering The Corporation: A Manifesto for Business Revolution*, New York: HarperBusiness.

Kaplan, R. S. and Norton, D. P. (1996). *The Balanced Scorecard: Translating Strategy Into Action*, Harvard University.

Kelly, S. and Allison, M. A. (1999). *The Complexity Advantage: How the Science of Complexity Can Help Your Business Achieve Peak Performance*, New York: Mc-Graw-Hill.

Labovitz, G. and Rosansky, V. (1997). *The Power of Alignment: How Great Companies Stay Centered*, New York: John Wiley & Sons.

Lewin, R. (1992-99). *Complexity: Life At The Edge Of Chaos*, Chicago: University of Chicago Press.

Lewin, R. and Regine, B. (2000). *The Soul At Work - Listen...respond...let go - Embracing Complexity Science for Business Success*, New York: Simon & Schuster.

Loehr, J. and Schwartz, T. (2003). *The Power of Full Engagement: Managing Energy, Not Time, Is the Key to High Performance and Personal Renewal*, New York: Free Press.

McMaster, M. (1995). *The Intelligence Advantage - Organizing for Complexity*, Douglas, Isle of Man, Great Britain: Knowledge Based Development.

Meyer, C. and Davis, S. (2003). *It's Alive: The Coming Convergence of Information, Biology, and Business*, New York: Crown Business.

Olson, E. and Eoyang, G. (2001). *Facilitating Organization Change: Lessons from Complexity Science*, San Francisco: Josey-Bass/Pfeiffer.

Peters, T. and Waterman, R. (1982). *In Search Of Excellence: Lessons from America's Best-Run Companies*, New York: Harper & Row.

Peters, T. (1982). *Thriving On Chaos: Handbook for a Management Revolution*, New York: Alfred A. Knopf.

Porter, M. (1985). *Competitive Advantage: Creating and Sustaining Superior Performance*, New York: Free Press.

Senge, P. (1990). *The Fifth Discipline: The Art and Practice of the Learning Organization*, New York: Currency Doubleday.

Treacy, M. and Wiersema, F. (1995). *The Discipline of Market Leaders: Choose Your Customers, Narrow Your Focus, Dominate Your Market*, Reading, MA: Addison-Wesley.

Waldrop, M. M. (1992). *Complexity: The Emerging Science at the Edge of Order and Chaos*, New York: Touchstone.

CHAPTER 8

UNRESOLVED ISSUES IN PROCESS-CENTRIC BUSINESS ANALYSIS: A CATHARTIC ROLE FOR COMPLEXITY

James Falconer

The business process approach, as an extension of the tradition of formal routines, had its noisiest of several incarnations in the early 1990s, and then survived a backlash that focused mainly on its narrow, inanimate, mechanistic posture to maintain a position of importance. While the approach has some positive attributes, it has many substantive flaws; these flaws are attributable more to a reliance on models than to a basis in process or any other characteristic, for conventional models are fundamentally at odds with understanding human organizations. A better approach to organizational analysis is one grounded in complexity science that embraces holism, organic precepts, and patterns.

Managing Organizational Complexity: Philosophy, Theory, and Application
A Volume in: Managing the Complex, pages 133-150.
Copyright © 2005 by Information Age Publishing, Inc.
All rights of reproduction in any form reserved.
ISBN: 1-59311-319-6 (cloth), 1-59311-318-8 (paper)

"It is but too easy to establish another durable and harmonious routine. Immediately all parts of nature consent to it. Only make something to take the place of something, and men will behave as if it was the very thing they wanted."

- Thoreau

A challenge to modelling

T his challenge to the enduring concept of modelling is already in progress. In a recent paper (Falconer, 2004), I unseat modelling elementally, and others (Lissack & Richardson, 2001; Richardson, 2005; Allen, *et al.*, this volume) have explored it framed by complexity. This chapter brings the challenge into the business domain. It weighs the balance with respect to 'business process' and, while largely descriptive rather than prescriptive, introduces opportunities that should be explored.

Here 'modelling' defines a traditional approach to enquiry, analysis and communication based on a simplified image of the world, with representational comprehensibility driven by quantification, reductionism and arbitrary objectivity. Many disciplines consider models so delineated to be sufficiently complex and representative abstractions of reality. While models can aid explanations, level the intellectual playing field, allow the untutored eye to see things unlooked-for, facilitate conceptual focus, and permit expression and analysis more conveniently and cheaply than working with actual systems, models inhibit true understanding (as well as facilitate) of represented phenomena. If applied indiscriminately to former or proposed contexts, models can be inappropriate, and can leave disciplines ill-equipped or exposed. Models can degrade the viability of human enterprise by discouraging innovation and self-improvement, stymieing development, restricting adaptiveness, and obviating serendipity.

The modelling paradigm as a pervasive part of enquiry methods translates as automatic deployment of models in response to phenomena. The model becomes the object of focus (Norman, 2001). As such the real object fades, model-driven interventions translate with less certainty into similar, desirable or known responses in the real world system, and the likelihood actually increases that unpredictable change will result there. Nonetheless, encouraged by the apparent simplification that models offer, researchers and practitioners propose predictable, familiar, descriptive / analytical models and consider them important and viable.

One of few the challengers to model-driven science, Checkland (Checkland, 1981; Checkland, 1985; Checkland & Scholes, 1990) extends Vickers's (1965; 1983) work into a 'soft systems methodology' that embraces the non-mechanistic character of human systems and emphasizes 'intellectual constructs' (patterns by another name) over models. Complexity science, more recently, has offered a new means to understand our world. Convergence in this discipline, however, has yet to emerge around the role of models: some (Wheatley, 1992; Kelly, 1998) embrace complexity science as a challenge to our comfortable, tired, inefficacious traditional methods, while other influential clusters paradoxically support traditional methods while contending that the domains under scrutiny are complex.

Precepts for the use of models include:

- a heuristic systemic meta-model;
- traditional underpinnings (linear causal analysis, mathematics, Newtonian physics, systems science, biological processes, econometrics, etc.);
- simple / linear systemic evolution;
- circumscribability of systemic evolution, and;
- reductionism.

Models give these embodied precepts reinforcement. Specifically, models:

- enforce process and structure though such may be fleeting, evanescent and / or nonexistent;
- oversimplify and overgeneralize;
- encourage prescriptiveness and bricolage;
- present an arbitrary / false / unattainable image of objectivity, and;
- claim hegemony over represented phenomena.

This behavior is suspect in complex human enterprise systems and exacerbated by myriad flawed analytical methods.

Herein modelling, provocatively, is a monolithic realm; any viable exceptions would call boundaries of 'modelling' more into question than the degree of generalization in the definition. Also, to suggest that it is not models *per se* that are problematic, but their application, fundamentally implies that the behavior of the modeler / model-user is detachable from that of the model, that different conditions can apply to subject and object. This thinking is flawed: understanding framed by models needs to consider modeler(s), modelling, model-user(s), model use, model(s), and represented reality as a complete, inviolate conceptual entity; applying reductionism here would be doubly problematic.

Formal routines and their application in the metaphor of business process in the modern corporation

Early formal routines were driven by survival, protection, and societal harmony. The oral tradition meant they were not consistent, reliably practised, or uniformly accepted, but simply adapted to circumstances, however fleeting the conditions or ephemeral the optimality. Superficially, formal routines supplant humanity's often maladroit self-organization, and that such metaphors persist over centuries shows our capitulatory affinity for them.

With civilization, formal routines inhered in institutions: agricultural societies, fiefdoms, churches, military organizations, etc. The command and control metaphor was therefore convenient for burgeoning industry. Management structures became necessary, with hierarchy the dominant form. Formal routines helped divide labour into manageable functions and allowed for worker specialization.

Business *analysis* is conducted to observe and understand organizational circumstances and consider effectiveness- and efficiency-based improvement interventions, test the interventions for efficacy, and realize them through strategy, tactics and / or operations. Formal routines in analysis originated with the 'scientific management' movement of the early 1900s, with such proponents as Taylor (1911) (and Ford, 1923) driving what could be termed the 'first wave' of formal routine based business analysis. At the core was efficiency, i.e., trying to extract maximum returns from mass production and division of labour. Some successes were attained through techniques such as time-and-motion studies and by considering work as mechanized routine. Identifying work inefficiencies through quantitative measures, however, was insufficient for creating more effective organizations: scientific management downgraded the human element in the work performed, and the picture was therefore incomplete and potentially misleading. Subsequently, humanism entered business thought, stewarded by such proponents as Mayo (1933), Roethlisberger, Dickson and Wright (1939), Maslow (1954, 1965), Trist (1978, orig. 1959), McGregor (1960), Cyert and March (1963), Leavitt (1965), Berger and Luckmann (1966), and Weick (1979), despite Simon (1945, 1960), Thompson (1967), and others simultaneously reviving formalism, mechanization, and reductionism.

Resurgence of these latter precepts in business analysis was surely abetted by the systems science approach of Ashby (1956), von Bertalanffy (1968), Forrester (1969, 1971), Ackoff and Emery (1972), and Beer (1972), which addressed multivariate, arguably complex, systems by modelling them using a precise approach and a formal discipline (despite sometimes advancing cautionary notes about exclusionary application of systems science methods to (human) social systems). This approach had adherents, and has latterly been revived by writers such as Senge (1990), but inadequacy of such models versus the actual systems has always been evident. Most pointed - and perhaps poignant - was the approach's late-1970s unseating (see Senge, 1990: 281-2) that in a more receptive community would have been a death-knell for systems science, if not model-driven science *in toto*. Despite the model-centric method, in that moment, revealing its inadequacy vis-à-vis complex systems, it continued forward.

There were also several pseudo-scientific approaches and methodologies based on models and quantitative measurement, such as operations management (especially the program evaluation and review technique / critical path method (Baker & Eris, 1964; Shafer, *et al.*, 1965)) and total quality management (Juran, 1964; Ishikawa, 1985). Business thinking has whipsawed between 'hard' and 'soft' preoccupations since, and while humanist, sociocultural concerns still find a receptive audience, 'scientific' approaches enjoy easier acceptance among the business community.

Distinct mechanistic analysis based on formal routines began with Schein (1969) and Anderson (1973), and continued with Porter's (1979, 1985) value chains, Rummler and Brache's (1991) influential diagrammatic approach, and other direct antecedents (Bower & Hout, 1988; Buboff, 1988; Colquhoun, *et al*, 1989; Scott Morton, 1991), and figured in such overarching approaches to business efficiency analysis as supply chain management. These prepared the way for the 'second wave' of formal routine based analysis to re-advance mechanistic methods and quantitative approaches and capture the spotlight in 1990. This movement, which reified the *business process*, and variously called *reengineering, redesign,* or *improvement*, was launched by Davenport (Davenport & Short, 1990; Davenport, 1993) and Hammer (Hammer, 1990; Hammer & Champy, 1993), and leading proponents (Harrington, 1991; Coulson-Thomas, 1994; Manganelli & Klein, 1994) advanced a similar approach to theirs. Business process, in the framing of the second wave writers, was a clear, direct descendent of the formal routine lineage - and as such freely (though not always forthrightly) borrowed from earlier thinking - while offering an ostensibly novel lexicon, representation, and methodology, packaged for the masses. This last aspect was important because, as several have vociferously noted (Earl, 1994; Earl & Khan, 1994; Mumford, 1994; Grover & Malhotra, 1997), the fundaments were not that novel.

A fuller understanding of the process approach arrived after the discipline matured and performance data existed. The results: determinants of success and failure (Grover, *et al*, 1995; Childe, *et al*, 1997; Al-Mashari & Sairi, 1999), classification frameworks (APQC, undated; Palmer, 1995; Malone, 1997; Ericsson, 2001) and generic structures (Brynjolfsson, *et al*, 1997; Melão & Pidd, 2000; Lin, *et al*, 2002), best practices (Povey, 1998), modelling guidelines (Becker, *et al*, 2000), and approaches for process / strategy alignment (Talwar, 1993).

Most proponents, academics-cum-consultants and firms offering methods, tools and / or services, though anxious to differentiate themselves from the competition, presented process approaches with key characteristics in common (see also Grint, 1994):

- *method-driven*: cannot be applied effectively in a haphazard, ad hoc fashion as other tactical evaluation mechanisms can;
- *mechanistic*: represent an 'engineering'-like (see Feiler, 1993) approach to 'white collar' business operations;
- *focused on the customer* in defining the domain of interest and setting the design priorities;
- *top-down*: expending minimal effort toward understanding current reality,

instead focusing on high-level process design and building from there;

- *broad* where functional approaches are deep, spanning functional and operational boundaries and attempting to galvanize organizations to a process purpose;

- a *clean slate* approach to analysis and design, where everything is subject to challenge, recrafting, replacement, or removal, and the focus is on 'starting fresh', as fresh as possible;

- *hierarchical*, open to 'drill down' process expansion; and

- promoting *information technology* (IT) as (at least) a key enabler of process renewal (see Henderson & Venkatraman, 1993; Venkatraman, 1994; Willcocks & Smith, 1995) and (more often) as renewal's objective (see Curtis, *et al*, 1992; Davidson, 1993; Keung, *et al*, 1996; de Vreede & van Eijck, 1998) or even as inextricably bound to it (see van Stijn & Wensley, 2001).

Business process approaches have consistently found a supportive audience, so clearly offer some value. Process:

- constitutes an aid to understanding how the work of a business enterprise is done, providing a common language and a level playing field for analysis / design participants;

- inherits many benefits from models, owing to its reliance on them, and therefore can allow hidden information to surface, focus a community of interest, and open up richer system analyses;

- abrogates the hierarchical / functional / traditional orientation that both dominates and hinders genuine improvement-seeking organizations, and allows a fresh and effective means of self-perception;

- disturbs complacency and acts as a catalyst for action;

- encourages process ownership to make accountability transparent through formalization;

- can free stifled / marginalized innovation by providing it fresh context in which to adhere; and

- raises the profile of organizational IT and frames it as strategic / enabling regarding transformative change.

While the process approach has these strong points in its favour, to understand it fully requires exploring its considerable methodological shortcomings.

First, the process approach summons the loathsome 'cult of measurement', a cabal that twists Haire's (1964: 221-223) observation about *measured* things getting attention to mean *measurable* things. This ethos frames the world only through time, cost and quality 'metrics' and is strongly reductionist, normative and quantitative; a perspectival triumvirate that has traditionally kept truths hidden in many disciplines. The weakness of such framing is most evident in human systems, such as business organizations.

Second, process is tightly focused, rather than holistic (see Harrison & Pratt, 1993, for an example). Resultantly, it focuses insufficiently on other change aspects, especially people and culture. Most of the backlash (Davenport & Stoddard, 1994; Strassman, 1994; Brown & Gray, 1995; Cooper & Markus, 1995; Davenport, 1995; Brown & Isaacs, 1996; Mumford & Hendricks, 1996; Eisenberg, 1997; Kleiner, 2000) that scuppered the second wave zeal came from this quarter, citing exclusionary focus as a primary cause for the high failure rate for process-driven initiatives. Even 1990s proponents of process (Davenport & Stoddard, 1994; Davenport, 1995; see Lancaster, 1995) eventually admitted this error of neglect.

Third, process approaches to change are rarely guided by an appropriately designed and integrated change management approach (see Padulo, 1994; Cooper & Markus, 1995; Kettinger & Grover, 1995; Stoddard & Jarvenpaa, 1995). Thus, often the resulting change is one-time or sporadic, removed from the broader change landscape, and unsustainable and / or neglected over time.

Fourth, in practice, a process approach is characterized by a clear absence of any consistent and identifiable method (see Coombes & Hull, 1997), a condition characterized by:

- vagueness around objectives or scope in design initiatives, and no evidence of an overall strategy;
- assumptions that method encapsulation within tools (see van Stijn & Wensley, 2001) obviates needing strong method(s) that transcend any particular tool;
- disconnection of the process approach used from the desired automation or extant supporting IT;
- considerable variance in skill / expertise levels among internal and external process and change consultants, often masked by a patina of professionalism;
- knowledge workers without particular process skills attempting process analysis / design;
- backsliding into outdated techniques, such as flowcharting or time-and-motion studies;
- employing a too mechanistic approach - in lieu of overarching method - that over-empowers 'engineers' (process analysts without engineering education) who are doing analysis / design; and
- high failure rates for process-based initiatives - 70-80% according to Hammer and Champy (Lancaster, 1995) - constitute extent not accounted for by normal project failures or expected process-associated challenges.

Fifth, there are business processes that cannot or should not be modelled (Churchman,1967, might have called them "wicked"), except when recast substantially. These processes are typically: creative; ad hoc or situation-dependent; characterized by unobtainable, evanescent, volatile / transient, and / or meaningless performance metrics; unimprovable; or informal (Charan, 1991; Krackhardt & Hanson, 1993) (arguably the core of how organizations actually work).

Sixth, replacing organizations' 'functional blinders' with 'process blinders' results in no better perspective than before, replacing one narrow view with another, rather than introducing a panoptic view.

Seventh, there is the problem of measurement skewing observations, not just focus. Heisenberg (1983, orig.1927) proffered a veritable symbiosis between measurement and measured phenomena, thereby calling all measurement into question. Roethlisberger, et al. (1939) observed a variant on the same phenomenon in the business context. Scrutinizing process causes an inevitable productivity uptick; therefore, already subjective choices about which processes to target for improvement become more contentious.

Eighth, there is still far too little method / tool convergence or interoperability. Process analysis tools are too often tied to particular methods or vice versa, so that use of one supports the use of the other. Vendors hoping to cross- or up-sell products and services are mostly to blame.

Ninth, there are hidden, endemic methodological shortcomings in the process approach, which would include:

- allowing unmodeled / unmodelable 'white space' (see Rummler & Brache, 1991) to exist in models;
- efficiency subverting effectiveness as a design objective;
- models biased by the underlying meta-model upon which the method is based;
- depicting process domains with hard, fixed boundaries - closed systems;
- unwieldy methods enforcing hierarchical capture and depiction metaphors;
- linear, single-threaded processes tritely cited as design objectives;
- tendency toward 'neat and tidy' models, promoting mechanism, reductionism, simplification, a technocratic view (i.e., process having a self-automation analysis / design goal), and hierarchical orientation (enforced in some methods or symbologies (IDEF, DFDs, etc.)); and
- flawed assumptions that organizational systems seek equilibrium and will remain in that state unless changed deterministically by design, which formalism-based approaches such as ISO 9000 promote, and which obviate natural organizational phenomena, such as continuous change in a 'stable system far from equilibrium' (see Prigogine & Stengers, 1984) or systemic recursion / adaptation through autocatalysis / optimization or in response

to environmental perturbations.

Whether the process approach's shortcomings caused its fall from favour or whether it was on a waning fad cycle is unclear. The second wave came and went with equivalent fanfare, though its artefacts persevere in the wake of de-cline / succession: many companies still focus on business process to catalyze analysis, improvement and transformation, and value related skills. What is also remarkable is the degree of persistence despite the both theoretical and practical counter-offensive from the 'soft' side of business thinking.

Process evolved beyond its initial fundaments and became a richer discipline of components and downstream infrastructure, an evolution from 'workflow' to 'process enactment' to 'business process management' (BPM). The latest incarnation incorporates earlier emphasis on corporate management of pro-cess as a resource (see Zairi & Sinclair, 1995) and grafts enterprise-computing capability onto the enactment metaphor. Proponents of BPM (Smith & Fingar, 2002; Smith, et al., 2002) call it the 'third wave' of business process work, align-ing it with concepts such as enterprise resource planning, enterprise resource management, customer relationship management, and e-commerce, as well as shared services and business process outsourcing. Shortcomings inherent in the process approach, however, cannot be assailed by announcing a 'third wave'; the issue still is process' reliance on models, and process models fall prey to the problems endemic to models, to perhaps the utmost extent.

Process-centric business analysis and reliance on models

Process-centric business analysis is dependent on and inseparable from its models, and is primarily flawed for this reason, not because of its basis in pro-cess. Without models, the process approach is untenable, like a story without a language in which to tell it. Process models do share models' positive attributes; however, process must also contend with models' flaws, which for process models translate into:

- a heuristic process meta-model;
- framing (complex) processes using traditional underpinnings;
- assumptions of defined process permanence;
- clear process boundaries; and
- reductionism in process analysis.

Grounding organizational analysis in the metaphor of model is emblematic of a widespread failure to acknowledge *organizational complexity*, an instance of systemic complexity that considers organizations as complex, rather than simple or merely 'complicated' (see Cilliers, 1998: viii-ix, and this volume), and with which traditional models are fundamentally incompatible as metaphors. Organizational complexity is typified by:

- intractably extensive interconnections between systemic nodes (roles, data, events, ideas, tasks, tools, etc.);
- systemic unpredictability and the inability of any and all actors to effect operational control;
- systemic boundaries that are evanescent, mutable, vague, and subjective; and
- the suitability and affinity of patterns, as emergent systemic properties, for encapsulating and revealing organizational essence.

Promising work has explored agent-based networks (Bonabeau, 1997; see Newman, 2003; see Robertson, this volume), and computational organizational theory in general (Carley, 1995; Weiss, 1999), ostensibly embracing social network analysis and connectionist network theory. While understanding systemic implications of organizations-as-complex-systems furthers the discipline, it is no more defensible that these experiments invalidate claims of disparity between models and complex organizations than that connectionist artificial intelligence (AI) work - vastly more cogent than was heuristic AI - invalidated legitimate concerns about models vis-à-vis human intelligence.

Process modelling is at odds with the target organizational systems: they are complex and it is not. Further, revelations about process offered above, applied generally to complex systems, might imply that:

- measurement of phenomenal aspects is misleading;
- better understanding comes from holistic approaches;
- continuous change is characteristic, so avoiding approaches based upon a linear metaphor for change and / or the precept that change can be 'managed' is advisable;
- flexible methods are preferred over formulaic approaches;
- analysis is subverted by approaches that bound the system;
- characteristic uncertainty defies traditional analytical methods, especially those based on models;
- full understanding requires an extensive array of methods and tools that is often challenging to weave together usefully; and
- effectiveness (rather than efficiency), networks (not hierarchies), messiness, disequilibrium, adaptation, emergence, and patterns are all, perhaps counterintuitively, part of cogent thinking.

Complex systems research, therefore, could illuminate the process approach to (business) organizational analysis. In exploring this possibility, the objective is to consider a still broader role for complexity theory in such analysis.

Recommendations: Steps to a more balanced approach and implications for process work

In recasting analytical business disciplines, their model-centric core should be replaced with complexity science tenets. Seeking an appropriate metaphor for 'organization science' reveals that management science, systems science, and computer science, all of which inhabit the business process space to varying degrees, are inappropriate for the job.

Considerable literature (Kay, 1984; Stacey, 1992; McMaster, 1996; Sherman & Schultz, 1998; Lewin & Regine, 2000; Wang & von Tunzelmann, 2000; Olson & Eoyang, 2001) advocates the application of complexity to business, and more general writing on complexity (Kelly, 1994; Holland, 1995; Kauffman, 1995; Holland, 1998; Heylighen, et al., 1999) provides useful background. Complexity as applied to business in general, and to the under-represented domain of process in particular (Bach, undated; Burkhart, et al., 1996) should continue to be research areas that receive due attention. Here, to conclude, are specific recommendations to guide both research threads.

First, a more holistic posture should be employed for business analysis, allowing richer knowledge of any situation. Holism begets patterns and frameworks, rather than models (see Figure 1 below). Extant holistic business frameworks (Hurst, 1984; Liker, et al., 1987; Scott Morton, 1991; Willcocks & Smith, 1995) might help in understanding a holistic orientation. Holistic approaches address more social concerns, only occasionally cogently explored with respect to business process (Bartlett & Ghoshal, 1995; Brown & Gray, 1995; Palmer, 1995; Brown & Isaacs, 1996; Melão & Pidd, 2000; Lin, et al., 2002), though there is research that connects such holistic domains as sociotechnical systems (Mumford, 1994; Biazzo, 2002) and soft systems methodology (Galliers & Baker, 1995; Patching, 1995) to process.

Second, less mechanistic approaches should be applied to organizational analysis. Two research strands already inform this space somewhat: first, considering organizations as organic, 'living' entities (de Geus, 1997; J. Richardson, this volume), which rejects the more traditional mechanistic view in favour of organizations as adaptive or resilient; and second, considering organizations as informal networks rather than functional hierarchies (Charan, 1991; Krackhardt & Hanson, 1993).

Third, patterns should be embraced as a metaphor for organizational analysis. A pattern is a knowledge metaphor that is closely analogous to tacit mental thought-patterns, and that attempts to encapsulate and articulate them. Patterns have a long history, providing underpinning metaphors for music, art, literature, cinema, sport, agriculture, policy-making, etc., but have only recently made incursions into such hitherto model-centric fields as business and IT (see Falconer, 1999). Table 1 depicts patterns as compared with models and frameworks. Patterns constitute a noteworthy foil for the hegemonic grip of the model in organizational analysis.

Regarding...	Model	Framework	Pattern
Goal	Explanation, encapsulation	Framing, contextualization	Illustration, reflection
What depicted	Generalized case to which specific cases are said to conform	Frame for all envisaged cases based on preceding cases	Generalizable case that emerges from an aggregated and evolving empirical reality
Basis	Mastery of phenomena through the scientific method	Desire for meaningful dialogue and understanding	A holistic worldview
Evolution	Drives toward order and simplification	Is as rich as the system dictates is necessary / possible, but tends toward circumscription	Maintains criticality
Soft / hard orientation	Largely quantitative	Quantitative and qualitative as system requires	Largely qualitative
Adaptiveness	Wants to fit empirical episodes into the prevailing exemplar	Organizes / positions empirical episodes for maximizing meaning	Adapts to empirical episodes and the emergence of knowledge

Table 1
Comparison of analytical metaphors and relevant aspects

An approach keyed off these three recommendations could eventually unseat a still pervasive - yet naïve - confidence in such model-centric disciplines as business process. Complexity, in this domain, is key: it permits analysis, improvement and transformation through more suitable framing, and fosters the emergence of an alternative, equally realized metaphor to support, complement, recast, or supplant process. Such re-examination could address the shortcomings of process enumerated here and envisage future evolution. It is hoped that such shifting of metaphor would enable more effective understanding of business organizations and other human-devised systems.

It is superficially encouraging that the espoused third wave of process work, BPM, embraces tenets of complexity, though I remain unconvinced it does so purposefully or authentically, and its clear basis in intentional control I find rather suspect in this regard. More encouraging would be a full and complete re-examination of process-driven organizational analysis, improvement and transformation, using the tenets of complexity science as catalyst. Recommended as part of this undertaking would be an exploration of pattern (especially) and possibly other alternative (complementary) metaphors to process for the purpose of describing organizational phenomena, and of frameworks that would be in harmony therewith.

References

Ackoff, R. I. and Emery, F. E. (1972). *On Purposeful Systems*, Chicago: Aldine-Atherton.

Al-Mashari, M. and Zairi, M. (1999). "BPR Implementation Process: An Analysis of Key Success and Failure Factors," *Business Process Management Journal*, 5(1): 87-112.

American Productivity and Quality Center. (undated). *Process Classification Framework*, APQC's International Benchmarking Clearinghouse summary report.

Anderson, R. G. (1973). *Organization and Methods*, London: MacDonald and Evans.

Ashby, W. R. (1956). *An Introduction to Cybernetics*, London: Chapman & Hall.

Bach, J. (undated). *Process Evolution in a Mad World* (Borland International white paper).

Baker, B. N. and Eris, R. L. (1964). *An Introduction to PERT-CPM*, Homewood, IL: R.D. Irwin.

Bartlett, C. A. and Ghoshal, S. (1995). "Rebuilding Behavioral Context: Turn Process ReEngineering into People Rejuvenation," *Sloan Management Review*, 37(1): 11-23.

Becker, J., Rosemann, M. and von Uthmann, C. (2000). "Guidelines of Business Process Modeling," in W. van der Aalst, J. Deseland and A. Oberweis (eds.), *Business Process Management: Models, Techniques and Empirical Studies*, Berlin: Springer-Verlag, pp. 30-49.

Beer, S. (1972). *Brain of the Firm: The Managerial Cybernetics of Organization*, London: Allan Lane.

Berger, P. L. and Luckmann, T. (1966). *The Social Construction of Reality: A Treatise in the Sociology of Knowledge*, Garden City, NJ: Doubleday.

Biazzo, S. (2002). "Process Mapping Techniques and Organizational Analysis," *Business Process Management Journal*, 8(1): 42-52.

Bonabeau, E. (1997). "From Classical Models of Morphogenesis to Agent-Based Models of Pattern Formation," *Artificial Life*, 3(3): 191-211.

Brown, J. S. and Gray, E. S. (1995). "The People Are the Company," *Fast Company*, 1(1): 78-82.

Brown, J. and Isaacs, D. (1996). "Conversation as a Core Business Process," *The Systems Thinker*, 7(10): 1-6.

Brynjolfsson, E., Renshaw, A. A. and Van Alstyne, M. (1997). "The Matrix of Change," *Sloan Management Review*, 38(2): 37-54.

Bower, J. L. and Hout, T. M. (1988). "Fast-Cycle Capability for Competitive Power," *Harvard Business Review*, 66(6): 110-118.

Carley, K. M. (1995). "Computational and Mathematical Organization Theory: Perspective and Direction," *Computational and Mathematical Organization Theory*, 1(1): 39-56.

Charan, R. (1991). "How Networks Reshape Organizations - for Results," *Harvard Business Review*, 69(5): 104-115.

Checkland, P. (1985). "From Optimizing to Learning: A Development of Systems Thinking for the 1990s," *Journal of the Operational Research Society*, 36(9): 757-767.

Checkland, P.B. (1981). *Systems Thinking, Systems Practice*, Chichester: Wiley.

Checkland, P. and Scholes, J. (1990). *Soft Systems Methodology in Action*, Chichester: Wiley.

Childe, S., Maull, R. and Mills, B. (1997). *UK Experiences in Business Process Reengineering*, University of Warwick Business Process Resource Centre Report 9, retrieved

August 9, 2003, from http://bprc.warwick.ac.uk/rc-rep-9.html

Churchman, C. W. (1967). "Wicked Problems," *Management Science*, 4(14): B141-142.

Cilliers, P. (1998). *Complexity and Postmodernism: Understanding Complex Systems*, London: Routledge.

Colquhoun, G. J., Gamble, J. D. and Baines, R. W. (1989). "The Use of IDEF0 to Link Design and Manufacture in a CIM Environment," *International Journal of Operations and Production Management*, 9(4): 48-65.

Coombes, R. and Hull, R. (1997). *The Wider Research Context of Business Process Analysis*, University of Warwick Business Process Resource Centre Consultancy Report, retrieved August 19, 2003, from http://bprc.warwick.ac.uk/umist.html

Cooper, R. and Markus, M. L. (1995). "Human Reengineering," *Sloan Management Review*, 36(4): 39-50.

Coulson-Thomas, C. (ed.) (1994). *Business Process Re-engineering: Myth & Reality*, London: Kogan-Page.

Curtis, B., Kellner, M. I. and Over, J. (1992). "Process Modeling," *Communications of the ACM*, 35(9): 75-90.

Cyert, R. M. and March, J. G. (1963). *A Behavioral Theory of the Firm*, Englewood Cliffs, NJ: Prentice-Hall.

Davenport, T. H. (1993). *Process Innovation: Reengineering Work through Information Technology*, Boston: Harvard Business School Press.

Davenport, T. H. (1995). "The Fad That Forgot People," *Fast Company*, 1(1): 70-73.

Davenport, T. H. and Short, J. E. (1990). "The New Industrial Engineering: Information Technology and Business Process Redesign," *Sloan Management Review*, 31(4): 11-27.

Davenport, T. H. and Stoddard, D. B. (1994). "Reengineering: Business Change of Mythic Proportions?" *MIS Quarterly*, 18(2): 121-127

Davidson, W. H. (1993). "Beyond Re-engineering: The Three Phases of Business Transformation," *IBM Systems Journal*, 32(1): 65-79.

de Geus, A. P. (1997). "The Living Company," *Harvard Business Review*, 75(2): 51-59.

de Vreede, G.-J. and van Eijck, D. T. T. (1998). "Modeling and Simulating Organizational Coordination," *Simulation and Gaming*, 29(1): 60-87.

Earl, M. (1994). "The Old and New of Business Process Redesign," *Journal of Strategic Information Systems*, 3(1): 5-22.

Earl, M. and Khan, B. (1994). "How New is Business Process Redesign?" *European Management Journal*, 12(1): 20-30.

Eisenberg, H. (1997). "Reengineering and Dumbsizing: Mismanagement of the Knowledge Resource," *Quality Progress*, 30(5): 57-64.

Eriksson, D. M. (2001). "Multi-modal Investigation of a Business Process and Information System Redesign: A Post-implementation Case Study," *Systems Research and Behavioral Science*, 18(2): 181-196.

Falconer, J. (2004). "Modelling Complexity: Is the Fly Out of the Fly-Bottle or Stuck on the Fly-paper?" in P. Sotolongo (ed.), *Proceedings of the Second Biennial Seminar on the Philosophical, Methodological, and Epistemological Implications of Complexity Theory*, Havana: Instituto de Filosofia.

Falconer, J. (1999). "The Business Pattern: A New Tool for Organizational Knowledge Capture and Reuse," in L. Woods (ed.), *Proceedings of the 62nd ASIS Annual Meeting*, Medford, NJ: American Society for Information Science, pp. 313-330.

Feiler, P. H. (1993). *Reengineering: An Engineering Problem*, Software Engineering Institute Special Report CMU/SEI-93-SR-5, Carnegie Mellon University.

Ford, H. (1923). *My Life and Work*, London: Heinemann.

Forrester, J. W. (1969). *Urban Dynamics*, Cambridge, MA: MIT Press.

Forrester, J. W. (1971). *World Dynamics*, Cambridge, MA: Wright-Allen Press.

Galliers, R. D. and Baker, B. S. H. (1995). "An Approach to Business Reengineering: The Contribution of Socio-technical and Soft OR Concepts," *INFOR*, 33(4): 263-278.

Grint, K. (1994). "Reengineering History: Social Resonances and Business Process Reengineering," *Organization*, 1(1): 179-201.

Grover, V., Jeong, S. R., Kettinger, W. J. and Teng, J. T. C. (1995). "The Implementation of Business Process Reengineering," *Journal of Management Information Systems*, 12(1): 109-144.

Grover, V. and Malhotra, M. J. (1997). "Business Process Reengineering: A Tutorial on the Concept, Method, Technology and Application," *Journal of Operations Management*, 15: 193-213.

Haire, M. (1964). *Psychology in Management*, New York: McGraw-Hill.

Hammer, M. (1990). "Reengineering Work: Don't Automate, Obliterate," *Harvard Business Review*, 68(4): 104-112.

Hammer, M. and Champy, J. (1993). *Reengineering the Corporation*, New York: HarperBusiness.

Harrington, H. J. (1991). *Business Process Improvement: The Breakthrough Strategy for Total Quality, Productivity, and Competitiveness*, New York: McGraw-Hill.

Harrison, D. B. and Pratt, M. D. (1993). "A Methodology for Reengineering Businesses," *Planning Review*, 21(2): 6-11.

Heisenberg, W. (1983). "The Physical Content of Quantum Kinematics and Mechanics," in J. A. Wheeler and W. H. Zurek (eds. and trans.), *Quantum Theory and Measurement*, Princeton: Princeton University Press, pp. 62-84 (translation of original 1927 article).

Henderson, J. C. and Venkatraman, N. (1993). "Strategic Alignment: Leveraging Information Technology for Transforming Organizations," *IBM Systems Journal*, 32(1): 472-484.

Heylighen, F., Bollen, J. and Riegler, A. (eds.) (1999). *The Evolution of Complexity: The Violet Book of "Einstein Meets Magritte"*, Dordrecht: Kluwer.

Holland, J. H. (1998). *Emergence: From Chaos to Order*, Reading, MA: Addison-Wesley.

Holland, J. H. (1995). *Hidden Order: How Adaptation Builds Complexity*, Reading, MA: Addison-Wesley.

Hurst, D. K. (1984). "Of Boxes, Bubbles, and Effective Management," *Harvard Business Review*, 62(3): 78-88.

Ishikawa, K. (1985). *What Is Total Quality Control? The Japanese Way*, Englewood Cliffs, NJ: Prentice-Hall.

Juran, J. M. (1964). *Managerial Breakthrough: A New Concept of the Manager's Job*, New York: McGraw-Hill.

Kauffman, S. (1995). *At Home in the Universe: The Search for Laws of Self-Organization and Complexity*, New York: Oxford University Press.

Kay, N. M. (1984). *The Emergent Firm: Knowledge, Ignorance and Surprise in Economic Organization*, New York: St. Martin's Press.

Kelly, K. (1998). *New Rules for the New Economy: 10 Radical Strategies for a Connected World*, New York: Viking.

Kelly, K. (1994). *Out of Control: The New Biology of Machines, Social Systems, and the Economic World*, Reading, MA: Addison-Wesley.

Kettinger, W. J. and Grover, V. (1995). "Toward a Theory of Business Process Change

Management," *Journal of Management Information Systems*, 12(1): 9-30.

Kleiner, A. (2000). "Revisiting Reengineering," *Strategy + Business*, 20: 27-31.

Krackhardt, D. and Hanson, J. R. (1993). "Informal Networks: The Company Behind the Chart," *Harvard Business Review*, 71(4): 104-111.

Kueng, P., Kawalek, P. and Bichler, P. (1996). *How to Compose an Object-oriented Business Process Model?* Informatics Process Group Working Paper, Department of Computer Science, University of Manchester.

Lancaster, H. (1995). "Reengineering Authors Reconsider Reengineering," *The Wall Street Journal*, January 17, p. B1.

Leavitt, H. J. (1965). "Applied Organizational Change in Industry: Structural, Technological and Humanistic Approaches," in J. G. March (ed.), *Handbook of Organizations*, Chicago: Rand McNally, pp. 1144-1170.

Lewin, R. and Regine, B. (2000). *The Soul at Work: Embracing Complexity Science for Business Success*, New York: Simon & Schuster.

Liker, J. K., Roitman, D. B. and Roskies, E. (1987). "Changing Everything All at Once: Work Life and Technological Change," *Sloan Management Review*, 28(4): 29-47.

Lin, F.-R., Yang, M.-C. and Pai, Y.-H.(2002). "A Generic Structure for Business Process Modeling," *Business Process Management Journal*, 8(1): 19-41.

Lissack, M. R. and Richardson, K. A. (2001). "When Modelling Social Systems, Models ≠ the Modelled: Reacting to Wolfram's A New Kind of Science," *Emergence*, 3(4): 95-111.

Malone, T. W., Crowston, K., Lee, J., Pentland, B., Dellarocas, C., Wyner, G. Quimby, J., Osborne, C., Bernstein, A., Herman, G., Klein, M. and O'Donnell, E. (1997). *Tools for Inventing Organizations: Toward a Handbook of Organizational Processes*, MIT Center for Coordination Science white paper.

Manganelli, R. L. and Klein, M. M. (1994). *The Reengineering Handbook: A Step-By-Step Guide to Business Transformation*, New York: Amacom.

Maslow, A. H. (1965). *Eupsychian Management: A Journal*, Homewood, IL: Richard D. Irwin, Inc.

Maslow, A. H. (1954). *Motivation and Personality*, New York: Harper.

Mayo, E. (1933). *The Human Problems of an Industrial Civilization*, New York: Viking.

McGregor, D. (1960). *The Human Side of Enterprise*, New York: McGraw-Hill.

McMaster, M. D. (1996). *The Intelligence Advantage: Organizing for Complexity*, Boston: Butterworth-Heinemann.

Melão, N. and Pidd, M. (2000). "A Conceptual Framework for Understanding Business Processes and Business Process Modelling," *Information Systems Journal*, 10: 105-129.

Minar, N., Burkhart, R., Langton, C. and Askenazi, M. (1996). *The Swarm Simulation System: A Toolkit for Building Multi-agent Simulations*, Sante Fe Institute overview paper, retrieved August 13, 2003 from http://www.swarm.org/archive/overview.ps

Mumford, E. (1994). "New Treatments or Old Remedies: Is Business Process Reengineering Really Socio-Technical Design?" *Journal of Strategic Information Systems*, 3(4): 313-326.

Mumford, E. and Hendricks, R. (1996). "Business Process Re-engineering RIP," *People Management*, 2(9): 22-29.

Newman, M. E. J. (2003). "The Structure and Function of Complex Networks," *SIAM Review*, 45(2): 167-256.

Normann, R. (2001). *Reframing Business: When the Map Changes the Landscape*, Chichester, UK: Wiley.

Olson, E. E. and Eoyang, G. H. (2001). *Facilitating Organization Change: Lessons from Complexity Science*, San Francisco: Jossey-Bass.

Padulo, R. (1994). "Reengineering for Long Term Survival: The 'Management-learning' Process," *Focus on Change Management*, July-August: 10-13,19.

Palmer, K. D. (1995). *Advanced Process Architectures*, hardcopy of presentation slides, source unknown.

Patching, D. (1995). "Business Process Re-engineering," *Management Services*, 39(4): 8-11.

Porter, M. E. (1979). "How Competitive Forces Shape Strategy," *Harvard Business Review*, 57(2): 137-145.

Porter, M. E. (1985). "How Information Gives You Competitive Advantage," *Harvard Business Review*, 63(4): 149-160.

Povey, B. (1998). "The Development of a Best Practice Business Improvement Methodology," *Benchmarking for Quality Management & Technology*, 5(1): 27-44.

Prigogine, I. and Stengers, I. (1984). *Order Out of Chaos: Man's New Dialogue with Nature*, New York: Bantam.

Richardson, K. A. (2005). "The Hegemony of the Physical Sciences: An Exploration in Complexity Thinking," accepted for publication in *Futures*.

Roethlisberger, F. J., Dickson, W. J. and Wright, H. A. (1939). *Management and the Worker: An Account of a Research Program Conducted by the Western Electric Company, Hawthorne Works, Chicago*, Cambridge, MA: Harvard University Press.

Rummler, G. A. and Brache, A. P. (1991). "Managing the White Space," *Training*, 28(1): 55-70.

Schein, E. (1969). *Process Consultation: Its Role in Organization Development*, New York: Addison-Wesley.

Scott Morton, M. S. (ed.) (1991). *The Corporation of the 1990s: Information Technology and Organizational Transformation*, New York: Oxford University Press.

Senge, P. M. (1990). *The Fifth Discipline: The Art and Practice of the Learning Organization*, New York: Doubleday Currency.

Shafer, L. R., Ritter, J. B. and Meyer, W. L. (1965). *The Critical-Path Method*, New York: McGraw-Hill.

Sherman, H. and Schultz, R. (1998). *Open Boundaries: Creative Business Innovation Through Complexity*, New York: Addison-Wesley.

Simon, H. A. (1945). *Administrative Behavior*, New York: Free Press.

Simon, H.A. (1960). *The New Science of Management Decision*, New York: Harper & Row.

Smith, H., Neal, D., Ferrara, L. and Hayden, F. (2002). *The Emergence of Business Process Management (Version 1.0)*, CSC's Research Services / BPMI online publication, retrieved August 13, 2003 from http://www.bpmi.org/bpmi-library/A8CC9383F9.CSC-BPM-Rpt-Jan2002.pdf.

Smith, H. and Fingar, P. (2002). *Business Process Management: The Third Wave*, Tampa, FL: Megan-Kiffer.

Stacey, R. D. (1992). *Managing the Unknowable: Strategic Boundaries Between Order and Chaos in Organizations*, San Francisco: Jossey-Bass.

Stoddard, D. B. and Jarvenpaa, S. L. (1995). "Business Process Redesign: Tactics for Managing Radical Change," *Journal of Management Information Systems*, 12(1): 81-107.

Strassmann, P. (1994). "The Hocus-pocus of Reengineering," *Across the Board*, June: 35-38.

Talwar, R. (1993). "Business Re-engineering—A Strategy-driven Approach," *Long*

Range Planning, 26(6): 22-40.

Taylor, F. J. (1911). *The Principles of Scientific Management*, New York: Harper.

Thompson, J. D. (1967). *Organizations in Action*, New York: McGraw-Hill.

Trist. E. L. (1978). "On Socio-technical Systems," in W. M. Pasmore and J. J. Sherwood (eds.), *Sociotechnical Systems: A Sourcebook*, reprinted from unpublished 1959 lecture, La Jolla, CA: University Associates, Inc., pp. 43-57.

Van Stijn, E. and Wensley, A. (2001). "Organizational Memory and the Completeness of Process Modeling in ERP Systems: Some Concerns, Methods and Directions for Future Research," *Business Process Management Journal*, 7(3): 181-194.

Venkatraman, N. (1994). "IT-enabled Business Transformation: From Automation to Business Scope Redefinition," *Sloan Management Review*, 35(2): 73-87.

Vickers, G. (1965). *The Art of Judgement*, London: Chapman & Hall.

Vickers, G. (1983). *Human Systems Are Different*, London: Harper & Row.

von Bertalanffy, L. (1968). *General System Theory: Foundation, Development, Applications* (rev. ed.), New York: George Braziller.

Wang, Q. and von Tunzelmann, N. (2000). "Complexity and the Functions of the Firm: Breadth and Depth," *Research Policy*, 29: 805-818.

Weick, K. E. (1979). *The Social Psychology of Organizing*, New York: Random House.

Weiss, G. (ed.) (1999). *Multiagent Systems: A Modern Approach to Distributed Artificial Intelligence*, Cambridge, MA: MIT Press.

Wheatley, M. J. (1992). *Leadership and the New Science: Learning about Organization from an Orderly Universe*, San Francisco: Berrett-Koehler.

Willcocks, L. and Smith, G. (1995). "IT-enabled Business Process Reengineering: Organizational and Human Resource Dimensions," *Journal of Strategic Information Systems*, 4(3): 279-301.

Zairi, M. and Sinclair, D. (1995). "Business Process Re-engineering and Process Management: A Survey of Current Practice and Future Trends in Integrated Management," *Management Decision*, 33(3): 3-16.

Zuboff, S. (1988). *In the Age of the Smart Machine: The Future of Work and Power*, New York: Basic Books.

CHAPTER 9

THE USE OF BYTES TO ANALYZE COMPLEX ORGANIZATIONS

Shann Turnbull

This chapter shows how a gap in organizational analysis can be filled by using the transaction of bytes to compare hierarchical organizations, controlled by a single control centre, with complex ones possessing distributed decision making with multiple communication channels and control agents. No social organization can exist without the transmission, reception and processing of bytes between and within biota. The ability of an organization to survive depends upon its communication and control architecture not requiring its components to exceed their ability to transact bytes. Bytes are represented by patterns in matter or energy. Data, information, knowledge and wisdom are composed of bytes. Transaction byte analysis provides an instrumental basis for evaluating, comparing and designing human organizations independently of the level of technology that may be employed. Transaction Byte Analysis is compared with Transaction Cost Economics that it subsumes when the social construct of cost becomes a proxy for bytes.

Managing Organizational Complexity: Philosophy, Theory, and Application
A Volume in: Managing the Complex, pages 151-165.
ISBN: 1-59311-319-6 (cloth), 1-59311-318-8 (paper)

Introduction

This chapter shows how a gap in organizational analysis can be filled by using the transaction of bytes to compare hierarchical organizations, controlled by a single control centre, with complex ones possessing distributed decision making, with multiple communication channels and control agents.

Nonhierarchical or 'network' social organizations introduce structural complexity as found within biota. Like biota, network organizations contain distributed control centres with a multiplicity of communication channels and control agents. The control channels in a hierarchy all centralize in a single control centre that limits structural variety.

According to the definition of complexity used by the by the London School of Economics (LSE, 2004), network organizations introduce two types of complexity. One type of complexity is structural as referred to above and the other is in the behavior of humans and their relationships.

The LSE defines organizational complexity as being "associated with the intricate inter-relationships of individuals, of individuals with artefacts (such as IT), and with the effects of interactions within the organization and between organizations and their 'environment' which includes related businesses" (LSE 2004).

Hierarchies largely depend upon establishing hegemony in the values of its members to produce consistent obedience to superiors and so conformity. Hierarchies suppress the complexity built into social animals to have contrary and changeable interactive behavior such as being competitive / cooperative, suspicious / trusting, self-interested / altruistic and so on. Theories about organizations, especially those of economists, typically assume that all humans behave in a consistent manner.

Theoretical gaps in analyzing complexity

A number of scholars have identified gaps in organizational analysis (see for example Falconer, this volume). Radner (1992: 1384) states that "I know of no theoretical research to date that compares the relative efficiency of nonhierarchical organizations within a common model". Jensen (1993: 873) observed that "we're facing the problem of developing a viable theory of organizations" while Zingales (2000) states that in regards to existing theories of the firm "they seem to be quite ineffective in helping us cope with the new type of firms that are emerging". It was the emergence of network firms that led Zingales (2000) to question accepted theories of the firm and to pose four questions that any new theory of the firm must answer. Transaction Byte Analysis (TBA) provides answers to all four questions (Turnbull, 2001).

TBA grounds organizational analysis in cybernetics or system science. Wiener (1948) defined cybernetics as "the science of control and communication in the animal and the machine." This definition can now be extended to include social organizations. TBA provides a basis for developing "the elusive science of organization" sought by Williamson (1991: 12). A science of organization grounded in system science might better be described as the 'science of governance' as according to the Oxford Dictionary the word 'cybernetics' means to 'steer' or 'govern' (Little, et al., 1956).

TBA was so named to indicate both its similarity and differences with Transaction Cost Economics (TCE) developed by Williamson (1975). Williamson used TCE to explicate the work of Coase (1937) as to why firms exist. He also used TCE to explain the development of different forms of firms but only in the context of them being a hierarchy or what Coase described as an "master and servant" or "employer and employee" relationship. Jensen and Meckling (1976) analyzed this relationship using the term "Principal and Agent" that assumed humans had a predictable and consistent self-interest.

Williamson (1985: 279–283) explains how US firms early in the 20th century divided into Multi-divisional (M–Form) hierarchies to mitigate information overload and bounded rationality. This change was explained by Chandler (1966: 382–83) who stated that "the operations of the enterprise became too complex and the problems of co-ordination, appraisal, and policy formulation too intricate for a small number of top officers to handle both long-run, entrepreneurial, and short-run operational administrative activities".

The development of M–Form from unitary (U–Form) firms increased as business organizations grew bigger and more dynamic to overload the data processing ability of individuals. But as businesses became even bigger, more dynamic and complicated, network (N–form) firms became increasing prevalent. Jones, et al. (1997) report that network firms are most likely to develop in the more dynamic industries like fashion textiles, construction, movie making, sound recording, financial services and high tech semi-conductor or biological industries.

Besides being more dynamic, the firms discussed by Jones, et al. (1997) are also more knowledge intensive. This makes the transaction of bytes relatively more important than the production and exchange of goods and services of less dynamic and knowledge intensive firms.

Context of the TBA framework

TBA is based on the limited ability of any biota to receive, store, process and transmit bytes by using what ever technology that is relevant. While bytes are the numaire of analysis, biota is the subject of analysis. TBA does not concern itself if the biota forming a social organization is human or another form of life. In this way TBA provides a common basis to compare social organizations between specie. When human organizations are being analyzed, TBA does not need to concern itself if it is a firm, how it is organized or what is the purpose of the organization. Because the subjects of analysis are individuals and their limited ability to transact bytes, it does not matter what technology is used to communicate bytes with other humans. It is the human interface with technology that creates limits on the design of organizations.

Ashby (1968: 4) anticipated the application of the science of control and communication to organizations when he wrote, "cybernetics is likely to reveal a great number of interesting and suggestive parallelisms between machine, brain and society". A common feature of complex machines / devices, brains and society is that they cannot operate without transacting data composed of bytes.

Information represents data that has meaning. For a person to associate meaning to data they must be able to relate it to data already stored in their brain. This requires associating the pattern of bytes stored in the brain with the bytes received. The stored bytes are the result of nature and nurture and are subject to neurological limits.

Knowledge is useful information. The recognition that information can be useful is likewise dependent upon associating the bytes stored with the bytes received. *Wisdom* is the knowledge of when to apply knowledge and so it is also subject to the physical limits of storing, receiving and associating bytes. In summary, data, information, knowledge and wisdom are constituted by bytes. Any changes in data, information, knowledge and wisdom requires perturbations in matter or energy. This introduces instrumental limits on any form of biota to acquire or process data, information, knowledge and wisdom.

In the following section, the limited ability of humans to transact bytes is identified. The section after, considers the inherent limitations of hierarchies in creating a communication and control architecture that can minimize the transaction of bytes while reducing errors. Design strategies that are found in nature, and in some social organizations, for overcoming the limited ability of biota to transact bytes are considered next. In the concluding section, TBA is compared with TCE, which TBA subsumes when costs become a proxy for bytes.

Limited ability of humans to transact bytes

The limited ability of humans to process information was noted by Hayek (1945: 527) who stated that "the problem of a rational economic order is trivial in the absence of bounded rationality limits on human decision makers". Williamson (1975: 21) explains that:

"The physical limits take the form of rate and storage limits on the powers of individuals to receive, store, retrieve and process information without error. Simon observes in this connection that 'it is only because individual human beings are limited in knowledge, foresight, skill and time that organizations are useful instruments for the achievement of human purpose'", quoting Simon (1957: 199).

Williamson went on to say "Bounded rationality involves neurophysiological limits on the one hand and language limits on the other". In other words, bounded rationality and information overload can be explained in terms of the limited ability of human physiology and neurology to transact bytes. In recent years it has become possible to quantify the limited ability of humans in this regard.

The research department of British Telecom has measured the rate that each of the five human senses can transact bytes. According to Cochrane (2000, 2004) the 'bandwidth' of smell is less than 10 bytes per second while taste and touch can provide up to 15 bytes per second. Sound is four orders of magnitude higher at 100 Kilobytes per second while sight is another four orders of magnitude higher at 1,000 Megabytes per second.

Humans have little control over their smell and taste. Touch is not a significant channel of communication in most organizations. This leaves body movements and sound as the principal means for humans to transmit signals directly to other or through the use of technology.

According to Kurzweil (1999: 103) the rate at which the human brain can sequentially process data through the neocortex is limited to around 200 calculations per second. This compares very poorly with desktop computers that operate a million times quicker. However, humans can still currently outperform computers in the recognition of speech, body movements and facial features because of their ability to recognize patterns. Pattern recognition depends upon the brain's massively parallel data processing ability. It is pattern recognition that provides the "foundations for most human thought" according to Kurzweil (1999: 79).

Kurzweil (1999: 103) points out that the human brain has around 100 billion neurons with "about 100 trillion connections, each capable of a simultaneous calculation... With 100 trillion connections each computing at 200 calculations per second, we get 20 million billion calculations per second" that far exceeds the ability of current computers. The relevance of this point is that the ability of social organizations to perform effectively is not just the limited capability of their human components, but on the architecture of their communication and control channels. It explains how ordinary people can achieve extraordinary results to out perform extraordinary people through adopting superior organizational architecture.

Beside limits in transacting bytes, humans have limits in storing information and knowledge. Kurzweil (1999: 119) estimates that "The number of concepts - 'chunks' of knowledge - that a human expert in a particular field has mastered is remarkably consistent: about 50,000 to 100,000". He went on to say that "This approximate range appears to be valid over a wide range of human endeavours: the number of board positions mastered by a chess grand master, the concepts mastered by an expert in a technical field, such as physician...". However, he points out that this knowledge is "only a subset of the knowledge we need to function as a human being". His rough estimate of the number of chunks - bits of understanding, concepts, patterns, specific skills - per human is 100 million.

The challenge for organizations is to coordinate human understanding, concepts, specific skills and abilities in the most effective way with their physical limitations to transact bytes and their contrary and inconsistent behavior. Nature has developed strategies for biota to transact bytes within their limited abilities to allow them to sustain their specie in unpredictable and ever changing environments. These depend upon adopting a special type of network architecture considered in the concluding section. To provide a comparison, the inherent problems in hierarchies to minimize the transaction of bytes on a reliable basis are next considered.

Inherent problems of hierarchies

Command and control hierarchies are the dominant strategy in modern societies to minimize information overload and bounded rationality. However, they have inherent problems when compared with network organizations. TBA provides a way to compare both on a common basis.

It is in an effort to reduce information overload that managers limit the number of subordinates who report to them. Hierarchies develop from subordinates repeating this process. This leads to the necessity for orders to be transmitted and interpreted through a number of levels down a hierarchy with reports on the consequences being condensed and reported back up the chain of command. The process creates errors in communications. It can also build in biases from the self-interest of the communicators not to implicate themselves in adverse reports and to promote good news.

The problem of generating communication errors is revealed in the game of 'Chinese whispers' when people are competing to be accurate. In this game equal teams of three or four people compete to transmit the same message for an audience that compares the results. The message almost invariable gets distorted, especially as the message gets longer and contains more information.

In a hierarchy, people may not be motivated to accurately communicate. This is because it is often not in the best interest of any subordinate to report any problem up the chain of command for which she or he could be held accountable. Downs (1969: 116-118) has shown that only a small fraction of information reported up a hierarchy is likely to be accurate. This explains why CEOs, company directors and heads of government departments may not be fully informed of problems within their organizations.

Newspaper reporters and crime investigators typically cross check information from a number of independent sources. As pointed out by Shannon and Weaver (1954), the reliability of communications can be increased as much as desired by increasing the number of channels. Because the span of control of CEOs is limited, their ability to obtain a number of independent channels of information from each division or person reporting to him or her is limited. While a Board of Directors is appointed (among other things), to monitor the CEO, they are typically not provided with any systemic process to undertake their legal responsibilities with multiple channels of communication independent of the CEO to check the veracity of communications.

Shareholders may have the technical right to appoint an auditor to cross check information but in practice the appointment, tenure and remuneration of auditors becomes subject to the grace and favor of management. As reported by Bazerman, *et al.* (1997), auditors become the representatives of management as demonstrated in recent high profile unexpected business failures. In any event, auditors have a very narrow remit on the information that they cross check.

Another inherent problem in the architecture of hierarchies is in regulating themselves to respond constructively and efficiently to changes in their operating environment. The problem arises because hierarchies lack requisite variety in control agents as required by Ashby's *Law of Requisite Variety* (Ashby, 1968: 206). This is because they have a centralized control system that inherently lacks variety. Another problem is the corollary of the Law of Requisite Variety that states that it is impossible to amplify regulation variety without "supplementation" (Ashby, 1968: 265). In organizations, supplementation would require the establishment of co-regulators. However, experience shows that hierarchies typically capture co-regulators like auditors to make them ineffective.

The lack of independent decision making in a hierarchy is another problem. Von Neumann and Morgenstern (1964) identified the advantages of introducing a variety of decision-making centers. Beer (1995: 448) describes this as the Neumann theorem, which states: "outputs of arbitrarily high reliability can be obtained from computing elements of arbitrarily low reliability if the redundancy is large enough". However, hierarchies are designed to condense information and decision making rather than to create redundancies.

While hierarchies are created to minimize the transaction of bytes they introduce errors, biases, missing information and inadequate decision-making. These problems can be accepted to some degree in many situations, but the problems become exacerbated as organizations grow in size, are exposed to increasing number of environmental variables, and rely more and more on quickly receiving, processing and reacting to information as reported by Jones, *et al.* (1997).

Jones, *et al.* reported that network organizations arise when environmental variables increase and / or change more rapidly. This is consistent with the ability of network organizations to introduce a requisite variety of communication and control channels to regulate variety as closely as required without error. It is also consistent with the decomposition of decision making to be decomposed into a requisite variety of centres to reduce information overload and bounded rationality to acceptable levels.

However, network organization need not necessarily economize the bytes transacted by their constituent components. The communication and control architecture of the network needs to be appropriate. The type of architecture that is appropriate is considered in the following section.

Network organizations

There are two important strategies to consider in the design of network organizations. One is the principle of "Subsidiary Function" (Schumacher, 1975: 203) which states that no higher order association should undertake any function that can be undertaken at a lower level. In this way the bytes transacted through an intermediate 'order of association' can be eliminated.

The second strategy is that each 'order of association' should become what Simon (1962) describes as "a nearly decomposable systems", in which "the interaction among the sub-systems are weak, but not negligible". It is the "weak but not negligible" interaction that is crucial to economize the transaction of bytes through individual components of the system. The weak interaction needs to be within the capabilities of individual components so that they can guide / steer the sub-system in such a way that it furthers the objectives of the whole system.

Koestler (1967) later identified the sub-systems described by Simon as being a 'holon'. For organizations, Mathews (1996: 34) adopts a stronger definition for a holon than used by Simon or Koestler. He states that "it is essential that each 'holon' be endowed with its own processing ability, its own autonomy, its own 'mind' or intelligence". Mathews (1996: 40) goes on to identify "holonic autonomy, system dependence and recursivity as the defining features of holonic organizational architectures". These three tests are met by a nested network of stakeholder-controlled cooperatives located around the town of Mondragón in Northern Spain (Turnbull, 2003). Thomas and Logan (1982: 109) reported that "the cooperatives are more efficient than many private enterprises", and "there can be no doubt that the cooperatives have been more profitable than capitalist enterprises".

There are almost 200 firms employing over 60,000 people in the Mondragón network. Each firm has the power to leave the network and be an independent self-governing unit and so meets the test of having 'holonic autonomy'. Each firm represents a 'sub-system' of the whole (holon) and so gives up some self-governing powers to join the network to provide 'system dependence". But also, as a result, "the interaction among the subsystems are weak, but negligible" in the words of Simon (1962).

A network of four independently constituted decision centers governs each firm (Turnbull, 2003). A dozen of so firms form a group that is governed by a similar pattern of four independently constituted decision centres to provide recursivity to meet the third Mathew test for a holonic system.

Bernstein (1980) provides further empirical evidence that self-governing organizations require internal division of powers and checks and balances. In a survey of nontrivial worker managed firms from many parts of the world, he reported that none was governed by a unitary board. A most compelling feature of this survey was that this fact was true even in countries where unitary boards were the dominant form, as found in the US and UK. The empirical evidence is supported by the ground-breaking theoretical work of Persson, *et al.* (1996). They showed how an appropriate separation of powers provides net advantages to all constituents stakeholders.

Mathews (1996: 41–44) describes holonic organizations as possessing the following characteristics: centralization / decentralization; bottom-up / top-down; autonomous / integrated; order / ambiguity. In comparing them with hierarchies, holonic organizations provide centralization and decentralization of control; systemic reliability and flexibility; systemic responsiveness; systemic learning and organizational innovations: autopoiesis. Mathews (1996: 41) claims that "holonic systems exhibit superior performance on all these points than conventionally structured hierarchical organizations". But it is their prodigious "reduction in data transmission and in data complexity", noted by Mathews (1996: 30) which is of special interest as this provides one basis for TBA to explain their 'superior performance' compared with hierarchies.

Another more familiar example of a holonic organization is VISA International, Inc. It demonstrates how it can operate locally on a global basis to illustrate the features described by Mathews. It also illustrates the competitive advantages of firms made up of a network of separate decision making centres. The founding CEO of VISA, Dee Hock (1996) explained that VISA International "has multiple boards of directors within a single legal entity, none of which can be considered superior or inferior, as each has irrevocable authority and autonomy over geographic or functional area".

Both VISA and Mondragón illustrate Hock's (1996) "second law of the universe: Nothing can be made simpler without becoming more complex." While the architecture of the whole / holon becomes more complex, the requirement for its components to transact bytes becomes less as shown by Turnbull (2003).

The paradox is that complexity in the communication and control network of organizations, when structured as a network of almost self-governing components, provides superior effectiveness than the simplicity of hierarchies because they prodigiously reduce the need for individuals in the system to transact bytes.

Hock concludes that society has "an institutional problem" from relying on simple hierarchies that should not, and cannot, be trusted whether they are in the private or public sector. This view is consistent with the findings of Dunbar (1993) on the limited capacity of individuals to establish close trusting relationships with more than 150 people.

It is the transaction of bytes rather than the social construct of cost that can explain the competitive advantages of complexity found in nature. In the next concluding section, TBA is compared with TCE for investigating and explaining the operations of organizations that operate as firms.

Comparison between TBA and TCE frameworks

In this section TBA is compared with TCE (which represents a leading framework for investigating firms). Williamson developed TCE by building on the theory of the firm developed by Coase. Coase (1937) only considered firms that had "some authority (an 'entrepreneur') to direct resources" in a "master and servant" or "employer and employee" relationship as noted in the first row of Table 1.

	Framework of analysis	TCE (Coase / Williamson)	TBA (Developed by the author)
1	Relationship of people	Master / servant, employer / employee	Any, eg., family, master / servant, cooperative, competitive, associative, etc.
2	Type of social institution	For-profit firms not labor managed	Any social organization, including any type of firm
3	Unit of analysis	Cost	Bytes
4	Subjects of analysis	Transactions and their costs	People and the bytes they transact
5	Objectives	Economizing costs	Anything. (For firms, economizing the transaction of bytes by people)
6	Basis for objective	Normative to reduce costs	Physiological limits in transacting bytes
7	People behavior	Independent variable. Constant self-interest, opportunism, competitiveness, etc.	Dependent variable. Changeable and contrary such as self-interested / altruistic, opportunistic / selfless, competitive / cooperative, etc.
8	Modes of governance	Markets, hierarchies and hybrids of both	Combination of clans / communities, associations, hierarchies and / or markets
9	Communication and control through:	Markets and hierarchies	Related mixes of senses, semiotics, words and numbers
10	Firms of two or more people exist because:	Markets fail to provide information economically	Complex tasks can be carried out with individuals transacting fewer bytes and / or need to exceed other limits of individuals.

Table 1
Comparison of TCE and TBA frameworks

Williamson (1985: 265) states that he "is mainly preoccupied with assessing capitalist modes of organization". He goes on to acknowledges the existence of Mondragón enterprises that he refers to as an 'experiment' but notes that labor managed firms require further study and so are excluded from TCE as noted in the second row of Table 1.

However, even with capitalist firms, Barney and Ouchi (1986: 8) state that there are "theoretical and empirical anomalies". They go on to say that "the search is on for a more general framework, a framework that will include the insights of the traditional theory, but will place those insights in a context that allows the theorist to explain a wider diversity of economic and, particularly, organizational phenomena". They identified the need for "a new paradigm for understanding and studying organizations". TBA is presented as such a framework grounded in the physiological and neurological limitations of people to transact bytes and the science of cybernetics.

Unlike TCE, TBA has universal application for investigating all social relationships and institutions as noted respectively in the first and second rows of Table 1. This is because no social relationship can be established without communication and so the transaction of bytes. It is the use of bytes to replace costs as listed in the third row of Table 1 that creates the fundamental difference between the two frameworks. It is in this way that TBA "involves the same bundle of data as before, but placing them in a new system of relations with one another by giving them a different framework" to quote Kuhn (1970: 80) who was describing a 'paradigm shift'.

The suggestion "that the transaction is properly regarded as the basic numaire of analysis" as presented in the fourth row of Table 2 was made by Commons (1934: 4–8). This suggestion was made some 14 years before Wiener (1948) identified the science of cybernetics. When Commons put forward his suggestion it was not practical to consider transactions involving bytes as this word was not coined by until 1946. In any event, the concept of a 'transaction' and its cost has changed over the years as described by Klaes (2000). There has been little agreement between various writers on what constitutes a transaction and so how its cost might be measured in some of its forms.

Not only are there ambiguities about what constitutes a transaction, there are also ambiguities about how to measure the social construct described as a cost. The determination of a cost depends upon many subjective factors such as what cost is fixed and what is variable and how they should be allocated. Overhead costs continue with the passage of time and the determination of relevant time intervals can be arbitrary. Costs are measured in another social construct called money. In modern societies money can no longer be defined in terms of any specified materials or services.

Bytes on the other hand are embedded as patterns in material or energy and their communication involves perturbations in materials or energy. As biotas have limited material and energy to store and transact bytes this creates an instrumental need to economize bytes. It also creates an instrumental need to economize the amount of materials and energy required by biota to store bytes. This is why TBA is concerned with the physical necessity to economize bytes rather than need to economize the social construct of cost used by TCE as noted in rows five and six of Table 1.

There could be many objectives in communicating bytes but in firms there would be an instrumental need to economize bytes to reduce costs and / or information overload and / or bounded rationality. However, the economizing of costs is a normative assumption for allocating resources within a firm as noted in row six of Table 1. Scholars such as Alchian and Demsetz (1972) and Dallas (1988) question this assumption because of the difficulty of senior managers in nontrivial firms to possess either the information or will to reduce cost.

As information can alter the behavior of people, individuals become both a dependent and independent variable in the TBA framework as indicated in row seven of Table 1. Because people have limited ability to receive, store, retrieve, analyze and transmit information, the effectiveness of firms becomes dependent upon keeping the capacity of people to transact bytes within their capabilities. Besides reducing the volume of bytes that individuals need to transact, the architecture of firms also require sufficient redundancy in transactions to overcome both the contrary nature of humans and their errors.

A feature of TBA noted in the introduction is that it accepts that people can act in a contrary manner to introduce an element of complexity not accepted by most other theories of organizations. TBA accepts both agency theory (Jensen & Meckling, 1976) and stewardship theory (Donaldson & Davis, 1994). TBA provides an explanation of why evolution has bred these characteristics into social animals. It is to minimize the transactions of bytes between social animals by building in checks and balances in each of them to facilitate their self-regulation to insure that the species is sustained. Command and control hierarchies inhibit the built-in characteristics of humans to be self-regulating.

The process of building in checks and balances within each member of a species to achieve regulation illustrates a process described as "supplementation" by Ashby (1968: 265). As discussed above, supplementation provides the only way to amplify regulation.

TCE is based on the "limited institutional repertory" (Hollingsworth & Lindberg, 1985: 221–2) that transactions can only be governed by markets and hierarchy as described by Williamson (1975) as noted in row eight of Table 1. TBA accepts that transactions can be governed by any combination of four different modes of governance described by Hollingsworth and Lindberg (1985). The recognition that clan and associative relationships can govern transactions provides a basis to analyze boards of directors. The TBA framework also provides a basis for developing a more comprehensive, compelling and relevant reasons why firms can exist in many forms (Turnbull 2001).

Consistent with its limited scope of governance mechanisms, TCE limits it methods of communication and control to markets and hierarchies as noted in row nine of Table 1. TBA accepts any method of communication and control through any governance mechanism.

Williamson developed the TCE framework based on the view by Coase that firms exist because market markets fail in organizing productive activities as efficiently as hierarchies. Coase (1937) stated "The most obvious cost of 'organizing' production through the price mechanism is that of discovering what the relevant prices are. This cost may be reduced but it will not be eliminated by the emergence of specialists who will sell this information." Coase was trained as an accountant, and so used costs to explain the existence of a firm. However, the costs that concerned him were a proxy for bytes that communicate prices. In other words firms exist because the price mechanism provides insufficient bytes to organize complex activities as noted in row ten of Table 1.

The TBA framework is universal. It can be applied independently of organizational form, structure, purpose or social context. By allowing organizational analysis to be grounded in the physiological and neurological characteristics of people and the laws of cybernetics, TBA provides a framework for evaluating or designing institutions. It shows how cybernetic principles provide a basis for identifying 'organizational advantage' which Nahapiet and Ghoshal (1998: 261) say is "as yet inadequately understood". TBA also provides design criteria for analyzing, evaluating and / or designing complex human social institutions or different social systems created by humans or other forms of biota.

Bytes provide a micro unit of analysis as sought by Williamson (1990: xi) to "find techniques for observing the phenomena at a higher level of resolution" as also proposed by Simon (1984: 40). As the ability humans to identify, store or transfer knowledge can be decomposed into bytes, this approach is consistent with the observation by Williamson (1991: 11) that "...Winter, like Demsetz, also emphasizes the importance of knowledge acquisition and its utilization in future work on the theory of the firm".

In discussing the theory of the firm Winter (1991: 179) referred to the "present theoretical chaos". Chaos was noted by Kuhn (1970: 77) as a "precondition for the emergence of novel theories" and for the need for finding a new paradigm, as proposed by Barney & Ouchi (1986). Winter (1991: 193) went on to observe, "[i]n the past half-century, it has been clearly demonstrated that the economy is much better at changing itself than economists are at changing their minds".

The acceptance of TBA by economists may need to wait for acceptance by other social or natural scientists. There are compelling reasons for them to do so as TBA provides a methodology to analyze and design social institutions grounded in the natural sciences. It also provides a way to compare human institutions with "the architecture of life" (Ingber 1998).

References

Alchian, A. and Demsetz, H. (1972). "Production, Information Costs, and Economic Organization," *American Economic Review*, 62: 777–795, reproduced in Barney and Ouchi (1986: 129–155).

Ashby, W. R. (1968). *An Introduction to Cybernetics*, London, England: University Paperback.

Barney, J. B. and Ouchi, W. G. (eds.) (1986). *Organizational economics: Toward a New Paradigm for Understanding and Studying Organizations*, Jossey-Bass, San Francisco.

Bazerman, M. H., Morgan, K. P. and Loewenstein, G. F. (1997). "The Impossibility of Auditor Independence," *Sloan Management Review*, 38: 4, <http://web.mit.edu/smr/issue/1997/summer/8/>.

Beer, S. (1995). *Decision and Control: The Meaning of Operational Research and Management Cybernetics*, England: John Wiley & Sons.

Bernstein, P. (1980). *Workplace Democratization: Its Internal Dynamics*, New Brunswick, New Jersey: Transaction Books.

Chandler, A. D. (1966). *Strategy and Structure: Chapters in the History of the Industrial Enterprise*, Cambridge, MA: MIT Press.

Coase, R. H. (1937). "The Nature of the Firm," *Economica*, 4: 386–405, reproduced in Barney and Ouchi (1986: 80–98).

Cochrane, P. (2000). "Hard Drive: Bandwidth and Brandwidth," *Telegraph*, April 6, London, http://www.cochrane.org.uk/opinion/papers/telegraph/2000/06-04-00.htm

Cochrane, P. (2004). Personal communication, 10 April.

Commons, J. R. (1934). *Institutional Economics*, Madison: University of Wisconsin Press.

Dallas, L. L. (1988). "Two Models of Corporate Governance: Beyond Berle and Means," *Journal of Law Reform*, 22(1): 19–116.

Donaldson, L. and Davis, J. H. (1994). "Boards and Company Performance: Research Challenges the Conventional Wisdom," *Corporate Governance: An International Review*, 2(3): 151–160.

Downs, A. (1967). *Inside Bureaucracy*, Boston, US: Little Brown & Co.

Dunbar, R. I. M. (1993). "Coevolution of Neocortical Size, Group Size and Language in Humans," *Behavioral and Brain Sciences*, 16: 681–735.

Hayek, F. A. (1945). "The Use of Knowledge in Society," *American Economic Review*, 35(September): 519–530.

Hock, D. (1996). "The Chaodic Organization: Out of Control and Into Order," <http://www.newhorizons.org/future/hock.htm>.

Hollingsworth, J. R. and Lindberg, L. N. (1985). "The Governance of the American Economy: The Role of Markets, Clans, Hierarchies and Aassociative Behaviour," in W. Streeck and P. C. Schmitter (eds.), *Private Interest Government: Beyond Market and State*, London, England: Sage, pp. 221–267.

Ingber, D. E. (1998). "The Architecture of Life," *Scientific American*, January: 30–39.

Jensen, M. C. (1993). "The Modern Industrial Revolution: Exit and the Failure of Internal Control Systems," *The Journal of Finance*, 48(3): 831–880.

Jensen, M. C. and Meckling, W. H. (1976). "Theory of the Firm: Managerial Behaviour, Agency Costs and Ownership Structure," *Journal of Financial Economics*, 3: 305–360.

Jones, C., Hesterly, W. S. and Borgatti, S. P. (1997). "A General Theory of Network Governance: Exchange Conditions and Social Mechanisms," *Academy of Management Review*, 22(4): 911–945.

Klaes, M. (2000). "The Birth of the Concept of Transaction Costs: Issues and Controversies," *Industrial & Corporate Change*, 9(4):567–593.

Koestler, C. O. (1967). *The Ghost in the Machine*, London, England: Hutchinson.

Kuhn, T. S. (1970). *The Structure of Scientific Revolutions*, Chicago, US: University of Chicago Press, 2nd edn.

Kurzweil, R. (1999). *The Age of Spiritual Machines: When Computers Exceed Human Intelligence*, New York, NY: Viking.

Little, W., Fowler, H. W. and Coulson, J. (1956). The Shorter Oxford English Dictionary, London, England: Oxford University Press, 3rd edition, p. 2487.

LSE. (2004). London School of Economics, http://www.psych.lse.ac.uk/complexity/lexicon.htm

Mathews, J. (1996). "Holonic Organizational Architectures," *Human Systems Management*, 15: 27–54.

Nahapiet, J. and Ghoshal, S. (1998). "Social Capital, Intellectual Capital and the Organizational Advantage," *The Academy of Management Review*, 23(2): 242–266.

Persson, T., Roland, G. and Tabellini, G. (1996). *Separation of Powers and Accountability: Towards a Formal Approach to Comparative Politics*, Innocenzo Gasparini Institute for Economic Research (IGIER), Working Paper, No. 100, July, Milan.

Radner, R. (1992). "Hierarchy: The Economics of Managing," *Journal of Economic Literature*, 30(September): 1282–1415.

Schumacher, E. F. (1975). *Small is Beautiful: A Study of Economics If People Mattered*, London, England: Abacus.

Shannon, C. E. and Weaver, W. (1949). *The Mathematical Theory of Communications*, Urbana, IL: The University of Illinois Press.

Simon, H. A. (1957). *Models of Man*, NY: John Wiley & Sons.

Simon, H. A. (1962). "The Architecture of Complexity," *Proceedings of the American Philosophical Society*, 106(December): 467–482.

Simon, H. A. (1984). "On the Behavioral and Rational Foundations of Economic Dynamics," *Journal of Economic Behavior and Organization*, 5(March): 35–56.

Thomas, H. and Logan, C. (1982). *Mondragón: An Economic Analysis*, London, England: George Allen and Unwin.

Turnbull, S. (2001). "Grounding the Theory of the Firm in the Natural Sciences," presented to the 13th Annual meeting of the Society for the Advancement of Socio-economics, University of Amsterdam, Amsterdam, The Netherlands, 30 June, <http://papers.ssrn.com/sol3/papers.cfm?abstract_id=283785>.

Turnbull, S. (2003). "Governing the Management of Complexity," *19th EGOS Colloquium*, European Group for Organizational Studies, Copenhagen Business School, Denmark, July 4, <http://ssrn.com/abstract=436380>.

Von Neumann, J. and Morgenstern, O. (1964). *Theory of Games and Economic Behavior*, 3rd ed., NY: John Wiley & Sons.

Wiener, N. (1948). *Cybernetics: Control and Communication in the Animal and the Machine*, MIT Press.

Williamson, O. E. (1975). *Markets and Hierarchies: Analysis and Anti–Trust Implications*, NY: Free Press.

Williamson, O. E. (1985). *The Economic Institutions of Capitalism*, NY: Free Press.

Williamson, O. E. (1990). *Industrial Organization*, London, England: Gower House.

Williamson, O. E. (1991). "Introduction," in *The Nature of the Firm: Origins, Evolution & Development*, O. E. Williamson, and S. G. Winter (eds.), NY: Oxford University Press, pp. 1–17.

Winter, S. G. (1991). "On Coase Competence and the Corporation," in *The Nature of the Firm: Origins, Evolution & Development*, O. E. Williamson, and S. G. Winter (eds.), NY: Oxford University Press, pp. 179–195.

Zingales, L. (2000). "In Search of New Foundations," *The Journal of Finance*, 55(4): 1623–1653.

CHAPTER 10

CHAOS-BASED PRINCIPLES OF FORECASTING

Liu Hong and Kurt A. Richardson

Ideas and thinking frameworks about nature and society based on chaos theory are quite different from those of conventional science, and are arguably driving a scientific paradigm shift. Chaos theory provides new insights and modeling methodologies for economic and technological forecasting, making the future of complex systems clearer. As an important part of complexity science, chaos theory opposes the traditional principles of economic and technological forecasting; its influence on forecasting is not only to patch-up traditional forecasting theory, but to support a forecasting paradigm shift well. So, what characterizes this supposed paradigm shift? Which solutions does chaos theory provide for the existing problems of forecasting? Following the results obtained by chaoticians in recent years, this chapter relates the concepts of chaos to forecasting and attempts to provide some answers to above questions. This chapter especially puts forward several new principles of forecasting.

Managing Organizational Complexity: Philosophy, Theory, and Application
A Volume in: Managing the Complex, pages 167-182.
Copyright © 2005 by Information Age Publishing, Inc.
ISBN: 1-59311-319-6 (cloth), 1-59311-318-8 (paper)

Introduction

Traditional methodologies of forecasting are derived from the Newtonian / mechanistic paradigm. The principles of *mechanism* include: the *principle of inertia*, the *principle of correlation*, the *principle of analogy*, and the *principle of probability* (Joseph, 1993). These principles have been widely applied to forecasting in the fields of the society, economy and technology, and have yielded many positive results. However, the forecasting theories based on these principles cannot reasonably explain and forecast numerous complex technological and economic phenomena. Forecasting for such complex phenomena often deviate from the real state of affairs. What can or cannot be forecasted? Why is the predictability of things that follow the same dynamics often so different? Why is the predictability of things different from time to time? To what extent is a certain thing predictable? Is the cost of forecasting certain complex things worthwhile? Traditional forecasting theories cannot provide reasonable answers to these questions. Therefore, some people do not consider forecasting a branch of science, and even blame these problems on researchers for supposedly not knowing the forecasting 'art' well.

In recent years, with the development of the complexity sciences, which provides a new perspective, economic and technological forecasting has become more problematic: forecasting for some things has become clearer, whilst forecasting for certain other things has become more difficult. The findings of chaos theory, which is an important component of complexity science, opposes the principles of traditional economic and technological forecasting as follows (Liu, 1999):

1. According to the principle of inertia, a system tends to maintain the same direction, cycle and properties of state, and we can predict the future of it through trend extrapolation. The force that determines the past also determines the future. According to chaos theory, the process of bifurcation is one of the ways for a system to evolve in a complex manner; there is a qualitative change in the system's trajectory that is quite different from the past trajectory. Furthermore, no matter how well a model fits past time series, extrapolations of the model tend to be qualitatively incorrect when the system moves towards a bifurcation point.

2. According to the principle of correlation, there is always a clear causal explanation for what happens and through the mathematical methods of regression and correlation analysis we have the means to uncover such explanations - *correlation equals causality*. On the other hand, according to pattern simulation based on chaos principles, in some contexts, there is no direct relationship between factors which may appear to correlate with each other very closely - *correlation does not equal causality*.

3. According to the principle of analogy, similar phenomena will have similar explanations, i.e., similar starting conditions will lead to qualitatively

similar results. Whereas, the butterfly effect of chaos theory illustrates that the future depends critically on initial conditions, i.e., two very similar contexts may evolve towards two (qualitatively) very different futures.

4. According to the principle of probability, discrepancies between a forecast and the actual time series data comes from random factors, or the co-effect of numerous little factors, that are exogenous to the system. Whereas, according to chaos theory, the apparent randomness of a system's behavior can come from both endogenous and exogenous sources.

The influence of chaos theory on forecasting is not to 'patch up' traditional forecasting theory, but to stimulate a forecasting paradigm shift (Howell, 1995; Liu, 2000). So, what form does this shift take? Which solutions does chaos theory provide for the existing problems of forecasting? According to the findings of chaos theory in recent years, this chapter attempts to provide answers to these questions, and put forwards several new forecasting principles for economic and technological systems.

The meaning of forecasting by chaos theory

In general, chaos theory states that: order comes from disorder, disorder comes from order; chaos comes from simplicity, simplicity comes from chaos (see, for example, Crutchfield, et al., 1986). The birth of chaos theory has challenged the Laplacian determinism based on the Newtonian paradigm. On the one hand, chaos theory expresses that simple rules could give rise to uncertain and complex phenomena, in which forecasting becomes difficult. On the other hand, chaos theory also suggests that uncertain and complex phenomena may only obey a simple and certain law, and therefore forecasting becomes quite possible. This statement seems contradictory. So, what is predictable by chaos theory? And what is unpredictable? The concept of forecasting in chaos theory must be clarified before exploring these questions. To do this, Liu and Li (1998) classifies forecasting into three categories: *trajectory predicting, range forecasting* and *qualitative futuring* (see Figure 1).

Generally speaking, forecasting is the process of deducing the future properties of a particular system, as well as estimating the future value of those properties, based on its past and present status. We can divide forecasting into two types according to the type of forecast provided: *qualitative forecasting* and *quantitative forecasting*. The former is concerned with the prediction of qualitatively different scenarios, or behavioral regimes. It usually provides predictions for the long-term future. Rather than being concerned with grossly different scenarios, the latter focuses on detailed quantitative prediction. Associated with such predictions are confidence measures which provide information regarding the accuracy of the predictions being made.

Chaos theory originates from physics. Much of the literature on chaos theory regards forecasting as the process of determining exactly how a particular trajectory of a particular system unfolds - this is known as *trajectory forecasting*. However, in economic and technological forecasting, because of the complex nature of these systems, exact trajectory information cannot be obtained. In such circumstances we might be able to extract information regarding a range of possible trajectories. Each trajectory would be different, but overall they would provide a range of possible future system states. This is so called *range forecasting*. For some systems, their future cannot be predicted by either trajectory or by range forecasting methods, but we can know their direction of motion - this is known as *qualitative futuring*. Both range forecasting and trajectory predicting are quantitative forecasting methods, even though their respective degrees of precision are different.

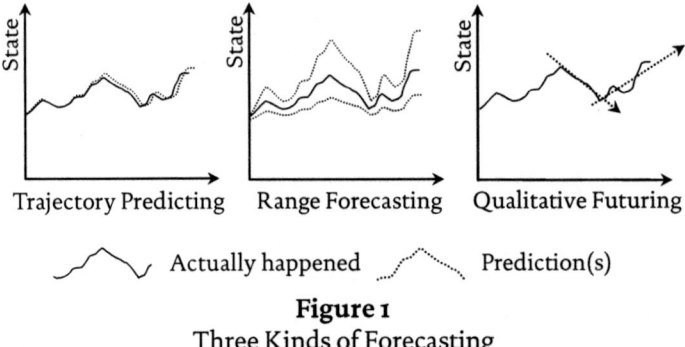

Trajectory Predicting   Range Forecasting   Qualitative Futuring

Actually happened   Prediction(s)

Figure 1
Three Kinds of Forecasting

Generally speaking, because of the sensitive dependency on initial conditions, a chaotic system is said to be unpredictable, i.e., an exact long-term quantitative forecast is impossible, although a relatively exact short-term forecasting is indeed possible. Moreover, the emergence of a chaotic behavioral regime in a complex system is rather well defined, and therefore the qualitative forecasting of the appearance chaos itself within a system is possible. Even though predicting the details of future trajectories and ranges is problematic in complex systems, predicting the onset of chaos itself is quite possible. For example, the *logistic mapping*, $X_{t+1} = RX_t(1-X_t)$: X_{t+1} is stable when R changes within the range 0 to 3; X_{t+1} is periodic when R is within 3 to about 3.56, and; X_{t+1} is chaotic and complex (as there exist nonchaotic, periodic windows) when R changes within 3.56 to 4 (Figure 2). Therefore, the often stated conclusion that chaotic systems are unpredictable comes from a focus on trajectory / range forecasting, which may lead people in the wrong direction when they try to make predictions for chaotic / complex systems.

In trying to make forecasts for particular systems we must be very selective in what forecasting methods we choose - the method must fit the system. If such a critical approach to forecasting method choice is not applied then we risk drawing unreasonable conclusions such as 'complex systems behaving chaotically are unpredictable'. Whether or not a system is predictable depends as much on our choice of forecasting method as it does on the system itself.

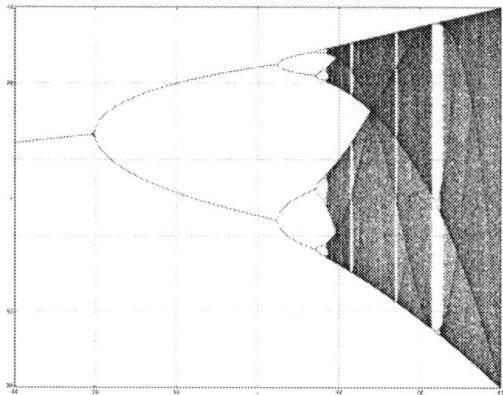

Figure 2
The Familiar Bifurcation Diagram for the Logistics Mapping
(R is along the x-axis, the y-axis show the different states the system
converges on for different values of R)

System forecasting using chaos theory

Underlying assumptions

Different system premises result in different forecasting attributes. The premises on which chaos theory is based are quite different from the ones on which traditional science is built. Classical science, which is based on the Newtonian / mechanistic paradigm, regards things as linear, explicable, tending towards equilibrium, well-behaved, certain, and analytical. Whereas, chaos theory regards the essential characteristics of the real world to be: system interactions are generally nonlinear, explanation is problematic (as a result of complex causality), unbalanced (far-from-equilibrium), anomalous and cannot be logically analyzed. Only when the relations between different systemic factors are weakly-nonlinear is a method called *linearization* (the process of approximating local nonlinearity linearly in order to find local solutions) effective. Otherwise, linearization becomes impractical.

The systems of interest for economic forecasting, technological forecasting or social forecasting, are dynamic, unstable, discontinuous and irreversible, and have many qualitatively different future possibilities. Despite the fact that many of the forecasting tools available cannot deal with discontinuity (qualitative change), and rely heavily on the past to predict the future, systems that yield to such analyses are few and far between. Discontinuous and un-expected change is the norm rather than the exception for complex systems. Complex systems are sensitive to context and so different contexts can lead to quite different behavioral regimes. Even if a system has been relatively stable for a reasonable period of time, certain contexts may trigger nonlinear, discon-tinuous change, which would not be predictable using simplistic forecasting methods that focus on system trajectories only. In table 1, the various possible behavioral types of a system are classified into order, disorder, chaos, anti-chaos and self-organized criticality. With each behavioral category a different kind of forecasting is required.

	Order	Disorder	Chaos	Anti-chaos	Self-organized criticality
Trajectory Predicting	Long	-	Short	-	-
Range Forecasting	Long	-	Middle	-	Short or long
Qualitative Futuring	Long	-	Possible	-	Possible

Long means the system can be forecasted in long-term
Short means the system can be forecasted in short-term
Middle means the system can be forecasted in medium-term
Possible means the system's qualitative futuring may be possible to a very limited extent

Table 1
Forecasting Characteristics of System under Different Status

What is predictable?

Some short-term futures are predictable. According to chaos theory, a nonlinear dynamical system's phase space (i.e., the space of all possible system states) is dominated by relatively few attractors, which include *common attractors*, i.e., *fixed-point* attractors, *periodic* attractors and *quasi-periodic* attractors, and *strange attractors* (which include *chaotic* attractors and *strange nonchaotic* attractors). This is quite different from a classical thermodynamical system in which the chances of a system being in any particular state is equal for all states, i.e., the phase space has no large-scale structure unlike the attractors present in a complex system's phase space.

Whatever attractor a particular system is following, a small change in its starting conditions, or a small external perturbation, hardly transforms the system's status in the short term when the system's structure remains fixed. Therefore, a relatively precise short-term forecast is feasible. The feasibility of short-term prediction can be judged by calculating a system's *Lyapunov exponents*, which is a measure of how fast two trajectories that start very close to each other diverge (see for example Wolf, 1986). In chaotic systems trajectories that originally began very close to each other tend to diverge at an exponential rate. When a system has a positive (> 0) Lyapunov exponent there is a *time horizon* beyond which quantitative prediction breaks down.

Suppose we measure the initial condition of an experimental system very accurately. No measurement is perfect so let us say that there is an error $|\delta_o|$ associated with our measurement. After a time, t, then our initial error $|\delta_o|$ has grown to $|\delta_o| e^{\lambda t}$, where λ is the largest Lyapunov exponent for this particular system. If we impose a level of tolerance to our prediction, a say, then our prediction becomes intolerable after a time of the order of $(1/\lambda)(\ln \{a/|\delta_o|\})$ (Liu & Li, 1998). So, no matter how hard we work to reduce measurement error, we cannot make accurate predictions longer than a few multiples of $1/\lambda$. As an example, if we reduced our measurement error a million fold then we could predict only 2.5 times longer!

Despite the limitations imposed on quantitative prediction by the existence of a time horizon, qualitative predictions regarding when a system will behave chaotically or not is less problematic. With the exchange of substance, energy and information between a system and circumstances, the system's behavior may transform qualitatively from simple to complex and from order to disorder. Moreover, in many nonlinear systems this process always follows a well-defined route such as *quasiperiodicity, intermittency* (alternation of phases of regular and chaotic dynamics), *period doubling* (period-1→period-2→period-4→period-8→chaos, see Figure 2), and *period-adding* (period-1→period-2→period-3→period-4→chaos). The developing pattern of a system is, therefore, *qualitatively* forecastable.

In many simple nonlinear dynamical systems, the rate at which different behavioral regimes give way to the next may be forecasted. When a period-doubling bifurcation appears in a system, the ratios of parameter distance between two successive period-doublings approaches a constant. This constant is known as the *Feigenbaum constant* and is approximately equal to 4.669201609. It is interesting to note that this constant is universal in the sense that it applies to a variety of dynamical systems. So, it seems that for some nonlinear systems, qualitative change is very much predictable.

Some researches have indicated that the dynamic pattern of a complex system is uncertain on the microlevel, but is relatively stable on the macrolevel. This is another way of saying that although quantitative prediction is limited beyond the time horizon, accurate qualitative prediction is quite possible. However, in some systems even qualitative prediction is problematic. Even in these systems, though, identifying the qualitatively different regimes is possible, even if determining when and where they will occur is not.

What is unpredictable?

If a system's dynamics is dominated by a strange (chaotic) attractor, then small changes in its original conditions will grow exponentially. As such, long-term forecasting for the system cannot be exact and trustworthy. As far as complex systems are concerned, new conditions (contexts) emerge continuously, which can affect the system's behavior in nonlinear ways. This makes exact long-term forecasting much more difficult, and in many cases, essentially impossible. If a system's dynamics is dominated by common attractors, then its long-term future behavior can be predicted, e.g., the time of sunrise everyday on Earth.

The appearance of different modes of behavior is determined by certain order parameters (e.g., R in the logistics model above). Order parameters for real systems are not easy to determine, however. In adaptive systems, qualitative changes in the system's structure may lead to the dominance of a different set of order parameters. If the order parameters change then predictions based on previous order parameters will, of course, not be valid. Even the determination of different regimes (phase space attractors) becomes difficult, let alone their position in phase space. Complex systems often self-organization into hierarchies. The relationship between macro and microlevels are just like the ones between wholes and their component parts. A change at the macrolevel may be the result of changes at the microlevel, but it is very difficult to ascertain which subsystem it happened in because of the complex causality that operates in complex systems. As we mentioned above, correlation does not necessarily lead to explanation.

The concepts of chaos / complexity theory and their implications for forecasting

Scientists have been concerned with the implications for forecasting from chaos theory since the discovery of chaotic behavior. In the 1960s MIT meteorologist Edward N. Lorenz discovered the *butterfly effect* whilst researching a grossly simplified model of a weather system (Lorenz, 1963). In the mid-1970s Princeton University biologist Robert R. May discovered the delicate relationship between complex / simple, and certainty / randomness in the research of particularly simple mathematical models with surprisingly complex dynamics (May, 1977). The reason that many people often associate chaos theory with issues in forecasting is that chaos theory led to some inescapable limitations on forecasting in the presence of nonlinearity. The following sections discuss how some of the concepts in chaos theory impact forecasting.

Nonlinearity and forecasting

The object researched in chaos theory is nonlinear dynamical systems containing at least three inter-dependent variables. The importance of nonlinearity is that an increment in an independent variable will result in a disproportionate change in the dependent variable. This disproportionality invalidates forecasting techniques based on forerunner index or variable substitution. For example, consider a company that employs 10 marketing people who sell 1 million units. If the relationship between input (number of marketing people) and out (units sold) is nonlinear then doubling the number of marketing people would not necessarily lead to a doubling of sales.

If the exact nature of the nonlinear relationship between input (independent variable) and output (dependent variable) then of course having knowledge of one would give us easy access to knowledge of the other. If nonlinear feedback exists between the variables, then because of the possible presence of sensitivity to initial conditions, prediction of the value of the dependent variable becomes limited to periods shorter than the system's time horizon (as defined above).

Feedback and forecasting

The relationship among system variables / factors may be linear or nonlinear, strong or weak, and positive or negative. When the relationship is defined by a single positive-feedback loop or negative-feedback loop, then forecasting by extrapolating the trend is easily done. However, in most cases, the relationship between system factors is rather more complex than the single feedback loop case. Each factor participates in a system of different feedback loops comprising both positive and negative feedback - the whole system is a compound of many positive and negative feedback loops. Because of complex dynamics that results from feedback loop interaction, the state of such systems is uncertain, although it may be forecasted with the use of computer simulation. For many nonlinear feedback systems of the form $y_{t+1} = f_j(y_t)$, the system's qualitative state y_{t+1} may change from simple to complex and from complex to chaotic as a result of external forces (such as flow of substance, energy and information, etc). In period-doubling systems, the pace at which qualitative change occurs will increase more rapidly as certain order parameters are changed. In such systems, making trajectory-based forecasts from one segment of data is not appropriate. What is needed is *rolling forecasting* in which the data used for prediction is updated with the most current observations. In this case, long-term forecasting is the net result of many, data-adjusted, short-term forecasts.

Attractors and forecasting

The most important property of systems that are characterized by a single common attractor is that, over the long-term, the system's trajectory will remain qualitatively similar and perfectly predictable, e.g., having moved quickly into the attractor basin of a period-4 attractor the system's trajectory will remain within that attractor indefinitely. Therefore, the long-term prediction of a system characterized by common attractors can be forecasted easily and exactly.

The presence of chaotic (strange) attractors would make only short-term forecasting possible, although long-term prediction would be prohibited because of the 'butterfly effect'. For longer-term predictions a different approach is necessary. The phase space of any nonlinear dynamical system might contain multiple attractor basins, which opens up the possibility that the system might be 'pushed' towards one particular attractor or another. Therefore, the basis of forecasting such systems is to identify the different attractors that cover state space and the conditions (contexts) under which the system will fall into the basins of these different attractors. Having such knowledge would allow us to make a range of predictions for each attractor, e.g., if a particular system's phase space is characterized by five different attractor basins, then we could produce five different forecasts, any one of which would be accurate at a particular future time.

Bifurcation and forecasting

Bifurcation, or forking, is a common phenomenon in the evolving process of nonlinear systems. The boundaries between different phase space attractors are referred to as *separatrices*. If a system trajectory crosses a separatrix then an abrupt (qualitative) change in the system's trajectory occurs. For example, in the simple logistics system above separatrices manifest as *bifurcation points* on the bifurcation diagram shown in Figure 2. Of course, in higher dimensional systems separatrices manifest as loci or surfaces, but in all cases they are the boundary between qualitatively distinct system behaviors, or regimes of operation.

In systems that approach chaos through the process of period-doubling. This particular route to chaos involves a doubling in the attractor period as the system bifurcates with the increase of certain order parameters. The rate of bifurcation is related to the Feigenbaum constant discussed above and is therefore a predictable aspect of certain systems. In between the bifurcation events, trend forecasting is a perfectly useful prediction tool, although there may be difficulties near bifurcation points / separatrices.

However, not all bifurcation processes involve period-doubling and so this type of forecast has its obvious drawbacks. As we've already mentioned matching the appropriate forecasting method to the corresponding system type is a critical prerequisite to forecasting itself.

Intermittence and forecasting

Intermittence is a pattern-alternating process in which a different pattern appears after a period of another pattern. There are two types of intermittence: (1) after a length of time of tracing a regular pattern (e.g., a period-2 cycle) the system's behavior changes abruptly into a disordered pattern and then returns to the former pattern, and; (2) a disordered pattern changes abruptly into a regular pattern before returning back to the disordered state.

The property of intermittence may be used to explain why history often replays in real life. For example, if an earthquake had happened in one region in the past, then it may happen again in the future; if someone had fallen sick last winter, then he or she may fall sick again this winter. Of course, both of these examples are speculative, and it would take considerable effort to confirm if intermittence did indeed explain the repetitive nature of these particular phenomena. Unfortunately, not all intermittent-like behavior are cases of intermittence (as it is defined here). Indeed, even if we are in a position to support the notion that a particular phenomena is an example of intermittence, there are significant difficulties in determining the intervals between the intermittent behavior. We can obtain knowledge of the different types of behavior that the system oscillates between, but we cannot know when each 'mode' will appear.

Synchronization lock-in and forecasting

"A surprising fact about chaotic attractors is their susceptibility to synchronization. This refers to the tendency of two or more systems which are coupled together to undergo closely related motions, *even when the motions are chaotic*" (Alligood, *et al.*, 1997: 387, original emphasis). When different systems influence each other, synergy can result. Synergy, or *lock-in*, is when different systems follow the same pattern and keep to this pattern for an extended period of time. If lock-in persists between a system of interest and other systems, forecasting the future of the system of interest is not only based on itself, but also on the other systems. In such situations there no certain method that can be used to distinguish the system of interest and the new system that comes into being through the interaction of the various systems. The reason is that any of the component systems may become the 'main' system, i.e., the system which dominates overall behavior. Any effort to 'push' the system of interest into a different attractor basin may fail because the system of interest is locked-in to another system which continues along its original trajectory. This creates a problem for forecasting.

Power laws and forecasting

Chaoticians discovered that the *frequency*, F(s), of change in a system is inversely proportional to the *scale*, s, of the change (see for example Bak, 1996). That is to say, the frequency of large-scale change is low, whereas the frequency of small scale change is high - this is an example of a *power law*. To be precise: $F(s) = s^{-\tau}$ where τ is a constant. Furthermore, the mechanism that drives both small- and large-scale change is identical. As a real life example, consider the magnitude of earthquakes in a region of the southwestern United States known as the New Madrid earthquake zone. It has been shown (Bak, 1996) that "every time there are about 1,000 earthquakes of, say, magnitude 4 on the Richter scale, there are 100 earthquakes of magnitude 5, 10 of magnitude 6, and so on" (p. 12). This is known as the Gutenberg-Richter law. In economics, the distribution of large and small enterprises also follows such a power law. According to this rule, it is possible to estimate the probability that great scientific discoveries and technological innovations happen.

Self-organization and forecasting

A major property of self-organizing systems is that the comprising agents can adjust their performance autonomously, which includes changing their relationship with other agents (according to the performance of other agents and circumstances) in order to adapt to new circumstances. Therefore, self-organizing system usually have a strong survival instinct and adaptation ability. At the macrolevel, the future of a self-organizing system lies in the variance of circumstances. At the microlevel, performance of an individual agent depends on the relationship between itself and other agents. For example, the short-term future of each vehicle on the traffic network may be predictable as we can focus on local considerations only. However, the long-term future of each individual is very difficult to ascertain as it depends upon global, as well as local, considerations.

Emergence and forecasting

The concept of emergence (which is discussed at greater length in Chapters 2 and 4) refers to the properties of a whole system that are not plainly apparent in the system's parts - in some sense, the properties of the whole (macrolevel) are novel in that they are not explicable in terms of the properties of the whole's parts (microlevel). Emergence is a direct consequence of the existence of multiply interacting feedback loops between agents; the ability of independent judgments and decision-making by each agent, and; the property of self-organization. Therefore, when considering such complex systems it is impossible to forecast the properties of the whole pattern from each agents' performance.

Individual coherence and global forecasting

If the behavior of the individuals that comprise a system is effectively uncorrelated and independent, or incoherent, then the behavior of the overall system will be simple, i.e., the system's phase space will contain no attractors. This sort of system is often referred to as a *thermodynamical* system in the classical sense. If, however, individual behavior is coordinated, correlated, dependent and coherent then the behavior of the whole may potentially be rather more complex, i.e., the system's phase space will contain attractors. As such, forecasting becomes rather more difficult as the methods that assume average values and equilbrium, which work perfectly well for thermodynamical-type systems, become ineffective.

Chaos-based principles of forecasting

In the opening section of this chapter the forecasting principles based on a Newtonian paradigm were presented. Now that the various elements of chaos theory have been explored, a revised set of forecasting principles are presented that are based on chaos theory itself.

Certainty principle

If a system can be perfectly described in mathematical terms; the change of system's order parameters is stable; the system state is either equilibrium, periodic or quasi-periodic (common attractors) then its future is easily forecasted. Small differences in initial conditions for this system will result in slightly different futures. External perturbations may be described by the inclusion of a random variable. The key to exactly forecasting such systems is to exactly describe the system model, its initial conditions and order parameters. If, however, the order parameters are unstable, the future will not always certain.

Intrinsic randomicity principle

Simple and well-defined systems do not lead only to simple and predictable patterns, but may also lead to much more complex patterns (such as the chaotic behavior displayed by the incredibly simple logistics system above). Complex phenomenon may indeed be the result of simple and certain rules, but seemingly correlating factors may not really be the reason behind the observed phenomenon. Therefore, variables obtained by correlation analysis alone may not actually be the relevant variables driving the observed phenomena. A major issue for forecasting is that there are many (possibly infinite) ways to explain a limited set of observations that result from nonlinear processes. Each explanation may make qualitatively different predictions in contexts not represented by our observed data set. The challenge for forecasters, then, is not only in finding a model that reproduces the observed behavior, but to choose among the multitude of different models that will fit our collected data equally well.

Attractors principle

How a system behaves depends upon the type and quantity of attractors that characterize the system's phase space. If the attractor is common, such as fixed point, limit cycle and quasi-periodic attractors, then the system's behavior can be predicted exactly over the long-term. If the attractor is chaotic, such as Lorenz's strange attractor, then exact long-term is impossible, although exact short-term forecasting is possible. If a system's phase space is characterized by more than one attractor, then the system's behavior depends upon which attractor the system is following at the time the forecast is made. Generally speaking, each attractor has associated with it its own range of contexts. That is to say, the range and position of initial conditions determines the future pattern of the system.

Fractal principle

The principle of analogy for traditional forecasting emphasizes the similarity (and therefore comparability) between different things at different times and in different space, and as such asserts that the future course or pattern of similar things accords with what has already passed. The fractal principle suggests that for some systems, both the whole and its parts share similar characteristics. This fractal similarity may occur in time (e.g., the pattern of stock price changes during a particular day is similar to those changes that occur of a particular week), or space (e.g., the pattern of a particular branch of a tree is similar to that of the whole tree). The reason why some some systems are fractal is that the behavior of the different parts that make up the whole, is determined by similar rules to the whole, but on different timescales. Therefore, the key to understanding the fractal characteristics of a particular system is to investigate its intrinsic running rules. For example, Liu (2001: 108-116) calculated the fractal dimensions of a time series, and by virtue of the similarities occuring at the local and global levels was able to develop a forecasting method.

System hierarchy principle:

For a system consisting of finite entities operating in a linear mode, the resulting behavior of the whole may be deduced from the sum of individual behaviors, and individual behavior may be also deduced from the behavior of the whole. However, if a system is nonlinear and complex, the behavior of the whole, which is different from constituent individuals' behavior, cannot be obtained by simply adding up individual behaviors. Individuals in such complex systems connect to each other and form different scales, entities, or hierarchical levels. Under certain conditions these emergent scales can organize into a system of subsystems. Lock-in between, and within, these different emergent subsystems may occur which can restrict the individuals' behavior to only a few qualitatively different modes. As such, the forecasting of properties at different hierarchical levels within a complex system is problematic.

Development and evolution principle

Any system must undergo a process of simplicity→complexity and birth→maturity→aging→rebirth. Accordingly, forecasting the future of complex systems needs to based on a viewpoint that evolves. Many systems have a natural fractal growth process (Liu & Li, 1996). That is, variables representing system states are unstable and slowly adapt. After the period of birth, the system enters into a period of rapid development. This is followed by a period system maturing. The pace of development slows and may even stagnate, becoming unstable again. The ending of this phase of increase becomes the beginning of a new phase, and these phases form a larger increasing phase. According to process of growth exhibited by the logistics model, as a system's order parameter is increased, the system's behavior undergoes a process of period-doubling from equilibrium→increase→period-2→period-4→...", and then enters into a phase of fractal chaos. This is of course, quite different from economic and technological systems in which the underlying rules and relevant order parameters can change frequently: a *meta-evolution* if you like. What is so interesting about such simple models as the logistics model is that all the different phases can appear in a system whose underlying rules and relevant order parameters are fixed.

Self-succeed and self-defeat principle

How do we know if a forecasting subject is self-organized or other-organized? Or, whether a forecasting variable is endogenous or exogenous? These properties of the forecasting subject determine its forecastability, and the forecasting approach we might employ. The fundamental factor that determines whether a particular forecast succeeds or fails is the resulting change in the system created by the forecast itself. This kind of forecasting is *endogenous forecasting*. If the forecast accords with the expectation of the system's individuals, then the system's individuals will adopt various measures in order to realize the forecast - the forecast will *self-succeed*. Whereas, if the forecast does not accord with the expectation of agents, then the system's individuals will adopt various measures to prevent the forecast from being realized - this forecast will *self-defeat*.

Conclusion

Economic and technological systems are complex systems, and their forecasting belongs to complex system's forecasting. The principles of chaos-based forecasting, which are quite different from those of traditional forecasting, help us to understand the rules behind complex phenomena and grasp some aspects of the future of economy and technology. Theories of complex systems provide a new paradigm for forecasting research. Far from being unpredictable, the forecasting of complex systems requires a critical examination of the relationship between the forecasting method / tool used and the system of interest itself. Just because a certain approach *can* be applied, does not mean that the resulting forecast is meaningful.

Acknowledgements

This chapter was partly supported by the National Natural Science Foundation of China (No. 70172012) and the Social Science Project of Ministration of Education of China (No. 03JB630015).

References

Alligood, K. T., Sauer, T. D. and Yorke, J. A. (1996). *Chaos: An Introduction to Dynamical Systems*, NY: Springer.

Bak, P. (1996). *How Nature Works: The Science of Self-Organized Criticality*, NY: Springer-Verlag.

Crutchfield, J. P., Farmer, J. D., Packard, N. H. and Shaw, R. S. (1986). "Chaos," *Scientific American*, 254(12): 46-58.

Howell, T. (1995). *Chaos and Forecasting*, Singapore: World Scientific.

Joseph, M. (1993). "Technological Forecasting: An Introduction," *The Futurist*, July-

August, 13-16.

Lorenz, E. N. (1963). "Deterministic Nonperiodic Flow," *J. of Atmos.*, 20: 130-141.

Liu, H. and Guo, Z. Y. (1998). "Chaos Paradigms of Forecasting," *Journal of Systemic Dialectics*, 6(4): 31-35 (in Chinese).

Liu, H. (1999). "Nonlinear System Theory and New Forecasting Paradigm," *Forecasting*, 18(2): 1-6 (in Chinese).

Liu, H. (2000). "A Review on Economic Forecasting Paradigm and Methodology of Chaos Theory," *Ziran Zazhi*, 22(6): 311-315 (in Chinese).

Liu, H. (2001). *Economic Chaos Management*, China Development Press (in Chinese).

Liu, H. and Li, B. Q. (1996). "Research and Application of Fractals in Natural Growth Processes," *Science & Technology Review*, 10: 21-24 (in Chinese).

May, R. M. (1977). "Simple Mathematical Models with Very Complicated Dynamics," *Nature*, 82: 8-167.

Wolf. A. (1986). "Quantifying Chaos with Lyapunov exponents," in A. V. Holden (ed.), *Chaos*, New Jersey, US: Princeton University Press, pp. 273-290.

CHAPTER 11

PREDICTING THE HUMAN WEATHER: HOW DIFFERENTIATION AND CONTEXTUAL COMPLEXITY AFFECT BEHAVIOR PREDICTION

Robert G. Jones and Gowri Parameswaran

Many organizational psychology practices rely heavily on the assumption of the predictability of individual behavior. In this chapter, we describe three perspectives on the predictability of individual behavior in social situations characterized by varying amounts of complexity. The perspective adopted integrates the Vygotskian and Wernerian perspectives to yield predictions concerning the degree and basis of predictability of individual behavior, particularly in rich organizational contexts. Implications for theory, research, and practice are drawn.

Managing Organizational Complexity: Philosophy, Theory, and Application
A Volume in: Managing the Complex, pages 183-199.
Copyright © 2005 by Information Age Publishing, Inc.
All rights of reproduction in any form reserved.
ISBN: 1-59311-319-6 (cloth), 1-59311-318-8 (paper)

Introduction

Attempts to understand and predict individual human behavior have changed little in method or approach since the work of Galton and Munsterberg in the late nineteenth and early twentieth centuries. Yet, if anything, the need for developing adequate predictive models of individual human behavior has grown, given the enormous tragedies of the twentieth century that might have been mitigated by early identification of problematic individual and group behaviors (Chiles, 2001). In an age of unprecedented scientific blossoming in other areas of inquiry, the failure of behavioral prediction to move beyond simplistic linear and interactive models can perhaps be attributed to the "quick fix" approach taken by mainstream behavioral scientists - the so-called *dust-bowl empiricism* that characterized American applied psychology for much of the twentieth century.

Moving beyond this inertia of expediency will require reconsideration of some of the radical voices in psychological science: Heinz Werner, Lev Vygotsky, and Max Wertheimer, among others. Following in the physical science traditions from which they came, these scientists attempted to construct unifying theories of behavior without the help of much of the empirical evidence available to scientific psychology today. Return to such theorizing has occurred sporadically, as in the person-situation debates of the 1970s in social psychology. This theorizing has come out of narrow areas and has tended not to account for changes in natural science. In short, the time is right for a further large scale theory-development in an attempt to understand how and when individual behavior can be predicted.

An initial attempt

Psychological practices in organizations rely heavily on the assumption of the predictability of individual behavior, based on either contextual or individual characteristics. In addition to developing large numbers of measures of individual characteristics for the purpose of prediction, attempts to define and measure context are not completely unheard of in behavioral science. For example, template matching techniques in applied social psychology (Highhouse & Harris, 1993), job analysis in industrial psychology (Harvey, 1992), and the task characteristics approach (Morris & Hackman, 1969) have attempted to clearly define and categorize situational characteristics which influence behavior. However, defining context has been far from the mainstream problem of organizational psychology.

Instead, organizational research has been concerned almost entirely with the use of aggregated relationships among human perceptions and stable characteristics to attempt to understand behavior. In fact, the so-called "ecological fallacy" is a basic assumption of much organizational practice. Here, aggregated information is used to reach decisions about individual cases. For example, if *growth need strength* has been shown in aggregated studies to predict work quality (cf. Hackman & Oldham, 1976), then increasing individual growth need strength (or selecting individuals high in it) is used by managers in local settings to increase quality.

Aggregation problems

Bridging the gap between aggregation-based theories (general principles) and individual behavior in a work context (local conditions) is one of the essential challenges of both researchers and practitioners in many areas of science (see Gleick, 1987). Most of us know from experience that general principles do not always apply well to local conditions, and that drawing broad conclusions based on local events is problematic. The title of this chapter refers to this problem in weather forecasting, which we believe is very analogous to the problem of predicting individual behavior in organizations. Clearly, the small portions of variability accounted for in most aggregated organizational research stand as an indicator of the gap between aggregated principles and individual phenomena. Similarly, problems of generalizing from case studies are strong indicators of this problem. Thus, the problem of reaching meaningful scientific progress and devising highly reliable practices is severely compromised by the gap between general principles and local contexts.

Analysis of contexts

The perspective of Vygotsky and his students (1978, 1987) argues for the inseparability of person from context. Vygotsky's *contextual theory* proposes that individual "behavior could be understood only as the history of behavior" (1978: 8). Vygotsky used Engels's (1940) notion of 'tools' and proposed that physical and mental tools that are created by societies over the course of history are used by individuals to change the context in which they live; this, in turn, transforms the societal 'tools' available for individuals to utilize, and a self-organizing cycle emerges. The internalization of one kind of tool - culturally produced mental symbols - brings about behavioral transformations and forms the bridge between early and mature forms of behavior. Thus, in this view, the individual and the context form a self-organizing whole or unit, through mutual development.

One of the logical extensions of this argument is that behavior can never be adequately predicted based on independent individual characteristics. That is, the internalized context is always a part of the individual's lawful behavior. This is a radical departure from the assumption of much organizational practice that behavior is lawful, based on stable individual differences that are treated as largely separable from the context in which behavior occurs. If this radical position is taken, then practices such as selection tests, training, and performance management systems, all of which rely on context-independent individual characteristics, would be at least complicated, and at worst invalidated. Beyond this, even job design, compensation systems, and other practices aimed at changing the general context of the organization could be compromised by local disturbances in individual context.

Contextual complexity

The more traditional view, that individual behavior in organizations can be lawfully manipulated through various interventions at the individual, group, and organizational levels can only be reconciled to this person-context view if the complexities of local contexts can somehow be accounted for. One way to do this is to better analyze the relationship between complex individual and contextual systems. This would allow for idiographic prediction based on local conditions and would recognize the self-organizing nature of these systems (see Jones, et al., 2000, for a similar argument).

An analysis of this sort is presented here. The radical contextual argument is clarified and modified in this chapter using the Wernerian concepts of *ontogenesis* and *differentiation* (Crain, 1992). We argue that, where contexts are relatively simple (so-called "strong situations"), behavior can be largely predicted by situational analysis. Where contexts are more complex, there is greater or less predictability of individual behavior based on whether the individual's own ontogenesis has occurred in the context in which behavior is to be predicted. Individuals who have developed within a given context will be more differentiated along the lines of the specific context. We suggest that, the more individual ontogenesis has occurred in a complex context, the less likely it will be that individual behavior will be lawful within that context. Instead, we argue that contextually random behaviors, based on individual volition and choice, are more likely under these circumstances. Thus, agency and self-organization occur most often in complex contexts within which individuals have operated for considerable periods.

In individuals with ontogenesis outside a given complex context, on the other hand, individual behavior will be predictable based upon the degree of complexity that an individual is able to perceive in the situation. This ability to accurately perceive the demands of the situation is also a basis of prediction of individual performance in less complex situations; hence the predictive accuracy of mental abilities measures. In the simplest situations, however, behavior is elicited lawfully based upon contextual stimuli. Thus, we argue that predictability is based on complexity in both person and context.

In this chapter, we will briefly review the views of Vygotsky and Werner as they pertain to the predictability of individual behavior. Next, we will describe how Werner's and Vygotsky's views can be used to interpret findings from the organizational literature on person-situation relationships. We then discuss definitions of contextual complexity. This leads us to propose a "person-situation" relationship which depends on the complexity of the situation, the ontogeny of the individual, and the relation between the two. Implications and research suggestions based on this relationship (imbedded in organizational paradigms) will be offered.

Vygotsky, Werner, and predictability of individual behavior

The *intrinsic teleology* of human behavior (Viney, 1993) is a continuing problem in psychology. Those in the behavioral tradition, on one extreme, argue that an understanding of the efficient and material causes of behavior (stimulus and response conditions, in particular) is adequate for explaining behavior (see Hill, 1996). At the other extreme, volitional theorists (see Howard & Conway, 1986) argue for the need to fully understand final and formal causes as objects of psychological science. This perspective places emphasis on such things as strategies, motives, and goals for predicting behavior.

Vygotsky's argument that behavior can only be understood or predicted at the contextual level of analysis provides an alternative to these views. The 'history of behavior' as Vygotsky viewed the term, included the physiological substrates of behavior, the immediate situation, as well as the historical and cultural context in which the individual developed. Vygotsky adopted the *historical materialist theory of society*, and attempted to relate it to concrete psychological questions. This view proposed that historical changes and trans-formations in people's material lives lead to individual changes in conscious-ness and behavior. On the face of it, this sounds like the environmentalist position of extreme behaviorism, but it evolved differently.

Instead of evolving into behaviorism, this early analysis of psychological change was later developed by Vygotsky's students and followers. Leontiev (1981) proposed that the unit of analysis in psychology should be 'the individual acting in and on the context', rather than the individual alone. Gibson (1966) argued against mental phenomena being a private affair, but instead proposed environmental 'affordances' that are interpreted and acted upon by the indi-vidual. Affordances are defined as "the reciprocal relation or 'fit' between the actor and the environment that is necessary to perform functional activities" (Thelen, 1995). In these theorists' extensions, causality is understood at the personal-contextual rather than the individual level of analysis. That is, any individual's behavior is no longer the primary focus of psychological prediction. Rather, defining the person-context unit becomes the essential job of behavioral sciences, in service of predicting behavior across individual-contexts.

Some examples of research studies that arose from Vygotsky's theory in-clude Gustafson's (1984) study of infants who began looking at far-away objects that they previously had not looked at, once they were provided with walkers. These pre-locomotive infants' perception changed with the changing environ-ment. Other researchers in the Vygotskian tradition (Rogoff, 1982; Lave, 1988; Bruner, 1983) focused on how children play an active role in engaging other 'experts' in their environment in order to further their own cognitive development. Cole (1985) and Lave (1988) explored differences between information processing in complex everyday environments as compared to less complex affordances in the learning context.

Person by situation interactions

A mainstream approach to dealing with person-context relationships comes from the social psychological research of the 1980's (Pervin, 1989; Mischel, 1990). The "person-by-situation" interactionist view of human behavior has been applied in principle to organizational practice (Moorehead & Griffin, 1995). Briefly, this approach supposes that individual behaviors are products of the interaction of individual and contextual factors. Several variants of this view have been articulated (see Pervin, 1989), but with mixed support for applying any principles broadly (Snow, 1989).

Part of the problem with applying person by situation interaction views is the lack of clear definition of situation (Hattrup & Jackson, 1996). Situational complexity (Wood, 1986) and so-called "strong situations" have been described (e.g., Blass, 1991; Mischel, 1977), but few operations adequately capture the richness of the variables associated with these constructs. In organizational science, complexity has been defined in terms of the diversity / homogeneity of a context (Katz & Kahn, 1966), as well as its clustering / randomness (Emery & Trist, 1965). Diversity / homogeneity is defined in terms of both the number of systems involved in the context and the congruence among these contextual forces. For example, a complex work context may include role demands from more than one source, and these sources may not provide consonant demands. Clustering / randomness is defined as the degree to which the context itself is organized in terms of its demands and constraints. At one extreme, a simple context would provide very clear demands, contingencies, and constraints for any "reasonable person." At the other extreme, complex contexts are very difficult to predict or control, and may appear to be largely random (Jones & Rittman, 2002). These conceptual definitions of complexity were originally devised to describe organizational environments, but they also resonate well with similar notions in complexity science.

Definitions of context and complexity at the job level also have been offered (see Morrison & Brantner, 1992; Hunter, 1980; Wood, 1986), and a literature dealing with the relationships among job experience, job performance, and job complexity has identified potentially important issues in this domain. The relationship between job experience and job performance has been explicated in two meta-analyses (McDaniel, et al., 1988; Quiñones, et al., 1995). These studies suggest that looking at different contexts (task, job, organization; Quiñones, et al., 1995), levels of experience, and levels of complexity (McDaniel, et al., 1988) influences the relationship between time on a job and the performance of that job. However, the operational definition of job complexity used in this research (a dichotomy based on Hunter's 1980 measure), did not take into account the sorts of complexities defined above, much less the sort of self-organizing that is used in complexity science (Gleick, 1987; Thelen, 1995). For this and other reasons, the observed moderating influence of context should be considered a low estimate (Kane, 1997; Aquinas & Stone-Romero, 1997). Still, the idea that these variables are interrelated in ways suggestive of Vygotsky's views argues for better accounting for these relations in organizational theory.

A small but widely recognized literature on the effects of job design on motivation also provides an approach to the Vygotskian person-context unit. This literature developed from early work by Turner and Lawrence (1965) and Hackman and Oldham (1976). It suggested that characteristics of the person (i.e., growth need strength and "critical psychological variables") and the context (task characteristics) influence behaviors. It is ironic in the context of the current discussion that this literature was criticized for inadequately separating individual and group views from job "realities" (Salancik & Pfeffer, 1978). That is, following Vygotsky's argument, individual behavior and perception could not be adequately separated from job context. Perhaps as a result of this sort of problem with defining context, attempts to describe its influences on behavior in organizations remain sparse.

For our purposes, we define context complexity with reference to both the salience of the affordances offered by the context, and by the feedback(s) that the actor strives towards. In a strong situation, the outcomes of actions and the paths toward the feedback(s) associated with these outcomes are clearly defined (Brown & Lovett, 2001). In a highly complex situation, neither the means nor the results of action are clearly specified, and many different behaviors may produce the same end (*equifinality* and lack of direct contingencies). In the strong situational context, small variations in behavior could produce big differences in outcome. In highly complex situations, it is not the *size* of variations in behavior on a single dimension, but *qualitative* differences (different behavioral dimensions) that lead to different outcomes. An analogous concept is the difference between ill-defined and well-defined problems. The latter can be resolved by following an algorithmic solution, while the former requires creative problem-solving procedures (Hunt & Ellis, 1999).

Individual differences.

In contrast, the influences of individual differences on behavior have received enormous research attention in applied organizational literature (see Cascio, 1998; Murphy, 1996 for examples). Unfortunately, this largely cross-sectional literature assumes that individual differences exert nearly universal influences on behavior across situations (see Pervin, 1989; Aquinas & Stone-Romero, 1997). It therefore does little to advance our understanding of the interplay between individual and situation over time.

One exception to the lopsided weighting of either context or individual influences on behavior in organizations comes from Schneider (Schneider, 1987; Schneider, *et al.*, 1995), who proposed the attraction-selection-attrition (ASA) model of organizational behavior. This model makes specific predictions about the influence processes that relate individual and organization characteristics to one another over time. People are attracted to organizations based on perceived similarities in various characteristics, in this model. Over time, through several hypothesized mechanisms, organizations come to be composed of similar individuals whose similarities define the social context over time. Unfortunately, only some of the tenets of this model have been supported in research (Jackson, et al., 1991; Schneider, et al., 1995; Jackson & Schuler, 1995).

Clearly, alternative approaches which integrate contextual definition and individual characteristics are warranted (Hattrup & Jackson, 1996). The next section will propose one such approach. This *ontogeny-complexity model* of behavioral prediction in organizations uses the initial and long-term knowledge of individuals about complex organizational situations as a basis for understanding self-organizing organizational systems. The predictability of behavior is thought to be based on both *individual* complexity (*á la* Cantor & Kihlstrom, 1987) and *situational* complexity. One major difference is that individual complexity is a function of individual differences not only in ability to comprehend situations, but also in ontogeny in a given complex situation. The influence of stable individual differences on behavior is posited to be greatest in complex systems where individuals have relatively less complex understandings of the situation. Volition plays a greater role when individuals have higher levels of complexity in their awareness of complex situations. Here, the Vygotskian view of the person-context as a self-organizing unit is most viable. The direct influence of situation on behavior is posited to be greatest when situations are relatively simple. These relationships are summarized in Figure 1 and explicated in the next section.

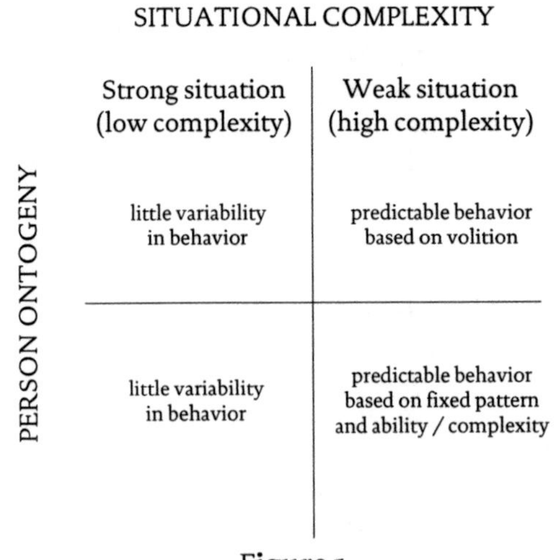

SITUATIONAL COMPLEXITY

	Strong situation (low complexity)	Weak situation (high complexity)
	little variability in behavior	predictable behavior based on volition
	little variability in behavior	predictable behavior based on fixed pattern and ability / complexity

PERSON ONTOGENY

Figure 1
Summary description of the person ontogeny, situation complexity model

Person ontogeny and situation complexity

The work of Heinz Werner (Crain, 1992) helps to provide a framework for understanding when individual behavior will be predictable. Werner argued that individual *ontogeny* (development within a context) follows the *orthogenic principle*. This principle states that, "Whenever development occurs, it proceeds from a state of relative lack of differentiation to a state of increasing differentiation" (Werner & Kaplan, 1956). "Differentiation" refers to the separation of global entities (including perceptions, cognitive structures, and variables influencing behavior) into separate, hierarchically integrated entities. This can be applied to change in a person's notions about context from simplistic to more complex. On average, people with greater *ontogenesis* in a situation will have developed greater differentiation in their understandings of that situation.

In the theory we will describe here, it is assumed that individuals' mental representations of context change from simplistic perceptions to more complex representations over time, through ontogenesis. In social development within a context, this would mean that people commonly dubbed "characters" respond the same way to all circumstances. This mode of responding is indicative of lack of recognition of contextual complexity. At the other extreme, career diplomats might respond to even slight variations in diplomatic protocol within the complex context of consular relations. Thus, Vygotsky's argument that the person cannot be separated from context holds only to the extent that the person has developed within a particular, complex context.

The differentiation argument is related to the work of Cantor and Kihlstrom (1987). These authors argue that people differ in their ability to recognize complexities in social contexts. Such an individual difference in *social intelligence* could plausibly derive from one's differentiated view, based on ontogeny in similar social contexts, such as those similarities created by cultural norms. This leads to a first proposition:

Proposition 1: Individual ontogeny within a context will predict social intelligence in that context.

This proposition provides for a modification of Vygotsky's view, since the "separability" of individual behaviors from context will be predicated on an individual's ability to accurately recognize the situation's contingencies. For individuals who have differentiated according to the demands of a complex context, behaviors will likely be based on informed choices. For those unable to recognize the situation's complexity, on the other hand, predispositions, including what Cialdini (1995) refers to as "fixed action patterns" will be the basis of behavior. Put another way, people will respond to complex situations which they do not comprehend using simplistic responses only to the most salient cues, and using behaviors that are well-learned. The situation, though complex, will be reduced to a few cues to which that person is predisposed to attend to. Behaviors that are "typical" for them based on experiences in other past circumstances will result. Thus, the peculiarities of past experience and stable individual differences will predict behavior of people who are exposed to complex environments which they do not comprehend. This is where information aggregated from groups about correlations among a set of variables can be used to predict behavior.

Proposition 2: In complex situations, people with social ontogenesis outside these circumstances will tend to behave in ways consistent with stable individual characteristics.

Related to this, most individual differences used in selection (e.g., mental abilities) will only predict behavior of people with initially undifferentiated understandings in complex circumstances. Over time, differences in ability to think in complex ways will determine the onset and speed of ontogenesis.

But what of people who are familiar with the complex contingencies of a context? Here, we argue, the primary individual differences which might predict behavior are differences in volition. If an individual is able to take into account specific characteristics of the context, then they need not rely on heuristic responses or on their ability to quickly learn to make sense of the circumstances. Instead, they will be more likely to recognize the range of appropriate behaviors available to them and can then choose from these the responses they prefer, including behaviors that will deliberately change the context in which they are operating. Such preferences are grounded in the peculiar objectives valued by an individual in that situation, as opposed to their propensities learned from other circumstances. Thus, motivation will be the basis of individual behavior in complex contexts which they can adequately discern.

Proposition 3: In complex situations, people with differentiated views of these complexities will tend to behave in ways consistent with their peculiar motivational propensities.

Thus, behavior will be less predictable for people acting in complex contexts with which they are well-acquainted. This is because motivations may not be as stable as the well-learned or predisposed behavior patterns used by people who are not familiar with contextual complexity. In addition, many of the deliberate, motivated behaviors of differentiated people behaving in complex contexts will have direct or indirect impacts on the nature of the situation. Thus, if one knows what to do in complex circumstances, s/he will be more likely to change those circumstances.

Proposition 4: In complex situations, people with differentiated understandings will tend to exert influences likely to change the situation and, ultimately, their own behaviors.

For less complex situations, there is ample evidence that human behavior is predictable based on the demands of the situation (see Cialdini, 2001; Blass, 1991). In particular, a long tradition of social psychological literature has shown the influence of conformity, obedience, and other "strong" situational influences. Here, behavior is predictable largely on the basis of relatively universal motives, rather than peculiar motives or individual propensities. Ironically, it may be the generally ambiguous nature of these situations that leads most people to respond in highly predictable ways. Thus, if there is no way to immediately interpret a situation (it is ambiguous for all observers), it is a "simple" situation. Differentiation in these circumstances is not possible, since the situation sends a clear "ambiguous" message to all observers. Consequently, individual responses follow others' (the person in power or the group's) responses.

Proposition 5: In simple situations, behavior will be predictable based on the demands of the situation, not on the basis of individual differences or peculiar motives.

Although the idea of a strong situation is not synonymous with the idea of a simple situation, we would argue that many of the strong situations in social psychological research do elicit very predictable responses because they are perceived as requiring clear responses. The findings that most people respond in very stereotypical ways to the demands of obedience and conformity suggest that deliberately disobeying these demands has very clear consequences in the minds of those confronted with them. That is, there is no great ambiguity or complexity in the responses to these demands.

Implications for the predictability of individual behavior

There is some evidence that this *ontogeny-complexity approach* to understanding human behavior in organizations is accurate. The first comes from the voluminous literature on prediction of performance from individual differences. While there is ample evidence that mental abilities measures are predictive of performance, the conditions placed on this generalization are highly suggestive of a complexity effect. First, the predictive accuracy of mental abilities measures is relatively greater in complex than in simple jobs (McDaniel, *et al.*, 1988). Since such measures are commonly used in lower level positions for more complex jobs, it is not surprising that they are predictive of performance-related behaviors. This suggests that stable individual differences, particularly in abilities to discern complexity, predict behavior of newcomers to complex situations.

A second limitation of using individual differences measures also supports the ontogeny-complexity approach. This is the tendency for predictive accuracy (operationally, the correlation between predictor and performance measures) to diminish over time on the job (Austin, *et al.*, 1989). This is explained by people's behavior no longer being predicted by their ability to perceive complexities differentially after some period of time on the job. There are other explanations for this effect, as well, most of which do not contradict an ontogeny-complexity view. For example, it has been suggested that the predictor-performance relationship is indicative of how quickly people learn the demands of the job (McDaniel, *et al.*, 1988). This is of course consistent with the view that there will be a reduction in variability of performance over time, as suggested in the ASA model (Schneider, *et al.*, 1995). Thus, ontogeny in the complex situation leads to a diminished role of stable individual differences in predicting behavior.

Equally interesting are the results from a few available long-term studies of predictability of behavior in higher level (and presumably more complex) jobs (Howard & Bray, 1988; Jones & Whitmore, 1995; Keller, 1997). In these studies, performance and promotion in organizations was predicted by motive propensities to a greater extent than it was predicted by individual abilities. This is consistent with the idea that volition is predictive of behavior of differentiated people in complex situations. Thus, individual behavior is least predictable on the basis of person or context alone when individuals are operating in complex, but familiar, contexts. An adjunct explanation which is more speculative also follows from this analysis. Motive-related variables may be indicative of greater effort expended in order to comprehend and master a situation. By putting forth greater effort to understand and master situations, people's behavior becomes *part of* the situation. That is, behavior can be understood only as a part of the self-organizing person-situation unit. Differentiated people and complex contexts can be thought of as exerting a reciprocal influence that makes behavior both inseparable from the situation and a function of the individual's volition (cf. Wood & Bandura, 1989).

The implications of this ontogeny-complexity approach for management theory are also somewhat striking. If organizational decision makers are attempting to control behavior, there are two general strategies available. First, attracting undifferentiated people with specific individual propensities will make behavior predictable in complex situations. This is of course the staffing solution. What must go along with this, in order to make people's behavior continuously predictable, is to alter the situation consistently, so that individual abilities are still predictive. The problems with this are several, including finding individual abilities which are applicable across situations, which may explain the popularity of validity generalization for mental abilities measures. Also, being able to alter the situation regularly may be unnecessarily disruptive. The second solution is to make the context fairly simple and constant. This approach is of course the basis of compensation, industrial engineering, and work design efforts.

A solution that has recently been proposed by Youngcourt and Jones (2002) applies the notion of self-organizing to performance management. This approach suggests that performance appraisal interviews be treated as opportunities for "position management." This approach argues that performance management, in addition to trying to change the job incumbent's behavior to meet job demands, is an attempt to improve performance by altering job demands to conform to individual strengths and weaknesses. This allows for individual differences in ontogeny-differentiation within the work context, and treats context and person as essentially a single unit.

Implications for theory and research are also interesting. In particular, conceptual development of the mechanisms of self-organization is an important next step. We suggest looking in two places for clues for further development. The first is in existing theories of work adjustment, such as Dawis and Lofquist's (1979). This model suggests that differences in contexts and individuals determine whether people and organizations attempt to influence one another or simply "react" to one another. This model therefore provides some clues regarding mechanisms affecting complexity matches and self-organization behaviors.

A second place to look for clues for mechanisms of self-organization in the workplace is at the confluence of learning and decision making models (see Horn, this volume; Van den Broeck & Mestdagh, this volume). When people learn through conscious processes of change, there is likely a self-organizing associated with their context. Here, the context is personified in the person's complex cognitive representations of it. Further, when people decide to take individual or collective action to change a context as a result of their learning, self-organizing may be seen in its most manifest form. Here, the context comes to reflect the person or group. In both instances, a person-context unit is derived. So, examining the relationship between learning and decision making, particularly in group level multiple cue probability learning (Ilgen, et al., 1995) may hold considerable promise for understanding the sort of ontogenic self organizing that occurs in complex systems.

Research under these circumstances evolves well beyond the usual individual difference and task characteristic measurement common in organizational science. At the same time, successful organizational researchers have used methods that implicitly account for parts of the problem of defining person-context units. For example, job analysis and culture assessment are common first steps in developing organizational interventions. Given some idea of the contingencies of the situation, interventionists develop methods for attempting to affect either people (e.g., selection, training, performance management) or the context within which they function (e.g., organizational development, job enrichment, and management change). Of course, we believe that assessment should include some idea of the complexity of contingencies with respect to some of the dimensions we have described. Given an understanding of the *strength* of organizational situations, interventions may attempt to reduce complexities (e.g., through bureaucratic rationalization, job re-engineering, team building, and group decision support), increase them (through certain types of organizational change initiatives), increase complexity of individual cognitive representations (which may be an implicit purpose of training currently), or affect volition at important decision points. Suggestions for dealing with this last approach are few and far between, but an emerging literature on creativity in organizations may help to inform these interventions (see for example Kawai, this volume). The point is that traditional interventions aimed at person or at organization are not adequate when the situation and person are complex, self-organizing units, for the reasons we have described.

Despite problems with research methodology (see Robertson, this volume), we believe that our central idea, that behavioral prediction is itself contingent on characteristics of situation, individual, and self-organizing person-context units is deserving of further attention. This is particularly so when we consider the likelihood that most individual differences, when used in aggregate, will be most predictive when the situation is relatively complex and the individuals placed in the situation undifferentiated (consistent with the strong predictive power of abilities in complex, entry level jobs). Understanding that people develop within their work contexts, that they may find ways to alter these contexts (e.g., through job promotion, job enrichment, team learning, and even dysfunctional activities), and that the person and context become inextricable as people develop complex constructions of their contexts, are all consistent with existing theories within organizational science. However, by integrating these components, we can see that, as an individual becomes more differentiated in a complex situation, it becomes necessary to take into account volition and the mutual influences of person and situation on each other in order to predict and control work behavior.

References

Aquinas, H. and Stone-Romero, E.F. (1997). "Methodological Artifacts in Moderated Multiple Regression and Their Effects on Statistical Power," *Journal of Applied Psychology*, 82: 192-206.

Austin, J. T., Humphreys, L. G., and Hulin, C. L. (1989). "Another View of Dynamic Criteria: A Critical Reanalysis of Barrett, Caldwell, and Alexander," *Personnel Psychology*, 42: 583-596.

Blass, T. (1991). "Understanding Behavior in the Milgram Obedience Experiment: The Role of Personality, Situations, and their Interactions," *Journal of Personality and Social Psychology*, 60: 398-413.

Brown, J. C. and Lovett, M. C. (2001). "The Effects of Reducing Information on a Modified Prisoner's Dilemma Game," proceedings of the *Twenty-Third Annual Conference of the Cognitive Science Society*, pp. 134-139.

Bruner, J. S. (1983). *Child's Talk: Learning to Use Language*, New York: Norton

Cantor, N. and Kihlstrom, J. F. (1987). *Personality and Social Intelligence*, Englewood Cliffs, NJ: Prentice-Hall.

Cascio, W. F. (1998). "The Theory of Vertical and Horizontal Individualism and Collectivism: Implications for International Human Resource Management," in J. L. C. Cheng and R. B. Peterson (eds.), *Advances in International Comparative Management*, Vol. 12., US: Elsevier Science/JAI Press.

Chiles, J. (2001). *Inviting Disaster: Lessons from the Edge of Technology*, NY: Harper Business.

Cialdini, R. B. (1995). "A Full-Cycle Approach to Social Psychology," in G. G. Brannigan and M. R. Merrens (eds.), *Social psychologists: Research adventures*, New York, NY:

McGraw-Hill Book Company, pp. 53-72.

Cole, M. (1985). "The Zone of Proximal Development: Where Culture and Cognition Create Each Other," in J. V. Wertsch (ed.), *Culture, Communication and Cognition: Vygotskian Perspectives*, New York: Cambridge University Press, pp. 146-151

Crain, W. (1992). *Theories of Development: Concepts and Applications*, Englewood Cliffs, NJ: Prentice-Hall.

Dawis, R. V. and Lofquist, L. H. (1976). "Personality Style and the Process of Work Adjustment," *Journal of Counseling Psychology*, 23(1): 55-59.

Emery, F. E. and Trist, E. L. (1965). "The Causal Texture of Organizational Environments," *Human Relations*, 18: 21-32.

Engels, F. (1940). *Dialectics of Nature*, New York: International Publishers.

Gibson, J. J. (1966). *The Senses Considered as Perceptual Systems*, Boston: Houghton-Mifflin.

Gleick, J. (1987). *Chaos: Making a New Science*, New York: Viking.

Gustafson, G. E. (1984). "Effects of the Ability to Locomote on Infants' Social and Exploratory Behaviors: An Experimental Study," *Developmental Psychology*, 20(3): 397-405.

Hackman, J. R. and Oldham, G. (1976). "Motivation Through the Design of Work: Test of a Theory," *Organizational Behavior and Human Performance*, 16: 250-279.

Harvey, R. J. (1992). "Job Analysis," in M. D. Dunnette and L. M. Hough (eds.), *Handbook of Industrial & Organizational Psychology*, Vol. 2. (2nd ed.), California: CPI, pp. 71-163.

Hattrup, K. and Jackson, S. E. (1996). "Learning About Individual Differences by Taking Situations Seriously," in K. R. Murphy (ed.), *Individual Differences and Behavior in Organizations*, San Francisco: Jossey, Bass, p. 507.

Highhouse, S. and Harris, M. M. (1993). "The Measurement of Assessment Center Situations: Bem's Template Matching Technique for Examining Exercise Similarity," *Journal of Applied Social Psychology*, 23: 140-155.

Hill, O. W. (1996). "The Internal/External Dimension in Psychoepistemic Orientation and Measures of Ability," *Perceptual & Motor Skills*, 82(3): 872-874.

Howard, A. and Bray, D. W. (1998). *Managerial Lives in Transition: Advancing Age and Changing Times*, New York, NY, US: Guilford Press.

Howard, G. S. and Conway, C. G. (1986). "Can There Be an Empirical Science of Volitional Action?" *American Psychologist*, 41: 1241-1251.

Hunt, R. R. and Ellis, H. C. (1999). *Fundamentals of Cognitive Psychology*, 6th ed., New York, NY, US: McGraw-Hill.

Hunter, R. H. (1980). "The Nature and Effects of Perceived Instrumentality in Relation to Academic Motivation and Achievement," *Dissertation Abstracts International*, 40(8-A).

Ilgen, D. R., Major, D. A., Hollenbeck, J. R. and Sego, D. J. (1995). "Raising an Individual Decision Making Model to the Team Level: A New Research Model and Paradigm," in R. A. Guzzo and E. Salas (eds.), *Team Effectiveness and Decision Making in Organizations*, San Francisco: Jossey-Bass.

Jackson, S. E., Brett, J. F., Sessa, V. I., Cooper, D. M., Julin, J. A., and Peyronnin, K. (1991). "Some Differences Make a Difference: Individual Dissimilarity and Group Heterogeneity as Correlates of Recruitment, Promotions, and Turnover," *Journal of Applied Psychology*, 76: 675-689.

Jackson, S. E. and Schuler, R. S. (1995). "Understanding Human Resource Management in the Context of Organizations and Their Environments," *Annual Review of Psychology*, 46, 237-264.

Jones, R. G., Stevens, M. J., and Fischer, D. L. (2000). "Selection in Team Contexts," in J. F. Kehoe (ed.), *Managing Selection in Changing Organizations*, San Francisco: Jossey-Bass, pp. 210-241.

Jones, R. G. and Rittman, A. (2002). "A Model of Emotional and Motivational Components of Interpersonal Interactions in Organizations," in N. Ashkanasy, C. Hartel and W. Zerbe (eds.), *Managing Emotions in the Workplace*, Armonk, NY: M.E. Sharpe.

Jones, R. G. and Whitmore, M. D. (1995). "Evaluating Developmental Assessment Centers as Interventions," *Personnel Psychology*, 48(2): 377-388.

Kane, J. (1997). "Assessment of Situational and Individual Components of Performance," paper presented at *Society for Industrial and Organizational Psychology*, St. Louis.

Katz, D. and Kahn, R. L. (1966). *The Social Psychology of Organizations*, Oxford, England: Wiley.

Keller, R. T. (1997). "Job Involvement and Organizational Commitment as Longitudinal Predictors of Job Performance: A Study of Scientists and Engineers," *Journal of Applied Psychology*, 82: 539-545.

Lave, J. (1988). *Cognition in Practice*, Cambridge: Cambridge University Press.

Leontiev, A. N. (1981). "The Problem of Activity in Psychology," in J. V. Wertsch (ed.), *The Concept of Activity in Social Psychology*, Armonk, NY: M.E. Sharpe, pp. 37-71.

McDaniel, M. A., Schmidt, F. L., and Hunter, J. E. (1988). "Job Experience Correlates of Job Performance," *Journal of Applied Psychology*, 73: 327-330.

Morris, C. G. and Hackman, J. R. (1969). "Behavioral Correlates of Perceived Leadership," *Journal of Personality & Social Psychology*, 13(4): 350-361.

Morrison, R. F. and Brantner, T. M. (1992). "What Enhances or Inhibits Learning a New Job? A Basic Career Issue," *Journal of Applied Psychology*, 77, 926-940.

Mischel, W. (1977). "The Interaction of Person and Situation," in D. Magnusson and N.S. Endler (eds.), *Personality at the Crossroads: Current Issues in Interactional Psychology*, Hillsdale, NJ: Erlbaum, pp. 333-352.

Pervin, L. A. (1989). "Persons, Situations, Interactions: The History of a Controversy and a Discussion of Theoretical Models," *Academy of Management Review*, 14: 350-360.

Rogoff, B. (1982). "Integrating Context and Cognition," *Advances in Developmental Psychology*, 2: 128-170

Quiñones, M. A., Ford, J. K., and Teachout, M. S. (1995). "The Relationship Between Work Experience and Job Performance: A Conceptual and Meta-Analytic Review," *Personnel Psychology*, 48: 887-910.

Salancik, G. and Pfeffer, J. (1978). "A Social Information Processing Approach to Job Attitudes and Task Design," *Administrative Science Quarterly*, 23: 224-253.

Schneider, B. (1987). "The People Make the Place," *Personnel Psychology*, 40: 437-454.

Schneider, B., Goldstein, H. W., and Smith, D. B. (1995). "The ASA Framework: An Update," *Personnel Psychology*, 48: 747-773.

Snow, R. E. (1989). "Aptitude-Treatment Interaction as a Framework for Research on Individual Differences in Learning," in P. L. Ackerman, R. J. Sternberg, and R. Glaser (eds.), *Learning and Individual Differences: Advances in Theory and Research*, New York: W.H. Freeman.

Thelen, E. (1995). "Motor development: A New Synthesis," *American Psychologist*, 50: 79-95.

Turner, A. N. and Lawrence, P. R. (1965). *Industrial Jobs and the Worker*, Boston: Harvard

University Press.

Viney, W. (1993). "A Study of Emotion in the Context of Radical Empiricism," in M. E. Donnelly, *Reinterpreting the Legacy of William James*, Washington, DC, US: American Psychological Association, pp. 243-250.

Vygotsky, L. S. (1978). *Mind in Society*, Cambridge, MA: Harvard University Press.

Vygotsky, L. S. (1987). *The Collected Works of L. S. Vygotsky, Vol. 1: Problems of General Psychology*, New York, NY, US: Plenum Press.

Werner, H. and Kaplan, B. (1956). "The Developmental Approach to Cognition: Its Relevance to the Psychological Interpretation of Anthropological and Ethnolinguistic Data," *American Anthropologist*, 58: 866-880.

Wood, R. E. (1986). "Task Complexity: Definition of the Construct," *Organizational Behavior and Human Decision Processes*, 37: 60-82.

Wood, R. and Bandura, A. (1989). "Social Cognitive Theory of Organizational Management," *Academy of Management Review*, 14: 361-384.

Youngcourt, S. S. and Jones, R. G. (2002). "Position Management: A Broader Definition of Performance Appraisal System Effectiveness," presented at the 17th Annual Conference of the Society for Industrial and Organizational Psychology, 12-14 April.

CHAPTER 12

DEALING WITH COMPLEXITY IN ORGANIZATIONAL CONTROL PROCESSES: DRAWING LESSONS FROM THE HUMAN BRAIN

Rajaram Veliyath and K. Sathian

Organizational control systems originated from simple cybernetic models. These had limitations such as fixed cause-effect linkages, an emphasis on stable equilibrium, efficiency maximization goals and ex-post corrective action. By contrast, organizations are complex adaptive systems characterized by large numbers of elements, non-linear interactions, positive and negative feedback, self-organization, changing cause-and-effect relationships and emergent phenomena. The authors propose the human brain with its properties of complex learning, iterative interactions, plasticity, self-organization, specialization with generalization, multiple approaches, redundancy and immediacy as an improved model for a complex control system. We suggest how some of these properties might be incorporated in organizations.

Managing Organizational Complexity: Philosophy, Theory, and Application
A Volume in: Managing the Complex, pages 201-216.
Copyright © 2005 by Information Age Publishing, Inc.
All rights of reproduction in any form reserved.
ISBN: 1-59311-319-6 (cloth), 1-59311-318-8 (paper)

Introduction

The early organizational control systems were based on cybernetic models derived from simple electro-mechanical systems. Because organizations are social systems of a much higher order of complexity, the application of such simple control models in organizational control processes resulted in numerous control problems. Behavior substitution, goal displacement and short-term orientation are examples of control problems that surfaced. In addition, the business press regularly reports numerous examples of strategic control and governance failures at companies (e.g., Adelphia Communications, Enron Corp., MCI / WorldCom, Tyco International). Given the complex nature of organizations, complexity theory and its application in organization science should better enable us to understand and begin dealing with these control failures (Anderson, 1999). Complex adaptive systems exhibit characteristic features such as the absence of a tight linkage between rules and agents' actions, co-evolution of the system to the edge of chaos, emergence and self-organization (op. cit.). Much of the prior work in complexity theory has been interdisciplinary in nature. Frameworks such as cellular automata, neural networks and genetic algorithms have been used to study complex adaptive systems.

Adopting a similar approach we study characteristics of the human brain and examine how some of these can be modeled in organizational control systems. The brain exhibits many of the characteristics of complex systems. In organizational control situations where adaptability and flexibility are important, some of the characteristics of the human brain may be appropriate. The brain has been previously used as a metaphor in the study of organizations (Beer, 1972; Garud & Kotha, 1994; Morgan, 1986).

The chapter is organized into four sections. The first section introduces literature in complexity theory including some work included in the current volume. The next section presents features and limitations of organizational control systems and examines how complexity theory may help deal with some of these limitations. The third section presents the human brain as an analogy for a complex adaptive system and discusses how the brain's features can be incorporated in organizations. The fourth section concludes by discussing the implications.

Properties of complex systems

The literature on complex systems discusses numerous concepts that provide a varied set of lenses for viewing organizations. Many of these concepts have been discussed in the different contributions in this volume. The properties of complex systems (Anderson, 1999; Cilliers, this volume; Gershenson & Heylighen, this volume) that are specifically applicable to organizations and therefore of interest in examining control systems are the following:

- Like complex systems, organizations consist of large numbers of elements (i.e., employees, organizational subunits) that dynamically interact with each other, resulting in complex processes with unpredictable outcomes.

- The complexity increases exponentially with the number of elements (i.e., determined by increased scope and size of the organization), the complexity of each individual element (i.e., the type of organizational structure and basis for organizational groups), the number of interactions between these elements, and the complexity of these interactions (i.e., nature of interdependencies between organizational subunits).

- As in complex systems, organizational interactions are nonlinear with many direct and indirect feedback loops. This is especially the case in network type organizations. These dynamic interactions result in emergent phenomena. Mintzberg & Waters (1985) and others have described emergent strategies and patterns of strategic behavior, in the strategic management literature.

- Like complex systems, organizations are open systems. The external environment affects organizations and determines their survival.

- Causality is unpredictable. Consequently, small events can have drastic organizational consequences (witness the crises that organizations sometimes are confronted with, described in the accompanying article by Gilpin, this volume), while sometimes big changes have little or no effect (examples being the frequent failures of major organizational restructuring to arrest declining performance). Thus cause-and-effect relationships are not completely known or predictable.

- Organizations, like complex systems, can be self-organizing. Traditional organizations were top-down, hierarchical, and stable. By contrast, today's networked organizations are flatter, team-based, process-oriented and fluid. Both team leadership and roles vary and are situation specific. The external relationships of these organizations also evolve and vary. Some of these organizations are virtual in nature (as described by Richardson, et al., this volume). Such self-organization is a characteristic of complex systems described by numerous authors including Allen, et al. (this volume).

In reality, organizations are nonlinear feedback systems (Stacey, 1995), where agents are free to vary, alter, or ignore the accepted decision rules and behavioral scripts. Given that human organizations exhibit the properties described, how appropriate are current organizational control systems? What modifications can be suggested to improve their effectiveness? Where would we look for alternative models? If the human brain is an alternative model, which of its desirable characteristics can be incorporated in organizational control systems? How can this be accomplished?

Organizational control systems

Most organizational control systems operate under the following assumptions:

- A pre-existing plan against which control is affected (Anthony, 1965).
- Benchmarks for performance are known, fixed and measurable.
- Corrective action is taken primarily after the transformation process is completed (i.e., ex-post).

These assumptions are from cybernetic models. However, they are restrictive and impose many limitations (Band & Scanlan, 1995; Flamholtz, 1979; Hofstede, 1978):

- Cybernetic models emphasize stability and do not adequately deal with uncertainty, complexity, and change.
- They do not recognize the capability of organizations as complex systems to self-organize and come up with emergent solutions
- Cybernetic approaches are susceptible to errors in interpretation, evaluation, and prescription.
- The goals adopted in control processes are frequently those of the more influential stakeholder groups. Because the aspirations of those with less influence are given less importance, goal setting is not holistic.
- Frequently, control processes occur after the fact (i.e., ex-post). They are adjunct to planning activity. This reduces their timeliness and effectiveness.

Today's organizational control systems have to accommodate multiple requirements. Basic operational control deals with questions of efficiency (Anthony, 1965). It preserves status quo and organizational stability. Management control emphasizes effective resource allocation to enhance business competitiveness (op. cit.). Strategic control checks the appropriateness of organizational goals, and monitors the nature of organizational competitive advantages (Schreyogg & Steinmann, 1987). It ensures long-term organizational survival through adaptation. Hence, organizational control systems have to ensure efficiency, effectiveness of resource allocation, as well as safeguard organizational adaptation and survival. Adaptation is linked to holistic learning. Using holistic approaches, the claims of both the organization's internal as well as external stakeholder groups (Freeman, 1984) are considered integral to problem definition and problem solving. This ensures the organization's internal as well as external legitimacy (Chakravarthy & Lorange, 1991).

Table 1 summarizes some of the arguments. Listed in the columns, from left to right, are characteristics of control models, the assumptions underlying these control characteristics, proposed modifications and the resulting advantages.

Model Characteristics	Existing Assumptions	Modified Assumptions	Resulting Advantages
Cause-effect Linkages	Cause-effect linkages known and fixed	Cause-effect linkages are modified based on changing conditions	Enhances organizational adaptation; enables double-loop learning
State of Equilibrium	Control promotes stable equilibrium; homeostasis	Control promotes dynamic equilibrium based on changing conditions; bounded instability	Enhances organizational adaptation, learning & resilience
Goals	Emphasize efficiency and effectiveness; optimize short and long term organizational performance	Holistic goal-setting	Accommodates needs of all stakeholder groups; ensures firm's legitimacy
Timeliness	Ex-post control; lagged response	Ex-ante control; anticipatory and concurrent control activity	Real-time responsiveness; enables successful control

Table 1

Existing Assumptions and Suggested Modifications in Organizational Control Models

Since control models are designed to seek stable equilibrium, they assume fixed cause-effect linkages. However a control model where these linkages are modified based on changing conditions is more appropriate. This facilitates double-loop learning (Argyris & Schön, 1981) and enables the organization to become more adaptable to changing circumstances. Agents in nonlinear feedback systems like organizations are free to change the rules of cause-and-effect, schemas or scripts that govern their behavior (Anderson, 1999). When all or many of the agents in a system keep changing the rules, there are many outcomes possible for any individual's actions, group behavior is more than simply the sum of individual behaviors and small changes can escalate into major outcomes. Cause-and-effect relationships become difficult to ascertain or predict. Thus a change in assumption to accommodate flexibility in cause-and-effect relationships, would enable organizational control systems to become more effective.

Second, the system property of homeostasis (Katz & Kahn, 1966) promotes a return to status quo. It preserves stable equilibrium. This assumption is ideal for most operational control systems and for organizations in industries with very little change or turbulence. Traditional control systems based on negative feedback sustain regular predictable behavior. This may be insufficient in industries which are experiencing high rates of change in customer tastes, technologies, and actions of competitors. Control systems that can handle such rapid and frequent changes and enable the organization to learn and adapt would be more appropriate.

Moreover, when human agents in organizations change the rules governing behavior, or when based on their schemata, these agents exhibit behaviors that are not in accordance with the rules (Anderson, 1999), the system is driven by amplifying positive feedback along potentially unstable equilibrium paths. Then the system exhibits a tendency for unstable behavior (Stacey, 1995). The literature on complexity discusses such systems that are characterized by bounded instability and emergent order. Such systems flip-flop between positive feedback that produces instability and negative feedback that restores stability, as Murray (this volume) describes. Such systems move far from equilibrium, often towards the edge of criticality (i.e., chaos). At the point of criticality enough common consciousness (schemas) and patterned behaviors (routines) keeps the system from tipping over into disequilibrium. Such processes that take organizations to the edge of chaos are necessary for innovation and creativity. Positive feedback enables behavior that is novel, unlike the routine, predictable behaviors that are manifested under pure negative feedback. These characteristics if present in control systems would increase the organization's adaptive capability. Bounded instability, accompanied by both positive and negative feedback also enables learning and promotes organizational resilience. All of these properties are necessary in fast changing environments.

Control models would better serve organizational needs if they could simultaneously ensure efficiency, promote effectiveness in resource allocation as well as holistically set goals. Holistic goal-setting accommodates not only the needs of the firm's dominant coalition, but also acknowledges the claims of all stakeholder groups in the firm's internal and external environments. Accommodating all these needs guarantees organizational legitimacy (Chakravarthy & Lorange, 1991). As Falconer (this volume) describes in a related article, a holistic approach moves beyond narrow frameworks, adopts healthier mental metaphors, and embraces more social concerns. Holistic goal setting also moves beyond a focus on solely financial measures to encompass a broader array of process and stakeholder-based measures of organizational effectiveness (Kaplan & Norton, 1992; Quinn & Rohrbaugh, 1983). Holistic goal setting in strategic control processes provides the organization with greater legitimacy.

Finally, control has to be timely. In operational control, the control process is activated at the end of the planning-implementation-performance cycle. While this lagged limited role is sufficient in operational control systems, strategic control necessitates continuously questioning the organizational mission, objectives and goals, in order to ensure appropriate, real-time organizational responsiveness. Therefore in order to be successful, control systems need to coexist with, instead of merely being adjunct to planning processes. Such properties would enhance the organization's real-time responsiveness.

Table 1 discussed the assumptions of traditional control models, and suggested modifications. The challenge lies in designing an organizational control system that can accommodate all these requirements. In looking for alternative metaphors, we turn to the human brain. In the interest of drawing practical analogies based on current neurological research, we model the brain as a system (i.e., an organ in the human body), separate from its cognitive aspects as a part of the mind or of human consciousness.

The human brain as an analogy for a complex control system

Some properties of the human brain that could be appropriately modeled in organizational control systems are:

- *Complex Learning*: Possesses double-loop learning as well as learning to learn capabilities.
- Framing of solutions through iterative interactions, not top-down executive fiat, includes top-down, bottom-up and interactive processes.
- *Self-organization*: Developing nerve networks make decisions and structure their own development.
- *Plasticity*: Moving to new states of equilibrium to ensure adaptability and resilience.
- *Multiple approaches*: Parallel and distributed computation.
- *Redundancy*: Redundancy of functions built into constituent components, specialization with generalization.

The human brain is more advanced than organizational control systems when it comes to adaptability, learning, and resilience. Its plasticity is one of the unique properties of the brain. Plasticity implies the middle ground between elasticity and brittleness. Following an impact, a plastic object does not stretch or shatter, but survives in a modified form. This property is instrumental in promoting dynamic equilibrium. The brain is capable of adjusting to trauma and learning through plasticity (Merzenich & Jenkins, 1993). Plasticity offers insights into the unique properties of the brain for self-organization, complex learning, resilience, and the capability to move to new states of equilibrium. The human brain also exhibits simultaneous specialization and generalization and redundancy of functions. We will take each of the control characteristics discussed in Table 1 and show how the human brain modifies the existing control assumptions.

Table 2 summarizes some of features of the human brain that might be applicable to complex systems and the benefits each provides. It also discusses how some of these features can be incorporated in organizations through the use of different types of control processes, scanning / forecasting techniques, and structural or systemic design attributes.

Brain Feature	Benefits	How Achieved in Organizations
Tuning operating parameters and framing solutions through iterative interactions	Enables modification of cause-effect linkages; furthers double-loop learning	Interactive control systems; dialectical inquiry
Self organizing / Plasticity	Enables modified states of equilibrium; enhances organizational adaptation, learning and resilience	Networked and virtual structures; self-organizing work groups; dynamic capabilities
Specialization with generalization / redundancy	Ensures holistic goal-setting	Dual responsibility for strategic and operating targets across hierarchy levels and Business Units; multi-tasking
Immediacy	Enables rapid responses; facilitates real-time responsiveness	Strategic Issue Management Systems; Strategic Leap Control

Table 2
Incorporating 'Brain-Like' System Features in Organizations

Cause-Effect Linkages: The human brain is extremely adaptable, through constant tuning of operating parameters. This is accomplished either via feedback about the consequences of actions or by commands from higher centers. It is capable of changing beyond narrowly defined boundary conditions and adjusting to new, unprogrammed stimuli. The modification of these schemas is accomplished through various mechanisms, which include changes in the signals at synapses (the connections between individual nerve cells or neurons) and also, in some instances, growth of new connections (Kaas & Florence, 1997).

In addition, the human brain also exhibits a tremendous ability to generate versatile responses and solutions in different contexts. The brain does this by coming up with appropriate solutions framed through iterative, nonlinear interactions that result in the selection of transient neuronal assemblies depending on the task at hand. The brain has a great degree of cross-connections and facility for exchanges between different components, and there is a degree of redundancy in its connectivity. There is evidence of bottom-up information flow from lower to higher levels of hierarchically organized sensory systems (Reed, 1999), top-down flow of information from higher to lower hierarchical levels (Hupé, *et al.*, 1998), and simultaneity exhibited through concurrent firing of neurons (Schecter, 1996). The huge numbers of neurons (upwards of 100 billion), the redundancy of connections among them and the frequency of firings enables the human brain to replicate properties of complex systems such as the presence of numerous elements and nonlinear feedback loops, both direct and indirect (see the descriptions of complex systems offered by Anderson, 1999; Cilliers, this volume; Gershenson & Heylighen, this volume). These properties facilitate versatility.

As is evident from the preceding discussion, the brain's capability to develop versatile solutions and responses through modifying cause-and-effect linkages, and its learning, are partly based on iterative interactions among networks of neuronal connections. Interactive control systems and dialectical inquiry are two examples of organizational processes that ensure iterative interactions. Interactive controls are the process by which top management uses planning and control systems to actively debate and challenge data, underlying assumptions and action plans (Simons, 1994, 1995). Interactive controls involve a combination of top-down as well as bottom-up communication as well as information flows. Different existing systems like project management systems, profit planning systems, brand revenue budgets, intelligence systems and human development systems can be used interactively (Simons, 1995). The selected interactive system can be used by top management in consultation with other key members at lower hierarchy levels as well as from different functional areas. Dialectical inquiry combines two different (and opposing) views—thesis and antithesis generated based on differing assumptions about a strategy—into a synthesis. The synthesis is accomplished through face-to-face debate to analyze the assumptions that must prove correct if each of the two opposing strategies is to be valid (Grant & King, 1982: 143).

Modified States of Equilibrium: The human brain is also self-organizing, a characteristic of complex systems - see Allen, *et al.* (this volume), Cilliers (this volume) and Murray (this volume). Self-organization (Gazzaniga, 1992) is critical to the normal development of the enormously complex structural and functional elements of the brain from a tiny speck consisting of just a few cells. As soon as sense organs become functional, physical stimuli from the environment can interact with the developing organism and influence its development (Gazzaniga, 1992). Thus, the eye, when it becomes active, transmits information to higher centers in the brain. This information can influence the developing dynamics of the basic neural circuits of the brain. All sensory stimuli that bombard the higher brain centers can modulate electrical activity in the brain, thus influencing its development. An initial overabundance of nerve fibers and their synaptic connections is pruned during subsequent development. In many cases, this paring-down process is guided by functional criteria that reflect sensory signals from the environment. If the sensory signals are altered, e.g., by preventing visual input arriving from one eye, the system develops abnormally. The resulting abnormalities become permanent if the manipulation is done during a critical period in early development (Hubel & Wiesel, 1970). Thus to some extent, the environment is selecting out and establishing neural connections from a larger set for a particular function.

Neuronal signaling underlies all decisions in the brain, whether these are conscious or unconscious. Thus, developing nerve nets can use their unique ability to perform logical operations to structure their own development. Neuronal connections get strengthened with use. Donald Hebb first proposed that when the axon of one neuron repeatedly and persistently takes part in firing a second neuron because the two are associated with a particular activity, over time some metabolic change or growth process occurs in one or both neurons, such that the first one's efficiency in firing the second is increased (Crick, 1995: 182-183). There is now ample evidence for Hebbian processes operating in the central nervous system, as in the changes in synaptic signaling, that contribute to learning and other forms of neural plasticity.

The brain is capable of shifting the locus of adaptation from one part of the system to another over time. In order to accomplish this, the human brain employs a dynamic network structure (Churchland, 1995). In addition to connections between individual neurons in a given brain region, there are also connections between neurons in different brain regions. These connections are activated depending on the complexity of issues being addressed. The selection of particular connections is not made by hierarchical fiat but is based on requirements. The process would be analogous to the activation of informal intra- and inter-organizational networks, based on the specific task at hand. The excess capacity enables the development of new activities and functions. This is similar to emergence, which a number of authors in this volume (Cilliers; Gershenson & Heylighen; Murray; Richardson, K.) have noted as a characteristic of complex systems. All the above features enable nonlinear positive feedback to occur, along with traditional negative feedback.

Self-organization and plasticity are the main properties that would also help organizations to enhance adaptation, improve learning and resilience. Self-organization is accomplished in organizations through networked and virtual structures. The network configuration enables the sharing and formation of information that starts positive feedback cycles. The enterprise as an open system takes on a self-renewing character when new information continuously enters from the market, creates fluctuations and generates a variety of problems and decision-alternatives (Nonaka, 1988). Some networked structures reorganize frequently to solve customer problems. Employees in such organizations also anticipate and embrace change (Burns & Stalker, 1961; Schoonhoven & Jelinek, 1990). The latter authors have also discussed self-designing as well as quasi-formal structures that are appropriate for organizations in high technology, fast-changing environments.

Self-organization can also be practiced internally through freeing employees to figure out how to get the job done without hierarchical fiat and control (Petzinger, 1997). Groups of people work together without supervisors to plan, coordinate, and evaluate their own work. Work options such as part-time work, job sharing, flextime, extended leaves, and contract work all fall within the ambit of self-organization. Self-organizing groups are characterized by autonomy, the ability to set challenging goals that transcend present ones and are typically multidisciplinary in composition (Nonaka, 1988). Many leading companies like Honda, Canon, Coca-Cola and Monsanto have adopted these practices.

Plasticity is enabled through dynamic capabilities. Here organizations continuously modify their capabilities, competencies, resources, routines and processes to stay abreast of requirements in changing markets (Teece, *et al.*, 1997). Examples are companies like Canon and Sharp Corporation. These companies have continuously reconfigured and parlayed their capabilities in specific areas to move into different markets over time. Over time, Canon has employed its capabilities in digital imaging to compete in different end-markets like calculators, cameras and copiers. Likewise, Sharp has used its capabilities in Liquid Crystal Displays (LCDs) to progressively enter markets in calculators, copiers, fax machines, VCRs and television sets. Sharp also employs other means like chemicalization. Chemicalization uses aggressive head-hunting for talent from outside of the company as well as transfers of the top 3 percent of all ranks of R&D researchers and marketing personnel across business groups and between functions every 3 years to enable cross-fertilization of innovation. Gold Badge Projects are another means of ensuring plasticity. They are multi-disciplinary teams funded by Corporate HQ and reporting directly to them, that work on projects in areas where Sharp does not currently offer products, but where market needs exist. Such processes when incorporated in organizations, enhance their plasticity, learning and extend their resilience.

Holistic Goal Setting: Holistic goal setting is aided through simultaneous specialization and generalization combined with some redundancy.

Organizational control systems exhibit a high degree of specialization in terms of responsibility and roles. Top management is most responsible for strategic control activities, middle management for management control activities and lower echelons for operational control (Hofstede, 1978). By contrast, the human brain functions through simultaneous specialization (viz., the brain has different mechanisms for short-term and long-term memory respectively) and partial redundancy (Eichenbaum, *et al.*, 1999). There is some degree of specialization, e.g., the prefrontal cortex plays the role of central executive with the pre-motor cortices being responsible for motor planning and the primary motor cortex (at a lower hierarchical level) being accountable for executing movement. However, there is also distributed responsibility with the overall response being a result of collaboration among these different areas of the brain.

There is no fixed locus of control. The brain's responses are based on collaborative activity among bunches of neurons. For example, complex functions such as face recognition are achieved through differentiation of patterns of responses in assemblies of neurons, or neural networks, within specialized brain areas. These patterned responses in specific neural networks arise through bottom-up and top-down information flows and learning (Churchland, 1995). The brain has massive descending axonal projections from later neuronal populations back to earlier populations. These are in addition to the normal ascending projections from earlier to later populations. This architecture enables the recurrent network to include endless patterns in time as well as space, thereby generating a wide variety of behaviors. These are similar to schemas and behavioral routines that have been noted in complex adaptive systems by Anderson (1999), Falconer (this volume) and others.

In addition, neurons in each area exhibit modular specialization with 'fine coding' of the specialized functions they are responsible for. But they also exhibit 'coarse coding' of non-specialized functions. For instance, the visual pathways of the brain show specialization for function, with some areas specialized for perception of form and color, and others for location in space and motion through space. Neurons in each area encode the relevant characteristic of visual stimuli. However, they also exhibit coarse coding of stimulus characteristics for which they are not specialized (Desimone & Duncan, 1995). This ensures redundancy of functions so that a given function is not exclusively dependent on a particular area of the brain. Through redundancy of functions, the brain adjusts in a top-down as well as in a bottom-up manner. It also gives the brain its property of plasticity, described earlier.

Enabling collaborative responsiveness in organizational control systems through simultaneous specialization and generalization and redundancy might help accomplish holistic goal setting. This can be accomplished through instituting dual responsibility assignments for individual managers (such as meeting strategic and operating targets), as well as for business units.

Dual structures involve a combination of strategic structures and operating structures. The strategic structure is a grouping (family) of businesses based on product / business segments which share commonalities in product use, customer segments, and functional resources utilized (Chakravarthy, 1984). An example would constitute the toiletry business family in a company like Proctor and Gamble, which would be a collection of the toothpaste, shampoo, and soap SBUs. This strategic structure is not permanent. However it provides a lens for the way these businesses can view their environment. The operating structure involves centralized control at the product or divisional level, of functions such as engineering, advertising, and distribution. The implementation of specific programs is the dual responsibility of both the strategy managers as well as the operating managers. In addition to the sharing of resources, the dual structure is more flexible than traditional hierarchies. The systems architecture (budgeting and planning systems, control systems, performance evaluation systems) should also have the flexibility to accommodate and support the structural attributes described above.

Business units are also specialized in terms of strategic imperatives. For example, in a corporation's portfolio of businesses, some are classified as growth businesses, others as stable, some needing strategic redirecting classified as reorient businesses, and finally, the dog businesses are categorized as harvest businesses. All of these types of businesses will have different sets of goals and strategies. This leads to specialization at a sub-systems level that in the brain is exemplified by different functions performed by different brain regions. However, for the survival and growth of the corporation as a whole, all these different businesses have to collaborate to achieve corporate level goals and objectives while pursuing their individual business goals and strategies.

At the individual level, the property of specialization with generalization and redundancy can be achieved through having employees who are multiskilled and multi-tasked, and who can be rotated through different departments and functions. Likewise, equipment too can be configured to perform more than one task.

Enhancing Timeliness: Ensuring a more timely responsiveness of the control system can be accomplished through immediacy.

The brain responds in real-time to stimuli through its property of immediacy (i.e., real-time responsiveness). An important feature of neural function is the extremely rapid signaling mechanism enabled by the use of electrical signals (action potentials). This enables the complex neural networks that comprise the brain and spinal cord to rapidly process inputs and generate appropriate outputs in real time. Such rapidity of response obviously has tremendous significance from an evolutionary perspective (as for instance in interactions between predators and prey). These properties of the brain enable real-time responsiveness.

Immediacy can be introduced in organizations through Strategic Issue Management Systems and Strategic Leap Control. Strategic Issue Management Systems help in early identification and management of signals and events that might adversely affect the organization (Ansoff, 1990: 370; Lorange, *et al.*, 1986). It is a real time continuous tracking and controlling system. The identified issues are continuously tracked and their potential impacts on the organization assessed based on: 1. their evolutionary patterns; 2. likely impact on the corporation, and; 3. probability of occurrence (Fahey & Narayanan, 1986). Strategic Leap Control assumes that the environment is changing so rapidly and discontinuously that normal evolutionary control processes are inadequate (Lorange, *et al*, 1986). The organization remains in a state of preparedness that is typically undertaken in times of war. These features in control systems enable an organization to ensure real-time responses to threats and unexpected contingencies.

Discussion

Organizations are undoubtedly complex adaptive systems that are in dynamic equilibrium. Small differences either in initial conditions or in the subsequent pattern of interactions can result in completely divergent outcomes. Positive nonlinear feedback drives these systems to the edge of chaos, where they are challenged to maintain the balance between stability and flexibility. Organizations also consist of large numbers of agents (i.e., employees, sub-units) each of whom acts in accordance with their individual schemas. These schemas may be very different from established practice or theory-in-use. Therefore, goals and intentions only loosely relate to behavior, and in the 'garbage can' model of organizational decision-making (Cohen, *et al*, 1972), there may be solutions chasing problems, instead of the other way around. Consequently, organizations exhibit emergent patterns of behavior. They are also self-organizing. Finally, organizations are also open systems whose environments are confronting them with a host of challenges such as globalization, the information revolution, demanding stakeholder scrutiny, and workforce diversity. The rate, scope, and threat posed by these changes in the environments have increased exponentially, further adding to the complexity of organizational challenges. These challenges put a premium on the organization's responsiveness to change, ability to adapt and capacity for learning. Complex adaptive systems approaches offer us an alternative to reductionist analyses, and an approach that is more appropriate for organizations in today's challenging conditions.

As compared to these complex models of organizations, control systems evolved from earlier cybernetic models that were used in simpler electro-mechanical systems. These simpler control models were initially the bases for organizational control systems. However, they contained many restrictive assumptions that were inappropriate for complex organizations. Recognizing and dealing with these inconsistencies might help improve control systems designed for contemporary organizations.

In an effort to understanding how a better control system can be designed, we examined the human brain as an example of an improved control model. The human brain has many of the same complex system characteristics that organizations manifest. We studied a few of these characteristics and examined how current neuroscience theory explains the brain's ability to exhibit these. Finally, we described how some of these characteristics might be replicated in organizations.

We provided examples of how complex system properties are manifested in business organizations. However, while each suggested example exhibits one or a few characteristics, no control system incorporates all these necessary properties (as discussed in Table 1). Many of the suggested recommendations cover areas outside of traditional control, such as organizational processes, structures, systems and management practices. While such distinctions may be useful for analytical purposes, in today's complex organizations no activity can be discretely and exclusively categorized. Each managerial activity contains to varying degrees, elements of planning, organizing, leading and controlling, the traditional functions discussed in the management literature. Moreover, controlling complex organizations operating in present-day dynamic global markets necessitates considering all organizational activities as being within the ambit of control. It is only through implementing the meta-level of control proposed in the paper that management can be certain that they are truly in control of the organization's well-being and destiny. Undoubtedly the many features that we have proposed would also involve large resource outlays and further compound the complexity of organizations. But today's brutal competitive conditions are so challenging in their scope and control implications, that they necessitate draconian and innovative solutions.

References

Anderson, P. (1999). "Complexity Theory and Organization Science," *Organization Science*, 10(3): 216-232.

Ansoff, H. I. (1990). *Implanting Strategic Management*, New York: Prentice Hall.

Anthony, R. N. (1965). *Planning and Control Systems: A Framework for Analysis*, Boston, MA: Harvard Business School Publishing.

Argyris, C. and Schön, D. A. (1981). *Organizational Learning*, Reading, MA: Addison-Wesley.

Band, D. C. and Scanlan, G. (1995). "Strategic Control Through Core Competencies," *Long Range Planning*, 28(2): 102-114.

Beer, S. (1972). *Brain of the Firm*, Chichester: John Wiley & Sons.

Burns, T. and Stalker, G. M. (1961). *The Management of Innovation*, London: Tavistock Publications.

Chakravarthy, B. S. (1984). "Strategic Self-Renewal: A Planning Framework for Today," *Academy of Management Review*, 9(3): 536-547.

Chakravarthy, B. S. and Lorange, P. (1991). *Managing the Strategy Process: A Framework for a Multibusiness Firm*, Englewood Cliffs, NJ: Prentice-Hall.

Churchland, P. M. (1995). *The Engine of Reason, the Seat of the Soul*, Cambridge, MA: MIT Press.

Cohen, M. D., March, J. H. and Olsen, J. P. (1972). "A Garbage Can Model of Organizational Choice," *Administrative Science Quarterly*, 17: 1-25.

Crick, F. (1995). *The Astonishing Hypothesis: The Scientific Search for the Soul*, New York: Simon & Schuster.

Desimone, R. and Duncan, J. (1995). "Neural Mechanisms of Selective Visual Attention," *Annual Review of Neuroscience*, 18: 193-222.

Eichenbaum, H., Cahill, L., Gluck, M., Hasselmo, M., Keil, F., Martin, A., McGaugh, J., Murre, J., Myers, C., Petrides, M., Roozendaal, B., Schacter, D., Simons, D., Smith, W. & Williams, C. (1999). "Learning and Memory: Systems Analysis," in M. J. Zigmond, F. E. Bloom, S. C. Landis, J. L. Roberts, L. R. Squire (eds.), *Fundamental Neuroscience*, San Diego: Academic Press, pp. 1455-1486.

Fahey, L. and Narayanan, V. K. (1986). *Macroenvironmental Analysis for Strategic Management*, St. Paul: West Publishing Co.

Flamholtz, E. (1979). "Organizational Control Systems as a Managerial Tool," *California Management Review*, 22(2): 50-59.

Freeman, R. E. (1984). *Strategic Management: A Stakeholder Approach*, Boston: Ballinger Publishing.

Garud, R. and Kotha, S. (1994). "Using the Brain as a Metaphor to Model Flexible Production Systems," *Academy of Management Review*, 19(4): 671-698.

Gazzaniga, M. S. (1992). *Nature's Mind*, New York: Basic Books.

Grant J. H. and King W. R. (1982). *The Logic of Strategic Planning*, Boston: Little Brown.

Hofstede, G. (1978). "The Poverty of Management Control Philosophy," *Academy of Management Review*, July: 450-461.

Hubel, D. H. and Wiesel, T. N. (1970). "The Period of Susceptibility to the Physiological Effects of Unilateral Eye Closure in Kittens," *Journal of Physiology*, 206: 419-436.

Hupé, J. M., James, A. C., Payne, B. R., Lomber, S. G., Girard, P. and Bullier, J. (1998). "Cortical Feedback Improves Discrimination Between Figure and Background by V1, V2 and V3 Neurons, *Nature*, 394: 784-787.

Kaas, J. H. and Florence, S. L. (1997). "Mechanisms of Reorganization in Sensory Systems of Primates After Peripheral Nerve Injury," in H. J. Freund, B. A. Sable and O. W. Witte (eds.), *Brain Plasticity: Advances in Neurology*, Vol. 73, pp. 147-158.

Kaplan, R. S. and Norton, D. P. (1992). "The Balanced Scorecard: Measures that Drive Performance," *Harvard Business Review*, Jan.-Feb.: 71-79.

Katz, D. and Kahn, R. L. (1966). *The Social Psychology of Organizing*, New York: J. Wiley & Sons.

Lorange, P., Morton, M. F. S. and Ghoshal, S. (1986). *Strategic Control Systems*, St. Paul, MN: West Publishing.

Merzenich, M. M. and Jenkins, W. M. (1993). "Reorganization of Cortical Representations of the Hand Following Alterations of Skin Inputs Induced by Nerve Injury, Skin Island Transfers, and Experience," *Journal of Hand Therapy*, 6: 89-104.

Mintzberg, H. and Waters, J. A. (1985). "Of Strategies, Deliberate and Emergent," *Strategic Management Journal*, 6: 257-272.

Morgan, G. (1986). "Towards Self-Organization: Organizations as Brains," in G. Morgan (ed.), *Images of Organizations*, Beverly Hills, CA: Sage Publications, pp. 77-109.

Nonaka, I. (1988). "Creating Organizational Order Out of Chaos: Self-Renewal in Japanese Firms," *California Management Review*, 30(3): 57-73.

Petzinger, T., Jr. (1997). "Self-Organization Will Free Employees to Act Like Bosses," *Wall Street Journal*, Jan. 3.

Quinn, R. E. and Rohrbaugh, J. (1983). "A Spatial Model of Organizational Effectiveness Criteria: Towards a Competing Values Approach to Organizational Analysis," *Management Science*, 29(3): 363-377.

Reed, R.C. (1999). "Vision," in M. J. Zigmond, F. E. Bloom, S. C. Landis, J. L. Roberts, L. R. Squire (eds.), *Fundamental Neuroscience*, San Diego: Academic Press, pp. 821-851.

Schecter, B. (1996). "How the Brain Gets Rhythm," *Science*, 274: 339-340.

Schoonhoven, C. B. and Jelinek, M. (1990). "Dynamic Tension in Innovative, High Technology Firms: Managing Rapid Technological Change Through Organizational Structure," in M. A. Von Glinow and S. A. Mohrman (eds), *Managing Complexity in High Technology Organizations*, New York: Oxford University Press.

Schreyogg, G. and Steinmann, H. (1987). "Strategic Control: A New Perspective," *Academy of Management Review*, 12(1): 91-103.

Simons, R. (1994). "How New Top Managers Use Control Systems as Levers of Strategic Renewal," *Strategic Management Journal*, 15: 169-189.

Simons, R. (1995). *Levers of Control: How Managers use Innovative Control Systems to drive Strategic Renewal*. Boston, MA: Harvard Business School Press.

Stacey, R. O. (1995). "The Science of Complexity: An Alternative Perspective for Strategic Change Processes," *Strategic Management Journal*, 16: 477-495.

Teece, D. J., Pisano, G. and Shuen, A. (1997). "Dynamic Capabilities and Strategic Management," *Strategic Management Journal*, 18(7): 509-533.

CHAPTER 13

THEORY OF INTEGRAL COMPLEX ORGANIZATION

Ronald C. Murray

The transformations organizations have been experiencing in recent decades differ fundamentally from the partial and incremental modifications to the mechanistic organizational model that constituted organizational change during the industrial age. While that incremental change generated variations on the predominant organizational theme of the age, the transformations many organizations have been experiencing recently involve changes to the theme itself. They are a part of countless intertwining social, cultural, psychological, scientific, and technological developments associated with the new consciousness, realties and patterned organizational behaviors that characterize Large-Scale Organizational Change (LSOC). This chapter describes and explains LSOC in terms of complexity theory concepts by developing a systems model of complex organization and a theory of integral complex organization. This model and theory distinguish LSOC from incremental change in terms of the systemic change that occurs in organizations when members' realities and associated patterned behaviors evolve; explain why LSOC is occurring now and the integral complex organizational model that is emerging through it; and provide a comprehensive, integrated and strategic approach to managing LSOC in order to accelerate and direct it.

Managing Organizational Complexity: Philosophy, Theory, and Application
A Volume in: Managing the Complex, pages 217-235.
Copyright © 2005 by Information Age Publishing, Inc.
All rights of reproduction in any form reserved.
ISBN: 1-59311-319-6 (cloth), 1-59311-318-8 (paper)

Introduction

Organizations have been experiencing rapid and fundamental change in recent decades on a scale not seen since the mechanistic organizational model emerged in the eighteenth century. Just as that earlier organizational transformation was a part of countless intertwining social, cultural, psychological, scientific, and technological changes that ushered in the modern era, so too today's transformation is part of multi-dimensional change. This complete organizational transformation differs fundamentally from the partial and incremental changes made to improve or customize the mechanistic model during the industrial age. While those changes generated variations on the predominant organizational theme of the age, the transformations many organizations have been experiencing over the last few decades involve changes to the theme itself.

Significant attempts have been made to describe and explain this change phenomenon as *Large-Scale Organizational Change* (LSOC) (Mohrman, *et al.*, 1990), in some cases linking LSOC to complexity concepts (Laszlo & Laugel, 2000). These authors have pointed out that leadership in LSOC requires an understanding of why and how this kind of change occurs, and how it can be accelerated and directed. This chapter builds on the ideas in these works by developing a systems model of complex organization and a theory of integral complex organization based on complexity theory concepts to:

- distinguish LSOC from incremental change in terms of the systemic change that occurs in organizations when members' realities and associated patterned behaviors evolve;
- explain why LSOC is occurring now and the integral complex organizational model that is emerging through it;
- provide a comprehensive, integrated and strategic approach to accelerating and directing LSOC.

The essence of social organization in current realities

All descriptions, explanations and predictions of phenomena and how they behave and change are based on explicit or implicit theories. Obviously, the concepts these theories include must be consistent with the meaning of the phenomena they are trying to explain, describe and predict or they will be disconnected from the reality the thinker is trying to understand. Therefore, complexity theory concepts must be consistent with the essence, or essential meaning, of social organization within current social realities if they are to be used to think about these organizations' characteristics, behavior and development.

The relationship between theoretical concepts and the reality in which they are found is evident in the consistency between mechanistic theories and organizations of the modern era of European civilization, and in the concurrent revolutionary changes that occurred in twentieth century realities and theories. Within the social realities of the modern era organizations were machine-like equivalents of the mechanical technologies they were created to serve. The consistency of these realities with Taylor's view of manual workers as replaceable automatons of a mechanical organization is evident in the high regard his time-and-motion studies enjoyed for so long, in spite of his distortion of data to fit the model (Wrege & Hodgetts, 2000).

Social thinkers of the modern era adopted the positivist viewpoint, theories and methods of the natural sciences and philosophical thought of the time. The themes running through the thought of Descartes, Hobbes, Adam Smith, Saint-Simone and Rousseau were consistent with the mechanistic world-view epitomized in Newtonian science and Weber's organizational theory. Since the universe and society were vast machines in the reality of the time, social scientists saw no reason why their application of the theories and methodologies of the physical sciences should not yield an equivalent understanding of social phenomena. The reality of mechanistic organizations and the theories created to study them were products of the same consciousness, or orientation towards the world, within which the natural sciences and mechanical technologies developed. Within this relating form of consciousness the existence and behaviors of discreet entities were understood in terms of their constituent parts and inter-relationships.

The attenuation of the modern era in the late nineteenth century is evident in the loss of consensus on relating consciousness and its associated reality. The radical transformation of scientific thought evident in Maxwell's recognition of the need to study phenomena as integrated wholes (Maxwell, 1920) revealed a new mental model of the material world on which consensus emerged in the physical sciences over the following decades. But just as the mechanistic models of modern science had been an integral part of relating consciousness and the physical and social realities of their time, the new scientific mental models were part of an emerging consciousness that became evident in every field of human thought and activity through the twentieth century. All forms of expression also began to challenge the consciousness of nature and society as an objective external world of interrelated entities. Through the paintings of the Impressionists and abstract art, the stream of consciousness novels of Joyce and Wolfe, the improvisation of Jazz, and the interpretative dance of Nijinsky and Diagelev run common themes of interdependence of the artist and the art, the viewer and the world, and the knower and the known.

If the world acquires meaning and thus becomes real for humans through their interdependence with the phenomena they experience, they are not isolated beings whose consciousness receives knowledge of an external, objective world. Rather, consciousness is an active, meaning-giving orientation towards the world through which phenomena acquire meaning as they become real for the knowing mind. Things cannot be thought of without the meaning that permeates them and which is acquired through the ongoing encounter between human consciousness and the world. This is an involved, unifying consciousness because it integrates what relating consciousness separated, including the observer and the world, to the point that it is impossible to think about involved consciousness without the world towards which it is oriented, or to think of the world without consciousness. Within this unifying consciousness it became natural to keep wholes together and think about them in all of their complexity, rather than fragment them in an effort to explain them in terms of their parts.

The reality of complex phenomena and methods of studying them in all of their complexity using concepts that support integrative holistic analysis gathered momentum in von Bertalanffy's General Systems Theory, cybernetics, and complexity theory. However, the implications of involved, unifying consciousness for the reality and study of social organizations developed slowly because, unlike physical and biological phenomena, they are self-reinforcing. Since organizations are entities of the social world that their members experience as reality, they reinforce members' existing consciousness and realties, thereby generating the patterned behaviors that constitute themselves. Since this self-reinforcement is not found in phenomena of the material world, the transformation of social realities, social organizations and social science methodologies lag changes in other fields of human thought and action.

This self-reinforcing nature of organizations highlights their essence in current realities that must be incorporated into complexity concepts when they are used to describe and explain complex social phenomena. Although every human being is a carrier of involved consciousness, individuals do not create it in isolation. They acquire it collectively as they experience the world as social beings, and since their behavior is part of the social context experienced by others, they simultaneously contribute to the development of common consciousness within which the world acquires meaning. We see this consciousness-development process when people join an organization. Until they have 'learned the ropes' they have to think about how to interact with others, but once they have acquired the common consciousness of the group they behave in ways that have become natural for them. This natural behavior within shared consciousness and shared realities generates the common patterned behaviors that constitute the organization as a unified whole. Hence, the essence of organization in current realities is patterned behavior that manifests its members' common consciousness and realities.

A change in the common consciousness and realities that are manifested in an organization's constituting patterned behaviors is the distinguishing feature of LSOC. This is consistent with the variety of definitions that have been proposed for this type of change in terms of its depth, pervasiveness and organizational characteristics (Mohrman, et al., 1990) and provides them with an underlying synthesis. Hence, LSOC is systemic change in that it permeates every element of an organization simultaneously as it generates new patterned behaviors, whereas partial and incremental changes to single elements do not involve new patterned behaviors and occur within existing consciousness and realities.

A systems model of integral organization

An organization as a social entity is described by its mission, processes, structure and culture. Its mission defines its reason for existence in terms of the difference it makes in the lives of consumers of its products and services - its added-value to them. The mission may serve others in the organization, external organizations or individual consumers. It may be very clear and consistent, or may become vague and inconsistent indicating a loss of commonality in the consciousness and realities of the organization's members.

The organizational capacity to achieve the mission is provided by the other elements of the socio-technical infrastructure. Processes provide a dynamic perspective on members working together using standardized procedures to create and deliver products and services for customers and to manage the organization. These processes must be consistent with the organization's structure which provides a static perspective on members working together within units, and a management hierarchy that arranges the organization's resources and focuses them on the work to be done. Fragmented processes of discrete steps carried out within units are consistent with impermeable structural boundaries, whereas streamlined and integrated processes require thin boundaries across which people work with ease. An organization's processes and structure are based on the shared attitudes, values and perceptions that constitute its culture. Attitudes and values in relation to the sharing of information, resources, clients and work have significant implications for the kinds of processes that can be effective, and for the nature of structural boundaries.

From the perspective of its members' interactions, an organization is described in terms of their roles, responsibilities, relationships and resource management practices. Every organization needs members to perform roles and to carry out specific responsibilities within these roles in order to achieve its mission. Such roles and responsibilities are interdependent with the organization's processes, structure and culture. If defined entirely within the context of an organization's units they are consistent with fragmented processes, thick boundaries, and a possessive culture, but these elements will be very different if roles and responsibilities are defined in relation to the organization as a whole. Similarly, members' working and reporting relationships within units, across the organization, and with other organizations must be consistent with their roles and responsibilities, as well as with the organization's culture, structure, and processes. The same is true of resource management practices. If they are used to control resources within organizational units, roles and responsibilities will be narrowly defined, working and reporting relationships will be confined to organizational units surrounded by thick boundaries, and processes will be fragmented.

When organizations are perceived as patterned human behaviors underlying their elements as social entities and as members' interactions, they can be described in terms of their internal and external information flow and the mental model that allow members to acquire a common reality. The flow of information depends to some degree on the technology available, in that a paper-based information flow imposes limitations on members' interactions that are minimized by electronic information technologies. However, organizations using similar technologies experience different information flows because their other elements open up some social communication channels and close others, thereby determining the patterned behaviors that can occur. Finally, the characteristics of the mental model and its consistency among members is interdependent with all of the other elements. If members' experiences of the other elements support a hierarchical command-and-control mental model they will behave accordingly. However, if some members have this model in their heads and others see the organization as a network of self-directed people with responsibility for managing their own work and relationships, they will not understand why their patterned behaviors are inconsistent.

These elements are naturally consistent with one another and with the environment because the organization is an integral whole within members' reality that encompasses the environment. Hence, organizations are naturally integral in two respects: all of their elements constitute an integrated whole and they form a unity with their environment. In this sense they constitute an open social system. Evolutionary change maintains this internal and external integrity in a gradually changing world. However, when organizations and the world of which they are a part go through fundamental and rapid change they lose some of their internal integrity or wholeness and their integrity with their environment. The integrated nature of these elements supports a theory of integral organization based on complexity concepts that describes and explains organizations as complex integrated wholes, and provides a comprehensive, integrated and strategic approach to managing LSOC.

Theory of integral organization based on complexity concepts

Attempts to think about complex phenomena as unified wholes were described by Ludwig von Bertalanffy as organismic: "The conception of the system as a whole as opposed to the analytical and summative points of view; the dynamic conception as opposed to the static and machine-theoretical conceptions; the consideration of the organism as a primary activity as opposed to its primary reactivity." (1960: 18-19). To further the holistic study of systems von Bertalanffy developed a General Systems Theory of universal principles of organization applying to systems in general. Such a theory, he claimed, was necessary for studying the essential problems of human knowledge which involve understanding the organizing principles of a system that make it more than the sum of its parts (1956: 1).

The systems approach has generated innovative thinking about socio-cultural phenomena, such as the concept of society as a complex adaptive system which is "open internally as well as externally in that the interchanges among their components may result in significant changes in the nature of the components themselves with important consequences for the system as a whole" (Buckley, 1968: 499). However, if societies and organizations are patterned behavior that occurs naturally within a common consciousness that evolves through members' experience of the world, they must be seen as complex evolving systems rather than adaptive. Otherwise the concept of system will not be consistent with the meaning of social organization in current realities and will fail to recognize the collective creativity they can exhibit. Concepts for studying complex systems have continued to develop in the physical, biological and social sciences, and constitute complexity theory that builds on systems theory. A complex, like a system, is a phenomenon the parts of which are entwined together such that they cannot be taken apart without destroying the whole.

Since an organization's elements constitute a unified whole, and since the loss of its internal and external integrity produces inconsistencies among these elements and with the environment, complexity concepts offer a means for expanding our understanding of integral organizations as social systems. However, these concepts must not reduce social systems to a lower level of complexity by carrying meanings appropriate to physical or biological phenomena rather than the essence of organization. This would render explanations of organizational existence, behavior and change meaningless.

Complexity theorists reject reductionism in the sense that whole systems must be described and explained in all of their complexity, rather than as parts linked together by causal relationships. They see complexity concepts as the means for avoiding the reductionism that characterized the modern era. However, that reductionism was two-fold. In addition to reducing wholes to their component parts, social phenomena were described and explained using concepts applicable to the material world. Unfortunately, this form of reductionism is sometimes repeated in the application of complexity concepts. Such reductionism destroys the meaning of organization and is contrary to the systems principle that each level of complexity has distinctive qualities that cannot be described and explained in terms applicable to lower levels. Furthermore, systems at each level of complexity have relationships with their environments that differ qualitatively from those at lower levels. For social systems this qualitative difference is based on the essence of organization defined above - patterned behavior that manifests members' common consciousness and realities. When complexity concepts incorporate this essence into their meaning social organizations and complex evolving systems become synonymous, allowing the concepts to enhance our thinking about organizations and how they can be managed.

Complexity concepts consistent with the essence of organization also overcome the dualism inherent in the perception that social systems are the product of cognitive thinking. Such perceptions are preferable to those that equate social and physical systems, since they recognize that behavior is based on the reality of the behaving individual, unlike the behavior of grains of sand or gas molecules. But organizations are not the result of individual decisions. People do not think continually about how to behave. They act in ways that are natural within their social realities. Hence, grounding complexity concepts in patterned behavior and common consciousness allows individuals and their social organizations to be considered as a unity. Social organizations become consciousness systems rather than cognitive systems.

Complexity concepts consistent with the essence of social organization can be used to describe and explain the existence, characteristics and behavior of integral organizations as complex evolving systems, and how and why these systems maintain their integrity in a changing environment through LSOC. This understanding provides the basis for a comprehensive, integrated and strategic approach to managing systemic LSOC that will rebuild organizational integrity to meet the challenges organizations are experiencing today.

Integral organizations as complex evolving systems

Several complexity concepts can describe and explain the existence, characteristics and behavior of integral organizations as complex evolving systems if they are defined in relation to common consciousness and realities, patterned behaviors, integral organization, and LSOC. These concepts include emergence and emergent properties, environment, boundaries, connectivity, self-organization, and subsystems.

Emergence and emergent properties

Emergence (which is also discussed in Chapters 2 and 4 in this volume) is the process through which collective patterned behaviors develop in all of a social system's elements simultaneously and interdependently as manifestations of members' growing common consciousness and realities. It occurs when organizations are established, their units become more integrated, they merge to form a new entity, or they form inter-organizational networks. A new social entity does not exist until a common consciousness emerges among its members to generate the patterned behaviors that make it more than the sum of its parts.

Since each organization element is one aspect of members' patterned behaviors, an organization's integrity increases as the common consciousness and realities that are manifested in these collective behaviors emerge. On the other hand, if an organization's internal and external integrity decline, the system decays as its emergent property dissipates. Its elements become inconsistent with one another and may also be individually fragmented because they take on many meanings in members' conflicting realities. This is the situation in which LSOC usually occurs in order to rebuild the organization's integrity and ensure its viability, although organizations vary in the degree to which decay sets in before LSOC occurs. If LSOC does not occur, the system may lose integrity to the point that it no longer has an emergent property - it is no longer a system.

Environment, connectivity and boundary

As a social system emerges it becomes distinguishable from its environment and at the same time its emergent property changes the environment for itself and for all other systems. The environment is not an objective situation in the sense that it comes with identical pre-determined meanings for every social system. Rather, each organization's environment carries meaning for its members within their common consciousness and realities. Hence, systems do not exist in identical environments, and the environmental phenomena relevant to a particular system's existence, characteristics, and behavior are determined by their relevance to its organizational elements within its members' common realities.

Connectivity refers to the interrelatedness among a social system's members and between a system and its environment, including other systems. The level of internal connectivity indicates the intensity of the interactions and interdependencies among members, as evident in the nature of organizational roles, responsibilities and relationships. External connectivity indicates the level of interaction and interdependence between a system's members and its environment. Integral organizations have a high degree of internal connectivity, since their members' common consciousness and realities that support consistency among their organizational elements also provide the basis for intense interactions and interdependence. Such systems also have a high level of external connectivity because of their unity with their environment.

A social system is distinguished from its environment by the interactions that, within the members' common consciousness and realities, are included in versus excluded from the patterned behaviors that constitute the system. Since the system exists within its members' shared meaning of the world, the boundaries between internal and external interactions are not physical, but are evident in members' common realities and associated behaviors such as their roles and responsibilities, their relationships, and how they manage the organization's resources. Such behaviors constitute patterned interactions among those within the organization's boundaries.

Boundaries vary in the degree to which they impede interactions and the flow of information. Closed systems with thick external boundaries that restrict interactions and information flow have a high level of internal integrity, but lack unity with their environment such that they cannot recognize significant environmental events and changes. At the other extreme, systems with boundaries that are permeable to the point of insignificance lack emergent properties, consistency among their elements and patterned behaviors. The interactions that constitute such a system are difficult if not impossible to distinguish from its environment, further undermining the system's integrity as its elements develop in many directions. Social systems with obvious but permeable external boundaries have integrity among their elements and within their environment. The emergent properties associated with a high level of internal integrity provide the basis for distinguishing between systems and their environment, and the consistency between their elements and environment provides the basis for its openness that allows the system to recognize and accommodate environmental events and changes.

LSOC through which every organization element changes simultaneously based on evolving realities and patterned behaviors involves the organization's environment, its internal and external connectivity, and its internal and external boundaries.

Self-organization

The concept of self-organization refers to the spontaneity found in the emergence of social systems and their self-differentiation to higher levels of complexity. A social system's self-organizing capacity is essential for its existence and its ability to evolve as it strives to maintain and enhance its internal and external integrity. Variations in self-organizing capacities among social systems indicate differences in internal organizational integrity and unity with their environment.

Self-organization is possible for social systems because phenomena and events shape and re-shape patterned behaviors as they acquire and change meaning within their members' common consciousness and realities. This is why two systems in the same apparent situation differ in their emergent properties, behavior, and evolution. The consistency in the meaning of events and phenomena found in systems with significant internal integrity based on their members' common consciousness and realities enhances the system's self-organizing capacity. This capacity is further enhanced by a system's external integrity with its environment, without which the consistent information about environmental phenomena and events needed to self-organize would not be available. To the extent that a system loses its internal and external integrity it exhibits self-fragmentation rather than self-organization, to the point that LSOC is necessary to regain sufficient integrity for the system's survival.

Subsystems

The incorporation of a number of social systems into a single system with an emergent property at a higher level of complexity does not destroy the lower level systems or their emergent properties. They continue to exist as subsystems with varying degrees of self-organization. This concept is based on the ability of members to identify with both their units and the larger organization. Systems at both levels of complexity consist of patterned behaviors manifesting a single common consciousness in which they are equally real. The changing strength of subsystems accompanies the development and decay of social systems as their emergent properties and their capacity for self-organization expand and contract.

A high degree of internal and external integrity occurs when the patterned behaviors that constitute an organization's units are fully consistent with and integrated into the patterned behaviors comprising the organization itself. There are no inconsistencies in the common consciousness and reality that underlie the organization and its units. Otherwise their missions, processes, structures and cultures would conflict, and members would experience inconsistent expectations. The emergent properties of such a system and its subsystems are consistent, the internal boundaries among subsystems are permeable, there is a high degree of connectivity within and among subsystems, and both system levels have a high degree of self-organization.

However, if an organization and its units carry a variety of meanings for their members, such as when change is experienced differently across the organization, the commonality of consciousness is weakened. The system loses some of its emergent property, and its subsystems become more cohesive. They expand their self-organizing capacity at the expense of the system, accelerating its decay as their missions, processes, structures and cultures become differentiated. As their significance increases, subsystems become part of a common consciousness that may not be supportive of the larger system's continued existence. The boundaries among such subsystems become less permeable, inhibiting interactions and information flow. Such change constitutes LSOC that must be managed if the appropriate balance between the system and its subsystems is to be maintained, or the system itself may disintegrate in its members' minds and patterned behaviors.

The evolution of complex evolving social systems in a changing environment

Complexity concepts can describe and explain how complex evolving systems maintain, lose and regain their integrity within a changing environment if they too are defined in relation to members' common consciousness, realities, patterned behaviors, organizational integrity, and LSOC. These concepts include equilibrium and far-from-equilibrium, edge-of-chaos, criticality, change of state, negative and positive feedback, and space of possibilities.

Equilibrium, far-from-equilibrium, edge-of-chaos, criticality and change of state

Complex evolving systems remain integral, both internally and externally, by maintaining their equilibrium while constantly exchanging information with a changing environment. This does not mean the system is unchanging. Even in a relatively stable situation complex systems maintain their state of equilibrium through adaptive equilibration that allows their elements to evolve incrementally so they can process information from the environment.

However, complex evolving systems with a capacity for self-organization have a much more sophisticated relationship with their environment and maintain their equilibrium through a process of self-differentiation through which they evolve to a higher level of complexity with new emergent properties. This capacity for self-organization and self-differentiation is essential when the environment exhibits discontinuous change because it enables the organization to engage in LSOC to change all of its elements simultaneously based on new common realities.

Social systems in a state of equilibrium internally and with their environments have a high level of organizational integrity. Consistency among their elements and with their environment provides experiences that reinforce existing realities and patterned behaviors. Elements change incrementally within the social realities of the time and place, thereby maintaining their consistency.

Systems move away from equilibrium as members' common consciousness fragments. When elements become incongruent internally and with their environment the system cannot adapt to external change or evolve incrementally to a higher level of complexity through self-differentiation because the common consciousness and patterned behaviors that provided its foundation have disappeared. When this happens a system goes through a change of state as it moves towards the edge-of-chaos where its emergent properties may undergo a radical change as part of a relatively minor change in the total situation. This is the system's point of criticality where there is enough common consciousness to keep it from disintegrating as its patterned behaviors weaken. Systems enter a state of chaos when a new common consciousness does not develop to produce the patterned behaviors required in a rapidly changing environment. At the edge-of-chaos organizations must engage in LSOC rather than incremental change to develop the common consciousness, realities and patterned behaviors that will change all of their elements simultaneously and interdependently.

Feedback processes

Negative feedback is information that maintains a system's current state by reinforcing its members' patterned behaviors. Since information acquires meaning within members' existing consciousness and realities, much of the information received by a system with significant internal and external integrity is negative feedback. As the literature on cognitive dissonance has long indicated, the meaning carried by information is strongly influenced by existing beliefs and attitudes. Such meaning is consistent with the common reality of the organization's members, and therefore reinforces existing behaviors. Hence, information that outsiders might see as supportive of organizational change may be interpreted as negative feedback by members, thereby reinforcing current patterned behaviors and resisting change. This raises significant issues for LSOC, since it is successful only when members exhibit new patterned behaviors based on new realities.

Positive feedback amplifies a complex evolving system's move away from equilibrium by changing patterned behaviors. The self-reinforcing nature of social organizations is a barrier to positive feedback. But in a time of discontinuous change when the present is not an extrapolation from the past and the future cannot be predicted from the present, people see the world in a variety of ways and information takes on different meanings, unconstrained by the meanings once provided by common consciousness. This drives the organization further from equilibrium. Feedback becomes positive as a system's internal and external integrity deteriorate and members' common consciousness becomes weakened through experiences that challenge existing social realities. For example, a single organization created through the merger of two with very different cultures and behavioral norms may experience communication problems because information and actions are interpreted differently. This undermines trust and organizational commitment which reinforces obstacles to communication. Such LSOC may so undermine the organization's integrity that it disintegrates unless planned interventions redirect the LSOC process by promoting different positive feedback based on an understanding of the members' current realities.

Space of possibilities

Social systems evolve by exploring their space of possibilities - new ways of organizing themselves to become more viable or to protect their viability in a changing world. The range of possibilities available to a system varies with its internal and external integrity. The high degree of connectivity and interdependence within an integral organization and with its environment ensure the system receives information about the consistencies between its environment and its elements as a whole. This promotes exploration of the system's space of possibilities, but limits it to those possibilities that make sense within existing realities. This maintains the system's stability by limiting incremental change to that which can be accommodated within existing realities.

When an organization's internal and external integrity break down, the system's space of possibilities changes significantly. Its elements relate differentially to the environment because they have become inconsistent, and because the system has lost its unity within the environment, allowing it to take on a variety of meanings within members' fragmented realities. The space of possibilities open to exploration by the system is both expanded and fragmented. If the system engages in a variety of incremental and disconnected internal changes that further decrease the connectivity among its elements it expands its space of possibilities as it moves further from equilibrium towards rapid uninhibited change. This situation is exemplified in the plethora of incremental changes implemented by organizations over the last few decades. At such times organizations must replace incremental change with LSOC that will change all of its elements simultaneously and interdependently as a new common consciousness and realities develop.

Using the theory of integral organization to understand and manage LSOC

Many organizations are currently far-from-equilibrium systems entering a transitional state of bounded instability at the edge-of-chaos. They are experiencing a number of discontinuous social, economic, political and technological changes, and have difficulty dealing with these challenges to their integrity because consensus on an organizational mental model to replace the mechanistic model has not yet formed. Hence there is no clear equilibrium point towards which they can direct incremental change. Instead, their elements are evolving in relation to several disparate environmental factors, increasing the inconsistencies among them. This is a process of systemic LSOC.

Left alone, these organizations will eventually evolve to new point of equilibrium and regain their integrity with emergent properties impossible to foresee in a world of discontinuous change, or they will disintegrate. But it will be a long, complex and tension-filled evolution. Hence, many are trying to accelerate and direct their change. Unfortunately, most change management tools in vogue today focus on accelerating and directing partial and incremental change appropriate for systems close to equilibrium that need to adjust one or two of their elements while the others remain constant. In that simpler situation broad consensus on an organizational mental model provided a paradigm that ensured all elements remained relatively constant or changed incrementally. But during a period of paradigm shatter when consensus on social and organizational models is lost and organizations are in a state of transition, incremental change management exacerbates the naturally-occurring inconsistencies among their elements, further reducing their integrity. This is why the LSOC that each organization is experiencing differently must be understood and then managed through a LSOC management process that mirrors the natural transformation it is trying to accelerate and direct. The theory of integral organization based on complexity concepts provides a framework within which comprehensive, integrated and strategic LSOC can be planned, designed and implemented.

Planning and designing LSOC

Evidence of the LSOC occurring among organizations today is found in the symptoms of declining integrity and the associated decay of their emergent properties as they move far-from-equilibrium. Some are losing congruence with their environment as customers no longer want the added-value they have always provided, or expect it to meet a number of their related needs through an integrated set of products and services. Others find their processes, structures and cultures that were developed for operating in protected markets are inconsistent with competitive global markets created by deregulation and trade agreements. Those that try to engage in e-business transactions with customers, suppliers and partner enterprises based on integrated real-time information find their processes, structures and cultures constitute a p-business infrastructure designed for paper-based information flow. The list goes on, but the theme remains the same - the integrity of many organizations in relation to their environments is declining. At the same time many are experiencing declining integrity among their elements. Some are acquiring new missions in response to environmental pressures but without developing the processes, structures, cultures or member interactions necessary to carry them out. Others are streamlining and integrating their processes to use new technologies, but within a hierarchical and silo-like structure with thick internal boundaries supported by a culture of hoarding rather than sharing. And some are defining new structures without changing their members' roles, responsibilities and relationships.

This loss of integrity is generating many of the challenges facing managers today. They need people to work together across the entire organization rather than within semi-autonomous units, and even to work closely with people in other organizations from whom they were once separated by thick boundaries, in order to achieve the integrative potential offered by electronic information technologies. They require employees of merged organizations with very different perspectives and values to work with a degree of harmony that usually evolves through years of collaborative experience. This pace and scope of change create confusion and undermine the clarity of roles, responsibilities and relationships, thereby weakening organizational commitment and promoting withdrawal behaviors such as tardiness, absenteeism, turnover, and loss of corporate citizenship. It can also increase resistance to the LSOC the organization needs as its members respond by reinforcing their current behaviors.

However, the roots of this LSOC lie far beneath these symptoms. The social systems in which these evolutionary changes and challenges are occurring are in a transitional state far-from-equilibrium, and lack the common consciousness and realities among their members that will allow new patterned behaviors to emerge. This loss of common consciousness, including consensus on the organizational mental model, is part of a the transformation from the relating consciousness of the modern era to a unifying form of consciousness described earlier. This transformation has been evident in many forms of human thought and action for some time, but is only now becoming manifested in new mental models of social organization. We have not experienced a paradigm shift. Rather, we are living in a time of paradigm shatter that denies organizations the common guidepost they need to integrate internal and external changes into all of their elements simultaneously and interdependently. Hence, each organization must develop and acquire consensus on its own paradigm by planning, designing and implementing LSOC without a ready-made set of tools such as those used for incremental change management.

The characteristics of LSOC provide guidance on the approach within which organizations can accelerate and direct their own change. LSOC is distinguished by a change in members' common consciousness and realities that are manifested in their patterned behaviors, thereby reconstituting all of the organization's elements into a new coherent whole. These new realities emerge through countless consistent experiences through which members' social world takes on new meaning. Therefore, managed LSOC must create the conditions within which the desired realities will emerge and be sustained. This requires a comprehensive, integrated and strategic approach to LSOC management as illustrated in the Large-Scale Organizational Change Framework shown in Table 1.

Organization Elements	Current Status	Change context	Future Scenarios	Visions and goals	Change Interven-tions
Elements of the organization as a social entity					
1. Mission					
2. Processes					
3. Structure					
4. Culture					
Elements of the organization as members' interactions					
5. Roles					
6. Responsibilities					
7. Relationships					
8. Resource manage-ment practices					
Elements of the organization as patterned behavior					
9. Information Flow					
10. Mental model					

Table 1
Large Scale Organizational Change Framework

The completion and maintenance of a LSOC Framework involves five ongoing, iterative and interrelated activities.

Assess the organization's current status in relation to each element

A LSOC management process requires an understanding of members' current realities in relation to all of the organization's elements because these realities provide filters through which information and events acquire meaning, and they are often very different from the realities of senior management. Without an understanding of current realities, change strategies and interventions may have unintended consequences. An accurate assessment reveals significant LSOC information about the organization such as: the degree of commonality in members' realities in relation to the organization's elements; the level of integrity among its elements and the congruence of these elements with the environment; the thickness of internal and external boundaries and the degree of autonomy among its subsystems; the strength of its emergent properties and where it lies on the continuum of states from stability to transitional to chaotic.

Assess the organization's change context in relation to each element

LSOC management must also take into account the implications of the discontinuous change occurring in the organization's environment and the implications of that change for each of its elements. At the edge-of-chaos where LSOC occurs, an organization is highly vulnerable to environmental changes. Therefore, it must be able to recognize key events and act early to turn threats into opportunities. A comprehensive environmental assessment identifies the external phenomena and events that collectively constitute a change context in relation to each of the organization's elements. Such an assessment identifies the negative and positive feedback the system is experiencing from its environment, and the space of possibilities it is able to explore.

Determine future scenarios for each element

Since the situation is characterized by discontinuous and inconsistent changes, the future characteristics of the organization's elements cannot be defined with certainty based on an analysis of current realties and environmental factors. However, a number of potential scenarios can be developed. Such scenarios define possible organization models that include every organization element, and identify the conditions under which each will evolve in the absence of change interventions. This analysis will indicate the conditions under which the system will: move beyond its point of criticality to a state of chaos where its emergent properties will dissipate as the connectivity among its elements collapses; remain at the edge-of-chaos in a transitional state where its effectiveness diminishes over time as members' commitment declines; or move to a new stable state where it will rebuild its integrity around a new point of equilibrium.

Define visions and goals in relation to all elements

An appropriate scenario can then be chosen as the organizational model on which managed LSOC will develop consensus among the members in order to transform their realities and collective patterned behaviors. This scenario provides a vision of each organization element and the goals that will turn that vision into reality. Such a vision and goals are essential for LSOC management because members can lose sight of where the organization is going when their realities, norms and behaviors are changing, particularly if the change process is protracted. This has serious implications for organizational morale and commitment. At the same time, a situation of discontinuous change where LSOC occurs requires flexibility in the organizational vision and goals.

Although each organization must define its own future elements, some general characteristics can be identified from the nature of the situation in which LSOC occurs and must be managed. Missions, for example, require some degree of durability because they are the organization's reason for existence and cannot change frequently. But in a situation of LSOC they must be responsive to discontinuous change or the organization may find itself in a business with no customers. Hence missions must be defined comprehensively in relation to customers' needs, and able to meet them through a variety of products and services. Fluid and flexible structures and process are needed to allow the organization to adapt quickly to discontinuous change. Members must manage their own relationships and information flow, pulling in the information they need rather than waiting for someone to push it to them. Responsibilities must be defined in relation to expected accomplishments for the organization rather than routine activities in job descriptions. And integrated, real-time information must be available throughout the organization to promote responsiveness.

Change interventions in relation to each element

With the elements of the future organization defined, a comprehensive, integrated and strategic set of change interventions can be identified in relation to all organization elements. The comprehensive quality of the interventions allows them to create a total situation within which the organization's members will, through daily experiences, acquire the common consciousness and realties needed to generate the patterned behaviors that will constitute the redesigned organizational infrastructure. Since these interventions are interdependent, they may generate positive feedback among themselves and hence drive further change.

Implementation

Since organizations in a transitional state vary considerably and respond to change differently, implementation must be customized to the organization's current status and change context. Although the implementation of LSOC must be customized to fit the circumstances of each organization that has entered a transitional state, a number of principles of such change can be identified from the characteristics of this state.

Since the situation is characterized by discontinuous change, the implementation of managed LSOC must be flexible to allow the organizational model to adapt to changing conditions, and must be iterative to allow organizations to learn from experience. The pace and scope of change during implementation must also take into account the organization's capacity to absorb change or it may be moved to a state of chaos. At the same time, implementation must be systemic rather than incremental, since changes depend on one another and they collectively create a total situation in which members' common consciousness and realities develop. Discrepancies among the organization's elements will promote confusion and prolong the LSOC process. For the same reasons change must be carried out system-wide, or at least in a way that indicates the entire organization will be transformed before the process is complete. Some changes may be sequenced, starting with interventions and methods consistent with the current organization to build momentum, but they must be part of a clear transition strategy, and if they are highly interdependent they must be introduced simultaneously. In any case, the time-frame and end state for the entire process must be clearly understood throughout the organization. The process may take years to complete but everyone must know where the organization is going because an organization cannot survive for long with lack of integrity among its elements and with its environment. Since LSOC requires changes to members' realities and patterned behaviors, their involvement in the process is essential to gain their commitment. Hence they must be involved in the development of change management tools appropriate to the organization's LSOC.

LSOC management is by nature extremely complex because it occurs when organizations have moved to a transitional state and are operating under conditions of discontinuous change. However, the concepts of integral organization and complexity theory provide a comprehensive and integrated approach to LSOC management that mirrors this complexity and allows organizations to be strategic in managing their own change.

References

Bertalanffy, L. von. (1956). "General Systems Theory," *General Systems*, 1: 1-10.

Bertalanffy, L. von. (1960). *Problems of Life*, New York: Harper Torchbooks.

Buckley, W. (1968). "Society as a Complex Adaptive System," in W. Buckley (ed.), *Moderns Systems Research for the Behavioral Scientist: A Sourcebook*, Chicago: Aldine Publishing Company.

Laszlo, C. and Laugel, J.-F. (2000). *Large Scale Organizational Change: An Executive's Guide*, Boston: Butterworth-Heinemann.

Maxwell, J. C. (1920). *Matter and Motion*, New York: Macmillan.

Mohrman, A. M., Mohrman, S. A., Ledford, G. E., Jr., Cummings, T. G. and Lawler, E. E., III. (1990). *Large-Scale Organizational Change*, San Francisco: Jossey-Bass Publishers.

Wrege, C. and Hodgetts, R. (2000). "Frederick W. Taylor's 1899 Pig Iron Observations: Examining Fact, Fiction, and Lessons for the New Millennium," *Academy of Management Journal*, 43(6): 1283-1291.

CHAPTER 14

SELF-REPRODUCTION OF THE ENTERPRISE: VON NEUMANN'S MODEL APPLIED

Pavel O. Luksha

A widely accepted notion of the enterprise as an evolving entity, taken from neo-Darwinian perspective, implies that enterprise is a self-reproducer. Evidently, self-reproduction of firm (and other similar institutions) is one layer between self-reproduction of social individuals and that of a society. However, mechanisms of self-reproduction until recently were not discussed explicitly. Application of von Neumann's model of universal self-reproducing automata allows the identification of four key elements that should exist in a self-reproducing firm: 1. technologies specific to the firm; 2. implementers transforming technologies into actions; 3. tutors, translating technologies to new (and existing) implementers, and; 4. a coordinator to ensure consistency and synchronization of these processes. A classification of self-reproducing firms, based on their complexity relative to their environment, is provided. A number of implications of a firm's self-reproductive nature are considered, including internal and external factors, and organizational change.

Managing Organizational Complexity: Philosophy, Theory, and Application
A Volume in: Managing the Complex, pages 237-252.
Copyright © 2005 by Information Age Publishing, Inc.
ISBN: 1-59311-319-6 (cloth), 1-59311-318-8 (paper)

Introduction

The enterprise, or the firm, is a key (and ubiquitous) element of the business world. For ages, it has attracted the attention of both economic and management theorists. Debates over its structure and functions continue, but there is hardly a unified theory. Intuitively, the firm is envisaged as an entrepreneurial or corporate enterprise for manufacturing and / or commercial activities, yet various suggestions have been made concerning the peculiarities of the firm that distinguish it from any other social institution.

The firm has been largely recognized as the cornerstone of socioeconomic evolution in market-type societies (Knudsen, 2002). Yet, little has been done to clarify the mechanism of what is known as the prerequisite to evolutionary processes: self-reproduction / self-maintenance of the individual firm. Ability to self-reproduce has emerged as a major type of self-sustenance for complex dynamic systems in highly turbulent environment, as a way to retain their function and structure (Kauffman, 1993).

As economic science strives to build a structured evolutionary theory of a firm (Rahmeyer, 2003), it cannot omit the concept of self-reproduction. It has been recognized that the firm should be considered as an evolving whole, a complex adaptive system (Montresor & Romagnioli, 2003; Morgan, 1997). The purpose of this chapter is to discuss possible mechanics by which enterprises (as systems) may reproduce themselves, and their implications.

Self-reproduction in the evolutionary context

The firm as an evolving entity has, in its evolutionary mechanics, notable resemblances with biological evolutionary mechanisms (Saviotti & Metcalfe, 1991). The key process of evolution, acquisition of new properties of the system (also called traits), typically occurs through R&D and internal optimization, but frequently also goes through introduction of new staff bringing in new corporate habits and behavioral practices (e.g., in M&A). In general, the firm may evolve

- either through internally caused changes in technologies: 'mutations' in technologies, or selection of best practices,
- or through externally caused changes in technologies (that include both value-chain processes and managerial practices): informational exchange with other firms ('crossing-over of technologies'), or acquisition of new practices (patents, licenses, consultancies, as well as recruitment of qualified staff).

Evolution, from a neo-Darwinian perspective, is driven by the following properties of systems evolving: openness, mutability, and heredity (Eigen & Schuster, 1979). The prerequisite of evolution is thus self-reproduction of the evolving entity. Self-reproduction of biological systems allows them to perpetuate their informational basis, while an individual may experience senescence and death. Similarly, the informational basis of an enterprise - the content of its routines - is retained through the self-reproduction process of the firm.

It is evident that, in socio-economic context, self-reproduction (SR) should be understood in its broad meaning: production of system copies, known as *outer self-reproduction*, and replacement of all elements inside the system, or *inner self-reproduction*. Both processes of outer and inner SR have similar mechanics: the latter case can be represented as production of a copy exactly at the location of an original, i.e., there is no spatial differentiation.

Self-reproduction of firms is one possible intermediate layer between reproduction of individuals and that of societies (as described for example in Luksha, 2001), and is a dominating form of such a layer in market economies. Societal self-reproduction requires simultaneous mass-like actions of large socio-economic groups. Yet, a social order does not emerge by itself, but only through emergence of order at the lower level of organization. Then, social self-reproduction in a modern 'economy-based' society can only be accomplished through 'isles' of organized and manageable socio-economic life: through firms and organizations. If there were only a system of free economic exchanges in a market, then a contact between each two individuals would always only be an occasional event, and links (especially in case of non-specialized goods and services) would not be sustainable - and thus, no regular reproduction would be possible. In other words, the firm is a 'cell' of social 'macro-organism': only through self-reproduction of 'cells' is an organism self-maintained as a whole. Evidently, much like in an organism, different types of cells have been developed to accomplish specific functions, different kinds of organizations have emerged, that support various social activities, and so the firm is not a unique type of institution that has to reproduce (other such institutions may include: governmental bodies, charity organizations etc.). The focus of this chapter, however, is on self-reproduction of enterprise, and the implications it might have for business.

Self-reproduction: von Neumann's formalism

To realize the key elements of the firm that support its self-reproduction, the theory of self-reproductive automata (see e.g., Sipper, *et al.*, 1998) can be applied. A basic model of a self-reproducing entity has been suggested by J. von Neumann (recognized also as a founding father of the game theory).

The management and organizational science of recent years has shifted away from a 'machine' metaphor of the enterprise towards a metaphor of organization as living, organic system. The use of an automata-based model in the present chapter, however, should not discourage the reader, primarily, for two reasons. First, a number of authors argue that the machine metaphor should not be abandoned, since organizations are complex entities that have mechanistic, as well as organic, properties (see for example Connor & Napolitano in this volume). Second, and more importantly, the model that has been suggested by von Neumann, intended to study the essential property of living matter, was one of the first attempts to tackle organism-type systems with mathematical formalism. The validity of von Neumann's model for both modeling of life and constructing of artificial self-replicators is now widely accepted (Freitas & Merkle, 2004).

Von Neumann proposed in his report (an extended version published in (von Neumann & Burks, 1966) that a self-reproducing automata (JVN automata) must incorporate four key elements, namely (see also Figure 1):

a. instructions that describe a structure and processes of an automaton;
b. a copying unit, that is capable of reading, and copying, instructions: it copies instructions into a new automaton, and it translates them as directions for a production unit;
c. a factory, or a production unit, that builds a new automaton based on instructions supplied by a copying unit, and;
d. a controller, that serves to coordinate the other three and ensures that both a new automaton is build and instructions are copied. This unit, as it has been suggested later, can be optional, as coordination between three units can be intrinsic.

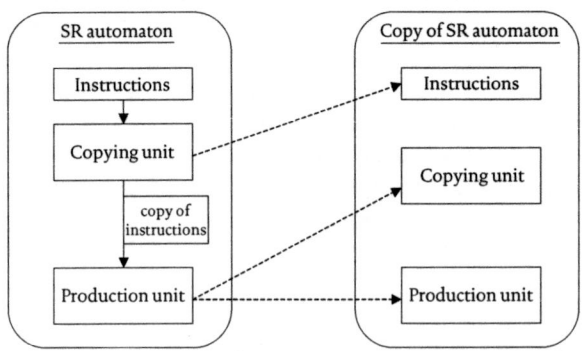

Figure 1
Structure and Operation of JVN Automaton

An feature of utmost importance for a JVN automaton is that it is the simplest structure capable not only of reproducing itself, but also to produce arbitrary additional (potentially constructible) components, or to perform arbitrary additional (potentially realizable) operations, provided they are described in instructions.

The JVN automaton should be looked upon more attentively for some other reason. Von Neumann was particularly interested in designing such a complicated model (as, evidently, more basic models of self-reproduction exist) because he wanted to scrutinize a system that has sufficient capabilities to evolve; and it has been shown that the JVN automaton is such a system. It is why this is a model that should be considered more closely for economic systems that exhibit evolution.

Key elements of the firm supporting self-reproduction

It is evident that the firm, much like the JVN automaton, possesses the following properties:

1. it reproduces itself:
    *   time-wise: many companies exist for decades and even centuries (the oldest family company in the world, Kongo Gumi, was founded in Japan in 578 AD); evidently, there is not a single person that stays with a company from its foundation day, and yet, the company's key knowledge is retained, as well as its brand, and its self-awareness ('corporate spirit');
    *   space-wise: companies develop not only by growing in size, but also by spreading in space, by opening offices in new locations, frequently in other countries, and establishing the same standards and organizational routines throughout all the offices;
2. the reproduction process is primarily based upon translation of core knowledge and competencies of the firm to new employees that replace, or add to, existing ones (Senge & Sternman, 1992; Bessy, 2000);
3. the firm is capable of handling functions, and maintaining structures, that are not reproduction-related, and yet which are preserved in the course of self-reproduction;
4. the firm is an evolving entity that evolves primarily through changes, both purposeful and unintended, in its core knowledge and competencies.

These properties suggest that the utilization of JVN automaton model could be potentially useful. Using the model, it is then possible to suggest elements that could accomplish similar functions in the course of firm self-reproduction.

A minimal self-reproducing structure of a firm then would include:

a. technologies: a body of knowledge, skills and codes (including machine codes) appropriate for production; may appear in formally codified (explicit) as well as in more intuitive (implicit) forms (Antonelli, 1999);
b. 'implementers': workers and / or machines (IT, robotics) transforming technologies into their operations and activities;
c. 'tutors', responsible for translation of technologies to new implementers, may appear in various forms, for instance:

- skilled workers educating new workers;
- training specialists;
- corporate knowledge databases for self-education;
- control centers for replication of machinery codes;

d. a 'controller': an executive, or an entrepreneur, or even an automatic device (such as a control center for robots), that coordinates activities of implementers and tutors.

Elements of a self-reproducing firm, that correspond to units in JVN automata, are presented in Table 1.

	Element of the JVN automaton	Element of the SR firm	Function of the element
1	instructions	technologies	a body of core knowledge (competencies, strategies, know-hows etc.) to define a system
2	production unit	implementers	actors that realize a body of knowledge in regularly repeated activities (routines)
3	copying unit	tutors	actors ensuring acquisition of key technologies by new implementers
4	controller	coordinator	actor establishing coordination in activities of all other actors to ensure consistency and synchronization

Table 1
Analogies Between a JVN Automate and a Self-Reproducing Firm

Application of this table may be broader than just outlining today's organization. If we assume that certain functions could be delegated to automatic and robotic devices then this table could also describe firms of the future: such as a fully automated self-reproducing and self-maintaining system, since its elements are not necessarily humans and knowledge, but machines and codes. Some projects such as Moon colonization (Freitas & Gilbreath, 1980) or flying systems (Moore, 1956) were suggested as engineering projects in the recent past; debates over these ideas continue. However, since an enterprise remains embedded in society, and it will still be in the future, replacement of all its human elements by machines will be doubtful. Despite a tremendous growth of mechanization in Western enterprise since the beginning of the Industrial Revolution, and especially over the last century, some essential human characteristics (e.g., creativity) have proven to be impossible to implement into machinery.

Functions of key elements of the firm

In a modern firm, its key elements of a self-reproductive structure are all human. Functions of implementers are typically taken over by a skeleton and supporting staff.

Technologies represent the 'knowledge essence' of evolutionary economics' routines, as they necessarily include a description of the main technological process, as well as supporting processes. However, they also include the codification (explicit and implicit) of corporate identity, known as a 'corporate culture', set-up of organization relationships etc. (Wilderom & Van der Berg, 2000). In terms of a general framework of social self-reproduction dynamics, as set out in Luksha (2001), technologies represent a stratified social memory attributed to different groups of enterprise employees and managers.

The function of tutors as a 'copying unit' of a firm can be elaborated further to explore the implications of the JVN model. It can be noted (based on JVN automaton analogy) that:

1. tutors do not necessarily have to remember all instructions, their main function is only to transfer instructions stored elsewhere (e.g., in a corporate book of standards) to implementers (as the copying unit itself does not 'remember' instructions), and;

2. tutors can transfer instructions to implementers by guiding / controlling them (as the copying unit is also transmitting a copy of instructions to 'the factory'). It appears that a self-reproducing firm needn't have an explicit institution of tutors; this function can be performed, e.g., by middle-management mentors, that direct and at the same educate a skeleton staff of implementers (a technique known as 'coaching').

Von Neumann assumed that each component of his 'automaton' was programmed, or determined, to accomplish its intended action, guided by instructions. In the firm, constituted of humans, employees may not always implement working routines in an accurate manner. Thus, the issue of conveying instructions, following them accurately, and reacting to employees' deviations from those instructions arises. The firm thus requires mechanisms of steering that are accomplished by junior and middle managerial staff.

The function of a coordinator is important, although a lot of activities can be synchronized through self-steering. It becomes critical in large organizations, where mass-like activities take place. There, coordination of activities is taken over by a CEO and senior managerial staff.

Classes of the firm by type of self-reproduction

A general classification of self-reproducing systems has been suggested in (Luksha, 2002). It follows the formal definition of self-reproduction by Löfgren (1972) as "the entity producing entity in the given environment." It is possible to point out that, for different classes of self-reproducing systems, the complexity of the environment relative to the entity is often different. The virus is evidently less complex than a cell that is required for its reproduction; and even more so is a computer virus relative to a computer. To the contrary, a bacteria reassembles itself from comparatively simple 'construction elements' of organic compounds, and thus it is more complex than the environment it uses to reproduce (a bacteria may also exchange part of its genetic material with other bacteria, that is a system of comparable complexity; however, this act is not necessary for reproduction, although it is advantageous for evolution). Sexually reproducing species, requiring a sexual partner (which is an entity of comparable complexity) are something in between. The strict application of this classification would require elaboration of one of the formal complexity measures (Edmonds, 1999); yet, intuitively it appears feasible.

Based upon this classification, it is possible to derive major types of self-reproducing firms (Table 2), characterized by different degree of complexity in respect to their environment. Three such types can be identified: an entrepreneurial idea, a company, and a self-reproducing corporation.

Type of enterprise	Formal class (Luksha, 2002)	Description
Entrepreneurial idea	quasi-self-reproducer: no formal internal structure responsible for reproductive function (system is less complex than its environment). Example: a virus	an individual, or a group of people, that center around the same idea or intent
Company, also, member of SR firm network	semi-self-reproducer: depends on internal reproductive structures as much as on outside structures (system is comparable in complexity to its environment). Example: organism of species with sexual divergence	an enterprise, operating through certain (formal and informal) processes, concentrated on certain core competencies and reproduction of core knowledge
SR corporation, or self-reproducing firm network	fully capable self-reproducer: produces many of its components inside itself, internalizes some functions of its environment (system is higher complex than its environment). Example: a bacteria, or a society	an enterprise (as previous), which also takes over (insources) some social functions (e.g., recreation and social memory replication for its personnel)

Table 2
Classification of Self-Reproducing Firms

From a business perspective, quasi-self-reproducers rely heavily on external resources, e.g., a start-up entrepreneur would try to look for personnel capable as 'jack of all trades', and exploit many non-business facilities (e.g., personal living quarters), and outsource anything possible. This is, so to say, one extreme of the classification scale.

On the other side, fully capable self-reproducers rely on their own capabilities. Large corporations may have a lot of highly specialized personnel, and may create specific business units to suit their every need. For example, Hershey, Pennsylvania, is a town of chocolate factory workers that has every facility for life and recreation: cottages, schools, hospitals and entertaining zones; the location has a large candy plant with a full cycle of production. As another example, Ford's River Rouge complex in Detroit operated much in the same manner (Forbes, 1998), being technically capable to produce anything from glass and steel to complete cars and battleships.

Most enterprises, however, are neither too small to outsource all their reproductive functions to other institutions, nor are they too big to insource these functions. They are in between, reproducing the company-specific knowledge and competencies within themselves, and placing anything else outside (sexual reproduction, general education of employees, etc.). Being comparative in their complexity with any other institution they depend upon, such firms can be called *semi-self-reproducers*.

All these types of firms reproduce themselves in the same manner, and should therefore have similar structural elements. Yet, for some of them, these elements are poly-functional, as well as some key functions of reproduction being placed outside the system. Generally, fully capable self-reproducers internalize reproduction processes (as bacteria do), and quasi-self-reproducers externalize them (as viruses do).

Processes in an enterprise
Self-reproduction in the firm

Self-reproduction of a firm was first explicitly emphasized in an evolutionary theory of a firm: firms survive in competition between themselves, and reproduce through reproducing routines, or 'a typical set of operations' (Nelson & Winter, 1982). It could be commented that, similar to the 'gene war' and 'meme war' suggested by Dawkins (1989) as the essence of biological and social evolution, respectively, on the individual level the 'routine war' constitutes the essence of competition on the organizational level. Yet, Nelson and Winter (1982) do not focus particularly on the reproduction of these routines (nor is this accomplished explicitly in consequent papers), associating them primarily with manufacturing technologies possessed by the enterprise.

The *resource-based* paradigm and its elaborated version, the *dynamic capability* approach, admits that each firm has certain relatively stable attributes that lead to its consistent heterogeneity regarding its market performance, and provision of resources: its market strategy, its internal management and organizational structure, and its specific competencies and capabilities (Penrose, 1959). The firm is looked upon as a bundle of productive physical and human resources (stocks) capable of internal development, whose produced results can be used in manufacturing purposes. Creation, use and dissemination of individual and organizational knowledge is the most important task of the firm. Furthermore, this approach can be extended to say that the firm is primarily a knowledge-integrating institution (Grant, 1996), thus yielding a *knowledge-based* theory of the firm.

Elaboration of the evolutionary-based approach can be accomplished when it is noticed that evolution may only occur through survival of individual beings constituting a population; in this case, a population of firms in the industry. Nelson (1995) recognizes that forces of persistence retain continuity in respect to which features survive in the selection process. Thus, a notion of survival, and thereby self-reproduction, has a prime importance.

It could be also argued that the process of self-reproduction should be considered in a broader context. It is possible to identify reproduction of activities, reproduction of roles and organizational structures, reproduction of working capital, reproduction of long-term types of capital (physical, intellectual and social) and that of work force.

The enterprise is therefore a set of interdependent processes directed towards reproduction of the entity, the 'wholeness' that it represents. This idea has been slightly touched on in 'regulation theories' (Jessop, 1990) and other social theories. An idea that firm tries to mitigate all disturbances through 'negative feedback loops', has earlier been considered by Beer (1988), who proposed his notion of the 'cybernetic firm', built in accordance with the principle of homeostasis.

The idea of considering the firm as self-sustaining and self-maintaining has also been considered in autopoietic theory (Bednarz, 1988). However, only particular aspects of self-reproduction have been examined: the firm represented as a structure of social relations that is maintained through regularly reproduced social interactions. Accordingly, less attention has been paid to the physical 'substance' of self-reproduction.

A key difference of a self-reproducing firm from other complex self-reproducing systems (e.g., living systems such as organisms), is that a firm can only exist within the bounds of structured social processes. Its main 'goal of operation' lies 'outside' of itself: a production / commerce beneficial to an owner. A process of self-reproduction then appears to be a 'supporting' process. This is different from biological self-reproduction: living systems do not live for something, they are just living. In this sense, a firm is neither 'autopoietic' nor it is 'homeostatic' in the strict sense, although it might contain some 'built-in homeostatic regulators' that increase its efficiency and accumulate results of its 'useful work' through, e.g., repetitions of a firm cycle.

Process-based view of the firm

The enterprise incorporates several different types of simultaneous processes, operating within a network of socio-economic relations. Using the process-based approach (Porter, 1985), three major types of processes can be identified in any enterprise that include:

- 'main' process (known also as 'primary activities'): manufacturing / commercial activity, intended to be beneficial to a firm's owner;
- self-maintenance / self-reproduction process (known also as 'supporting activities'): restorative activities, costly to a firm's owner;
- through processes (also considered as 'supporting activities'): processes of management regulation and control through information processing and exchange: finance, administration, IT, legal etc. (coordination activities, implicitly or explicitly, present in virtually any process of the firm; they might either be undertaken by skeleton staff in the form of self-steering, or accomplished by managerial staff).

These processes are repeatedly accomplished by any enterprise in the creation of relations with its environment: clientele, suppliers, workforce and stakeholders: see Figure 2.

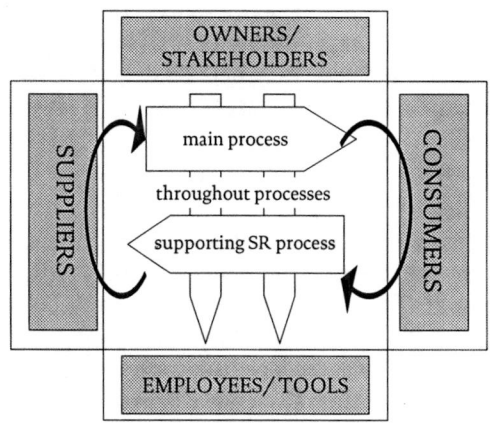

Figure 2
Processes of an Enterprise
(black arrows indicate transactions occurring at the boundary of the 'firm',
and 'closing' processes within the firm)

A firm may exist without running its 'useful action' (as malfunctioning firms sometimes do); but it will not exist without maintaining itself. And thus self-reproduction should be considered as a central process to any firm (accomplished through participation in market activities with the firm's specific competencies).

A firm is a self-reproducer first - a tool for collective survival (including that of capital owners) - and only then it is a tool for benefit generation. Metaphorically, this makes the firm a modern analogue of what tribes used to be thousands of years ago: a way to sustain a group in an aggressive environment. When a group is relatively small, self-reproduction processes may well be quite implicit. But, as the firm grows in size, this function increases in importance and may even become overwhelming - destroying innovation capabilities (that is, adaptation ability) by its large self-reproducing bureaucratized structure.

Evidently, in financial terms, a successful self-reproducing firm must operate at least at the break-even point: otherwise it does not have enough resources to restore its structure (including depreciated tangibles and intangibles). Thus, such a firm is also a profit-maker - but its target is not for profit maximization per se, but a maximal length of survival. Dutta and Radner (1996) demonstrate that in an uncertain world, the decision rules that maximize long term survival are not those that maximize expected (short-term) profits. It may be argued that enterprises are not *profit-maximizers* as they are considered by the conventional theory (due to factors such as bounded rationality and cognitive capabilities), but *self-reproducing lifespan maximizers*.

Implications of firm self-reproduction

As social systems are self-reflective, a concise understanding of a property in a social system changes a system's behavior towards this property (Geyer & van der Zouwen, 1990). Therefore, realizing that the self-reproduction property is a dominating property of a firm may help to shape its practical applications. Several important implications are evident here.

Internal factors in 'routine' operation

The first set of implications regards the internal factors driving firm dynamics. As products become increasingly knowledge-rich (a growing share of compensations attributed to the factor of knowledge and skills), qualified workers become a key, and most valuable, manufacturing resource of the firm (Sveiby, 1997). Firms can no longer be considered as purchasers of unskilled labor from households, as was the case with the classical firm of nineteenth and twentieth centuries. There need for a workforce with specific competencies forces firms to establish and maintain the process of *competence management*. As both supply and demand for such competencies can frequently be unique, firms look for ways to retain competent employees (either by bounding contracts, or by incentive programs).

As a consequence of their technological specialization (or, their knowledge heterogeneity) firms get involved in personnel development: personnel training, coaching, and building of social capital. This means that firms are driven to become more explicitly focused on their own self-reproduction. Accordingly, firms gradually turn from a classical role model of selfish profit-makers into a community partner entities.

Not surprisingly, firms frequently start to take over some traditionally 'social' functions such as education (social reproduction) and even recreation (social self-maintenance) of their employees. Practical examples may include Japanese companies retaining their employees ('company-family' model), or transnational consulting companies preserving their competencies (such as the Big Four, international management / IT consultants, and others).

External factors

Another group of consequences is related to external factors of firm dynamics. Today's business thinking may still be dominated by either classical or institutional paradigms, assuming that either scale effect must be achieved (therefore enlarging and specializing) or that efficiency of production should be comparable to market benchmarks, therefore reducing size and outsourcing (Slywotzky, et al., 1998). Firms 'exploit' human capital and knowledge while allowing other institutions to produce them (much as natural resources are exploited), thus placing them as part of the external environment. Suppliers and consumers are also addressed as external factors.

A process that has occurred in recent years is *internalization of the environment*. It has been realized that outsourcing per se is not favorable; companies have to establish long-term non-market relations, and although each of them might have different ownership, they have to coordinate activities so tightly that in fact they act as a whole. Such cases fall outside of the institutionalism approach, but they are quite relevant to self-reproduction. Firms, especially those in hi-tech industries (automotive, space and aircraft, computer and electronics, etc.), tend to integrate (at least through informational exchange) with their customers and suppliers. Customers become part of the reproduced system through methods such as branding and 'demand generation' activities; feedback firms also them informed of their future needs. Similarly, suppliers are informed about a firm's own needs, and joint programs are developed to satisfy these needs, e.g., in machinery design nowadays part of the design may be done in parallel at supplier's premises.

Firms may insource various activities that will be important in the long-term, instead of dropping them to realize short-term benefits. Limits to such in-sourcing will be determined by the ability to remain in the market (e.g., a function of recreation can only be taken over if it is performed more efficiently than in the market). As qualified personnel have become a key production factor, enterprises tend to enter in long-term partnerships with producers of new qualified workforce (such as universities), and institutions for human restoration (such as communities with budget-financed hospitals and cultural institutions, or commercial healthcare / recreation companies). Social responsibility standards have been introduced in many of the largest companies, and a growing number of companies obtain certification for attaining international social standards (such as SA8000).

Organizational change

A third group of issues is related to firm evolution. As firms change, their main problem becomes to preserve the key resources and capabilities that constitute themselves. Companies have realized that in the course of change they might lose their key knowledge - this has been called 'a boiled frog problem' by some authors (as a frog can slowly be boiled without noticing it, if it is put into cold water and the temperature raised slowly) (Hoffman & Hanes, 2003).

It becomes evident that the deposits of firm technologies (e.g., corporate knowledge databases), and institutionalized ways of translating / transferring these technologies (e.g., corporate training), are both critical for consistent self-reproduction. Many companies have introduced a position of Chief Knowledge Officer (or Chief Learning Officer), to facilitate the process of knowledge preservation (Pringle, 2003).

In terms of organizational design, from the perspective of the self-reproducing model introduced, the proper identification of tutors should be a key step for any organizational re-engineering: until tutors take on newly re-designed practices for replication, firms may frequently keep on reproducing the old procedures and old corporate culture which organizational engineers try to eliminate.

Concluding remarks

The notion that certain processes in the enterprise serve its self-maintenance and self-reproduction is not new to economic and management theory. It was the resource-based approach that emphasized reproduction of a firm's key capabilities and resources. The model outlined in this chapter allows us to consider in more detail how this reproduction is accomplished. Identification of the main elements of the self-reproduction process, and major types of self-reproducing entities, may have interesting implications for both a firm's routinized dynamics and evolution. In its turn, the general theory of self-reproduction, a part of modern complexity theory, finds interesting groundings in a subject that has been traditionally alien to it - theoretical economics and organization theory.

Acknowledgements

Earlier versions of this paper have been presented at the Sociocybernetics Conference in Corfu, Greece, SABI SIG of ISSS'03 Conference in Hersonissos, Greece, and at the EAEPE'03 Conference on Infonomics in Maastricht, Netherlands. The author would like to thank the participants of these meetings for their comments. The author also expresses his gratitude to the referees for their valuable remarks and suggestions.

References

Antonelli, C. (1999). "The Evolution of the Industrial Organization of the Production of Knowledge," *Cambridge Journal of Economics*, 23: 243-260.

Bednarz, J. (1988). "Autopoiesis: The Organizational Closure of Social Systems," *Systems Research*, 5(1): 57-64.

Beer, S. (1988). *Brain of the Firm*, 2nd edition, London: John Wiley Press.

Bessy, C. (2000). "Is the Reproduction of Expertise Limited by Tacit Knowledge?" *Danish Research Unit for Industrial Dynamics Conference Learning Economics Proceedings*, Aalborg.

Dawkins, R. (1989). *The Selfish Gene*, Oxford: Oxford University Press.

Dutta, P. and Radner, R. (1996). *Profit Maximization and the Market Selection Hypothesis*, NY: New York University.

Edmonds, B. (1999). *Syntactic Measures of Complexity*, PhD Thesis, University of Manchester.

Eigen, M. and P. Schuster (1979). *Hypercycle*, Berlin: Springer-Verlag.

Forbes (1998). "Looking Back: River Rouge," *Forbes*, 161(18 May): 122, 124, 128.

Freitas, R. and Gilbreath, W. (eds.) (1980). *Advanced Automation for Space Missions*, Proceedings of the NASA/ASEE Study.

Freitas, R. and Merkle, R. (2004). *Kinematic Self-Replicating Machines*, Georgetown, TX: Landes Bioscience.

Geyer, F. and van der Zouwen, J. (eds.) (1990) *Self-referencing in Social Systems*, Salinas, CA: Intersystems Publications.

Grant, R. (1996). "Toward a Knowledge-Based Theory of the Firm," *Strategic Management Journal*, 17: 109-122.

Hoffman, R. and Hanes, L. (2003). "The Boiled Frog Problem," *IEEE Intelligent Systems*, August-September: 68-71.

Jessop, B. (1990). "Regulation Theories in Retrospect and Prospect," *Economy and Society*, 19(2): 153-216.

Kauffman, S. (1993). *The Origins of Order: Self-Organization and Selection in Evolution*, NY: Oxford University Press.

Knudsen, T. (2002). "Economic Selection Theory," *Journal of Evolutionary Economics*, 12: 443-470.

Löfgren, L. (1972). "Relative Explanations of Systems," in G. J. Klir (ed.), *Trends in General Systems Theory*, NY: John Wiley & Sons.

Luksha, P. (2001). "Society as a Self-Reproducing System," *Journal of Sociocybernetics*, 2(2): 13-36.

Luksha, P. (2002). "Formal Definitions of Self-Reproductive Systems," *Proceedings of 8th Artificial Life World Conference*, Sydney, Australia.

Montresor, S. and A. Romagnioli (2003). "Modeling Firm From a System Perspective: Some Methodological Insights," PRIN Working Paper AT1 5/2003

Moore, E. (1956). "Artificial Living Plants," *Scientific American*, 195: 118-126.

Morgan, G. (1997). *Images of Organization*, London: Sage Publications, Ltd.

Nelson, R. (1995). "Recent Evolutionary Theorizing about Economic Change," *The Journal of Economic Literature*, 33: 48-90.

Nelson, R. and Winter, S. (1982). *The Evolutionary Theory of Economic Change*, Harvard Univ. Press.

Penrose, E. (1959). *The Theory of the Growth of the Firm*, NY: John Wiley & Sons.

Porter, M. (1985). *Competitive Advantage*, New York: Free Press.

Pringle, D. (2003). "Learning Gurus Adapt to Escape Corporate Axes," *The Wall Street Journal*, 7(Jan): B1.

Rahmeyer, F. (2003). "Towards an Evolutionary Theory of the Firm," *Proceedings of 3rd European Meeting of Applied Evolutionary Economics*, Augsburg, Germany.

Saviotti, P. and Metcalfe, J. (1991). "Present Development and Trends in Evolutionary Economics", in P. Saviotti and J. Metcalfe (eds.) *Evolutionary Theories of Economics and Cultural Change*, Chur: Harwood Academic.

Senge, P. and Sternman, J. (1992). "Systems Thinking and Organizational Learning: Acting Locally and Thinking Globally in the Organization of the Future," *European Journal of Operations Research*, 59(1): 137-150.

Sipper, M., Tempesti, G., Mange, D. and Sanchez, E. (eds.) (1998). *Artificial Life: Special Issue on Self-Replication*, 4(3).

Slywotzky, A., Morrison, D. and Quella, J. (1998). "Achieving Sustained Shareholder Value Growth," *Mercer Management Journal*, 10: 7-22.

Sveiby, K.-E. (1997). *The New Organizational Wealth: Measuring and Managing Knowledge-Based Assets*, San Francisco: Berrett-Koehler Publishers.

Von Neumann, J. and Burks, A. (1966). *Theory of Self-Reproducing Automata*, University of Illinois Press.

Wilderom, C. and Van den Berg, P. (2000). "Firm Culture and Leadership as Firm Performance Predictors: A Resource-Based Perspective," Center for Economic Research Working Paper No. 2000-003.

CHAPTER 15

THE OBSERVATION, INQUIRY, AND MEASUREMENT CHALLENGES SURFACED BY COMPLEXITY THEORY

Eric B. Dent

Traditional (reductionist) science has not done an adequate job of establishing effective processes for observation, inquiry, and measurement. The domain of interesting organizational phenomena that can be adequately addressed by arms-length, objective measurement has been relatively exhausted. An exploration of most topics of appeal, such as strategy, innovation, leadership, communication, and so forth has been stunted by an inadequate depiction of how they operate. A more comprehensive approach to observation, inquiry, and measurement is perspectival observation, a term adapted from Schwartz and Ogilvy (1979), which connotes not anything-goes-subjectivity, but the differences in perspective which arise when observing from a different 'place'. This chapter will: 1. gather in one place, the measurement and inquiry challenges - such as the issue of proxy, beta change, and knowing subjects - surfaced by complexity theory, and; 2. offer insights into how complexity theory can better inform both organizational researchers and practitioners as they deal with these measurement challenges. In addition to typical organizational examples, this chapter uses illustrations from newspaper stories, movies, and other pedestrian sources to demonstrate the real-world pervasiveness of the difficulty of observation and measurement in contemporary social science issues.

Managing Organizational Complexity: Philosophy, Theory, and Application
A Volume in: Managing the Complex, pages 253-268.
Copyright © 2005 by Information Age Publishing, Inc.
All rights of reproduction in any form reserved.
ISBN: 1-59311-319-6 (cloth), 1-59311-318-8 (paper)

Introduction

One of the contributions of the work in complexity theory is its demonstration that traditional (reductionist) science has not done an adequate job of establishing effective processes for observation, inquiry, and measurement. The domain of interesting organizational phenomena that can be adequately addressed by arms-length, objective measurement has been relatively exhausted. An exploration of most topics of appeal, such as strategy, innovation, leadership, communication, and so forth has been stunted by an inadequate depiction of how they operate.

A more comprehensive approach to observation, inquiry, and measurement is *perspectival observation*, a term adapted from Schwartz and Ogilvy (1979), which connotes not *anything-goes-subjectivity*, but the differences in perspective which arise when observing from a different 'place' - 'place' meaning everything from geographical position to psychologically-embedded history. Consequently, two different people viewing the videotape of the beating of Rodney King by the Los Angeles police can reasonably see different things - depending on their views of race relations, past experiences with police, knowledge of what it takes to subdue a belligerent person, and so forth. They could not, however, reasonably see a reenactment of the musical "Chicago" in the tape. This distinction is succinctly captured by Stewart and Cohen (1997):

"The message is not that reality doesn't exist, nor that it can be anything you want it to be. The message is that reality is not the same as your observation of it: that is just one shadow out of many. Reality is whatever casts all those interrelated shadows, and you can infer some aspects of its structure by looking at how different shadows are interrelated." (p. 200)

Perspectival observation also connotes that the measuring process may alter the phenomenon being measured (Dent, 1999). This dilemma can be illustrated with a thermometer and a bucket of water. If the water is 'cold' and the thermometer is at room temperature, when the thermometer is inserted into the water it will raise the temperature of the water, slightly. There is no way to get around this effect. The thermometer would need to be at precisely the same temperature as the water not to change the temperature. However, a circularity arises since the only way to know the temperature is to measure it. For most everyday purposes, though, the change in temperature caused by the measurement process is insignificant and irrelevant to the purpose of the measurement. In the organizational and other social sciences, however, this effect is often not negligible.

The purpose of this chapter is twofold.

1. to gather in one place, the measurement and inquiry challenges surfaced by complexity theory. Most of these have been addressed, separately,

elsewhere.

2. to offer insights into how complexity theory can better inform both organizational researchers and practitioners as they deal with these measurement challenges.

In addition to typical organizational examples, I will use illustrations from newspaper stories, movies, and other pedestrian sources to demonstrate the real-world pervasiveness of the difficulty of observation and measurement in contemporary social science issues.

Observation, inquiry, and measurement challenges

The following proposed taxonomy is one way of framing a discussion of the observation and measurement challenges. The seven headings are merely illustrative. There is no suggestion that these categories are the most significant of all possible categories or even all inclusive. Although I have endeavored to make them as distinct from each other as possible, there is some overlap. Seven categories of problems inherent in observing and measuring complex phenomena are.

*   Even the most straightforward rules or definitions require interpretation
*   How and what to measure
*   Unintended projection of those conducting the measurement
*   The phenomenon of interest is never directly measured (the issue of proxy)
*   Recalibrated understanding of measurement instruments (beta change)
*   Awareness of being measured (knowing subjects)
*   The act of measurement inevitably changes the phenomenon being measured

Even the most straightforward rules or definitions require interpretation

Put aside, for the moment, the measurement of leadership, spirituality, or attitudes. What could be more straightforward than the measurement of height? As it turns out, there is controversy in determining which building is the tallest in the world. The determination of height is so sticky that in 1969 the Council on Tall Buildings was established to make judgments about height. The two leading contenders are the Petronas Towers in Kuala Lumpur, Malaysia and the Sears Tower in Chicago, USA. The Sears Tower has 110 stories while the Petronas Towers has 88. The highest occupied floor of the Sears Tower is some 200 feet above that of Petronas. However, Petronas has a 'spire' which raises its crown to 1,483 feet. The roof of the Sears Tower is at 1,450. The Sears Tower has antennas which extend to 1,703 feet. By decree of the Council, though, spires count and antennas don't (Haggerty, 1996). The problem is not so neatly solved at this point. There can be at least several steps of regress as the definitions of 'spire' and 'antenna' are interpreted, their sub-elements defined and interpreted, and so on.

A similar story is charmingly told in the movie *The Englishman Who Went Up a Hill but Came Down a Mountain* starring Hugh Grant. The film tells the story of British cartographer Reginald Anson who in 1917 was charged with surveying the height of Ffynnon Garw, the esteemed 'mountain' in Wales. Unfortunately, for the proud Welsh of the area, Ffynnon Garw measures 984 feet, 16 feet short of a 'mountain' designation and would have to be re-classified as a hill. Horrified by the thought that their 'mountain' will be lost, the locals decide to increase the height of Ffynnon Garw by twenty feet (which they do by delaying Anson's departure while they add dirt to the top). So, not only is height a factor, but so is the timing of the measurement since the height of mountains can apparently change (see the section on "Awareness of being measured" below).

How and what to measure

Before the 1998 season the American major college football teams launched a ranking system known as the Bowl Championship Series (BCS). The BCS was installed to ensure that the best two teams each year would ultimately play each other in a bowl game, resulting in a clear *best* team of the year. It was also supposed to minimize the subjectivity of coaches' or sportswriters' opinions in the rankings. The BCS uses a computer average of information compiled by eight 'experts'. Each expert has a different formula which may include factors such as schedule strength, margin of victory, early-season-results vs. late-season-results, opponents' winning percentage, among others. Ironically, the BCS has generated as much, if not more, controversy than it was intended to resolve. About every two or three seasons, fans have generally agreed that the BCS "didn't get it right."

Perhaps, having more commercial implications than the Bowl games are the 'hits' to web sites. Advertisers are paying for 'eyeballs captured', so measuring web *traffic* is an important activity. The three major internet rating firms are Media Metrix, Nielsen / NetRatings, and PC Data. During one three month period, PC Data reported a 21 percent increase in people visiting About.com. Media Metrix showed traffic remaining the same and Nielsen / NetRatings claimed a 12 percent drop (Cha, 2001). A variety of explanations account for some of the differences. For example, some rating firms don't count users who are younger than eighteen, others count PC users and not Mac users, and still others treat web hits from a work location differently from those made on a home computer. Although some of these differences will be sorted out in time, the *interpretation* issue muddies the water. As I write, I am 'working', but I am at home and it is Saturday. Should a rating firm categorize my web activity in support of this chapter as 'work' or not?

Most people probably do not realize that there are competing philosophies about how statistics on crime, unemployment, head-count, and many other important public policy characteristics are measured. In May 2001, the Federal Bureau of Investigations (FBI) released its year 2000 crime figures which showed no change from 1999. The media generated headlines about the end of the seven-year decline in crime and the need for greater law enforcement strategies. A month later, the Justice Department released its figures showing that crime in general had decreased 10 percent from 1999 to 2000 (Murray, 2001). Why the difference? The FBI tabulates crimes reported to law enforcement agencies. The Justice Department surveys a representative sample of homes and asks them crime-related questions (not including whether the crime was reported). Likewise, some government agencies count the actual employment in the United States while others survey households about the employment, or lack thereof, by those in the household.

Perhaps the greatest source of statistical controversy in the United States is the decennial census. The results of this census determine congressional representation, the flow of federal dollars into social programs, and other important allocation of resources. Federal law requires that each person be counted. Some people assert that the census results in an under-count because it may miss those who are homeless, those who are illegal immigrants, etc. (even though these groups are pursued by census takers). Interestingly, those who assert an under-count can offer what they describe as a fairly precise measure of the under-count (often based on representative sampling).

Unintended projection of those conducting the measurement

What people actually 'see' is to some degree determined by their belief systems. The movie *Contact* based on Carl Sagan's best-selling 1985 novel nicely illustrates the tension between prior belief and observation. Jodie Foster plays Ellie Arroway, once a researcher for the SETI (Search for Extraterrestrial Intelligence) Institute and then a free-lance extraterrestrial intelligence searcher, who has an experience that contradicts her scientific beliefs. The final storyline of the movie is Foster's attempt to rationalize or reconcile her scientific training with her actual experience.

A 'real' version of *Contact* occurred after moon samples were brought back by the Apollo astronauts. Prior to the initial moon landing, scientists had spent decades developing a comprehensive body of theoretical work. Mitroff (1974) interviewed 42 leading scientists of the Apollo space program at four intervals before and during the collection of moon samples. These samples would provide strong evidence in favor of and in opposition to a number of the theories at the time concerning topics such as age of the moon, general geochemical and petrological results, and seismic and magnetic results. In general, in spite of the evidence accumulating to strengthen the evidence for the work of certain scientists, those who became out of favor continued to hold their prior beliefs.

"In the words of a number of the respondents: 'They [referring to the other scientists] just don't change, do they? But then, perhaps if I were honest with myself I'd say I haven't changed much either and again I'm not so sure that it is always bad for science for scientists not to change easily, although it can be extremely dangerous and irritating at times'" (Mitroff, 1974: 167). Consistent with the notion of perspectival observation, Mitroff makes the case that it is important for scientists to have strong emotions and commitment to ideas in order to be most effective. James Falconer's chapter, "Unresolved Issues in Process-Centric Business Analysis: A Cathartic Role for Complexity," (this volume) provides greater detail about how academics, researchers, and practitioners all easily embrace models even though aspects of the modeled phenomenon depart from the model's predictions.

Max Planck (1949) is famous for writing, "a new scientific truth does not triumph by convincing its opponents and making them see the light, but rather because its opponents eventually die, and a new generation grows up that is familiar with it" (pp. 33-34). His assertion is that it is unlikely that unintended projections can be removed by training or evidence. The new 'truth' is accepted when the preponderance of old adherents die.

The phenomenon of interest is never directly measured (the issue of proxy)

As pointed out in "How and what to measure," in the social sciences, we never directly measure the phenomenon of interest. We measure a proxy. The critical issue in every measurement, therefore is, how well the proxy represents the phenomenon of interest. In the past, some proxies provided fairly good estimates. Now, these have broken down. For example, former United States Senator Daniel Patrick Moynihan focused at the end of his career on inaccuracies in the consumer price index (CPI). This index is incredibly important to economic activity. A commission of scholars in the mid 1990s concluded that if the "CPI overstates inflation by one percentage point per year through 2005, this will add almost $140 billion to the deficit that year and $634 billion to the national debt" (Will, 1996). The CPI is an attempt to measure the 'cost of living'. In fact, it measures a fixed 'market basket' of goods updated infrequently. Although there have been improvements since Moynihan's work, the CPI still does not accurately reflect how people live, the value of products with changing features (when CD players become standard in cars, for example), and substitutions (if beef prices skyrocket people buy less).

The proxy issue is important in assessing the effectiveness of teachers. How are great teachers identified? The 1985 and 1986 Florida Teacher of the Year recipients were both denied merit increases under the merit pay program in place at the time. The awards were given because of the teachers' enthusiasm, dedication, involvement with students, and innovation in the classroom. The merit pay formula heavily emphasized factors such as how promptly a teacher begins and ends class, whether the lesson plans are properly designed, whether there are quantifiable learning objectives for each class and so forth. The merit pay program apparently makes the common error of measuring what is easy to measure, which is often a poor proxy for the phenomenon of interest.

Nielsen Media Research is the world's leading company in measuring television viewers. The Nielsen ratings are extremely important, essentially dictating which shows continue to be aired and determining the price of commercial advertisements. Nielsen measures TV viewership in a variety of ways including electronic meters (People Meters) on the sets of 5,000 representative homes requiring viewers to press an 'I'm watching' button, instruments that record to which station the set is tuned in other homes, and diaries kept by viewers of the shows they watched in still other homes. Measuring TV viewing, as with most other social phenomena of interest, has become increasingly more complex and controversial. Years ago, when only diaries were used, the system was very reliable because TV viewing consisted of discrete events. Viewers turned on their sets at an appointed time to view a particular show(s) drawn from a limited set of choices. Journalers were also much more diligent about accurately recording their viewing. Today, even with electronic People Meters, there are several issues that confound accurate measurement. In many homes, the TV(s) is on for extended periods of time even though it is not actually being watched. People are less diligent about record keeping and pressing the 'I'm watching' button. Finally, the development of remote control has created the sport of channel surfing, viewers are using a variety of devices to record a show and (possibly) watch it later, and inventors have created various products so that commercials may be muted or not viewed at all.

Recalibrated understanding of measurement instruments (beta change)

Beta change is a term that reflects a change in the measurement instrument during an inquiry process (Golembiewski & Munzenrider, 1976). In other words, the 'yardstick' for the measurement is not the same when used to take measurements at two different times. Imagine a three-day training course on managing diversity. On Monday morning, the participants, predominately white males, are given a pre-test with questions such as, "in your business dealings, how frequently do you discriminate against women and people of color?" The most frequent responses are "never" and "rarely." Then the participants go through a three-day experience in which their awareness is raised so that they can see their behaviors in ways that they previously could not. When responding to the same question Wednesday evening, the most frequent responses are "rarely" and "occasionally." The conclusion drawn from a classic experimental design would be that the training increased prejudice in the participants. Anyone familiar with these training courses knows that is not what happened. In fact, the shift in awareness meant the yardstick did not measure on Monday what it measured on Wednesday.

Beta change is apparently also a factor in the reporting of crime statistics as discussed in "How and what to measure". In addition to the difference in the data collected by the Justice Department and the FBI, there has been a difference in the percentage of crime reported over time. Hispanic women, for example, reported only 47 percent of the violent crimes against them in 1999, but reported 61 percent in 2000 (Murray, 2001). In the span of one year, reporting rates increased in virtually every demographic category. The beta change that took place was a change in the extent to which people viewed victimization as inherent in their way of life. When people do not believe that the police are effective against crime, they do not report crimes, treating them instead as 'personal problems'. However, when crime rates drop, people believe that the police can do something about what is happening to them. Consequently, they report more crimes. The possibility of beta change exists in nearly all social studies and must be addressed by serious researchers.

Awareness of being measured (knowing subjects)

For several years, Business Week (BW) magazine biannually has been conducting research in order to rank the top business schools in the country. BW takes the 'customer's' point of view and asks students and the companies that hire them to rate their experiences with the business schools. In its 1998 ranking of MBA programs, BW complained that the students had not participated fairly because students at some schools had circulated memos saying "If you have complaints about your program, the BW survey is not the place to air them." Rather than create a research design that accounted for knowing subjects, who have an incentive for their schools to rank highly, BW described the students' behavior as 'cheating'.

In the "How and what to measure" section I discussed measuring web site hits. Another factor in that measurement is the wide range of screen refresh times employed by web page providers. A frequent refresh rate is necessary for changing data such as sports scores or stock prices. Static web pages, however, do not need refreshing. Each refresh is counted as an additional web site hit. Sites such as AltaVista and Lycos have been accused of inflating their web hits by using a refresh rate of only five minutes (Cha, 2001). NetRatings has assigned staff solely to the problem of web site hit manipulation.

A special case of 'knowing subjects' is induced measurement. An effort is made to predict a measurement based on very precise and careful current measurements. However, all things do not remain the same so that the predicted measurement is impacted by the unanticipated actions of agents. Perhaps, the most well-known induced measure is that of traffic. Urban planners can measure fairly accurately the amount of traffic in a given area. They then determine how much traffic a new road could accommodate. However, that factor has to be adjusted because additional traffic is generated by the new road. People who took the subway because it was incrementally better for them now find that driving is better. People who limited trips because of waiting in traffic now take the additional trips. To account for induced traffic, planners often include a 30 percent increase factor.

Making a simple 30 percent adjustment is not always successful, as hydrologists in charge of measuring flood levels of the Red River learned in the spring of 1997. Computer models account for some sandbagging on the part of people threatened by flood. What the modelers didn't realize, though, is that the higher the water level rises, the more people fear damage and loss to their property. Consequently, they will participate in even more sandbagging, which causes the water level to rise higher still. As the modelers began to understand the unprecedented volume of sandbagging that was taking place, they adjusted their initial expected crest level from 49 feet on April 13th to 50 feet on April 14th. However, news that the water height was expected to be even higher caused people to sandbag even more. On April 16th the prediction was changed to 50.5 feet. On April 17th, 52 feet. On April 18th, the final prediction was 53 feet ("Sandbagging," 1997). The crest was actually 54.11 feet. The volume of water was accurately projected on April 13th. The ongoing sandbagging and height of the water was never accurately projected. The induced effect was always underestimated.

The act of measurement inevitably changes the phenomenon being measured

I have never had my blood pressure measured accurately. To be more precise, my blood pressure in the presence of medical professionals is higher, I sense, than it is nearly all of the rest of the time. Essentially, though, the attempt to measure the phenomenon of interest (my blood pressure) changes the phenomenon of interest. The movie *Patch Adams* starring Robin Williams is an example of this dynamic with consequences in the opposite direction. *Patch Adams* is the true story of a physician who has a positive impact on people simply in the way that he intervenes with them. Adams' foil in the movie is his roommate who aces every exam and has the most book knowledge of medicine. He engages in the traditional objective, arms-length relationship with his patients. The roommate (played by Daniel London) has his epiphany when he realizes that although he knows what to prescribe to help a patient, the prescription requires the patient to follow the doctor's instructions, and she won't do so. London's character concedes to Patch Adams's approach while lamenting that although he knows everything that needs to be done for this woman, he cannot get her to eat.

I recently experienced this dynamic in a more (economically) painful way. While purchasing a home, I used an internet service which shopped my potential mortgage among a number of companies. I also engaged in my usual financial activity that has allowed for a consistently high credit score. As it turns out, my car died and I needed to purchase a new car the day after I bought the house. The home mortgage came with a rebate if I also applied for and used a credit card. I applied for the credit card, but was denied. The reason: too many recent credit checks about me. American credit bureau scores are FICO (Fair Isaacs and Company) scores. One element of the score is the number of credit checks in a certain period of time. Consequently, simply checking someone's credit can lower their credit rating. The same phenomenon is true of the CPI discussed above. Some elements in the market basket of goods and services are themselves dependent on the CPI level. So increases in the CPI boosts the cost of those items which increases CPI and the index ratchets inaccurately higher and higher.

A complexity science approach to scholarship with perspectival observation

Complexity theory has opened up a number of new approaches to scholarship for researchers. Two methods will be briefly discussed here.

- discovering patterns in 'footprint' data
- looking for and expecting mutually causal phenomena, employing an interaction model rather than one of cause and effect

Footprints

Ken Wilber has proposed a two-by-two matrix with axes of interior-exterior and individual-collective. It provokes a very comprehensive approach to research that matches the method (and validity assertions) to the type of information sought. For purposes of this section, I will focus on Wilber's upper left quadrant, the interior of the individual. Wilber (2000) claims, "the only way you can know my interior, my depth, is by asking me, by talking to me... And when I report on my inner status, I might be telling you the truth, but I might be lying. You have no other way to get at my interior except in talk and dialogue and interpretation, and I might fundamentally distort, or conceal, or mislead - in short, I might lie" (p. 99).

Complexity theory has suggested that the focus in research should now be on pattern (Bailey, 1996). Wolfram (2002) has written a tome that demonstrates the usefulness of pattern identification as a research method for a variety of phenomena that cannot be understood by other methods. I am suggesting that there is an intriguing opportunity at the intersection of Wilber's interiors and complexity theory's patterns. In Wilber's quote above, he allows for the spoken word to be the research data in the upper left quadrant.

It is unclear, though, at what point an inquiry becomes one of an exterior nature. When does 'I' data become 'it' data? The 'I' language is about depth and meaning. I assert that individuals' interiors can be accessed as well through other methods as they can by talking and that those methods pose less of a threat of misrepresentation. Both methods described below use interpretation and claim to provide understanding about meaning and depth. As equally problematic as misrepresentation, which Wilber focuses on, is the issue of retrospective sense making, in which there is no intended misrepresentation, but simply that human reports do not reflect the relatively spontaneous actions and manifestations of unconscious energy that characterize activity.

Two methods which reflect the interior as good as, or better than, talking, are McClelland's work with *thematic apperception tests* (TAT) and Jaques' work with *coding for human capability*. Speech is only one way in which humans reveal their interiors. They also write, draw, communicate non-verbally, and so forth. In fact, it is harder to 'lie' through body language than it is through speech. The best poker plays are experts at identifying the 'tells' which less capable players exude. The communication sent by the 'tell' is more accurate than the betting words, which may be a bluff. In fact, both McClelland and Jaques have tested to see if respondents can 'fake' their behaviors to produce a higher reading than would otherwise be accurate, and found that people cannot. An analogy would be to a cognitive test. One cannot outguess the test by performing better than she innately would. She can, however, perform worse than her capability. So, McClelland and Jaques (and other methods focused on patterns) seem to have developed methodologies which surface the depth and address the meaning of the 'I' language, with fewer validity threats because they take advantage of the fact that speech is not the only way people reveal their interiors.

McClelland's (1953, 1961) primary focus has been on researching the achievement desires of individuals. Typically he has used TATs in which individuals are shown pictures that are open to wide interpretation, and asked to describe what they see and what the person in the picture is thinking. McClelland and his colleagues then developed a valid and reliable coding method for determining the types of stories respondents would tell that would indicate whether the respondents would likely be high achievers. Of even greater interest is the work in which valid coding has been developed on data sets that do not have to be derived for the research. Studies have correlated doodling and achievement; also, vase designs from archeological findings. If an individual is creating a vase, producing a scholarly article, or arguing a case, without being studied, he has little or no incentive to be anything other than genuine in his behavior.

In his book *Human Capability*, Elliott Jaques suggests a valid, unobtrusive method for determining an individual's complexity of mental process. Jaques and Cason (1994) discovered that individuals use their highest level of mental process whenever they are speaking passionately about a topic. Their method involves having respondents make the case for an issue. They then employ a coding process on the transcript of the argument. Like McClelland, Jaques has been able to generalize this method to other arenas such as developing a valid way of determining the complexity of mental process of an artist. In my own work, I have developed a coding process for surfacing the worldview assumptions of academic and practitioner authors of articles in journals such as *Administrative Quarterly* and *Harvard Business Review* (Dent & Powley, 1999).

Expecting mutually causal phenomena: The interactional model

Complexity theory is being applied to a number of social science questions which contain mutually causal phenomena, those in which variables of interest "evolve and change together in such a way (with feedback and feedforward) as to make the distinction between cause and effect meaningless" (Guba, 1985: 88). If variables cannot be discretely identified as 'independent' and 'dependent', traditional models of causality become inappropriate, and worse, misleading.

An alternative is for complexity theory researchers to use the *interactional model*, shown in Figure 1, to depict the interrelationship among variables (Dent, 2003). This model has interaction as the unit of analysis. Rather than the simplistic formulation of X causes Y, it includes X (the cause), Y (the effect), A (the perpetrator of the cause), and B (in the social sciences, the manifestor(s) of the effect), as well as E (the embeddedness or context of all this) and T (interaction over time).

The example in Figure 1 is of a manager (A) announcing a request to work overtime (X), with the expectation that the employees (B), will be more productive (Y). In the classic experimental design, X and Y are carefully specified. Little or no attention is paid to A, B, E, and T. When A is specified, it is usually in terms of demographic information such as age and gender. What is likely more significant is information about *interiors* (Wilber, 2000). Typically, time factors, such as those of Figure 1 are never specified - did the request come early or late in the work group's formation, has there been an established pattern of such requests, and so forth.

Since the traditional model of causality has been dominant for hundreds of years, the beginning of attempts at alternatives, such as the interactional model are necessarily crude and cumbersome. Complexity theory either needs to develop more elegant models of interrelationship, or be more rigorous in the specification of additional variables so that the coevolution and emergence of social phenomena can be better understood.

A complexity science approach to practice with perspectival observation

Complexity theory has also opened up a number of new approaches to more effective performance for organizational practitioners. Two methods will be briefly discussed here.

- Pursue personal development
- Develop an understanding and appreciation for paradox

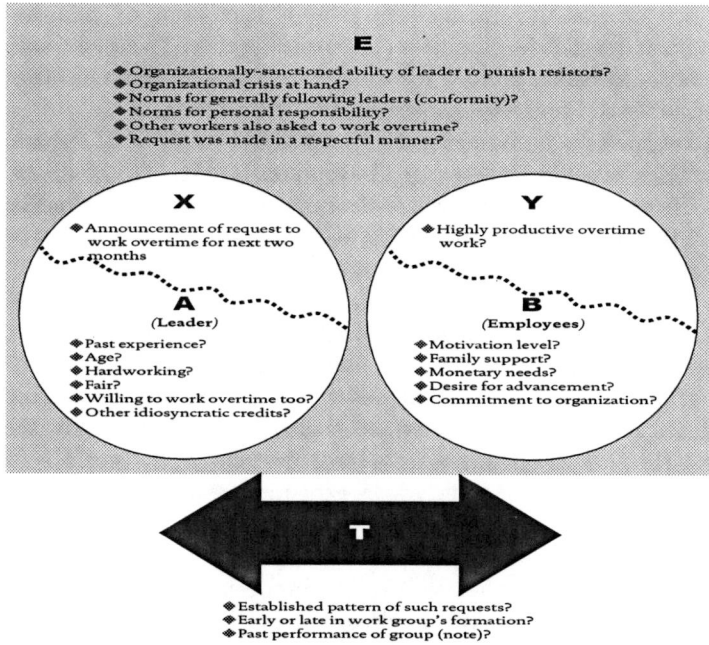

Figure 1
The Interactional Model (adapted from Dent, 2003, 304)

Pursue Personal Development

People in Western society are so steeped in objective observation that perspectival observation feels foreign and wrong. However, although research in adult development is still in its infancy, it seems clear that the ability to take multiple perspectives is consistent with higher levels of adult development. In Veliyath and Sathian's chapter, "Dealing with Complexity in Organizational Control Processes: Drawing Lessons from the Human Brain" (this volume) the authors go into greater detail about positive attributes of the brain such as the ability to take multiple perspectives and plasticity.

Kohlberg and Hersh (2001) have found that one of the most dramatic steps in development is between stage 4 and stage 5. Although as few as nine percent of the American population may achieve this step, it results in a radical widening of perspective. Once someone has achieved this broader frame of reference, she cannot 'lose' it. The world has been permanently changed. Consequently, if someone can hasten his or her own development, she is likely to increase personal effectiveness.

Research in adult development has not reached the point of offering definitive guidance about how individuals can trigger their own advancement. It seems clear that movement occurs once someone's worldview has been shattered or comes up lacking in a life challenge. However, "society and its institutions provides little incentive for people" to go beyond the Conventional (stages 3 and 4) level of development (Thompson, 2000). I have employed some techniques in consulting which have resulted in participants reaching the "ah ha" experience and possibly increasing their perspective.

I call the primary method I use the 'O. J. activity', after O. J. Simpson. I was too busy with other matters to pay attention to the trial of football and movie star O. J. Simpson who was alleged to have murdered his wife. Whether or not he was guilty was a major topic of discussion in 1995-97 as criminal and civil trials were held. I had friends and colleagues whom I admired and thought were brilliant who believed Simpson was innocent. I also had friends and colleagues whom I admired and thought were brilliant who believed Simpson was guilty. Consequently, I became interested in how this difference could be explained. In asking people why they held their belief, I discovered their conclusions were based on quite different assumptions such as the trustworthiness of police, the fairness of the judicial system, whether wealthy people can 'buy' their way out of trouble, whether a man could murder the mother of his children, the rigor and interpretation of DNA and other lab tests, and so forth.

In organizations, I divide a group of people into those who believe he is innocent and those who believe he is guilty. The 'innocent' group then must identify what assumptions a person must hold in order for them to rationally and reasonably believe Simpson to be guilty. The 'guilty' group works conversely. I use this activity on whatever topic is timely such as a 30 percent tuition increase in a university setting, whether Bill Clinton should have been impeached, whether George W. Bush was rightfully elected in 2000, and so forth. Participants report that this exercise forced them to challenge their own assumptions, and to be more facile in understanding a variety of perspectives.

Develop an understanding and appreciation for paradox

An important partner of objective observation is the universal applicability of logic. Complexity theory work, however, has suggested that paradox may provide greater explanation than logic in an increasing number of situations. Paradoxes should not be seen as implausible. Rather, they "create a tension from which creative solutions emerge" (Regine & Lewin, 2000: 19). Some see the concept of paradox as so important that they now define leadership as essentially the management of paradoxes (Lewin & Regine, 2000; Farson, 1996). Peck (1987) asserts that "if a concept is paradoxical, that itself should suggest that it smacks of integrity, that it gives off the ring of truth. Conversely, if a concept is not in the least paradoxical, you should be suspicious of it and suspect that it has failed to integrate some aspect of the whole" (p. 238).

Handy (1994) has identified nine principal paradoxes he feels are critical for anyone wanting to understand societies or organizations. These range from the *Paradox of Intelligence* to the *Paradox of the Individual.* Farson (1996) identifies as most significant an understanding of the paradoxes of human relations, communication, the politics of management, organizational predicaments, change, and leadership. In the paradox of human relations, for example, research suggests that once a manager finds a technique that works, he must abandon it in order to maintain effectiveness.

Stewart and Cohen (1997) offer the novel *Empire Star* by science fiction writer Samuel R. Delany as an example of the importance of thinking *multiplexually* (which is similar to the *critical pluralism* discussed in Chapter 2). In this book, the multiplex mind is one that can simultaneously accept multiple sides of a paradox. "It sees not just one interpretation of reality, but many, yet it sees them as a seamless whole. Such a mind is untroubled by mere inconsistency; it is comfortable with a mutable, adaptive, loosely coherent flux" (p. 289).

Effectiveness in a Perspectival World

My conclusion is the same as Delany's - the universe is better understood through the multiple lenses of paradox and perspective. Facility with these lenses will greatly increase the effectiveness of individuals in- and outside of work. The science of inquiry needs to develop in different directions. Mihnea Moldoveanu, in his chapter "An Intersubjective Measure of Organizational Complexity Grounds: A New Approach" (this volume) describes a promising avenue of exploration. An ideal measure is a predictively competent, intersubjectively agreeable algorithmic representation (or computational simulation) of the phenomenon. This measure captures both subjective and objective concerns about the definition of a complexity measure.

Jerry Harvey has described the work of the National Training Laboratory (NTL) in the late 1950s and early 1960s as the "Manhattan Project" of group dynamics (Dent, 2002). Conditions are ripe for the emergence of an effort that would be the equivalent of the Manhattan Project in the areas of perspectival observation, emergence, coherence, paradox, and interrelatedness.

References

Bailey, J. (1996). *After Thought,* New York: BasicBooks.

Cha, A. E. (2001, February 4). "Counting Web Traffic; Which Internet Sites Have the Most Visitors? It Depends on Whom You Ask," *The Washington Post,* H01.

Dent, E. B. (1999). "Complexity Science: A Worldview Shift," *Emergence: A Journal of Complexity Issues in Organizations and Management,* 1 (4): 5-19.

Dent, E. B. (2002) "The Messy History of OB&D: How Three Strands Came to be Seen as One Rope," *Management Decision,* 40(3): 266-280.

Dent, E. B. (2003). "The Interactional Model: An Alternative to the Direct Cause and Effect Construct for Mutually Causal Organizational Phenomena," *Foundations of Science,* 8(3): 295-314.

Dent, E. B. and Powley, E. (1999). "Administrative Sciences Quarterly: Canary of Worldview Shift?" in A. M. Castell, A. J. Gregory, G. A. Hindle, M. E. James, and G. Ragsdell (eds.), *Synergy matters: Working with Systems in the 21st Century,* Norwell, MA: Kluwer Academic Publishers.

Farson, R. (1996). *Management of the Absurd: Paradoxes in Leadership,* New York:

Simon and Schuster.

Golembiewski, R. & Munzenrider, R. (1976). "Measuring Change by OD designs," *Journal of Applied Behavioral Science*, 12 (April-June): 133-157.

Guba, E. G. (1985). "The Context of Emergent Paradigm Research," in Y. S. Lincoln (ed.) *Organizational Theory and Inquiry*, Beverly Hills: Sage Publications.

Haggerty, M. (1996, April 16). "The Heights of Pride," *The Washington Post*, D1.

Handy, C. (1994). *The Age of Paradox*, Boston: Harvard Business School Press.

Jaques, E. and Cason, K. (1994). *Human Capability: A Study of Individual Potential and its Application*, Arlington, VA: Cason Hall & Co.

Kohlberg, L. and Hersh, R. (2001). "Moral Development: A Review of Theory," *Theory in Practice*, 16(2): 53-.

Lewin, R. and Regine, B. (2000). *The Soul at Work: Listen... Respond... Let Go: Embracing Complexity Science for Business Success*, New York: Simon and Schuster.

McClelland, D. C. (1961). *The Achieving Society*, New York: The Free Press.

McClelland, D. C., Atkinson, J. W., Clark, R. A. and Lowell, E. L. (1953). *The Achievement Motive*, New York: Irvington Publishers, Inc.

Mitroff, I. I. (1974). *The Subjective Side of Science: A Philosophical Inquiry into the Psychology of the Apollo Moon Scientists*, Amsterdam : Elsevier.

Murray, I. (2001, July 15). "Good News! More People are Reporting Crimes," *The Washington Post*, B03.

Peck, M. S. (1987). *The Different Drum: Community-Making and Peace*, New York: Touchstone.

Planck, M. (1949). *Scientific Autobiography and Other Papers*, trans. by Frank Gaynor. New York: Philosophical Library

Regine, B. and Lewin, R. (2000). "Leading at the Edge: How Leaders Influence Complex Systems," *Emergence: A Journal of Complexity Issues in Organizations and Management*, 2 (2): 5-23.

Sandbagging Skewed Computer Flood Model. (1997, April 27). *The Washington Post*.

Schwartz, P. and Ogilvy, J. (1979). *The Emergent Paradigm: Changing Patterns of Thought and Belief*, Menlo Park, CA: SRI International.

Stewart, I. and Cohen, J. (1997). *Figments of Reality: The Evolution of the Curious Mind*, Cambridge: Cambridge University Press.

Thompson, M. C. (2000). *The Congruent Life: Following the Inward Path to Fulfilling Work and Inspired Leadership*, San Francisco: Jossey-Bass.

Wilber, K. (2000). *A Brief History of Everything*, 2nd edition, Boston: Shambhala.

Will, G. (1996, September 30). "Inflation Inflated," *Newsweek*, 92.

Wolfram, S. (2002). *A New Kind of Science*, Champaign, IL : Wolfram Media

CHAPTER 16

AN INTERSUBJECTIVE MEASURE OF ORGANIZATIONAL COMPLEXITY: A NEW APPROACH

Mihnea Moldoveanu

This chapter attempts to accomplish the following goals:

a. *formulate and elaborate the epistemological problem of studying organizational complexity qua phenomenon and of using "organizational complexity" qua analytical concept in the study of other organizational phenomena;*
b. *propose and defend a solution to this epistemological problem by introducing a definition of complexity that: 1. introduces the dependence of 'complexity of an object' on the model of the object used, without either; 2. falling into a fully subjective and relative view of complexity or; 3. falling into a falsely subject-independent view thereof and thus; 5. making precise the subjective and objective 'contributions' to the definition of complexity to the end of; 5. making 'complexity' tout court a useful analytical construct or hermeneutic device for understanding organizational phenomena;*
c. *show how the new view of complexity can be usefully applied in conjunction with classical, well-established models of organizations to understand the organizational phenomena that are paradigmatic for the research tradition of each of those models;*
d. *derive the implications of the new view of organizational complexity for the way we study and intervene in organizational life-worlds.*

Managing Organizational Complexity: Philosophy, Theory, and Application
A Volume in: Managing the Complex, pages 269-299.
ISBN: 1-59311-319-6 (cloth), 1-59311-318-8 (paper)

"The study of organizational complexity faces a difficult epistemological problem"

O*rganizational complexity* has become a subject of study in organizational research (see, for example, Anderson, 1999). Researching 'organizational complexity' requires one to confront and ultimately resolve, dissolve or capitulate to the difficulties of defining the property of complexity of an organizational phenomenon and (often) defining and defending a complexity measure for organizational phenomena, which allows one to declare one phenomenon more complex than another. This minimal conceptual equipment is necessary in view of the age-old concern of scientifically minded researchers to turn qualitative impressions into quantitative measures and representations, but faces a serious epistemological problem that is connected to the basic ontology of proposed 'complexity metrics' and 'complexity spaces'. Here is an exposition of that problem, in brief.

Outline of the epistemological problem of talking about 'complexity' and using the term 'complexity'

As with all measures that can be used as research tools, we would like our measures of complexity to be intersubjectively valid: two observers A and B ought, through communication and interaction, to come to an agreement about 'the complexity of object X', in the same way that the same two observers, using a yard stick, can come to an agreement about the 'length of this football field'. The epistemological problem I would like to draw attention to is that of achieving such an intersubjectively valid measure. Of course, questions such as 'how would we know a complex phenomenon if we saw it?' and 'how can complexity of different phenomena be compared?' would also be resolved by a solution to the core epistemological problem.

Various definitions of 'complexity' in the literature can be understood as purposeful attempts to come to grips with the problem I have outlined above. Thus, consider:

Complexity as structural intricacy:
The 'strong' objective view of complexity

The outcome of an era of greater 'self-evidence' in matters epistemological, the structuralist view of complexity is echoed (as we shall see, with a twist) in organizational research in Simon's (1962) early work and in Thompson's (1967) seminal work on organizational dynamics. It is not dissimilar from structuralist analyses of physical and biological structure and function (D'Arcy Thompson, 1934; von Berthalanffy, 1968). It is based on a simple idea: complex systems are structurally intricate. Structural intricacy can best be described by reference to a system that has (a) many parts that are (b) multiply interconnected. In the years since Edward Lorenz's discovery in 1963 of chaotic behavior in simple dynamical systems, we have come to know both: that there exist simple (by the structuralist definition) systems that nevertheless compel us to classify them as complex (such as chaotic systems) ,and complex systems (by the structuralist definition) that behave in ways that are more characteristic of simple systems (large modular arrays of transistors, for instance). A finer set of distinctions was called for, and many of these distinctions can be perceived from a more careful study of Simon's work.

Simon (1962) did not leave the view of complex systems at this: he postulated that complex systems are made up of *multiply-interacting multitudes of components* in such a way as to make predictions of the overall behavior of the system starting from knowledge of the behavior of the individual components and their interaction laws or mechanisms. Unwittingly (to many of his structuralist followers), he had introduced the predicament of the observer, the predictor, the modeler, the forecaster, perhaps the actor him / herself into the notion of complexity of a phenomenon. But this slight sleight of hand remained unnoticed, perhaps in part due to Simon's own emphasis on the structural component of a definition of complexity in the remainder of his (1962) paper. The (large, and growing) literature in organization science that seeks to understand complexity in structuralist terms (as numbers of problem, decision, strategic or control variables and number of links among these variables, or number of value-linked activity sets and number of links among these activity sets - Levinthal & Warglien, 1999; McKelvey, 1999) attests to the fruitfulness of the structuralist definition of complexity (NK(C) models of organizational phenomena can be deployed as explanation-generating engines for product development modularization, firm-level and group-level strategic decision processes, the evolutionary dynamics of firms, products and technologies, and many other scenarios), but does not fully own up to the cost that the modeler has to make in the generalizability of his or her results.

These costs can be understood easily enough if one is sufficiently sensitive to: (a) the relativity of ontology, and; (b) the effects of ontology on model structure. There is no fact about the identity and the number of interacting components that we may use in order to conceptualize an organizational phenomenon. (Alternatively, we may think of the problem of establishing an ontology as self-evident as an undecidable problem.) We may think of organizations as interacting networks of people, behaviors, routines, strategies, epistemologies, emotional states, cultural traditions, and so forth. Moreover, we may expect that within the same organizational phenomenon, multiple such individuations may arise, interact with one another and disappear. This leaves in doubt both the essence of the modules or entities that make up the part-structure of the organizational whole, and the law-like-ness of the connections between these entities. Surely, phenomena characterized by shifting ontologies, changing rule sets and interactions between co-existing, incommensurable ontologies exist (consider cultural transitions in post-communist societies) and are complex, but are not easily captured in NK(C) models or other models based on networks on simple modules interacting according to locally simple rules. Thus, in spite of the very illuminating analysis of some complex macro-structures as nothing but collections of simple structures interacting according to simple local rules, the structuralist analysis of complexity imposes a cost on the modeler because of an insufficient engagement with the difficult epistemological problem of complexity.

Complexity as difficulty: The subjective view

Running parallel to the structuralist approach to the definition of complexity is a view that considers the complexity of a phenomenon to be related to the difficulty of making competent, valid or accurate predictions about that particular phenomenon. This view was certainly foreshadowed in Simon's (1962) work, when he stipulated that structurally complex systems are complex in virtue of the fact that predicting their evolution is computationally nontrivial. Of course, he did not consider the possibility that structurally simple systems can also give rise to unpredictable behavior, as is the case with chaotic systems (Bar-Yam, 2000). A system exhibiting chaotic behavior may be 'simple' from a structuralist standpoint (a double pendulum is an example of such a system), but an infinitely accurate representation of its initial conditions is required for an arbitrarily accurate prediction of its long-time evolution: phase space trajectories in such a system diverge at an exponential rate from one another (Bar-Yam, 2000). Thus, Simon's early definition of complexity needs to be amended so as to uncouple structural intricacy from the difficulty of making predictions about the evolution of a system.

This difficulty - of predicting the evolution of complex systems - may not be purely informational (i.e., may not merely require a theoretically infinite amount of information about initial or boundary conditions). Thus, Rivkin (2000) shows that the problem of predicting the evolution of Boolean networks made up of simple nodes coupled by simple causal laws (NK(C) networks) is computationally intractable when the average number of connections per node in the system increases past a (low) threshold value. And, simple paradoxes in second-order logic highlight the fact that undecidability can arise even in logical systems with a very small number of axioms (e.g., deciding on the truth value of "I am telling a lie").

The subjective difficulty of predicting the evolution of a complex phenomenon thus seems to be connected to structural complexity in ways that are significantly more subtle and complicated than was pre-figured in Simon's early model. This situation has led some to treat complexity as a purely subjective phenomenon, related to predictive or representational difficulty alone (Li and Vitanyi, 1993). This has made 'complex phenomena' natural candidates for study using paradigms for the study of judgment and decision making under uncertainty.

This tendency is easy enough to understand: an uninformed, computationally weak observer will find interaction with a complex phenomenon to be a predicament fraught with uncertainty and ambiguity (as he or she will not be able to predict its evolution). What matters then is not whether or not a phenomenon is complex in some objectively or intersubjectively valid way, but rather whether or not it is difficult for the observer that must interact with this phenomenon, to make competent predictions about it, and how such an observer makes his or her predictions. Thus, the very large literature on cognitive *biases* and *fallacies* human reasoning under uncertainty and ambiguity (Kahneman, *et al.*, 1982), or of heuristic reasoning in foggy predicaments can be understood as a branch of the study of complexity, as it studies the ways in which people deal with a core characteristic of complex phenomena, namely, the predictive fog with which they confront human intervenors and observers.

This state of epistemological affairs will hardly be satisfying to those who want to study essential characteristics of complex phenomena - characteristics that are invariant across observational frames, cognitive schemata and computational endowments of the observers of these phenomena. Such researchers will want to cut through the wealth of complexity-coping strategies that humans have developed over the millennia to the core of what it means for a phenomenon to be complex, and to investigate complexity per se, rather than complexity relative to the way of being-in-the-world of the observer. Such an ambition is not, on the face of it, ridiculous or misguided as many useful strategies for dealing with complex systems can be discerned from the study of prototypical, simplified, 'toy' models of complexity. For instance, the study of chaotic systems has given rise to approaches to the harnessing of chaos for the generation of secure communications systems that use chaotic waveforms to mask the secret data that one would like to convey across a wire-tapped channel; and the study of computationally complex algorithms (Cormen, *et al.*, 1993) has given rise to strategies for distinguishing among computationally tractable and intractable problems, and finding useful tractable approximations to intractable problems (Moldoveanu & Bauer, 2004).

Nevertheless, purely structural efforts to capture the essence of complexity via caricaturized models have failed to achieve the frame-invariant characterization of complexity that some researchers have hoped for. Structurally intricate systems can exhibit simple-to-predict behavior, depending on the interpretive frame and computational prowess of the observer. Difficult-to-predict phenomena can be generated by structurally trivial systems. All combinations of structural intricacy and predictive difficulty seem possible, and there is no clear mechanism for assigning complexity measures to phenomena on the basis of their structural or topological characteristics. An approach that combines the felicitous elements and insights of both the objective and subjective approaches is called for. I will now attempt to provide such a synthetic view of complex phenomena.

"The fundamental problem of complexity studies can be dissolved if we look carefully into the eye of the beholder" The phenomenon never speaks for itself by itself

A solution to the epistemological problem of speaking about 'the complexity of a phenomenon' is provided by looking carefully at the eye of the beholder. It is, itself, a 'difficult-to-understand' entity, because it is intimately coupled to the cognitive schemata, models, theories and proto-concepts that the beholder brings to his or her understanding of a phenomenon. It is through the interaction of this 'eye' and the phenomenon 'in itself' that 'what is' is synthesized. In Hilary Putnam's words (1981), "the mind and world together make up the mind and the world." Thus, whatever solution to the epistemological problem of complexity is proposed, it will have to heed the irreducibly subjective aspect of perception, conceptualization, representation and modeling. But there is also an irreducibly 'objective' component to the solution as well: schemata, models and theories that are 'in the eye of the beholder' cannot, by themselves, be the foundation of a complexity measure that satisfies minimal concerns about intersubjective agreement because such cognitive entities are constantly under the check and censure of 'the world', which provides opportunities for validation and refutation. This suggests that a fruitful way to synthesize the subjective and objective viewpoints on complexity of a phenomenon is to measure the complexity of intersubjectively agreed-upon or 'in-principle' intersubjectively testable models, representations and simulations of that phenomenon.

This presents us with a problem that is well-known to epistemologists, at least since the writings of Kuhn (1962). It is the problem of coming up with a language (for referring to the complexity of a model or theory) that is itself outside of the universe of discourse of any one model, theory or representation. Kuhn pointed to the impossibility of a *theory-free observation language*, a language that provides observation statements that are not sullied by theoretical language. Putnam (1981) pointed to the impossibility of a *theory-free meta-language*, a language that contains statements about other possible languages without itself being beholden to any of those languages. Both, however, remained in the realm of language as it is understood in everyday parlance, or in the formal parlance of the scientist. To provide a *maximally model-free conceptualization of complexity*, I will instead concentrate on 'language' as an algorithmic entity, a program that runs on a universal computational device, such as a Universal Turing Machine (UTM). Admittedly, UTM's do not exist in practice, but the complexity measure I put forth can be particularized to specific instantiations of a Turing Machine. (The costs for doing so, while not trivial, are not prohibitive of our effort).

If we allow this construction of a language in which a complexity measure can be provided, the following way of conceptualizing the complexity of a phenomenon suggests itself: *the complexity of a phenomenon is the complex-*

ity of the most predictively competent, intersubjectively agreeable algorithmic representation (or computational simulation) of that phenomenon. This measure captures both subjective and objective concerns about the definition of a complexity measure. It is, centrally, about predictive difficulty. But it is also about intersubjective agreement, about both the semantic and syntactic elements of the model used, about the purpose, scope, scale and accuracy required of the predictions, and therefore about the resulting complexity measure. Thus, the complexity of a phenomenon is relative to the models and schemata used to represent and simulate that phenomenon. It is 'subjective'. But, once we have intersubjective agreement on ontology, validation procedure and predictive purpose, the complexity measure of the phenomenon being modeled, represented or simulated is intersubjective (the modern word for 'objective').

We now have to show how 'difficulty' can be measured, in a way that is itself free of the subjective taint of models and schemata that are used to represent a phenomenon. To do so, I break up 'difficulty' into two components. The first - *informational complexity*, or *informational depth* (Moldoveanu & Bauer, 2004) - relates to the minimum amount of information required to competently simulate or represent a phenomenon on a universal computational device. It is the working memory requirement for the task of simulating that phenomenon. The second - *computational complexity*, or *computational load* (Moldoveanu & Bauer, 2004) - relates to the relationship between the number of input variables and the number of operations that are required by a competent representation of that phenomenon. A phenomenon is 'difficult-to-understand' (or, to predict): if its most predictively competent, intersubjectively agreeable model requires an amount of information that is at or above the working memory endowments of the modeler or observer; if the computational requirements of generating predictions about such a phenomenon are at or above the computational endowments of the modeler or observer, or both together. To make progress on this definition of complexity and, especially, on its application to the understanding of the complexity of organizational phenomena of interest, we need to delve deeper into the nature of computational load and informational depth.

The informationally irreducible: What informational depth is and is not

The view of informational depth presented here does not differ from that used in the theory of algorithms and computational complexity theory (Chaitin, 1974). The *informational depth* of a digital object (an image, a representation, a model, a theory) is the minimum number of elementary symbols required in order to generate that object using a general purpose computational device (Chaitin, 1974). Without loss of generality, we shall stipulate that these symbols should be binary (ones and zeros), knowing than any M-ary alphabet can be reformulated in terms of a binary alphabet. Of course, it matters to the precise measure of informational depth which computational device one uses for representational purposes, and, for this reason, we stipulate that such a device be a Universal Turing Machine (UTM). I do this in order to achieve maximum generality for the measure that I am proposing, but at the cost of using a physically unrealizable device. We achieve maximum generality because a UTM can simulate any other computational device, and therefore can provide a complexity measure for any simulable digital object. If that object is simulable on some computational device, then it will also be simulable on a UTM.

Admittedly, the cost of using an abstract notion of a computational device (rather than a physically instantiable version of one) may be seen as high by some who are minded to apply measures in order to measure that which (in reality) can be measured, rather than in order to produce qualitative complexity classes of phenomena. In response, we can choose to relax this restriction on the definition of 'the right' computational device for measuring complexity, and opt to talk about a particular Turing machine (or other computational device, such as a Pentium or PowerPC processor, powering IBM and MAC clone machines). This move has immediate consequences in terms of the resulting definition of informational depth (a digital object may take fewer symbols if it is stored in the memory of a Pentium processor than if it is stored in the memory of a PowerPC processor), but this is not an overpowering argument against the generality of the measure of informational depth I am putting forth. It simply imposes a further restriction on the computational device that is considered to be 'the standard' for the purpose of establishing a particular complexity measure. To achieve reliability of their complexity measures, two researchers must agree on the computational platform that they are using to measure complexity, not just on the model of the phenomenon whose complexity they are trying to measure, and on the boundary conditions of this model (the class of observation statements that are to be considered legitimate verifiers or falsifiers of their model).

What is critically important about the informational depth of a digital object is its irreducibility: it is the minimum length (in bits) of a representation that can be used to generate a digital object given a computational device, not the length of any representation of that object on a particular computational device. Informational depth is irreducible, as it refers to a representation that is informationally *incompressible*. The sentence (1) 'the quick brown fox jumped over the lazy dog' can be compressed into the sentence (2) 'th qck brn fx jmpd ovr lzy dg' without information loss (what is lost is the convenience of quick decoding) or even to (3) 't qk br fx jd or lz dg', but information is irretrievably lost if we adopt (4) 't q b fx jd or lz dg' as shorthand for it. Correct decoding gets increasingly difficult as we go from (1) to (2) to (3), and suddenly impossible as we go from (3) to (4). We may say, roughly, that (3) is an irreducible representation of (1), and therefore that the informational depth of (1) is the number of symbols contained in (3). (Note that it is not a computationally easy task to establish informational irreducibility by trial and error. In order to show, for instance, that (3) is minimal with regards to the 'true meaning' of (1) (given reliable knowledge of the decoder, which is the reader as s/he knows her / himself), one has to delete each symbol in (3) and examine the decodability of the resulting representation. The computational load of the verification of informational minimality of a particular representation increases nonlinearly with the informational depth of that representation.)

Informational irreducibility and the commonality of a platform for representation together are necessary conditions for the objectification of informational depth as a complexity measure. The first guides the observer's attention and effort towards the attainment of a global informational minimum in the representation of the effort. The latter stipulates that observers use a common benchmark for establishing informational depth. The informational depth of a phenomenon, the informational component of its complexity measure, can now be defined as the *minimum number of bits that an intersubjectively agreeable, predictively competent simulation of that phenomenon takes up in the memory of an intersubjectively agreeable computational platform*. All the platform now needs to do is to perform a number of internal operations (to 'compute') in order to produce a simulation of the phenomenon in question. This takes us to the second component of our complexity measure:

The computationally irreducible: What computation is and is not

As above, we will consider to have fixed (a) our model of a phenomenon, (b) the boundary conditions for verification or refutation of the model and (c) the computational device that we are working with. We are interested in getting a measure of the computational difficulty (i.e., computational load) of generating predictions or a simulation of that phenomenon using the computational device we have used to store our representation of it. If, for example, the phenomenon is the market interaction of oligopolistic firms in a product or services market and the agreed-upon model is a competitive theoretic one, then the representation (the informational component) of the phenomenon will take the form of a set of players, strategies, payoffs and mutual conjectures about rationality, strategies and payoffs, and the computational component will comprise the iterated elimination of dominated strategies required to derive the final market equilibrium. The most obvious thing to do to derive a complexity measure is to count the operations that the computational device requires in order to converge to the required answer. Two problems immediately arise:

P1. The resulting number of operations increases with the number of data points or input variables even for what is essentially 'the same' phenomenon. Adding players, strategies or conjectures to the example of game-theoretic reasoning above, for instance, does not essentially change the fact of the matter, which is that we are dealing with a competitive game. We would surely prefer a complexity measure that reflects the qualitative difference between solving for the Nash equilibrium and solving (for instance) for the eigen-values of a matrix (as would be the case in a linear optimization problem);

P2. Many algorithms are iterative (such as that for computing the square root of N) and can be used *ad infinitum*, recursively, to generate successively sharper, more accurate approximations to 'the answer'. Thus, their computational load is in theory infinite, but we know better: they are required to stop when achieving a certain level of tolerance (a certain distance from the 'right answer', whose dependence on the number of iterations can be derived analytically, on *a priori* grounds).

Both (P1) and (P2) seem to throw our way of reasoning about computational difficulty back into the realm of arbitrariness and subjectivity, through the resulting dependence on the precise details of the problem statement (P1) and the level of tolerance that the user requires (P2). To rectify these problems, we will require two modifications to our measure of computational load:

M1. I shall define computational load relative to the number of input variables to the algorithm that solves the problem of simulating a phenomenon. This is a standard move in the theory of computation (see, for instance, Cormen, *et al.*, 1993);

M2. I shall fix (or require any two observers to agree upon) the tolerance with which predictions are to be generated. This move results in defining computational load relative to a particular tolerance in the predictions that the model or representation generates.

Qualitative complexity classes: The simple, fathomable, unfathomable, tractable, intractable, complex, complicated and impossible defined

We are now in a position to give some objective (i.e., intersubjectively agreeable) content to various subjectively suggestive or evocative ways of describing complex phenomena. I will show that common sense approaches to the description of complex phenomena are rather sharp when it comes to making distinctions among different informational and computational complexity differences.

Distinctions in informational space: Fathomable and unfathomable phenomena

A laboratory experiment studying the results of a two-player competitive bidding situation is a fathomable phenomenon, if we stick to some basic assumptions that the subjects will follow basic rules of cooperative behavior relative to the experimenter, and of incentive-driven behavior relative to one another. We can create a representation of the situation that is workable: storable in a reasonably-sized computational device. The same experiment, when conceived as an open-ended situation in which the turmoils and torments of each of the subjects matters to the outcome, along with minute differences in their environmental conditions, upbringing or neuropsychological characteristics, becomes unfathomable: its representation exceeds not only that of an average observer, but also can easily overwhelm the working memory of even very large computational devices. Unfathomability can also result from too little information, as makers of movies in the 'thriller' genre have discovered. A sliced-off human ear sitting on a lawn on a peaceful summer day (as in *Blue Velvet*) is unfathomable in the sense that too little context-fixing information is given for one to adduce a plausible explanation of what happened (or, a plausible reconstructive simulation of the events that resulted in this state of affairs). Thus, (1) 'the quick brown fox jumped over the lazy dog' is fathomable from (2) 'th qck brn fx jmpd ovr lzy dg' or even from (3) 't qk br fx jd or lz dg', but not from (4) 't q b fx jd or lz dg'. Compression below the informational depth of an object can also lead to unfathomability, in the same way in which informational overload can.

Distinctions in computational space: Tractable, intractable and impossible

Along the computational dimension of complexity, we can distinguish between three different classes of difficulty. *Tractable* phenomena are those whose simulation (starting from a valid model) is computationally simple. We can predict rather easily the impact velocity of a coin released through the air from a known height, to an acceptable level of accuracy, even if we ignore air resistance and starting from the constitutive equations for kinetic and potential energy. Similarly, we can efficiently predict the strategic choices of a firm if we know the subjective probabilities and values attached to various outcomes by its strategic decision makers, and we start from a rational choice model of their behavior. It is, on the other hand, much computationally harder to predict with tolerable accuracy the direction and velocity of the flow of a tidal wave run aground (starting from an initial space-time distribution of momentum (the product of mass and velocity), knowledge of the Navier-Stokes equations and a profile of the shore). It is, similarly, computationally difficult to predict the strategic choices of an organization whose output and pricing choices beget rationally targeted reaction functions from its competitors, starting from a competitive game model of interactive decision making and knowledge of the demand curve in their market.

Computation theorists (see, for example, Cormen, *et al.*, 1993) distinguish between computationally easy (tractable) and difficult (intractable) problems by examining the dependence between the number of independent variables to the problem and the number of operations required to solve the problem. They call tractable those problems requiring a number of operations that is at most a polynomial function of the number of independent or input variables (*P-hard problems*) and intractable those problems requiring a number of operations that is a higher-than-any-polynomial function of the number of independent or input variables (*NP-hard problems*). This demarcation point provides a qualitative marker for computation-induced complexity: we might expect, as scholars of organizational phenomena, different organizational behaviors in response to interaction with P and NP-complex phenomena, as has indeed been pointed out (Moldoveanu & Bauer, 2003b).

Of course, not all problems are soluble, and not all phenomena are simulable or representable on a finite state computational device. Impossible phenomena are precisely those that cannot be so simulated, or, more precisely, whose simulation gives rise to a provably impossible problem. The problem of deciding whether or not 'I am telling a lie' is true or false, for instance, is provably impossible to solve; so is the problem of predicting, to an arbitrary accuracy and at an arbitrarily distant point in time, the position and velocity of the endpoint of a double pendulum described by a second order nonlinear equation exhibiting chaotic behavior, and starting from a finite-precision characterization of the initial conditions (displacement, velocity) of the different components of the pendulum.

Distinctions based on interactions between the informational and computational spaces: Simple, complicated and complex

I have, thus far, introduced qualitative distinctions among different kinds of complex phenomena, which I have based on natural or intuitive quantizations of the informational and computational components of complexity. Now, I shall introduce qualitative distinctions in complexity regimes that arise from interactions of the informational and computational dimensions of complexity. I intuitively call complicated those phenomena whose representations are informationally shallow (or, simple) but computationally difficult (but not impossible). The Great Wall of China or the Egyptian pyramids, for instance, are made up of simple building blocks (stone slabs) that are disposed in intricate patterns. One way in which we can understand what it is to understand these structures is to imagine the task of having to reconstruct them using virtual stone slabs in the memory of a large digital device, and to examine the difficulties of this process of reconstruction. In both cases, simple elementary building blocks (slabs and simple patterns of slabs) are iteratively concatenated and fit together to create the larger whole. The process can be represented easily enough by a skilled programmer by a series of nested loops that all iterate on combinations of the elementary patterns. Thus, the digital program that reconstructs the Great Wall of China or the Pyramids of Egypt in the memory of a digital computer does not take up a large amount of memory (and certainly far less memory than a straightforward listing of all of the features in these structures as they appear to the observer), but are computationally very intensive (the nested loops, while running, perform a great number of operations). In the organizational realm, complicated phenomena may be found to abound in highly routinized environments (such as assembly and production lines) where the overall plans are informationally highly compressed but drive a high computational load.

I propose calling complex those phenomena and structures whose *representations are informationally deep but computationally light.* Consider an anthill exhibiting no correlations among the various observable features that characterize it. Using the method of the previous example, consider the process of reconstructing the anthill in the memory of a digital device. In the absence of correlations that can be exploited to reduce the information required to represent the anthill, the only way to achieve an accurate representation thereof is to store it as a three-dimensional image (a hologram, for instance). The process of representing it is computationally simple enough (it just consists of listing each voxel - three-dimensional 'pixels'), but informationally it is quite involved, as it entails storing the entire structure. Complex phenomena in the organizational realm may be found wherever intelligibility of overall behavioral patterns is only very slight, as it is in securities trading and complex negotiations within and between executive teams.

By analogy, I propose calling simple those phenomena whose representations are computationally light and informationally shallow. These phenomena (such as frictionless pulleys and springs and point masses sliding down frictionless incline planes in physics, choice and learning phenomena in low stakes environments in economics and psychology, mimetic transfer of knowledge and routines in sociology) are usually 'building blocks' for understanding other, more complicated phenomena (collections of pulleys making up a hoist, the suspension system of a car, market interactions, organizational patterns of knowledge diffusion). They often constitute the 'paradigm' thought experiments around which disciplines (i.e., attempts to represent the world in words and equations) are founded (Kuhn, 1990). We will interact with such 'simple' phenomena in greater detail in the subsequent sections, which aim to show how our measure of complexity cuts across various ways of looking at organizations and modeling their behavior.

"The new conceptualization of complexity helps us see our way through any organizational model to the complexity of the underlying phenomenon"

The benefit of this new representation of complexity does not lie purely in the fact that it can make precise lay intuitions about various terms that have been (loosely) used to describe the user's predicament when faced with a complex phenomenon (as shown above), but also in the fact that it can provide a model-invariant approach to the representation and measurement of the complexity or organizational phenomena. Model-invariant means that the representation of complexity can be used in conjunction with any model of organizational phenomena that is amenable to algorithmic representation (a weak condition, satisfied by all models that are currently in use in organization science, studies and theory). To substantiate this claim, I will now analyze the models of organizational phenomena that have come to dominate the literature during the past 20 years, and show how the complexity measure that I have developed here can be used to quantify the complexity of the paradigmatic phenomena that these models were meant to explain.

It is important to understand what 'quantifying the complexity of a phenomenon' is supposed to signify here. As shown above, 'the complexity of a phenomenon' is an ill-defined concept, unless we make reference to a particular (intersubjectively tested or testable) model of that phenomenon, which we will agree to provide the basis for a replication of that phenomenon as a digital object (i.e., to provide a simulation of that phenomenon). The phenomenon enters the process of complexity quantification via the model that has been chosen for its representation. Hence, the subjective analytical and perceptual mindset of the observer of the phenomenon is incorporated into the complexity measure of the phenomenon, and the intersubjective (i.e., objective) features of the phenomenon are taken into consideration via the requirement that the model used as the basis of the complexity measurements be intersubjectively agreeable (i.e., that two observers using the model to represent or predict a phenomenon can reach agreement on definitions of terms, the relationship of raw sense data to observation statements, and so forth). The models that will be analyzed below are already, in virtue of their entrenchment in the field of organizational research, well-established in the intersubjective sense: they have been used as coordinative devices by researchers for many years, and have generated successful research programmes (i.e., research programmes well-represented in the literature). Thus, I are justified in studying the complexity of phenomena that are paradigmatic for the use of these models via studying the (informational and computational) complexity of the models themselves, and remain confident that we are not just engaging in the measurement or quantification of pure cognitive structures. Moreover, the complexity measures that will emerge are intersubjectively agreeable (i.e., 'objective') in spite of the fact that the inputs to the process of producing them have a subjective component.

Organizations as systems of rules and rule-based interactions

Recent efforts at modeling organizations have explicitly recognized them as systems of rules and rule-based interactions among multiple agents who follow (locally) the specified rules. The modeling approach to organizations as rule-based systems comprises three steps: a. the specification of a plausible set of micro-rules governing interactions among different agents; b. the specification of a macro-level phenomenon that stands in need of an explanation that can be traced to micro-local phenomena, and; c. the use of the micro-local rules, together with initial and boundary conditions, to produce simulations of the macroscopic pattern that emerges. Simple local rules (such as local rules of deference, cooperation, competition and discourse) can give rise to complex macroscopic patterns of behavior which may or may not be deterministic (in the sense that they vary with the nature of the micro-local rules but do not change as a function of changes in initial and boundary conditions). A simple micro-local rule set that is plausible on introspective and empirical grounds, such as Grice's (1975) cooperative logic of communications (which requires agents to interpret each others' utterances as being both informative and relevant to the subject of the conversation, i.e., 'cooperative') can, for instance, lead to organizational patterns of herd behavior in which everyone follows the example of a group of 'early movers' without challenging their assumptions.

The rule-based approach to modeling organizational phenomena is congenial to the computational language introduced in this paper, and lends itself to an easy representation in complexity space. A rule is a simple semantic-syntactic structure of the type 'if A, then B', 'if not A, then not B', 'if A, then B, except for the conditions under which C occurs', or, 'if A, then possibly B'. Agents, acting locally, ascertain the 'state of the world' (i.e., 'A') and take action that is deterministically specified by the rule that is deemed applicable ('if A, then B', for instance). In so doing, they instantiate a new state of the world ('C'), to which other agents react using the appropriate set of rules. (I shall leave aside, for the purpose of this discussion, the very important questions of ambiguous rules, conflicts among rules, and rules about the use of rules, but they are discussed in Moldoveanu and Singh (2003). Sets of agents interacting on the basis of micro-local rules (statistical or deterministic) can be represented as cellular automata (Wolfram, 2002) with agents represented by nodes (completely described each by a set of elementary states that change as a function of rules and the states of other agents) and a set of rules of interaction (denumerable, finite and either statistical or deterministic). This clearly 'computational' (but quite general, see Wolfram, 2002) interpretation of organizations-as-rule-systems is easily amenable to an application of the complexity measures that I have introduced above. First, the informational depth of a phenomenon explained by a valid rule-based model is the minimum description length of a. the agents; b. the micro-local rules, and; c. initial and boundary conditions required to suitably simulate that phenomenon. The computational load of such a phenomenon is the relationship between the number of input variables (agents, agent states, rules, initial conditions boundary conditions) that the model requires to produce a successful simulation (i.e., a successful replication of the macroscopic pattern that stands in need of explanation). Thus, when seen through the lens of rule-based systems of interactions, the 'measure' of organizational phenomena in complexity space is easily taken - a fortunate by-product of the universality of cellular automata as models of rule-based interacting systems of micro-agents. (Note that the applicability of the complexity measure phenomena seen through a rule-based interacting system lens depends sensitively on the universality of the cellular automata instantiation of rule-based systems).

The complexity measures that I have introduced can also be used to ask new questions (to the end of garnering new insights and exploring - or generating - new phenomena) of rule-based models of organizational phenomena, such as:

1. How does the informational depth of micro-rules affect the computational load of the macro-phenomena that depend causally on them? Is there a systematic relationship between the complexity of micro-rules and the complexity of macro-patterns?

Answering such questions could lead to the articulation of a new, intelligent craft of organizational rule design.

2. How does macroscopic complexity affect the design of micro-local rule sets? What are the conditions on the rationality of individual rule designers that would be required for them to purposefully alter macroscopic patterns through the alteration of micro-local rules?

Answering these questions could lead to a new set of training and simulation tools for organizational rule design and rule designers, and would also point to the bounds and limitations of the 'engineering' approach to rule system design.

Organizations as spatio-temporally stable behavioral patterns (routines and value-linked activity chains)

Organizations can also be modeled as systems of identifiable routines or activity sets, according to a dominant tradition in organizational research that dates back to at least the seminal work of Nelson and Winter (1982). A routine is a stable, finite, repeated behavioral pattern, involving one or more individuals within the organization. It may or may not be conceptualized as a routine (i.e., it may or may not have been made explicit as a routine by the followers of the routine). Being finite and repeated, routines are easily modeled either as algorithms or as the process by which algorithms run on a computational (hardware) substrate. Because an algorithm prescribes a sequence of causally linked steps or elementary tasks, wherein the output of one step or task is the input to the next step or task, the language of algorithms may in fact supply a more precise definition of what a routine is: it is a behavioral pattern that is susceptible to an algorithmic representation (Moldoveanu & Bauer, 2004). For example, an organizational routine for performing due diligence on a new supplier or customer might include: a. getting names of references; b. checking those references; c. tracking the results of the evidence-gathering process; d. computing a weighted decision metric that incorporates the evidence in question, and; e. making a go / no go decision regarding that particular supplier or customer. The steps are linked (the output of one is the input to the other) and the process is easily teachable and repeatable.

Understanding routines as algorithms (or, as the running of algorithms) allows us to easily apply our complexity measures to routine-based models of organization. Specifically, we map the number of linked steps involved in the algorithmic representation of a routine to the computational load of the routine. The informational depth of routine is given by the size of the blue-print or representation of the routine *qua* algorithm. These modeling moves together allow us to investigate the complexity of organizational phenomena through the lens provided by routine-based models thereof. Routine sets may be more or less complex in the informational sense as a function of the size of the memory required to store the algorithms that represent them. They may be more or less complex in the computational sense as a function of the number of steps that they entail.

Given this approach to the complexity of routines, it becomes possible to examine the important question of designing effective routines in the space spanned by the informational and computational dimensions of the resulting phenomena. Here, the language of algorithm design and computational complexity theory proves to be very helpful to the modeler. For example, algorithms may be defined recursively, to take advantage of the great sequential speeds of computational devices. A recursive algorithm is one that takes, in successive iterations, its own output at a previous step as its input at the next step, converging, with each step, towards the required answer or 'close-enough' approximation to the answer. Examples of recursive algorithms include those used to approximate transcendental numbers such as π or e, which produce 'additional decimals' with each successive iterations, and can be re-iterated *ad infinitum* to produce arbitrarily close approximations to the exact value of the variable in question. Defining algorithms recursively has the advantage (in a machine that is low on memory but high on sequential processing speed) that costly storage (and memory access) is replaced with mechanical ('mindless') raw (and cheap) computation.

Organizational routines may, following the analogy of algorithms, be usefully classified as 'recursive' or 'non-recursive', depending on their structure. Some organizational tasks (such as the planning of inventories of products, assemblies, sub-assemblies and components) may be seen as successive (recursive) applications of a computationally intelligible 'kernel' (matrix multiplication or matrix inversion, Moldoveanu & Bauer, 2004) at successively 'finer' resolutions (or levels of analysis), in such a way that 'high-level' decisions (regarding product inventory, say) become inputs to applications of the algorithm at lower levels of analysis (regarding assemblies or components). Other organizational tasks (such as reasoning by abduction in order to provide an inference to the best explanation of a particular organizational or environmental phenomenon are not susceptible *prima facie* to a recursive algorithmic interpretation and entail a far greater informational depth.

Mapping routines to algorithms allows us to consider both the evolution of routines (from a structural or teleological perspective) and to incorporate the phenomenological aspect of the complexity of the resulting phenomena into the routine-based analysis of organizational phenomena. In particular, we can produce a canonical representation of different routine-based phenomena in the language of algorithms whose informational depth and computational load can be quantified, and ask:

1. How do routine sets adapt to their own complexity? Are there canonical self-adaptation patterns of routine sets to increases in computational load or informational depth?

2. How should routine designers trade-off between informational depth and computational load in conditions characterized by different configurations of (informational-computational) bounds to rationality? How do they make these trade-offs?

3. Are there general laws for the evolution of complexity? How does the complexity of routine sets evolve over time?

Organizations as information processing and symbol manipulation systems

Perhaps the most congenial of the classical traditions to the study of organizations to the computational interpretation being put forth in this chapter is that originating with the Carnegie School (March & Simon, 1958; Cyert & March, 1963; Simon, 1962). In that tradition, organizations are considered as information processing systems. Some approaches stress the rule-based nature of the information processing task (Cyert & March, 1963), but do not ignore the teleological components thereof. Others (Simon, 1962) stress the teleological component, without letting go of the fundamentally rule-based nature of systematic symbolic manipulation. What brings these approaches together, however, is a commitment to a view of organizations as purposive (but boundedly far-sighted) symbol-manipulation devices, relying on 'hardware' (human and human-created) and a syntax (grammatical syntax, first-order logic) for 'solving problems' (whose articulation is generally considered exogenous to the organization: 'given', rather than constructed within the organization).

There is a small (but critical) step involved in the passage from a view of organizations-as-information-processing-structures to an algorithmic description of the phenomena that this view makes it possible for us to represent. This step has to do with increasing the precision with which we represent the ways in which organizations process information, in particular, with representing information-processing functions as algorithms running on the physical substrate provided by the organization itself (a view that is strongly connected to the 'strong-AI' view of the mind that fuelled, at a metaphysical level, the 'cognitive revolution' in psychology, a by-product of the Carnegie tradition). This step is only possible once we achieve a phenomenologically and teleologically reasonable partitioning of problems that organizations can be said to 'solve' or attempt to solve into structurally reliable problem classes. It is precisely such a partitioning that is provided by the science of algorithm design and analysis (Cormen, et al., 1993), which, as we saw above, partitions problems into *tractable*, *intractable* and *impossible* categories on the basis of structural isomorphisms among solution algorithms. 'What the organization does', *qua* processor of information, can now be parsed in the language of tractability analysis in order to understand: a. the optimal structure of information processing tasks; b. the actual structure of information processing tasks, and; c. structural, teleological and phenomenological reasons for the divergence between the ideal and the actual.

That we can now do such an analysis (starting from a taxonomy of problems and algorithms used to address them) is in no small measure due to the availability of complexity measures for algorithms (and implicitly for the problems these algorithms were meant to resolve). Informational and computational complexity bound from above the adaptation potential of the organization to new and unforeseen conditions, while at the same time providing lower bounds for the minimum amount of information processing required for the organization to survive *qua* organization. In this two-dimensional space, it is possible to define a structural 'performance zone' of the organization seen as an information processing device: it must function at a minimum level of complexity (which can be structurally specified) in order to survive, but cannot surpass a certain level of complexity in order to adapt (which can also be structurally specified and validated on teleological and phenomenological grounds). Adaptation, thus understood, becomes adaptation not only to an exogenous phenomenon, but also to the internal complexity that efforts to adapt to that phenomenon generate. This move makes complexity (informational and computational) a variable whose roles as caused and causer must be simultaneously considered.

Organizations as systems of interpretation and sense-making

It may seem difficult to reconcile the starkly algorithmic view of complexity that I have put forth here with a view of organizations as producers and experiencers of the classical entities of 'meaning': narrative, symbol, sense, interpretation and meaning itself (Weick, 1995). This is because it does not seem an easy (or even possible) task to map narrative into algorithm without losing the essential quality of either narrative or algorithm in the process. It is, however, possible to measure (in complexity space) that which can be represented in algorithmic form, not only about narrative itself, but also, perhaps more importantly, about the processes by which narratives are created, articulated, elaborated, validated and forgotten. These processes (describing the processes by which organizations interact with the narratives that they produce and how they 'live' these narratives) are often more amenable to algorithmic interpretation than are narratives themselves and equally important to the evolution of the organizations themselves.

To see how narrative and the classical structures of meaning can be mapped into the algorithmic space that allows us to measure the complexity of the resulting phenomena, let us break down the narrative production function into three steps. The first is an ontological one: an ontology is created, and comes to inhabit the 'subjects' of the narrative. The organization may be said to be populated by 'people', by 'embodied emotions', by 'transactions', by 'designs and technologies', and so forth, These are the entities that do 'causal work', in terms of which other entities are described. Surely, the process by which an ontology is created cannot (and should not) be algorithmically represented, but this is not required for the algorithmic representation of this initial ontological step. Every algorithm begins with a number of 'givens' (which factor into its informational depth) which are 'undefined' (either because they have been implicitly defined or because there is nothing to be alarmed about in leaving them undefined). That which does matter to the algorithmic representation of this first narrative-defining step is precisely the process of mapping of ontological primitives to other primitives, over which most narrative-designers (like any other theorist) often fret, and in particular: how deep is it? How many times does the question 'what is X?' have to be answered in the narrative? For instance, does (one particularly reductive kind of) narrative require that organizations be analyzed in terms of individuals, individuals in terms of beliefs and desired, beliefs and desires in terms of neurophysiological states, neurophysiological states in terms of electrochemical states … and so forth? Or, rather, does the analysis stop with beliefs and desires? The articulation of the ontological first step in the production of narrative can, it turns out, be analyzed in terms of the complexity metrics I have introduced here. At the very least, we can distinguish between informationally deep ontologies and informationally shallow ones, with implications, as we shall see, for the computational complexity of the narrative-bearing phenomenon that we are studying.

The second important step is that of development or proliferation of a narrative: the process by which, through the purposive use of language, the filtering of relevant from irrelevant information and the use of the relevant information to give words meaning, narratives 'take over' a particular component of organizational life. It is the case that the subjective experience of 'living a story' cannot be precisely algorithmically replicated, but each of the steps of this experience, once we agree on what, precisely they are, can be given algorithmic interpretation whose complexity we can measure (in both the informational and computational sense). The process of 'validation' of a story for instance, can be easily simulated using a memory-feedback filter, a comparison and a decision based on a threshold comparison (regardless of whether the narrative validator is a justificationist or falsificationist). Of course, validation processes may differ in computational complexity according to the design of the filter used to select the data that purports to 'make true' the narrative. Abductive filters (based on inference to the best explanation) will be computationally far more complex than inductive filters (based on straight extrapolation of a pattern, Bylander et al., 1991), just as deductive processes of theory testing will be more computationally 'heavy' than will inductive processes that serve the same purpose.

Thus, we can distinguish usefully between simple and complex narratives (and even among, simple, complicated, tractable, intractable and impossible ones) and examine the effects of the complexity of these narratives on the evolution of the organization (and on the narratives themselves) as long as we are willing to make a sacrifice in the phenomenological realm and allow that not all components of a structure-of-meaning can be usefully represented in algorithmic form, in exchange for being able to cut more deeply and narrowly into a set of variables that influence the evolution and dynamics of such structures in organizational life.

Organizations as nexi of contracts and as competitive and cooperative (coordinative) equilibria among rational or boundedly rational agents

Not surprisingly, approaches to organizational phenomena based on economic reasoning (Tirole, 1988) are congenial to an algorithmic interpretation and therefore to the measures of complexity introduced in this chapter. One line of modeling considers firms as nexi of contracts between principals (shareholders) and agents (managers and employees) (Tirole, 1988). A contract is an (implicit or explicit) set of contingent agreements that aims to credibly specify incentives to agents in a way that aligns their interests with those of the principals. It can be written up as a set of contingent claims by an agent on the cash flows and residual value of the firm (i.e., as a set of 'if ... then' or 'iff ... then' statements), or, more precisely, as an algorithm that can be used to compute the (expected value of) the agent's payoff as a function of changes in the value of the asset that he or she has signed up to manage. In the agency-theoretic tradition, the behavior of the (self-interested, monetary expected value-maximizing) agent is understood as a quasi-deterministic response to the contract that he or she has signed up for. Thus, the contract can be understood not only as an algorithm for prediction, by the agent, of his or her payoff as a function of the value of the firm in time, but also as a predictive tool for understanding the behavior of the agent tout court.

The (informational and computational) complexity components of principal-agent agreements can be understood, *prima facie*, as the informational depth and computational load of the contractual schemata that form the governance 'blueprint' of the organization: the *de facto* 'rules' of the organizational game, which become wired into the behavior of the contractants. Such an interpretation is straightforward, and can be expected to yield clean measures of contractual complexity, and, implicitly, of the complexity of organizational phenomena understood through the agency-theoretic lens. On deeper study, however, it is clear that the complexity of a contract is not an immediate and transparent index of the complexity of the organizational phenomena that are 'played out' within the confines of the contract, as the problems of performance measurement, specification of observable states of the world, and gaming by both parties of the contractual schema have to also be taken into consideration. Thus, measuring the complexity of contracts (conceptualized *qua* algorithms) provides us merely with a lower bound of the complexity of the phenomena that are understood through a contractual lens.

A more complete reconstruction of self-interested behavior in organizations, which is no less amenable to an algorithmic interpretation than is the agency-theoretic approach is that based on game-theoretic methods. In such an approach, organizational phenomena are understood as instantiations of competitive or cooperative equilibria among members of the organization, each trying to maximize his or her welfare. What is required for the specification of an intra-organizational equilibrium (competitive or cooperative) is a representation of the set of participants ('players'), their payoffs in all possible states of the world, their strategies and their beliefs (or conjectures), including their beliefs about the beliefs of the other participants. These entities together can be considered as inputs to an algorithm for the computation of the equilibrium set of strategies, through whose lens organizational phenomena and individual actions can now be interpreted. It is the complexity of this algorithm (backward induction, for instance) that becomes the *de facto* complexity measure of the organizational phenomenon that is represented through the game-theoretic lens.

Some work has already started on understanding game-theoretic models through a computational lens (Gilboa, 1989), and the basic idea is to consider individual players (participants) as computational devices attempting (but not always succeeding, depending on their informational and computational constraints) to solve for the equilibrium set of strategies and to compute the expected value of their payoff in the process. These approaches have focused predominantly on computational complexity, and have attempted to model the influence of bounded rationality on the resulting equilibria by iteratively reducing the computational capabilities of the players in the model (i.e., by placing upper bounds on the computational complexity of the problems they attempt to resolve or on the algorithms that they use). The complexity measures introduced here add texture to this computational modeling paradigm, by introducing a set of useful distinctions among different problem classes in the space of computational load (tractable, intractable, impossible) and by introducing an informational component to the complexity measures used to date, which has not always been taken into consideration (and corresponding to the 'working memory' of each individual player).

What does the new operationalization of complexity mean for how we carry out 'organization science' and 'organizational intervention'?

The complexity measures that have articulated above make it possible to develop a research program that combines three ways of representing organizations (phenomenological, teleological, structural) that have until now generated separate (and largely incommensurable) ways of knowing and ways of inquiring about organization. I will examine in this final section the ways in which the new measure of complexity (and the implicit space in which this complexity measure 'lives') enables insights from structural, teleological and phenomenological studies of organizational and individual behavior to 'come together' in a research programme that examines how complexity (as a dependent variable) emerges as a discernible and causally powerful property of organizational plans, routines and life-worlds and how complexity (as an independent variable) shapes and influences organizational ways of planning, acting and being.

Contributions to the structural perspective

Structural perspectives on organizations (such as many of the ones analyzed above) conceptualize organizations in terms of causal models (deterministic or probabilistic). These models refer to organizations as systems of rules, routines, capabilities or value-linked activities. As I already showed, any such model, once phrased in terms of algorithms (whose convergence properties are under the control of the modeler) can be used to synthesize a complexity measure for the phenomenon that it is used to simulate. Complexity (informational and computational) emerges as a new kind of modeling variable - one that can now be precisely captured. It can be used within a structuralist perspective in two ways:

i.   As a dependent variable, it is a property of the (modeled) phenomenon that depends sensitively on the algorithmic features (informational depth, computational load) of the model that is used to understand that phenomenon. In this sense, it is truly an emergent property, in two ways:

   1.   It emerges from the non-separable combination of the model and the phenomenon: it a property of the process of modeling and validation, not merely of the model alone or of the phenomenon alone;

   2.   It emerges from the relationship between the observer / modeler and the phenomenon, in the sense that it is a function of the interaction of the observer and the phenomenon, not of the characteristics of the observer alone or of the phenomenon alone.

Thus, it is now possible to engage in structuralist modeling of organizational phenomena which can explicitly produce complexity measures of the phenomena in question (as seen through a particular structural lens). Such measures can then be used both in order to track variations in 'organizational complexity' as a function of changes in organizational conditions (new variables, new relationships among these variables, new kinds of relationships among the variables, new relationships among the relationships...) and to track variations in 'organizational complexity' as a function of changes of the underlying structural models themselves (it may turn out that some modeling approaches lead to lower complexity measures than do others, and may for this very reason be preferred by both researchers and practitioners).

ii. As an independent variable, complexity (as operationalized above) can be used as a modeling variable itself: the complexity of an organizational phenomenon may figure as a causal variable in a structural model of that phenomenon. This maneuver leads us to be able to consider, in analytical fashion, a large class of reflexive, complexity-driven phenomena that have the property that their own complexity (an emergent feature) shapes their subsequent spatio-temporal dynamics. Such a move is valuable in that if, as many studies suggest (see Miller, 1993; Thompson, 1967; Moldoveanu & Bauer, 2004) organizations attempt to adapt to the complexity of the phenomena that they encounter, it is no less true that they try to adapt to the complexity of the phenomena that they engender and that they themselves are, in which case having a (sharp) complexity measure that one can 'plug' into structural models as an independent variable makes it possible to examine:

1. organizational adaptation to self-generated complexity, by building temporally recursive models in which complexity at one time affects dynamics at subsequent periods of time;

2. the evolution of complexity itself, by building behaviorally informed models of the complexity of various adaptations to complexity.

Contributions to the teleological perspective

The teleological perspective conceptualizes organizations as adaptive, cost-benefit computing and optimizing structures that adopt and discard structures and structural models as a function of their contribution to an overall utility function. They have a purpose (*telos*) which may be to maximize profits, predictability or probability of survival (instantiated in an overall fitness function). The computational perspective on complexity and the algorithmic measures of complexity that I have introduced allow us to study - within teleological models of organizations - the effects of phenomenal complexity on the trade-offs that decision-takers make in their organizational design choices.

Even more importantly, we can deploy the apparatus developed by algorithm designers and computational complexity theorists to study the coping strategies that managers to deal with organizational complexity. To understand how this analytic apparatus can be usefully deployed, it is essential to think of the organization as a large scale universal computational device (such as a Universal Turing Machine, or UTM), of organizational plans and strategies as algorithms and of organizational activities and routines as the processes by which those very same algorithms run on the UTM. Now, we can distinguish between several strategies that managers - qua organizational designers - might adopt in order to deal with complexity in both computational and informational space, drawing on strategies that algorithm designers use in order to deal with large-scale problem complexity.

Computational space (K-space) strategies: Structural and functional
partitioning of intractable problems.

When faced with computationally intractable problems, algorithm designers usually partition these problems using two generic partitioning strategies (Cormen, *et al.*, 1993). They can split up a large scale problem into several smaller-scale problems which can be tackled in parallel; or, they can separate out the process of generating solutions from the process of verifying these solutions. Either one of these partitionings can be accomplished in a more reversible ('soft') or irreversible ('hard') fashion: the problem itself may be split up into sub-problems that are tackled by the same large-scale computational architecture suitably configured to solve each sub-problem optimally (functional partitioning), or the architecture used to carry out the computation may be previously split up into parallel sub-architectures that impose pre-defined, hard-wired limits on the kinds of sub-problems that they can be used to solve.

These distinctions can be used to make sense of the strategies for dealing with K-space complexity that the organizational designer can make use of. Consider the problem of system design, recently shown to be isomorphic to the intractable (NP-hard) 'knapsack problem'. Because the problem is in the NP-hard class, the number of operations required to solve it will be a higher-than-any-polynomial (e.g., exponential) function of the number of system parameters that enter the design process as independent variables. Solving the entire system design problem without any partitioning (i.e., searching for the global optimum) without the use of any simplification may be infeasible from a cost perspective for the organization as a whole. Partitioning schemata work to partition the 'problem space' into sub-problems whose joint complexity is far lower than the complexity of the system design problem taken as a whole.

Consider first how functional partitioning works for the designer of a system-designing organization. S/he can direct the organization as a whole to search through the possible subsets of design variables in order to achieve the optimal problem partitioning into sub-problems of low complexity, sequentially engage in solving these sub-problems, then bring the solutions together to craft an approximation to the optimal system design problem. Alternatively, the systems-designing organization designer can direct the organization to randomly generate a large list of global solutions to the system design problem taken as a whole in the first phase of the optimization task, and then get together and sequentially test the validity of each putative solution *qua* solution to the system design problem. In the first case, optimality is traded-off in favor of (deterministic and rapid) convergence (albeit to a sub-optimal, approximate) answer. In the second case, certainty about convergence to the global optimum is traded off against overall system complexity.

Such partitioning schemata can also be achieved structurally. The systems-designing organization designer can pre-structure the organization into sub-groups that are bounded in K-space as to the computational load of the problems they can take on. This partitioning can be 'hard-wired' into the organization through formal and informal rule systems, contracts, and organizational fiat. Now faced with the overall (NP-hard) system design problem, organization will adapt by splitting it up spontaneously into sub-problems that are matched to the maximum computational load that each group can take on. Alternatively, the organizational designer can hard-wire the solution-generation / solution verification distinction into the organizational structure by outsourcing either the solution-generation step (to a consulting organization, to a market of entre-preneurial firms, to a large number of free-lance producers) while maintaining the organization's role in providing solution validation, or by outsourcing the solution validation step (to the consumer market, in the form of experimental products with low costs of failure) while maintaining its role as a quasi-random generator of new solution concepts.

Information-space (I-space) strategies

Of course, hard problems may also be 'hard' in the informational sense: the 'working memory' or 'relevant information' required to solve them may exceed the storage (and access-to-storage) capacities of the problem solver. Once again, studying the strategies used by computational designers to deal with informational overload gives us a sense of what to look for as complex-ity coping strategies that organizational designers use in I-space. As might be expected, I-space strategies focus on informational reduction or compression, and on increasing the efficiency with which information dispersed throughout the organization is conveyed to decision-makers to whom it is relevant. I will consider compression schemata first, and access schemata second.

Compression Schemata. Lossy compression achieves informational depth reduction at the expense of deletion of certain potentially useful information or distortion of that information. Examples of lossy compression schemata are offered by model-based estimation of a large data set (such that the data is represented by a model and an error term) and by *ex ante* filtering of the data set with the aim of reducing its size. In contrast to lossy information compres-sion, lossless compression achieves informational depth reduction without the distortion or deletion of potentially useful information, albeit at the cost of higher computational complexity of the compression encoder.

Consider, as an example of how these strategies might be deployed within an organization, the problem a top management team faces in performing due diligence on a new market opportunity for a product manufacturer (instanti-ated as the appearance of a new technology within the firm, or a new niche within the market). There is a large amount of information readily available about competitors, their technologies, products, intellectual capital, market-ing and distribution strategies, marginal and fixed costs, about customers and their preferences, about the organization's own capabilities and competitive advantages in different product areas, about long-term technological trends and the effects of short-run demand-side and supply-side discontinuities in the product market. This information comes from different sources, both within the organization and outside of it. It has various levels of precision and credibility, and can be used to support a multiplicity of possible product development and release strategies. Let us examine how complexity management of the due diligence problem mimics I-space reduction strategies pursued by computational system and algorithm designers.

First, lossy compression mechanisms are applied to the data set in several ways: through the use of *a priori* models of competitive interaction and demand-side behavior that limit the range of data that one is willing to look at, through the specific *ex ante* formulation of a problem statement (or a set of hypotheses to be tested on the data) which further restricts the size of the information space one considers in making strategic decisions, and through the application of 'common sense' cognitive habits (such as data 'smoothing' to account for missing points, extrapolation to generate predictions of future behavior on the basis of observations of past behavior, and inference to the best explanation to select the most promising groups of explanatory and predictive hypotheses from the set of hypotheses that are supported by the data). Lossless (or, quasi-lossless) compression of the informational depth of the remaining relevant data set may then be performed by the development of more detailed models that elaborate and refine the most promising hypotheses and explanations in order to increase the precision and validity with which they simulate the observed data sequence. They amount to high resolution elaborations of the (low resolution) approaches that are used to synthesize the organization's basic 'business model' or, perhaps more precisely 'model of itself'.

Access Schemata. The second core problem faced by the organizational designer in I-space is that of making relevant information efficiently available to the right decision agents. The designer of efficient networks worries about two fundamental problem classes: the problem of network design and the problem of flow design (Bertsekas, 1985). The first problem relates to the design of network topologies that make the flow of relevant information maximally efficient. The second problem relates to the design of prioritization and scheduling schemes for relevant information that maximizes the reliability with which decision agents get relevant information on a timely basis.

The organizational designer manages network structure in I-space when s/he structures or tries to shape formal and informal communication links among individual members of the organization in ways that minimize the path length (or geodesic) from the transmitter of critical information to the intended receiver. Such 'wiring' of an organization can be performed through either reversible ('working group') or irreversible ('executive committees') organizational mechanisms. It can be achieved through either probabilistic (generating conditions for link formation) or deterministic (mandating link formation) means. The organizational designer manages information flow when he (she) designs (or attempts to influence) the queuing structure of critical information flows, and specifically the prioritization of information flows to different users (as a function of the perceived informational needs of these users) and the scheduling of flows of various priorities to different users, as a function of relative importance of the information to the user, the user to the organizational decision process, and the decision process to the overall welfare of the organization.

Let us examine the proliferation of I-space network and flow design strategies with reference to the executive team and their direct reports discussed earlier, in reference to the management of a due diligence process in I-space. First, network design. The team comprises members made up of members of independent functional specialist 'cliques' (product development, marketing, finance, business development) that are likely to be internally 'densely wired' (i.e., everyone talks to everyone else). The executive team serves as a bridge among functionalist cliques, and its efficiency as a piece of the informational network of the firm will depend on the reliability and timeliness of transmission of relevant information from the clique that originates relevant information to the clique that needs it. 'Cross-clique' path lengths can be manipulated by setting up or dissolving cross-functional working groups and task groups. Within-clique coordination can be manipulated by changing the relative centrality of various agents within the clique. These effects may be achieved either through executive fiat and organizational rules, or through the differential encouragement of tie formation within various groups and subgroups within the organization.

Second, flow design. Once an informational network structure is 'wired' within the organization, the organizational designer still faces the problem of assigning different flow regimes to different users of the network. Flow regimes vary both in the informational depth of a transmission and in its time-sequence priority relative to the time at which the information was generated. The assignment of individual-level structural roles with formal and informal groups within the organization can be seen as a way of shaping flow prioritization regimes, as a function of the responsibility and authority of each decision agent. In contrast, the design of processes by which information is shared, deliberated, researched and validated can be seen as a way of shaping flow scheduling regimes, as a function of the relative priority of the receiver and the nature of the information being conveyed.

Contributions to the phenomenological perspective

The proposed approach to the measurement of complexity started out as an attempt to reconcile the subjective view of complexity as difficulty with various objective views of complexity, which conflate complexity with one structural property or another of an organizational phenomenon. The synthesis between the objective and subjective views was accomplished by making explicit the contribution that the observer's models, or cognitive schemata, used to understand a phenomenon makes to the complexity of the phenomenon, by identifying the complexity of a phenomenon with the informational depth and computational load of the most predictively successful, intersubjectively validated model of that phenomenon. This move, I argue, makes the complexity measure put forth applicable through a broad range of models to the paradigmatic phenomena they explain.

But, it also opened a conceptual door into the incorporation of new subjective effects into the definition of complexity. In our informational and computational dimensions, 'complexity' is 'difficulty'. A phenomenon will be declared by an observer to be complex if the observer encounters a difficulty in either storing the information required to simulate that phenomenon or in performing the computations required to simulate it successfully. Such difficulties can be easily captured using the apparatus of algorithmic information theory (Chaitin, 1974) and computational complexity theory (Cormen, et al., 1993). Are they meaningful? And, do they allow us to make further progress in phenomenological investigations of individuals' grapplings with 'complex' phenomena?

Earlier in the chapter it was shown that the vague concepts that individuals use to describe complex phenomena, such as 'unfathomable', 'simple', 'intractable', 'impossible' and 'complicated' can be given precise meanings using one, another or combinations of both of the informational and computational dimensions that I have defined for the measurement of complexity. These distinctions make it possible for us to separate out the difficulties that observers of complex phenomena have, and enables the articulation of a research programme that facilitates the interaction between the mind and the 'complex'. They also make it possible for us to quantitatively investigate three separate phenomena that have traditionally been interesting to researchers in the behaviorist tradition:

a. The informational and computational boundaries of competent behavior, and in particular the I-K-space configurations that limit adaptation to complexity. Here, the use of simulations of cognitive function and the ability to model the algorithmic requirements (informational depth, computational load) of any model or schema make it possible to break down any complex predicament along an informational and a computational dimension and to hypothesize informational, computational and joint informational / computational limits on intelligent agent adaptation and adaptation potential;

b. The trade-offs between informational and computational difficulty that intelligent adaptive agents should make when faced with complex phenomena, which can be studied by simulating the choices that intelligent adaptive agents make among different available models and schemata for understanding complex phenomena, which in turn enables the study of:

c. The trade-offs between informational and computational difficulty that intelligent adaptive agents actually do make when faced with complex phenomena, which, in the time-honored tradition of behaviorist methodology applied to decision analysis, could be studied by measuring departures of empirically observed behavior of agents faced with choosing among alternative models and schemata from the normative models discovered through numerical and thought experiments.

References

Anderson, P. (1999). "Introduction to Special Issue on Organizational Complexity," *Organization Science*, 10: 1-16.

Bar-Yam, Y. (2000). *Dynamics of Complex Systems*, NECSI mimeo.

Bertsekas, D. (1985). *Data Networks*, Cambridge: MIT Press.

Bylander, T., Allemang, D., Tanner, M. C. and Josephson, J. (1991). "The Computational Complexity of Abduction," *Artificial Intelligence V*, 49: 125-151.

Chaitin, G. (1974). "Information-theoretic Computational Complexity," *IEEE Transactions on Information Theory*, 20:10-30.

Cormen, T. H., Leiserson, C. E. and Rivest, R. L. (1993). *Introduction to Algorithms*, Cambridge: MIT Press.

Cyert, R. M. and March, J. G. (1963). *A Behavioral Theory of the Firm*, New Jersey: Prentice Hall.

D'Arcy Thompson, R. (1934). *Structure and Form*, New York: Basic Books.

Gilboa, I. (1989). "Iterated Dominance: Some Complexity Considerations," *Games and Economic Behavior*, 1.

Grice, H. P. (1975). "Logic and Conversation," in P. Cole and J. Morgan (eds.), *Syntax and Semantics*, New York: Cambridge University Press.

Kahneman, D., Slovic, P. and Tversky, A. (1982). *Judgment Under Uncertainty: Heuristics and Biases*, New York: Cambridge University Press.

Kauffmann, S. (1993). *The Origins of Order: Self-Organization and Selection in Evolution*, New York: Oxford University Press.

Kuhn, T. S. (1962). *The Structure of Scientific Revolutions*, Chicago: University of Chicago Press.

Kuhn, T. S. (1990). *The Road Since Structure*, Cambridge: MIT Press.

Levinthal, D. and Warglien, M. (1999). "Landscape Design: Designing for Local Action in Complex Worlds," *Organization Science*, 10: 342-357.

Li, M. and Vitanyi, P. M. B. (1993). *An Introduction to Kolmogorov Complexity and Its Applications*, New York: Springer Verlag.

March, J. G. and Simon, H. A. (1958). *Organizations*, New York: Wiley.

McKelvey, B. (1999). "Avoiding Complexity Catastrophe in Coevolutionary Pockets: Strategies for Rugged Landscapes," *Organization Science*, 10: 294-321.

Miller, D. (1993). "The Architecture of Simplicity," *Academy of Management Review*, 18: 116-138.

Moldoveanu, M. C. and Bauer, R. (2004). "On the Relationship between Organizational Complexity and Organizational Structuration," *Organization Science*, 15: 98-118.

Moldoveanu, M. C. and Singh, J. V. (2003). "The Evolutionary Metaphor: A Synthetic Framework for the Study of Strategic Organization," *Strategic Organization*, 1: 439-449.

Nelson, R. and Winter, S. (1982). *An Evolutionary Theory of Economic Behavior*, Cambridge: Harvard University Press.

Putnam, H. (1981). *Reason, Truth and History*, New York: Cambridge University Press.

Rivkin, J. (2000). "The Imitation of Complex Strategies," *Management Science*, 46: 8.
Simon, H. (1962). "The Architecture of Complexity," reprinted in H. Simon (1982). *The Sciences of the Artificial*, Cambridge: MIT Press.
Thompson, D. (1967). *Organizations in Action: Social Science Basis of Administrative Theory*, John Wiley, 1967.
Tirole, J. (1988). *The Theory of Industrial Organization*, Cambridge: MIT Press.
Von Bertalanffy, L. (1968). *General System Theory: Foundations, Development, Applications*, New York: Braziller.
Weick, K. E. (1995). *Sensemaking in Organizations*, Beverly Hills: Sage.
Wolfram, S. (2002). *A New Kind of Science*, Wolfram Research.

CHAPTER 17

IMAGINING COMPLEX PARTNERSHIPS

Will P. Medd

This chapter aims to show how understanding complex social systems requires a conceptualization of both openness and closure. The chapter does this through a focus on the concept of 'partnership' working, and argues that there are strong affinities between the aspirations of partnership as a holistic practice and the emphasis on holism in complexity science. Such an approach emphasizes the open nature of complex systems. However, the chapter asks, how can we understand the boundaries of a partnership? Since it is impossible for everything to be incorporated into a partnership, we need to have some understanding of how the boundaries are made. The chapter argues two quite distinct perspectives are on offer from complex social science. First, a 'pure' approach that seeks to identify what is purely social. This approach sees the partnership as a system of communication that defines the system / environment relationships of the partnerships. The second perspective, a 'hybrid' perspective, by contrast, seeks to expose the always open character of a partnership being remade on different locations. This approach sees the partnership as a distributed hybrid system that is multiple in form. The chapter concludes by arguing the need for recognizing the necessity of both closure and openness and with this the need for complexity analysis to incorporate multiplicity.

Managing Organizational Complexity: Philosophy, Theory, and Application
A Volume in: Managing the Complex, pages 301–311.
Copyright © 2005 by Information Age Publishing, Inc.
All rights of reproduction in any form reserved.
ISBN: 1-59311-319-6 (cloth), 1-59311-318-8 (paper)

Introduction

This chapter aims to show how understanding complex social systems requires a conceptualization of both *openness* and *closure*. The chapter does this through a focus on the concept of 'partnership' working and argues that there are strong affinities between the aspirations of partnership as a holistic practice and the emphasis on holism in complexity science. There are many ways in which complexity could be applied to partnerships working. Complexity could be applied to the 'wicked issues', those deeply embedded and perpetuating social problems, for example explaining the complex dynamics of the life-course or of inner city decline (consider applications in Byrne, 1998). Complexity could also be applied to the very dynamics of institutional fragmentation, exploring, for example, the historical contingencies and path-dependencies of institutional divides. Both of these are important. However, I want to focus more specifically on the problem of 'partnerships' *per se*. What can complexity tell us about what they are?

The chapter argues that we need to take issues of openness and closure as central to understanding partnership working. Having introduced the approach of this chapter to complexity, I then develop three perspectives on partnership working. The first, the holistic approach, shows the similarity of partnerships to complexity science, drawing attention to the ways in which models from complexity science offer interesting metaphors for describing partnership dynamics. The problem with this approach, however, is that it leaves us still unclear of what actually constitutes 'the partnership'. The second strategy I highlight, with an emphasis on the singularity of the partnership, concerns closure of the 'pure' partnership constituted in communications. This strategy involves positing complexity within the world itself exploring not just how partnership arise out of the problems of complexity, but also how partnerships deal with problems of complexity. What then of openness? This is the third strategy, one which emphasizes the multiplicity of partnerships. This 'hetero-geneous' approach to partnerships involves looking to the detail, to the social and material aspects that enable partnerships to happen. It is exploration of the singular (closed) and the multiplicity (openness) that I think we need to undertake to understand the complex dynamics of partnerships.

Approaching complex partnerships

"Much of the challenge for institutions lies, not in understanding and managing something qualitatively new called 'complexity', but in positively acknowledging their already-present complexity and 'messiness' and coping mechanisms. More ambitiously, policy and user-institutions need to be directly encouraged, not only to talk *complexity, and then to pretend to manage it as before, but also to* embody *its realization in developing institutional relations, mediations and identities"* (Shackely, *et al.*, 1996: 221, emphasis in original).

The quotation by Shackley, *et al.,* points towards two sensitivities that I want to highlight in this chapter. The first is to recognize that there are limits to the extent to which complexity provides methodological and managerial solutions to inevitably contested terrain. Models of complexity cannot be expected to resolve the problems of institutional dynamics which, for a long time now (from street-level bureaucrats - Lipsky, 1980 - to network governance - Amin, 1997) are known not to adhere to the formal protocols, procedures, standards etc. that policy sets down - be those characterized by bureaucratic rules, performance management or evidence-based practice . Secondly, there is a tension often within the management literature on complexity which is about whether, on the one hand, organizations are already complex systems and hence we need to realize that in order to manage them more effectively, or whether on the other hand, organizations need to become complex systems in order to function more effectively. For analytical purposes I want to argue we need to think of organizations and partnerships between organizations as already complex and we need to explore what we can learn about that complexity rather than imposing models of complexity onto already messy processes. To imagine complexity we need to explore how the world deals with complexity, copes with complexity, and in doing so, embodies complexity. Then we can more adequately relate the models from complexity science to the issues of partnership working.

One of the paradoxes of complexity science is that it can be presented in terms of rather simplistic models. It has of course been a fascinating journey to explore the ways in which the simple interactions can lead to complex dynamics and how complex interactions can lead to simple dynamics (Cohen & Stewart, 1994). However, applying these insights directly and uncritically to understanding organizations means making a number of assumptions of simplicity - as the starting point for interactions or the emergent outcome - in ways which may overlook some of the more subtle aspects of organizational life. This has of course been the concern of a growing body of literature concerned with the theoretical, methodological, and epistemological role that complexity science can offer for social science, including overcoming the barriers between the social and 'natural' sciences (see Byrne, 1998; Eve, *et al.,* 1997; Kiel & Elliot, 1996; Urry, 2003). In exploring the ways in which 'social' and 'natural' worlds can be subject to similar dynamic behavior - for example Urry (2003) suggests it is better to think in terms of 'material' or 'hybrid' worlds rather than distinct 'social' and 'natural' worlds - a key question remains about the extent to which (and how) the intentionality of human activities may or may not be incorporated within models from 'complexity science'. This is an inherent problem for any models of the social world, namely, the ultimate test of whether models from complexity science can accommodate within them the effects of their own appropriation for human action (cf. Medd, 2001a).

The argument that I want to develop in this chapter is that the central problem we are dealing with is one of understanding the dynamics of 'openness' and 'closure', and of course, their co-relationship. Often complex systems are described as being open, in so far as they exchange energy and matter with their environment. But there is also closure. This point is often neglected though it is developed by Capra (1996) who argues that as well as understanding the dynamics of openness, as modelled for example by Prigogine's *dissipative structures* (Prigogine & Stengers, 1984), so too we need to understand the dynamics of closure, as conceptualized by autopoiesis (Maturana & Varela, 1980). Capra develops this as an analytical strategy to suggest that complex systems are structurally open, exchanging energy and matter, yet organizationally closed, referring to their form, that is determining their own relations which maintain their continuity and identity. He adds to this a process of cognition referring to the process of life through which the organization becomes structurally embodied. The problem is, how to deal with this and what this means we look for.

One of the problems of the literature on partnership working is that it tends to work with normative and teleological assumptions. Normative in so far as definitions of 'partnership' are derived from what are taken to be 'good' partnerships, and teleological in so far as the assumption follows that moves towards partnerships, joint-working etc. are moves towards progress. It may seem rather counterintuitive to critique notions of 'working together'. After all, who would suggest partnerships are a bad thing? However, assumptions of partnership working can carry with them limits to what is possible and what questions are asked. For example, if it is assumed that a partnership decision represents consensus then there is no need to examine the extent to which dissent or controversy is hidden, overlooked, even ignored. Certainly we can apply models from complexity science to partnership working in terms of what we think partnerships should be doing (cf. Pratt, *et al.*, 1998, 1999; who draw on Wheatley, 1999). But important work needs to be done in exploring the role of complexity science from an explanatory point of view of partnerships, one which does not try to understand partnerships by criteria that prejudge how partnerships work in terms of success and failure. It is then we can then turn to examining the implications and possibilities for managing partnerships.

My argument is that just as we need to understand the dynamics of openness and closure in complex systems, then, so too we need to explore partnerships in this way. My aim in this chapter is then to contribute to an approach that uses the insights of complexity science to complexify thinking (cf. Chia, 1998). An approach which is not about seeking methodological simplicity but is rather about developing our imagination, complexifying our thinking, about 'partnerships'. For those who ask the 'so what' question this chapter will disappoint. I make no apology for this. How we think about partnerships, how we imagine them, will impact on what we expect from them, what we want them to do and, indeed, how we see our relationships to them.

The holistic approach

There is a strong affinity between the promise of complexity and the desires of partnership working. Partnerships are often and most broadly defined as 'working together', as a 'collaborative'. In similar way this is often emphasized by complexity scientists emphasizing interdependency and 'coevolution' (e.g., Goodwin, 1994). Complexity science is also often described as *holistic*. Not in the sense that everything can be reduced to the whole (Price, 1997: 10) but in the sense that understanding the whole cannot be attained through understanding the parts or the original conditions of the system (Byrne, 1998: 15; see also Capra, 1996). Partnership working too emphasizes the notion of 'holism' (see for example, Wilkinson & Applebee ,1999; Pratt, *et al.*, 1999 who draw on Wheatley, 1999). Partnerships tend to be seen to address the whole, for example the whole needs of the community or individual through organizational collaboration. They bring everything together. All is shared, inclusive, collaborative, consensual etc. The point of working together is indeed to achieve things that working alone cannot achieve. In this sense the whole becomes greater than the sum the of parts.

We could develop this perspective, but this holistic, and indeed romantic view of complexity that is developed here is problematic. The key problem is what constitutes the 'whole' of the partnership. What are the elements that interact to form an emergent whole? Can we identify the rule-based parts or elements that we find in models of complexity? When we think about the complexity of the different organizations involved in the partnerships, can it really be described as holistic? How should we define the boundaries of the partnerships as a complex system? The holistic approach assumes that complex dynamics can be made explicit. The holistic perspective represents a paradox in complexity science. One the one hand, complexity science embodies a 'romantic' imagination (Kwa, 2002), which invites expression of, and gives value to, the non-verbal, the emotional, the spiritual, and the artistic. The romantic vision suggests a view in which complexity cannot be grasped, we need art, poetry, emotions to express it. On the other hand, however, we find the models of complexity science embodying strategies that want to make complexity explicit by emphasizing abstraction over material form (cf. Hayles, 1999), it privileges 'looking up' (rather than down) and, in doing so, assumes the possibility of an 'overview'. So the romantic vision is one which seeks the whole and sees it as somehow knowable.

The search for an overview is tinged with a rather impossible quest, one that highlights the limits of 'the whole' that can be assumed in complexity and, in our case, partnerships. The vision of the whole seems to be one that emphasizes openness. In blurring the boundaries between partnership agencies the whole becomes qualitatively different, as something more than the sum of its parts. Law (2004) points out, however, that this view "in practice means ... a continuing invitation to step up the size of the model. To take in more". Yet it is precisely this dynamic which is impossible. Partnerships cannot incorporate everything. The limits of time, among other things, mean that distinctions have to be made, that partnerships must draw boundaries, set limits, they must exclude (see Medd, 2001b).

The pure partnership

If stepping up the size of the model is problematic, we need to ask how we can understand drawing boundaries. This requires a different approach. It requires asking what is the partnership? Consider this first methodological move:

"Whether the unity of an element should be explained as emergence 'from below' or as constitution 'from above' seems to be matter of theoretical dispute. We opt decisively for the latter. Elements are elements only for the system that employs them as units and they are such only through this system. This is formulated in the concept of autopoiesis. One of the most important consequences is that systems of a higher (emergent) order can possess less complexity than systems of a lower order because they determine the unity and number of elements that compose them; thus in their own complexity they are independent of their material substratum. This also means that the complexity that is necessary or sufficient to a system is not predetermined 'materially', but rather can be determined anew for every level of system formation with regard to the relevant environment." (Luhmann, 1995: 22-3)

This shares then the idea of an emergent order, but not an holistic order because the emergent system is not all inclusive but forms complexity 'anew'. The implication is to ask, not how partnerships are all inclusive but rather, what is the complexity they form? What is this new complexity? In other words we look to the relations, rather than emergent whole, that form the partnership, that is, a move from 'wholes and parts' to 'system / environment differences'.

What then might those relations be? Interestingly models from complexity science tend to be concerned with emergent spatial patterns. Of course spatiality is important to partnerships - as in the social world generally. However, what might be the relations that constitute the social world? When we think of partnerships through the romantic imagination in which the whole is emergent from the parts, our tendency (as humans and probably in some form humanists) is to see the parts as humans and the whole as some sort of collective dynamic. For the 'pure' approach, by contrast, we need to ask what the relationship between humans and the partnership is because the partnership, remember, forms complexity anew. This is powerful; by separating partnership organization from humans we can then ask important questions about how they come to relate rather beginning with *a priori* assumptions of that relationship. Of course it also enables us to think beyond humans (with the terror and pleasure this can bring out (Hayles, 1999), to think about how the other organizations come to relate (or not relate) to the relations that constitute the partnership.

The issue here is about how to understand 'sociality'. The typical view (which is quite compatible with the holistic view) is that social systems are composed of actions. In this sense, people come to play a part in the system through their social actions. However, as a second methodological move:

> "...one can ask whether this accurately grasps the relationship between action and sociality, above all, whether it grasps the relationship in a sufficiently productive way ... If one begins with the possibility of a theory of self-referential systems and with problems of complexity, there is much to suggest simply reversing the relationship of constraint. Sociality is not a special case of action; instead, action is constituted in social systems by means of communication and attribution as a reduction of complexity, as an indispensable self-simplification of the system." (Luhmann, 1995: 138).

This suggests we understand 'partnerships' as an emergent set of relations that constitute a system in terms of meaningful communications. The communications are self-referential in so far as they determine what is and is not the partnership through their codes. The conceptualization of communication, however, is not what we would normally expect. Communication is not about an actor-agent-human transferring knowledge to another, or 'interpersonal' understanding. The process is more difficult. Communication works back-to-front. By definition for communication to take place it requires receipt. Such receipt does not depend on understanding - misunderstanding also forms communication. The crucial points is, for communication to take place, an effect must be produced (Luhmann, 1995: 154). Here 'observation' is embedded as key within the dynamic of the system; it is observation (as listening, (mis)understanding) that constitutes the communication.

What does this mean for the pure partnership? The emerging partnership constitutes a difference that defines the partnership as the partnership. At the general level it works with a communication code of 'partnership / non-partnership'. The 'pure' partnership is a system of communications that refer to the relationships between the organizations that are said to be in the partnership. Said to be is important for this highlights the point that the description of a set of relations as 'partnership' is a simplifying strategy; it simplifies the complexity of various sets of possibilities into particular relations called 'partnership'. The implication is that the 'partnership' creates a new form of complexity. What this approach brings to our attention is the way in which the complexity of a partnership involves the constitution of communications that form a new strata of complexity, a complex system in the environment of other systems. The partnership here is not one based on a whole in which there is value consensus, order, necessity, or intersubjectivity. The partnership becomes a self-referentially ordered (out of disorder) system motivated by complexity and contingency (it could have been otherwise).

The emphasis of this approach is on the closure of the communications that define the partnership as partnership. Conceptualizing such closure, however, does not mean assuming that agreement, or consensus, is actually achieved but leads us to examining how decisions are made that constitute communications within the partnership. The emphasis is on reading the simple from the complex in so far as it is about understanding how the problems of complexity are dealt with in the world, in the partnership. The problem is the identification of the partnership in terms of the formal constitution, which leaves us with questions about what such a partnership means in practice.

The hybrid partnership

The pure approach says little about how we would understand the detail of a partnership in practice. And yet it is the specificity of the detail of partnerships that is so important, for that is where decision with real implications take place. What partnerships do locally is ultimately where they make the differences that matter. While the pure approach emphasizes how partnerships read simplicity from disorder, the points of disorder are important. While the pure approach privileges selections that are made, negotiation, mediation, translation are lost. Indeed, the complexity of these things, we might say is lost. To look to the detail means to look down into the partnership. Looking down involves a more 'Baroque' approach to complexity which has three key characteristics relevant here:

"*First the historic baroque insists on a strong phenomenological realness, a sensuous materiality. Second this materiality is not confined to, or locked within, a simple individual but flows out in many directions, blurring the distinction between individual environment. And third, there is also the baroque inventiveness, the ability to produce lots of novel combinations out of a rather limited set of elements*" (Kwa, 2002: 26)

This baroque imagination is about the distributed embodiedness of a complex system. Importantly though, it does not require us to define such embodiedness in terms of particular types of elements, as implied in the pure approach, and nor does it refer to an integrated whole implied in the holistic approach. Instead, understanding the complexity of partnerships through a baroque imagination means exploring the heterogeneity of the constitution of partnerships and the multiplicity this entails. It means that there can be no overview (Law, 2004). The global (the partnership in this case) becomes something that is always situated, is always specific and must, therefore, always be accomplished.

This version of complexity (though not addressed specifically to debates in complexity science) is demonstrated in Dugdale's account of what we can call a 'partnership' committee in Australia, whilst exploring the health dangers of intrauterine contraceptive devices (IUD) and which, as one outcome, produced a leaflet to inform women of some of the issues (Dugdale, 1999). She argues against approaches that assume that such a committee, which includes representation from science, industry, government, health services and herself (as a lay member), a partnership, can be understood to achieve closure on issues of controversy. There is no emerging whole, based on a consensus. But nor are there dynamics that could be described as purely social. Dugdale's account examines the shifting negotiations of power; how through those negotiations the very identity of the participants are negotiated, and how it is through the 'practical materiality' of such partnerships that makes them possible. Materials are important. For example, Dugdale points to the variety of heterogeneous materials - from her first class air tickets to her the architecture of the building where they meet - that form relations that constitute the subjectivities and identities of participants. The paradox is that while the partnership is represented as a singular body concerned with a singular issue, this occurs through the construction of a multiplicity of subjectivities with different constructions of the issue. Both singularity and multiplicity, sameness and difference, openness and closure, become important; it is the oscillation between them that enables the partnership to work, to make decisions.

When we consider that the idea of complexity science is an idea about distributions, about distributed systems, then if we consider 'partnerships' as distributed complex systems it seems necessary to explore the local constitution of the partnership. Since there are multiple locations the partnership would seem to become multiple. When we think of such multiple locations we can also start to see how much less than 'everything' can be included in the partnership (contra the 'holistic' approach) but at the same time, much more than 'communications' (contra the 'pure' approach) seems to matter. Indeed, the approach suggests the need to explore the heterogeneous entities and relations that are a part of partnership formation. When we allow ourselves to see such complexity, then many things come into play that are important: computer technologies, telephones, policy documents, evidence based reports, transports, the settings for meetings and so on. These things all become significant for a distributed partnership. What then of closure and openness? The answer seems to imply the need to have both, with each, as we would expect with complexity, depending on the other. Hence, Dugdale's point that the decision about the IUD (i.e., closure) was made possible by different constitutions of that devise (openness). It means not only introducing multiplicity about our understanding of the partnerships, but also introducing multiplicity into the partnership such that recognizing the multiple ways the partnership constructs its object, and the hidden ways in which this can take place.

Conclusion

In this discussion of partnership working I have argued that we need to do more work than simply align complexity to partnership working. Complexity needs to have more explanatory power in assessing the very dynamic in which solutions are continually prescribed while the tensions of partnership working continue. Complexity suggests that partnerships will always be local and that local history will matter. But focusing on the local this does not mean in contrast to the global. This is not about micro versus macro. It is about how, within the local the global is always present, being played out, being 'performed' (Law, 2004). To understand 'partnerships' we do not begin with ready made (globalizing) definitions of what constitute 'good' partnerships. Instead, we examine the dynamics that come to define partnerships as partnerships. And, which I think is crucial, there is a role here for suggesting that a complexity perspective may help in developing partnership working when the 'perfect' model cannot be achieved. A complexity perspective, for example, may offer insight into why a partnership is not working well, but also how to make it work better without the assumption that there will be shared understanding, shared information and so on.

My suggestion then is that we make the link between complexity and partnerships, but that we do not do this with a 'romantic' holistic pre-occupation. Instead of claims to such openness, we recognize the necessity of closure where such closure means *disintegration* as much as *integration*, *exclusion* as much as *inclusion*, *ignorance* as much as *information*. To help see these dynamics I have played with the idea of the 'pure' partnership to explore closure and the formation of a complex dynamic that becomes 'the partnership' as a distinct entity. This helps us understand the selectivity of partnerships faced with complexity and the constitution of the partnership in terms of communications, which attribute decisions as action within the partnership. By contrast, however, I have also played with the idea of a 'hybrid' partnership which points more to ideas of openness. This approach, instead of searching for a purely social emergent order, examines the detail of practices and materials through which partnerships are continually constituted and distributed. It offers an almost fractal-like gaze to explore the detail within the particular (e.g., 'a decision') through which the global (e.g., 'the partnership') is constituted and located.

References

Allen, C. (2001). *Desperately Seeking Fusion: On 'Joined-Up Thinking', 'Holistic Practice' and the New Economy of Welfare Professional Power*, Centre for Sustainable Urban and Regional Futures, University of Salford.

Amin, A. and Hausner, J. (eds.). (1997). *Beyond Market and Hierarchy: Interactive Governance and Social Complexity*, Cheltenham: Edward Elgar.

Byrne, D. (1998). *Complexity Theory and the Social Sciences: An Introduction*, London: Routledge.

Capra, F. (1996). *The Web of Life: A New Synthesis of Mind and Matter*, London: Harper Collins.

Chia, R. (1998). "From Complexity Science to Complex Thinking: Organization as Simple Location," *Organization*, 5(3): 341-369.

Cohen, J. and Stewart, I. (1994). *The Collapse of Chaos: Discovering Simplicity in a Complex World*, Harmondsworth, Penguin.

Dugdale, A. (1999). "Materiality: Juggling, Sameness and Difference," in J. Law and J. Hassard, *Actor Network Theory and After*, Oxford: Blackwell.

Eve, R. A., Horsfall, S., and Lee, M. E. (eds.) (1997). *Chaos, Complexity and Sociology: Myths, Models, and Theories*, London: Sage.

Goodwin, B. (1994). *How the Leopard Changed Its Spots*, London: Phoenix Giants.

Hayles, K. (1999). *How We Became Posthuman: Virtual Bodies in Cybernetics, Literature, and Informatics*, Chicago: Univ. of Chicago Press.

Kiel, D. L., Elliot, E. (eds.) (1996). *Chaos Theory in the Social Sciences: Foundations and Applications*, Michigan: University of Michigan Press.

Kwa, C. (2002). "Romantic and Baroque Conceptions of Complex Wholes in the Sciences," in J. Law and A. Mol (eds.), *Complexities: Social Studies of Knowledge Practices*, London: Duke University Press.

Law, J. (2004). "And if the Global Were Small and Non-Coherent? Method, Complexity and the Baroque," *Environment and Planning D: Society and Space*, 22: 13-26

Lipsky, M. (1980). *Street-level Bureaucracy: Dilemmas of the individual in public services*, New York: Russell Sage Foundation.

Luhmann, N. (1995). *Social Systems*, Stanford: Stanford Uni. Press.

Maturana, H. R. and Varela, F. J. (1980). *Autopoiesis and Cognition: The Realization of the Living*, Dorderacht: D.Reidel.

Medd, W. (2001a). "What is Complexity Science? Toward an 'ecology of ignorance'," *Emergence: Journal of Complexity Issues in Organizations and Management*, 3(1): 43-60.

Medd, W, (2001b). "Complexity and Partnership," in D. Taylor (ed.), *Breaking Down Barriers: Reviewing Partnership Practice*, Brighton, HSPRC University of Brighton.

Pratt, J., Gordon, P. and Plamping, D. (1999). *Working Whole Systems: Putting theory into Practice in Organizations*, London: Kings Fund.

Pratt, J., Plamping, D. and Gordon, P. (1998). *Partnership: Fit for a Purpose?* London: Kings Fund.

Price, B. (1997) "Myth of Postmodern Science," in R. A. Eve, S. Horsfall and M. E. Lee (eds.), *Chaos, Complexity and Sociology: Myths, Models, and Theories*, London: Sage.

Prigogine, I. and Stengers, I. (1984). *Order Out of Chaos: Man's New Dialogue With Nature*, London, Heinemann.

Shackley, S., Waterton, C. and Wynne, B. (1996). "Imagine Complexity! The Past, Present, and Future Potential of Complex Thinking," *Futures*, (28): 201-225.

Urry, J. (2003). *Global Complexity*, Cambridge: Polity.

Wheatley, M. J. (1999). *Leadership and the New Science: Discovering Order in a Chaotic World*, San Francisco: Berrett-Koehler.

Wilkinson, D. and Applebee, E. (1999). *Implementing Holistic Government: Joined-Up Action on the Ground*, Bristol: Policy Press.

CHAPTER 18

THE IMPROVISED-ORCHESTRATION MODEL OF ORGANIZATIONAL EVOLUTION

Tadahiko Kawai

The excellent results of some large Japanese companies in the 1990s including Sony and Honda were not due to characteristics of the so-called Japanese type of management including 'kaizen', 'keiretsu', multifunctional teams and such. Neither were they the core competencies such as Sony's miniaturization technology or Honda's engines and power trains. Rather, the critical factors were top and middle management's strong and autonomous strategic initiatives, and collaboration in those initiatives. This chapter sets forth a model of organizational evolution for large, complex firms, which involves strong, autonomous strategic initiatives of both top and middle management, and linkages between them. It will be developed based on a CAS (complex adaptive system) paradigm. Then, the proposed model will be illustrated by the cases of Honda and Sony. Reconciling a dispute between the continuous and discontinuous change paradigms and formulating a modified version of the existing CAS paradigm on which a dynamic theory of strategy-making can be built are other significant objectives of this chapter.

Managing Organizational Complexity: Philosophy, Theory, and Application
A Volume in: Managing the Complex, pages 313–329.
ISBN: 1-59311-319-6 (cloth), 1-59311-318-8 (paper)

Introduction

Although many Japanese industries lost their international competitiveness in the 1990s, some large companies including Sony and Honda have achieved excellent results. The key factors for their success, however, were not due to characteristics of the so-called Japanese type of management including quality control or *kaizen*, product development based on supplier (or *keiretsu* firm) involvement, cross-functional teams and such. Neither were they the core competencies such as Sony's miniaturization technology or Honda's engines and power trains as many researchers have pointed out (e.g., Prahalad & Hamel, 1990; Stalk, *et al.*, 1992; Hayes & Pisano, 1994). Rather, the critical factors were top and middle management's strong and autonomous strategic initiatives, and collaboration in those initiatives. This collaboration was achieved intentionally and / or unintentionally, and cross-sectionally and / or longitudinally, realizing a kind of 'improvised-orchestration'.

The autonomous strategic initiatives observed involved more aggressive initiatives than those that are normally conceptualized in the relevant literature. More specifically, in the case of middle management, they involved more aggressive initiatives than 'normal championing'. One typical type of initiative taken was a 'rebellious championing' (Bower, 1970; Kanter, 1983; Floyd & Wooldridge, 1992), meaning, for example, the development of new products without the approval of superiors. In the case of top management, they involved more aggressive initiatives than 'normal strategy-making', which is based on the approval of the top management team. One typical type of such initiatives was an *autocratic strategy-making* where a CEO enforces 'personal' strategies irrespective of opposition by other team members, or by overruling the majority-based decisions (Noda & Bower, 1996).

These types of initiatives had been rare in large Japanese firms where 'consensus' had been the pervasive method of decision-making. More importantly, although these two types of initiatives were usually taken separately, one was sometimes followed by the other, producing an orchestrated strategy with improvisation.

Thus, in order to explain the results of excellent Japanese companies such as Sony and Honda, it is necessary to develop a framework of organizational evolution that involves top and middle management's strong strategic initiatives and 'collaboration' between them. And more importantly, this framework appears to apply not only to Japanese firms but also to any firm in an uncertain or turbulent environment.

This chapter sets forth a model of organizational evolution for large, complex firms, which involves strong, autonomous strategic initiatives of both top and middle management, and linkages between them. It will be developed based on a complex adaptive system (CAS) paradigm. Although several researchers tried to apply the complexity theory to strategy-making, the results were not satisfactory. Formulating a modified version of the existing CAS paradigm applicable to the theory of strategy-making is another significant objective of this chapter.

The chapter is divided into four sections. The next section examines existing literature that is closely relevant to this theme, focusing mainly on the continuous change paradigm regarding organizational change and the adaptation of large, complex firms to turbulent environments. In the second section, a general model is proposed, namely the *Improvised Orchestration* (IO) model of organizational evolution, based on the modified CAS paradigm. The third section presents the cases of Sony and Honda, which illustrate the proposed model. The final section discusses some of the implications of the model, both theoretical and practical.

Previous research

Let us examine the relevant existing literature with respect to the following requirements of the IO model that will be presented later. First, both top management's autocratic and middle management's rebellious initiatives are conceptualized. Second, collaboration between these two types of initiatives is conceptualized.

Continuous vs. discontinuous schools

The most relevant field dealing with the theme of this chapter is the organizational (including strategy) change or evolution, and there are two types of paradigm. One is the *discontinuous change paradigm* and its most representative model is the *punctuated equilibrium theory* (Tushman & Romanelli, 1985; Tushman & Anderson, 1986; Gersick, 1988, 1991; Romanelli & Tushman, 1994). It asserts that organizations evolve through "relatively long periods of stability (equilibrium), punctuated by compact periods of qualitative, metamorphic change (revolution)" (Gersick, 1991: 12). Organizations evolve only incrementally during periods of equilibrium because they are the organic wholes or configurations in which all the parts are so closely integrated that they cannot be changed independently even in the face of environmental changes. However, if the environment changes drastically, incremental change is insufficient and an overall organizational change must be introduced through strong initiatives by top management.

This paradigm is not enough for our purposes because it does not fulfill the requirements of the IO model. First, it does not involve rebellious initiatives by middle management and although it involves top management's strong initiatives, they are quite exceptional and appear only in revolutionary periods. Second, collaboration between the initiatives of top and middle management is not conceptualized.

Another field is the *continuous change paradigm*, which asserts that changes or evolution in strategy and / or structure are continuous and incremental, and are chiefly made by the autonomous initiatives of middle level management (Quinn, 1981; Johnson, 1988; Quinn & Cameron, 1988). Although there are many variations of this paradigm, the following two representative works are the most relevant here.

Burgelman model

The first is Burgelman's model, which consists of two types of corporate strategic behavior (Burgelman, 1983, 1991). One is the *induced strategic behavior* that is made based on the firm's current concepts of corporate strategy including new product development of existing product lines. The other is *autonomous strategic behavior*, which is entrepreneurial behavior by individuals at the operational and middle levels of organizations such as seen in conceiving and championing new products or businesses that are not in line with the existing strategy concepts.

Based on this distinction and in light of the findings of research on internal corporate venturing, Burgelman asserts that strategic renewal of large, complex firms requires the interlocking of autonomous strategic behavior of middle management with the two selection mechanisms. One is the *internal mechanism* within the company by which only promising autonomous strategic behavior is selected from among competing initiatives. The other is the *external mechanism* by which the business created through such behavior competes with those of other companies in the market. Top management's role is restricted to the retroactive rationalization of the autonomous strategic behavior of middle management that has been selected by both internal and external selection mechanisms.

One example is found in Intel's transformation from dynamic random access memory (DRAM) to microprocessor unit (MPU) maker, which was achieved not by a top management decision, namely 'induced strategic behavior', but by the 'autonomous strategic behavior' of middle management. One typical case is that of the RISK processor (a kind of MPU) business. L. Kohn, an astute technologist, had been trying to get Intel into this business ever since he joined the company due to his firm belief in its potential. However, since the CISK (the existing MPU) business was very successful, the official corporate strategy was not to enter the RISK business. Knowing that a formal request would never be accepted, Kohn took a 'disguised strategy' as a last resort. That is, although he designed the RISK processor as a stand-alone processor, he made it applicable to some CISK processors as an accessory and sold it to the top management as a 'co-processor'. Thus, "by the time top management realized what their 'co-processor' was, Kohn, with the help of two other champions, had already lined up a customer base for the stand-alone processor ..." (Burgelman, 1991: 247) and ultimately succeeded in broadening Intel's business base.

Burgelman's model is very important in that it reveals the possibility of a model different from a traditional model that can be depicted as an *orchestration model* in which the conductor presents the theme and requests the full adherence to it by all members. More specifically, the Burgelman model succeeded in attaching a flavor of *improvisation* to the orchestration model. It is also important to note that Burgelman referred to the notion of *self-organization* in introducing the notion of autonomous strategic behavior.

However, it does not satisfy the requirements of the IO model mentioned earlier. It lacks the autonomous strategic initiatives of top management and, accordingly, it cannot deal with collaboration in initiatives. In addition, Burgelman's concept of autonomous strategic initiatives of middle management does not have a very high level of rebelliousness in its championing.

Brown=Eisenhardt model

Another approach is the model developed by Brown and Eisenhardt (1997) concerning multiple-product innovation. They assert that in fast-moving markets, such as the computer industry, it is vital for companies to change continuously through multiple-product innovation. One of the key points that successful managers follow is in combining limited structures (namely, the rules concerning priorities and responsibilities, etc.) with extensive interaction. It is because this combination not only effectively motivates members and helps them understand the rapidly changing environments, but it also allows for improvisation. Improvisation in jazz is sometimes misunderstood to be the result of free playing by all players. However, real improvisation is made possible by *real time extensive communication among players bound by a few rules.*

This model of improvisation seems appropriate as a model of multiple-product innovation in a turbulent environment and it is interesting to note that, in contrast to Burgelman's reference to self-organization, it refers to the complexity theory as follows. "Continuously changing organizations are likely to be complex adaptive systems with semi-structures that poise the organization on the edge of order and chaos, and links in time that force simultaneous attention and linkage among past, present, and future. These organizations seem to grow over time through a series of sequenced steps, and they are associated with success in highly competitive, high-velocity environments" (Brown & Eisenhardt, 1997: 32).

Although the Brown=Eisenhardt model is quite appealing, we can not utilize it because it is a model developed for small R&D teams, and so is not applicable to large organizations, and therefore cannot satisfy the requirements of the IO model. In addition, the following points need to be noted regarding its interpretation of improvisation. First, although the Brown=Eisenhardt model focuses on speedy adaptation to environments, as if it is the only merit of improvisation, creative collective outcome is another, and often more important, merit of improvisation as far as *group improvisation* is concerned (Bastien & Hostager, 1988). Second, although one member usually plays a dual role as both a (substantial) leader and a player in group improvisation, this point is not addressed in the above model.

Improvised orchestration (IO) model

The next step is to build a model of IO by extending Burgelman's model based on the modified CAS paradigm and through the introduction of the notion of improvisation that was mentioned above.

Complex adaptive system (CAS) paradigm

Although researchers differ considerably in how they differentiate or relate such concepts or paradigms as the complex system (CA), CAS, chaos, and self-organizing (e.g., Anderson, 1999; Morel & Ramanujyam, 1999), I consider the CS paradigm to consist of the self-organization and the (deterministic) chaos sub-paradigms, and the discussion below is restricted to the former. (Concerning the application of the latter, see, for example, Levy (1994); Thietart & Forgues, 1997; Dooley & Van de Ven, 1999.)

According to this view, the CAS paradigm is seen as a predominant variant of the self-organization paradigm, which emphasizes the *adaptive* aspects of CS. That is, it postulates that CAS is adaptive not only because its agents exhibit adaptive behavior, but because the CAS as a whole (or its emergent structure) responds and adapts to its environment (e.g., Waldlop, 1992: 149; Anderson, 1999: 223).

What should be noted here, however, is that, in existing literature, adaptation of CAS as a whole is considered to arise not as a result of *purposive* adaptive behavior of CAS as a whole, but as a result of adaptive behavior of its interactive agents. And this is implied by the basic premise of emergent characteristics of CS and hence that of CAS, stating that CAS consists only of interactive agents and does not involve such entities as hierarchical organizations that represent the whole system and exhibit purposive adaptive behavior. (Incidentally, when Buckley used the word CAS, he emphasized the adaptive aspect of the system as a whole. However, his conceptualization was based on the framework of the (general) systems theory and the emergent aspect of the system was not considered - Buckley, 1998.)

Other than this existing view of the CAS paradigm, however, it is possible to postulate that adaptation of CAS is made possible not only by adaptive behavior of its agents, but also by purposive adaptive behavior of CAS as a whole if the following assumptions are posited. First, the agents of CAS take autonomous (adaptive) behavior as postulated in the existing CAS paradigm. Second, however, the agents are not perfectly autonomous, and, when necessary, they can take concerted actions and build a hierarchical organization for that purpose and perform *role behavior* directed by that organization as postulated in the traditional *formal* organization theory (e.g., Barnard, 1938). Finally, the agents behave as role players and their aspect as the agents of CAS becomes latent as far as their needs are fulfilled, but, once that condition is lost, that aspect is evoked and the agents again become autonomous players.

This view - which I call the *modified CAS paradigm* - may be unacceptable for the proponents of both the existing CAS and the formal organization paradigms since it seems to imply the juxtaposition of two antithetical paradigms. However, the assumption of the agent who can take two types of behavior such as autonomous and role behavior is not only non-contradictory but also entirely consistent with our recognition of the real world. And this might be one example of the assertion that "[g]iven that no one perspective can capture the inherent intricacies of complex systems, the analysis of complex systems requires us to consider a number of perspectives" (Richardson, *et al.*, 2001: 13) It is also consistent with Dent's chapter in this volume stating that "Complexity theory work ... has suggested that paradox may provide greater explanation ... [T]he universe is better understood through the multiple lenses of paradox and perspective."

Applying the modified CAS paradigm to the strategy-making processes

Now, let's consider that one CS is poised in an certain environment and has to survive against the threat from that environment. Then it would be quite natural that this system (or its members) considers that some level of concerted member action is necessary, and introduces some kind of hierarchical organization within it. This means that the system now has come to have a dual structure consisting of a CS and a hierarchical organization. I call this type of CS a CAS, since it is a complex system that is poised within the environment and tries to adapt to it.

An important characteristic of this system is that each member also comes to have a dual membership: as a member of the CS as well as of a hierarchical organization. The individual is considered to perform not only a role assigned to him as a member of the organization, but also to exhibit autonomous behavior as a member of the CS.

If this is applied to a middle manager, it first follows that the individual performs strategic behavior that has been assigned. Since this behavior is deduced from the corporate strategy conceived by top management, it can be called *orchestrated behavior* by middle management. This behavior can be represented as O_M, where 'O' stands for orchestration and the 'M' for middle management.

On the other hand, the individual also initiates autonomous strategic behavior and this can be called *improvised behavior* of middle management. This can be represented by I_M, where 'I' stands for improvisation. One conspicuous example of this improvised behavior is that of Kohn of Intel as seen with regards to the RISK processor.

The important point is that this logic should be applied to all members of the system, including top management, and we can consider top management's orchestrated behavior as O_T as well as their improvised behavior as I_T, where 'T' stands for top management. O_T is a basic function of top management in orchestrating the organization according to the conceived theme and eliciting the concerted action of all members. On the other hand, I_T is the autonomous strategic behavior of top management. It is top management's behavior, taken irrespective of the opposition of other members of the top management team or the whole company. Examples are the CEO's approval of middle management's strategic behavior or behavior enforcing 'personal' strategies against the strong opposition of other top management (or by overruling the majority-based decisions). The former may be represented as I_T <approval> and the latter as I_T <enforcing>.

Improvised orchestration (IO)

Given the above set of behaviors of top and middle management, IO can be postulated based on this behavior. The basic elements of IO are the four types of behavior mentioned above, namely, O_M, O_T, I_M and I_T. And the basic patterns of IO can be defined as the following patterns of interaction among these basic elements.

Pattern 1: $[I_M \rightarrow I_T$<approval>] This pattern implies that improvisation by middle management is followed by improvisation by top management in such a way that, for example, the CEO approves the autonomous strategic behavior of middle management, such as that exhibited by Kohn.

Pattern 2: $[I_M \rightarrow I_T$<approval> $\rightarrow O_T]$. This is an extension of Pattern 1 and implies that top management not only approves autonomous strategic behavior by middle management, but also incorporates it into formal corporate strategy, namely orchestrating a theme. This can happen when the initiative by middle management is very promising.

Pattern 3: $[I_M \rightarrow I_T$<approval> $\rightarrow (O_T \rightarrow) I_T$ <enforcing>]. This is a pattern in which improvisation by middle management evokes not only improvisation by top management as approval of the former but also (via or not via O_T) more aggressive improvisation by top management of enforcing a personal strategy against the opposition of other members of the top management team

These are the basic elements and patterns of improvisation and more complicated patterns can be conceptualized, for example, by classifying I_M (as done with I_T), by combining Patterns 1-3, or by adding other patterns starting with I_T. However, the above patterns would be enough for the purpose of this chapter in exemplifying the possibilities of the IO model.

Illustrations

Let's demonstrate how the IO model is useful in explaining actual facts by applying it to the cases of Honda and Sony. Although the entire histories of these companies could be explained using the IO model, such an extensive work is beyond the scope of this article and thus we will only deal with a few conspicuous events at both companies. (The cases are based on Kawai, 1999 and Tateishi, 2002.)

Case 1: Odyssey and the creative mover series (Honda)

Honda is one of the world's major automakers and one of the few Japanese businesses that were internationally competitive through the 1990s. However, it experienced a rather radical decline in performance in the early 1990s despite doing very well in the U.S. and Canada. One of the major reasons for this was the bursting of the economic bubble, which was unavoidable. However, the decline in its market share was inexcusable and there were two reasons for this. One was that Honda's strategy had placed an emphasis on the development of 'world-cars' due to its long time goal to be a worldclass automaker. Moreover, this strategy had been successful as far as the North American market was concerned. Nevertheless, it had the side effect of making light of the domestic market and the 'world-cars', such as sedans, were not popular in Japan's automobile market. Another reason for the decline was that Honda did not have RVs (recreational vehicles), which started to become fashionable in the domestic market.

Honda's formal corporate strategy was not to enter the RV market. The main reason was Honda's above-mentioned goal. There was another reason; it could not afford the huge investment required for entering that market. That is, although the production of RVs required a production line with the same height as that of a truck production line, Honda did not have any truck production lines. So, for Honda to enter the RV market, the introduction of a new production line that would cost more than $8 million was necessary. But this was inconceivable at the time.

In the midst of a worsening situation, N. Kawamoto became the President of Honda in 1993. He succeeded the 'world-car' strategy and talked about RVs in such a way that 'there is no space to drive big RVs (in a small country like Japan)'. And he energetically pursued an organizational transformation to reinforce the company's ability to develop new sedans that could succeed both globally and locally. He literally pushed his way through *autocratically*, irrespective of strong opposition and criticism from both within and outside the company, and changed many traditional ways of doing things that had been effective when Honda was struggling to become a major four-wheeled automaker from a two-wheeled vehicle venture company. That was why Kawamoto was referred to as 'Hitler'.

Under such circumstances, T. Sugiyama, a senior car-development engineer, began to seek the potential of entering the RV market without a huge investment, considering that RVs were vital for the revival of Honda in the domestic market. His idea was to introduce a Japanese type of small RV, which could be assembled on the existing production line for sedans with their low height. He personally studied this possibility in the factory and subsequently verified it. Then, with the help of other engineers, he made a mock-up of the RV, presented it to top management, and finally got the approval from President Kawamoto to develop that automobile, later named the Odyssey.

On the other hand, recognizing the possibility to assemble small RVs on existing production lines, Kawamoto launched a very aggressive strategy in 1994. The aggressive strategy was a sales target of 800,000 vehicles in the domestic market in 1998 for which most people were quite wary, since the sales volume in 1994 was only 610,000. However, Kawamoto was confident of achieving this target because he was sure that his strategy of introducing a series of small RVs would succeed. It was the Creative Mover Series consisting of two minivans, one station wagon, and one four-wheeled vehicle. He delegated a large portion of the power in the development to the younger generation.

Odyssey was placed on the market in October 1994 and the four Creative Mover Series vehicles were released between October 1995 and November 1996. The result was that not only the Odyssey, but all of the Creative Mover Series vehicles were a huge hit. Honda's market share sharply rose and became second to Toyota in November and December 1997 for the first time in its history. In addition, the sales target of 800,000 vehicles was achieved in 1997, one year earlier than targeted. Odyssey and these other cars not only became the savior of Honda in the domestic market but also laid the foundation for further growth as a global player thereafter.

Analysis of case 1

Let's analyze the above case. First of all, Sugiyama's behavior in proposing and verifying the creative idea of small RVs was clearly an I_M - improvisation by middle management - since it was autonomous strategic behavior and carried out against the official corporate strategy.

Second, President Kawamoto's behavior seems to be a pattern of $[I_T$ <approval> $\rightarrow O_T]$. Although there is no clear information about the attitudes of other members of the top management team, his recognition of Sugiyama's proposal can be strongly guessed as being an I_T<approval> - an *approval* type of improvisation by top management - judging from his autocratic behavior in those days. That is, it is an autonomous strategic behavior as a member of a CAS. It is also clear that this behavior was followed by O_T - orchestration by top management - meaning that the Odyssey was incorporated into Honda's official strategy. Thus, the process from Sugiyama's Odyssey proposal to Kawamoto's approval, to its subsequent incorporation into official strategy by Kawamoto can be interpreted as Pattern 2: $[I_M \rightarrow I_T$<approval> $\rightarrow O_T]$.

Third, launching the Creative Mover Series by Kawamoto is clearly an I_T<enforcing> - an *enforcing* type of improvisation by top management - because it was carried out by him in spite of strong criticism from within and outside the company. So, if this strategy is added to the process mentioned above, the total process can be described as Pattern 3: $[I_M \rightarrow I_T$<approval> $\rightarrow O_T \rightarrow I_T$<enforcing>]. That is, the whole process of IO in the case of Honda can be described as Pattern 3. It was started by Sugiyama's (individual) improvisation and echoed by Kawamoto's (individual) improvisation.

Finally, the following points should be mentioned as characteristics of the above IO. First, it was a very creative strategic move in that the Odyssey and other vehicles created a new small RV market that is quite adequate for the Japanese people. Second, that creative move functioned as a proactive strategy for Honda in that it substantially absorbed uncertainty with which Honda was faced. That is, it was uncertain at that time whether or not RVs would become a clear trend in the near future. In such a situation, the Odyssey helped Honda reduce this uncertainty by creating a new market in which it had strong competitiveness. Finally, although Honda was late in entering the normal RV market, its action in opening and establishing a small RV market was quite speedy.

Case 2: PlayStation (Sony)

Sony is another company that achieved excellent results in the 1990s. Sony's success can be explained very well using the IO model. For example, the Walkman was produced through improvisation of the president at the time, M. Morita. Furthermore, entering the movie business through the acquisition of Columbia Pictures was the result of Morita's personal aspiration to combine 'hardware' and 'software' (he was the chairman at that time). The proposal for the acquisition was first rejected at the board of directors' meeting. It was the strong persuasion of then president Ohga, at the next meeting, which opened with strong solicitation by Morita, which made the acquisition possible. These initiatives of Morita and Ohga can be interpreted as I_T<enforcing>.

Another conspicuous example is the development of PlayStation (PS), the game console business. It was initiated by the strong personal ambition of K. Kutaragi, a technologist, who had a firm belief that the game console with 3D technology could be profitable in the near future. He first proposed the idea of making a joint venture with Nintendo and succeeded in concluding a contract in spite of the strong opposition by the top management team.

Nintendo, however, suddenly changed its new console development partner from Sony to Philips, the Netherlands' electronics giant and the contract with Sony was broken. Then, Kutaragi began to force the development of a game console within the company. However, the opposition to this proposal was very strong and, when discussed at the top management meeting, it was almost decided not to enter that business. At that moment, Kutaragi, who had been allowed to attend the meeting, stood up and began to persuade the members. His final words to President Ohga were the following. "How can you put up with such humiliation as the contract you signed is being broken so easily? You wouldn't just be silent if we were treated as children, would you? Wouldn't this hurt the glorious brand of Sony?" Hearing this, it is reported, that Ohga slammed the table and left the room, saying that "If you are going to say that much, verify the possibility of your plan on your own. Do it!" Thus, the development of PS was approved. It subsequently became a very big hit and grew to be one of Sony's major sources of profits along with its succeeding PS2.

Kutaragi's behavior was undoubtedly that of I_M and Ohga's was that of I_T, creating Pattern 2: $[I_M \rightarrow I_T\text{<approval>} \rightarrow O_T]$. Furthermore, it is to be noted that the game business was quite uncertain and the key success factor was the creative and autonomous decisions made by both top and middle management and the unintentional collaboration between them.

Discussion

The above illustrations can be discussed from several theoretical and practical viewpoints as outlined below.

Continuous 'and' discontinuous change model

The first theoretical implication is that the possibility of the IO model reveals that of a reconciliation of the dispute between the continuous and discontinuous change paradigms mentioned at the beginning of this article. It is because the improvisation involved in the IO model enables the continuous changes emphasized by the continuous change paradigm, while, at the same time, enabling overall radical changes when necessary, which were considered as important in the discontinuous change paradigm. Put differently, the IO model can be seen as a general model of organizational evolution which includes as its specific models both the continuous change models including Burgelman's and Brown=Eizehardt's and the discontinuous change models.

Moreover, the IO model makes it possible to deal with the changes that the dichotomous paradigms cannot. For example, it can conceptualize repetition of radical changes in a relatively short period of time, which are required in truly turbulent periods. In a dichotomous view, radical changes are conceptualized only in a discontinuous paradigm as exceptional events following long periods of stability.

Dynamic theory of strategy-making

The second theoretical implication as a corollary to the one stated above is that the IO model can be a basis of a dynamic theory of strategy-making that is effective in a turbulent environment. Most of the existing theories of strategy-making including the positioning and the resource-based theories, which are consistent with the concept of orchestration, are not useful in that environment since they posit a static environment where consumers' needs and / or technologies are relatively stable. In sharp contrast to this, the IO model can lead to the construction of a more dynamic theory of strategy-making, since the proactive strategies by the IO model can change or affect environments themselves, thereby 'absorbing' uncertainty itself.

Relating to this point, it is noteworthy that the above discussion is consistent with the recent trend in strategy-making research that the option-based theories emphasizing the importance of flexibility in strategy-making are welcomed. This is because improvisation, and in consequence IO, can produce diverse strategy options and therefore flexibility in strategy, which is a basis of option-based theories aimed at longitudinal risk dispersion (e.g., Sanchez, 1995; Amram & Kulatilaka, 1999).

Complex 'and' adaptive system models

The third theoretical implication is that the CAS paradigm presented earlier - which was named the 'modified CAS paradigm' - is better than the existing CAS paradigm in that it enables the construction of the IO model which is applicable, in principle, to any size of organization, while the models and the metaphors based on the existing CAS paradigm are mostly restricted to the explanation of organizing aspects of the organization (e.g., Weick, 1998; Hatch, 1998) or of small groups like R&D teams. In addition, it is important to note that it was made possible by the explicit introduction of the dual structure of CAS and "purposive adaptive behavior of CAS as a whole" into the existing CAS model.

In conjunction with this implication, two points merit attention. One is that Stacey (1995) also posited the dual structure of organization in his framework of strategic change so that the concept of the *edge of chaos* could be applied. However, it is a structure consisting of formal and informal organizations and is quite different from our conceptualization, in which both CAS and the hierarchical organization are formal. It is true that the Stacey type of conceptualization is possible and somewhat useful in explaining self-organization in informal organizations (a good example is McMillan, this volume).

It seems to be doubtful, however, that Stacey's concept of dual structure would give us a new insight beyond what is given by the traditional organization theories. It is because in this type of conceptualization formal and informal organization are tend to be treated separately, and an explanation of how self-organization in informal organizations would transform or affect formal organizations is hard to give. Edge of chaos should be sought not between formal and informal organizations, but between CAS and hierarchical organizations.

Another point is that Goldstein's (this volume) self-transcending construction (STC) paradigm presented in this book seems to have something in common with the modified CAS paradigm or the IO model built on that. It is because the STC paradigm posits that emergence requires some constructional resources and produces radically novel outcomes, while the IO model satisfies these conditions in that the output of IO is usually quite innovative and the hierarchical organization involved in it might be interpreted as one of Goldstein's 'constructional resources'.

New insights concerning championing and improvisation

The fourth theoretical implication is that the IO model gives the concept of 'rebellious championing' a more positive meaning than that given in the existing leadership theories. It has been treated as rather an aberrant and ad hoc phenomenon in those theories, though it is considered useful, 'as a result', for organizations. By contrast, in the IO model, it is treated as the integral part of the organizational evolution and survival, which should always be mobilized when necessary.

The final implication is that 'improvisation' involved in the IO model is different from that in jazz improvisation widely discussed in organization research literature (see for example the Special Issue of *Organization Science*, Vol.9, No.5, 1998). First, although the application of the metaphor of jazz improvisation in existing literature is restricted to small groups or organizations like R&D teams, improvisation in the IO model is applicable to any size of organization from small groups to large hierarchical organizations like Honda or Sony. Second, although jazz improvisation in the existing literature is mostly a 'metaphor', improvisation involved in the IO model is a testable theoretical concept. (Accordingly, in order for the existence of improvisation to be verified, one must give it a more operational definition than was given in this chapter and examine whether it is satisfied or not.)

IO as a useful strategy in uncertain environments

Turning to the practical implication of the IO model for the organization, the most important point is that IO in strategy-making is vital for their survival in uncertain environments since it enables them to absorb uncertainty. In order for the organizations to realize that, however, the following points must be addressed by the organizations and elaborated on by the researchers.

First, although the flexibility of organizations is important in uncertain environments, it must be more than simply 'organic', as discussed in existing literature including Weick's theory of loose-coupling (Weick, 1976). More specifically, it must also be an organization in which all of the members including top and middle management take autonomous strategic initiatives. Put differently, it must be an organization that can elicit their creativity, energy and risk-taking behavior to the maximum extent possible as *dissipative energy*. We can call this type organization as the one that involves an 'emergent (organizational) infrastructure'. It would be realized when the organization has such characteristics as flat and flexible structures, a personnel management system based on the merit system, a high level of power delegation or empowerment, and an open and challenging organizational climate.

Second, in order for the organization to elicit only the merits of IO while avoiding its dysfunctional side effects, it must guard against the risk of disorderly expansion of the activities of the organization. Although a detailed discussion on this point is beyond the scope of this chapter, the organization must evaluate the results of the autonomous behavior and hold the members who exhibit that behavior accountable. The members' sense of taking responsibility for their own autonomous initiatives is very important since those initiatives are widely accepted only when they are accompanied by responsibilities. Honda and Sony have this type of emergent infrastructure and are quite eager to maintain it.

New management logic

This concludes the discussion of the IO model and suggests the possibility of quite a different management logic than the existing one. Lewin expressed his view of the 'new management logic' that would become possible by applying the complexity theory to management as follows.

"... *managers should facilitate, guide, and set the boundary conditions within which successful* self-organization *can take place. In the language of open system and complexity, the new management logic requires managing all the organizational levers of* dissipative energy... *The new management logic also requires internal processes that facilitate all kinds of emergent processes as self-generated sources of dissipative energy, such as* improvisation, product champions, *and* emergent strategies. *In addition, the new management logic requires openness to* bottom-up processes *and acceptance of effective equifinal outcomes. Finally, the new management logic also requires* leadership styles *that moderate dysfunctional tension and forestall the emergence of chaos.*"

Many of these ideas are not new. However, they do not simply represent old wine in new bottles. What is appealing about the reframing that the science of complexity is provoking is that ideologically rooted managerial advice, such as empowerment, *emerges from theoretical foundations in complexity. This reframing gives me reason to believe that complexity science has much to recommend to organization science* (Lewin, 1999: 215 - highlights added).

As the highlighted words show, the IO model is seen to have systematically satisfied many of the requirements of Lewin's new management logic in a single concrete model.

References

Anderson, P. (1999) "Complexity Theory and Organization Science," *Organization Science*, 10(3): 216-232.

Amram, M., and Kulatilaka, N. (1999). *Real Options: Managing Strategic Investment in an Uncertain World*, Harvard Business School Press.

Barnard, C. I. (1938). *The Functions of the Executive*, Harvard University Press.

Bastien, D. T. and Hostager, T. J. (1988). "Jazz as a Process of Organizational Innovation," *Communication Research*, 15(5): 582-602.

Bower, J. L. (1970). *Managing the Resource Allocation Process*, Irwin.

Brown, S. L. and Eisenhardt, K. M. (1997). "The Art of Continuous Change: Linking Complexity Theory and Time-paced Evolution in Relentlessly Sifting Organizations," *Administrative Science Quarterly*, 42: 1-34.

Buckley, W. (1998). *Society: A Complex Adaptive System: Essays in Social Theory*, Gordon and Breach Publishers.

Burgelman, R. A. (1983). "A Model of the Interaction of Strategic Behavior, Corporate Context, and the Concept of Strategy," *Academy of Management Review*, 8(1): 61-70.

Burgelman, R. A. (1991). "Intraorganizational Ecology of Strategy Making and Organizational Adaptation: Theory and Field Research," *Organization Science*, 2(3): 239-262.

Dooley, K. J. and Van de Ven, A. H. (1999). "Explaining Complex Organizational Dynamics," *Organization Science*, 10(3): 358-372.

Floyd, S. W. and Wooldridge, B. (1992). "Middle Management Involvement in Strategy and Its Association with Strategic Type: A Research Note," *Strategic Management Journal*, 13: 153-167.

Gersick, C. J. G. (1988). "Time and Transition in Work Teams: Toward a New Model of Group Development," *Academy of Management Journal*, 31(1): 9-41.

Gersick, C. J. G. (1991). "Revolutionary Change Theories: A Multilevel Exploration of the Punctuated Equilibrium Paradigm," *Academy of Management Review*, 16(1): 10-36.

Hatch, M. J. (1998). "Jazz as a Metaphor for Organizing in the 21st Century," *Organization Science*, 9(5): 556-568.

Hayes, R. H. and Pisano, G. P. (1994). "Beyond World-Class: The New Manufacturing Strategy," *Harvard Business Review*, January-February: 77-86.

Johnson, G. (1988). "Rethinking Incrementalizm," *Strategic Management Journal*, 9: 75-91.

Kanter, R. M. (1983). *The Change Masters*, Simon & Schuster.

Kawai, T. (1999). *Leadership in Complex Adaptive Systems*, (in Japanese) Yuhikaku.

Levy, D. (1994). "Chaos Theory and Strategy: Theory, Application, and Managerial Implications," *Strategic Management Journal*, 15: 167-178.

Lewin, A. Y. (1999). "Application of Complexity Theory to Organization Science," *Organization Science*, 10(3): 215.

Morel B. and Ramanujam, R. (1999). "Through the Looking Glass of Complexity: The Dynamicis of Organizations as Adaptive and Evolving Systems," *Organization Science*, 10(3): 278-293.

Noda, T. and Bower, J. L. (1996). "Strategy Making as Iterated Processes of Resource Allocation," *Strategic Management Journal*, 17: 159-192.

Prahalad, C. K. and Hamel, G. (1990). "The Core Competence of the Corporation," *Harvard Business Review*, May-June: 79-91.

Quinn, J. B. (1981). *Strategies for Change: Logical Incrementalism*, Irwin.

Quinn, R. E. and Cameron, K. S. (eds.) (1988). *Paradox and Transformation: Toward a Theory of Change in Organization and Management*, Ballinger.

Richardson, K. A., Cilliers, P. and Lissack, M. (2001). "Complexity Science: A 'Grey' Science for the 'Stuff in Between'," *Emergence*, 3(2): 6-18.

Romanelli, E. and Tushman, M. L. (1994). "Organizational Transformation as Punctuated Equilibrium: An Empirical Test," *Academy of Management Journal*, 37(5): 1141-1166.

Sanchez, R. (1995). "Strategic Flexibility in Product Competition," *Strategic Management Journal*, 16: 135-159.

Stacey, R. D. (1995). "The Science of Complexity: An Alternative Perspective for Strategic Change Processes," *Strategic Management Journal*, 16: 477-495.

Stalk, G., Evans, P. and Shulman, L. E. (1992). "Competing on Capabilities: The New Rules of Corporate Strategy," *Harvard Business Review*, March-April: 57-69.

Tateishi, Y. (2002). *Sony Revolution*, (in Japanese) President.

Thietart, R. and Forgues, B. (1997). "Action, Structure and Chaos," *Organization Studies*, 18(1): 119-143.

Tushman, M. L. and Anderson, P. (1986). "Technological Discontinuities and Organizational Environments," *Administrative Science Quarterly*, 31: 439-465.

Tushman, M. L. and Romanelli, E. (1985). "Organizational Evolution: A Metamorphosis Model of Convergence and Reorientation," in L. L. Cummings and B. M. Staw (eds.), *Research in Organizational Behavior*, 7: 171-222. JAI Press.

Waldrop, M. M. (1992). *Complexity: The Emerging Science at the Edge of Order and Chaos*, Sterling Lord Literistic.

Weick, K. E. (1976). "Educational Organizations as Loosely Coupled Systems," *Administrative Science Quarterly*, 21: 1-19.

Weick, K. E. (1998). "Improvisation as a Mindset for Organizational Analysis," *Organization Science*, 9(5): 543-555.

CHAPTER 19

STORYTELLING AND THE COMPLEX EPISTEMOLOGY OF ORGANIZATIONS

Ken Baskin

This chapter uses a complexity perspective to argue that, in addition to the traditional management picture of organizations as coherent entities, organizations are cultural ecosystems in which their members work together to create the knowledge they need to survive and meet other 'personal' needs. In doing so, the author suggests that human beings transform information into knowledge by fitting it into the stories they tell themselves to reduce the complexity of the world to manageable dimensions. Organizations, then, can be viewed as ecosystems of story creating local workgroup cultures in which employees develop the knowledge they need to meet their needs, rather than the knowledge management believes they should be developing. The author illustrates these ideas drawing on an original research study he conducted in 2001. He concludes that senior managers have a particular responsibility to think of their organizations as cultural ecosystems, as well as coherent wholes, so that they can take advantage of the insights thus provided.

Managing Organizational Complexity: Philosophy, Theory, and Application
A Volume in: Managing the Complex, pages 331-344.
Copyright © 2005 by Information Age Publishing, Inc.
ISBN: 1-59311-319-6 (cloth), 1-59311-318-8 (paper)

Introduction

"Out here you always fight for survival. You have to be part of a gang just to stand a chance. Slowly, your gang becomes your family." Lo, *Crouching Tiger, Hidden Dragon* (2000)

I began thinking about the issues explored in this essay in 1991, when I was writing speeches at Bell Atlantic, now Verizon. I noticed that people in work units that were absolutely dependent on each other for success, Engineering and Marketing, for example, seemed to be in constant battle with each other. This was a far cry from the picture of corporate culture holding people together that I was reading in the literature, and I began to wonder if the group cultures of people who worked with each other every day effected them far more powerfully than the company's corporate culture.

Even now, more than a decade later, the literature continues to focus on organizational culture as a unifying force that can be managed to improve corporate performance. From the first popular discussion of the topic, Peters and Waterman's *In Search of Excellence* (1982), through Schein's classic *Organizational Culture and Leadership* (1985) and the dozens of volumes that followed, only one that I know gives serious consideration to what I am calling local workgroup cultures, Parker's *Organizational Culture and Identity* (2000). In it, he writes, "organizational culture should be seen as 'fragmentary unities' in which members define themselves as collective at some times and divided at others." In complexity terms, the vast majority of those writing about organizations appear to see them only as coherent wholes operating in market environments.

In this chapter, I would like to build on this traditional conception of the organization as a coherent whole. Complexity thinking - and for me complexity is much more a way of thinking than a "theory" or "science" - suggests that any complex system can be viewed from three perspectives:

1. as a coherent whole, for example, a fish;

2. as an agent in a more inclusive environment, the fish in the ecosystem of its stream; and

3. as an environment in which its agents operate, the fish as the system in which its cells, organelles and molecules exist.

Traditional organizational theory treats the first two of these perspectives, but ignores the third. For me, organizations also exist as environments - I think of them as *cultural ecosystems* - that people in them are continually re-creating in order to survive in a world of constant change.

To further this volume's goal of applying complexity thought to our understanding of organizations, I want to examine the epistemological implications of this view. Specifically, I want to consider organizations as if they were *human ecosystems that enable those in them to generate knowledge to be used for their own purposes*, as well as those of their organizations. In doing so, I address three questions:

- What, specifically, does a complexity perspective bring to this examination?
- What does such a perspective suggest about the dynamics of human storytelling and its relationship to generating knowledge?
- What happens when we place this conception of storytelling / knowledge generation in the context of the organization as a cultural ecosystem?

Two challenges from a complexity perspective

For me, the field of complexity studies the patterns that emerge as complex adaptive systems coevolve in their environments. An enormous amount has been written about such systems - from their nonlinearity to their rule-based agent behavior and emergence (see, for example, Holland, 1995; Battram, 1996; as well as many of the chapters in this volume). Two implications of this perspective, however, have been overlooked: 1. that, in the continually evolving world of complexity, the survival of any complex adaptive system depends on its ability to recognize current conditions and implement behaviors that enable it to adapt appropriately, and; 2. that, for human beings, this capability arises largely from the ability to tell stories. So I want to start by examining these implications.

First of all, knowing how to behave appropriately presents significant challenges in a world where new conditions can emerge. I would suggest that complex adaptive systems have evolved a series of structures to generate such knowledge, from atomic / molecular structure to DNA, nervous systems, and mind. In living systems, as Plotkin (1993) puts it, "knowledge" is "the relationship between the organization of *any* part of a living creature's body and particular aspects of order in the world outside that creature" (author's italics). Through knowledge, he adds, living things adapt and therefore survive. In the course of evolution, adaptive structures have become increasingly varied. Bacteria have proteins that grab passing food molecules and drag them inside. Some flowers mimic the sexual parts of bees so those bees will fertilize them. Multi-cellular organisms eventually developed nervous systems, spinal chords and, finally, the brain, from which mind emerged.

Mind and conscious learning distinguish human life. Many animals - paramecia, ants, or dogs, for instance - can learn new tasks; some can even create new ways of eliminating obstacles from their paths. A few can create tools. However, only the human being seems able to imagine new futures and change the world so that they can realize such futures. Fisher (1987) suggests that we human beings are essentially storytellers, *Homo narrans*. Stewart and Cohen argue that the ability to tell the stories that envision new worlds was the key difference that allowed *Homo sapiens* to triumph over other forms of man (Pratchett, *et al.*, 2002). At the same time, this need to interpret the world as stories has important implications for how each of us act, experience the world, and generate knowledge.

This brings me to the second issue a complexity perspective creates, stories as an adaptation to what I have called "the dilemma of the two worlds" (Baskin, 2003). Humans must live simultaneously in two coevolving, yet very different worlds. First, we must live in the external world of people, things, and events, where we participate in the life around us. This external world is always beyond our ability to perceive. Complexity suggests, moreover, that this external world is so woven through with multiple causes and complex feedback loops that the human mind cannot fully comprehend it. Bohm (1980), in his work prefiguring complexity thought, suggested that the external world - the "implicate order" - is so rich that we can only perceive selected elements of it - the "explicate order". As a result, we must also live in a second world, the internal world our minds create in order to navigate the external world. This internal, perceptual world is the 'map' that enables us to navigate the 'territory' of the external world, to use Alfred Korzybski's well known formulation. It is in this world that we understand life around us.

These two worlds are deeply interconnected. The details of anyone's perceptual world are *selectively* taken from the external world. Like other living things, our perception filters out significant amounts of information, "skewered toward the features of the world that matter" most to our survival (Clark, 2001). In addition, cultural environment strongly shapes the world picture anyone develops. As a result, "our sense organs do not show us the real world. They stimulate our brains to produce, to invent if you like, an internal world made of the counters, the Lego set, that each of us has built up as we mature" (Pratchett, *et al.*, 2001). The interaction of this created world picture with the external world forms a powerful feedback loop. Consider, for instance, how Einstein's articulation of Relativity, a product of his inner, perceptual world, created immense shifts in the external world.

The vehicle with which humans most often organize the external world is the story. A story is, as Bateson (1979) notes, a "little knot" of relevance, providing the context with which we create meaning, drawing on our "patterns and sequences of childhood experience." Thus, in Kauffman's (2000) terms, stories are "how we tell ourselves what happened and its significance." To accomplish this end, the storyteller must choose and order events for inclusion, put them in sequence, and indicate cause-and-effect relationships. Stories thus enable us to reduce the external world to comprehensibility. Because of that reduction, we can construct apparently incompatible stories from the same events. For Cohen (2003), this ability to create such different meanings from the same reality is a central quality of all complex systems. Meaning emerges from the storyteller's choosing and sequencing events (see, for example, Weick, 1995; Boje, 2001.)

Storytelling and knowledge

Knowledge, I've come to believe, is one product of the self-reinforcing feedback loop by which human beings connect their internal perceptual worlds with the external world. In this way, each of us generates knowledge as we test the images of our internal worlds in the external world. Knowing occurs as people interact with the external world, including, of course, each other. In such interactions, people respond on an unconscious level, and if the response creates the desired results, they will repeat that response in similar situations (Powers, 1998, examines this dynamic). Then, they tell stories about their interactions so that each is consciously able to explain what might have happened. At first, such stories are what Boje (2001) calls *antenarrative*. That is, they are tentative attempts to find meaning; the events of the stories are still dynamic. Boje notes that "people live in the antenarrative"; in other words, each of us experiences life as the ongoing stories we tell ourselves in order to explain what is happening around us.

Once a person has created a story to explain an event, he or she will act on the basis of that story, most often without being conscious of the process. If this action doesn't produce the results predicted in the story, the person will create a new, perhaps more accurate, antenarrative. When the action does produce desired results, the person will continue to enact that story in his or her life. At some point in reiterating this feedback loop, the antenarrative – what *might have* happened - becomes fixed as narrative - what *did* happen (see Bal, 1997, for a full definition of "narrative"). With time and further successful reiteration in different situations, the story can become mythic and begin to signify, not merely what happened, but *the way things are*. As Campbell (1968) pointed out, such *personal* mythology is especially important in Western society.

Much of the literature on the subject of storytelling - White and Epston (1990) in therapy, for example, or Weick (1995) in organizations - discusses it in terms of *sensemaking*. What I am talking about is subtly different, and, I think, more elemental. The need that drives human beings to tell stories is not merely the need to make sense out of the world. Rather, we tell stories to help us *discover the actions we must take in order to survive*. To put it another way, stories enable people to transform information - Bateson's (1979) "difference that makes a difference" - into the knowledge we need to survive in our continually changing world. This is the power of storytelling.

What any of us 'knows' about any information depends largely on the stories through which that information is processed. For example, the information that the Sun rises on one side of the sky and sets on the other has generated a variety of knowledge. At various times people have 'known' that Apollo drives his chariot across the sky; that the Earth rotates around the Sun; or that the Sun rotates around the Earth. So important is such knowledge - it is, if I'm correct, experienced as a matter of survival - that much of history is about people killing each other over the differences in what they know from the same information. Whether we consider today's Palestinians and Israelis, 16th Century Protestants and Catholics, or 12ᵗʰ Century Crusaders and Muslims, these people believed that their stories were identical to the external world and died to defend them. Moreover, it appears that knowledge derived from mythic stories is more deeply held than that derived from narrative, which is more deeply held than that from antenarrative.

As note in an earlier article (Baskin, 2003), this storytelling begins in the context of the family, which is, after all, our first model of social interaction, the model for the way we experience all organizations. Three issues raised there are critical:

- The family is the vehicle by which young children absorb culture-specific stories, in media and ritual for example, leading those in our culture to such 'Western' experiences as post-Renaissance perspective or consumerism;

- Most people adopt behavior patterns as they interact with other family members and, then, construct stories to explain the habitual behavior patterns (their 'personalities') that they will bring into other contexts;

- Because young children are entirely dependent on their parents for survival, these unconsciously developed behavior patterns become extremely powerful, so that the stories they tell function like the attractors of complexity studies.

Knowing in organizations

If the model I am developing here is accurate, then this self-reinforcing cycle of storytelling and knowledge generation continues in every organization that any of us belongs to, with our local groups - those in which we interact on a daily basis - functioning much like the family. To get a better picture of how this works, I would like to turn now to the results of a research study I performed in 2001, with funding from the Institute for the Study of Coherence and Emergence. In this project, I interviewed more than 100 workers in 27 workgroups in three American hospitals. In the interviews, I asked participants to tell stories about such subjects as their most notable successes and difficulties, working to create a picture of their local group cultures.

In all cases, those I spoke with experienced their work worlds more strongly in terms of their local group cultures than their hospital's organizational cultures. As a result, people in different groups 'know' very different things about common experiences and, not surprisingly, tell very different antenarratives to explain them. For example, one hospital had recently implemented a service quality program. The final document included more than 45 behaviors grouped to reflect five core values. Employees were required to sign this document as a condition of employment. As an outsider, my immediate reaction was that it seemed overly long, including behaviors that seemed common sense - "Adhere to the hospital smoking policy" - and others that were highly sophisticated - "Act as a teacher and role model." None of these sophisticated behaviors were defined; no training was provided; and the consequences of following or ignoring them were not articulated.

People in different groups experienced the program differently. For a senior manager responsible for the program, it represented a significant success. She told me:

"We were careful to design it in a way that reflected employee empowerment, following the guidelines in the literature. We chose a committee representing a cross-section of the organization to develop our agreement defining service excellence. We had them work together to identify and define five key values and then list the behaviors that demonstrate those values. Rather than a management pronouncement, it was designed to represent an employee initiative."

A group of nursing coordinators responsible for implementing this program among the nurses in their clinical departments told different stories. They explained that the program seemed like a good idea but had been implemented in a way that had reduced it to "a piece of paper." One coordinator was angry that the program didn't help her with significant professional matters that might have had affected the quality of service:

"I looked at a patient's room and noticed that the commode was dirty. I told the aide, but she just said, 'What do you want me to do? Lick the bowl?' I was furious at her attitude. I wanted to get an immediate suspension. But when I went to Human Resources for a high level punishment, they seemed mostly afraid that she would sue the hospital. With the way the service excellence program is being implemented, I could send her home if she wears the wrong color pants. But when this nurse's aide was insolent, I couldn't do anything."

The differences in these two antenarrative stories reflects the respective position and concerns of those telling them. The senior manager was responsible for designing and implementing the program to increase the level of service quality in a way employees would embrace. In her story, she focused on the design process and her efforts to make sure it was performed suitably. When I told her about the concerns of the nursing coordinators, she replied that management had decided to start enforcing those behaviors that were easiest to identify and discipline. As one would expect, her story reflects the need to justify her decisions and judgment. The nursing coordinators, on the other hand, were responsible for making their departments in the hospital function smoothly day-to-day. As a result, their stories reflected the difficulties that the service excellence program was creating for them. These stories were also tinged with some resentment at having to sign a document that required them to do things, such as "Use 'please' and 'thank you' as a matter of course," that they expected of themselves. People in a number of the workgroups with whom I spoke shared the attitude of the nursing coordinators. As antenarrative, the perceptions embodies in these stories are still negotiable. But if management does not address this divergence in what people 'know' about the program, problems seem inevitable, as such stories deepen into narrative.

The shift from antenarrative (what *might have* happened) to narrative (what *did* happen) is subtle, and deciding whether stories are one or the other is a subjective judgment. At one hospital, however, I spoke to a group of nurses from three floors of the hospital, whose stories seemed on the verge of turning into narratives of victimhood. A number of factors seemed responsible for this shift, including the weakness of their nurses' union and a lack of leadership from their immediate supervisors. But their comments and, especially, the stories they told made it clear that the sense of victimhood had become the context in which they worked. Perhaps the most indicative was one nurse's comment: "Everybody has problems about what we do, but no one supports us." Other nurses talked about this treatment from doctors, administrators, and nursing supervisors. As one said of the doctors, "Sometimes I think they're just waiting for us to drop a pen so that they can yell at us."

One story, in particular, suggested to me that the nurses' stories of victimization were becoming fixed as narrative. The nurse had been discussing how patients sometimes blamed them for the patients' own behavior:

"One patient came in drunk after rolling over his car. He'd become paralyzed and was suing the hospital. I had to sit through a five-hour deposition with his lawyer, who wanted to make me seem stupid and negligent. It was one of the most upsetting experiences of my life. But no one in management supported me. No thanks. No note of appreciation. Nothing. No one cared."

Whether this story is antenarrative or narrative is a subjective judgment. But in the context of the conversation with these nurses, it gave me the feeling that the speaker had negotiated this story with others in the group, more a statement of what had actually happened than a guess. They 'knew' that they had been isolated and victimized. It's worth noting that the senior managers in this hospital were surprised to learn how deeply this sense of victimhood had grown.

None of the stories I heard during these interviews seemed to have become mythic. That may have been because, like most hospitals, these three were undergoing significant changes internally and externally. Mythic stories tend to reflect conditions that are somewhat more settled. I heard one of my favorite examples of a story that had become mythic when I was teaching quality improvement at a cola bottling warehouse about ten years ago. One afternoon, a mechanic with more than 20 years on the job was telling me why he and his coworkers liked their current manager, who'd gotten the group involved with the quality training:

"The manager before this one came to us right after his MBA. He thought he knew everything. So he never came down on the floor to talk to us about how we did our jobs. One time, I had this problem and went to talk to him about it. I explained

the problem and how we could solve it. He turned to me and said, 'Thanks for coming in to tell me about this. But workers work and managers think. Go back to your job'. We got rid of him in six months."

That final sentence, delivered with a smirk, suggested to me that this was a mythic story. The mechanic and his coworkers had processed the information that their new manager was making their jobs more difficult through a series of similar stories and, acting on those stories, were able to get rid of him. What they 'knew' was that they understood the system in which they worked better than the manager and that they could manipulate it more successfully. The story, then, was not so much about what happened, as the way things were. It was mythic.

One key point here is that people will 'know' what they believe they have to know to survive and meet their most important needs, not what management thinks they should know. To the extent that any management is ignorant of the storytelling / knowledge generation in an organization's workgroups, they are operating without vital information.

Organizations as cultural ecosystems

What all this suggests to me is that, culturally, organizations can be profitably viewed as if they were *ecosystems*. I don't mean to imply that they are not also held together by a corporate culture. Each of the three hospitals where I interviewed had a culture that reflected its unique history and position in the community. However, for managers, understanding the organization as a cultural ecosystem may prove at least as valuable as understanding its corporate culture.

Before examining what I mean by organizations as cultural ecosystems, I need to state a couple of caveats. For one thing, I have presented the fiction that people in any organization belong to only one workgroup. This is clearly untrue. In my research I spoke to several people who belonged to three or four such groups. For another, I would have liked to include a much wider collection of stories in the previous section. As a result, my choices there overemphasize the unique position of upper management as a local workgroup. Other stories could have shown differences between people in radiology and physical therapy groups, for example. Still, I believe that my analysis holds true, even with these limited examples.

Why, then, do I identify organizations as cultural ecosystems? A biological ecosystem is a dynamic network of diverse living agents (Kelley, 1994). Ecosystems are further characterized by niches, the 'professions' that species develop to survive. Because the species in any ecosystem are coevolving - that is, each species must change to adapt to the changes in other species - new niches are continually forming (Rothschild, 1990). The complex dynamics of any ecosystem results from the interactions of different species - predators and their prey, for example - as they respond to each other. In recent years, both specific markets (Moore, 1996) and the economy as a whole (Rothschild, 1990) have been compared to such systems. My research on cultures in workgroups has convinced me that the ecosystem is also a valuable way to think about organizations.

Let me emphasize that this is a metaphor. No ecosystem has a niche for managing the whole system, as organizations have senior management. Nonetheless, the idea of an organization, and especially a hospital, as an ecosystem of local workgroup cultures (cardiac nurses) and the larger niches to which they belong (nursing) has unexplored value. For instance, hospitals have great diversity of personnel - from analytical doctors oriented toward solving healthcare problems to nurturing nurses who want to care for people, from analytical hospital administrators oriented toward solving business problems to rule-oriented people in human resources. People in local workgroups tend to share similar natures and needs. As a result, they are likely to draw similar knowledge from the storytelling they do together. Moreover, the interactions between people in different groups will reflect the differences in the way those in each create different knowledge from shared experiences. Over and over, in my research study, I saw people in different groups coming into conflict for exactly this reason - nurse coordinators and human resources people in one hospital, radiologists and nurses in another, nurses and those in the pharmacy at the third. These groups, I believe, are what Lo, in the epigraph I use from the film *Crouching Tiger, Hidden Dragon*, refers to as 'gangs', the families we depend on for survival out in the world. It was this realization, finally, that enabled me to understand the antagonism between people in Marketing and Engineering at Bell Atlantic.

In addition, the complex dynamics of an organization are very much like those of a biological ecosystem. Consider the effects of the culture of victimhood forming in one of the hospitals where I conducted my research. As morale dropped and the nurses felt more and more victimized, many of the experienced nurses began to think about leaving. Moreover, the overall feeling was so negative that student nurses from local colleges rarely wanted to be hired. Especially at a time when the nation faces a nursing shortage, the hospital faced significant problems in providing adequate care, which, in turn effected everything from the attitudes of technical employees to the hospital's bottom line. This dynamic reminded me of the dynamics of predator and prey populations that Cohen and Stewart (1994), for example, discuss, as changes in the population of one species spread, first to those other species most dependent on it, and then through the system as a whole.

Implications for management

Viewing organizations as cultural ecosystems can benefit managers in a variety of ways. First of all, it suggests, as I've demonstrated, that people in different groups are likely to know different things about the same situations. Until people recognize this dynamic and make the effort to understand the viewpoint of people in other groups, misunderstandings are all but unavoidable. The inability to recognize that different workgroups develop different cultures, different stories for explaining their workplaces, and therefore different knowledge sets, can be especially problematic in senior management. In all three hospitals, most of the workgroups composed of people below middle management were convinced that senior management was indifferent, incompetent or misguided. In most cases, these people liked the hospitals where they worked and wanted to contribute. But management consistently took action without understanding how people at this level were transforming that information into knowledge. As a result, employees often 'knew' that these actions meant something very different from management's intentions. This is what happened at the hospital whose senior managers were so proud of the new service quality program, while its nurse coordinators felt demeaned and confused. Yet senior management absolutely need the support of these coordinators if the program is to succeed. Unless those senior managers can understand how different their knowledge of the program is from that of the coordinators, this difference is likely to create all sorts of problems. Once senior management does understand, it can take remedial action.

Paying attention to the stories told in different group cultures can do more than help management avoid this kind of mixed message. It can also enable management to identify a variety of opportunities to encourage employees to contribute more fully to the goals of the organization. At one hospital in a rural area, I interviewed members of the Information Technology (IT) group. Members of the group told me stories about how much they enjoyed their successes in solving the difficult problems presented by doctors. In addition, they told me about their activities consulting with smaller area hospitals that didn't have their own IT groups. On the other hand, they complained that budget cuts were making it impossible for them to attend the seminars they needed to stay current, even though they earned the hospital significant income from their consulting. That income went to the department to which the IT group reported. Once management recognized what was going on at the level of this group culture, it had the option to encourage members of the IT group to make a greater contribution to the organization. For instance, if it had set apart a portion of the income the IT group produced as a fund its members could use for travel and education, management could have encouraged members of this group to focus on solving healthcare information management problems that the hospital could have marketed to other hospitals.

I don't pretend that it would be easy to manage an organization as a cultural ecosystem. It would demand that managers stop acting on the assumption that people in the organization are a homogenous group. It would demand regular inventories of group cultures throughout the organization. It would demand working to help people in all groups meet their legitimate personal needs, because only then are they likely to make the full contribution to the organization of which they are capable. Most of all, it would demand that senior management listen to the stories of those people throughout the organization. Judging from much of the literature on storytelling in organizations (see, for example, Denning, 2001; Neuhauser, 1993), which advises senior management on the use of storytelling as a way to manipulate employees, this is a radical idea.

Closing thoughts

My argument, thus far, is fairly simple. It suggests that:

- The process by which human beings create stories and then transform information into knowledge is driven by our deepest needs, including survival;

- This process occurs as we interact with others, especially in small groups - family, peer groups, workgroups - of those with whom we spend significant amounts of time;

- Employees will develop knowledge about their products and customers, but also about their managers, and will focus their attention on that knowledge which most helps them meet their needs;

- This process can be influenced by what is happening in any person's environment, but cannot be controlled;

- Organizations are organic engines of knowledge creation because they are structured in relatively small workgroups of people developing shared meaning;

- When organizational pressures make it difficult for people to meet their legitimate needs, they are likely to develop knowledge about how to protect themselves, rather than how to help the organization meet its needs;

- By understanding the stories and culture of any group, management can encourage people to develop and use knowledge that will contribute to an organization's welfare.

From this point of view, organizations are epistemological ecosystems by which people in large groups learn to survive. This is a radical expansion of the traditional definition of an organization and, for that reason, demands further study. For instance, a thorough ethnological study of an organization, followed by an analysis of the dynamics of interaction among people in different local workgroups, could create a detailed map of organizational dynamics, of that organization's challenges and opportunities. Such a map of dynamics could have enormous value for our understanding of the nature of organizations in general, as well as for that organization's managers. Other possible avenues of exploration may have even more value to both students of organization and those who manage them.

References

Bal, M. (1997). *Narratology: Introduction to the Theory of Narrative*, 2nd ed., Toronto: University of Toronto Press.

Baskin, K. (2003). "Complexity and the Dilemma of the Two Worlds: The Dynamics of Navigating Fantasyland," *Emergence*, 5(1): 36-53.

Bateson, G. (1979). *Mind and Nature: A Necessary Unity*, New York: E. P. Dutton.

Battram, A. (1996). *Navigating Complexity: The Essential Guide to Complexity Theory in Business and Management*, London: The Industrial Society.

Boje, D. M. (2001). *Narrative Methods for Organizational and Communication Research*, London: SAGE Publications.

Bohm, D. (1980). *Wholeness and the Implicate Order*, London: ARK Paperbacks.

Campbell, J. (1968). *The Masks of the Gods: Creative Mythology*, New York: The Viking Press.

Clark, A. (2001). *Being There: Putting Brain, Body, and World Together Again*, Cambridge, MA: MIT Press.

Cohen, J. (2003). "Why Is Negentropy, like Phlogiston, a Privative?" *International Nonlinear Sciences Conference*, Vienna, Feb. 9.

Cohen, J. and Stewart, I. (1994). *The Collapse of Chaos: Discovering Simplicity in a Complex World*, New York: Penguin Books.

Crouching Tiger, Hidden Dragon (2000). DVD, Sony Pictures Classics.

Denning, S. (2001). *The Springboard: How Storytelling Ignites Action in Knowledge-Era Organizations*, Boston: Butterworth Heinemann.

Fisher, W. R. (1987). *Human Communication as Narration: Toward a Philosophy of Reason, Value, and Action*, Columbia, SC: The University of South Carolina Press.

Holland, J. H. (1995). *Hidden Order: How Adaptation Builds Complexity*, Reading, MA: Perseus Books.

Kauffman, S. (2000). *Investigations*, New York: Oxford University Press.

Kelley, K. (1994). *Out of Control: The Rise of Neo-Biological Civilization*, Reading, MA: Addison Wesley.

Moore, J. F. (1996). *The Death of Competition: Leadership and Strategy in the Age of Business Ecosystems*, New York: Harper Business.

Neuhauser, P. C. (1993). *Corporate Legends & Lore: The Power of Storytelling as a Management Tool*, Austin, Texas: PCN Associates.

Parker, M. (2000). *Organizational Culture and Identity: Unity and Division at Work*, London: Sage Publications.

Peters, T. J. and Waterman, R. H., Jr. (1982). *In Search of Excellence: Lessons from America's Best-Run Companies*, New York: Harper & Row.

Plotkin, H. (1993). *Darwin Machines and the Nature of Knowledge*, Cambridge, MA: Harvard University Press.

Powers, W. T. (1998). *Making Sense of Behavior: The Meaning of Control*, New Caanan, CT: Benchmark Publications.

Pratchett, T., Stewart, I. and Cohen, J. (2002). *The Science of Discworld II: The Globe*, London: Edbury Press.

Rothschild, M. (1990). *Bionomics: Economy as Ecosystem*, New York: Henry Holt and Company.

Schein, E. H. (1991). *Organizational Culture and Leadership: A Dynamic View*, San Francisco: Jossey-Bass.

Weick, K. E. (1995). *Sensemaking in Organizations*, London: Sage Publications.

White, M. and Epston. D. (1990). *Narrative Means to Therapeutic Ends*, New York: W.

W. Norton & Company.

CHAPTER 20

ANCIENT INSIGHTS INTO THE MODERN ORGANIZATION

Julie Richardson

This chapter compares emergent thinking about the nature of organizations from contemporary science with ancient insights about the organization of nature. It traces the development of organizational theory and practise from the metaphor of the machine to the living organism and takes the next step by asking how healthy is the living organization? Drawing from ancient insights about holistic health, it suggests a way forward to diagnose the health of organizational patterns at different levels - from individual characteristics; team dynamics, leadership qualities; management structures and processes and design of the working environment. Its potential is to diagnose and catalyze change in organizational patterns towards more sustainable and healthy states.

Managing Organizational Complexity: Philosophy, Theory, and Application
A Volume in: Managing the Complex, pages 345-360.
Copyright © 2005 by Information Age Publishing, Inc.
All rights of reproduction in any form reserved.
ISBN: 1-59311-319-6 (cloth), 1-59311-318-8 (paper)

Overview

T his chapter explores the changing nature of human organizations from the metaphor of the *machine*, to contemporary understanding of the organization as a *living system*, to offer new insights into healthy living organizations.

Insights are drawn from emergent thinking about the nature of organizations in terms of self-organizing, adaptive and creative systems. Complexity science offers a new understanding of organizations in terms of patterns and relationships and refocuses organizational strategy towards the emergent characteristics of whole systems rather than reducing it to its individual parts.

The move towards a more holistic understanding of organizations in terms of patterns and relationships also has ancient roots. In the West, the pre-Darwinian worldview reasserts the primacy of processes over events, of relationships over entities and of development over structure. In the East, the School of Naturalists developed a system of pattern recognition based on elemental energetic fields observed from natural systems.

This chapter compares emergent thinking about the nature of organizations with ancient insights about the organization of nature. It suggests a way forward to recognize energetic patterns within organizations at different levels - individual characteristics, team dynamics, leadership qualities, management structures and processes, and design of space. Its potential is to diagnose and catalyze change in organizational patterns towards more sustainable and healthy states.

In this chapter I use a series of scientific metaphors to explore the behavior of human organizations - from the machine to living organisms. If human organizations are indeed alive, then they will display patterns of health and disease like any living organism. The final section of the chapter draws from holistic health approaches to explore the characteristics of a healthy living organization and how we might diagnose and catalyze change in organizational patterns towards more sustainable and healthy states.

Organizations as machines

"We have learned to use the machine as a metaphor for ourselves and our society and to mould our world in accordance with mechanical principles. This is nowhere more evident than in the modern organization." (Morgan, 1997: 12)

The conventional organizational map portrays the mechanistic organization as a set of clearly defined parts or functional departments, joined together by formal rules and relationships. Management plans, coordinates, commands and controls. Problems or constraints to achieving stated goals were conceived largely as technical problems for which technical solutions were sought. In its idealized form, commands were issued from the top and would be executed by the parts in a clearly defined way to achieve a predetermined and predictable outcome. Failure or breakdown could be located to an identified part - whether it is a department, product, or individual - and dealt with in isolation. The organization was regarded as a well-defined closed system reinforced by and reflecting obligations and accountability as defined by law.

This deterministic and linear world of management, hierarchy and control reflects the dominant mode of organizational theory and practise in the latter half of the 20th century. This model proved popular across management and had some operational and economic success in times of relative stability. However, as we enter the 21st century, its inflexible and rigid structures cannot respond to the rapid pace of social, economic and environmental change. In addition, the model is collapsing under the stresses and strains of internal dynamics that fail to take account of the human or living aspects of human organizations. Morgan (1997: 30) asserts that the apathy, carelessness and lack of pride encountered in the modern workplace is directly attributable to the mechanistic approach. The inflexible and controlling structures stifle creativity and create a deadening and subversive sub-culture that undermines the ability of the organization to meet its primary objectives.

Organizations as living systems

The limitations of the mechanistic metaphor has unleashed a whole industry in organizational change theorists and practitioners. The observation that organizations have behaviors and 'personalities'; that they have proved difficult to 'control' in a mechanistic fashion; and that different species of organizations have evolved in response to their external environments, has led to a series of organizational metaphors based on living systems.

Capra (2002) distinguishes between the living and nonliving aspects of organizations whereas others have defined legitimate shadow networks (Stacey, 1996). The shadow networks are spontaneous and informal and develop their own codes of practise and informal rules for interacting with each other. These networks emerge and serve a myriad of purposes, which may or may not be aligned with the stated objectives and rules and relationships defined by the formal organization (the 'legitimate network').

The informal or shadow aspects of human organizations operate as if they were 'alive' displaying complex, nonlinear, and creative behaviors characteristic of living systems. Many authors have characterized human organizations as living systems with these complex behaviors (see for example, Stacey, 1996; Morgan, 1997; Reason & Goodwin, 1999).

Drawing from these studies, this chapter briefly reviews the key features of complex, nonlinear, self-organizing systems that characterize the living organization. Living systems are open to the external environment. This means that they are in a dynamic process of interaction and mutual dependence. They also self-regulate which means maintaining internal equilibrium in response to a changing external environment. Over time, they may also proactively seek to influence or co-create more favorable external environmental conditions - acting alone or in collaboration with others.

The characteristics, outcomes and qualities of a whole system (such as a human organization) cannot be understood from the individual parts alone. They emerge from the underlying pattern of relationships that connect the parts to the whole. The dynamic relationships between the parts that make up the properties of the whole may take many different forms. For example, if we map the dynamic relationships between a highly ordered and stable system we would see that the system eventually converges to a single point, known as a *point attractor*. Other systems may show completely random behavior having no discernible pattern of relationships. Chaotic systems sit somewhere in-between order and randomness. If we map the relationships of a chaotic system we observe highly patterned, bounded but unpredictable shapes known as *strange attractors*.

In an organizational context, strange attractors can be thought of as a field that attracts, concentrates and inspires the energy of people (Dimitrov & Naess, 2002). This may be a person, an event, a policy or an idea. Sometimes the strange attractor will manifest behaviors which are detrimental to the organization, its members and the surrounding environment. In other cases the strange attractor will catalyze behaviors, which enhance life and vitality. Re-configuring the pattern of organizational relationships will create new strange attractors with different emergent behaviors. In the dance of organizations, the attractor and the organization co-evolve and are created together.

The phenomena of emergence means that organizations operate under conditions of uncertainty and vagueness, where no ultimate answers or best solutions exist. This strongly counters the traditional view of management as requiring strong direction and control from above. Greater legitimacy is given to management philosophy and practise rooted in a bottom-up and participatory approach that genuinely values dialogue and consensus building. Such an approach recognizes that complex systems can only be 'disturbed' and not controlled or directed.

When organizations operate like living systems, the task of management becomes more like an organizational doctor than an engineer. I image the role to be like an acupuncturist or the conductor of an orchestra. Being in tune with the coherence and dynamics of the whole system, detecting signs of disharmony and disconnection, and responding with appropriate signals, intervention or stimulation. The living system manager becomes a highly tuned and skilled facilitator, drawing on his or her whole self (mental, intuitive, emotional, and physical) to create the conditions for coherence and self-organization to emerge.

Organizations as 'healthy' living systems

If organizations are alive, then they will display patterns of health and disease like any living system. According to Capra (2002) the 'aliveness' of an organization depends on the qualities and behaviors of the informal networks - are they flexible, adaptable and creative? The formal structures may also be alive to different degrees depending on how much they are in tune with the informal networks. Others suggest that healthy systems naturally evolve towards a regime that is delicately poised between order and chaos. Organizational health has also been interpreted as the harmonious and dynamic balance between the internal and external environment. This is where the complexity of the internal environment reflects the complexity of the external environment.

"The internal diversity of any self regulating system must match the variety and complexity of its environment if it is to deal with the challenges posed by that environment." (Morgan, 1997: 112).

Conversely, organizational disease manifests when the organization either becomes too ordered for purpose (displaying resistant, stuck and habitual behaviors) or too disordered (lacking coherence and connectivity). Understanding organizational health and disease in this way provides an exciting avenue to deepen our understanding of organizational dynamics.

But historical insights from within our own and other cultures also offer a deep vein of knowledge about the health and dynamics of organizational patterns. In fact, many influential thinkers have found Eastern natural philosophies hold important insights consistent with the swing in science from an atomistic and mechanical mode to an organicist and holistic worldview. The most well-known study that linked developments in Western physical science with a more holistic world-view from the East was Frijof Capra's *The Tao of Physics*, first published in 1975.

In China, the scientific School of Naturalists[1] developed a system of pattern recognition over a 3000 year period to diagnose patterns of health and disease at different levels - from the individual, to social organization to environmental systems. The basic principle of healthy systems was the ability to adapt and creatively respond to change in either the internal or external environment whilst maintaining system integrity. Disease occurs when the underlying pattern of organization connecting different elements of the system becomes too rigid and habitual or too disconnected and disintegrated.

In China, the pattern of relationships was known as *li*, and the medium linking these relationships was known as *qi*. This medium can be thought of as a flow of energy, matter or information. The continuous and dynamic process in which the pattern of organization becomes embodied gives form and qualities to the individual or organization. Depending on the emergent properties arising out of the pattern of organization, this may imbue life, health and vitality or may manifest as pathology and disease.

The linking medium (*qi*) has both a qualitative and a flow dimension. The qualitative dimension relates to the overall resonance or tone. Five essential qualities were defined corresponding to energetic tones observed in natural systems - such as the five seasons (winter, spring, summer, late summer, and autumn) as well as the five essential elements (water, wood, fire, earth, and metal). The flow dimension relates to observed deficiencies or excess in the presence of these essential elements in an individual, society or environment.

The pattern of organization refers to how these essential elements relate to each other in terms of positive and negative feedback processes. Positive feedback symbolizes a reinforcing or supporting relationship whereas negative feedback refers to a dampening or diffusing relationship.

This system was developed into a highly refined body of knowledge about health and disease, known as *Chinese medicine*. This chapter applies some of the knowledge from this holistic system of health to give insight into patterns of health and disease within human organizations. This requires defining the energetic qualities of the organization in terms of the five elements and diagnosing the pattern of relationships that connect these elements. The principles for catalyzing change by disturbing the organizational pattern are now discussed below.

Elemental qualities

The challenge is to define a useful set of organizational qualities over which there is consensus, as well as specifying how these qualities relate to the specific aspect of the organization.

In this chapter, I use the archetypes of the five elements as a framework to organize and cluster organizational characteristics and qualities. These qualities are used to uncover the nature or personality of an organization as they reveal themselves in different ways, from the quality of the working environment, to leadership style and structures and processes.

Some of the essential characteristics of the five elements (Beinfield & Korngold, 1991: 140-141) and their correspondences with the ancient Chinese worldview are reviewed in Table 1.

The water element corresponds to the deep reservoirs of energy in the rivers, seas and oceans that function as a vital store-house for energy and as the source of potentiation and impetus for action. In Chinese medicine the water element is associated with the kidney and bladder. These organs govern the transportation and transformation of bodily fluids and also relate to impetus and the seed of action, activated through the hormonal and autonomous nervous systems. In terms of health, if the water element is weak, there is no impetus to respond to information received from hormonal or nervous impulses whereas hypersensitivity causes stress and the inability to relax and replenish essential reserves.

Aspect	Water	Wood	Fire	Earth	Metal
Archetype	Philosopher	Pioneer	Wizard	Peacemaker	Alchemist
Season	Winter	Spring	Summer	Late summer	Autumn
Cycle	Consolidation and potentiation	Expansion and initiation	Completion and fulfillment	Stability and poise	Contraction and release
Values	Knowledge	Action	Compassion	Service	Mastery
Talent	Imagination	Initiative	Communication	Negotiation	Discrimination

Table 1
Elemental associations

The wood element is about directing life's creative force to achieve our goals and aspirations. In Chinese medicine, wood corresponds to the liver. The liver derives from the adjective 'to live'. It is about living life to the full by directing our efforts towards realizing our potential. The liver directs the smooth flow of blood to the muscles, allowing activity and action. In terms of health, wood affects the quality and smooth release of blood to where it is needed for action. Imbalance may manifest as muscle pain and stiffness; dizziness and mood swings.

Nourishment, support and fecundity are associated with the soil and the earth element. In Chinese medicine, earth corresponds to the digestive organs of the stomach and spleen. In terms of health, an earth imbalance manifests at the physical level as digestive orders and at the emotional level as feeling under-supported and unnourished.

Fusion and integration is the organizing principle for the fire element. The power of fire overcomes separation by welding divergent elements into one. It has the capacity to transform, quickly and irreversibly. In Chinese medicine, the heart is the primary fire organ. At a physical level it provides the pulse that integrates the body through the circulation of blood from the core to the periphery and back again. At a psychological level, the heart represents our central consciousness and awareness of ourselves as an integrated being.

The metal element is about boundaries and interfaces between internal and external environments. In Chinese medicine, the metal element governs the lung and large intestine. The lungs are the membrane through which breathing takes place and the function of the large intestine is to eliminate unwanted waste. Metal imbalance manifests as problems in our exchange with the outside world. For example, respiratory problems at a physical level, and feelings of isolation and depression at an emotional level indicate problems in the metal element.

The elements and their associations can then be applied to the modern day organization. The emergent elemental signature of the organization is used as the basis for diagnosing the underlying pattern of organizational health.

Organizational water: Genius or just dreamy?

Water is associated with winter, the season of deep inward movement, rest and regeneration before the outward thrust of spring. The water element can be thought of as the store house of the organization which provides essential reserves in times of stress or crisis. The quality of water is endurance, courage and determination, and the energy behind it is the will to survive. The dynamics of the water element can be likened to the 'rest before the storm' or the potential energy contained in the pendulum as it rests between the upward and downward swing. Rest and fallow periods allow excitement and the motivation for action to build. It is this aspect of water that is associated with inspiration and potentiation - the raw conception of an idea before it is put into action.

Water refreshes an organization with imaginative and original ideas. Water structures, processes and people enable the genius of the organization to flourish if given the space and channelled in the right direction. More often than not, the power of water is dissipated and dissolved and the potential genius of an organization remains a dream. At the physical level, water spaces allow for rest, regeneration and reflection - real retreats from everyday frenetic activity. Water processes and polices generate long-term vision, incorporate time for retreat and reflection, and are unbounded. The water leader is an enigmatic type - original and visionary but difficult to fit into timetables and everyday concerns.

An organization with a water imbalance may be found in risky areas of business (such as the stock market) where courage and risk taking are highly rewarded, but the potential costs are high. This is life on the edge where high stress, adrenaline and another cup of black coffee is the order of the day. There is no time for relaxation, retreat and replenishing vital resources – here today, gone tomorrow is the motto. The importance of slowing down in order to see the primary threat to survival is stressed by Peter Senge in the Fifth Discipline.

"The primary threats to our survival, both of our organizations and of our societies, come not from sudden events but from slow, gradual processes. Learning to see slow, gradual processes requires slowing down our frenetic pace and paying attention to the subtle as well as the dramatic." (Senge, 1997: 22-23).

Organizational wood: Strategic or just stressed?

The wood aspect relates to spring and its associations with new creation, growth and the initiation of action. Whereas the water element provides the impetus or initial conception of the idea, it is the wood energy that allows it to manifest and be put into action. A healthy wood aspect captures the outward, vigorous and smooth flowing energy of the spring as well as the yielding nature of wood. This ensures the adaptation and flexibility needed for the creative resolution of conflicts that may arise as new plans are implemented.

Strategy, goal setting, negotiation and conflict resolution provide a buzz-ing, action-orientated environment conducive to growth. Many organizations are built around a strong (often over-bearing) wood element. Good strategy building and planning processes are signs of strength in this element. Wood leaders provide strategic direction and motivation to get things done. The feel of a wood environment is one of movement, negotiation and growth.

Blockages in the wood element may manifest as authoritarian, top-down, rigid management structures that suffocate creativity and disable the orga-nizations ability to creatively respond to change. The organization may be characterized by stop-start cycles indicating bouts of high energy followed by collapse - with impatient, impulsive and non-participatory decision-making. Weakness in the wood element manifests as a lack of direction and timidity around decision-making. The pervasive working climate will be one of frustra-tion or boredom, as creative energies are never realized.

Organizational fire: Communicating or just chaotic?

Fire provides the heart of the organization. This is about the passion of the organization that inspires and motivates. It is like a deep pulse that connects and integrates across departments, location and status. Good, open and honest communication is critical for re-kindling the spark and overall coherence of the organization. Walking into an organization and hearing people chatting and laughing, feeling openness in the way the space is organized for good commu-nication indicates that a healthy fire element is present. A 'fire type manager' will be inspirational, uplifting and passionate. A strong presence of fire is crucial for keeping spirits high, good open communication and motivating staff.

An organization suffering from a fire imbalance may loose its sense of inte-gration and community, becoming chaotic and fragmented with each person or department operating independently. Satellite departments may get separated from the core leading to communication breakdown at different levels: between policy formulation and implementation; and between senior management and employees. Open communication breaks down fostering hostility and the development of over-defensive and protective barriers, fuelling mistrust, lack of transparency and accountability.

Organizational earth: Lean or just anorexic?

The earth element is about resources that nourish and support the organization. Earth is about remaining lean and agile - avoiding slipping into stagnation and obesity but at the same time not starving the organization of essential resources and support. A strong 'earth element' is about the quality of organizational life and all the components that go into creating this quality. Does the organization feel well grounded, nourished and nourishing? Critically important are staff welfare policies and having the resources necessary to carry out your work effectively. An organization that feels homely and well cared for indicates the presence of a strong earth element. Leadership will be approachable and supportive, striving for harmony and peace throughout the organization.

An organization suffering from an earth imbalance may have the general air that the key resources of the organization are not properly cared for or nurtured - whether it be people, equipment, buildings, or relationships with customers. There may be a sense that the policies or strategy of the organization is not rooted in practical reality and day to day concerns. The pot plants are dying, the photocopier does not work and staff are starved of the basic resources needed to carry out their work effectively - whether it be training, information or equipment.

Organizational metal: Cutting through or just cutting?

The metal element is about the efficient use of resources and the elimination of wastes that are no longer useful. An over-active metal element will be clearing out and cutting back before the real fruits have manifested or been 'digested'.

The metal pulse cuts through to the basic core and essence - it brings clarity, precision and quality to an organization. You can feel the presence of metal through its order, structure and routines. At the physical level, spaces that are uncluttered and clean have a strong metal quality. This presence of a strong metal element is most important when clarity and precision is required, such as in accounting offices or in the surgeons operating theatre. A 'metal type manager' is a familiar breed: someone that can cut through the confusion and irrelevant details and get straight to the point. Accountability, trustworthiness and precision are typical qualities of a metal manager.

An organization out of balance in the metal phase may be living in the glory of past success, ceremony and tradition. Images of traditional accountancy or legal offices spring to mind. There may be an air of moral superiority or detached indifference with an almost clinical separation from the affairs of the world 'out there'. Security is gained from holding onto old ideas, whereas new concepts, technologies and people seem invasive and threatening. Fastidious attention to detail and tidy controlling structures create an overall rather depressing and isolated air of nothing really happening - no creativity, no interaction, no exchange.

Pattern

The underlying pattern of an organization is the configuration of relationships among the systems essential elements or components. The structure of the organization can be thought of as the material embodiment of this pattern of organization. Conventionally, we have used the metaphor of the machine to describe the structure and parts that make up the modern organization. The health of an organization is then measured in terms of quantifiable outputs. This approach is also reflected in modern medicine that measures health in terms of structural and bio-chemical change.

If we see the organization through a more holistic worldview then we shift our perspective from parts to wholes and from material objects to patterns and relationships. This perspective is not only consistent with recent advances in complexity theory but also reflects more holistic views of health and disease. For example, in Chinese medicine the emphasis has been on diagnosing the pattern of relationships between the different elemental components. A disharmonious relationship between these components will manifest as discernible patterns in the signs and symptoms of disease.

Hence, understanding patterns is crucial to diagnosing organizational health from an holistic perspective. In the ancient Chinese system, the relationships between the elements originate from environmental observations which show how each element is connected to all other elements.

- Water is nourished by wood, restrained by fire, revitalized by metal and controlled / absorbed by earth.
- Fire generates earth, melts metal, is fuelled by wood and is quenched / restrained by water.
- Metal vitalizes water, cuts wood, is formed by earth and is melted by fire.
- Wood generates fire, is stabilized by earth, nourished by water and is cut / restrained by metal.
- Earth forms metal and minerals, absorbs / dams water, is generated by the ashes from fire and is stabilized by wood.

All the elements are inter-connected and related to each other through a dynamic pattern of support and control relationships. The support relationships (Figure 1) show how one element nourishes and fuels the next element in the sequence. These linkages provide a series of positive or reinforcing relationships (positive feedback loops). For example, water nourishes wood, which in turn fuels fire and so forth. The control relationships (negative feedback) provide a counter-balancing force to negate or control their respective

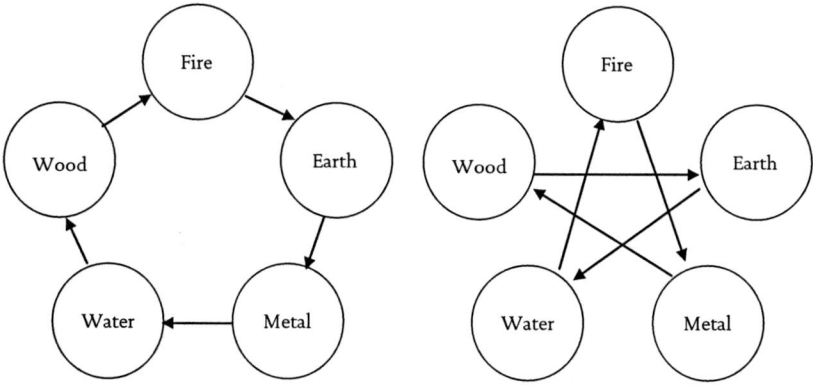

Figure 1: Support Cycle   **Figure 2:** Control Cycle

elements. For example, water restrains fire, which in turn melts metal. Figure 2 shows the control relationships that provide a series of negative, diffusing or reducing forces.

Being able to see the pattern of organizational relationships has various dimensions:

Connectivity: what aspects of the organization are most connected and which are relatively isolated and disconnected? Which elements are over-represented and excessive and which are weak and under-represented? Often the most obvious signs and symptoms relate to areas of congestion, but any symptoms of excess are generated by, and reflect areas, of weakness elsewhere in the system. Thinking about what is missing is just as important as taking account of those signs and symptoms that shout the loudest.

Overlapping patterns: are their elemental signatures that are common to different aspects of the organization (such as space and leadership) or do these complement or balance each other?

Dynamic feedback: The concept of working with, rather than against feedback cycles is central to working with complex systems. Strategic interventions that take account of positive feedback allow the potential of small changes to have large impacts. Positive feedback reinforces change, whereas negative feedback dampens and diffuses any intervention.

Diagnosis

Diagnostic questioning, observations and perceptual maps can be used to identify the qualities of the elements within the organization at different levels; from the working environment; to leadership competencies; to team dynamics. The exercise can be undertaken with individuals, teams or with the organization as a whole. The elemental signature of the organization will emerge, showing where and how the different elements manifest and their relative strengths and weaknesses.

At the simplest level, organizational disease is characterized by one or more elements dominating or over-controlling the others. When this happens, the associated elements in the support and control sequences are weakened and if the pressure continues, ultimately may collapse. Without corrective action the spiral of disharmony continues as the weakened elements fail to provide nourishment along the support sequence. At this stage in the cycle, the signs and symptoms will already be apparent in the organization but may be manifesting a long way from the root cause of the imbalance. Addressing these superficial signs and symptoms may provide a short-term solution, but long-term sustainable transformation requires a systemic approach that identifies and corrects the root cause of disharmony.

Figure 3 illustrates how an initial weakness in the water element, leads to a spiral of disharmony manifesting as symptoms in the elements throughout the organization.

Figure 3 shows how water fails to nourish wood, manifesting as a weakness in the wood element. The organization suffers from a lack of collective vision and purpose, with management characterized by vagueness, timidity and indecision. The depleted wood energy fails to stoke up the fire energy in the support cycle of the organization. Without a clear sense of purpose and vision, the human contact and relationships begin to suffer. The organization fragments and internal and external communications break down. The fire of the organization rapidly fades as projects never reach fruition and consequently satisfaction and completion are never realized. Without the creative tension of an active wood energy, the earth element remains unchecked in the control cycle. The nurturing and grounding aspects of earth become overbearing and suffocating, further dampening the dynamic tension essential for movement and change. Finally, the metal element in the control cycle becomes overactive and domineering, with its fastidious attention to detail, tight controlling structures and rigid adherence to rules, procedure and protocol.

This snapshot in the five element process shows how a simple deficiency or collapse in one aspect of the 'energetic organization' can devolve into systemic patterns of disharmony throughout the organization. Without corrective intervention, the organization will spiral further into degenerative patterns of 'organizational disease'.

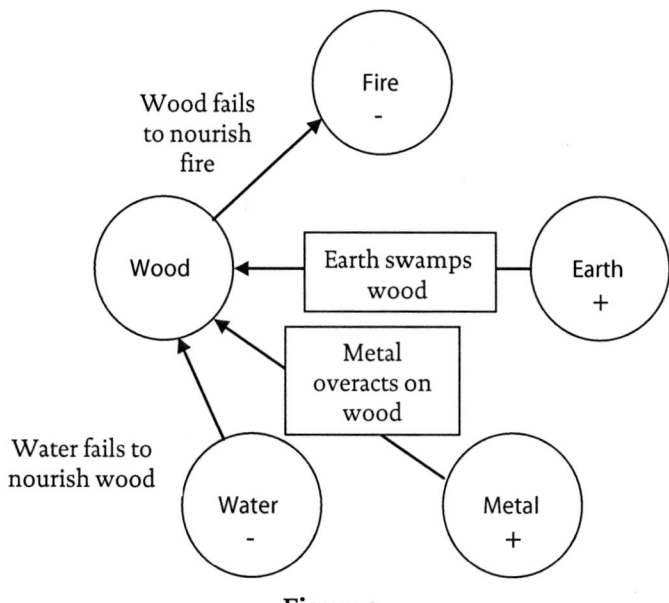

Figure 3
Spiral of Disharmony

Catalyzing change

Holistic health systems work on the principle that small, strategically targeted interventions can disturb the underlying pattern of organization and shift it towards healthier and more harmonious states. In Chinese medicine the signs and symptoms of disease can be disturbed, essentially through three routes:

- *Flow*: The acupuncturist uses her needles to re-connect and disperse. Having a picture of the organism as a coherent whole, she disperses, reduces and contracts congested elements and connects, stimulates and supports weak and disconnected elements. She knows that excess and deficiency go hand in hand and so works with both to avoid re-emergence of the problem in a different form elsewhere.

- *Quality*: The herbalist catalyzes change by introducing new energetic qualities that nudge a disturbed rhythm. The skill is in matching the energetic pattern of the individual with the known energetic qualities of herbal remedies. In this way excess is dispersed and deficiency supported.

- *Pattern*: All holistic health practitioners' work with the enormous capacity for self-regulation. Working with dynamic feedback, small strategic interventions can have large effects by stimulating virtuous cycles of self-healing. In holistic health this is known as the *homeopathic principle*, in holistic science it is the *butterfly effect*.

Various insights can be drawn from holistic medicine to catalyze change towards healthier states in human organizations:

- Build awareness of where and how the elemental qualities manifest within the organization.
- Link different aspects of the organization (such as management, structures and processes, and space) using the five elements.
- Identify which element(s) is most present or dominant and which are weak or absent.
- Develop strategies to enhance the flow by strengthening weak or absent elements and reducing the dominant elements.
- Work with feedback cycles rather than against. The homeopathic, or butterfly, principle enables large effects to be achieved with small interventions or disturbances.
- Recognize the role of the 'organizational doctor' as a co-creator of change and not as an independent observer.
- Work at different levels and away from where the 'problem' manifests. For example, changing the organization of working space can have profound

affects on staff morale and team dynamics.

Conclusions

Contemporary thinking on leadership, change-agency and sustainability is increasingly pointing to the need for people to be able to work holistically and with a greater understanding of complex and dynamic systems. At one level this means being in tune with the dynamic relationships between economic, environmental and social systems. At another level, it means working simultaneously with personal and organizational dynamics.

The application of chaos and complexity theory to organizational change means working with whole systems in which unexpected properties and characteristics of organizational behavior emerge from the configuration of relationships between the parts. This requires deepening our knowledge of patterns, drawing insights from both contemporary science and ancient practises. This chapter has explored the use of the five element framework as a way of engaging participants in a form of systems thinking and practice that has evolved over millennia.

The power of the framework is its application to any aspect of an organization - whether it be at the material (such as the design of the working environment); emotional (such as understanding team dynamics), or spiritual (such as values and vision) level. It works with the organization as an inter-connected whole - recognizing that changes at one level will have ramifications throughout the organization. Not only is it multi-dimensional, it also offers limitless combinations of change management strategies to meet the needs of diverse organizations. Hence, any aspect of an organization can be viewed through the lens of the five elements.

References

Beinfield, H. and Korngold, E. (1992). *Between Heaven and Earth: A Guide to Chinese Medicine*, New York: Ballantine Books.

Capra, F. (1975). *The Tao of Physics*, Shambala, Boston

Capra, F. (2002). *The Hidden Connections: A Science for Sustainable Living*, London: Harper Collins.

Dimitrov, V. and Naess, T. (2002). *Health Ecology: Learning to Cope with Complex Realities*, The National Centre for Nature-Culture-Health.

Morgan, G. (1997). *Images of Organization*, London, UK: Sage Publications Ltd.

Reason, P. and Goodwin, B. (1999). "Towards a Science of Qualities in Organizations: Lessons from Complexity Theory and Postmodern Biology," *Concepts and Transformations*, 4(3): 281-317

Senge, P. M. (1997). *The Fifth Discipline: The Art and Practice of the Learning Organization*, Century Business.

Stacey, R. (1996). *Complexity and Creativity in Organizations*, San Francisco: Berrett-Koehler Publishers.

Notes

1. The earliest reference to the school of naturalists is to Tsou Yen between 350BC and 270BC in the eastern States of Chhi and Yen in China.

CHAPTER 21

MACHINES OR GARDENS... OR BOTH?

Patrick E. Connor and Carole S. Napolitano

Organizations have been thought of in machine-like terms for more than a century. Grounded in a Newtonian view of the universe, classical organization theorists argued that organizations should be orderly, predictable, and designed for maximum control. This metaphor has come under heavy attack by those who prefer language that reflects the organic nature of organizations. Organizations, in this view, are more accurately thought of as living systems, and managers should view their role more like gardeners than mechanics. But is the machine metaphor really defunct? The authors have been hearing and reading language that is eminently machine-like: leverage, drivers ('create and drive a vision'), and knowledge depot are just a few. We ask, therefore, are these kinds of references still useful even if they are not adequate? And if so, in what relation to organic, organization-as-garden, metaphors? In short, can machine metaphors be coupled with organic ways of thinking and talking about organizations to achieve more holistic - and realistic - understanding?

Managing Organizational Complexity: Philosophy, Theory, and Application
A Volume in: Managing the Complex, pages 361-372.
Copyright © 2005 by Information Age Publishing, Inc.
All rights of reproduction in any form reserved.
ISBN: 1-59311-319-6 (cloth), 1-59311-318-8 (paper)

Introduction

In her closing keynote at the 1996 *Systems Thinking in Action* Conference, Meg Wheatley, author of *Leadership and the New Science* (1999), delivered a bald challenge to the audience of 1200 consultants and practitioners gathered to hear her latest thinking about organizational systems. Describing the audience as 'pathfinders', she proposed that in their efforts to diagnose and work with organizations they were vulnerable to the trap of becoming as controlling - albeit with new approaches, techniques, and structures - as anything they might be seeking to supersede. A case of new wine in old wineskins as it were. Wheatley, in fact, cautioned her audience about "tinkering at the level of structure and form rather than at the organization's core." In the broader sense one could hear Wheatley's message as a call to greater mindfulness about the subtle (or not so subtle) ways that we inadvertently reinforce old structures, notwithstanding our intent to transform them.

Her advice seems especially apt in light of current theory and practice with respect to the metaphors we choose to describe organizations. Proponents of organizations as living systems have, for several years now, called for the use of more organic metaphors that reflect the complex and dynamic quality of human organizations. Wheatley (1996), for example, continually reminds us that human organizations are living systems that ultimately defy the kind of precision machine metaphors imply. Peter Senge (1990, 1999), an acknowledged guru of systems-and-learning-organizations theory, exhorts that we must become "less like mechanics and more like gardeners." Yet the present authors have observed that the language broadly used among contemporary systems-thinking and learning-organization communities - in both conferences and the literature - continues to be eminently machine-like, including such frequently used terms as drivers ("create and drive a vision"), engines, and leverage. In that vein, a popular book is titled, *Building the Learning Organization* (Marquardt, 1996). The purpose of this essay is to explore this phenomenon with respect to our evolving understanding of the nature of organizations, the transition to new ways of thinking about and describing them, and the larger implications of these kinds of choices.

Generative power of language, especially metaphors

We can hardly begin an exploration of metaphors and organizations without first addressing the role of language in the broadest sense. There is a view (philosophers call it *naïve realism*, see the introductory remarks to section 1) that posits that reality is objective - is "out there" - and that the role of language is to report it. But as early as 1927 Werner Heisenberg demonstrated that whenever we take an accounting of the world we necessarily change it - that is, we actively participate, in spite of ourselves, in shaping the world we perceive (Wheeler

& Zurek, 1983: 62-84). This is especially true with respect to language. The Sapir-Whorf hypothesis, for example, pointed out the influence that cultural differences have in framing the perceptions of its users (Whorf, 1956). Moreover, the generative power of language is central to the growing body of social constructionist thought that has emerged in recent decades. As Cunliffe (2002: 128) says, "we create our social realities, meaning, and selves in embodied and situated dialogue." Thus, language does not just describe reality, language defines reality or, *our words create our worlds*. The colloquial illustration of this concept is the three umpires' exchange about calling balls and strikes: says the first, "I call 'em as I see 'em." To which the second responds, "I call 'em as they are." But the third has the last word - so to speak: "They ain't nothin' till I call 'em."

What does all this imply about metaphors? First, that they are surely more than just literary devices that serve to ornament our prose. As expressions of our conceptual systems, metaphors influence not only how we construct reality, but how we function in relation to it as well (Lakoff & Johnson, 1980). Consider the war metaphor that governs our approach to argument: Lakoff and Johnson (1980: 4) point out that such terms as "winning / losing," "indefensible," "strategy," "shoot down," "right on target," etc., are not just semantics - they actually determine, at least in part, the things we do when we argue: such as attack, defend, and counterattack our "opponent." Similarly, "war," "rapists," "raiders," and "casualties" - as compared with, for example, "partnership" - typify the language of mergers and acquisitions(which, perhaps not surprisingly, fail 70% of the time - Mirvis, 1999). Thus, metaphors are not just things we *think* by; they are things we *live* by. Metaphors represent an unconscious framework for perceiving, analyzing, and responding to our experience - and for developing any number of implicit assumptions about the things around us. Yet despite the generative power of metaphors, they are somewhat arbitrarily conceived, varying by culture, and thus are subject to reconsideration. Lakoff and Johnson (1980) imagine a culture where argument is viewed not as war but as dance, with behaviors that correspond to performing something that is balanced and aesthetically pleasing (see also Vaill, 1989).

Notwithstanding that metaphors are more than literary devices, the fact that metaphors are literary devices in the first place has significance for this exploration as well, since the role metaphors play in the scheme of discourse is to focus attention and heighten the impact of an utterance through a succinct comparison. Thus, metaphors have the power to distill complex or abstract ideas into striking, memorable images that can easily become governing ideas. Metaphors represent a catalytic force: because they "instantly fuse two separate realms of experience" (Barrett & Cooperrider, 1990), they have a presumptive, self-fulfilling quality that is, indeed, transformational. Senge's (1999) juxtaposition of mechanic and gardener illustrates the capacity of two simple, contrasting images to frame a fundamental shift: from our deeply-embedded view of organizations as machines that need to be fixed, discarded, or periodically 're-engineered', to the notion of organizations as living systems - complex and dynamic - that can be cultivated in ways that allow them to adapt and thrive as their environments evolve.

Moreover, the power of metaphors lies not just in their vividness and succinctness, but as well in their density and richness. Metaphors are potent precisely because they imply so much by saying so little. The metaphor has more than face value; the many connotations it carries can, by implication, be assumed to apply to the object of comparison. As Ortony (cited in Weick, 1979) points out, metaphors both invite and direct embellishment.

The value of metaphors as a means of understanding the complex universe of organizations and organizational life can hardly be overstated. We need a way to simplify and make sense of a phenomenon that is complicated, multidimensional, even paradoxical, yet central to our modern culture and to our personal and professional lives. The risk is that in choosing a metaphorical scheme we impose an oversimplified way of thinking - and of functioning - that, depending on the nature of the metaphor, limits our sense of possibilities or, worse, does damage to our very humanness.

Historically: Organizations are machines

It is no secret that organizations have been thought of in machine-like terms for the better part of a century. Grounded in a Newtonian view of the universe, classical organization theorists argued that organizations should be orderly, predictable, and designed for maximum control. In such a scheme the function of "management" then becomes ensuring routine, eliminating variation as much as possible; keeping the trains running on time, as it were, through conformity to mechanistic responses. Max Weber, the so-called father of bureaucracy, said it clearly (1958: 214):

"The decisive reason for the advance of bureaucratic organization has always been its purely technical superiority over any other form of organization... Precision, speed, unambiguity, knowledge of the files, continuity, discretion, unity, strict subordination, reduction of friction and of material and personal costs - these are raised to the optimum point in the strictly bureaucratic administration."

Weber's concept of bureaucratic rationality - central to all of classical organization theory - was that an organization that minimized uncertainty and ambiguity, while maximizing certainty and predictability, was a good thing in its service to the fundamental goal of productivity. The obvious means to achieve such control was to operate the organization (and its workers) like machines, which presented a challenge: how to wrest efficiency from the essentially inefficient human being? *Scientific Management* addressed this challenge by developing rules of behavior for workers that emphasized repetition, low discretion, a narrow range of tasks, and a large number of cyclical repetitions - all of which regulated and regimented activity in much the way a machine works. Accordingly, workers were evaluated in terms of their capacity, speed, durability, and cost (March & Simon, 1958: 15-19). One of the best examples of this perspective is the list developed by Frank and Lillian Gilbreth (1917), an engineer and psychologist respectively, specifying 18 classes of basic activities in the performance of tasks (e.g., 'reach', 'turn', 'grasp', 'release').

It is not surprising, then, given this perspective of organization, work, and workers, as well as the factory model of organization that dominated the late 19th and early 20th centuries, that the classicists focused their energies on time-and-motion studies, the arrangement of the work place, the design of tools and equipment, and the assembly line. Rationality was the objective, and efficiency the mantra. In the classic *Papers on the Science of Administration*, Lyndall Urwick (1937) described the matter of organizing as a technical problem, whose solution would maximize organizational goal attainment. To repeat: metaphors are more than just literary devices.

Organization-as-machine today

The foregoing suggests that organization-as-machine resides in the past. Not true. The metaphor is very much alive and well here at the beginning of the 21st century. The ideal organizational state continues to be described as the "well-oiled machine"; people still feel as if they are cogs in a wheel. Even organizational change efforts are often dubbed 're-engineering'.

A popular example of this sort of expression is the well-traveled phrase, "If it ain't broke, don't fix it!" The "it" in this cliché usually refers to some organization, system, policy, process, or the like. The problem with applying this cliché and similar references to organizations is that doing so renders the organization as mechanical object, because it is mechanical objects that get broken and need fixing. And the reason that rendering the organization in such a way is a problem is, "If [the organization] is a machine, then things should be smooth-running, predictable, efficient, and designed such that all the parts fit together to fulfill a single, unambiguous function or purpose" (Marshak, 1993: 45).

To take this argument a step further, if that which ain't broke is a machine, then organizational members are objectified as some of those parts making up that machine. And when a part is defective, it is either fixed or replaced by an identical part. Moreover, machines are about control and rigidity, not flexibility or adaptability. One would hardly want a lathe to adapt to the wood it is shaping. Thus systems and structures are formalized, and procedures are standardized. Tasks performed by machine parts are necessarily specialized and routinized. Yet today's rapidly-changing environment requires increasingly high levels of flexibility and adaptability. And though we talk of work-life balance, workers at all levels of all types of organizations find that expectations and pressures for performance continue to escalate with no apparent regard for the toll on what we continue to say is our most important resource; as if by ratcheting up the pressure we can simply put people into overdrive or recalibrate them for higher and higher levels of productivity.

There has got to be a better way of thinking about - and talking about - organizations. Fortunately, there is.

Current realities: The garden metaphor

The use of organic metaphors to describe organizations is hardly new, and links back to the etymological origins of the word most often used for business organizations: 'company'. As de Gues (2002) points out, the root of the word 'company' is the same as that of the word 'companion' which means 'the sharing of bread'. This relational orientation contrasts with the basis of that other common term, the 'firm', which is a pseudo-legalistic notion of confirming or ratifying an agreement by one's signature (Oxford English Dictionary). Rather, it jibes with the notion that organizations, including companies, are places where - unlike in the case of a machine - trust, influence, and a variety of dynamic interactions are central to the performance of work. So although companies became synonymous with machines for making money during the Machine Age, this was at odds with their fundamental nature. Today organic metaphors are taking on new significance. In his analysis of governing metaphors for organizations Morgan (1997) describes organic metaphors as focusing attention on organizational needs and environmental relations, on the life cycles of organizations, on organizational species, and on evolutionary patterns found in interorganizational ecology.

Similarly, the so-called new sciences - chaos theory, field theory, evolutionary biology, complexity theory - make a compelling case for viewing organizations as living systems and for considering the potentially rich applications that derive from recent discoveries in the living systems of the physical universe. For example, consider that organizations exhibit all the traits of complex systems: symbols and images are agents, interactions are governed by schema that require adaptation and learning, and the organizational system is embedded in co-evolving economic, social, and political supra-systems (Stacey, 1996: 10). The self-organizing property of systems provides additional evidence. Based on observations that certain creatures (e.g., birds and termites) are able to synchronize behavior around a shared goal spontaneously - without benefit of managers, organization charts, or other such organizational infrastructure - there is a growing belief across many disciplines that in living systems there is "order for free" (Kauffman, 1995: 71) and that human living systems could experience a much more sustainable kind of order if they were able to behave more naturally; more like the living systems that they fundamentally are. In so doing, they could integrate, much in the way a stream or river does, the diversity and flexibility so critical to effectiveness in the current environment. The notion that "life wants to happen" (Wheatley, 1999) speaks on the one hand to the futility of trying to ultimately control and direct human systems, and on the other to the potential for possibility, for discovery - for spontaneous collaboration and leadership (Napolitano & Henderson, 1998). In fact, the shift away from confining machine metaphors may be part of a global shift in society away from a materialist view of the universe (Harman, 1999). An alternative and more expansive perspective describes the organization as a living value system: "a multi-perspective colloquy of valuing" (Srivastva, *et al.*, 1999: 6) that has the potential to fundamentally transform the world.

Whatever the full dynamics of the shift, the price for these gifts is a greater tolerance for the kind of ambiguity and messiness that has nothing to do with machines, but everything to do with living systems as, like a river or stream, they find their path; learning as they go, finding alternative routes, making new connections along the way. Such a perspective leads us to a new metaphorical framework: instead of pistons and gears running in lockstep fashion, we conjure up a garden - the organization as a fertile place - where possibilities are seeded and where the role of manager is to cultivate the conditions within which varieties of potential can thrive.

Current realities: Are we sure?

So far, so good. It would appear that we've come a long way since Weber and others argued that the best organization was the one that most closely resembled the proverbial clock. Indeed, it would appear that we have come to a much more enlightened view. Many current scholars and practitioners, especially those in the learning-organization community (e.g., Senge, 1999; Wheatley, 1999; Brown & Isaacs, 1997), are calling for a more organic, i.e., garden-like, way of understanding organizations.

Or have we in fact come such a long way? Based on the authors' observation of organizational literature in general and learning-organization verbiage in particular, the answer is no. At this point we invite the reader to consider the following language drawn from recent publications, conference presentations, and common organizational parlance.

drivers - in the sense that *x* drives *y*

> example: create and drive a vision
> example: drive your strategy
> example: drive participation
> example: we need to drive our leadership principles deeper into the organization

funnels ("Wrong metaphor," said a conference presenter. "Venturi tube is much better.")

innovation engines

innovation pipelines

knowledge: treated as if it were a thing – for example, something to be captured

knowledge depot

lever / leverage
>   example: leverage knowledge across the company
>   example: the cultural transformation lever(!)

moving the needle

platforms

put systems in place to ...

search engine

traction
>   example: mobilizing the high-potential group will give this initiative more traction

As we have noted, a popular book on the subject is titled, *Building the Learning Organization* (Marquardt, 1996). And our personal favorites:

1. In *The Systems Thinker* journal, there is a standard feature called Toolbox; and;
2. one of the leading journals in organizational learning is actually called *Leverage*.

We submit that not one of the above terms is compatible with a garden view of organizational systems. In the case of the two journals mentioned, 'toolbox' speaks for itself, and not one of the various definitions of 'leverage' offered by the Oxford English Dictionary suggests that the term has any relevant meaning other than mechanical. So have we really come that far from Weber, the Gilbreths, Urwick, and the other classicists? More significantly, does this language reflect the same old instrumental view of organizational systems and their members? Consider:

>   Is a person's knowledge merely some thing to be captured? And by whom? More importantly, for whose purposes?
>
>   Is a person's participation something to be driven? Again, by whom and for what purpose?
>
>   Is innovation an engine? Is it driven by something? And how does creativity get inserted into a pipeline?
>
>   Does one build a garden?
>
>   ... and so forth.

As we acknowledged at the outset, language informs thinking. Shouldn't the language used to describe organizational systems today do more than inform mechanistic, instrumental thinking? Do we need to reconsider our metaphors? Yes, and yes. And in that reconsideration should we purge mechanistic references altogether? Or should we rethink how and where they most usefully, most appropriately, apply?

Machines AND gardens?

Perhaps we are being too critical. Organizations are complex entities, to say the least; paradoxical, even. It could be argued that organisms and ecological systems do have some mechanistic properties; that is, they have properties that can roughly (and for short-term prediction) be captured in explicit models. So let us say that they are both organic *and* mechanical. As Weick (1979) has cautioned, there are no wrong metaphors; metaphors merely differ as to the qualities or characteristics that they call out. To describe an organization as a runaway train careening down a mountainside may be useful in understanding the actions of its members. To describe it as a new sapling, struggling to find its place in the ecology - well, that too may be useful in understanding why certain decisions are being made in the enterprise. If it is true that organizations have both organic and mechanistic characteristics, then metaphorical language that calls out any of those characteristics has merit.

Still, why does mechanistic language have such a hold? And with what consequences? In response to the first part of the question, several possible explanations suggest themselves. First, notwithstanding the organic character of a human institution, perhaps organization-as-machine is an especially useful model. If the primary purpose of the organization is to do work and produce outcomes, then conceiving of organizations in terms that highlight the capabilities that machines represent makes some sense.

Second, it may be that the operating language of scholars and practitioners has not caught up with their rhetoric. That is, at a conceptual level, scholars and practitioners are comfortable with describing organizations organically. But at the level of action, any language that seeks precision may tend to produce mechanistic constructions - thus, 100+ years of attempting specificity and explicitness has such force as to make mechanistic references simply too instinctive and natural to be easily revised.

Thus, the use of machine metaphors may be more habit than intention at this point, a case of *theory-in-use* vs. *espoused theory* (Argyris, 1982). This explanation seems highly plausible at a time when we are in transition from a firmly entrenched view of the organization to what some would consider a radical reconceptualization (Ancona, *et al.*, 1999: 4-18). Change theorists have long known that behavior modification is the last and most difficult stage in what is typically a multi-phased, protracted process (Connor, *et al.*, 2003). Bridges (1991) in particular has argued that transition is a three-phase process, in which, ironically, *beginnings* (the appropriation of new behaviors, or, in this case, language) occur at the final stage of a process that starts with *endings* (a letting go of the old), and proceeds through a *neutral zone* - a kind of limbo between the old and new. In thinking about organizations, we believe that scholars and practitioners are in the neutral zone, in which historical language has not yet given way to contemporary - despite philosophical rhetoric to the contrary. Given the long history and cultural reinforcement of mechanistic metaphors, it makes sense that practice would lag behind theory. Parenthetically, it may be worth noting that the authors found it difficult in writing this paper to avoid using words like function and operate which come so automatically (pun intended) to mind.

A third explanation may offer the richest possibility: perhaps it is not a question of accomplishing a shift from one model or metaphor to another, but rather of developing a more holistic integration of the two valid aspects of human organizations. Even if organizations are fundamentally organic, there may well be elements that are most aptly described in machine-like terms (even gardeners use tools). In this scheme the issue would be relegating machine metaphors to their proper place, so to speak, and bringing forward metaphors that acknowledge the living qualities of the system and the importance of cultivating the conditions within which living things can thrive and grow.

In response to the second part of the question posed at the beginning of this section (what are the consequences of the prevailing machine metaphor for organizations?), we must reiterate the profound ability of metaphorical choices to influence thought and behavior. The fact that machine metaphors are so dominant takes them out of the category of merely one among many ways to highlight organizational properties and gives them primacy. If organizations are talked about in largely mechanistic terms, they will be thought about as machines, and they will be operated as machines, with their attendant dehumanizing. Alternatively, if organizations are described in ways that acknowledge their qualities as living systems and consign mechanistic terms to a utilitarian role, they gain the capacity to evolve in ways that are dynamic and that more fully realize human potential - both individually and collectively.

Concluding thought

Why care if operational language is still stuck in the old-model, mechanistic-metaphor rut it has been in for more than a century? The most compelling reason has less to do with getting the language right for the sake of intellectual integrity than for restoring the original character of organizations and catalyzing the latent possibilities of human collectivity. As we have been saying throughout, we believe that language informs thinking, which in turn informs action. Choosing the right language, then, may well be a fateful act. To the extent that organizations are value-seeking entities capable of learning, of choice, of flexing and changing, and of responding in novel ways, they gain the capacity to realize their larger purpose, which is to further society's aims. There may be no time in our history when developing this systemic capacity is more critical - and intentional language choices are a powerful means to that end.

References

Ancona, D., Kochan, T. A., Scully, M., Van Maanen, J. and Westney, D. E. (1999). *Managing for the Future: Organizational Behavior & Processes*, Cincinnati, Ohio: South-Western.

Argyris, C. (1982). *Learning and Action: Individual and Organizational*, San Francisco: Jossey-Bass.

Barrett, F. J. and Cooperrider, D. L. (1990). "Generative Metaphor Intervention: A New Approach for Working with Systems Divided by Conflict and Caught in Defensive Perception," *The Journal of Applied Behavioral Science*, 26 (2): 219-239.

Bridges, W. (1991). *Managing Transitions, Reading*, Massachusetts: Addison-Wesley.

Brown, J. and Isaacs, D. (1997). "Start Talking and Get to Work: Conversation as a Core Business Process," *Systems Thinking in Action Conference* presentation, Orlando, Florida.

Connor, P. E., Lake, L. K. and Stackman, R. W. (2003). *Managing Organizational Change*, 3rd ed., Westport, Connecticut: Praeger Publishers.

Cunliffe, A. L. (2002). "Social Poetics as Management Inquiry: A Dialogical Approach," *Journal of Management Inquiry*, 11(2): 128-146.

de Gues, A. (2002). *The Living Company: Habits for Survival in a Turbulent Business Environment*, Cambridge, Massachusetts: Harvard Business School Press.

Gilbreth, F. B. and Gilbreth, L. M. (1917). *Applied Motion Study*, New York: Sturgis and Walton.

Harman, W. W. (1999). "Shifting context for Executive Behavior: Signs of Change and Revaluation" in S. Srivastva, D. L. Cooperrider, and Associates (eds.), *Appreciative Management and Leadership* (revised edition), Bedford Heights, Ohio: Williams Custom Publishing, pp. 37-54.

Kauffman, S. (1995). *At Home in the Universe: The Search for the Laws of Self-organization and Complexity*, New York: Oxford University Press.

Lakoff, G. and Johnson, M. (1980). *Metaphors We Live By*, Chicago: University of Chicago Press.

March, J. G. and Simon, H. A. (1958). *Organizations*, New York: John Wiley.

Marquardt, M. J. (1996). *Building the Learning Organization*, New York: McGraw-Hill.

Marshak, R. J. (1993). "Managing the Metaphors of Change," *Organizational Dynamics*, 22(1): 44-56 .

Mirvis, P. H. (1999). "Merging of Executive Heart and Mind in Crisis Management," in S. Srivastva, D. L. Cooperrider, and Associates (eds.), *Appreciative Management and Leadership* (revised edition), Bedford Heights, Ohio: Williams Custom Publishing, pp. 55-91.

Morgan, G. (1997). *Images of Organizations*, 2nd ed., Beverly Hills, California: Sage Publications.

Napolitano, C. S. and Henderson, L. J. (1998). *The Leadership Odyssey: A Self-Development Guide to New Skills for New Times*, San Francisco: Jossey-Bass.

Senge, P. M. (1999). "Learning for a Change," *Fast Company*, 24: 178-188.

Senge, P. M. (1990). *The Fifth Discipline: The Art and Practice of the Learning Organization*, New York: Doubleday.

Srivastva, S., Fry, R. E. and Cooperrider, D. L. (1999). "Introduction: The Call for Executive Appreciation," in S. Srivastva, D. L. Cooperrider, and Associates (eds.), *Appreciative Management and Leadership* (revised edition), Bedford Heights, Ohio: Williams Custom Publishing, pp.1-33.

Stacey, R. (1996). *Complexity and Creativity in Organizations*, San Francisco: Berrett-Koehler Publishers, Inc.

Urwick, L. F. (1937). "Organization as a Technical Problem," in L. Gulick and L. Urwick (eds.), *Papers on the Science of Administration*, New York: Institute of Public Administration.

Vaill, P. B. (1989). *Managing as a Performing Art: New Ideas for a World of Chaotic Change*, San Francisco: Jossey-Bass.

Weber, M. (1958). *From Max Weber: Essays in Sociology*, H. H. Gerth and C. Wright Mills (eds.), New York: Oxford University Press.

Weick, K. E. (1979). *The Social Psychology of Organizing*, 2nd edition, Reading, Massachusetts: Addison-Wesley.

Wheatley, M. (1999). *Leadership and the New Science* (revised), San Francisco: Berrett-Koehler.

Wheatley, M. (1996). "Understanding Organizations as Living Systems," *The Systems Thinker*, 7 (9): 5.

Wheeler, J. A., and Zurek, H. (eds.) (1983). *Quantum Theory and Measurement*, Princeton: Princeton University Press.

Whorf, B. L. (1956). *Language, Thought, and Reality: Selected Writings*, Cambridge: MIT Press.

CHAPTER 22

A COMPLEXITY-BASED SCRUTINY OF LEARNING FROM ORGANIZATIONAL CRISIS

Dawn R. Gilpin

As a means of exploring and embracing uncertainty and ambiguity in an organizational context, complexity theories would appear to be especially suited to the study and management of organizational crises, defined as unpredictable, though not altogether unfamiliar events that threaten the legitimacy of an organization. Organizational crises are often touted as potential learning experiences for the parties involved, but the traditional approach to crisis management may actually inhibit opportunities for learning and, paradoxically, increase the likelihood of subsequent crises. This paper draws on the fields of knowledge management, organizational learning and crisis management, explores the nexus among the three disciplines and examines possible barriers to learning inherent in the current dominant managerial and crisis management models. Finally, it suggests that a complexity-based approach to learning may prove more effective in dealing with the unpredictable events that threaten organizational legitimacy.

Managing Organizational Complexity: Philosophy, Theory, and Application
A Volume in: Managing the Complex, pages 373–388.
Copyright © 2005 by Information Age Publishing, Inc.
All rights of reproduction in any form reserved.
ISBN: 1-59311-319-6 (cloth), 1-59311-318-8 (paper)

Introduction

As a means of exploring and embracing uncertainty and ambiguity in an organizational context, complexity theories would appear to be especially suited to the study and management of organizational crises, defined as unpredictable, though not altogether unfamiliar, events that threaten the legitimacy of an organization. Organizational crises are often touted as potential learning experiences for the parties involved, but the traditional approach to crisis management may actually inhibit opportunities for learning and, paradoxically, increase the likelihood of subsequent crises.

The current dominant approach to crisis management is heavily linear and generally focused around the creation and execution of a detailed set of procedures known as the crisis management plan (CMP). Changing to a complexity-based viewpoint of crises requires a dramatic shift in perspective with far-reaching implications for managers, including how crisis-related information is handled and stored, and how learning processes are conducted.

The complex organization

Much of today's management science still bears the strong imprint of the scientific management and behaviorist approaches popular in the first part of the twentieth century. Efficient, linear causality is assumed, in which managers intervene as needed to control the dynamics within the system (Farquhar, 1919; Stacey, *et al.*, 2000). Classic systems theory focuses its attention on the parts, reifying the organization / system to simplify it for study, while simultaneously detaching it from the web of relationships that make it unique (van Uden, *et al.*, 2001).

Theories of complexity conceive of the 'system', including social systems such as organizations, in quite a different manner. We may arrive at a portrait of complex systems by combining and summarizing the characteristics identified by a variety of authors (Cilliers, 1998; McKelvey, 1999; Richardson & Lissack, 2001; Stacey, 1996; Stacey, *et al.*, 2000; Stacey, 2001; van Uden, *et al.*, 2001). Once we understand what a complex system is and how it behaves, we may begin to develop a coherent theory of how such systems acquire and process knowledge, and thus how they learn. This in turn will allow us to examine the role played in this learning process by crisis events.

Complex vs. complicated

Definitions of complex systems vary to some degree, even within this volume. However, there does appear to be some consensus that such systems present the characteristics below. Paul Cilliers provides a more complete set of descriptors in Chapter 1 (this volume), but for our purposes here the following should suffice.

Complex systems contain large numbers of individual elements. Although the number of parts is significant, it is not sufficient to identify a system as complex. A system such as a space launcher may consist of a large number of parts and yet be defined as merely complicated, rather than complex, since it does not meet the other essential criteria.

Complex systems are irreducible. In other words, they may not be accurately and exhaustively described in a less complex form. If it is possible to explain and predict the entirety of the range of behaviors of a given system, for instance in an instruction manual, then the system is complicated rather than complex.

The elements of a complex system interact locally and dynamically in an ongoing and nonlinear manner, and alter the fundamental composition of the system itself over time. This property is known as self-organization or emergence, and is perhaps the single most distinguishing feature that identifies a complex system as such. The elements, or agents, learn from their interactions and both generate and adapt to changes based on the feedback received, in a process called coevolution. Emergence results in unpredictable yet recognizable patterns of order, but since a complex system is never completely static, these patterns do not remain permanently stable.

There are no absolute boundaries in a complex system. Social scientists who adopt a complexity perspective view the human universe as a fluid array of groupings defined by the observer wishing to study a particular problem or situation. This grouping process recognizes that boundaries are not permanent and unchanging entities, but instead similar to Weick's (1995) definition of framing as "a generalized point of view that directs interpretations" (p. 4).

It logically follows that such a system, which evolves by means of constant internal and external interaction, experiences learning as an ontological necessity rather than an acquired skill.

Learning as an intrinsic property of organizations

There has been a great deal of attention in recent years focused on how organizations acquire information, process knowledge, and learn. Learning is said to have taken place when an individual's or group's attitudes, perspectives, or behaviors change (Blackler & McDonald, 2000), when it acquires new potential for change (Cope & Watts, 2000), or when it establishes new rules or changes existing ones in response to a perceived need to codify lessons drawn from experience (Beck & Kieser, 2003). In an organizational setting, learning may be said to have taken place when environmental cues are read and interpreted correctly and the learner acquires the ability to respond in a manner that benefits the individual, group, organization, or "system" as a whole. We might say then that the final purpose of learning is to provide the learner with the knowledge and skills necessary to make sense of the environment, draw accurate conclusions, and take appropriate action.

As the foregoing definition illustrates, however, from a complexity standpoint the 'learning organization' is a redundant term, since learning is a fundamental trait of all surviving complex systems and not something enforced by management. Organizational learning is a "multilayered intersubjective phenomenon" (Oswick, et al., 2000: 888) that is contextual in terms of both place and time, and demonstrates properties of emergence (Nidumolu, et al., 2001). The organization learns by acquiring information and negotiating meaning through situated interaction and both individual and group sensemaking.

Weick (1995) identified certain occasions or conditions as particular triggers for sensemaking activity. Three of the most significant such occasions for the present purposes are situations of high information load, complexity, and turbulence.

As information load increases, people neglect large portions of it. They adopt a variety of strategies to reduce the pressure, and these strategies affect what information is then available for sensemaking. Increased complexity tends to lead to narrow specialization and thus self-censoring of cues, or filtering of how those cues are interpreted. Finally, turbulence may be defined as "a combination of instability (frequency of change) and randomness (frequency and direction of change)" (Weick, 1995: 88).

Thus it would seem that organizational crises should constitute prime opportunities for learning by organizations, and indeed various authors urge managers to view them as such (see Caponigro, 2000; Coombs, 1999; Mitroff, et al., 1996). Yet empirical evidence seems to suggest that organizations do not take advantage of the learning opportunities afforded by crises, for a variety of reasons examined below.

Current model of crisis management

Before we can profitably explore how and what organizations learn from crises, it is necessary to have a general understanding of how crisis events are described in the literature, and the basic approach advocated by scholars and practitioners of crisis management. The most logical starting point is to explain specifically what a crisis is, and is not.

Pearson and Clair (1998) proposed the following comprehensive definition of organizational crisis:

"An organizational crisis is a low-probability, high-impact situation that is perceived by critical stakeholders to threaten the viability of the organization and that is subjectively experienced by these individuals as personally and socially threatening." (p. 66)

One critical distinction to be made, when defining a crisis and what is meant by crisis management, is that between a natural disaster, emergency or technological crisis and a "crisis of legitimacy" (Massey, 2001). Coombs (1999) equated *organizational legitimacy* with meeting stakeholder expectations, and thus a *crisis of legitimacy* results when the organization fails to meet the expectations of a significant portion of its internal and / or external stakeholders. Much of the writing on crisis planning and management seems to blur and confuse the line between emergency events and organizational crises of legitimacy, sometimes in unproductive ways. The practice of crisis management as discussed in this chapter does not refer to situations in which human lives are at immediate risk, and the crisis plan is intended as a communication tool rather than a substitute for emergency intervention.

Coombs (1999) prepared a comprehensive synthesis of the current state of the art in crisis management research and practice that reflects what most of those who work in, and study, the field consider to be best practice. Coombs developed his framework around a series of stages conceived as an endlessly looped process. In essence, he envisioned the crisis management function as requiring constant watchfulness on the part of the organization, with specific needs that change as the crisis process evolves through the various stages, which he identified as follows.

Signal detection involves seeking and identifying cues within the organizational context that may be indicative of an impending crisis, while *crisis prevention* attempts to stem the crisis through targeted actions and monitoring. *Crisis preparation* is the focal point of much of the literature on crisis management, emphasizing as it does central concerns such as diagnosing vulnerabilities, assessing crisis types, selecting and training the crisis team, selecting and training the spokesperson, developing the CMP, and reviewing the communication system (Coombs, 1999). The crisis plan has long been the centerpiece of prescribed crisis management strategies. The plan consists of a series of procedures for gathering, processing and divulging information to various stakeholder groups, ranging from organizational members to the media (see for example Caponigro, 2000; Coombs, 1999; Fearn-Banks, 1996). *Crisis containment* is essentially the stage at which the preparations are implemented, and *post-crisis concerns* refer to the aftermath during which the organization evaluates the impact of the crisis and determines how well it has handled the situation. This is the moment at which the organization is expected to learn from its experiences (Coombs, 1999; Mitroff, *et al.*, 1996).

Although the ongoing crisis management approach may seem to be coherent with the basic tenets of complexity by providing an adaptive model that includes monitoring and reacting to changes in the environment, a closer look reveals that the underlying assumptions of the current crisis management methodology reflect instead a mode of response some authors have characterized as 'complexity reduction', described in greater detail in the next section.

Modes of organizational response to turbulence

Organizational scholars have identified two broad categories of reactions to turbulent environments. The first approach seeks to impose order by deliberately limiting the boundaries of information gathering, minimizing and narrowing goals, formalizing and centralizing decision-making processes, and making stability top priority. Organizations that adopt this method - which is the predominant strategy taught by most western business schools and management guides - define successful crisis management as a means of minimizing the impact of crisis events on the organization. Such a response, referred to in the literature as *complexity reduction* (Ashmos, *et al.*, 2000), seeks to maintain an even keel and restore public legitimacy as quickly as possible following a crisis.

The second, less widespread philosophy is known as *complexity absorption* (Ashmos, *et al.*, 2000). As the name implies, complexity absorption is a strategy that does not attempt to control and predict events, but accepts the conflicts and uncertainty inherent in any organizational context and adapts as needed to ensure the long-term survival of the organization. While little empirical research has been conducted in this area, there is some evidence that organizations which take a complexity absorption approach to management handle unforeseen events more effectively (Ashmos, *et al.*, 2000; Daft & Weick, 2001). Among other things, such a strategy radically changes how organizations prepare for crises, how information is gathered, how decisions are made, as well as how - and what - organizations learn from crises that affect them.

Learning from organizational crisis

Once the crisis itself has blown over, most authors propose some form of post-hoc evaluation process. The primary purpose of the evaluation is generally considered to be a learning exercise: to gain insight into the crisis management process (Caponigro, 2000; Coombs, 1999; Mitroff, *et al.*, 1996). Evaluation is also used to calculate the approximate impact of the crisis on the organization, and thus offer tangible evidence of the relative success of the crisis management effort.

There are two main aspects of learning to be considered in the aftermath of a crisis. The first involves learning about the crisis event, exploring its various causes as well as any aggravating or precipitating factors that may have influenced its evolution. The second refers to learning about the crisis management process itself, a debriefing process that allows managers and others involved in handling organizational crises to review the steps taken, identify any mistakes made, and evaluate individual and team performance. Process-related evaluation also examines the barriers to learning that may be implicit in the crisis management procedures themselves.

Despite recommendations by various crisis management authors (see for example Caponigro, 2000; Mitroff & Anagnos, 2001; Pearson & Clair, 1998), neither area has received much attention from scholars or practitioners. One reason for this may be that both forms of learning must overcome a number of significant obstacles and are subject to the same difficulties that afflict crisis research in general, such as limited access to information (Pearson & Clair, 1998). In addition, there are a number of reasons why organizations that do not understand the principles of complexity simply refuse to learn from their own crises or those experienced by others.

Learning by crisis

It is not surprising that many people favor learning from experience, presuming 'hands-on' learning to be somehow more authentic than reflexive processes. However, there are drawbacks to this approach. Benjamin Franklin said, "experience keeps a dear school, but fools will learn in no other." One problem with learning from experience in real-world settings is that feedback cues are not always detected, unambiguous in meaning, and correctly interpreted. Learning may indeed take place, but it may involve the wrong lessons. Two negative learning patterns relevant to organizations and crises are *neurotic* and *superstitious* learning.

A neurotic symptom may be defined as persisting in an action that is no longer appropriate in given circumstances (Watzlawick, 1976). By examining the outcomes of our past choices, we decide which have been successful and thus which behaviors to reinforce (Gavetti & Levinthal, 2000). However, we do not always take changing circumstances into consideration when repeating the behavior, and may persist with actions that are no longer necessary or even counter-productive.

It is also possible to learn compulsive superstitious behavior, which may be particularly insidious for organizations wed to a culture of careful planning and control. Superstitions are generally considered to represent an attempt to exert control and make order in one's environment, and often reflect a deeply rooted belief in the direct causality of one's actions (Watzlawick, 1976; Weick, 2001). Various experiments have found that people will tend to generate superstitious rules to guide their behavior in uncertain situations, even when outcomes are entirely non-contingent (Rudski, *et al.*, 1999; Watzlawick, 1976). Given the high level of ambiguity in most organizational settings, with very loose coupling between outcomes and causal events, such faulty inferences may occur more frequently than is realized (Weick, 2001). The rationalist standard of encoding lessons in generalized procedures and rules (Beck & Kieser, 2003) may further exacerbate this tendency and thus magnify its negative consequences.

Whereas learned neuroses and superstitions are a result of learning the wrong lessons from experience, there may also be barriers in place that prevent people from learning anything of value. One obstacle that can distort experiential lessons is *causal attribution*, also known as *attribution bias*. Causal attribution indicates that decision makers "attribute good outcomes to their own actions and qualities while attributing poor outcomes to external factors such as environmental events and bad luck" (Schwenk, 1995: 476). Causal attribution has persistently emerged in empirical studies examining how people evaluate prior experiences. For instance, executives have been found to remember past strategies and outcomes as being more closely correlated to current positions than objective data demonstrate (Schwenk, 1995).

Various other forms of hindsight bias may also negatively affect the value of retrospective sensemaking and learning. Hindsight bias means that once an outcome is known, it appears to be the sole rational and obvious consequence of what came before. This belief affects how people interpret prior events, and evaluations of behavior are likely to be influenced by outcomes (Weick, 2001). If a rogue cop in an action movie defies his superiors' orders and saves the day, the positive outcome will result in his behavior being judged as courageous and morally correct, and he is likely to be rewarded and celebrated as an icon of courage and independent thinking. If the same behavior leads to the death of innocent victims, it will be judged as reckless and criminal, and the offender is likely to be punished and scorned as evidence of what can happen when individuals fail to follow the superior group wisdom. The behavior is evaluated not on its own merits but based on its outcome, despite the fact that in real-world settings any outcome tends to be the result of a complex web of circumstances rather than a single action or course of action.

The ramifications of biased sensemaking and neurotic learning from crisis situations are clear. In both successful and unsuccessful circumstances, attempts to draw on past behaviors and generalize from them (perhaps even formalizing them into procedures) based on the outcome of one situation may lead to disastrous error in future situations. Erroneous, incomplete or outdated conclusions may find themselves embedded in the crisis plan, the document at the heart of mainstream crisis management that provides a template for action based on existing organizational knowledge to save time in the heat of a crisis.

The perils of planning

Due to the tightly coupled nature of dense interrelationships in complex systems, plans are likely to have unforeseen side effects (Dörner, 1996). The long-term consequences of our plans may be quite unlike what we anticipated. As mentioned earlier, crisis plans have traditionally formed the centerpiece of crisis management as presented by scholars and practitioners, but some researchers have begun to question their part in the crisis response.

The classic analytical decision-making and planning model involves setting goals, deciding courses of action, taking action, reviewing feedback, and making corrective adjustments as needed in an ongoing loop until the goal is reached (Dörner, 1996). Crisis situations, however, pose a dilemma since the primary aim in managing them is not to attain a certain objective, but to abolish or evade undesirable circumstances. This is what is known as a *nega-*

tive goal. Negative goals tend to be vague, based simply on the realization that things cannot remain as they stand, but without setting specific conditions for a desirable outcome. This situation creates a problem up front in designing a strategy (Dörner, 1996).

To further complicate matters, the goals of most crisis situations are also unclear, defined by Dörner (1996) as lacking an unambiguous measure by which one can determine whether or not the goal has been reached. There are also generally multiple goals: resolving a crisis may mean having to satisfy various internal and external stakeholders (who often have conflicting interests), take corrective action, attempt to limit negative media coverage, and so on. Some of these circumstances can only be known once the crisis itself has begun. The variables involved in a crisis situation may be linked in a variety of complex ways that only become apparent as the situation unfolds - or even long after the crisis appears to be over.

Crisis planners are therefore expected to develop detailed procedures to meet complex, multiple, unclear, negative goals in relation to an event that has not yet occurred.

This emphasis on planning is primarily an attempt to reduce ambiguity and assert control. The mechanistic approach of detailed planning deliberately over-simplifies what is an extremely complex situation: by reducing the uncertainty of circumstances to a set of defined rules and steps, the perceived risk is diluted and the world is made to appear more controllable. This is a classic technique for coping with uncertainty (Dörner, 1996; Mitroff, *et al.*, 1996).

A little planning may be a dangerous thing. Coombs (1999) warned that managers may derive a false sense of security from a CMP. Pearson and Clair (1998) agreed, and cautioned that this exaggerated sense of complacency may be reinforced if organizations overcome various problems with minimal preparation. Furthermore, like other organizational rules and procedures, crisis plans offer additional opportunities to encode superstitious or neurotic learned behaviors.

Most researchers recognize that the messiness of organizational crises of legitimacy means they do not lend themselves easily to rote repetition of procedures, and include disclaimers about the need for crisis teams to remain flexible (Coombs, 1999; Pearson & Clair, 1998). Regardless of these warnings, however, institutionalization and the illusion of control may narrow the vision of crisis managers, limiting their flexibility and ability to adapt to rapidly evolving situations. Researchers have identified certain phenomena that may produce distortions of a given course of action when faced with a crisis situation, or when there is negative feedback to the first steps taken in the response process. The two most important such phenomena within the context of organizational crisis management are *threat-rigidity* and *escalating commitment*, both of which fall under the rubric of complexity reduction strategies.

Studies of threat-rigidity responses suggest that meticulous planning may be counter-productive. Barnett and Pratt (2000) described the effects of a threat as causing an organization to adopt a defensive pose, leading it to self-limit its information gathering and processing capacity and narrow decision options as a means of reducing uncertainty. Other researchers have also found evidence to support this position (D'Aveni & Macmillan, 1990; Penrose, 2000). It would seem to logically follow that if an organization has deliberately limited its options *a priori* by specifying a fixed set of procedures, it may fail to absorb information or consider decisions that fall outside this predetermined range of options (Pfeffer & Sutton, 1999).

Psychologists have also documented a phenomenon known as escalating commitment, in which people cling to previously made plans with increasing tenacity even when faced with evident failure (Edwards, 2001; Ross & Staw, 1993). Escalating situations are aggravated by a high perception of behavioral control, in which the decision maker is convinced that he or she has the skills, tools, and will to overcome any potential obstacles to success. Linear causality is assumed, and procedures become entrenched due to this confluence of internal and external pressures to maintain a given course of action despite negative feedback (Ross & Staw, 1993). One might describe escalating commitment as the opposite of learning.

Refusing to look and learn

Many managers decide that crisis events are too unique and infrequent to make close examination and change worthwhile (Elliott, *et al.*, 2000; Roux-Dufort, 2000). This was the same logic followed by the supporters of the Shoreham nuclear power plant on Long Island, who pressed forward in the wake of Three Mile Island, claiming that such accidents were so rare as to be practically unique. Amid various other problems that beset construction and commissioning of the plant, the coup de grace for the project was delivered by the Chernobyl explosion in 1986 which demonstrated that the disaster was not, in fact, an unrepeatable occurrence (Ross & Staw, 1993).

Alongside the perception of crises as too unusual to merit significant attention, Roux-Dufort (2000) identified another main culprit of the failure to learn as the urge toward *normalization,* or a return to conditions as similar as possible to those existing prior to the crisis. This drive reflects an outlook in which the organization is thought to exist in a stable, bounded state, only occasionally interrupted by exceptional crisis events. In other words, a push to 'return to normal' assumes that there exists a 'normal' status quo to which the organization can return - a position distinctly at odds with a complexity view of the constantly evolving organization.

Although a complexity perspective implies that most, if not all, crises will have ambiguous, complex causes that require careful investigation of multiple interlinked dynamics, organizations tend to hurry to identify the proximate, linear cause - very frequently 'human error' - as an attempt to assign blame and take prompt, visible action as a message to stakeholders. This cycle of culpability is especially insidious within business organizations, which tend to adhere to a rationalist philosophy that "presumes that actions based on knowledge and undertaken with skill are supposed to turn out right" (Mirvis, 1996: 20). The natural conclusion of this rationale is that if something goes wrong, it is due to a deficit in knowledge, competency, or both, hence one or more persons are to blame. It is not difficult to understand why many in such a context become socialized to cover up not only their own errors, but those of others.

Elliott, et al. (2000) concurred that oversimplification of complex circumstances is one factor that inhibits learning from crises; they also blamed a general inability to define problems clearly and a pervasive sense of complacency within many organizations which, taken together, may lead to a hasty search for scapegoats (often a result of the aforementioned simplistic review of circumstances). This attitude is clearly a complexity reduction coping technique that refuses to account for the subtleties of the crisis situation.

In Wicks's (2001) analysis of the Westray mine disaster in Nova Scotia, he focused on examining both the endogenous and exogenous factors of institutionalization that facilitated the crisis. In doing so, he made a careful distinction between the unsafe practices that were the direct causes of the disaster, and the contextual factors that led to those unsafe practices. This approach reflects a complexity-based worldview that declines to divorce single events from their broader context, but it is rare among scholars of organizational crises and rarer still within organizations themselves

By searching for proximate causes rather than broad contributing factors organizations hasten their return to 'normalcy' but may overlook numerous issues that play significantly into creating the conditions for crisis. Indeed, Elliott, et al. (2000) suggested that organizations can truly learn from crises only by taking a holistic approach, examining various aspects of the situation with an awareness of hidden interrelationships and the emergent qualities therein. This conclusion is echoed by Veliyath and Sathian (Chapter 12, this volume). Such an approach is obviously compatible with a complexity-based understanding of how organizations, their stakeholders, society, the environment, and other elements interact to form a complete, complex whole.

Scapegoating and superficial behavioral change are not merely barriers to learning from an individual crisis situation, but may also prove counter-productive in the long run. When scapegoats are sought within the organization, members may feel vulnerable and respond by making a greater effort to hide or cover mistakes, drawing the organization into a dangerous spiral.

The problem of learning from crises and understanding is a serious one. Although the dominant paradigm focuses on taking steps to regain legitimacy, from a complex perspective action, knowledge and understanding are closely intertwined. Corrective measures are not taken in a vacuum, but each step has short- and long-term consequences within the framework of complexity.

The difference complexity makes

Managers who accept a complexity-based view of the organization and its evolution are likely to take a radically different approach to managing organizational crises than the one advocated in the mainstream literature. Complexity shifts attention from the individual stages and steps to the role of knowledge, learning and communication throughout the duration of the crisis. Learning ceases to be viewed as a separate (and optional) stage that takes place only after the crisis is over, and is instead conceptualized as a process intimately intertwined with the organization's evolving response to the situation before, during and after the crisis event.

The problem of acquiring and synthesizing knowledge in an organizational context can be approached from a relational perspective. Becker (2001) identified three key problems created by the dispersal of knowledge. The first is the problem of large numbers, due to fragmentation that taxes organizational resources and prevents members from having a clear overview. Dispersed knowledge also creates asymmetries, or unequal distribution of knowledge which leads to uneven development of learning and, in turn, irregular constraints on further development. Finally, dispersal accentuates the problem of uncertainty, signifying that neither the available options nor their consequences may be known in advance, since they constitute emergent properties of the unfolding situation, and decisions must therefore be made without a complete or clear overview of context.

All three of these factors are characteristics typical of real-world situations, and as such correspond to features of complex systems as defined previously. All three are also likely to be aggravated in a crisis situation, and align neatly with Weick's (1995) sensemaking triggers of high information load, complexity, and turbulence. It may be possible to work with these constraints rather than against them by embracing a strategy of complexity absorption as opposed to reduction. The solutions Becker (2001) suggested to ameliorate these difficulties focus not on capturing and storing commodified information, but on facilitating access to knowledge through the enhancement of social networks. He described this strategy as "a shift from direct knowledge - 'know how' or 'know what' - to indirect knowledge: 'know whom'" (p. 1041).

In terms of reducing uncertainty, Becker (2001) recognized that it is necessary to distinguish between two fundamentally different types of uncertainty in devising the appropriate information strategy to adopt. *Stochastic uncertainty*, defined as a situation in which the probabilities for an array of possible outcomes are known, may be effectively reduced by increasing the amount of information available to the decision maker. The other form of uncertainty is known as *structural uncertainty*, often referred to in the literature as 'ambiguity'; in these situations, there is no certainty regarding the probabilities of various potential outcomes. Contrary to stochastic uncertainty, ambiguity is generally believed to be exacerbated by an increase in information (Becker, 2001; Weick, 1995). The most appropriate strategy for reducing this form of uncertainty is therefore through a process of individual and collective discussion and interpretation, or sensemaking. In other words, crisis managers should concentrate less on amassing large quantities of information and attempting to develop specific plans, and more on creating knowledge and relational networks in and around the organization, and developing effective communication and sensemaking skills.

Conclusion

The mainstream approach to crisis management is contrary to the principles of complexity. It prescribes a rapid return to a perceived state of stability, attempts to reduce or control ambiguity and uncertainty, and sees the future as relatively predictable. This presumption of linear effects also supports a framework based on the assumption that crisis managers can exercise control by taking local-ized action. If one accepts the perspective of complexity, in which the norm is not stability, but the ongoing emergence of recognizable (but unforeseeable) conditions, such an approach is clearly impractical.

Furthermore, the current paradigm is set up in such a way as to inhibit learning. When it comes to exploring the causes of a crisis, the linear rationale predominant in management in general - and crisis management in particular - may pose a serious hindrance to full comprehension of the occurrence. It fails to question the norms within an organization that may lead to crises or interfere with their management. The push for 'normalization' is a barrier to learning, as it encourages managers to seek the most proximate cause rather than reflexively examine complex causal interrelationships, including institu-tionalized dysfunctions. Its reliance on prepackaged rules and procedures may lead organizational members to ignore cues outside the prescribed framework instead of developing awareness and expertise. The entire crisis management process represents a potentially self-perpetuating negative cycle that can lead to the institutionalization of solutions that appear to work without understanding their long-term effects, and attempts to regain superficial legitimacy through means such as scapegoating. Once such a solution has been identified and the relevant corrective measures taken, the crisis is filed away as 'resolved' and the organization continues with 'business as usual', having publicly restored its semblance of legitimacy.

Finally, the dominant model's focus on superficial legitimacy may, through the cycle described above, paradoxically damage that legitimacy and thus harm the organization in the long term. Such an approach is clearly self-limiting from the standpoint of both complexity and communication, and fails to address potential problems that may be inherent in the organization's own procedures or its general operational context. These problems thus persist and may lead to subsequent, even recurring, crises that eventually tarnish the very legitimacy the organization has been striving to protect.

Reframing the crisis management process according to the principles of complexity, and forming a new understanding of how and what organiza-tions learn from crisis experiences, may help overcome some of the barriers to learning posed by the current dominant methodology. These areas remain as yet unexplored and thus are rich with opportunities for future study. Poten-tial areas of research and inquiry in this regard, to name just a few, include the role of communities of practice in forging relational and information-sharing bonds within, across and between organizations and their internal divisions; non-proceduralized problem solving and training methodologies such as those suggested by research on naturalistic decision making; the development of intuition and improvisation skills for use in crisis management (and here the *improvised-orchestration model* discussed by Kawai (Chapter 18, this volume) offers promising insights); and the use of scenario planning and similar techniques to overcome barriers to perception and imagination when faced with unforeseen circumstances within a complex organizational setting. As Dörner (1996) noted, "If we expect the unexpected, we are better equipped to cope with it than if we lay extensive plans and believe that we have eliminated the unexpected" (p. 165).

References

Ashmos, D. P., Duchon, D. and McDaniel, R. R., Jr. (2000). "Organizational Responses to Complexity: The Effect on Organizational Performance," *Journal of Organizational Change Management*, 13(6): 577-594.

Barnett, C. and Pratt, M. G. (2000). "From Threat-Rigidity to Flexibility: Toward a Learning Model of Autogenic Crisis in Organizations," *Journal of Organizational Change Management*, 13(1): 74-88.

Beck, N. and Kieser, A. (2003). "The Complexity of Rule Systems, Experience and Organizational Learning," *Organization Studies*, 24(5): 793-814.

Becker, M. C. (2001). "Managing Dispersed Knowledge: Organizational Problems, Managerial Strategies, and Their Effectiveness," *Journal of Management Studies*, 38(7): 1037-1051.

Blackler, F. and McDonald, S. (2000). Power, Mastery and Organizational Learning," *Journal of Management Studies*, 37(6): 833-851.

Caponigro, J. R. (2000). *The Crisis Counselor: A Step-By-Step Guide to Managing a Business Crisis*, Lincolnwood, IL: Contemporary Books.

Cilliers, P. (1998). *Complexity and Postmodernism*, London: Routledge.

Coombs, W. T. (1999). *Ongoing Crisis Communication: Planning, Managing and Responding*, Thousand Oaks, California: Sage Publications.

Cope, J. and Watts, G. (2000). "Learning By Doing: An Exploration of Experience, Critical Incidents and Reflection in Entrepreneurial Learning," *Journal of Knowledge Management*, 6(3): 104-124.

Daft, R. L. and Weick, K. E. (2001). "Toward a Model of Organizations as Interpretation Systems," in K. E. Weick (ed.), *Making Sense of the Organization*, Oxford: Blackwell Publishers Ltd, pp. 241-257.

D'Aveni, R. A. and Macmillan, I. C. (1990). "Crisis and the Content of Managerial Communications: A Study of the Focus of Attention of Top Managers in Surviving and Failing Firms," *Administrative Science Quarterly*, 35: 634-657.

Dörner, D. (1996). *The Logic of Failure: Recognizing and Avoiding Error in Complex Situations*, Reading, MA: Perseus Books.

Edwards, J. C. (2001). "Self-Fulfilling Prophecy and Escalating Commitment," *Journal of Applied Behavioral Science*, 37(3): 343-360.

Elliot, D., Smith, D. and McGuinnes, M. (2001). "Exploring the Failure to Learn: Crises and the Barriers to Learning," *Review of Business*, 21(3): 17.

Farquhar, H. H. (1919). "Positive Contributions of Scientific Management," *The Quar-*

terly Journal of Economics, 33(3): 466-503.

Fearn-Banks, K. (1996). *Crisis Communications: A Casebook Approach*, Mahwah, NJ: Lawrence Erlbaum Associates, Inc.

Gavetti, G. and Levinthal, D. (2000). "Looking Forward and Looking Backward: Cognitive and Experiential Search," *Administrative Science Quarterly*, 45(March): 113-137.

Massey, J. E. (2001). "Managing Organizational Legitimacy: Communication Strategies for Organizations in Crisis," *Journal of Business Communication*, 38(2): 153-183.

McKelvey, B. (1999). "Complexity Theory in Organization Science: Seizing the Promise or Becoming a Fad?" *Emergence*, 1(1): 5-32.

Mirvis, P. H. (1996). "Historical Foundations of Organizational Learning," *Journal of Organizational Change Management*, 9(1): 13-31.

Mitroff, I. I. and Anagnos, G. (2001). *Managing Crises Before They Happen*, New York: AMACOM.

Mitroff, I. I., Harrington, L. K. and Gai, E. (1996). "Thinking About the Unthinkable," *Across the Board*, 33(8): 44-48.

Nidumolu, S. R., Subramani, M. and Aldrich, A. (2001). "Situated Learning and the Situated Knowledge Web: Exploring the Ground Beneath Knowledge Management," *Journal of Management Information Systems*, 18(1): 115-150.

Oswick, C., Anthony, P., Keenoy, T. and Mangham, I. L. (2000). "A Dialogic Analysis of Organizational Learning," *Journal of Management Studies*, 37(6): 887-901.

Pearson, C. M. and Clair, J. A. (1998). "Reframing Crisis Management," *Academy of Management Review*, 23(1): 59-76.

Penrose, J. M. (2000). "The Role of Perception in Crisis Planning," *Public Relations Review*, 26(2): 155.

Pfeffer, J. and Sutton, R. (1999). *The Knowing-Doing Gap*, Boston, MA: Harvard Business School Press.

Richardson, K. A. and Lissack, M. R. (2001). "On the Status of Natural Boundaries, Both Natural and Organizational: A Complex Systems Perspective," *Emergence*, 3(4): 32-49.

Ross, J. and Staw, B. M. (1993). "Organizational Escalation and Exit: Lessons from the Shoreham Nuclear Power Plant," *Academy of Management Journal*, 36(4): 701.

Roux-Dufort, C. (2000). "Why Organizations Don't Learn from Crises: The Perverse Power of Normalization," *Review of Business*, 21(3): 25.

Rudski, J. M., Lischner, M. I. and Albert, L. M. (1999). "Superstitious Rule Generation is Affected By Probability and Type of Outcome," *The Psychological Record*, 49(2): 245-260.

Schwenk, C. R. (1995). "Strategic Decision Making," *Journal of Management*, 21(3): 471.

Stacey, R. D. (1996). *Complexity and Creativity in Organizations*, San Francisco: Berrett Koehler.

Stacey, R. D. (2001). *Complex Responsive Processes in Organizations: Learning and Knowledge Creation*, London: Routledge.

Stacey, R. D., Griffin, D. and Shaw, P. (2000). *Complexity and Management*, London: Routledge.

van Uden, J., Richardson, K. A. and Cilliers, P. (2001). "Postmodernism Revisited? Complexity Science and the Study of Organisations," *Tamara: Journal of Critical Postmodern Organization Science*, 1(3): 53-67.

Watzlawick, P. (1976). *How Real is Real?* New York: Random House.

Weick, K. E. (1995). *Sensemaking in Organizations*, Thousand Oaks, CA: Sage Publications.

Weick, K. E. (2001). *Making Sense of the Organization*, Oxford, UK: Blackwell Publishers Ltd.

Wicks, D. (2001). "Institutionalized Mindsets of Invulnerability: Differentiated Institutional Fields and the Antecedents of Organizational Crisis," *Organization Studies*, 22(4): 659-692.

SECTION THREE

APPLICATION

Section introduction
Using complexity thinking

In this section introduction I will briefly outline three approaches for how complexity thinking might support organizational management. These different approaches are derived from three different schools of thinking within the complexity movement. Like the divisions in this particular volume (refer to my introductory remarks on page v) these three schools are not isolated from each other, but themselves form a complex system of interrelationships. Despite their interdependence I still find it useful to divide the complexity movement into these divisions. The three schools / themes / divisions that I identify and discuss are: the neo-reductionists, the 'metaphorticians', and the critical pluralists.

The neo-reductionist school

The first theme is strongly associated with the quest for a theory of everything (TOE) in physics, i.e., an acontextual explanation for the existence of everything. This sub-community seeks to uncover the general principles of complex systems, likened to the fundamental field equations of physics[1]. The search for such over-arching laws and principles was / is one of the central aims of the general systems movement. Any such Theory of Complexity, however, will be of limited value. In Richardson (2005) I suggest that even if such a theory existed it would not provide an explanation of every 'thing' in terms that we would find useful. If indeed such fundamental principles do exist they will likely be so abstract as to render them practically useless in the everyday world of human experience - a decision-maker would need several PhDs in pure mathematics just to make the simplest of decisions.

This particular complexity community makes considerable use of computer simulation in the form of bottom-up agent based modeling (see for example, Robertson, this volume). The complexity perspective presented in Chapter 2 suggests that the 'laws' such nonlinear studies yield provide a basis for a modeling paradigm that is considerably broader than just bottom-up simulation, or any formal mathematical / computer-based approach for that matter.

The neo-reductionist school of complexity science is based on a seductive syllogism (Horgan, 1995):

- *Premise 1*: There are simple sets of mathematical rules that when followed by a computer give rise to extremely complicated patterns.

Managing Organizational Complexity: Philosophy, Theory, and Application
A Volume in: Managing the Complex, pages 391-396.
Copyright © 2005 by Information Age Publishing, Inc.
All rights of reproduction in any form reserved.
ISBN: 1-59311-319-6 (cloth), 1-59311-318-8 (paper)

- *Premise 2*: The world also contains many extremely complicated patterns.
- *Conclusion*: Simple rules underlie many extremely complicated phenomena in the world, and with the help of powerful computers, scientists can root those rules out.

Though this syllogism was definitively refuted in a paper by Oreskes, *et al.* (1994), in which the authors warned that "verification and validation of numerical models of natural systems is impossible," this position still dominates the neo-reductionist school of complexity. The recursive application of simple rules, is certainly not the only source of complex behavior, and should not be seen as the only legitimate way to study complexity in human organizations (or any where else for that matter).

Despite all the iconoclastic rhetoric about reshaping our worldview, taking us out of the age of mechanistic (linear) science into a brave new (complex) world, many complexity theorists of this variety have actually inherited many of the assumptions of their more traditional scientific predecessors by simply changing the focus from one sort of model to another. There is no denying the power and interest surrounding the new models (e.g., agent-based simulation, genetic algorithms) proposed by the neo-reductionists, but it is still a focus on the model itself. Rather than using the linear models associated with classical reductionism, a different sort of model - nonlinear models - have become the focus. Supposedly, 'bad' models have been replaced with 'good' models. The language of neo-reductionism is mathematics, which is the language of traditional reductionist science - although it should be pointed out that neo-reductionist mathematics is rather more sophisticated than traditional reductionist mathematics.

The metaphorical school

Within the organizational science community, complexity has not only been seen as a route to a possible theory of organization, but also as a powerful metaphorical tool (see, for example, Lissack, 1997, 1999; Richardson, *et al.*, Chapter 26, this volume). According to this school, the complexity perspective, with its associated language, provides a powerful lens through which to 'see' organizations. Concepts such as *connectivity, edge-of-chaos, far-from-equilibrium, dissipative structures, emergence, epi-static coupling, co-evolving landscapes*, etc., facilitate organizational academics and practitioners in 'seeing' the complexity inherent in socio-technical organizations. The underlying belief is that the social world is intrinsically different from the natural world. As such, the theories of complexity, which have been developed primarily through the examination of natural systems, are not directly applicable to social systems (at least not to the practical administration of such systems), though its language may trigger some relevant insights to the behavior of the social world which would facilitate some limited degree of control over the social world.

Using such a 'soft' approach to complexity to legitimate this metaphorical approach, other theories have been imported via the 'mechanism' metaphor into organization studies; a popular example being quantum mechanics (see McKelvey, 2001 for example). While new lenses through which to view organizations can be very useful (see Morgan, 1986 for an excellent example of this) the complexity lens, and the 'anything goes' attitude that often accompanies this perspective, has been abused somewhat. My concern is not with the use of metaphor *per se*, as I certainly accept that the role of metaphor in understanding is ubiquitous and essential. Indeed, in Richardson (2005) it is argued that in an absolute sense all understanding can be no more or less metaphorical in nature. My concern is with its use in the absence of criticism - metaphors are being imported left, right and center with very little attention being paid as to the legitimacy of such importation. This may be regarded as a playful activity in academic circles, but if such playfulness is to be usefully applied in serious business then some rather more concrete grounding is necessary. As van Ghyczy (2003) warns, "Instead of being seduced by the similarities between business and another field, you need to look for places where the metaphor breaks down... [M]etaphors are often improperly used" (p. 87-88).

I refer to this school of complexity, which often uncritically imports ideas and perspectives via the mechanism of metaphor from a diverse range of disciplines, as the *metaphorical school*, and its adherents, *metaphorticians*. It is the school that perhaps represents the greatest source of creativity of the three schools classified here. But as we all know, creativity on its own is not sufficient for the design and implementation of successful managerial interventions.

The critical pluralist school

Neo-reductionism with its modernistic tendencies can be seen as one extreme of the complexity spectrum, whereas *metaphorism* with its atheoretical acritical relativistic tendencies can be seen as the opposing extreme. In my view the complexity perspective (when employed to underpin a philosophical outlook) both supports and undermines these two extremes. What is needed is a middle path.

The two previous schools of complexity promise either a neat package of coherent knowledge that can apparently be easily transferred into any context or an incoherent mish mash of unrelated ideas and philosophies - both of which have an important role to play in understanding and manipulating complex systems. In my opinion, not only do these extremes represent overly simplistic interpretations of what might be, they also contradict some of the basic observations already made within the neo-reductionist mold, i.e., there are seeds within the neo-reductionist view of complexity that if allowed to grow lead naturally to a broader view that encapsulates both the extremes already discussed as well as everything in between and beyond.

One of the first consequences that arise from the complexity assumption is that as we ourselves are less complex than the Universe (The Complex System), as well as many of the systems we'd like to control / affect, there is no way for us to possibly experience 'reality' in any complete sense (Cilliers, 1998: 4; see also my introductory comments for Section 2 regarding incompressibility). We are forced to view 'reality' through categorical frameworks that allow us to 'fudge' our way through life. The critical pluralist school of complexity focuses more on what we cannot explain, rather than what can be explained - it is a concern with limits. As such, it leads to a particular *attitude* towards models, rather than the privileging of one sort of model over all others. And, rather than using complexity to justify an 'anything goes' relativism, it highlights the importance of critical reflection in grounding our models / representations / perspectives in an evolving reality. The keywords of this school are *open-mindedness* and *humility*. Any perspective whatsoever has the potential to shed light on complexity (even if it turns out to be wrong, otherwise how would one know that it was wrong?), but at the same time, not every perspective is equally valid. Complexity 'thinking' is the art of maintaining the tension between pretending we know something and knowing we know nothing for sure.

The three schools and management

Now that we have identified and discussed the three schools of complexity, how does each one contribute to the management of human organizations? The first one, neo-reductionism, is the easiest as it simply adds a new collection of analytical tools to the decision-makers tool set. These tools will probably impact the fields of management science and operations research the most, providing some very powerful tools to facilitate the decision-making process surrounding larger strategic questions. Indeed such models are ideal for exploring that class of question where individual behaviour matters only as a contribution to group behaviour. They will probably not contribute to rather more mundane day-to-day management activities - it is unlikely that the development of an agent-based model will help much in deciding if to promote someone or not, or whether to change the supplier for the hallway coffee machine. There are certain types of problems that can benefit from nonlinear analytical models and some problems that will not. This school of complexity seems to be the most visible at present, and is probably to easiest of the three to apply. Given the immense computational resources needed to utilize the neo-reductionist's tools, there is also a certain level of glamour and excitement associated with this sort of complexity application; this seems to have captured the imagination of the management world, even though the problems it can useful be brought to bear on are rather limited.

The metaphorical school of complexity can certainly play a part in the day-today activities of management. Given that our personal worldviews determine to a large extent what we 'see' and how we 'manage' what we 'see', replacing / enhancing that worldview with a perspective that is rather more sensitive to the complexities that are inherent in daily experience, can have a profound affect. Chapter 25 begins with an exploration that considers project management through the lens of complexity-inspired metaphors. It is difficult to fully appreciate the influence the widespread usage of complexity-inspired metaphors will have, but I would like to think that many of the shortcomings of the dominant command and control metaphor (which has become rather more than a metaphor) will be mitigated. Of course, replacing one worldview with another creates as many new problems as it solves. It'll be interesting to see what these new problems will be. (Although, seeing management as a problem solving process is itself a feature of the command and control attitude).

The metaphorical school does not only legitimate the use of complexity-inspired metaphors though; it is often used to justify a fully blown pluralism in which anything goes. We have to be careful that our wish to explore all possibilities does not lead to chaos (and I don't mean this in the mathematical sense). Quoting van Ghyczy (2003) again, "It's tempting to draw business lessons from other disciplines - warfare, biology, music. But most managers do it badly" (p.87).

The critical pluralist school of complexity also has implications for all aspects of management, although it is possibly one of the hardest to 'teach'. It encourages not only management, but all participant members of an organization, to approach everything they do in a critical way and to maintain some ontological distance from their ideas, i.e., to not take our ideas of organization too seriously - use our ideas to guide, or initiate, our thinking about organizations, not to determine our thinking. Complexity 'thinking' is a particular attitude towards our ideas of the world and the world itself, not a particular tool / method, or even a particular language.

The remaining papers in this volume look at the application of complexity in human organizations. Some are particular case studies that illustrate the direct application of complexity ideas - these cases are not post-hoc analyses of past cases in terms of complexity, but cases in which complexity ideas were explicitly employed from the very outset. Some deal with particular organizational activities, such as strategy making and project management, and offer frameworks for the direct application of complexity ideas in those activities. Together they offer only but a taste of how complexity theory / science / thinking might be realized in human organizations. I hope they will sufficiently illustrate that managing the complex has evolved from the 'blue sky' activity it was ten years ago, to an emerging set of practical tools, processes, and attitudes that have the ability to not only make organizations more sustainable (not necessarily profitable), but also to make organizational life more bearable!

References

Cilliers, P. (1998). *Complexity and Postmodernism: Understanding Complex Systems*, Routledge.

Ghyczy, T. von (2003). "The Fruitful Flaws of Strategy Metaphors," *Harvard Business Review*, September: 86-94.

Horgan, J. (1995). "From Complexity to Perplexity," *Science*, 272: 74-79.

Lissack, M. R. (1997). "Mind your Metaphors: Lessons from Complexity Science," *Long Range Planning*, April: 294-298.

Lissack, M. R. (1999). "Complexity: The Science, Its Vocabulary, and Its Relation to Organizations," *Emergence*, 1(1): 110-126.

McKelvey, W. (2001). "What Is Complexity Science? It Is Really Order-Creation Science," *Emergence*, 3(1): 137-157.

Morgan, G. (1986). *Images of Organization*, California, USA: Sage Publications.

Oreskes, N., Shrader-Frechette, K. and Belitz, K. (1994). "Verification, Validation, and Confirmation of Numerical Models in the Earth Sciences," *Science*, 263: 641-646.

Richardson, K. A. (2003). "On the Limits of Bottom-Up Computer Simulation: Towards a Nonlinear Modeling Culture," *Proceedings of the 36th Hawaiian International Conference on System Sciences*, Jan 7-10, 2003, IEEE: California.

Richardson, K. A. (2005). "The Hegemony of the Physical Sciences: An Exploration in Complexity Thinking," *Futures*, accepted for publication.

Notes

1. It is likely that these two research thrusts, if successful, will eventually converge if it is assumed assume that some kind of complex systems representation of the Universe as a whole is valid.

2. They may actually tell us more about the foundations and logical structure of mathematics than the 'real' world.

CHAPTER 23

THE IMPLICATIONS OF COMPLEXITY FOR BUSINESS PROCESS AND STRATEGY

Peter M. Allen, Jamie Boulton, Mark Strathern and James Baldwin

In this chapter we first demonstrate that complexity is really just reality without the simplifying assumptions that we make in order to understand it. We show that any clear understanding of a situation is probably quite misleading. It is just a snapshot description in terms of the main interactions between a reduced number of typical elements. This is important because it means that any business operation, or product, is conceived of in the simple, pure terms of the simple, mechanical description. It is only following implementation that we must be ready to deal with the inevitable contingencies and adaptations that will be required for our 'operation' to survive in the real, evolving world in which it has been launched. This is contrary to natural evolution of ecological systems, in which natural diversity occurs among individuals, with no particular 'purpose' in view, and what survives, survives, and what doesn't, doesn't. On the contrary, the human world of 'design' and of 'intent' leads us to launch entities and organizations that must 'learn' about the complex, changing world into which they have been introduced. This is illustrated using the example of the evolution of internal practices, routines and skills within manufacturing firms, showing where strategic decisions were made, and how agility and lean features are included structurally during the evolutionary process. The chapter ends by showing that complexity leads to the idea that the evolution and change of organizations and structures is about the successive instabilities that lead from one 'structural attractor' to another.

Managing Organizational Complexity: Philosophy, Theory, and Application
A Volume in: Managing the Complex, pages 397–418.
Copyright © 2005 by Information Age Publishing, Inc.
All rights of reproduction in any form reserved.
ISBN: 1-59311-319-6 (cloth), 1-59311-318-8 (paper)

Introduction: What is complexity?

Complexity is about the behavior of interacting entities, and the evolution of collective structure and behaviors over time. It arose as soon as science turned its attention to *open* systems as opposed to *closed* ones, and when the development of computers allowed us to study the behavior of nonlinear systems instead of simple, linear ones. Since the "invisible hand" of Adam Smith, the idea of self-organization has been present in economic thought, but unfortunately, economics evolved in a very particular way, one that attempted to transfer ideas from equilibrium physics as the basis for understanding. This led to classical and neo-classical economics that was strong on very general and rigorous theorems for completely artificial systems and weak on dealing with reality in practice. Today, with the development of evolutionary complex systems and the arrival of computers able to 'run' systems instead of us having to solve them analytically, interest is burgeoning in complex systems simulations and modelling. And this major advance can help us improve our quality of life and the functioning of our organizations and social institutions, and help to mitigate against anticipated problems such as climate change or the pensions crisis.

We need to understand how socio-economic systems 'work' and to be able to explore the probable consequences of different possible policies or interventions. And this means that we need to 'understand' how the underlying causality of a current social situation is operating, and how that compares with what the mechanical system predicts. But the difficulty with this approach is that it fails to recognize the essentially fluid nature of human behavior, and the ability of actors to modify their previous habits in response to the new opportunities or constraints of the situation.

Let us consider the initial question - what is a complex system? It can best be answered by turning the question around. We can *deconstruct* complexity by considering first what is *not* a complex system (Allen, 1999, 2001a, 2001b). The simple answer is that a *mechanical* system is not a *complex* system, and therefore if we can identify precisely the simplifying assumptions that allow us to write down a mechanical representation of a real system - an organization, an ecosystem, an economic market etc. - then we will have the defining aspects of a complex system. This will allow us to see what the key attributes of the properties of complex systems are, the factors on which they rely, and how in practical terms to make an organization evolve and change over time, adapting to and creating new opportunities and threats.

Let us consider carefully the successive assumptions that would be involved in building a mechanical representation of an ecosystem, an economic market, or an organization, and what the meaning of these simplifications is. The assumptions are:

1. That we can put a boundary around some 'system of concern,' and try to understand what it will do as a result of what is inside, and in the context

of what is outside

2. That we know how to classify the different types of interacting entities within the boundary, and therefore that we have an adequate 'dictionary' of possible terms.

3. That we can consider the actual entities present currently, and through their dynamic interaction understand what may happen

4. That we can consider the interactions in terms of their average values, smoothing what would otherwise be marked by irregularities due to their discrete and individual nature.

In making these successive assumptions we pass through successively more 'constrained' representations of reality. Initially, when no assumptions are made, we are in full (*skeptical*, as opposed to *affirmative*) *postmodernism*, where there is only a 'stream of consciousness' available, and no transferable knowledge is present. All individual situations are unique, and no lessons can be learned because every day is a new day and the internal workings of any of the participating elements are a continuing mystery. Unfortunately, this is what reality is like!

If we assume that we can classify the elements within a system then we can map out its evolutionary history. In some ways there is a degree of 'tautology' about this, because we have to assume that we know the key differences

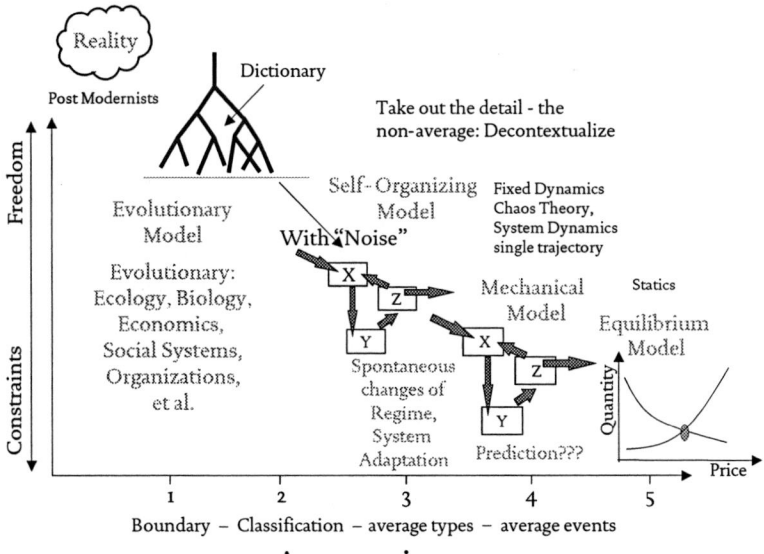

Assumptions

Figure 1
The overall conceptual scheme of increasingly simplified representation of a situation, as increasingly strong and limiting assumptions are made.

between elements so that it enables us to 'make-sense' of its evolution - in terms of the constituents that we have ourselves defined. This is related to the idea that sensemaking is an experimental process in which we are searching for self-consistency between the classification rules, and the sense that appears to result from their application. Hopefully, then, one obtains an *evolutionary tree* of some kind that captures the occurrence of innovations over time, leading to the current situation. The most obvious results of such a tree is that over time some things have disappeared, but more importantly various innovations have occurred - new entities and elements, providing new capabilities, attributes and properties for the system as a whole. The system has evolved - that is, it has changed both qualitatively and quantitatively; over time it has developed, transformed and pushed into new dimensions.

The next assumption shown in Figure 1, the *self-organization* model, takes us from the historical perspective of an evolutionary tree to that of the behavior of the current system. By considering the interactions of the current types, we freeze their identities, but consider the future as the result of their interaction. The crucial assumption is that there is no *micro-diversity* within the interacting types that have been defined. Without micro-diversity, there is no differential dynamics over time, leading to the adaptive and learning behavior of the inter-acting elements. However, there is still no constraint placed on the occurrence of the interactions between individual elements. This means that micro-events that underlie the dynamics such as birth, death, production, sales, etc. happen according to some probability function, with periods of high and low activity, of good and bad luck. The probabilistic dynamics of this approximation provide a representation that corresponds to that of self-organizing systems. The interactive terms may define a set of dynamical equations that have several possible long-term outcomes. These latter are called *attractors* of the dynamics, and if there were no probabilistic fluctuations present the system would simply move to the attractor of the particular basin that it is in. There will in general be more that one basin and these are separated by so-called *separatrices* as shown in Figure 2. These separatrices accord, one could say with the notion of the *edge of chaos* (Kauffman, 1995; Langton, 1991). With the presence of 'luck' and of high and low rates of activity the system can spontaneously jump between *attractor basins*, thus moving from one attracting configuration to another, and giving the impression of self-organization, although of course in practice the move to a new attractor is catalyzed by some interference with the system, be it noise, luck or more proactive intervention and so self-organization may be somewhat of a misnomer.

The final assumptions that takes us from a self-organizing system to a me-chanical one, is that of 'smooth' interactions. Not only do we assume that our system can be represented by the interaction of average elements, but now we assume that the micro-events that constitute the interactions occur at their average rate. Our representation is now average types interacting in an average way. Not surprisingly, we find a mechanistic outcome in which the future of the system is completely deterministic, and hence allows our model to provide

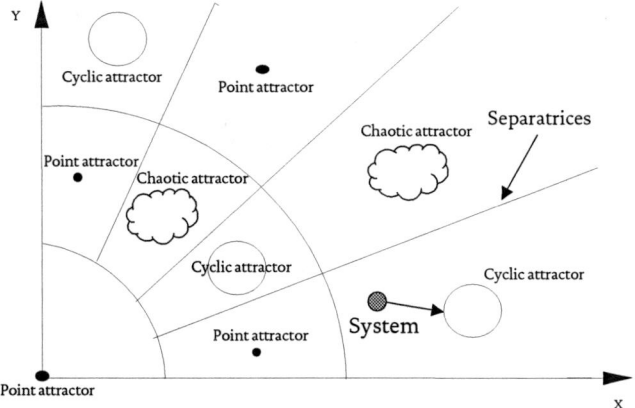

Figure 2
For a system of two variables x and y, we may have several different
possible final states

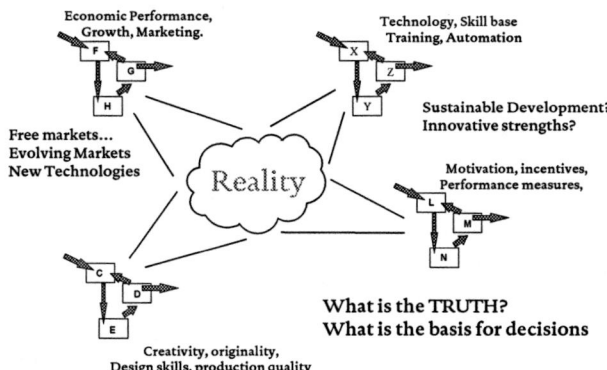

Figure 3
Different people see the same system in different ways. Each can however be
rational and self-consistent, whilst implying different actions or policies.

predictions. Of course, these predictions are indeed precise, but only for the simplified representation we have used. In real life, adaptive behavior, learning and even creativity can occur and so the real system will take a different pathway into the future than its simplified, mechanical representation. This effectively 'deconstructs' complexity. It corresponds to reality, while mechanical representations of reality are merely simplified, current snapshots of that reality, created by us to provide an illusion of understanding and control.

In reality, complex systems thinking offers us a new, integrative paradigm, in which we retain the fact of multiple subjectivities, and of differing perceptions and views, and indeed see this as part of the complexity, and a source of creative interaction and of innovation and change. The underlying paradox is that knowledge of any particular discipline will necessarily imply 'a lack of knowledge' of other aspects. But all the different disciplines and domains of 'knowledge' will interact through reality - and so actions based on any particular domain of knowledge, although seemingly rational and consistent, will necessarily be inadequate.

Management, or policy exploration, however, requires an integrated view. These new complexity ideas encompass evolutionary processes in general, and apply to the social, cultural, economic, technological, psychological and philosophical aspects of our realities. Often, we restrict our studies to only the 'economic' aspects of a situation, with accompanying numbers, but we should not forget that we may be looking at very 'lagged' indicators of other phenomena involving people, emotions, relationships, and intuitions, to mention but a few. We may need to be careful in thinking that our views will be useful if they are based on observations and theories that refer only to a small sub-space of reality - the economic zone. The underlying causes and explanations may involve other factors entirely, and the economic "effects" of these may be only delayed, ripples or possibly tidal waves. What matters over time is the expansion of any system into new dimensions and conceptual spaces, as a result of successive instabilities involving dimensions additional to those the current 'system' appears to occupy. These ideas form the basis of so-called evolutionary economics.

This idea of evolution as a question of 'invadeability', with respect to what was not yet in the system, was the subject of a very early paper by Allen (1976). Essentially then, systems are seen as temporary, emergent structures that result from the self-reinforcing, nonlinear interactions that result from successive 'invasions' of new characteristics or entities. History is written not only by some process of 'rational improvement' in its internal structure but more fundamentally by its dialogue with elements that are not yet in the system - successive experimental linkages that either are rejected by the system, or which 'take off' and modify the system irreversibly (see Figure 4).

Rational improvement of internal structure, the traditional domain of 'systems thinking', supposes that the system has a purpose, and known measures of 'performance' which can indicate the direction of improvements. But, this more fundamental structural evolution of complex systems that results from successive invasions of the system by new elements and entities, is characterized by emergent properties and effects, that lead to new attributes, purposes and performance measures. In the next sections therefore, we attempt to show that this structural evolution is not in fact 'random' in its outcome, as successful invasions of a system are always characterized by the revelation of positive feedback and synergy, creating particular new, internally coherent, structures from a growing, explosively rich set of diverse possibilities.

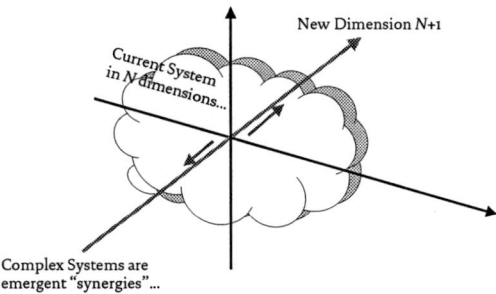

Figure 4
The evolution of complex systems, at different possible levels within
structures, is a 'dialogue' with the aspects and factors that are not playing an
active part within it, at present.

The complexity matrix

What are the implications of this new understanding of complexity for management? Indeed, is there any role for management in a complex world? After all, if the world is truly 'post-modern', and each of us is in a unique, novel and incomparable situation, then maybe there is no advice or method that can be laid down?

Our position however, is not so extreme. We believe that are lessons to be learned and a method that can be followed, questions that can be helpfully asked, which increase the chance of an adaptive, evolutionary management process. All systems that emerge, persist and wish to grow must deal with the fact that by their present actions they must attract resources, and they must also change their actions to fit into the future.

In this connection we can re-write our deconstruction of complexity on a two by two matrix that looks at the short and the long term, and at the closed and open nature of the dimensions considered. The matrix is shown in Figure 5.

Lower left quadrant:

If we consider the problem of the short term and of the business processes that are present, and which are designed to turn input materials and labour into output products and services, and in so doing to provide the resources to pay for the whole organization. This is a structurally fixed system that functions on basis of certain fixed assumptions about the environment. So, it assumes, for example, that the input resources are available as required at a given cost, and that customers will buy the production at a given price. It assumes that employees will have the appropriate skills and will work at the wage levels provided, and it assumes that the machines, the power supply, the waste disposal, water supply etc. all function without problems. If all these elements could be guaranteed constant and uninterrupted, then the process could be 'tuned' to peak efficiency, and minimum cost.

Unfortunately, this guarantee cannot be given, and in addition, the resources, technologies, customers and competitors will all be subject to change over time. In the short term, we will have the response of the overall manager to the fact that the business is open to the environment.

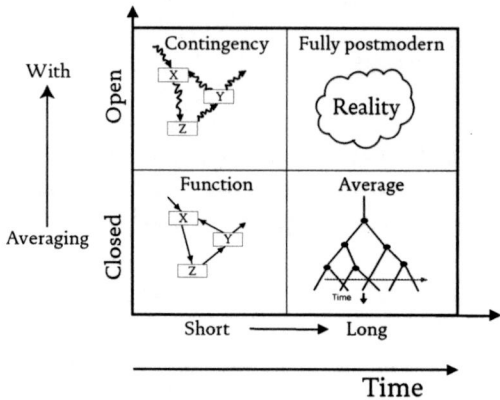

Figure 5
The Situation Matrix expresses our understanding of the system is
in each quadrant.

Upper left quadrant

In reality, in the short term, there are still a series of factors that come from outside the closed set of routines and processes defining the business and that can affect the smooth running of the business process. So, the upper left quadrant shows us that the prudent manager needs to allow for 'contingency' and for dealing with breakages, wear and tear, accidents and possible problems with resources, or with the customers for the activities of the system. Clearly, fires arise because of such things as careless disposal of smoking materials, or some electrical fault. Both of these events are not part of the business processes, but come into the system from dimensions that are 'outside' the processes. They are however, foreseeable. The development of a fire alarm system, of a machine monitoring service, the use of security companies and of insurance policies would cover quite a lot of the calculable risks that would be foreseeable in the running of a typical business. Providing the business was typical then these would be relatively easy to establish and plan on the basis of the statistical experience of other companies. Obviously, however, if there were some special circumstances like a terrorist threat associated with the particular characteristics of the owner, or the location of the business, then contingency plans and insurance could only be worked out in a specific project designed to 'model' and simulate possible events, and to estimate their probabilities.

An important point however, is that, whatever the routines that constitute the normal business processes, they will actually follow a trajectory in time that will take the business to its functional dynamic attractor. With the additional presence of the fluctuations and noise associated with this contingency quadrant, the system may well re-configure itself and flip between different regimes of operation, representing other possible attractors, as in Figure 6.

Lower right quadrant

In the lower right quadrant, we have the 'sense-makers' and research department thinking about the history of the business, and of the sector in which it has evolved. A picture of the past can be drawn, in which key innovations can perhaps be identified and the 'future direction' of the products and of the business organization can also be reflected upon. This R&D department, will be attempting to improve the products and services delivered by the company, both by designing better products, and by designing better business processes and organizational structures. The development process undertaken in the R&D department will both be subject to agreement from the management concerning the 'fit' of a new product or process with the aims and goals of the organization, and also will be subject to the experiences encountered when the new products, business processes or organizational forms are tried out in reality in the left hand quadrants.

This lower right quadrant is really the place where an initially open set of possibilities is turned into concrete innovations and developments, and these passed on to become a short-term reality. Clearly, one could also reflect on new designs and processes that decreased the 'contingency' requirements by being inherently less vulnerable to particular dangers. In fact the system shown in the lower left quadrant corresponds to the end of the evolutionary tree shown here. This quadrant is therefore about the past, the present and the next step.

Upper right quadrant

This is the quadrant in which Management must encounter new aspects of reality. It may be new opportunities posed by new technologies, or new competition from different directions, changing patterns and costs of necessary resources, or of customers. There may be emerging environmental issues like pollution of the atmosphere or of the local river, or the long-term risk of climate change. There may be changing trends occurring in the economic sector, and in customer needs and competitors' capabilities. These will all need to be noticed by an attentive management process, made sense of in terms of type of threat or opportunity and degree of urgency, and turned into strategy concerning the 'positioning' of the business, its internal resources and its emergent capabilities.

This can only occur if there is a sensemaking process that looks out at the opportunities or threats and tries out possible responses, and a set of diverse

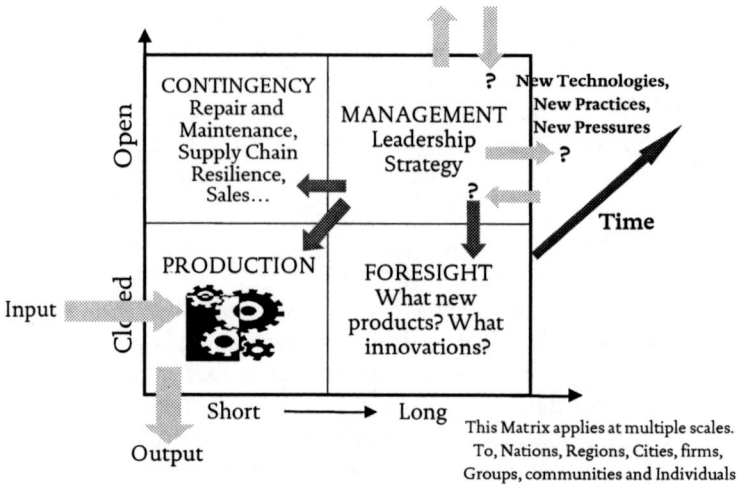

Figure 6
The "activity matrix" for a complex system.

options in the minds of the management as to where and how they wish to modify the current functional processes of the business.

In the short-term, a set of efficient processes must operate to achieve the multiple dimensions of performance that are required for the business to pull in resources to live and grow. It must also formulate the necessary contingency plans and actions to survive foreseeable events that may disrupt it. Such questions as designing resilient supply chains, and rapid customer care would be part of such a system. However, with part of this 'surplus' it must also pay for the right hand quadrants in which the future business processes, and their contingency plans are also cooked up, hopefully providing a smooth transition from one structure to the next.

This leads us to a different version of the matrix.

Our matrix describing the 'evolution' of a complex system now shows four aspects:

- Production
- Contingency
- Sensemaking
- Management

The *production* box describes the organized activities that are currently bringing in the necessary resources to maintain, run and potentially grow the system. This is a closed set of actions, that pull in inputs, convert them to outputs that are sent into the environment, and in so doing allows resources to be brought into the system. This is how you currently earn your living.

The *contingency* box of the upper left, takes into account that in the short-term, any such system will in fact encounter fluctuations and accidents within it and in its environment, and that a service of repair and maintenance, of supply chain repair and customer care will be needed to keep it running. We will also see insurance policies for possible accidents and contingencies and also have a prepared set of emergency services ready to intervene in the event of fire, flood or some other crisis. Over time, the 'contingencies' that are encountered by the fixed process will be characterized by increasingly long time-scales, and at some point will require not just a repair mechanism, but a real restructuring of the process itself. We shall move from the 'maintenance' of the chosen production process to the need for a real innovation and for a new process to replace it. If this doesn't occur, then the system will be eliminated. The source of innovation and structural change comes therefore from the *sensemaking* lower right hand box that considers the relative merits of possible futures that may arise from available innovative options and their possible 'fit' with the current internal structure.

Strategy will consist in looking for future success in a particular direction, and therefore guiding the lower right hand box, R&D, to search for changes in those directions. Clearly, this strategy must take into account messages from the environment about potential markets for potential products, and also the internal resources of the firm, that both limits and enables its capabilities. These internal resources must include an adequate population of all four quadrants, otherwise the organization will simply fossilize, and be eliminated.

Clearly, the vital issues are those of deciding how to 're-design' the production processes of the lower left, so that they will work better in the circumstances of the future. This introduces a range of possibilities, among which must figure the idea of a portfolio of 'new products' that are grown from a small initial size, and either succeed in taking over from the previous dominant form, or fail. Another important issue will be the stage in the life-cycle of a sector or industry in which the system is operating. If it is very new, with an explosion of new technologies, products and customer needs, then rapid and open exploration and innovation will be required, and sensemaking may not be easy. If the sector had a fundamental permanence, but nevertheless undergoes regular changes (as in the fashion industry for example) then the ability to adapt rapidly to emerging fashion will be crucial and very short design and delivery times required. If the sector is mature, then only process innovation and economies of scale will really be important, and so the sensemaking will be basically linked to increasing efficiency, volume and reducing costs.

In order to conceive of 'possible innovations' that might be successful in future circumstances we can use complex / evolutionary systems models. After all, if we don't even know what possible new configurations are even 'functional' then we can only leave it all to chance. So, strategic modelling can help us reflect on possible designs for the future. It can help us by indicating the emergent attributes, strengths and weaknesses of the new system, and different possible configurations that might emerge with or without our action. Unless we engage on this *exploratory* modelling, we shall do this, then we will simply be engaging in an exercise with no real basis.

The use and abuse of models

Any definition of strategy implies some conscious link between action and outcome. This could either be a direct link - the positioning of an organization within some market structure - or less direct - when some changes in internal structure are designed to lead to more effective operation, and to greater performance than otherwise. But this implies some knowledge of the future, of cause and effect, on the part of those proposing a particular strategy, which in its turn implies that the strategist has a model that allows such 'projection' into the future. Of course, this model may be purely intuitive, based on some perceived similarity between the current situation and some others in the past; it could be a more formal representation of the situation underpinning the beliefs about actions and consequences, or it may be a very formal, mathematical model that explicitly represents the behavioral rules and interactions of the components of the situation, and allows 'what if' experiments to be performed, and strategies to be tested and evaluated before implementation.

From our deconstruction of 'complexity' however, what we know is that all these approaches have their limitations. Firstly, the 'intuitive' approach relies on the idea that this situation is not unique, but is one of a type – *and* that you know the key factors that label it as such. Obviously, it will be difficult to know whether this is true, and luck, and creative post-rationalization will play a considerable part in the winning of reputations. The more formal 'working' models of a situation, as we have shown, will only be created by discarding internal diversity and fluctuations, and so will lack the capacity for players whose behavior is represented in the model to 'learn' or to respond creatively to their experiences. Such models are therefore potentially useful in pointing out what may happen if nothing changes, and certainly what may happen if the agents stick to their prescribed routines and job descriptions. Whilst pointing out the shortcomings of such models, it must be noted that any discussion of

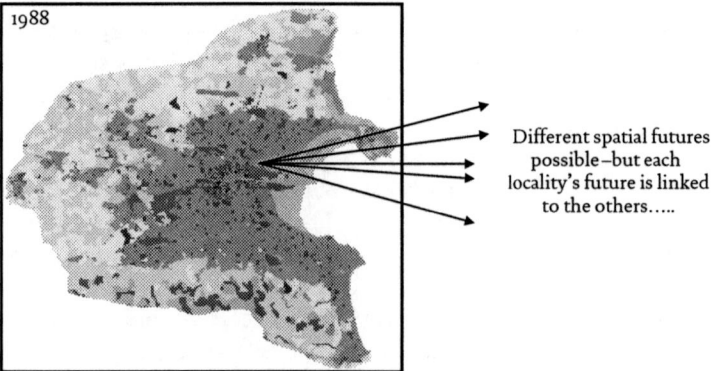

Figure 7: A spatial, dynamic model of Dublin that can be used to explore the many different possible future pathways (White & Engelen, 2000).

strategy that is ignorant of the current attractor that existing routines and job descriptions will lead to, nor what other attractors may exist for these same behavioral rules and what their properties might be, is surely not really able to discuss strategy at all. However, strategy development is really much more difficult than this, because in general the landscape of attractors will change over time and today's strategy, fitted to today's environment, may not lead to success tomorrow.

If you do not know 'where' your current system is going, and you do not know what alternative destinations might exist, then what are you discussing? In the early evolutionary, spatial urban models developed over 20 years ago (Allen, 1997) the possible trajectories of distributed, interacting multiple agents were made explicit, and their properties estimated (see Figure 7). From these, strategic choices could be made that might avoid some of the unhelpful strategic directions that led to problems. Obviously, the models were subject to the limited ability to imagine new technologies, new types of agent and new phenomena in general. However, in terms of what was known they did allow different possible attractors to be revealed, and gave an indication of the qualitative advantages and disadvantages that might characterize them. Without any such model (which is what really happened since these models have not been used) what can be said of the planners or the politicians, the lobby groups, the environmentalists etc.? On what did they base their (often contradictory) assertions? The answer is either that they based them on their honest but unsupported beliefs, or on their perceptions of their own interests.

So, even though we must recognize the imperfections of any such model, and we must be ready to modify it and reconfigure it as we move through time, it still remains the only way that we can project coherently the possible implications of our assumptions about how things work. Mathematical models are therefore not *the* representation of a situation, but are the way that we can explore the possible consequences of our own beliefs about how things operate, and explore whether or not we find them to be consistent with what we observe. It is therefore an 'abuse' of modelling to claim that this represents the system and how it will behave, since players within it may well change their behavior. However, it is equally an 'abuse' of modelling to say that a model has no value or legitimacy at all. It has the legitimacy of considering the coherence of the assumed behavior of micro-actors with the observed, emergent structures and flows. It is this link between levels that is vital, and that distinguishes a model that seeks a degree of explanation underneath what is observed, and one that is merely a description of what is observed.

In considering the meaning of strategy we can also look at it in terms of whether it is about creating an organization that can learn and adapt successfully in a changing world, which of course means that it is about how distributed intelligence can be successfully coupled by an organizational form. This is the territory of the fourth quadrant in Figure 6. This is because organizations themselves clearly do not 'know' anything, or 'learn' anything. It is the individuals within them that know and learn, and it is through the articulations provided by the organizational forms and practices that the organizational capabilities emerge and evolve. We can build models that help us understand how behavior can be successfully modified and adapted over time, and these can help to reveal which methods and structure work better than others.

Manufacturing evolution

The previous section briefly presented how models can be useful in helping us understand the possible outcome of different strategies. The changing patterns of practices and routines that are observed in the evolution of firms and organizations can be looked at in exactly the same way as that of 'product' evolution above.

We would see a *cladistic* diagram (a diagram showing evolutionary history) showing the history of successive new practices and innovative ideas in an economic sector. It would generate an evolutionary history of both artifacts and the organizational forms that underlie their production (McKelvey, 1982, 1994; McCarthy, 1995; McCarthy, *et al.*, 1997). Let us consider manufacturing organizations in the automobile sector.

With these characteristics (Figure 8) as our 'dictionary' we can also identify 16 distinct organizational forms:

- Ancient craft system
- Standardised craft system
- Modern craft system
- Neocraft system
- Flexible manufacturing
- Toyota production
- Lean producers
- Agile producers
- Just in time
- Intensive mass producers
- European mass producers
- Modern mass producers
- Pseudo lean producers
- Fordist mass producers
- Large scale producers
- Skilled large scale producers

The evolutionary tree of Figure 9 can be deduced from cladistic theory, and this shows the probable sequence of events that led to the different possible organizational forms. However, in the spirit of complex systems thinking and that of the formation of networks, we want to consider the synergy or conflict that different pairs of attributes actually have. Instead of only considering the different list of characteristic features that constitute the different organizational forms, we also look at the pair-wise interactions between each pair of

Standardization of Parts	1	TQM sourcing	27
Assembly Time Standards	2	100% inspection sampling	28
Assembly line layout	3	U-Shape layout	29
Reduction of Craft Skills	4	Preventive Maintenance	30
Automation (Machine paced shops)	5	Individual error correction	31
Pull Production System	6	Sequential dependency of workers	32
Reduction of Lot size	7	Line balancing	33
Pull procurement planning	8	Team Policy	34
Operator based machine maintenance	9	Toyota verification of assembly line	35
Quality circles	10	Groups vs. teams	36
Emloyee innovation prizes	11	Job enrichment	37
Job rotation	12	Manufacturing cells	38
Large volume production	13	Concurrent engineering	39
Mass sub-contracting by sub-bidding	14	ABC Costing	40
Exchange of workers with suppliers	15	Excess capacity	41
Training through socialization	16	Flexible automation of product versions	42
Proactive training programmes	17	Agile automation for different products	43
Product range reduction	18	In-Sourceing	44
Automation (Machine paced shops)	19	Immigrant workforce	45
Multiple sub-contracting	20	Dedicated automation	46
Quality Systems	21	Division of Labour	47
Quality Philosophy	22	Employees are system tools	48
Open Book Policy with Suppliers	23	Employees are system developers	49
Flexible Multifunctional workforce	24	Product focus	50
Set-up time reduction	25	Parallel processing	51
Kaizen change management	26	Dependence on written rules	52
		Further intensification of labour	53

Figure 8
53 Characteristics of manufacturing Organizations

practices, in order to examine the role of 'internal coherence' on the organizational performance. In this *complex systems* approach, a new practice can only invade an organization if it is not in conflict with the practices that already exist there. In other words, we are looking at 'organizations' not in terms of simply additive features and practices, but as mutually interactive *complexes* of constituent factors.

From a survey of manufacturers (Baldwin, *et al.*, 2003) concerning the positive or negative interactions between the different practices, a matrix of pair interaction was constructed allowing us to examine the 'reasons' behind the emergent organizational forms, with successful forms arising from positive mutual interactions of constituent practices. This is shown in Figure 10.

We have then been able to develop an evolutionary simulation model, in which a manufacturing firm attempts to incorporate successive new practices at some characteristic rate. There is an incredible range of possible structures that can emerge, however, depending simply on the order in which they are tried. But, each time a new practice is adopted within an organization, it changes the *invadeability* or *receptivity* of the organization for any new innovations in the future. This is true illustration of the *path dependent evolution* that characterizes organizational change. Successful evolution is about the 'discovery' or 'creation' of highly synergetic structures of interacting practices.

In Figure 11 we see the changing internal structure of a particular organization as it attempts to incorporate new practices from those available. In the simulation, the number available start from the ancient craft practice on the left, and successively add the further 52 practices on the right. At each moment in time the organization can choose from the practices available at that time, and its

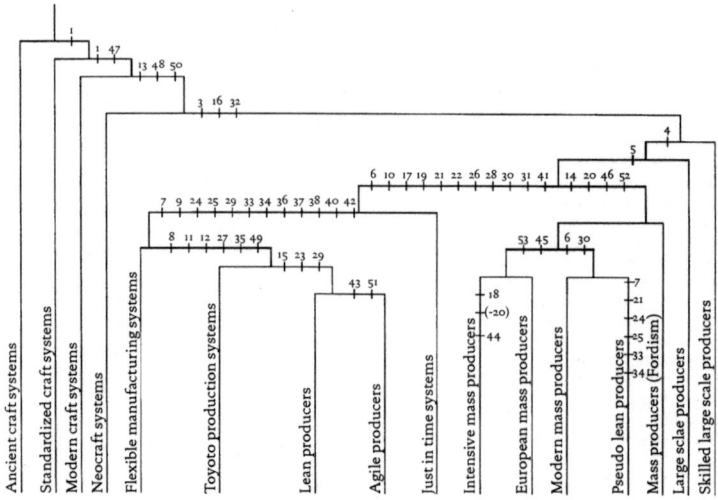

Figure 9
The cladistic diagram for automobile manufacturing organizational forms.
(McCarthy, *et al.*, 1997

53x53 Pair Interactions

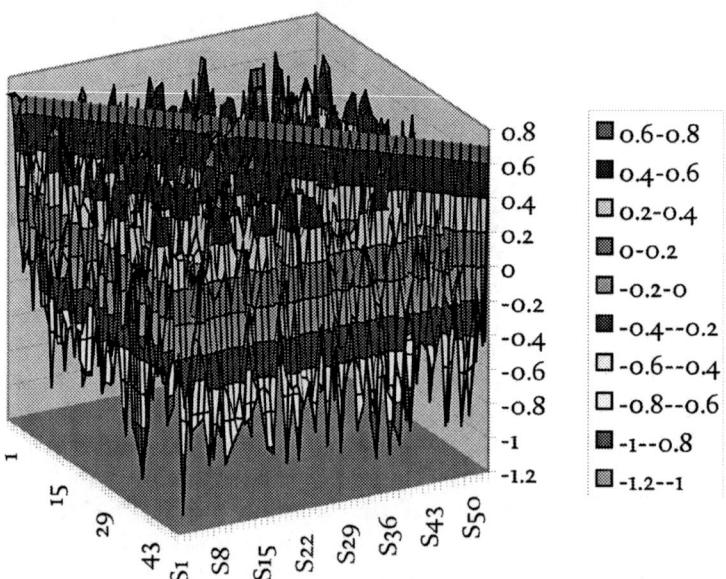

Figure 10
The 53x53 matrix of pair interactions of the characteristic practices. It allows
us to calculate the net attraction or conflict for any new practice depending
on which ones are present already.

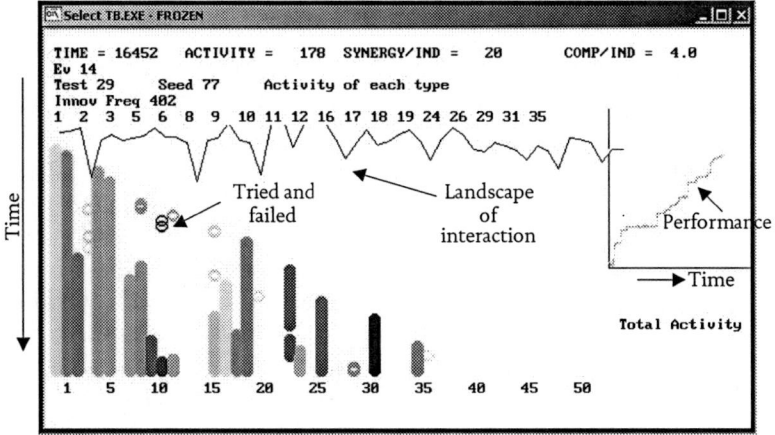

Figure 11
An evolutionary model tries to "launch" possible innovative practices in a random order. If they invade, they change the "invadability" of the new system.

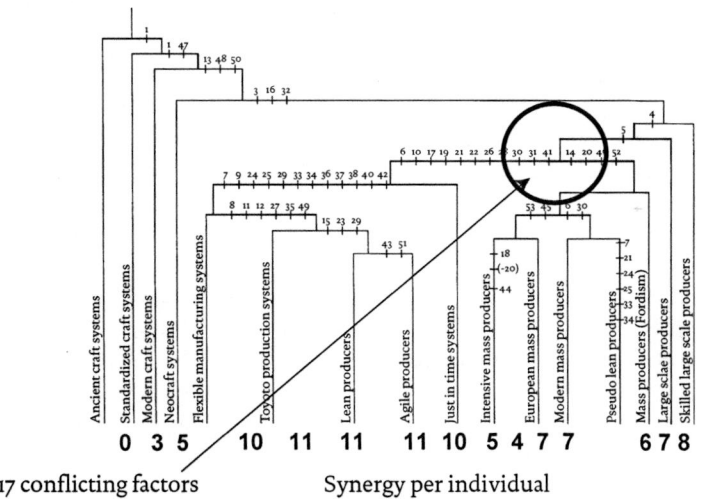

Figure 12
Knowledge of the pair matrix for the different characteristics allows us to calculate the synergy / individual in the different organizations.

overall performance is a function of the synergy of the practices that are tried successfully. We see cases where practice 4, for example, is tried several times and simply cannot invade. However, practice 9 is tried early on and fails, but does successfully invade at a later date. The particular emergent attributes and capabilities of the organization are a function of the particular combination of practices that constitute it.

The model starts off from a craft structure. New practices are chosen randomly from those available at the time and are launched as a small 'experimental' value of 5. Sometimes the behavior declines and disappears, and sometimes it grows and becomes part of the 'formal' structure that then conditions which innovative behavior can invade next.

Different simulations lead to different structures, and there are a very large number of possible 'histories'. This demonstrates a key idea in complex systems thinking. The explorations / innovations that are tried out at a given time cannot be logically or rationally deduced because their overall effects cannot be known ahead of time. Therefore, the impossibility of prediction gives the system *choice*. In our simulation we mimic this by using a random number generator to actually choose what to try out, though in reality this would actually be promoted by someone who believes in this choice, and who will be proved right or wrong by experience, or in this case by our simulation. In real life there will be debate and discussion by different people in favour of one or another choice, and each would cite their own projections about the trade-offs and the overall effect of their choice. However, the actual success that a new practice meets with is pre-determined by the *fitness landscape* resulting from the practices already present and what the emergent attributes and capabilities encounter in the marketplace. But this landscape will be changed if a new practice does successfully invade the system. The new practice will bring with it its own set of pair interactions, modifying the selection criteria for further change. So, the pattern of what could then invade the system (if it were tried) has been changed by what has already invaded successfully. This is technically referred to as a *path dependent* process since the future evolutionary pathway is affected by that of the past.

Our results have already shown, Figure 12, that the evolution through the tree of forms corresponds to a gradual increase in overall *synergy*. That is, the more modern structures related to 'lean' and to 'agile' organizations contain more 'positive' links and less 'negative' links per unit than the ancient craft systems and also the mass-producing side of the tree. In future research we shall also see how many different structures could have emerged, and start to reflect on what new practices and innovations may be available today for the future.

Our work also highlights a 'problem' with the acceptance of complex systems thinking for operational use. The theory of complex systems tells us that the future is not completely predictable because the system has some internal autonomy and will undergo path dependent learning. However, this also means that the 'present' (as described by existing data) cannot be proven to be a *necessary* outcome of the past - but only, hopefully, a *possible* outcome. So, there are perhaps so many possible structures for organizations to discover and render functional, that the observed organizational structures may be 16 in several hundred that are possible. In traditional science the assumption was that 'only the optimal survive', and therefore that what we observe is an optimal structure with only a few temporary deviations from average. But, selection is effected through the competitive interactions of the other players, and if they are different, catering to a slightly different market, and also sub-optimal at any particular moment, then there is no selection force capable of pruning the burgeoning possibilities to a single, optimal outcome. Complexity tells us that we are freer than we thought, and that the diversity that this freedom allows is the mechanism through which sustainability, adaptability and learning occur.

This picture shows us that evolution is about the discovery and emergence of structural attractors (Allen, 2001a, 2001b) that express the natural synergies and conflicts (the nonlinearities) of underlying components. Their properties and consequences are difficult to anticipate and therefore require real explorations and experiments, to be going on, based in turn in diversity of beliefs, views and experiences of freely acting individuals.

Conclusion

This chapter has explored some of the implications of complexity for management and in particular for strategy. The deconstruction of complexity allows us to clarify what a complex system is, and how exactly it differs from a mechanical system. It allows us a proper differentiation between evolutionary, self-organizing, dynamic and equilibrium representations of real situations. This leads us to our 'complexity matrix' which must characterize any organization in the real world if it is persist in the future. This results ultimately from the Second Law of Thermodynamics, which states that the maintenance or growth of any structure or organization requires a flow of negative-entropy. Energy, matter and information must flow if the structure is to persist. The short-term side of the matrix will largely be concerned with 'wear and tear', mechanical failures, and depreciation. However, this is merely about maintaining the existing business process and production. In a changing world, there is a need to evolve and adapt the business process, production and products so as to maintain and grow their ability to attract the necessary resources from the environment.

This makes the implications of complexity very clear indeed. While everyone may agree that increasing efficiency, and cutting costs in an existing production process is useful, it must not be the only 'changes' occurring. There is a need to use resources to explore possible new processes, products and structures that will be needed over the longer term. Only management can allocate resources to these activities, and only management can set a frame for possible innovations. Clearly, management needs to take a strategic view on what 'kind' of company they wish to be. This limits and channels the exploration of new products, new practices and innovations that need to be considered for possible adoption. So, the cladistic model allows a re-construction of history in terms that are understandable, possibly excluding some of the failed even non-occurring innovations that might have been. This consideration shapes the choice of possible changes that might be adopted, as a degree of suitability and fit may perhaps be calculable.

However, this still leaves the central mystery of how genuinely new phenomena can be 'dealt with' by management. It would still appear true that ultimately, the diversity of firms faced with the issue, or the diversity of ideas present within firms facing the issue will lead to ill-informed but diverse responses, some of which may show the way that the new phenomena can be dealt with, and eventually incorporated into the 'closed' dimensions of current knowledge and practice. This is really just like natural evolution, in which underlying genetic and situational diversity leads to the amplification of individuals / groups with appropriate attributes, and the decline of the others. This fundamental recognition of the impossibility of 'knowing' or calculating what to do when faced with a novel situation means that for long-term survival we must allow more diversity that can currently be 'justified', as a storehouse of possibilities and options for an unknown future.

Similarly, at the level of the market place, firms with different strategies or capabilities also try to 'invade' and remain in the system. Exploratory changes lead to a divergent exploration of possibilities. New elements are amplified or diminished as a result of the dual selection processes operating on one hand 'inside them' in terms of the synergies and conflicts of their internal structures, and also 'outside them', in their revealing of synergy or conflict with their surrounding features in the market. So, a new practice can 'invade' a system if it is synergetic with the existing structure, and this will then either lead to the reinforcement or the decline of that system in its environment if the modified system is synergetic or in conflict with its environment. Because of the difficulty of predicting both the emergent internal and external behaviors of a new action, the pay-off that will result from any given new action can therefore generally not be anticipated. It is this very ignorance that is a key factor in allowing exploration at all. Either the fear of the unknown will stop innovation, or divergent innovations will occur even though the actors concerned do not necessarily intend this. Attempting to imitate another player can lead to quite different outcomes either because the internal structure or the external context is found to be different.

Throughout the economy, and indeed the social, cultural system of interacting elements and structures we see a generic picture at multiple temporal and spatial scales in which uncertainty about the future allows actions that are exploratory and divergent, which are then either amplified or suppressed by the way that this modifies the interaction with their environment. Can a new behavior form a self-reinforcing loop of mutual advantage in which entities and actors in the environment wish to supply the resources required for the growth and maintenance of the system in question.

Complex systems thinking is not simply telling us that we are forever doomed to evolve into an unknown future, with sometimes interesting, sometimes painful consequences. Rational thinking has revealed the limits to rational thinking. Our actions and explorations are necessarily creative, and as soon as science deals with non-equilibrium systems of biological and social situations then it also is forced to recognize the essentially creative nature of the universe. Discovering a law such as that of 'gravity' could not change that law. But in the social or economic sciences discovery of patterns of behavior will, if communicated or used for decision-making will change them. In these fields then, research and knowledge generation are simply part of the evolutionary processes of the system - part of an ongoing cultural evolution - and only the 'rules' of change that govern evolutionary complex systems can be said to transcend phenomenology. Most research and knowledge will simply reflect what happens to be the case in any particular instance under study, and to attempt to classify cases into apparently different groups. But such knowledge will be dependent on an assumption of stationarity, which in an evolutionary world will necessarily fail at some point in time. Such studies and classifications will really be a reflection of the kind of questions that society is interested in addressing, and the values and problems that are of current importance. In this way they are as much a part of the cultural landscape as literary, artistic and theatrical productions.

Acknowledgement

This work was supported by the ESRC NEXSUS Priority Network.

References

Allen, P. M. (1976). "Evolution, Population Dynamics and Stability," *Proc Nat Acad Sci, USA*, 73(3): 665-668.

Allen, P. M. (1994) "Evolutionary Complex Systems: Models of Technology Change," in L. Leydesdorff and P. van den Besselaar (eds.), *Evolutionary Economics and Chaos Theory: New Directions in Technology Studies*, New York: St. Martin's Press, pp. 1-17.

Allen, P. M. (1997). *Cities and Regions as Self-Organizing Systems: Models of Complexity*, Amsterdam: Gordon and Breach.

Allen, P. M. (2001a). "Knowledge, Ignorance and the Evolution of Complex Systems," in J. Foster and S. Metcalfe (eds.), *Frontiers of Evolutionary Economics: Competition, Self-Organization and Innovation Policy*, Cheltenham, UK: Edward Elgar.

Allen, P. M. (2001b). "A Complex Systems Approach to Learning, Adaptive Networks," *International Journal of Innovation Management*, 5(2): 149-180.

Kauffman, S. (1995). *At Home in the Universe: The Search for Laws of Self-Organization and Complexity*, Oxford, UK: Oxford University Press.

Langton, C. (1991). "Computation at the Edge of Chaos: Phase Transitions and Emergent Computation," in S. Forest (ed.), *Emergent Computation*, Boston, MA: The MIT Press.

McCarthy, I. (1995). "Manufacturing Classifications: Lessons from Organizational Systematics and Biological Taxonomy," *Journal of Manufacturing and Technology Management: Integrated Manufacturing systems*, 6(6): 37-49.

McCarthy, I., Leseure, M., Ridgeway, K. and Fieller, N. (1997). "Building a Manufacturing Cladogram," *International Journal of Technology Management*, 13(3): 2269-2296.

McKelvey, B. (1982). *Organizational Systematics*, California: University of California Press.

McKelvey, B. (1994). "Evolution and Organizational Science," in J. Baum and J. Singh (eds.), *Evolutionary Dynamics of Organizations*, Oxford: Oxford University Press, pp 314-326.

White, R. and Engelen, G. (2000). "High-Resolution Integrated Modeling of the Spatial Dynamics of Urban and Regional System," *Computers, Environment and Urban Systems*, 24: 383-400.

CHAPTER 24

AGENT-BASED MODELS TO MANAGE THE COMPLEX

Duncan A. Robertson

This chapter introduces agent-based models and their application to management. The use of agent-based models is especially beneficial in situations where there are a number of inter-connected agents forming a complex system, be they firms, employees, customers, or other entities. We discuss the concept of agent-based modeling, building on an example model of interacting firms and customers. We discuss how this model was developed using the agent-based modeling toolkit RePast. We describe not only the advantages but also the disadvantages of agent-based models over more traditional techniques. We introduce several other agent-based models from the more general social science literature, discuss the level of complexity that should be introduced into an agent-based model, and discuss how such a technique may make an impact on the manager or organization whose strategy is to endeavor to manage the complex.

Managing Organizational Complexity: Philosophy, Theory, and Application
A Volume in: Managing the Complex, pages 419-432.
ISBN: 1-59311-319-6 (cloth), 1-59311-318-8 (paper)

Introduction

The use of agent-based models is fast becoming an indispensable tool for studying complex systems. Over the past few years, this technique has been applied to the social sciences and more recently these models have found themselves used within mainstream management research. Their application towards business and management is relatively new, and is an area where great potential exists for studying firm behavior in complex environments.

Agent-based modeling has variously been described as the 'third way' of carrying out research (Gilbert & Terna, 2000), Axelrod (1997) describing agent-based modeling as differing from inductive and deductive methods, while Epstein and Axtell (1996) refer to agent-based modeling as 'generative' social science. But just how does this relatively new methodology differ from traditional methods? And how is it being used within organizations and management?

The terms agent-based modeling, individual-based modeling (Hiebeler, 1994), or bottom-up modeling (Pratt, *et al.*, 1992) all refer to the concept of redefining the way we model systems, differing from traditional techniques which may assume homogeneity of actors, with their focus on rationality and equilibrium, or traditional techniques that may impose rules on the system in a 'top-down' fashion. Agent-based modeling changes this approach. It has been suggested that agent-based modeling is a better method of modeling complex social systems, such as those encountered by managers within firms and other organizations. Whilst such approaches are being recognized in a wide range of social science disciplines, their application to mainstream management has been less prevalent. This chapter introduces the concept of agent-based modeling to business problems, while being wary of the potential pitfalls of applying the concept without critical thought or reservation.

Even though managers may be used to modeling within their corporations, the use of agent-based modeling can at the very minimum provide a new technique for modeling - one that is not predisposed to equilibrium solutions, perfect rationality, or optimization algorithms that many other models may be predicated upon.

Models and modeling within business and management

When faced with the problems of a complex world, we can try and understand them using models that we are familiar with in order to codify and analyze these problems. For example, we may rely on insight from similar situations that we have confronted in the past, or we may analyze the situation using techniques that are familiar to us, such as statistical methods. Whilst such methods may be appropriate in situations where the environment is stable and where processes are linear, such techniques can be augmented by new methodologies, especially in situations of instability and nonlinearity. Agent-based modeling, which we describe in this chapter, offers the opportunity to study systems of interrelated 'agents' in a new way - a technique that may help our understanding of inter-firm and intra-firm processes, and may give us new insights into managerial problems that are considered too complicated to be modeled by traditional means.

Modeling as a technique is certainly not new - we can understand complicated data by using mathematical or statistical models to determine how variables interact, we may set up formalized relations between players, as in game theory, or we may use econometric models to forecast the trajectory of a system. However, each of these paradigms relies to a greater or lesser extent upon restrictions imposed by the modeling technique. For example, game theoretical approaches have been criticized for their assumptions of rational actors, and their usual limitation on the number of players (typically two) that are part of the system. Econometric models may be over-complicated, while mathematical models can typically be 'solved' in order to produce a closed form or analytical solution to a problem thereby being predicated on a solution being able to be found.

While agent-based modeling also relies on certain assumptions about how the model is constructed, the flexibility in the technique allows us to model a wide range of systems of inter-connected agents, as we shall demonstrate below.

Agent-based models: An example

In order to demonstrate the components of an agent-based model, we now review the construction of a typical model. We review a model constructed in *RePast* (a toolkit for constructing agent-based models) of inter-firm competition (Robertson, 2003). The basic premise of the model is that different firms compete for customers as shown in Figure 1. Each of the entities shown in Figure 1 is an *agent*.

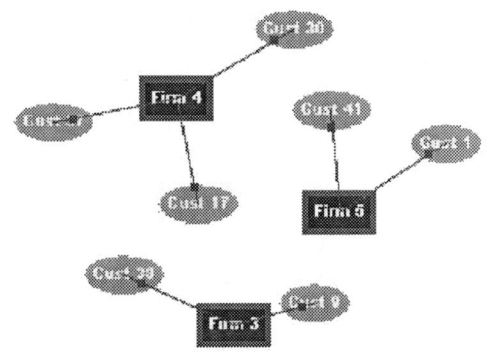

Figure 1
Firm and Customer Agents (after Robertson, 2003)

Agent-based models require several components for their construction. The most fundamental components of an agent-based model are the agents themselves. Agents are the fundamental 'building blocks' of the system; the behavior of these agents drives the behavior of the model. In the example above, the agents include customer agents and firm agents. The linkages between agents are themselves agents, and are constructed in a similar way to the customer and firm agents.

We can think of an example of modeling firms within an industry. What agents do we need to create - to model - in order to produce an overall model of these firms? Firstly we need to define an agent type that represents the firm itself. The properties of the agent are governed by the parameters that we ascribe to an agent. In the case of a firm agent, its parameters could include the firm's size, profitability, number of employees, and several other parameters that we may be interested in investigating. Some of the parameters that are used to specify this particular model are shown in Figure 2.

In Figure 2, we see some of the parameters that are used to construct the model. These represent the *model parameters* - those that are used to describe the initial construction of the model. For instance, we see that we can set parameters for the number of firm and customer agents within our industry, and

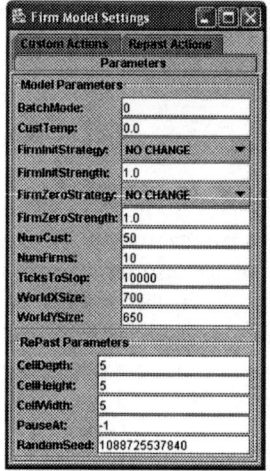

Figure 2
RePast Parameters Panel

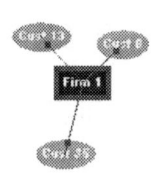 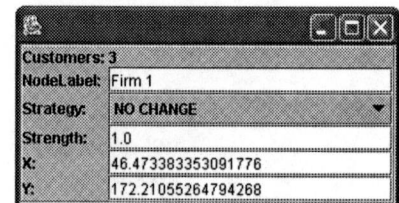

Figure 3
Probed Agent (after Robertson, 2003)

indeed how such firms move around in the industry (we specify strategies for each firm, for example a 'no change' strategy). However, one of the key reasons that we use agent-based modeling rather than other types of simulation is that it allows us to treat each agent as a heterogeneous, autonomous 'being'. We are not restricted to identical agents - we can specify the behavior and parameters of individual agents (which may be different to the behavior and parameters of other agents). We can demonstrate these individual parameters by 'probing' an individual agent as in Figure 3.

As can be seen, each individual agent has parameters associated with that agent, for example the x and y co-ordinates of the agent, the 'strength' of the velocity at which it moves, and its individual strategy (in this case, the agent has a 'no change' strategy). Such *agent parameters* may be inherited from the model parameters, or changed as the result of a rule being executed in the model.

Agent-based models are notable in that agents can themselves be comprised of agents. For instance, the firm agents shown in Figure 1 could themselves be further comprised of other agents - for example individual employees within a firm. Such *nesting* of agents is an important phenomenon that can be achieved by the use of agent-based models. Such *sub-agents* can themselves take on heterogeneous properties that in turn contribute to the heterogeneity of the firm. Unlike other models, each agent can take on differing parameter values, thereby giving inter-agent heterogeneity. Whereas for instance in macroeconomic models, a 'representative firm' notion could be used (where all firms within an industry could be considered homogeneous), in an agent-based model the heterogeneity of different agents can be captured. An agent-based model could treat each individual firm or customer as a separate entity with different characteristics as defined by the parameters of that agent.

The modeler must then define how the agents interact - for instance how customers interact with firms, and how these actions influence the firms' behaviors. This is done by means of the model itself - this defines how, at each time step, the agents change their parameters (for example their location within space). By this process, the parameters of the agents can change and evolve over time. Such *rules* of agent behavior are at the heart of the model itself: without specifying the rules of interaction of agents, the model is not fully specified. In the example above, agents each have a *strategy* that is operationalized by the rules that the agent adopts. For example, a firm agent may adopt a strategy of simply remaining still; a more sophisticated strategy would be to imitate the lead firm in the industry, which could be operationalized by determining rules that specify a movement strategy that is derived firstly by determining the number of customers of each competitor, and then moving towards the lead competitor with a speed defined by the agent parameter 'strength'. By determining similar rules for other agent behaviors, we are able to model the strategies of the agents.

Why use agent-based models?

What are the advantages of using such an approach over traditional modeling techniques? Agent-based models differ from traditional models that look at system-wide behaviors such as systems dynamics models (Forrester, 1961). In such systems dynamics models, the unit of analysis is the macroscopic output of the system. The individuality and heterogeneity of the components flowing through the system are compromised for the macro level results.

In agent based modeling, spatial interaction between individual agents can be included in the model. Models that include a notion of proximity (whether geographical or otherwise) are well suited to agent-based modeling; each agent can have differing preferences as to when to act, and this can be determined by the proximity to other agents.

One of the most important features of agent-based models is that they need not be in equilibrium. While economic models aim to produce a 'solution', whether this be of a closed form type (i.e., by solving a set of differential or difference equations), or by finding an outcome where there is no incentive for players to change their strategies (such as discovering Nash equilibria in game theoretic models), this presumption of equilibrium is not required for agent-based models. Traditional game-theoretical models and other economic models may assume rationality of actors, whereas agent-based models are more suited to modeling boundedly rational behavior where agents adapt to their environment. Agent-based models *can* reach such states of equilibrium, for example where emergent properties are apparent where the system becomes stable over time. This is however not a requirement of an agent-based model, and in this respect, agent based models can be considered more general than equilibrium-based models.

Of course, the use of agent-based modeling will not eclipse the use of statistical, mathematical, and other types of modeling. Some of the drawbacks of using agent-based models are set out below.

Drawbacks of the agent-based paradigm

The use of agent-based modeling has disadvantages that are side-effects of its very advantages. Firstly, the models that are created do not lend themselves to analytical solution: there may be no 'solutions' to the model as there may be for a macro-economic model. Macro-economic modelers would naturally lead themselves to finding a solution whereby equilibrium is established: in the simplest models of supply and demand, this would be where the supply curve and the demand curve meet - the point of equilibrium. However, in dynamic systems that have a stochastic element, there may be no equilibrium (dynamic or otherwise), and in this regard the quest of searching for equilibrium may in fact be futile. If a model can be solved analytically, then this may be the best way of modeling a system - the results produced by an analytical model can be far more elegant than the potentially rather inelegant results from an agent-based model (of course, agent-based models that exhibit emergence may be exceptionally elegant). However, the social and business world is inherently 'messy': we should be rather wary of basing our actions on analytical models if we assume that their results may be applied in the business world without reservation.

A further drawback of agent-based models is that it is necessary to be able to program the behavior of the agents, whether this is done via a graphical interface to software that determines the behavior of 'ready made' agents, or whether this is at a deeper level where it is necessary to include all details of the agent behavior. The use of in-depth programming requires knowledge but can enable the user to create tailored agents, whereas use of pre-defined agent types allows ease of set up of the model but with the inability to tailor the model to particular modeling requirements. While it is possible for personal computers to run models with potentially unlimited number of agents, there are practical problems that limit the number of agents that can be successfully modeled, restrictions as to the memory and processor capacities of the computer. Of course, such limitations will become less important given advances in technology, but such considerations still need to be borne in mind during the construction of the model. The limitation on the number of agents, as well as being related to the absolute number of agents required to be modeled, also depends on the level of complexity and amount of interaction between agents. If all agents act independently, this requires less resource than agents that act based on the properties of other agents, for example the behavior of an agent depending upon the states of other agents within a social network. The interrelation of agents requires more resources to be used, and consequently restricts the number of agents that can be modeled effectively.

Complexity of the agent-based model

Whereas in a statistical model there is the presumption that the more simple or parsimonious the model the better, this is not necessarily the case for an agent-based model. The level of complexity that is used in developing the model is very much dependent on the use that the model is to be put to, described by Carley (2002) as the 'veridicality' of the model. At one extreme, agent-based models can be used to model situations where the object is to 'recreate' the characteristics of the real world. Such models tend to use a large number of agents, and require significant computing power in order to create an environment that mirrors the real world.

Agent-based models fall into two broad categories - those that intend to demonstrate a particular phenomenon, particularly those that demonstrate a feature such as the emergence of a macro-level property by virtue of micro-level rules. The other group of models includes those that attempt to model reality, where the models tend to be complicated in their nature. It is important that these different types of models are distinguished and not confused; models should be explicit at their outset as to whether they purport to model the real world or whether they are to be used for theory building. If however the model falls between these two extremes, there is potential criticism from both sides: that it does not reflect reality nor does it contribute to theory building.

Agent-based models in action

We can demonstrate several properties of agent-based models by looking at the features exhibited by some further examples of agent based models that have been used within the social sciences. One of the most interesting models within the social sciences that demonstrate such macro-level phenomena from micro-level rules is the segregation model developed by Schelling (1971, 1978). Although the model was originally demonstrated without the use of a computerized model (rather using a checkerboard and different colored counters to demonstrate the phenomenon), it is an ideal candidate to be converted into an agent-based model. The Schelling model is of interest in that it produces outcomes from the micro-level moves of the agents, so called *emergent* (Holland 1998) behavior. In Schelling's model, the agents represent people with preferences to be located near neighbors of the same color as themselves. However, even when the level of other-color tolerance is high, segregation is found to take place at the macro level, with clustering of people of different colors (Figure 4, implemented using *NetLogo*).

This result, which is not intuitive, can be investigated by the use of an agent-based model by changing the parameters of the model (for example varying the agents' tolerance for agents of a different color). The effect on the macro level properties that manifest themselves in the form of the level of segregation can then be studied.

In other examples of agent-based models, such as Epstein and Axtell's (1996) *SugarScape* model (Figure 5, implemented using *RePast*), where agents are trying to capture sugar (represented by the background color density) the rules of the agents (shown as circles in the figure) may be of the form 'look around n spaces to the north, east, south, and west, and move to the closest vacant space with the highest concentration of sugar, and collect all the sugar at that site', where n in this case would be a parameter of the agent, representing the 'vision' of that agent. A version of Epstein and Axtell's (1996) *SugarScape* model includes agents that are located within a grid, who can 'trade' with their neighbors, trading one of two goods: sugar or spice. Agents can move around the grid, either moving to collect a commodity or to trade with the agent's neighbors. Now, as each agent acts autonomously, any behavior at a macro level is made up of the interactions at the individual agent level. Epstein and Axtell (1996: 35) note that emergent properties can come out of these simple interactions, emergence being defined by them as 'stable macroscopic patterns arising from the local interactions of agents'. Such emergent properties - that can generate unexpected macro-level characteristics - are one of the most unusual properties of complex systems. Whilst previous approaches to complex behaviors such as chaos theory have been overstated as providing insights to

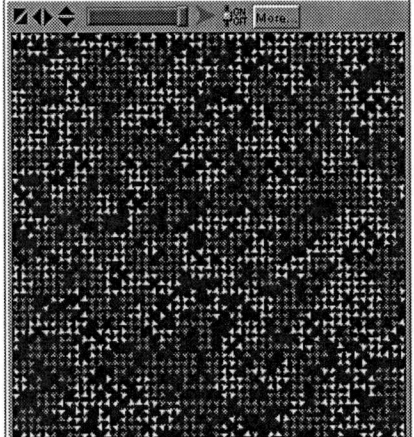

Figure 4
Model of Segregation implemented in *NetLogo* (Wilenksy, 1998; after
Schelling, 1971, 1978)

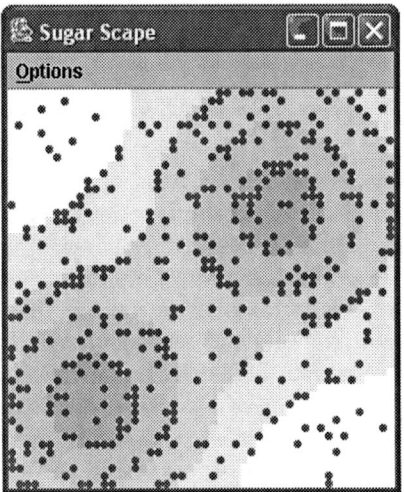

Figure 5
SugarScape Model (Collier, 2004; after Epstein & Axtell, 1996)

real systems, the complexity-based approaches to management have a greater
potential (Robertson, 2004).

Most agent-based models can be visualized on some sort of space - for example a map of the geographical location of the agents, whether this is where
employees are located in an organization in a geographical space or where the
employees are located in abstract space, for example a space representing the
employees' social network. The space in which agents move is important, as it
defines the proximity of the agents to each other. If this affects the network of

how agents interact, then it is important to specify carefully the properties of the space. For instance, if the space is purely geographic, it may be important to have clearly defined boundaries (i.e., the space is bounded). However, in models such as the *SugarScape* model, it may be important to not constrain the agents, in which case the topology of a torus - a donut-shaped 'world' - may be used so that the space in which the agents are located has no boundary.

The techniques have been applied to real and theoretical situations within management. Southwest Airlines have used an agent-based model to improve the operational efficiency of airfreight routing (Seibel & Thomas, 2000); excess inventories of Proctor & Gamble have been investigated by introducing an agent-based supply chain model (Siebel & Kellam, 2003) while researchers from France Télécom are using agent-based models to simulate the interaction of the behavior of their customers (Ben Said, *et al.*, 2001), while Axelrod, *et al.* (1995) have used agent-based models to investigate the formation of alliances. On the theoretical side, agent-based models have been used to study adaptive strategies on rugged fitness landscapes (Rivkin, 2001), Rivkin's agent-based model is predicated on Kauffman's (1993, 1995) *NK* model to generate 'tunable' fitness landscapes. Richardson, *et al.* (this volume) discuss landscape 'metaphors' as one example of where agent-based models could be used to explore the group decision support systems of complex projects.

Simple and complicated agent-based models

The construction of agent-based models can be grouped into those that purport to present a simple model, and those that attempt to produce a complicated model which is designed to reflect reality. The first type of model, of which the Schelling model is an example, uses a simple model with relatively simple agents in order to provide an illustration of a property, in this case the emergence of macro-level segregation from the micro-level interaction between agents. The power of such models is in their ability to develop theory as opposed to offering a predictive model. Such theory, so developed, can be used for example to test empirical data and to test hypotheses generated from the model, such modelers subscribing to the kiss ('keep it simple stupid') principle (Axelrod, 1997: 5). Agent-based models can be used to demonstrate emergence (Holland, 1998) whereby macro-level properties are discovered by micro-level interactions. The Schelling result of agents grouping into segregated colors is an example of an emergent phenomenon, such an outcome being not immediately apparent from the micro-level rules that are included in the model. In some regards, we can think of emergent phenomena as being long-run equilibria of the model: in the case of the Schelling model, the segregation result can be thought of as such. It is therefore possible - in principle at least - to define analytically the conditions by which the model results in emergent characteristics being presented.

However, not all agent-based models exhibit emergent properties. One can contrast simple agent-based models with agent-based models that aim to reflect the reality of an environment. This class of models has been used to model power grids, ecological environments, or stock markets. Real world data reflecting the structure of the environment, for example the precise interconnections between power distribution networks or the topological properties of a landscape can be incorporated into the model (for example using GIS data to recreate a geographical landscape or to incorporate every pylon and transmission wire in a power grid). With this real data being reflected accurately in the model environment, the user of the model can simulate the effects of power outages occurring in one part of the grid, this having the immediate benefit that the ability of the network to cope with an emergency can be simulated without the inconvenience and expense of testing the robustness of the system by actually exposing the system to an event such as a failure of one connection within the network. The advantage of using an agent-based model over a system wide model is that the researcher (whether they be an academic or a practitioner) may manipulate individual agents within the system to determine the effect that this individual agent has to the stability of the system. Such changes within the model may take the form of changes of parameters or rules in order to investigate whether the stability of the system is influenced by such changes. While such models are not full representations of the 'real world', their use is designed to give insight into a practical problem of relevance to managers and therefore are not 'designed' to produce macro-level properties of for example emergent behavior.

Of course, whether the model reflects the actual performance of such an event depends upon whether the model has been constructed appropriately. In order to discern whether a model is of use within an applied setting, it is important to 'dock' or calibrate such models with observed data and with other models of the same phenomenon (Axtell, *et al.*, 1996). While this is less applicable to theoretical models that are designed for theory-building, it is vital for models that are designed to reflect real world behavior.

The use of agent-based models may be particularly useful when environments in which firms operate are complicated and not able to be explained adequately by means of a traditional analysis. One of the great achievements of the community of researchers and practitioners involved in the agent-based modeling community is that models that seem applicable to, say a problem in biology (Levinthal, 1997), can potentially be transferred over to the domain of management, where it can provide an insight into managerial problems and those related to business applications.

Resources for agent-based modeling

The creation of modeling toolkits has allowed researchers to build agent-based models without the requirement of knowledge of detailed programming languages. The rise in popularity of agent-based modeling can in part be attributed to the fact that modeling resources have become easier to use. There is a rapidly growing array of toolkits available for agent-based modeling, for example the software packages *Ascape*, *NetLogo*, *RePast* and *Swarm*. However, at the time of writing there is no generally acceptable interface that allows users to develop tailored agent-based models without at least a minimal knowledge of programming. Of course, as more users are attracted to the field, it is only a matter of time until a suitable interface can be found to allow managers to set up their own agent-based models, apply the dynamical properties of their own firm or industry, and experiment with the model to see the effects of changes in parameters or assumptions as to how the model operates. Toolkits include sample models, including the *SugarScape* and *Schelling* models, which can demonstrate some of the potential of agent-based modeling. From the point of view of enabling models to be viewed without installing computer languages, *NetLogo* is of use in allowing models to be run from within a web browser. The use of *NetLogo* is however limited by the very ease with which it can be run: more advanced models that require more complex agent behavior will find that they require toolkits such as *RePast*. *RePast* has the advantage that it allows a large amount of flexibility in construction of the agents and the agent environment. At the time of writing, the *RePast* platform appears to be the platform that enables both the flexibility of application, but also has a following in both the social science and increasingly the managerial regimes. Therefore, for business applications that require a more detailed level of sophistication, the *RePast* platform should be considered seriously to start the journey into agent-based modeling.

Conclusions

The technique of agent-based modeling has great potential, to enable managers to understand the complex world in which they operate. Potential uses are wide, and encompass models that attempt to replicate the real world, to simpler models that exhibit emergent behavior. Agent-based models should however be introduced with several caveats. Emergent properties that may be seen within a model may not be experienced in a real world situation - changes in the parameters can knock the simulation from an emergent trajectory and thus the modeled results may not transpire in reality. Furthermore, the investment in setting up the model may outweigh the potential gains that are brought about from changing the configuration of a firm to incorporate findings from the model. However, the actual process of constructing a model of the environment - specifying which agents are most important to the operation of your firm - is a worthwhile process: but are people, machines, processes, or ideas the most important agents? In reality, it may be a combination of all these and more that are drivers of profitability. We should not forget that the active process of management itself provides a tangible effect on competitiveness of the firm. Agent-based models can add to the inventory of tools available in the manager's portfolio. Whether their utilization causes beneficial effects on competitiveness and profitability depends critically on how they are designed and implemented.

Acknowledgements

The author would like to thank Bill McKelvey and one anonymous referee. Errors remain the responsibility of the author.

References

Axelrod, R. (1997). *The Complexity of Cooperation: Agent-Based Models of Competition and Collaboration*, Princeton NJ: Princeton University Press.

Axelrod, R., Mitchell, W., Thomas, R. E., Scott Bennett, D., and Bruderer, E. (1995). "Coalition Formation in Standard-Setting Alliances," *Management Science*, 41: 1493-1508.

Axtell, R., Axelrod, R., Epstein, J. M., and Cohen, M. D. (1996). "Aligning Simulation Models: A Case Study and Results," *Computational and Mathematical Organization Theory*, 1(2): 123-141.

Ben Said, L., Drogoul, A., and Bouron, T. (2001). "Multi-Agent Based Simulation of Consumer Behaviour: Towards a New Marketing Approach," *Proceedings of the International Congress on Modelling and Simulation*, Canberra, Australia.

Carley, K. (2002). "Simulating Society: The Tension between Transparency and Veridicality," *Presentation to the Agent 2002 Conference*, Chicago IL, USA.

Collier, N. (2004). *SugarScape Model Implementation in RePast, Social Science Research Computing*, University of Chicago.

Epstein, J. M. and Axtell, R. (1996). *Growing Artificial Societies: Social Science from the Bottom Up*, Washington DC: Brookings Institution Press.

Forrester, J. W. (1961). *Industrial Dynamics*, Portland OR: Productivity Press.

Gilbert, N. and Terna, P. (2000). "How to Build and Use Agent-Based Models in Social Science," *Mind and Society*, 1" 57-72.

Hiebeler, D. (1994). "The Swarm Simulation System and Individual-Based Modeling," *Proceedings of Decision Support 2001: Advanced Technology for Natural Resource Management*, Toronto, Canada.

Holland, J. H. (1998). *Emergence: From Chaos to Order*, Reading MA: Addison-Wesley

Kauffman, S. (1993). *The Origins of Order: Self-organization and Selection in Evolution*, New York NY: Oxford University Press.

Kauffman, S. (1995). *At Home in the Universe: the Search for Laws of Self-organization and Complexity*, New York NY: Oxford University Press.

Levinthal, D. A. (1997). "Adaptation on Rugged Landscapes," *Management Science*, 43(7): 934-950.

Pratt, D. B., Mize, J. H., and Kamath, K. (1992). "A Case for Bottom Up Modeling," in 2*nd* *Industrial Engineering Research Conference Proceedings*, pp. 430-434.

Rivkin, J. W. (2001). "Reproducing Knowledge: Replication without Imitation at Moderate Complexity," *Organization Science*, 12(3): 274-293.

Robertson, D. A. (2003). "Agent-Based Models of a Banking Network as an Example of a Turbulent Environment: The Deliberate vs. Emergent Strategy Debate Revisited," *Emergence: A Journal of Complexity Issues in Organizational Management*, 5(2): 56-71.

Robertson, D. A. (2004). "The Complexity of the Corporation," *Human Systems Management, Special Issue: Corporation: An Intelligent Complex Adaptive System*,

23(2): 71-78.

Schelling, T. C. (1971). "Dynamic Models of Segregation," *Journal of Mathematical Sociology*, 1: 143-186.

Schelling, T. C. (1978). *Micromotives and Macrobehavior*, New York NY: Norton.

Seibel, F. and Kellam, L. (2003). "The Virtual World of Agent-Based Modeling: Proctor & Gamble's Dynamic Supply Chain," *Perspectives on Business Innovation*, 9: 22-27.

Seibel, F. and Thomas, C. (2000). "Manifest Destiny: Adaptive Cargo Routing at Southwest Airlines," *Perspectives on Business Innovation*, 4: 27-33.

Wilensky, U. (1998). *NetLogo Segregation Model*, Center for Connected Learning and Computer-Based Modeling, Northwestern University, Evanston, IL.

CHAPTER 25

THE COHERENT MANAGEMENT OF COMPLEX PROJECTS AND THE POTENTIAL ROLE OF GROUP DECISION SUPPORT SYSTEMS

Kurt A. Richardson, Andrew Tait, Johan Roos and Michael R. Lissack

This chapter argues that group decision support tools represent a valuable addition to the project manager's toolbox in that they facilitate the management of project complexity and encourage coherence within the project team. In addition, the role that virtual community applications may play in facilitating the operation of dispersed project teams will be briefly discussed. It will be argued that such communities are likely to be the form in which most temporary organizations, or teams, will embody themselves during the next few decades.

Managing Organizational Complexity: Philosophy, Theory, and Application
A Volume in: Managing the Complex, pages 433-458.
Copyright © 2005 by Information Age Publishing, Inc.
All rights of reproduction in any form reserved.
ISBN: 1-59311-319-6 (cloth), 1-59311-318-8 (paper)

Introduction
What are complex projects?

Project management is becoming more difficult. An obvious statement perhaps to the day-to-day project manager, but the changing operating environment is uncovering some genuinely novel challenges for the project manager. The modern organization can no longer be viewed as a group of loosely related departments with specific formal links, but as a series of highly interconnected business processes. The increased use of information technology, and the resulting interconnectivity, from local area networks, through intranets, the Internet, and now extra-nets of business-associated organizations, has increased the capability for individuals and groups to exchange information rapidly. This increased connectedness has meant that the identification of causal links, and where identified, the affect of such links on organizational behavior, is also increasingly difficult, making it more problematic to take informed decisions. This is the complex organization, and, rather than being an exception, it is becoming more common with the current trends in globalization and associated business fragmentation. In association with this higher level of organizational complexity we are also witnessing, unsurprisingly, a corresponding rise in project complexity. But what exactly do we mean by the term 'complexity'?

Recently a review of project complexity by Baccarini (1996) proposed a definition of project complexity to be "consisting of many varied interrelated parts", which he operationalized in terms of *differentiation* - the number of varied elements - and *interdependency* - the degree of interrelatedness between these elements (or connectivity). These measures are to be applied in respect to the various project dimensions, and he discusses two of them:

1. In terms of organizational complexity, differentiation would mean the number of hierarchical levels, number of formal organizational units, division of tasks, number of specializations, etc.; interdependency would be the degree of operational interdependencies between organizational elements.

2. In terms of technological complexity, differentiation would mean the number and diversity of inputs, outputs, tasks or specialities; interdependency would be the interdependencies between tasks, teams, technologies or inputs.

This clearly defines an important element of project complexity, perhaps the element that we think of most often when we consider a 'complex' project. There are, however, a variety of other meanings associated with the term that may prove useful in appreciating what is meant when a project is said to be *complex*. Table 1 summarizes these different modes:

	MODES OF COMPLEXITY Epistemic modes: formulaic complexity
Descriptive	Length of an account that must be given to provide an adequate description of the project of interest.
Generative	Length of the set of instructions that must be given to provide a recipe for producing the project of interest.
Computational	Amount of time and effort involved in resolving a problem.
	ONTOLOGICAL MODES: COMPOSITIONAL COMPLEXITY
Constitutional	Number of constituent elements or components. (Compare for example computers, people and communication lines.)
Taxonomical	Variety of the constituent elements: numbers of different components in their physical configurations. (Compare for example different cultures and different communication channels.)
	ONTOLOGICAL MODES: STRUCTURAL COMPLEXITY
Organizational	Variety of different possible ways of arranging components in different modes of interrelationship. (Compare a bureaucratic organization with an 'organic' organization.)
Hierarchical	Elaborateness of sub-ordination relationships in the modes of inclusion and subsumption. Organizational disaggregation into subsystems. (For example: individuals, teams, departments, sectors, companies, etc.) Here the higher-order units are, for this very reason, always more complex than the lower-order ones.
	FUNCTIONAL COMPLEXITY
Operational	Variety of modes of operation or types of functioning. (Teams have a more complex lifestyle than individuals. The processual structure of chess is vastly more elaborate than checkers.)
Nomic	Elaborateness and intricacy of the laws governing phenomena at issue. (Matrix management structures are more complex in this manner than vertical management structures.)

Table 1
Different Modes of Complexity (adapted from Rescher, 1998)

It is clear that these different views of complexity are interrelated (as you might expect) - it might be that greater organizational complexity goes hand in hand with hierarchical or operational complexity for example. In general, however, we can distinguish between the 'complicated' - more items, events or parts - and the more 'complex' - more interactions and emergent products of those interactions amongst the items, events, and parts. Thus, the initial research question: does the increasing complexity often associated with modern projects signify a need for change in project management style?

A paradigm shift?

In the not too distant past, it was an adequate approximation to assume that each department, sector, etc., could actually operate almost unawares of the other departments except for the odd transfer of information once in a while.

This of course is an over-simplification, but given the diminished complexity of the business environment, it seemed a reasonable and effective assumption to make. This is the (quasi-) complicated world. In this world, time seems to run slower (the business tempo was more sedate than the hectic pace in many industries today). Thus when errors in judgement occurred, there was more time to recognize the effects of the error; more time to understand how the error arose; and more time to take corrective action. All this was possible simply because the business environment was less complex - it was for most intents and purposes *complicated*. In the complex environment, however, life is less user-friendly, particularly if one merely pays lip service to the complexity. In this economy-in-overdrive, there is less time to recognize errors, but, because of the sometimes apparent disassociation between cause and effect, it can be very difficult to even recognize an error by its effects. Furthermore, if the error is caught there is little time for corrective action. This is more than mere speculation. Williams, *et al.* (1995) describes a case study in which a large engineering company was held hostage to just such an exceptionally complex environment.

Sometimes the error might not be life threatening (in an organizational sense), other times it might be - it is difficult to tell which beforehand, as complexity also significantly hinders our ability to predict. This shift in organizational form from (quasi-) complicated to complex is fundamental, and it is not controversial to suggest that a paradigm shift within the management sciences is necessary to continue managing effectively in this new (newly labeled at least) environment (Williams, 1999).

It is interesting to note that many companies themselves are actually *striving* to become more complex, in the name of competitive advantage. The scale of modern companies is serving as a driver on complexity. In the past, large companies were like Ford - put together like a *machine* with a given aim. However, modern companies like IBM, Microsoft, consulting house, etc. are more like *societies*. Arguably, the management of these societies has not evolved to meet this changing reality. It also, eventually, serves to isolate such companies from their customers. How does someone find the right person to do a job in IBM, for example?

Despite the difficulties that confront project teams in this (post) modern environment, there exists a wealth of evidence demonstrating the benefits of working in teams. Benefits that are frequently attributed to teamwork include: higher productivity, improved quality, enhanced employee quality or work life, lower costs, reduced turnover and absenteeism, reduced conflict, increased innovation, and better organizational adaptability and flexibility (Stewart, *et al.*, 1999). Not all evidence however, especially in more rigorous academic research, is completely supportive of these claims. If project managers are to give themselves and their teams the best opportunity of realizing these benefits and, in so doing, meeting customer requirements they must update their techniques and attitudes, which are currently guided by the principles of the command and control perspective.

Analysis in the past has, at best, tended to reduce project management to formal communications, pre-defined informational pathways and reporting structures to create the first order system dynamics. The insight generated, in comparison to the complex enterprise modelled, is small. Projects are far more than the doctrine, strategy or formally defined structures, it is the people within, and their behaviors that create, define, and run the endeavour. People do not work mechanically in their business nature; they work by experience, instinct and analysis. Therefore, the study of projects should be less about predictive certainty, and more about the insight and broad understanding that exploration using the complexity metaphor can bring. The uncertainty inherent to project management must be understood and managed rather than linearized and ignored - which is essentially the command and control doctrine.

Ten components of coherent management

Lissack and Roos (1999), propose a possible framework that claims to support this paradigmatic shift. This framework recognizes that in this new environment the perspective that the project team adopts, through which a representation is made, and on which decisions are based, is critical in the development of a 'coherent' strategy. By coherent we simply mean that the strategy is aligned with requirements defined from within and without the project team, i.e., it is 'situated'. In order to achieve such a strategy the interactions between the different team members and the team environment must be rich. Interaction and exploration are key features of this framework. In essence, what is proposed is a control strategy (without the 'command'). Such control is not prescriptive (that would comprise of commands) but instead is of the specify, observe, test, and respond variety such as adjusting the temperature of your shower. The framework is based upon the following ten basic building blocks:

1. *Use simple guiding principles*: Project management is complex enough without making it more so. The guiding principles that work are those that are aligned around basic values. It works much better to help people work efficiently than to have a 20-page prescription on how. Prescription inevitably limits personal creativity in providing each team member with insufficient breathing space to apply his own initiative. If instead the team can first understand, then agree, with a simple phrase like "the customer is always right," "keep on talking," or "exploration is king," then this will subtly underpin the teams' attitude towards how it goes about its day-to-day business thereby providing a level of guidance. The 'spirit' of the prescription is captured, but the details of how it is realized are left to the individual. This necessary relaxation of detailed rules is articulated in the patchiness principle from systems theory which states that "rule-bound systems, stipulating in advance the permissible and the impermissible are likely to be less stable than those that develop pell-mell" (Skyttner, 1996).

In the examples given "keep on talking" may be an attempt to promote group interactivity, or cohesion whereas "exploration is king" may be an attempt to encourage out-of-the-box thinking, or attune the team to its environment. There is no set guideline as to how many guiding principles are required - this is determined within the team, which improves teams members' buy-in and commitment to such principles. For short-term projects, it might be seen to be impractical to spend time developing such universally (as far as the group is concerned) accepted guiding principles (which might not be necessary if the team has been brought together previously for other projects, for example). On these occasions the project manager will necessarily take the lead in articulating what he sees as the important principles, and in so doing quickly setting the tone and style of how he believes the team should function - in a sense the PM would be defining the team *culture*. Of course, the language used to articulate such principles is important, the same message requiring different presentation for different teams (see 'use aligned words to fuel coherence'). However, once the essence of the concept is reflected in team behavior, each member will adopt his own personal variation of the simple guiding principles, interpreting them through his / her own particular mental model.

2. *Respect mental models (and interact with them)*: Each of us possesses a mental model that we employ to interpret our surroundings. These models are not static, but are amended and refined daily as we live our lives. Given that our personal history plays a central role in the details of this model (or 'paradigm' in a general sense) it is not surprising that our personal models are unique. This means that when two people look from the same point in the same direction they will 'see' different things (e.g., Kuhn, 1996), sometimes entirely differently. For example, when articulating 'simple guiding principles' the language used will provoke different interpretations in different team members. This is a fact of life and cannot be changed. It is not, however, a bad thing. Different interpretations can, and often do, result in misunderstandings. The meaning conveyed in a request from one individual to another might not be interpreted as originally intended by the requestor. The recipient may then act inappropriately in the eyes of the requestor. Sometimes this failure to carry out requests is easily rectified, but on other occasions the consequences might be considerably worse. An ability to empathise, therefore, is essential. However, being able to empathise with others requires access to their mental model. This can only be achieved through careful observation of behavior, and through interaction.

In multi-cultural groups a level of appreciation can be developed by considering the empirical behavioral characteristics of each culture involved and associating each cultural portrait with the relevant team member. This is not sufficient, however, as one must be careful not to 'tar everyone with the same brush'. An effort has to be made to understand the individual's viewpoint, not just general ethnic characteristics which can be misleading - generalizations through stereotyping in this context can be quite offensive to the individual. An appreciation of another's culture simply helps prevent insulting that individual, but this is no more than a starting point. A quote from the psychotherapist Carl Jung serves to illustrate this point by considering how a therapist might go about attending to his / her patient:

"The uniqueness of the individual and of his situation stares the doctor in the face and demands and answer. His duty as a physician forces him to cope with a situation swarming with uncertainty factors. At first he will apply principles based on general experience, but he will soon realize that principles of this kind do not adequately express the facts and fail to meet the nature of the case. The deeper his understanding penetrates, the more the general principles lose their meaning... With the growth of what both patient and doctor feel to be 'understanding', the situation becomes increasingly subjectivised. What was an advantage to begin with threatens to turn into a dangerous disadvantage" (Jung, 1958).

Critical thinking provides a useful process by which such appreciation can be harvested. For readers unaware of this mode of thinking, asking yourself the following questions during your interactions with your 'world', taken from *Asking the Right Questions: A Guide to Critical Thinking* (Browne & Keeley, 1998), may prove useful:

- What are the issues and the conclusions?
- What are the reasons?
- What words or phrases are ambiguous?
- What are the value conflicts and assumptions?
- Are there any fallacies in the reasoning?
- How good is the evidence?
- Are there rival causes?
- Are the statistics deceptive?
- What significant information is omitted?
- What reasonable conclusions are possible?

Of course, when teams are not co-located such interaction becomes very difficult, but all the more important given the disparate working environments. However, low-cost collaboration tools, such as video conferencing, can help in this area. Conferencing, however, should not be seen as a replacement for face-to-face interaction: the dynamics are quite different. It is important, whenever possible, for team members to meet in each other's working environments to fully appreciate their colleagues' priorities.

The diversity of views can be managed to minimize misunderstandings and potential conflicts. This diversity of views, however, is a powerful resource when operating within a complex environment. Different individuals 'see' different things, and by pooling these differing views a richer appreciation of the individuals' environment is developed, resulting in more informed decision making - there is a necessary balance between homogeneity and heterogeneity of views.

3. *Use landscape images*: The increasingly complex environment that project teams operate within, make deciding what action to take, and when, problematic. What we need is the means to recognize patterns in our complex environment to facilitate the decision making process. The 'means' comes in the form of an interface that can be used to take advantage of our considerable pattern recognition skills. The metaphor of landscapes can provide this interface in the very same way that Windows provides the interface between the OS and IS of computers and ourselves. The reason for choosing the landscape metaphor is simple - humans have very good spatial awareness, or 'spatial intelligence' (Gardner, 1993). In allowing the project team to construct a landscape image of how it perceives the project 'space', it can better recognize the important issues. Constructing a landscape need not require fancy technology; it could simply be the creation of a rich picture, or a causal map (which can be achieved in a group video conferencing mode - taking full advantage of technology where appropriate), on a whiteboard. In addition, the process of constructing the landscape will further provoke interaction between the team members, which will give each individual the opportunity to further develop their appreciation of the other members' mental models, and the convergence toward a project 'language'.

4. *Combine and recombine*: We have already mentioned that humans have a considerable ability to recognize patterns in complex situations and that this skill can be enhanced by presenting the situation in different forms. In constructing our personal pictures of our environment we rely on the brain's ability to recognize boundaries and, therefore, distinct 'parts' or elements that make up the environment. Relationships are then proposed between the 'parts' and, in so doing, creating 'wholes'. Again, our mental models play a central role in determining which 'parts' we acknowledge as real, and therefore the 'whole' that is generated.

There has been much written in the management literature suggesting that operation within a complex environment requires holistic thinking, as opposed to reductionist thinking . This perspective is valuable (and synthesizing the different perspectives of the project team will result in a more 'complete' picture), but it is not the be all and end all. Taking the whole apart and rethinking the ways in which the parts might be defined and recombined to create new wholes can also provide valuable insights into how one might operate within the complex environment. In short, combine and recombine is a process that allows the team to see the same things in different ways, which might result in novel procedures, ideas, concepts, etc. Few creative ideas originate out of whole cloth - they are the products of thinking about existing things in new ways and recombining old parts to make a new whole.

5. *Recognize your multiple roles, don't hide from them*: In the modern organization the identity of each individual is written out explicitly in the company's operating procedures, along with the roles and responsibilities that the iden-

tity should be associated with. For instance, in a project team there might be the Project Manager, Quality Manager, Technical Manager, Project Secretary, Technical Support, Subject Matter Expert, and so on. The problem with such distinct, and unchanging identities, is that context is omitted. We all have multiple roles, in the same way we possess multiple intelligences - at one moment one might be a subject matter expert, or a computer operator, the next one might be a friend, or a listener - it all depends upon the context. The context determines which role we adopt. Though this dynamic nature is not reflected in most operating procedures it is important to recognize it, and not be shy of breaking the mold determined by the organization's 'operating plan' when the context demands. This is a very human feature, and should be taken advantage of rather than restricted through detailed job descriptions. The team culture should support such a chameleon-like attitude towards roles. This freedom will allow the individual team members greater flexibility, which is essential as the operating environment becomes more complex (the patchiness principle strikes again), as well as putting them at ease when 'shape-shifting'.

6. *Create canyons, not canals*: The patchiness principle and the need for a certain level of team member freedom in order to endow the team, not only with the flexibility necessary to adapt to changing requirements, but with the inquisitiveness to explore their surroundings has already been mentioned. This inquisitiveness contributes to the successful development of a coherent strategy, and also gives the team a capacity to pre-empt changes to the strategy as necessary. It is difficult, if not impossible, to build such features into the fabric of the project team through the application of extensive procedures. So, why the 'create canyons, not canals' metaphor? Rivers need lots of room, yet when bounded by canyons (the metaphorical equivalent of simple guiding principles, and mental models) they are still free to explore. Tributaries are formed, and as the river meanders new places are explored. A canal on the other hand has fixed walls. A lot of time and effort (and therefore money) is spent keeping the flow within the canal exactly the same. The view from the canal, however, is limited and it becomes impossible to explore other regions. The creation of flow controls, through the construction of canals, is an attempt to control outcomes. Of course, control does affect outcome, but such restrictions can frequently result in the 'wrong' outcome, i.e., an incoherent outcome.

As mentioned above, exploration is key to remaining coherent, but this is exploration within limits - limits imposed by the guiding principles chosen, the individual mental models, the customer requirements, etc.

7. *Tell stories*: Team interactivity is essential in allowing individuals to learn to appreciate others' mental models, and to take advantage of the different perspectives brought to bear on a particular problem. Furthermore, it helps in the development of a project language. During the interaction between two or more persons, simply stating facts, quoting one-liners, opinions, etc., is a rather dull and uninformative way to communicate. Such impersonal presentation

of ideas and concepts are easily misinterpreted, as meaning is not easily conveyed. Telling stories is about allowing others the benefit of shared experiences. Stories allow others to relate to fact, context, emotion, and to bring their own interpretation to what they hear or read. This richer mode of interaction also enables others to obtain further insight into how an individual sees the world, and in what contexts they use certain words. Meaning happens from interaction, not from blind passive reception; encounters are memorable when they are infused with emotion. Stories not only allow emotions to be expressed by the teller but also to be inferred by the listener. When was the last time a set of bullet points carried lasting emotion? By contrast, the best speeches by both politicians and judges are centred around stories. Even Monica Lewinsky can attract a large audience for telling her story despite the fact that nearly everyone listening already knew all the details! Telling stories allows the listener to effectively put themselves into the teller's shoes.

8. *Send out scouting parties*: In order to remain coherent the team must have a clear understanding of what is going on in its environment, and how different events might impact the team's operations. It is arrogant to believe that the team knows everything there is to know about the subject matter it is working on, customer politics, etc. By sending out scouting parties to probe the environment, vital stories might be found that would be of great value to the team in achieving its goals. In a recent technology project designed by the first author, exploration time was explicitly built into the project plan. The guidelines to the team members were that if they came across an idea that they wanted to take further, they had the support of the project. At first, the exploration was initialized by the project manager as team members were wary of such freedom. As the project progressed, this type of exploration was seen as legitimate and the team felt more comfortable in pursuing paths, even though most of the time the journeys ended with no obvious returns (in terms of that particular project). However, in this particular project, not only was the technical standing of the work improved, but a change in customer politics was also recognized, resulting in a significant shift in the focus of the work. There is an obvious trade-off between staying focussed and exploring, and only through experiencing such practices can the appropriate balance for different projects be achieved.

As with most of the building blocks in this framework, the exploration results in further interaction as the stories are relayed back to the team and discussed, improving working relations further.

9. *Post and attend to road signs*: No project team will maintain coherence if the varied contributions of its members and of the team itself are not recognized with sufficient attendant notice such that the members involved can develop pride with regard to their activities. Such acts of recognition and notice function as 'road signs' within a community or housing development. Not only do such signs allow for recognition, but they also allow for meaningful directions to be communicated to others who are not part of the team. In the absence of

road signs not only might previously covered territory be remapped, but so too might previously encountered and easily avoided mistakes. The hoarding of such information within the team has thus two potentially negative effects: a possible feeling among team members that their contribution is being "hidden" from the outside world (either as an embarrassment or to prevent others from realizing the member's value) and the inability for others to learn from the (rather than of) the activities of the team. Unless a team is engaged by the intelligence services, it seems foolish to risk such ill-effects. The power of team behavior, learning, and coherence comes from the interactions that all three promote. Only if the environment and context in which the team operates is set up to promote recognition and further interaction can increasing returns result. Perhaps the most important aspect of coherence to the project team manager is the prospect of increasing returns.

10. *Use aligned words to fuel coherence*: In a number of the elements described thus far, mention has been made of the importance of language and the development of a project language. Despite the many supporters of a definitive English language, words do not have absolute meaning (Aitchison, 1997) - that would require the omission of context. The meaning of words depends strongly on the context, i.e., the meaning of words depends upon its usage. Given our different mental models, our personal context, the same word will mean something slightly different. In effect, the words we each use determine what we 'see'. If, then, we all use words differently how can we convey our thoughts to others without a common comprehension of what the words mean? We can't, for sure. However, through word usage, through story telling for example, an appreciation of how individual team members use words and associate meaning with them can be developed (which in turn provides insight into their mental models). This is what is meant by a project language.

Consider the development of a causal map in a group environment. The concepts that are generated will have been discussed and debated over, and through this interaction a shared appreciation of what the concept means will be created. Once a map has been developed one cannot simply show it to another team and expect them to associate the same (quasi-consensual) meaning to the concepts. There will be tacit understanding that results from the familiar, and agreed, usage of the words that cannot be conveyed through the map alone.

The project language will be specific to the project. The language will evolve in the project context, thereby instilling a shared appreciation of the 'project space' within the project members. Having such a common, context-specific, language increases the chances that a communication between members of the project team is interpreted in the same, or very similar, way thus limiting misunderstandings. It also promotes coherent action. This is because the language would have been developed in the project setting and so the meaning associated with words would convey images and impressions that are project specific.

Obviously, not all words carry the ability to promote coherent action. It is important to recognize which words have the potential to shape thinking and actions. These are words, or memes, which:

- align with existing values and impressions within the team;
- recur frequently;
- resonate with the situation and the context;
- create meaning.

Language and word choice form a manager's primary tool. At the lofty heights of grand strategy, Phil Conduit of Boeing recognized this. In the most recent reorganization he suggested banning certain words and encouraging others - as a means of helping to reshape the ecology of Boeing's workplace. Disney does it by insisting that its customers are 'guests' and that its employees are all 'hosts'. AOL does it by having 'members' not customers. In brief, words can seem like little things, but they are the vehicles for both transmitting and shaping our thoughts. Thoughts in turn breed actions. Coherent actions demand a context, which is itself coherent. Words, in this context, have the power to drive such coherent actions.

Now that we have considered the ten basic building blocks necessary to drive coherent actions within a project environment, we need a unifying framework that brings these blocks together.

The five steps

There are five simple steps that utilise the ten building blocks described above and are key to realizing the 'next common sense' in any project environment. They are:

1. Identify yourself and your goals;
2. Use the right language;
3. Create the right context;
4. Turn people loose and then get out of the way, and;
5. Use communication that works.

It is important to realize that these steps come as a package. For example, leaving out the final, communication, step is an invitation for an initially coherent program to dissolve into incoherence. The team members that were turned loose in step four may well have very different destination in mind and, without communication among them, will go in different directions. So, none of the steps can be omitted completely, but the effort expended in taking individual steps will vary from project to project. It is also important to recognize that once a step is taken it will be necessary to take it again at some other point in the project life cycle. For example, as the context changes, so individuals' identities will need to be reviewed which may result in amendments to the project language.

An inability to take these steps and review their status must be seen as a risk to the successful completion of the project. Of great benefit to the project manager is that the leadership is in some way distributed. Having confident team members, and an interactive environment, mean that the team will learn to recognize for itself the need to take a step back. In order for this mode of operation to be successful the role of manager as facilitator, rather than 'God-father', becomes central. The idea that the project manager is the 'boss', 'senior person', 'technical lead', etc. is outdated. Of course this may be one role, but the project manager's main job is to make things flow. More and more, project management is about coordination and facilitation not direction and control. 'Project manager' is a *role* not a *rank*. A project manager could be the most junior person on the team. The key is that all team members must respect the authority of the *role*. As an example, if a junior project manager asks a senior technical officer to switch tasks, he / she must do so.

In the previous section we presented and discussed, in the context of project management, a framework that facilitates the coherent management of complex projects. In the following section we will revisit each the constituent components of the espoused framework in developing a case for the potential role of group decision support in coherent project management.

The role of group decision support in coherent project management

The premise of this section is simple. Interaction and exploration are vital in modern management endeavours, group decision support (GDS) tools are based upon these same two concepts, and so GDS tools, by definition, should be an effective tool in the struggle to coherently manage complex projects.

After a brief introduction to what participative decision support tools are and their mode of application, their potential contribution to each of the ten building blocks will be discussed in an attempt to support the chapter's premise. A secondary aim of the chapter is to add to the body of literature concerning the GDS techniques and technologies. More than a dozen years of research in the lab and in the field have shown that GDS can substantially improve group productivity. There are now several thousand GDS installations worldwide, and that number is growing, but GDS has not yet achieved a mass market (Briggs, *et al.* 1998). This may simply be through a lack of awareness concerning the existence of such methods. It might be a reluctance to accept the paradigm-shift as real and necessary, in which case many might find it hard to class such techniques as 'scientific' and therefore be unprepared to take the plunge. Whatever the reasons, it is hoped that this chapter will add to the growing literature supporting the use of such approaches.

What is group decision support?

Group decision support systems

Group decision support systems (GDSS) facilitate the sharing of information and expertise to improve the quality of group decision making. The full benefits of such approaches accrue in decision-making contexts where the problem situation is 'messy'. One of the most pervasive characteristics of messy problems is that people hold entirely different views on: a. whether there is a problem, and if they agree there is, and; b. what the problem is. In that sense messy problems are quite intangible and as a result various authors (see for example Checkland & Scholes, 1990) have suggested that there are no 'objective' problems, only situations defined as problems by people. Given the increasing complexity of the project teams and their operating environment more and more decisions of this type arise. These varying perceptions of whether a problem might or might not exist, and what might constitute the problem, derive from the different mental models each project member is endowed with. Indeed, the starting point of any group decision analysis will be based on the different perceptions of the participants. We have already stated that the use of GDSS facilitates the sharing of information and expertise. Another way of stating this is that GDSS systematically elicits and shares mental models within teams - with the aim of developing a 'negotiated reality' as a basis for decision-making. The underlying assumption being that this interactive process will inevitably lead to better decision-making, as the problem space would be better explored and the participants would buy into the decision resulting in greater success for decision implementation.

Working in team environments is not always easy, and is not always effective. For instance, the team members may simply follow the lead of the senior member (*conformance*), or the team members may be more concerned with reaching agreement than with the quality of the final decision (a process known as *groupthink* - refer to Janis, 1982). GDS researchers claim that GDSS overcome these limiting factors (Vennix, 1996), and in so doing contribute significantly to the value of group decision exercises. Figure 1 summarizes both the potential losses and gains to the group decision process that result from the use of GDSS. The numbers in Figure 1 identify the GDSS features that prior research suggests contribute to increasing (numbers enclosed in parentheses) or decreasing (numbers enclosed in brackets) the specific processing gains and losses.

Figure 2 illustrates a 'typical' GDS intervention. A group of decision-makers (e.g., members of a project team needing to adopt a key supplier) are gathered together, either physically or, via technology, virtually. They are supplied with a facilitator who manages that decision making process for the group, but (generally) does not contribute to the content of the decision. At various stages of the intervention, the decision-makers are asked to contribute to an evolving group database that, over time, begins to define the problems and their solutions. For example, as an initial task, the group might use a networked

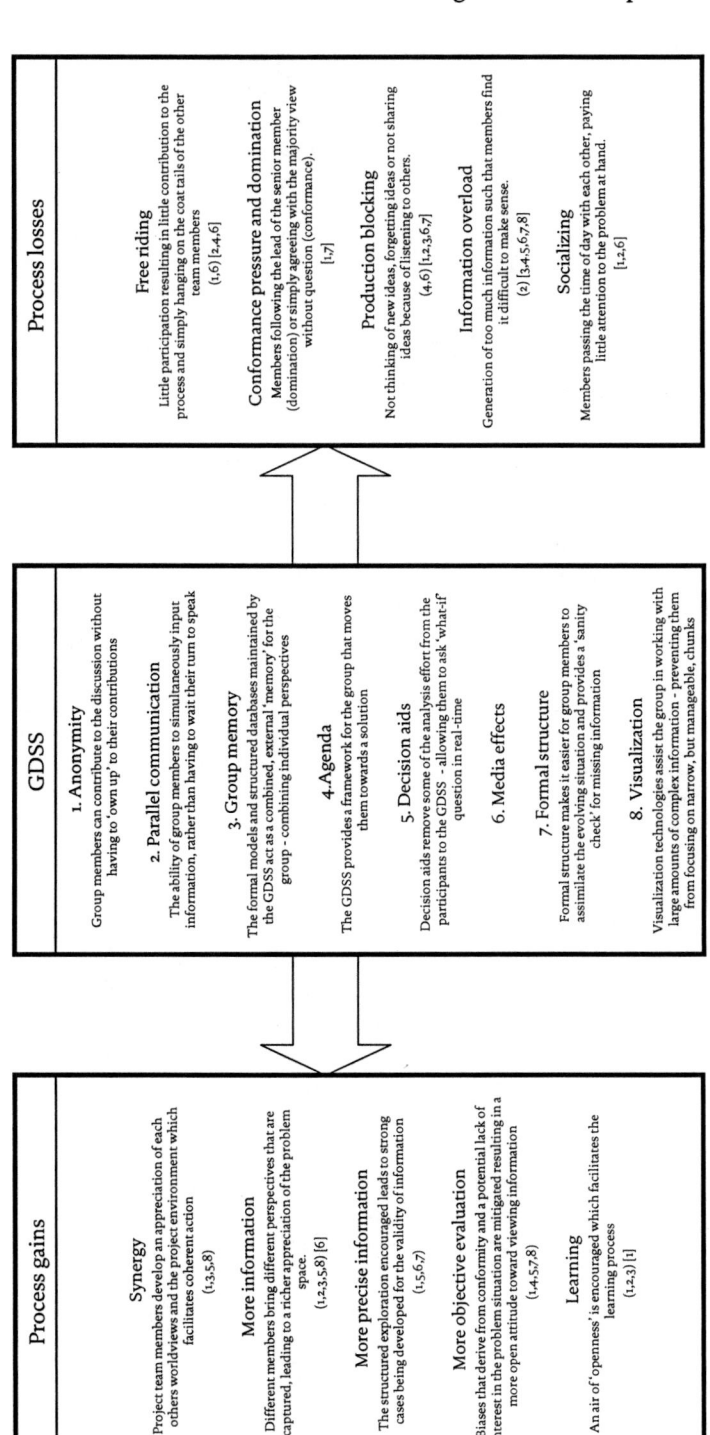

Figure 1
GDSS features
(Adapted from J. Nunamaker, Jnr, *et al.* 1993)

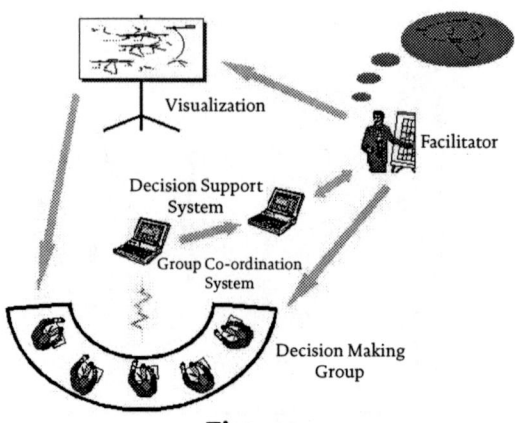

Figure 2
The GDSS process

computer system to brainstorm the key issues currently confronting their organization. This information would be collected by the facilitator (in real time) and given a rudimentary structure (e.g., encoded as an interrelated map of ideas), potentially using a specialized decision support system linked to the database. The facilitator's initial attempts at structuring the information would then be relayed to the group, via interactive visualization technologies and restructured to reflect the group's own understanding of the situation. The group would then use this understanding in the next stage of the process (e.g., evaluation of priorities).

The crux of the GDS approach lies not in the, often impressive, technology, but in the way the decision process is managed. GDSS allows a group to document and manage the complexity of its situation. This complexity can often paralyze a group into inaction, or lead it to continually revisit the same issues in a frustrating re-enactment of (the film) *Groundhog Day*. Successful systems encourage groups to interact with the information they are creating, altering it and questioning assumptions as they move towards an enhanced understanding of the situation. Rather than leaving key parts of the puzzle in the heads of individuals GDSS elicits that information, structures it and presents in a manner that allows groups to work with the full complexity of the problem - as opposed to oversimplifying it into unreal, but manageable, chunks.

GDSS provides a suite of powerful tools to assist groups making decisions in a complex environment - all designed to aid understanding and exploration, rather than produce formulaic 'answers'. Some of these tools include: electronic brainstorming; idea mapping; electronic voting; interactive simulation models; cluster mapping; interactive questionnaires and; conflict identification and resolution systems. With all these tools at their disposal, facilitators can approach a problem from multiple angles - often widening the perspectives of the decision-makers in the process.

Virtual communities

One of the most exciting developments in the area of global team working is the rise of the virtual community concept. Virtual communities have grown out of the explosive growth in the use of the Internet. Like so many Internet-based initiatives, society has stolen a march on 'big business'. Many have advocated this global communications framework as the vehicle upon which to build a new organizational model. However, while companies have harnessed its power as an information delivery and communications mechanism, they have singularly failed to harness its infinitely more potent potential as a knowledge creation tool. Meanwhile, community organizations like The Motley Fool have become big businesses by being able to nurture online communities.

A virtual community is an online meeting and collaboration space, where individuals can identify common interests, share ideas and collectively solve problems. Newsgroups are a simple, but extremely effective, example of a virtual community in action. More sophisticated systems have been developed for specialized areas. For example, The Motley Fool focuses on financial information and includes articles on personal investment, assessments of investment opportunities and private areas where groups can set up their own global 'investment clubs'.

Virtual communities may provide the mechanism for the new organizational model that Internet advocates have been predicating for the past few years. A virtual community can be used to create organizations based on the complexity principles advocated by modern organizational theorists (see for example, Baskin, 1998; Haeckel, 1999). Rather than applying isolated complexity concepts to outmoded organizations (as tends to happen), and watching as the 'innovative new idea' inevitably crumbles, virtual communities allow a complete, parallel, complexity-based organization to be overlaid on the existing organizational structures.

The virtual community concept presents a particular opportunity for the operation of project teams. Due to its independence from traditional organizational structures and geographical boundaries, it allows teams to be formed based solely on the profiles of individuals. Project managers no longer have to make do with local resources, truly global resources pools can be tapped for the smallest projects. Management thinkers, such as Handy (1996), have forecast an increase in the use of project teams comprised of independent, self-employed specialists - such as the model used in the film industry. Simultaneous forecasts for the rise in knowledge working suggest that tomorrow's successful organizations will be temporary affairs that can support efficient collaboration between the best expertise, wherever it is located. Virtual community technologies excel at such tasks.

Over the past few years, the GDS community has begun to see the potential of virtual communities as collaborative decision making environments. As a result, some of the most innovative GDSS now combine the formation of community with powerful analysis and visualization tools developed from years of organizational decision-making research. Such hybrid systems can tap vast reservoirs of global knowledge, over extended periods of time, and efficiently turn this vast knowledge base into enhanced organization understanding and timely, up-to-date, decisions.

In the remainder of this chapter, GDSS will be taken to refer to the wider class of group support facilities that includes virtual communities and associated technologies (such as online 'chat-rooms').

GDSS and coherent project management

The second half of this chapter will consider how the different attributes of the GDS process contribute to the ten building blocks that are seen as necessary components in the development of coherent project management strategies. The essence of each building block that was introduced in the first half of the chapter will be expressed, with further details being found in Lissack and Roos (1999).

GDSS and "Use simple guiding principles"

"Project management is complex enough without making it more so. The guiding principles that work are those that are aligned with basic values. Using guiding principles is much better in helping people work efficiently that having a 20-page prescription." The fundamental guiding principles in GDSS are exploration and interaction, and as expressed in the first half of this chapter, these key ingredients are essential in the process to develop coherent project management strategy. The group decision process could be utilized to explore further and assist in the identification of simple guiding principles. However, the guiding principles intrinsic to GDSS are very powerful in themselves. Rather than specifying the determined guiding principles, team members can experience the manifestations of adopting these principles through everyday use of GDSS. Given the previously reported successes of those who have taken advantage of GDSS for complex decision-making, the team would experience for themselves the benefits of working in such an interactive mode and buy into the underlying principles (consciously or sub-consciously). Through their continued use the simple guiding principles of exploration and interaction would become internalized as part of the individuals' mental models, encouraging each of them to carry these principles into other areas of their work where a GDSS might not be obviously employed. Experience has shown us that the individual may be unaware of this transition, but a change in behavior is instigated.

GDSS and "Respect mental models (and interact with them)"

"Each of us possesses a mental model that we employ to interpret our surroundings. These models are not static, but are amended and refined daily as we live our lives. Given that our personal history plays a central role in the details of this model it is not surprising that our personal models are unique. This means that when two people look from the same point in the same direction they will 'see' different things, sometimes entirely different." Generally, a mental model can be considered to be anything that helps an individual to answer questions, and a model can be seen to be good to the extent that one finds it useful for answering questions. We have already suggested that GDSS can affect the aspects of individuals' mental models that guide how they go about investigating a problem, but can it help to enable individuals to develop appreciations of their colleagues' mental models? Given that GDSS, an example being electronic brainstorming, encourages interaction and facilitates the visualization of the problem space, one would expect it to be invaluable in helping each member develop such an appreciation.

A major selling point, though, of GDSS is that contributions to the analysis are anonymous. Anonymity mitigates the effects of free riding, conformance pressure and domination, but at the same time it prevents the source of the contributions from being known. This can hinder the direct sharing of opinions that would yield insight into the contributors' perspective. This in turn would affect 'group memory' or the group's mental model. However, without the anonymity feature a very relaxed and open atmosphere would already have to exist within a team so that free riding, conformance pressure, and domination were not important issues. There exists the potential for trade-off. Is awareness of individuals' mental models more important than overcoming negative group processes which limit problem exploration? The answer to this is not black and white, like most answers to many questions concerning complex problems. In some teams continued practice of the simple guiding principles encourages an atmosphere in which anonymity is no longer necessary. Of course, debating the value of different concepts and how they might relate to each other will draw out the opinions of individual contributors so all is not lost, even in quite dysfunctional teams.

GDSS and "Use landscape images"

"The increasingly complex environment in which project teams operate, makes deciding what action to take, and when, problematic. What is needed is the means to recognize patterns in our complex environment to facilitate the decision-making process. The 'means' comes in the form of an interface that can be used to take advantage of our considerable pattern recognition skills." GDSS can form an integral part of this interface. For example, the development of a qualitative system dynamics model (influence diagram, or causal map) within a group setting, which is an effective way of synthesizing the project members' different perspectives, will facilitate the visualization of the problem space, which will enable coherent manoeuvring within the project 'landscape'. Furthermore, quantitative system dynamics modelling will provide further input into the development of the operating landscape by allowing real-time investigations into how the landscape might evolve in response to the implementation of different project strategies.

It is important to be aware of how the different elements of a GDSS bind the exploration of the landscape, and not to become too dependent upon one approach.

GDSS and *"Combine and recombine"*

"There has been much written in the management literature suggesting that operation within a complex environment requires holistic thinking, as opposed to reductionist thinking. This perspective is valuable (and synthesizing the different perspectives of the project team will result in a more 'complete' picture), but it is not the be all and end all." Sometimes, in simply reorganizing the elements that make up the current perspective, new, and potentially valuable, interpretations of the 'landscape' are uncovered. Most of the GDSS available provide a facility to visualize the problem space, also providing a variety of powerful tools to manipulate the representation to allow viewing from different positions. The ability to identify leverage points, potent concepts, and hiersets, etc. are central features of the Group Decision Explorer tool, for example. GDSS is very much attuned to assisting in the identification of what makes up the 'whole' and how those parts interact with each other by encouraging both bottom-up and top-down perspectives in the development of the 'landscape'.

GDSS and *"Recognize your multiple roles, don't hide from them"*

"In the modern organization the identity of each individual is written out explicitly in the company's operating procedures, along with the roles and responsibilities that the identity should be associated with. For instance, in a project team there might be the Project Manager, Quality Manager, Technical Manager, Project Secretary, Technical Support, Subject Matter Expert, and so on." The problem with such distinct, and unchanging identities, is that context is pre-defined, i.e., the rules of engagement are determined beforehand not taking into account local conditions. As with most teams the roles and responsibilities, though initially based on the company 'operating plan', evolve as the team evolves so the recognition of multiple roles will inevitably occur. To allow this evolution to occur team members must feel comfortable about stepping over the boundaries described by their formal job description. This can help lever creativity that would be otherwise suppressed through the detailed definition of roles and responsibilities. Although GDSS does not explicitly address such issues (though the generation of the project 'landscape' may shed light on the importance of members' role(s)), the spirit of exploration and interaction endorsed will encourage an atmosphere in which members will feel comfortable in exploring the boundaries of their own roles. GDSSs also tend to normalize roles (for the duration of the activity). For example, everyone has an equal voice. The process itself tends to pull people out of their role for a short period - introducing a new perspective to them.

GDSS and "Create canyons, not canals"

"The need for a level of team member freedom in order to endow the team, not only with the flexibility necessary to adapt to changing requirements, but also with the inquisitiveness to explore their surroundings, is essential when operating as part of a complex project. This inquisitiveness contributes to the successful development of a coherent strategy, and also enables the team to pre-empt changes to the strategy as necessary. It is difficult, if not impossible, to build such features into the fabric of the project team through the application of extensive procedures." The whole underlying philosophy of GDSS has developed to support such requirements. Not only are previously untapped sources of creativity levered by addressing and reversing many of the negative performance features of project teams, but they also provide a structured way of exploring the complex problem space. GDSS very much supports the creation of canyons by not placing rigid boundaries around the team. (Indeed, GDSS could itself actually be regarded as a canyon as its processes and technology provide a framework in which the team charts its direction). Naturally, the team's endeavours are bounded by the GDS paradigm but this is a very large 'space' to traverse. If the GDSS being employed is used appropriately then any limitations defined by the tool will be uncovered, and the team can, informed by their already developed understanding of the situation, look elsewhere for the necessary support.

GDSS and "Tell stories"

"Telling stories is about allowing others the benefit of shared experiences. Stories allow others to relate to fact, context, emotion, and to bring their own interpretation to what they hear or read. This richer mode of interaction also enables others to develop insight into how an individual sees the world, and in what contexts they use certain words." In some ways the computer-based GDSS can limit the telling of stories by reducing 'socializing' within the team, which is seen as a negative attribute, and by channelling much communication (at least during the early stages of process of decision-making) through the technology. Telling stories plays an important part in the creation of a cohesive (or synergic) team. The stories not only convey important information regarding the problem space, but also allow others to sympathise with the storyteller's perspective and appreciate how the storyteller uses language (which will mitigate the chances of misunderstanding and conflict when members interact). During the debating stage of group decision-making, stories concerning relevant experiences can be important in legitimizing certain concepts and relations that might have been proposed during the brainstorming session. GDSS by no means wholly prevents story telling, and the process can certainly benefit from the telling of stories. It is up to the facilitator to judge whether the story is 'valuable', or whether it is simply causing the team to defocus.

In actual fact, the 'lack of direct communication' problem arises mainly from an overly technological mindset on the part of the GDSS designers or operators. Just because its technology, it does not follow that computer experts are needed to use it. When GDSS gets in the way of telling stories it is generally the result of misuse or misdesign.

GDSS and "Send out scouting parties"

"In order to remain coherent the team must have a clear understanding of what is going on in its environment, and how different events might affect the team's operations. It is arrogant to believe that the team knows everything there is to know about the subject matter it is working on, customer politics, etc. By sending out scouting parties to probe the environment, vital stories might be found that would be of great value to the team in achieving its goals." One of the great benefits of GDS is that it quickly highlights areas where a group's knowledge is too weak to make an accurate decision. By structuring the issues faced by an organization, and the strategies required to tackle these issues, visualization tools can be used to accurately pinpoint missing information. This provides an agenda for a team's scouts. Ideally, scouting parties would be given a completely open agenda, ensuring that they do not focus on certain issues prematurely. However, the temporal and financial constraints of business life often make this an unrealistic ideal. By focusing the scouting activity, GDS maximizes the benefit of this investment.

GDSS documents the ongoing decision process within a group and sets up a dialogue between the project group and this documented understanding. When scouts report back to the group, their insights can be fed directly into the group's evolving 'organizational memory', allowing them to be assimilated by the other group members. In addition, the information obtained by the scouts is unlikely to be neatly packaged. They will have ill-defined experiences and perceptions, just as the decision-makers have of their own organization. The GDS framework will assist in extracting this tacit knowledge and determining what is of value to current requirements.

Finally, virtual communities can be used to provide vast numbers of scouts who report on a regular basis. As virtual communities make it easy for many individuals to participate in a project (by allowing multiple simultaneous communications channels and removing geographical barriers) an extended project team can be recruited, comprised of anyone who may have useful information to contribute. One example of this approach is the formation of an industry discussion group associated with a given project, where people from different organizations meet to swap ideas. Such groups are time consuming to operate in practice - not least because they require regular meetings to be organized. Virtual discussion groups operate continuously, with minimum maintenance, and support collaboration between hundreds of individuals. Each member of this group effectively becomes part of the project team, surveying the environment for pertinent information.

GDSS and "Post and attend to road signs"

"No project team will maintain coherence if the varied contributions of its members and of the team itself are not recognized with sufficient attendant notice such that the members involved can develop pride with regard to their activities. Such acts of recognition and notice function as 'road signs' within a community or housing development. Not only do such signs allow for recognition, but they also allow for meaningful directions to be communicated to others who are not part of the team."

One of the concerns often voiced about GDSS is their anonymity. This allows individual members of a team to express their true feelings without fear of reprisals. However, this strength can become a weakness when people want to be recognized for their contribution. Criticisms of this kind, however, tend to be based on a misunderstanding of the practice of GDS. Those who contribute key ideas tend to explicitly note the fact that it is their idea - either verbally or though the use of the technology used to support the team.

In fact, GDSS tends to reinforce the contribution of individuals by clarifying the role of the project and the individuals' activities within it. By helping to nurture a team memory, or negotiated reality, each person's role is unambiguously recognized across the team, and the significance of his / her assigned tasks is explicitly mapped back to the success of the entire project. This reduces the potential for others to downplay the activities of an individual. If they do not agree with the task, which was explicitly documented by the GDS exercise, why did they not bring it up at the time?

Many GDS approaches begin by placing the project in context, i.e., determining how it supports the wider organizational goals. This context is essential in providing a full understanding of the project. As a by-product of this process, individuals can trace the benefits of their activities through to the goals of the wider organization. This allows these individuals to demonstrate their worth to the organization and, as a result, senior management.

GDSS and "Use aligned words to fuel coherence"

"In a number of the elements described thus far, mention has been made of the importance of language and the development of a project language. Despite the many supporters of a definitive English language, words do not have absolute meaning – which would require the omission of context. The meaning of words depends strongly on the context, i.e., the meaning of words depends upon usage. Given our different mental models, our personal context, the same word will mean something slightly different. In effect, the words we each use determine what we 'see'. If, then, we all use words differently, how can we convey our thoughts to others without a common comprehension of what the words mean? We can't. However, through word usage, through story telling for example, an appreciation of how individual team members use words and associate meaning with them can be developed (which in turn provides insight into their mental models). We call this a project language." This language acts as a shorthand for the team, relieving the members of the need to provide complicated explanations to each other, and helping to develop a unique team culture. Anyone who has ever worked in a military environment will recognize the role of acronyms in developing an efficient, if exclusive, organizational language.

As with posting road signs, the focus of GDSS on the development of a common team mental model provides the basis for a shared vocabulary. In fact, the technical terminology of a given GDS process can help to form part of that vocabulary. An obvious example is in scenario planning, where a team is asked to define a set of 3-4 scenarios which represent possible future environments in which the team may have to operate. Each of these scenarios is purposely given a snappy, memorable title so that the group can integrate the scenarios into their everyday language. The titles are given their meaning by the group, from the shared process of constructing the various scenarios. In another example, taken from a GDSS used by one of the authors, ideas generated by the group have associated numbers that allow them to be quickly referenced by the software. These ideas have no meaning beyond this housekeeping activity. However, groups quickly adopt the numbers as a team vocabulary and months after a GDS session can be heard asking, "How are we doing on 67?"

Summary and conclusions

This chapter has attempted to open up a debate about the role of GDSS (and virtual communities) in the coherent management of complex projects. It has argued that modern projects are complex environments and introduced ten building blocks that are important facets in the successful management of complex project. It was then argued that GDSS can assist in the application of each of these building blocks.

Perceptual Control Theory suggests that projects can be viewed as 'control' hierarchies. "In a control system hierarchy ... the higher systems, rather than telling the lower ones how to act, tell the lower systems what to perceive. It is up to the lower systems to produce whatever actions are required to make the real perception match the reference perception. This means that the higher systems don't have to plan what to do in the case of disturbances; the lower systems will do so without being told if they can, and will notify the higher systems if they cannot" (Powers, 1998). The higher systems function to alter the reference perceptions. Management consists of guiding what team members perceive rather than instructing them on how to act. The ten building blocks, supported by GDSS, function as an effective means of providing such guidance and of providing the monitoring system for when actions at lower levels are not aligned with reference perceptions. While there is little proof, to date, that control hierarchies function better than command and control hierarchies, the many documented failures of the latter suggest that in the face of complexity something different is needed.

Projects will continue to become more complex. The march of technology, and its influence on global financial and business activities will ensure that this is the case. Society is also evolving, leading to significant changes in the way we work. If managers continue to use traditional project management processes, these societal changes will compound the complexity they face. Only by adopting new participative and exploratory project management practices will it be possible to effectively manage the projects of the future.

The challenge falls on two sides. GDS researchers and practitioners must turn their attention to providing ongoing support to project teams. For too long have they focused on, arguably more glamorous, 'one-off' strategic decisions. Project teams need processes and systems that are easy to set up and maintain over extended periods of time. Conversely, project teams need to adopt group decision technologies in managing their projects. The tools already exist to allow them to manage more effectively. Teams need to become less focused on predictive, command and control approaches and adopt the flexible, exploratory (and sometimes scary) approaches necessitated by the complex environment they now face.

References

Aitchison, J. (1997). *The Language Web: The Power and Problem of Words*, Cambridge University Press.

Baccarini, D. (1996). "The Concept of Project Complexity: A Review," *International Journal of Project Management*, 14: 201-204.

Baskin, K. (1998). *Corporate DNA: Learning from Life*, Butterworth Heinemann.

Briggs, R. O., Mittleman, D. D., Weinstein, N., Nunamaker, J. F. and Adkins, M. E. (1998). "Collaborative Technology for the Sea-Based Warfighter: A Field Study of GSS Adoption and Diffusion," *proceedings of the 31st Annual Hawaii International Conference on System Sciences*, Hawaii.

Browne, M. N. and Keeley, S. M. (1998). *Asking the Right Questions: A Guide to Critical Thinking*, Prentice Hall.

Checkland, P. and Scholes, J. (1990). *Soft Systems Methodology in Action*, Wiley.

Gardner, H. (1993). *Frames of Mind: The Theory of Multiple Intelligences*, Fontana Press.

Haeckel, S. H. (1999). *Adaptive Enterprises: Creating and Leading Sense-and-Response Organizations*, Harvard Business School Press.

Handy, C. (1996). *Beyond Certainty: The Changing Worlds of Organizations*, Harvard Business School Press.

Janis, I. L. (1982). *Groupthink: A Psychological Study of Foreign-policy Decisions and Fiascoes*, Houghton Mifflin Company, 2nd Edition.

Jung, C. G. (1958). *The Undiscovered Self*, Penguin Books.

Kuhn, T. S. (1996). *The Structure of Scientific Revolutions*, University of Chicago Press, 3rd Edition.

Lissack, M. R. and Roos, J. (1999). *The Next Common Sense*, Nicholas Brealey Publishing.

Nunamaker, J., Dennis, A., Valacich, J., Vogel, D. and George, J. (1993). "Group Support Systems Research: Experience From the Lab and Field," in L. M. Jessup and J. S. Valacich (eds.), *Group Support Systems: New Perspectives*, Macmillan.

Powers, W. T. (1998). *Making Sense of Behavior: The Meaning of Control*, Benchmark Publications, pp. 40-41.

Rescher, N. (1998). *Complexity: A Philosophical Overview*, Transaction Publishers, pp. 9.

Skyttner, L. (1996). *General Systems Theory: An Introduction*, Macmillan Press Ltd.

Stewart, G. L., Manz, C. C. and Sims, H. P. (1999). *Team Work and Group Dynamics*, Wiley, pp. 10-11.

Vennix, J. A. M. (1996). *Group Model Building: Facilitating Team Learning Using System Dynamics*, Wiley.

Williams, T. M., Eden, C., Ackermann, F. and Tait, A. (1995). "Vicious Circles of Parallelism," *International Journal of Project Management*, 13: 151-155.

Williams, T. M. (1999). "The Need for New Paradigms for Complex Projects," *International Journal of Project Management*, 17: 269-273.

CHAPTER 26

THE COMPLEXITY OF COMPLEX SYSTEMS CONFERENCES: REFLEXIVITY AND WALKING THE TALK

Michael R. Lissack

Complexity conferences may be an ideal expression of what the study of complex systems is about: a 'collective' which in totality can only be properly approached as 'an ensemble' is sought to be 'understood' by an observer in a manner such that the resultant understanding can be communicated to others without the necessity of a repetition of the total experience. The very heterogeneity of the attendees of these conferences demands that boundaries, uncertainty, emergence, dialogue and context be carefully attended to if the conference is to be labeled a 'success' by the majority of those attending. Indeed, the feedback effects of models, labels, and stories about complex social systems mean that simple characterizations - often the heart and soul of conference organizing - will leave out much more than they will capture. What complexity theory teaches us, is to try and describe activity while being aware of the power of the 'weak signals'. Different degrees of abstraction, attention to different components of a system, are appropriate to our varying pragmatic goals and conceptual and computational abilities. Thus, complexity conferences demand many characterizations and their interweaving into complex stories before something actionable can be understood. At conferences, persons share complex structures of cognition, and relate to one another from their shared rhetorical circumstance. A successful conference is a conference, which has embraced the possibilities for emergence and attempted to create the affordances those possibilities require.

Managing Organizational Complexity: Philosophy, Theory, and Application
A Volume in: Managing the Complex, pages 459-472.
Copyright © 2005 by Information Age Publishing, Inc.
All rights of reproduction in any form reserved.
ISBN: 1-59311-319-6 (cloth), 1-59311-318-8 (paper)

Introduction

"We should view organizations as complex cognitive systems, made up of people who see and interpret the world around them, and who strive to create values which have meaning to them and coherence with the group. Our corporations are populated with individuals who are striving for meaning, trying to understand what the company is about and what they have to do to succeed. If we view organizations in this way, we must have an acute awareness of how we create meaning in our organizations, of the messages which are sent, the symbols which define our organizations, and the cues given by the policies and practices." (Gratton, 2000).

Conferences are a strange but ubiquitous form of organization. Temporary in nature, they bring together anywhere from dozens to thousands of attendees whose goals are to extract meaning in some form from the fleeting organization of which they are momentarily a part. Conferences are filled with signs and symbols, formality and informality, drama and ritual. Conferences are stage settings for displays of meaning. And, often, for its lack. This chapter examines a subset of conferences - those claiming some link with complex systems - but its observations and conclusions are not limited to that subset. In many ways the 'beast' we label a 'conference' displays species behavior regardless of its particular form of embodiment or instantiation. Complex systems conferences are distinguished by their topic perhaps but seldom by the behavior which occurs in their temporary environment.

During the past decade I have attended perhaps thirty conferences whose stated aim was to explore the world of complex systems. Many of these conferences were held with a complexity oriented title by groups which attempt to address and discuss complexity as part of their regular practice. The setting is usually a prominent academic institution. The gatherings are often billed as a 'unique' opportunity for hard and soft scientists to engage in significant dialogue and are advertised as being full of 'meaningful contributions' from both groups as well as from the 'lay' people in attendance. The design of the meeting - the program, the interactions amongst speakers, and the physical setting - has much to do with this 'potential' being realized. Unfortunately oft times much too much is left to 'self -organize', environments are non-accommodating (both physically and structurally), or the organizers have 'over-structured' such that no free time is available for informal dialogue. In the absence of meaningful boundaries and a supportive environment, self organization is unlikely to be fruitful. In the presence of too much structure (be it physical, organizational, emotional, or content driven) the opportunities for self organization are illusory.

A retrospective study of these gatherings suggests that they are themselves an ideal expression of what the study of complex systems is about: a 'collective' which in totality can only be properly approached as 'an ensemble' is sought to be 'understood' by an observer in a manner such that the resultant understanding can be communicated to others without the necessity of a repetition of the total experience. An effective conference is one where emergence happens - where something new (be it learning, relationships, communication, ideas) is a byproduct of the interactions of the ensemble. (Notice that this method of evaluation is not limited to complex systems conferences but applies to most forms of gatherings). The goal of a retrospective study of these conferences would be to explore what it is about them which allows / fosters / guides / helps such emergence to occur. The study must also ask: can the emergence be ensured or caused or self-organized?

The ensemble that is in existence at a complex systems conference is more than just the individual attendees. It includes the environment for the meeting and the sub-meetings, the manner by which interactions are facilitated or structured, the goals of the attendees and the organizers, the content of material presented formally and informally at the meetings, the history (both actively attended to and the unattended to) of the participants, of their many interactions, and of their knowledge bases and memory thereof. Boundaries and their lack, semiotic systems and their display, the wide range of human emotions - all are present in the environment temporarily summoned into existence by the conference. Conferences are complex systems and the totality of the system is resistant to compression or dimensionality reduction. What follows is in the spirit of 'what can we learn from this' both with regard to conferences and with regard to complex systems.

Findings

The findings below are those of an only semi-detached observer - the present author. They do not purport to represent a scientific 'measurement' of the world of complexity conferences.

Complexity conferences, despite their chosen topic, are not all that distinguishable from the typical academic gathering. Some are run as very closed lectures-only events with informal gatherings restricted to meals and 'unofficial' time. Others are run as 'open space' events with no fixed agendas other than the very rules of 'open space' itself. If there is any lesson these conferences have in common it is that too much of anything (be it lectures, open space, creativity exercises, or coffee) is not a good thing. One does not need the study of complex systems to be aware of the value of moderation, but taking a complex systems approach does allow one to see some of the many facets of the ensemble at work.

Most books on management are constructed around a particular point of view. So too are most conferences. Whether deliberate or not, the implication of developing such single perspective theories is that there does in fact exist some all-embracing theory of management that can be applied globally to all management issues. Complexity conferences (especially when organized from a quantitative perspective) all too often fall into this trap. In an alternative view, organizations can be viewed as systems of interpretation and constructions of reality (Berger & Luckmann, 1967). In order to survive, organizations must find ways to interpret events so as to stabilize their environments and try to make them more predictable; organizations must also find ways to interpret events so as to be one with the environment, an environment that they choose. In conference terms, this alternative suggests that the complex systems, which are the study object of the complexity conference, include the conferees, their backgrounds, and their interactions. From this perspective, the conference is about making sense - though of *what* may differ radically from attendee to attendee.

Many organizers of complexity conferences mistakenly assume that a focus on 'hard methods' is a necessary component of any such conference. They look at academic approaches to business where models, analysis, and statistical research - the tools of hard sciences such as physics - are espoused as the tools of businessmen and infer a need for similar approach. Science uses such tools to reduce complexity in the objects of its study. What allows management academics to refer to their field as scientific is the reliance on models, on analysis, and on the compartmentalization of problems into smaller discrete units for study; the exact same tools and methods used traditionally in the natural sciences. There are many types of complexity, but science mainly deals with those complex problems that are amenable to formal simplifications. Not all complex problems can be so easily simplified however. Many problems resist such approaches; science, however, considers a particular set of problems which are relatively easily reduced. Easy problems, however, are not why conference attendees attend conferences. And so, to focus on methods which work with easily 'simplified' problems is to miss what might of most interest to the attendees.

Consider if you will Henry Mintzberg's classic comment: "If you ask managers what they do, they will most likely tell you that they plan, organize, coordinate and control. Then watch what they do. Don't be surprised if you can't relate what you see to those four words." If organizing is an emergent social process of discussion (as Mintzberg has recorded), then its point of departure is its interactive processes and not any first principle or basic managerial thesis of action. What one should do, see, understand, or communicate are not governed by absolutes, but by the demands of the local situation rooted in an understanding of that situation's innate complexity. Conferences are a bringing together of many such local situations and as such are an interweaving of immense complexity. A 'successful conference' will provide opportunities for sensemaking with respect to the complexity brought to the conference by the participant.

In this manner a conference is echoing a tenet of organizational life. A central concern of organization science is that of understanding how people construct meaning and reality, and exploring how that enacted reality provides a context for action. When managers 'enact' the environment, they as Weick (1995) put it: "construct, rearrange, single out, and demolish many 'objective' features of their surroundings ... they unrandomize variables, insert vestiges of orderliness, and literally create their own constraints." Through this process of sensemaking and reality construction, people at a conference give meaning to the events and actions of the conference as it unfolds. Success may be measured against some predefined objective (if the conference is from the single theory perspective) or may be a socially constructed variable. Its definition will vary much as the conferences themselves vary. Despite these variances, organizers will often attempt a single perspective theory definition of 'success'. The measure might be quantity of attendees, quantity of papers presented, quality of attendees, ratio of practitioners to academics, amount of dollars grossed etc. It is the rare conference that adjusts its definition of success on the fly as the conference unfolds; the reverse holds true, however, for many conference attendees - what they hoped to gain and what they gained are often disparate.

The contrast between the desire for 'hard' discussion and 'hard results' and the rhetoric about *openness, emergence* and *self-organization* is itself a motif for many conferences. It is not that complexity conference organizers are unaware of the paradoxes which they embody in their conference designs. Instead, the contrasts are themselves turned into an object of study - though the reflexivity is rarely of the immediate conference environment at hand, but rather of the 'theoretical' conference with which many of the attendees are presumed to be familiar.

Conference organizers have the supposed advantage of many studies of how to do things at conferences. Common to many analyses of 'how to run a successful conference' are observation of two orthogonal dimensions of a participant number (low / high) and topical diversity (low / high). These dimensions then suggest to four general conference archetypes:

	Low Topic Diversity	High Topic Diversity
Many Participants	Academic Conference	Ecology
Few Participants	Workshop	Critical dialogue

Complexity conferences are no different and many examples exist drawn from the four archetypes. Conferences can range the gauntlet from a free form open space event (where the participants determine the agenda and the method of delivery and meeting on the fly in accordance with a small set of rules) to a tightly controlled event with speakers in the front of the room and no time for conversations marching through a tightly packed agenda. All too often, conference organizers believe that by making adjustments in accord with the archetypes above they can ensure the 'success' of their event. What the archetypes leave out, however, is the weak signals embodied by the rest of the ensemble: backgrounds, language use, expectations, historical interactions, etc. Thus, I am going to suggest a few more categories that might be considered (this list is not all inclusive).

Perhaps we should look at the nature of the conference environment and whether the participants are there to learn new material or deliver existing material to an audience.

	Deliver Existing Material	Learn New Material
Closed Environment	Lecture	How-To Seminar
Open Environment	Happening	Self Help Group

Or perhaps we should look at the background characteristics of the participants and the quantity (or depth) of their previous interactions.

	Same background	Differing backgrounds
Many Interactions	Tribe	City
Few Interactions	Labeled As a Group	Cacophony of Strangers

Or perhaps whether the participants are experts or novices and whether their focus is on quantitative material or qualitative.

	Quantitative Focus	Qualitative Focus
Expert Participants	Model Presentations	Critical Dialogue
Novice Participants	Receive Lecture	Metaphor Development

Each of these perspectives is important in looking what might happen at a given conference. Depending upon the goals of the organizers and the participants some aspects of any given cell might be more or less appropriate for a particular activity.

Conference organizers are thus faced with a lengthy series of choices as partially shown in Table 1.

The complexity conferences I have attended have ranged across the full range of these choices. What is worth pondering is the multitude of choices to be made and the inherent variety of possible outcomes.

Some choices do not work well together. For example, if the organizer's goal is to draw out generative thinking then organizing lectures in a closed environment to a set of experts who arrived thinking they were all going to have an opportunity to deliver presentations on their work is unlikely to be very effective. Similarly, organizing an open space workshop for a collection of novices who have no history of prior interactions and little common background is unlikely to lead to advances in group knowledge and competency.

Just because the stated topic is 'complex systems' does not mean that the organizers wish to recreate a complex system in the conference itself. As Henry Mintzberg remarked at one such event, "For a complexity conference, this is the most militaristic, linear, over-organized event I have ever been to."

Control style
- Controlled and managed by organizers
- Self-ordering among participants

Agenda
- Tightly managed to minimize what might go wrong or out of order
- Semi-permeable boundaries that create conditions for self organization

Information Sources
- Expert-driven lectures
- information flow among participants

Content
- Narrow specific content to each discipline
- Explore span or transcend disciplines

Segregation
- Keep learners and experts segregated
- Mix learners and experts

Finding Direction
- Meet pre-determined expectations; alignment is valued
- Explore a broad landscape that accepts diverse, unfolding interests; coherence is valued

Continuity
- Focus on shared values to provide stability
- Focus on differences to evoke new insights

Purpose
- Sharpen critical thinking and judgment
- Provide expert information
- Draw out generative thinking
- Connecting people

Defining Success
- Individual achievement and mastery;
- Group competency building
- Social sense-making in communities of practice;
- Creative advances

Table 1
Choices to Be Made In Conducting a 'Complexity Conference'
(Adapted from McCandless, 2003)

Perspective

The attendees at complex system conferences arrive with a high degree of heterogeneity regarding academic background, occupations, expectations, goals, and use of language. Boundaries, uncertainty, emergence, dialogue and context are more than just intellectual constructs floating through the written work of the complexity community. They get embodied and enacted in our daily activities. They demand respect. The very heterogeneity of the attendees demands that boundaries, uncertainty, emergence, dialogue and context be carefully attended to if the conference is to be labeled a 'success' by the majority of those attending.

Complex systems can only be adequately described, modeled, or characterized by other complex systems - anything else is merely a label, a facet, or a situated event of the system in question. This is especially true when we think about social systems. As Kurt Richardson (private correspondence) notes:

"*A major difference between social systems and natural systems is that natural systems generally don't behave differently just because we think about them differently. A good model is a good model because it reflects some essential aspects of reality to a degree that facilitates successful action. Social systems can be considered a non-trivial sum of all our models of them. Social reality is co-determined by our thoughts about social reality - this is not such a big deal (one might even go as far as to suggest that it is mostly an irrelevant concern) in physics.*"

The feedback effects of models, labels, and stories about complex social systems mean that simple characterizations will leave out much more than they will capture. Only will many such characterizations and their inter-weaving into complex stories can something actionable be understood.

When complex systems research supposedly reveals power laws, CA formulations, nk models, phase space attractors, managed chaos or other mathematical or statistical properties we need to recognize that these are themselves labels describing situated events or facets and are not the essential characteristics of the system. It may be interesting to know that Zipf's law can plot city size but that tells you little about any given city or their many comprising networks. It may be convenient to know that the social network of company G is a scale free network but you really need to know who is a critical node and what the effect will be of removing some of the 'at this time' critical people.

The complexity of complexity means that these labels are factors in a larger story and the skill to be learned from complexity research is to tease out enough labels and enough factors so as to tell a complex story about the complex system. The complex story need not be as complex as the system to convey enough of the systems character so as to educate the observer about system potentials. An understanding of the potentialities of the system rather than predictions of system state are the goal. Such understandings allow for considerations of robustness, interference, and constraints to have context and meaning. Roger Bradbury (2000) tells us: "We need to build a model complex adaptive system in order to model a complex adaptive system." Conferences about complex systems are such models. They demand a similar attention to the multi-level interweavings of the very subjects of their study: the field of complex systems and the interests and goals of the attendees.

Consider a typical well intentioned failure: One runs into the conference organizer a few hours before the start of the event - relaxed and looked totally unconcerned. It is of course dangerous for organizers to be prematurely relaxed. If you are an organizer and are relaxed several hours before your event is beginning: worry, something bad is likely to happen. Then one enters the conference hall to find a raised stage for the 'speakers', tables and chairs at a lower level for the 'participants', and a microphone where participants ere to go to address questions to the stage. The traditional academic conference model of all learning is broadcast from the stage is not a physical format which allows for and encourages interactions amongst the participants. Participants at a complexity conference are likely to be as interesting and knowledgeable as the 'speakers'. More serious problems are built into the conference schedule itself. A fabulous keynote speaker is not followed by interaction or dialogue but by a panel of unrelated speakers. Worse, the panel has not met before nor interacted, in the absence of any foreknowledge has nothing to say regarding the keynote, and their facilitator has never interacted with them prior to their arrival on stage. Dialogue and group interaction are restricted by both physical environment and the structure of the program. Complexity and emergence place a central role on loose coupling. If the conference environment and structure is tightly coupled there is limited room for emergence and an active suppression of complexity.

What the failed conference has not considered is the very heterogeneity which attracts its attendees and speakers. The ensemble of interests backgrounds and knowledge does not easily lend itself to compression - especially the compression implicit in the traditional academic conference format. The ensemble demands an environment which is supportive of participation. As Ashmos, *et al.* (2002) phrase it:

"Participation, as a social process, creates a platform such that self-organizing becomes an expression of organizational learning and sense making... Participation facilitates the creation of 'meaning', a collective sense of what is real and true... Enhancing connections, however, is potentially problematic for managers who have become accustomed to the search for the stability, predictability, and orderliness the machine-model of organizations promises. Encouraging connections can subject open systems to confusion, messiness and inter-agent conflict because connections increase the amount and complexity of information with which the agent must cope. Encouraging connections creates intra-agent conflict because it will require agents to cast aside the assumptions of the machine model that lie at the heart of many organizations; letting go of practices which, even if not entirely satisfactory, are at least familiar and habitual... Encouraging connections through participation is essentially an exercise in complexifying everyday life in an organization because it encourages people to enter unknown areas, unfamiliar roles, new patterns."

Take the conference failure outlined above. What could been done? The same keynote speakers could have been followed by one or two discussants who were familiar with the material. This could then have been followed by group discussion. The panelists could have exchanged their presentation materials with each other and with some discussants (whose job would have been to interject potential relevance into the dialogue). Written papers could have been distributed for our reading in advance rather than our being subjected to a series of 'readings'. Concepts of open space and dialogue could have been embraced rather than ignored.

Paradoxically what may work best sometimes is for the conference organizers to select attendees who will function well together given the remaining choices the organizers have made regarding goals, environment, topic, etc. rather than having the organizers adjust their expectations to fit the attendees. Indeed, the very notion of open space presumes that the attendees have a pre-existing commitment to the topic / problem space being explored and a commonality of backgrounds and language so as to minimize the amount of time and effort which must be spent correlating varying conceptions of meaning, words, symbols, and purpose. Workshops for experts to discuss nagging problems at the edges of theories are not the place to have more than a token amount of novices. Conferences intended to 'spread the word' about some idea metaphorically are unlikely to be the appropriate place to have large numbers of quantitatively oriented computer programmers.

What complexity theory teaches us, is to try and describe activity while being aware of the power of the 'weak signals'. The most 'powerful' factors (forces) are not always determinant, the results of action do not follow simple linear patterns. Organizations, even more than individuals, have the ability to make and remake the cognitive connections, which define and constrain their world (see for example Clark, 1993; Fodor, 2001; Horgan & Tienson, 1996; Macdonald, 1995.) Prigogine suggested that self-organization was really organization by a system, once in a container, i.e., for 'self' one should substitute 'self-contained' or 'constrained'. For organizations, as for brains, some aspects of the container are the attentions, affordances and cognitive connections, which they bring with them and are attuned to. Social interaction is a constantly changing process of emergence, wherein 'organizing' leads to an ever evolving situation of 'organization'. At conferences, persons share complex structures of cognition, and relate to one another from their shared rhetorical circumstance. A successful conference is a conference, which has embraced the possibilities for emergence and attempted to create the affordances those possibilities require.

This embrace itself is dependent upon an implicit or tacit understanding of the difference between treating the conference experience as a set of codes, semiotic signs whose meaning can be in some manner derived from a 'look-up' table, and treating it instead as an elaborate network of 'cues', semiotic signs whose meaning is not derived but rather experienced by the schemas, interpretations, stories and codes that the encounter at a given moment between the cue and the interpreter triggers. When one is bound by the first definition then success is in some way defined by the extent to which attendees have had successful decodings. Objective measurement purports to be possible because the efficacy of decodings is measurable. By contrast, in a conference world defined by the 'cuing' definition there is no comparable notion of efficacy and no objective standard to measure. The ability of a speaker to transmit meaningful signals which have been correctly decoded by the listeners has relevance in the first definition and only minor significance in the second. The old standard of 'a conference is successful if you have made one new acquaintance and had one new idea' has meaning in the second definition and little meaning in the first. It must be noted that many conferences are described by both organizers and attendees as being in a world bound by the first definition, while the very behavior of the attendees suggests at least a tacit understanding of functioning in a conference world better described by the second definition.

Contrast the failure, if you will, with a proven at least partial success, the *Managing the Complex* conference series. In the initial version of the series, participants were asked to write down on three index cards topics they wished to have discussed in breakout groups at the conference. Each breakout group was given wall spaces where the participants spent an hour posting and reshuffling the posted cards. The breakout groups then were 'self-organized' around common self-selected subjects. Later versions of the conferences substituted a company with a stated problem as the focus for each breakout group. In both instances the group activities relied on the idea of an underlying commonality.

If a group, be it the secretarial pool or a top management team or a conference breakout group, shares some basic views, it is the interactions among those group members which allows for the others to make sense of any particular individual's actions or statements of intellectual positions. This sensemaking will occur only if indeed the group members both share a set of views (on why they come to work each day, what their work is about, on competition, collaboration, or even the impact of e-commerce on their business) and if they see themselves as a group. Without both the group identity and the shared views, the sensemaking is usually absent. It is sensemaking that is the key to further action, and the feeling of empowerment ("I am able to act.") which often creates a 'successful' conference.

At the *Managing the Complex* series, the sensemaking procedures within the breakout groups followed amazingly similar paths. An initial effort to work top-down rationally from first managerial principles were discarded rapidly and procedures of rich description and analysis were embraced. The manager and academics present opted for 'storytelling' (see Baskin, this volume) when they wanted to understand and act on a concrete situation. The context set out by the storyteller will conjure up a new set of 'related ideas' in the minds of each listener. Meaning emerges from the combination of what the storyteller supplies and what the listener's mind now adds. Stories suggest new images, combinations of old and new ideas, and allow the listener to place him / herself in a simulacrum of related action. Meaningful stories are not made up of isolated words. They too must evoke deeply held values and images. To offer up isolated words is to evoke a shallow stream of water in a hot desert. Whatever value there is dries up quickly.

In management theory terms the breakout groups sought coherence as socially co-validated narratives of activity. If the group could fit the statement into its collective narrative of the organization (the group, the problem), the statement was accredited 'truth status'. 'Truth' was the growing consistent web of the story, wherein the elements seemed to 'fit'. The criteria for making the 'fit' were periodically reviewed and examined. The ability of any particular element of discussion to join in an ever more complexifying web with the rest, was constantly examined. The groups spontaneously adapted a cognitive concept of managing. That concept demanded an interaction between what the participants heard from those presenting as experts, the opportunity to engage in serious dialogue, time out for reflection, and the 'walk-away' of feeling newly empowered in some direction.

Keith McCandless (2003) reflected on three types of interactions at complexity conferences (one-to-many, many-to-many, and one-to-self) while commenting on one such success at a complexity conference run by the Plexus Institute and offered potential organizers this advice:

- try to balance the three primordial forms of learning [one-to-many, many-to-many, and one-to-self] - don't offer too much [one to many] content and expertise, it can block learning and overwhelm participants

- make formal use of messy [many-to-many] exchanges - making sense together will reveal better questions, local talent, unexpected momentum, and new frames for decision-making

- build-in [one-to-self] time to deepen experience and spark imagination - interweaving the arts and reflective pauses can be very effective learning elements that invigorate participants

- draw out more difference in perspective as the meeting unfolds - don't cover-up diverse views, they lead to novelty and insight

- seek out the BIG questions and curiosities in the room - don't worry about answering all the questions, they become worthy attractors for future exploration

- trust that the participants will makes sense of difference and complex content - believe in participants' resilience more than they believe in it themselves

- create ways to amplify emergent themes and build them into unfolding conversations - don't miss opportunities for transcendent learning-in-the-moment with the imaginations at hand

As Sandra Mitchell (2003) puts it, "The suggestion that our current best theories exactly capture the world in all its details is hubris. The idealized and partial character of our representations suggests that there will never be a single account that can do all the work of describing and explaining complex phenomena. Different degrees of abstraction, attention to different components of a system, are appropriate to our varying pragmatic goals and conceptual and computational abilities." The same holds true for conferences as well as for theories - there is no single 'best way' and the sum total of the environment will dictate what is a success to each attendee.

I end this piece with a minor rewrite of Carnap's analysis of the acceptance of different linguistic forms within science substituting the language of conferences:

The acceptance or rejection of particular conference methodologies, just as the acceptance or rejection of any other methodologies in any branch of science, will finally be decided by their efficiency as instruments, the ratio of the results achieved to the amount and complexity of the efforts required. To decree dogmatic prohibitions or endorsements of certain conferencing methods instead of testing them by their success or failure in practical use is worse than futile; it is positively harmful because it may obstruct scientific progress. The history of science shows examples of such prohibitions based on prejudices deriving from religious, mythological, metaphysical, or other irrational sources, which slowed up the developments for shorter or longer periods of time. Let us learn from the lessons of history. Let us grant to those who work in any special field of investigation the freedom to use any form of expression which seems useful to them; the work in the field will sooner or later lead to the elimination of those forms which have no useful function. Let us be cautious in making assertions and critical in examining them, but tolerant in permitting a variety of conferencing methodologies (Carnap, 1950).

Complexity demands no less and no more.

References

Ashmos, D. P., Duchon, D., McDaniel, R. R. and Huonker, J. W. (2002). "What a Mess! Participation as a Simple Managerial Rule to 'Complexify' Organization," *Journal of Management Studies*, 39(2): 189-206.

Berger, P. L. and Luckmann, T. (1967). *The Social Construction of Reality: A Treatise in the Sociology of Knowledge*, Anchor.

Bradbury R. (2000). "Futures, Prediction and Other Foolishness," Plenary address to the *Conference of the International Society of Ecological Economics* in Canberra on 8th July.

Carnap, R. (1950). "Empiricism, Semantics, and Ontology," *Revue Internationale de Philosophie*, 4: 20-40.

Clark, A. (1993). *Associative Engines*, Cambridge: MIT Press.

Fodor, J. (2001). *The Mind Doesn't Work That Way: The Scope and Limits of Computational Psychology*, Cambridge: MIT Press.

Gratton, L. (2000). *Living Strategy: Putting People at the Heart of Corporate Purpose*, London: Financial Times-Prentice Hall.

Horgan, T. and Tienson, J. (1996). *Connectionism and the Philosophy of Psychology*, Cambridge: MIT Press.

Macdonald, C. (ed.) (1995). *Connectionism: Debates on Psychological Explanation*, Oxford: Blackwell.

McCandless, K. (2003). A Primordial Pedagogy: Caves, Campfires and Watering Holes at the Mayo Clinic/Plexus Summit.

Mitchell, S. (2003). *Biological Complexity and Integrative Pluralism*, Cambridge University Press.

Weick, K. (1995). *Sensemaking in Organizations*, Beverly Hills, CA: Sage.

CHAPTER 27

PARAMETERS FOR SUSTAINED ORDERLY GROWTH IN LEARNING ORGANIZATIONS

James K. Horn

The new sciences of complexity seek to understand both qualitative and quantitative changes that occur in systems whose identities and adaptations emerge from self-instructed interactions of system components. This chapter offers an inside look at a learning organization based on self-production and emergent behavior, two aspects of complex human social systems that exhibit both stability and growth in the human components whose interactions sustain system boundaries. In the example offered here, four parameter values are identified as crucial for the sustained growth of learning organizations and the individuals that comprise them: support, challenge, openness, and integration. The mechanics and characteristics of this particular example are presented alongside theoretical considerations that continue to inform the empirical research for the new sciences of complexity.

Managing Organizational Complexity: Philosophy, Theory, and Application
A Volume in: Managing the Complex, pages 473-491.
Copyright © 2005 by Information Age Publishing, Inc.
All rights of reproduction in any form reserved.
ISBN: 1-59311-319-6 (cloth), 1-59311-318-8 (paper)

"...the spirit of re-creation which masters this earthly form loves most the pivoting point where you are no longer yourself."

- Rilke

Introduction

The potential value of complexity science to management practice will likely become a measure of how the study of autonomous, adaptive systems can contribute to the scientific understanding of the social systems we know as learning organizations, i.e., those social entities capable of interactions that generate and sustain internal order and transitions resonant with environmental conditions. The realization of this potential requires an expanded conceptualization of science to include, not only the understanding of measurable, quantitative changes based within established scientific law, but the understanding of qualitative changes in system behaviors that are contingent upon, yet not reducible to, the physical components that constitute them. It will be a new science that is as rigorously attentive to acknowledging, describing, and mapping emergent, or creative, properties of complex social networks as has been, historically, traditional sciences to predicting the causal linkages between physical changes in the world that lend themselves more readily to mathematical and statistical models.

While it is obvious that such a science does not yet entirely exist, there is a growing acknowledgement that traditional science, though strong in explaining the interactions or relations among objects, is severely limited in mapping the myriad patterns of change that emerge within learning organizations. Without a fully-developed scientific alternative, however, there remains a strong propensity to sustain the familiar, though inadequate, methodologies in studying how organizations order themselves and evolve. And though some have begun an active search for alternative ways to more fully understand organizational change, others remain reluctant explorers, sometimes experiencing a type of 'Cartesian anxiety' (Varela, *et al.*, 1991: 140) that results when the foundations of traditional science are seen as an insufficient fulcrum from which the world may be leveraged.

Providing a full background for this problem is far beyond the purview of this chapter, but it is here worth remembering that, indeed, the history of science reflects a very early capitulation in attempting to understand the dynamics of change "as having its own reality" (Packard, 1992):

"From the Greeks to the present - because science got tied up in deriving things from fundamental law - the idea of change as having its own reality got left by the wayside. There was an intellection bifurcation, and the creative aspects of the world became religious questions" (p. 97).

That long-standing bifurcation has yet to be mended. In fact, the development of the social sciences, with a justifiable impetus for understanding the mechanics of social change, has made the separation even more prominent. It is unfortunate that management science, too, in its relative infancy, has been prone to the *physics envy* (Gould, 1983) that historically moved social sciences toward mathematical and statistical methodologies more appropriate for generating explanations of physical phenomena. The result has been a reduction of the complex data arising from social phenomena to an *abstracted empiricism* (Mills, 1959) that can be depicted by the available mathematical treatments and probability formulae to resemble, at best, a crude type of experiential shorthand. The fact remains, unfortunately, that there is little in the standard repertoire of traditional science that allows for the understanding of change as emergent phenomena that signal transitions within social organizations.

For management scientists, then, the capacity for understanding the reasons for creative change within the organizations they study remains, ironically, beyond the purview of the empirical methods that sustain their search. If a methodology were contrived to study just the emergent behaviors that drive living systems toward continuing sustainability within a world increasingly complex, then actual management practices may come to resemble the commonly espoused theories (Argyris & Schön, 1992) of openness and autonomy that often mask more rigid practices that now become driven in circular fashion by a traditional science of prediction and control that, in turn, is used to justify such authoritarian practices as scientifically grounded.

A new science of change

Only recently have the emerging sciences of complexity (Wolfram, 2002) brought empirical credibility to the claim that fine-grained predictions of predefined outcomes based on external controls may be inappropriate expectations for managing learning organizations. This is particularly true in light of human organizational needs for autonomy, creative problem resolutions, and adaptability within changing economic, political, and cultural environments. Acknowledgement of this limitation now spawns empirical and theoretical research of organizational dynamics, and these investigations span a wide range of venues, from artificial life environments (Langton, *et al.*, 1992) to human learning organizations (von Foerster, 1984; Stacey, 1996; Senge, *et al.*, 1999; Axelrod & Cohen, 2000) - with many stops in between.

The potential benefits accruing from these new models, simulations, and theories generate exciting possibilities; for they offer legitimacy, i.e., a scientific basis, to the search for organizational paths that suggest an understandable and sustainable route to orderly organizational change. Rather than focusing on the traditional scientific goals of prediction and control, however, complexity sciences adopt, perhaps, a more challenging agenda of comprehending and explaining general laws of pattern formation (Waldrop, 1992) that are manifested in the transitional phases, or phase shifts, within autonomous systems. Concerned with pattern formation and the conditions that are likely to initiate changes in these formations, complexity researchers continue to study the dynamics that provide the markers for growth, change, or learning. In short, these new explorations are concerned with scientific understanding of phenomena that, heretofore, have been ignored for their scientific unmanageability.

Two compelling characteristics and persistent themes run through the growing body of complexity literature. One concerns the common feature of complex autonomous systems to maintain interaction levels at a poised equilibrium that are both ordered and flexible between stasis and chaos (Kauffman, 1995). The other concerns the self-producing mechanics of emergent behaviors exhibited by autonomous (Varela, 1979), or self-organizing (Thompson & Varela, 2001), systems. These will be examined in the following two sections.

Interaction levels for stability and growth

Observations regarding optimal parameters for stability and growth within autonomous systems have been studied by a number of researchers, including Stephen Wolfram, Norman Packard, and Chris Langton (Waldrop, 1992: 225-34). In experimenting with initial interaction parameters for the spawning and growth of self-organizing systems within the digital world of cellular automata, Langton discovered, through a glitch in his computer program, what he termed the *lambda parameter*. He found the lambda parameter to be a level of interaction on either side of a mid-point between no interactions and an avalanche of interactions among the components of the system. When interactions were absent, the cellular automata exhibited zero growth. When interactions were sparse, some coalescence was apparent, but soon the self-organizing dots on the computer grid coalesced into static blobs. When the interactions between components were extremely numerous, the computer grid became chaotic, with cycles of accelerated growth followed by mass extinctions. But when the parameter for interactions was established just before or slightly past the mid-point, the automata exhibited "coherent structures that propagated, grew, split apart, and recombined in wonderfully complex ways" (p. 226). This was the lambda parameter, the boundary condition that produced continued growth, transformation and, in computer science terms, maximum computation. What became most interesting to both Packard and Langton was the repeated tendency for these systems to experience growth, transformation, or phase transitions, and then to reorganize at the same point.

Sometimes referred to as the *edge of chaos* phenomenon (Langton, *et al.*, 1992), complex autonomous systems occupy a state that is neither static nor chaotic but, rather, characterized by a level of interactions poised between order and disorder. This kind of self-organizing and adaptive behavior signifies an interactive state that preserves the potential for growth of a system and its members that constitute its autonomy, while extending a level of order that sustains, and becomes sustained by, the interactions of those same components. The organizational space between order and disorder, or between order and stasis, represents a coherent field that is stable, yet sensitive to transitional shifts that further enhance growth within a state of poised equilibrium. As Stacey (1996: 72-106) concludes in his review of this artificial life research with adaptive feedback networks,

"... a system occupies the space of endless variety, novelty, and creativity only at critical points in parameter values with enough disorder to prevent the system from becoming trapped in some local equilibrium ... but also with sufficient containing structure and order to prevent it from falling apart into patternless behavior." (p. 99).

In terms of learning systems, we may view the edge of chaos phenomenon as a pivot point between the novel and the confirmatory, or we may choose to think in terms of a sensitively-poised stability balanced between openness and integration, between the centrifugal (open) and the centripetal (integrative) movements of learners interacting within human social systems. Kuppers (1990) notes that "the optimum of production of information may be presumed to lie at the point where there is as much novelty as possible and no more confirmation than is necessary" (p. 56). Though more difficult to locate perhaps, outside of Langton's self-organizing computer simulations, it is not difficult to imagine a learning organization that takes advantage of the matching capacity toward the openness and integration that signifies poised equilibrium. Such a history would reflect a harmonious, heightened awareness with growth and stability needs in balance, just as it would engender a robust efficiency, in that large infusions of energy would not be necessary to move the system from either a static or a chaotic regime. This learning history would be maintained by taking full advantage of the balanced boundaries of openness and integration that characterize autonomous, interactive learners; and it would be accomplished by offering the appropriate levels of support and challenge that are required to obtain, over time, the balance of openness and integration that assure continued novelty and confirmation. The art and science of managing would, then, involve the continuing adjustment of support and challenge to fit the shifting needs of learners, whose learning histories are defined by alternating movements between these divergent and convergent needs for openness and integration.

These dynamics of conservation and growth, of centripetal and centrifugal directedness, respectively, comprise the inhibitory and the expansionary aspects exhibited by social entities capable of autonomous, self-organizing behavior. From a management perspective, the central issue is how to establish and adjust parameters or organizational boundary conditions that act together to de-center, or challenge, the essentially conservative phenomenon that sustains an entity's "budget of flexibility" (Bateson, 1972), while offering a space of safety from within which to support the exploratory forays that signal the beginnings of new growth trails. Understanding the organizational dynamics that sustain such changes will be greatly enhanced if we are able to identify and study authentic attempts to bring forth such parameters or boundary conditions that are focused on creating organizational health through the sustained renewal of individual human components. Therefore, the identification and systematic study of sustained, orderly growth within organizations offers a clearer understanding of the conditions and control parameters (Stacey, 1996) that are necessarily in place as phase transitions occur. This, of course, does not allow leaders and managers to predict the exact timing, direction, or consequences of particular transitions, but it does offer valuable information regarding the identification and adjustment of critical control parameters for the likelihood that subsequent phase transitions will occur.

Emergence within autonomous systems

My own research (Horn, 1995, 1999) of complex, autonomous learning organizations has focused on individual growth within learning communities of K-12 educators, selected as Fellows for a five-week personal and professional development opportunity centered on interdisciplinary liberal arts learning within a non-traditional academic setting. Remembered by some as an 'academic boot camp' or as an 'Outward Bound for the mind', these residential institutes functioned as outreach efforts by the College of Liberal Arts of the University of Tennessee to trigger personal renewal and professional growth in the lives of the fortunate teachers selected to participate. These summer institutes were crafted to create collegial, interdisciplinary, and interactive learning communities that would re-invigorate the personal and professional lives of those receiving fellowships to attend. Known as the Stokely Institute for Liberal Arts Learning, hereafter referred to as Stokely, this renewal program brought together twenty teachers each summer from 1985 to 1994 to become "immersed in learning and scholarship" (Fellows Program, 1988: 7). During this time of intense study, interaction, and reflection, Stokely provided a broad range of activities that included plays, concerts, dinner parties, films, field trips, banquets, and visiting lecturers. These activities were in addition to the primary learning activity, a series of interdisciplinary seminars conducted in a collegial setting under the direction of three university teacher-scholars and based upon an intensive, challenging set of readings that bridged the natural sciences and the humanities.

As we examine a concrete example of autonomous learning systems, it is important to flesh out the second compelling feature of these systems to self-produce themselves from interactions within boundaries that are brought forth by those interactions. Even as the Stokely Institutes maintained the same sustaining boundaries of organizational relations, or relational space, among administrators, faculty, and Fellows as collegial forums for personal and professional growth, each Institute was unique, with new participants (structural components) and new sets of interactions that determined each year the "texture of the space" (Varela, 1979: 261) in which each Institute would operate. These learning communities, then, emerged as autonomous social entities formed of a relational space that shaped, while being shaped, by the unique interactions among the persons, texts, events, and ideas that constituted each Institute. Though this conception of circular causation originated in the studies of Maturana and Varela to understand the mechanics of biological origins (Maturana & Varela, 1980, 1987, 1998), I am using a similar conception here of reciprocal causation (Thompson & Varela, 2001) to signify the self-generation of systems based on structural interactions by components within an organizing boundary that enables the interactions that, in turn, sustain the "organizational closure" (Varela, 1979) of the defining boundary.

Though it may seem paradoxical to conceive of such open interaction systems as being characterized by organizational closure, it nonetheless remains an interlocking feature of this and other self-referential groups of individuals that constitute autonomous systems, biological or otherwise: "autonomous units can be constituted by any processes capable of engaging in organizational closure, whether molecular interactions, managerial manipulations, or conversational participation" (Varela, 1979: 269). In fact, change within an autonomous system (resulting from structural interactions of components) can only occur within organizational parameters whose constancy distinguishes that system as a specific unity. Within the organizational boundary (relational space) that characterizes or defines an autonomous system as itself rather than as something else, the structural components (in this case, Stokely Fellows) that reside within those boundaries engage in interactions that maintain system identity, while bringing about changes that remain consistent with, but unspecified by, the larger environment.

The organizational closure of autonomous systems may be contrasted to the organizational openness of allonomous systems, or systems instructed by outside stimuli that we see in input-output models. Autonomous systems, significantly, are not instructed from the outside, but rather, respond to environmental perturbations in ways that are specified by the interactions of the components of the system itself. The openness, then, that we often associate with interacting social systems comes in the form of a multitude of possible meanings that are generated within the defining boundaries of language. The parameters of language, then, provide the closure that characterizes autonomous social systems that direct themselves in ways that preserve their integrity as systems, while maintaining an adaptive capacity that signifies an openness to change. Here, Luhmann (1990) helps to clarify this seeming contradiction:

"The autopoiesis [self-production] of communication by communication requires closure. Meaning, on the other hand, is a completely open structure, excluding nothing, not even the negation of meaning... As [social] systems of meaning-based communication [,] societies are closed and open systems. They gain their openness by closure" (p. 147).

The myriad meanings, and the possible shifts in these meanings, that derive from communication in learning organizations occur only within boundaries that are defined through the communication whose parameters are consensually understood in communicating. In short, communication is defined by communication. If this were not case, then communication would either require an externally-imposed meaning, or it would end up with no meaning at all as the parameters become so fluid (open) that meaning is disallowed by the missing consistency that organizational closure guarantees. This multitude of meanings derived from communicating requires the element of closure for the consensual domain (Maturana, 1978) to remain as the boundary that defines autonomy.

The 'Stokely experience'

The transformative realities of the Stokely Institutes provide classic cases for understanding the dynamics of self-organizing and adaptive organizational environments that offer strong clues as to the mechanics involved in re-creating such environments, or learning ecologies. After participating in one such Institute in 1988, I was granted access in the early 1990s for the only research study of Stokely to be conducted in its ten-year history. My focus (Horn, 1999) was on the transformative nature of changes in the personal and professional lives of the Institutes' Fellows. In-depth interviews with Fellows from seven of the ten Institutes yielded fascinating views of the synergy emerging within the groups that had lasting impacts as individuals came to reflect upon their participation as persons and as professionals who would, long after, keep alive the 'Stokely experience'. A full appreciation of wider implications of Stokely to understanding change in organizations requires attention to: 1. the organizational relations, or relational space, that provided the operational closure necessary for self-organized learning to occur, and; 2. the structural components that provided the network of interactions and transformations that constituted this learning community from year to year. The following discussion is grounded in the attempt to unravel Stokely's mutually-shaping relational space and structural components, two aspects of a unitary phenomenon that characterizes the self-sustaining and self-generating behavior of dynamic and self-referential systems.

From its inception in 1983, the Institute quickly evolved the relational space that remained consistent over the years. In doing so, it provided the closure necessary for autonomous systems, while remaining capable of expansion and contraction as the interactions of components exerted centrifugal or centripetal pressures that signal movement between expansionary and confirmatory modes of learning. An exhaustive examination of the interview data indicated that the ongoing interactions of the components (Fellows, Faculty, and Program) show moving centers of balance within four parameter values that characterized the relational space: 1. *support*, 2. *challenge*, 3. *openness*, and 4. *integration*. These adjustable, yet, ever-present parameter values enabled Fellows each year to experience the professional growth and personal renewal that became typical outcomes. Perhaps more importantly, the act of living within these parameters that, indeed, adjusted according to the interactions among the Program, Faculty and Fellows, lent new levels of understandings among Fellows regarding the processes for bringing forth (Maturana & Varela, 1980) and sustaining learning in such communities. It was, after all, the Fellows, Faculty, and Program that determined "the possible interactions the system [could] enter into" (Varela, 1979: 261); and the empowerment that resulted from learning about the active, creative nature of their own learning emboldened many of these Fellows to take charge of their personal lives and to shape their professional practices in ways that, heretofore, had been viewed as simply out of reach, or beyond their power to enact.

Stokely Fellows who reported transitions were those who were able to sustain a balance between support and challenge, and between openness and integration. While it is clear that challenge without an equal amount of support holds the potential for intimidation and withdrawal, it is clear, too, that support without challenge may create complacency and a false immodesty. A balance of support and challenge allowed Fellows to interact openly with people and ideas in ways that were neither self-deprecating nor grandiose. This opening up, then, was sustained by the many reflective opportunities to integrate new in-formation, as integration was modeled each day in the seminars and actively constructed in the many study group conversations. Confidence, accomplishment, and an expanded sense of self often resulted from this sustained balance.

Support and challenge

In the balanced pairing of complementary dyads, support / challenge and openness / integration, a Bateson (1979) aphorism would seem to apply: "Rigor alone is paralytic death, but imagination alone is insanity" (p. 219). Clearly, we can see in the relational space of Stokely the necessary balance achieved between support and challenge, and between openness and integration. We can see, too, that there was a conscious effort toward collegiality to balance the professorial expertise and positions of power with the less-esteemed roles of teachers, now turned Fellows. Foremost, perhaps, there existed an implicit assumption that learning communities could grow in proportion to the growth of individual members, whose own growth is proportionate to the sharing of that growth within the community that enabled it.

Support

Support represents the order parameter of the Institute's relational space that provided for the comfort and safety, both physical and psychical, for Fellows to venture into novel modes of thought and expression within a diverse group of individuals who shared a common career culture. In the residential setting of the Institute, Fellows found freedom to explore connections among disciplines, just as they found in Stokely's residential requirement a respite from the mundane responsibilities and normal distractions associated with everyday family living. As with the other relational boundaries, support came about and was sustained by the interactions and transactions among program, faculty, and participants - those components that each year consistently generated the network of interactions that provided the realization of these autonomous and generative learning communities (Horn, 1999).

In talking about the planning that preceded each Stokely Institute, one Fellow referred to "the stage being set for personal thinking, for personal reflection about teaching, about philosophy, about history, and science." It is clear that setting the Stokely stage was a complex process that sought to sustain the opportunity for autonomous, yet interdependent actors, to come together within a creative dialogue marked by a thorough collegiality that "made everyone a star."

As metaphor, setting the stage seems particularly appropriate, for each Institute encountered logistical problems that would be faced in preparing for a theatrical production. There were professors to be contacted from previous Institutes, and in some years tryouts were conducted for new ones. Once these key roles were filled, an intellectually-rigorous curriculum had to be written that would provide an integrated structure and maximum latitude for improvisation by the professors and the other actors. It was necessary to order books and journal articles for all participants. Seminar rooms had to be arranged so that each participant could share the stage. Scheduled appearances by guest lecturers were lined up. Visits to other departments and colleges within the university had to be arranged.

Participant tryouts came next, followed by the careful selection process. Accommodations for a five-week run were ordered, with two participants sharing a small university apartment. Stipend checks of five hundred dollars each were written to each Fellow to cover meals and incidental expenses. University Records office had to be contacted to record six semester hours of 4.0 graduate credit for each Fellow. Beyond these preparations, there was the need to provide tickets for cultural events. Transportation had to be arranged for field trips, as well as for any participant who could not walk to and from seminars. Opening and closing dinners at the faculty club had to be orchestrated. Catering had to be ordered to celebrate any participant birthdays that coincided with the Institute. Personalized certificates and plaques had to ordered and inscribed.

Upon arrival, Stokely Fellows found everything in place for an uninterrupted immersion into learning, both inside and outside the boardroom that had been reserved for the seminars. Apartments and keys were ready for them, with name tags, pens, paper, books, fruit baskets, and stipend checks to cover the cost of incidentals. There was a "vibrancy" in the air, as one Fellow described the initial atmosphere; and this anticipatory air was reinforced the first evening when Fellows and Faculty mingled and dined, thus establishing a collegial, personalized, and mutually-supportive rapport prior to any seminar sessions. As one Fellow said, "they made us their equals."

The Fellows warmed quickly to this new collegiality, which quickly engendered a stronger sense of self-worth and confidence. In short, they came to see themselves worthy of the respect and confidence that had been extended to them. This new confidence was reinforced by the encouragement toward personalized expression that the Faculty provided as the weeks of seminars, lunches, and dinner parties progressed. Because grades were not a consideration, professors and the curriculum were seen as less threatening, and the neutralization of the grade issue eliminated grade competition and the accompanying potential for self-distancing or withdrawal or 'hoarding of information'. Another consequence of all participants receiving "A's" can be seen in some participant's renewed commitment to give an equal amount in effort to fit what each felt she had been given. Because every participant's contribution was respected, and because perspectives were not validated by how well they matched those of the faculty, the temptation to establish a pecking order was minimized. This, in turn, left participants with the freedom to share and contribute, since respect was achieved through contribution to the dialogue; and contributions could only be measured in terms of their own learning. With these relations established, collegiality could be taken seriously, and collaboration within the group could coalesce as a natural alternative to competition.

Not everyone was immediately comfortable with the new sense of autonomy. The difficulty of adjusting to this new relational space was, for some, associated with previous educational experiences and with the perceived restrictions normally associated with the organizational limits of schools. For some of the participants, the introduction of non-specific learning goals, or goals with unspecified objectives, was a new experience; and to some degree it contributed to a sense of confusion and inner conflict regarding expectations. In a real sense, it brings into focus the other vector in this dyadic parameter relationship of support and challenge; for accompanying new autonomy is the personal responsibility to define a purpose that, heretofore, had been provided by someone else. Those, however, who were able to share their 'what are we doing here?' attitude with other Fellows found new possibilities generated from their interactions. The collegial, ungraded forum led many of the Fellows to reflect more deeply upon their own learning purposes, since it was obvious that none of the professors was going to define that for them.

Challenge

The more potent forms of mutual support arising from the interactions of Fellows bring challenge into even closer focus. The supportive relations that were manifested in interactions among Fellows were attributable, in large part, to the challenge presented by a very ambitious seminar agenda and three extensive sets of interwoven readings from the humanities, social sciences, and the natural sciences. While the initial reaction among some Fellows was disorientation and intimidation, the associated anxiety soon became transformed into a sense of sustained challenge as informal, interdependent reading and study groups formed that gave responsibility and voice to each participant, who in turn found solace and support in the work of others in their small groups. The sharing of ideas then created an intellectual intimacy that provided a bridge for the introduction of professional and personal concerns, thus breaking ground for new friendships and a broader sense of caring that came to permeate these groups.

A corollary to those supportive relations that allowed for the comfort and safety of the participants is the aspect of challenge that all participants identified as a primary characteristic of the Stokely Program. In many cases, it was the establishment of comfort and safety through support that allowed participants to quickly transform their initial sense of intimidation or threat to one of challenge. For most participants this transition occurred during the first week. While the intensity, breadth, and pacing of the program provided intellectual challenges to all Fellows, the wide-ranging topics proved equally challenging to many closely-held belief systems, both religious and ideological. As already indicated, the transition to challenge and openness appears to depend partially upon the state of readiness of each Fellow, and their willingness and ability to engage in interactions that helped form, coalesce and sustain the community.

According to Maturana (1980), the coalescence of community occurs when "certain contingencies are given that force them [people] to survive by integrating through their behavior a network of interactions that becomes a medium for the realization of their individual autopoiesis [self-production]" (p. 12). This characterization of self-created community aptly applies to the relational space that was in place as participants began to realize the 'Stokely experience'. It may seem paradoxical to talk of forced contingencies when referring to self-organized communities, but continued existence of such communities depends upon the creative and adaptive capacities of the components that constitute them. Indeed, it was the forced contingency of challenge that helped shape the relational space toward a level of interactions that hastened the emergence of the Stokely communities, built upon interdependence and autonomy.

Each Fellow recognized and refined his own unique challenge as the Institutes proceeded. As participants explored their own limitations, expectations were as high as they were unspecified; and in a very real sense, challenge from without became challenge from within. As one participant said, the Institute was "an opportunity to explore ... discovering yourself in other ways." All Fellows felt challenged by the amount of readings (over three thousand pages of text), the complexity of interwoven ideas within the readings, and the subsequent seminars that discussed and probed the linkages, some of them emerging in Aha! experiences that were enthusiastically shared. For many of the participants, the challenging nature of Stokely, itself, was a recognition of their potential to contribute, and the high expectations of Stokely indicated a belief in their capacities to operate within the collegial learning environment that the Fellows, themselves, helped form. This sense of recognition through challenge became fully enabled by the support that provided a moving point of equilibrium between the two complementary parameters that form this relational dyad, support / challenge.

Openness and integration

Openness

During these annual Institutes, openness enabled the centrifugal surges as Fellows began to explore the novel learning terrains that became visible as the fog of threat and intimidation began to dissipate. The permeating atmosphere of collegiality and equality contributed to the Fellows' sense of professionalism and self-worth; and that, in turn, helped to sustain conditions whereby participants felt safe enough to open themselves to the active examination of novel ideas and to the creation and sharing of new perspectives. The expectation that each Fellow could contribute was matched by supportive conditions that allowed each to do so. While highly structured with a rigorous set of readings and seminars, Stokely provided enormous latitude for personal exploration by assigning loosely-structured reaction papers that encouraged divergent responses and novel interpretations that were personally significant.

What is clear is that the degree of openness was related to the extent that the participants viewed themselves as being treated as valued professionals within a safe, diversion-free environment from which they were free to explore personal meanings related to novel concepts and ideas. The early validation of the Fellows' contributions and potential contributions to the seminars and study groups tended to minimize defensive stances that would "keep you to your inner vision." At the same time, the Fellows felt that their ideas were of value, thus leading one participant to conclude, "if my ideas are worth something, you know... I'll open my window a little bit more."

Openness was an attribute that permeated the Institute and the descriptions of experiences by former Fellows. With a rigorous set of readings and full schedule of lectures, seminars, and events, Stokely nonetheless carried on within a relaxed, collaborative environment that was maintained by Faculty who modeled the open exchange of ideas. The openness of the professors allowed many, otherwise reticent, Fellows to interact more freely and to establish their own sense of openness among others. The sharing of divergent views was a figural aspect for Fellows, who "always felt like we were free to ask questions, free to contribute." This kind of open forum for in-formational exchanges remained crucial in the subsequent transitions that Fellows experienced.

Openness among groups of Fellows varied from year to year. In groups whose members attempted to restrict interactions by limiting discussion of topics that appeared to conflict with certain values, group cohesiveness and individual openness became threatened. It is interesting to note that, on multiple occasions, Fellows took an active stance in maintaining the spirit of open inquiry by openly challenging censorial attacks and by seeking to reassure those Fellows who felt threatened. On such occasions, we see system components acting in ways to preserve the parameters that allowed for autonomous thought and actions.

Integration

In discussing the degree of openness necessary for optimal learning to occur, a Fellow noted that "the trouble with open-mindedness is that your brains can fall out." After days of exposure to ideas that challenged some of the foundational ideas of Western culture, many Fellows were attuned to the need to re-integrate, to restore order. Fellows, indeed, were discovering what Eleanor Duckworth (1987) meant when she said, "the discovery of something new throws into confusion something that was certain before" (p. 25).

The centripetal element of the relational space that provided the counterbalance for openness formed from the integrative boundary conditions that Stokely enabled. Many Fellows saw Stokely as a harmonizer of the cognitive and the affective, a social blender of the intellectual and the emotional; for it was within these communities that many ideas became suffused with personal meaning, and many personal values came under the bright light of intelligent scrutiny and reflection. Integration, then, is used here to point to the imbrication of ideas and overlapping of disciplinary perspectives that emerged by an active and reflective search for encompassing patterns formed from the sharing of distinct perspectives among Fellows and Faculty.

The Stokely Program was designed to accommodate multiple perspectives from various disciplines. For some, this search for connections was a new experience, and for others it served to focus and provide a path for what had previously been an intuitive longing for understanding 'the big picture'. The proximity and interweaving of ideas from the humanities, sciences, and the social sciences provided a rich source of interactions and potential insights regarding the connectedness of seemingly disparate disciplines, and it was the search within these interwoven disciplines that fostered the insights that signaled transitional states of understandings among Fellows. The feeding forward, or recursion, of these shared insights into subsequent reading and discussion set the stage for the emergence and integration of new understanding and meanings that had personal significance and professional implications.

In the opening up of disciplinary boundaries through the scope and sequence of topics and readings, Stokely encouraged the intermingling of ideas and concepts that provide the breeding ground for new insights. While the focus of the Institute was on interdisciplinary inquiry, participants found value in the wide range of specialties and styles that the professors brought to the seminars. This diversity of style and viewpoint provided multiple sources for connections across disciplines. By maintaining open interactions among a multiplicity of disciplinary and personal perspectives, Stokely demonstrated how engagement within such diversity of ideas may initiate successful challenges to unexamined suppositions or dogmatic contentions. For many Fellows, this individual and communal reflection resulted in the exposure of blind spots and to compelling new visions of the interrelatedness of human knowledge and communication as an expanded human ecology that remained alive long after Stokely.

Discussion

The brief analysis offered here provides a small textual edifice that signifies a description of a description of an experience, but it is the experience itself that remains alive, elusive, and compelling for former Fellows, as well as for our understanding of how creative change may be sustainable in learning organizations. A full appreciation of the multiple implications of Stokely will continue to focus on how the relational space of the Institutes was constituted in ways that enabled the renewal and growth of the participants whose interactions formed and maintained that space. What began for many Stokely Fellows as an intimidating prospect became, for most, a transformative learning experience that brought them closer to their own potential, to others in their diverse groups, and to larger worlds. Uncertainty and intimidation were transformed to challenge through collegiality, collaborative interactions, and careful attention to personal well-being. Sustaining the rigorous intellectual and emotional challenges required a commitment to a degree of open exchange. Openness required a sense of well-being, minimal distractions, and the capacity to interact within a collaborative framework. Those who were not open or never experienced the transition to openness did not have available to them the level of interactions necessary for further phase transitions to occur (Horn, 1999).

The intensity of the workload sharpened the focus on challenge and encouraged collaboration among Fellows. The resulting interdependency based on shared responsibility helped to enhance the support that the Program initiated. The diverse perspectives that were voiced within this community of learners provided potential sources for insights, new in-formation, and emergent meanings. Bridging disciplines required new connections among ideas and people. To balance the rigorous demands of the readings, seminars often took imaginative, exploratory turns; and loosely-specified response papers introduced the reflective turn through which personal meaning coalesced. Confidence grew with acknowledged accomplishment, and both fed forward into renewed immersion within a collegial atmosphere of integrative diversity. The degree of caring that defined group closeness was enhanced by continuing interactions that were both intellectual and social, thus encouraging personal and shared reflection. Enlargement of self was realized through new connectedness with ideas and with others in worlds co-constructed within the broader expanses of new experiential possibilities, both personal and professional in nature.

While the goals of renewal and learning were clearly delineated from the inception, the Stokely Institute never took on the characteristics associated with motivational seminars that use staged excitation to bring participants to pre-established levels of enthused readiness or agitated action. Clearly, the continuing influence of these Stokely experiences speaks to the power inherent in self-sustaining, interactive communities from which individual meanings are derived through discovery and invention rather than from "persuasion and propaganda" (Stacey, 1992: 125). These participant descriptions highlight the bitter irony that stems from the inadvertent stifling of learning that often occurs in organizations when attempts are made to insure that learning proceeds along pre-determined paths toward pre-defined outcomes. By directing learning only toward pre-defined ends, potential novelty and creativity are sacrificed in favor of confirmation, and the goal of processing and storing information replaces the opportunity to bringing forth new in-formation and meaning. If we accept the statement by Minsky (1986) that "the principle activities of brains are making changes in themselves" (p. 288), then the goals of information storage and retrieval appear dubious at best, as the principles of closure (Maturana & Varela, 1987) make clear in emphasizing the biological and cognitive imperatives that underpin autonomous human systems:

"... the nervous system does not 'pick up information' from the environment, as we often hear. On the contrary it brings forth a world by specifying what patterns of the environment are perturbations and what changes trigger them in the organism. The popular metaphor of calling the brain an 'information processing device' is not only ambiguous but patently wrong" (p. 169).

Concluding Remarks

The ethical dimensions associated with autonomous learning communities and the study of them are implicit within the ontology from which the principles of autonomy are derived. Inasmuch as realities are grounded in the acts of bringing forth worlds (Maturana & Varela, 1998) within consensual domains (Maturana, 1978), the opportunity to organize our individual lives becomes inextricably linked with the opportunity for others to do likewise. Much of the inequity among social organizations reflects a lack of understanding of this basic premise. The conditions prevailing in many enterprises and organizations that make the Stokely Institute sometimes appear as an aberration are conditions witnessed when organizations attempt to preserve themselves by restricting the necessary dynamics of the interacting members that comprise them. As the underlying principles of autonomous systems remind us, however, if the interactions that sustain the organization's unity are interrupted, "after a while you don't have any more unity to talk about" (Maturana & Varela, 1987: 46). What remains may certainly be a social system, but one without potential for transformative growth.

A further distinction is needed here in regards to comparing biological organisms to human social systems. Within a biological organism, it is, indeed, the case that the diminution of individual entities occurs as the plasticity of the organism's components are sacrificed in favor of the overall well-being of the organism. However, this loss of autonomy of components contrasts sharply to human social systems in that "... coherence and harmony in relations and interactions between the members of a human social system are due to the coherence and harmony of their growth in it, in an ongoing social learning which their own social (linguistic) operation defines…" (Maturana & Varela, 1998: 199). In social organizations that "embody enforced mechanisms of stabilization in all the behavioral dimensions of their members," we witness the loss of energy and vitality that characterizes "impaired human social systems" (p. 199).

Despite efforts to predict and control autonomous social organizations, the nature of autonomous change guarantees that "there are certain points beyond which you can't derive what is going to happen at the next level of complexity" (Packard, 1992: 97). What we can predict with some confidence is that subsequent levels will emerge if networks of interactions are allowed to generate themselves and if known parameters remain adjustable to the be-haviors of the entities comprising the system. Whether or not we choose to successfully engage the possibilities for self-organizing and adaptive behavior in learning organizations will determine if our institutions come to experi-ence change as cycles of enforced stasis with periods of cascading destructive avalanches, or as a continuing poised equilibrium, punctuated by successive shifts that characterize orderly growth of the systems and the individuals that comprise them.

In closing, managers and leaders should note that the acknowledgement of emergence as a phenomenon within self-organizing systems does not imply a rudderless capitulation of their own capacities to effect change or, otherwise, influence the systems they lead. Change does not only bubble up from the in-teractions of system members. After all, the interactions that sustain a system's survival occur only within the organizational closure that the parameters en-able, those boundary conditions that have been formed and sustained as con-sensual acts by the agents that characterize the system. These two co-defining elements constitute autonomous systems engaged in the "reciprocal causality" that results from "downward causation," or "changes in [order] parameters and boundary conditions," and "upward causation," which results from behavior of the agents to "generate and sustain the order parameters" (Thompson & Varela, 2001: 421). This downward causation that occurs from the adjusting of order parameters may, indeed, be viewed as the primary activities of managers and leaders; but this important and achievable goal can only be accomplished if managers and leaders are, and see themselves as being, interactive agents, albeit with distinct roles, within the systems they lead and manage. Arguably, the cultivation and adjustment of the support / challenge and open / integrative parameters will present formidable challenges to managers and leaders who have, heretofore, focused their efforts on direction-setting and instructive steering of the systems they manage and lead, systems whose human com-ponents, we now learn, determine their own learning. The consequences and potential rewards of this still-startling realization, or this "gestalt switch" (Varela, 1979), will be played out as leaders from many fields of organizational endeavor develop and interpret strategies to take full advantage of this capac-ity for autonomy that originates in our biology and that is recapitulated in the social systems we help to create, maintain, and grow.

References

Argyris, C. and Schön, D. (1992). *Theory in Practice: Increasing Professional Effectiveness*, San Francisco: Jossey-Bass.

Axelrod, R. and Cohen, M. D. (2000). *Harnessing Complexity: Organizational Implications of a Scientific Frontier*, New York: Free Press.

Bateson, G. (1972). *Steps to an Ecology of Mind*, New York: Ballantine Books.

Bateson, G. (1979). *Mind and Nature: A Necessary Unity*, New York: E. P. Dutton.

Duckworth, E. (1987). *The Having of Wonderful Ideas and Other Essays on Teaching and Learning*, New York: Teachers College Press.

Fellows Program: June 19-July 22, 1988. (1988), Unpublished, University of Tennessee, Knoxville.

Gould, S. J. (1983). *The Mismeasure of Man*, New York: W. W. Norton & Company.

Horn, J. (1995). *The Emergence of Meaning in an Interdisciplinary Learning Environment: A Qualitative Study of the James R. Stokely Institute for Liberal Arts Education*, Unpublished doctoral dissertation, University of Tennessee.

Horn, J. (1999). "Teacher Renewal and Transformation through Interdisciplinary Learning Experiences: A Study of Meaningful Learning in an Interdisciplinary Environment," *Teacher Development*, 3(2): 309-336.

Kauffman, S. A. (1995). *At Home in the Universe: The Search for Laws of Self-organization and Complexity*, New York: Oxford University Press.

Kuppers, B.-O. (1990). *Information and the Origin of Life*, Cambridge: MIT Press.

Langton, C., Farmer, D., Taylor, C., and Rasmusen, S. (eds.) (1992), *Artificial Life II*: Proceedings of the Workshop on Artificial Life Held February, 1990 in Sante Fe, New Mexico, Redwood City, CA: Addison-Wesley.

Luhmann, N. (1990). *Essays on Self-reference*, New York: Columbia University Press.

Maturana, H. R. (1978). "Biology of Language: The Epistemology of Reality," in G. Miller and E. Lenneberg (eds.), *Psychology and Biology of Language and Thought: Essays in Honor of Eric Lenneberg*, New York: Academic Press, pp. 27-63.

Maturana, H. R. (1980). "Man and society," in F. Benseler and W. Koch (eds.), *Autopoiesis, Communication and Society: The Theory of Autopoietic Systems in the Social Sciences*, Frankfurt: Campus Verlag, pp. 11-31.

Maturana, H. R. and Varela, F. J. (1980). *Autopoiesis and Cognition: The Realization of the Living*, Boston: Reidel.

Maturana, H. R. and Varela, F. J. (1987). *The Tree of Knowledge: The Biological Roots of Human Understanding*, Boston: New Science Library.

Maturana, H. R. and Varela, F. J. (1998). *The Tree of Knowledge: The Biological Roots of Human Understanding*, rev. ed., Boston: Shambhala.

Mills, C. W. (1959). *The Sociological Imagination*, New York: Oxford University Press.

Minsky, M. (1986). *The Society of Mind*, New York: Simon and Schuster.

Packard, N. (1992). "Norman Packard," *Omni*, 14 (January): 85-89.

Senge, P. M., Kleiner, A., Roberts, C., Roth, G., Ross, R., and Smith, B. (1999). *The Dance of Change: The Challenge to Sustaining Momentum in Learning Organizations*, Refern, AU: Currency.

Stacey, R. D. (1992). *Managing the Unknown: Strategic Boundaries between Order and Chaos and Organizations*, San Francisco: Jossey-Bass.

Stacey, R. D. (1996). *Complexity and Creativity in Organizations*, San Francisco: Berrett-Koehler.

Thompson, E. and Varela, F. J. (2001). "Radical Embodiment: Neural Dynamics and Consciousness," *Trends in Cognitive Sciences*, 5(10): 418-425.

Varela, F. J. (1979). *Principles of Biological Autonomy*, New York: North Holland.

Varela, F. J., Thompson, E. and Rosch, E. (1991). *The Embodied Mind: Cognitive Science and Human Experience*, Cambridge: MIT.

von Foerster, H. (1984). "Principles of Self-organization: In a Socio-managerial Context," in H. Ulrich and G. G. Probst (eds.), *Self-organization and Management of Social Systems: Insights, Promises, Doubts, and Questions*, New York: Springer-Verlag, pp. 2-24.

Waldrop, M. M. (1992). *Complexity: The Emerging Science at the Edge of Order and Chaos*, New York: Simon and Schuster.

Wolfram, S. (2002). *A New Kind of Science*, Champaign, IL: Wolfram Media.

CHAPTER 28

COMPLEXITY AND SPATIALITY: REGIONS, NETWORKS AND FLUIDS IN SUSTAINABLE WATER MANAGEMENT

Will P. Medd and Simon Marvin

This chapter argues that complexity analysis needs to explicitly examine the constitution of different spatial forms and the interdependencies between them in order to understand the emergence of complex socio-technical dynamics. While complexity analysis has often pointed to the importance of interaction between scale, we argue that complex socio-technical dynamics involve more than inter-scalar interaction, but also the interaction between different spatial forms. Building on literature from social studies of technology we argue for the need to examine the interactions between regional, networked and fluid spaces. The argument uses a case study on sustainable water as an illustrative example. By understanding the complex interactions across different spatial topologies we can gain a better understanding of the ways in which recursive relations between local and regional processes occur and the hidden work this can involve.

Managing Organizational Complexity: Philosophy, Theory, and Application
A Volume in: Managing the Complex, pages 493-504.
ISBN: 1-59311-319-6 (cloth), 1-59311-318-8 (paper)

Introduction

T his chapter argues that complexity analysis needs to explicitly examine the constitution of different spatial forms and the interdependencies between them in order to understand the emergence of complex socio-technical dynamics. The imagery surrounding the notion of emergent dynamics, for example, typically invokes a sense of an overarching emergent dynamic, qualitatively different to the characteristics of the parts 'below', a dynamic, in other words, whose spatiality transcends that of the parts. Allen's (1997) work on the relationship between individual decisions, urban growth and regional form is exemplary of this. Here we find the emergence of a self-organized space - the city or the region - constituted through smaller scale interacting entities, operating according to their own rules and within their own spatial parameters. The focus of such work then becomes on the nested and cascading relationships of interactions across different spatial levels or scales. Understanding interactions across spatial levels is important for understanding the dynamics of form (Cohen & Stewart, 1994). However, as we shall argue in this chapter, the spatial interactions that are important to complex socio-technical dynamics involve more than inter-scalar interaction, but also the interaction between different spatial forms. This requires paying closer attention to the topological characteristics of the dynamics, which means looking at the different spatial forms that are constituted through different types of relationships between objects (Mol & Law, 1994).

Our argument is developed through research on sustainable water management and questions about the boundaries upon which water management should be based. Such questions are not surprising when we consider how the hydrological cycle "carries water on an unending journey through streams, rivers and oceans, the atmosphere, the ice sheets, living systems and the deep earth" (Ball, 1999: 24). This cycle is only further complicated when one adds the reservoirs, treatment works, pipelines, drains, sewers and taps of infrastructures guiding water that have become so taken for granted in the modern world (Illich, 1986). Increased concerns about water quality in itself, as well as the impact of polluted water on the wider environment, have brought to the fore questions about the appropriate boundaries upon which water management should take place. Consequently the European Union Water Framework Directive (WFD), which came into force in December 2000 (European Community 2000) is an attempt to develop a more integrated approach to water management through the 'natural' space of a river basin. As such, integrated river basin management (IRBM) is, in principle, defined by an ecosystem boundary, a bio-physical region rather than other institutional or infrastructural boundaries. Such an approach is attractive and by and large welcomed within the water management community, though the extent to which institutional decision making will be able to adapt to these 'natural' boundaries remains to be seen (Moss, 2003; White & Howe, 2003). Complexity analysis could be useful here in seeking to develop the co-evolution of institutional dynamics around the river basin level. However we want to argue that the development of sustainable water practices and technologies within the river basin level, as an emergent 'regional space', will require more than improving alignment between institutional boundaries. We want to argue, first, if it will require understanding the interactions across socio-technical 'network spaces' that stretch beyond and through the river basin level, and second, the role of a 'fluid space' in-between such regions and networks. It is in this fluid space that a key role for intermediary organizations emerges that enables the translation of sustainable water practice and technologies into local contexts

The chapter is set out as follows. In the first section we outline our approach to complexity that builds upon social studies of technology and the application of complexity to social dynamics in order to understand the complex socio-technical assemblage of water management. This approach points to the significance of the spatial topology of the water management sector as a complex system, and in the second section we draw upon approaches to the spatiality of socio-technical systems to highlight different forms of spatiality. Through these approaches we demonstrate the regional, networked and fluid spatiality of water management and the particular significance of intermediary organizations operating in fluid space through which interactions of the regional and networked space take place. The final section concludes arguing for the development of a more spatialized understanding of complex dynamics.

Water as a complex spatial hybrid

One of the difficulties for understanding the possibilities of sustainable water management is how to conceptualize the relationships between the natural water cycle, technological infrastructures and social dynamics. One possibility is to focus on one dynamic - say the social as conversation (cf. Fonseca, 2002) - and treat the others, in effect, as environment. Alternatively, one could see them in terms of a co-evolving dynamic in a way similar to Rycroft and Kash's (1999) analysis of the significant role played by the complexification of social organization in enabling technological innovation in the United States. These approaches tend towards positioning clearly defined boundaries between the different dynamics - between the social, technological and natural. The emergent hybrid nature of such dynamics is neglected. This hybrid nature of socio-technical systems has been the subject of analysis within the broad disciplines of social studies of technology (see Mackenzie & Wajcman, 1999; Bjiker, et al., 1987, Bjiker & Law 1994). In the application to infrastructure (see Chappells, 2003; Graham & Marvin, 2001; Guy, et al., 2001) the emphasis is placed on the highly distributed nature of socio-technical dynamics, the importance of history and local context in determining emergent forms.

Through such a perspective there are no absolute definitive boundaries of 'water management' and analysis needs to understand the ways in which different boundaries - social, technical, natural, and hybrid - become constituted, changed, interact, dissolve, and are enmeshed. As Swyngedouw

(2004: 28) notes, "If I were to capture some urban water in a glass, retrace the networks that brought it there and follow Ariadne's thread through the water, 'I would pass with continuity from the local to the global, from the human to the non-human'" (Latour, 1993: 121). We might argue that the glass of water may be emergent from interactions between natural, technological and social dynamics in the past, but it becomes a hybrid actor in the present, one that is "simultaneously material, discursive, and symbolic" (Swyngedouw, 2004: 28). Hybridity is often hidden but becomes acutely revealed during times of crises, as Urry (2003) cites, for example, in relation to turbulent cities (Clark, 2000), global viruses (van Loon, 2002) and the character of 'normal accidents' (Perrow, 1999). When it comes to sustainable water management the effects of pollution, drought or flooding, for example, similarly reveal the complex interdependencies of natural, technical and social worlds in the emergent hybrid water crises.

The complex web of interconnectivities constituted by hybrid relations also invokes new spatial interdependencies. The ways in which socio-technical systems have come to involve new forms of spatial connectivity have been well documented. Formulations such as "time-space distantiation" (Giddens, 1984) or "time-space compression" (Harvey, 1989) point to the ways in which space is not an abstract container within which events happen, but time-space relationships are constituted through the orderings of social-technical relations. Through telecommunication networks you may be in closer contact to a friend on the other side of the globe than to your next door neighbor, for example. Importantly such spatial temporal orderings of infrastructure also involve the formation of new forms of inclusion and exclusion (Sibley, 1995). Urry's (2003) work develops an understanding of spatial-temporal relations through his analysis of global complexity. Urry argues that while 'the global' can be thought of as a 'regional' space, this tends to detract attention from the varied spatial patterns of global systems and the iterative character of the global processes. Instead, he proposes the need to understand the character of global networks that "consist of complex, enduring and predictable networked connections between people, objects and technologies stretching across multiple and distant spaces and times" (Urry, 2003: 56-57). In addition to such networks, however, are *global fluids* that "result from people acting upon the basis of local information but where these local actions are, through countless iteration, captured, moved, represented, marketed and generalized within multiple global waves (Urry, 2003: 60). Such global fluids include, travelling peoples, the internet, information, world money, global brands, automobility, environmental and health hazards, world's oceans and social movements.

In this chapter we want to develop this approach to hybrid spatiality to examine how the hybrid nature of the water sector reveals a regional, networked and fluid spatiality. The analysis of global complexity could be developed in relation to the emerging global water markets in which dominant multinational companies are expanding their reach into new water territories or the effects of global climate change on local hydrological cycles. Our focus is different however, and is concerned with particular questions about how sustainable water practices and technologies are developed and our examples concern experiences emerging from research within the North West of England. In doing so we want to argue that it is not just through iterative processes that local actions form part of emergent forms, but that through the often hidden work of intermediation in a fluid space, that sustainable water practices and technologies can move between the regional and the networked spaces of water.

Water regions, networks and fluids

Our study of sustainable water management is based in the North West of England (NW) which is distinctive to other countries because of early privatization in 1989 (see Kinnersley, 1994). We use the study to illustrate the significance of opening up analysis to the spatial dynamics of complex systems rather than to make claims about the specificities of sustainable water management generally. Urry's (2003) analysis of global complexity develops a framework based on a topological distinction drawn by Mol and Law (1994):

"First, there are regions in which objects are clustered together and boundaries are drawn around each cluster. Second, there are networks in which distance is a function of the relations between the elements and difference a matter of relational variety ... [and fluids, where] boundaries come and go, allow leakage or disappear altogether, while relations transform themselves without fracture" (Mol & Law, 1994: 643).

In this section we describe the spatial character of the NW water sector in relation to the three spatial forms of regions, networks and fluids.

Regional Water Space

The water system in the North West of England is defined by boundaries established in the 1973 Water Act that lead to a regional level of water management (Chappells, 2003; Kinnersley, 1994). These boundaries are in place today and define the water responsibilities of United Utilities, a private sector company who own the assets and operating rights for water in the North West. The boundaries of the water sector in the North West incorporate the apparent seamless flow (Chappells, 2003) of 2 billion liters of a day and 2.2 billion liters of wastewater water a day through its "192 reservoirs, 453 service reservoirs and towers, 40,000 km of water mains, 1,200 km of aqueduct, 137 water treatment works, 39,000 km of sewers, 600 wastewater treatment works" (United Utilities, 2003). Also working within this regional space, as well as the water company, are the regulators (for the environment, economic efficiency, customer services) and some private forms of operation (for example, using boreholes). And within the boundaries of the North West Region are various other, lower level, regional spaces, for example area offices for the regulator and water management zones of the utilities company.

For sustainable water management there are problems of defining water by such a regional space. This has been highlighted by considerations of the potential impact of the European Union Water Framework directive (European Community, 2000). The WFD defines the river basin level as the unit of water management in order to privilege an ecosystem definition over existing institutional boundaries. Within the North West pilot, work is currently being undertaken to explore the implications of such River Basin water management. Such work, however, highlights the nested character of multiple spaces that we can characterize as 'regional', for example the water companies management boundaries, local government boundaries, regional government, national government boundaries, non-governmental organizational boundaries, local communities, urban boundaries, rural boundaries and so on. Thus, while strategies for sustainable water management tend to represent particular regions (Europe, nation state, region, sub-region, river basin etc.), difficulties soon emerge about the interconnections and nestedness between regional spaces. Indeed, as institutions adapt towards a river basin model as the territorial unit of water management, 'problems of interplay between water and other relevant institutions - such as for spatial planning, agriculture or nature conservation - may be exacerbated' (Moss, 2003: 86).

A focus on the multiple and nested regional boundaries itself raises important questions about the interactions of emergent dynamics across different spaces. This is important to understand. However, what is missing if we remain within a regional imagery alone, is the ways in which these other spaces are also important and through which regional entities are constituted. Much work, in particular, has argued for the importance of network spaces in the constitution of regional spaces, for example through the road networks, telecommunications and, of course, water (Graham & Marvin, 2001).

Networked water space

Mol and Law argue, "the space in which regions can be drawn and differentiated exists ... is an effect or a product that depends another quite different kind of space, the space of networks" (1994: 648-9). The formation of the North West Regional Water management was premised on the notion of generating an "integrated zone" (Chappells, 2003). However, if we take the perspective of network space we see the distribution of water throughout the north west through a vast array of all-channel networks incorporating a complex assemblage travelling in all directions, more or less tightly coupled at different points. While such a network may appear, or indeed be represented by corporate bodies as an integrated whole, it is also characterized by fracture, disruption and differentiations. The people in the City of Manchester, for example, use a large supply of drinking water supplied from the Lake District which travels through large scale pipelines running for over 60 miles. Yet as the water also passes through, that water supply remains untouchable for people inbetween whom the pipeline runs nearby (see Graham & Marvin, 2001 on these 'by-pass' issues). Importantly then, the network space of the water infrastructure is one that disconnects as much as it connects.

Networks then cut across regional spaces and complexify our picture of the North West Regional water sector. Network space is a space that splinters the apparent integrated regional space (Graham & Marvin, 2001). The infrastructure of water networks connects and disconnects asymmetrically different locations, differentiating, for example, between industrial sites and domestic homes, supplying water from parts of the region to other parts of the region, discharging waste water in some areas and not others. Such splintering is multiplied. Just as there are different and overlapping regional spaces, so too there are networks among networks. There are networks of local water supply, for example, but also interlinkages between water supply and electricity (to drive pumps and treatment works), between waste water and rivers. These spaces are significant for they point to the limitations of a perspective that seeks to integrate water management at a river basin level, adding to the problem of overlapping regional boundaries the fragmentation of linkages across, through and in-between different networked spaces.

For sustainable water management this interdependence of regional and network spaces is made further problematic by the widespread distribution of different types of water users. Within a regional spatial framework patterns of water consumption and waste-water production can be aggregated. Such aggregation can include some differentiation of types of users, for example households, industrial users, small to medium enterprises and public sector organizations. However, within these groups we find their geographical dispersal involves quite different linkages to the networks of infrastructure enabling the supply water or taking away waste-water. As we start to look to the networked sets of relationships that connect different users then we move down in scale to the intricacies of local networks that reveals sets of interdependencies otherwise not visible. Here we want to focus on one particular example, the position of Small to Medium Enterprises (SMEs). In contrast to large-scale industrial users whose activities are easily identifiable by the water companies and the regulators, the activities of SME organizations often remain harder to identify. Individually their water consumption is marginal, such that changes in individual water usage would not have a huge impact on water resources in the North West Region. Collectively, however, their individual iterations through the networks lead to an significant impact to North West Regional level both in terms of water usage and waste-water disposal. For the environmental regulator the geographical distribution of SMEs across the region poses particular problems for introducing sustainable water management. In their solution to the problem, which we explore in the next section, we find a further space articulated, that of a fluid space working inbetween networks and regions that enables the translation of sustainable water management from the strategic level into these specific contexts (cf. Hayes, 2001).

Fluid water spaces

Introducing fluid space in a chapter about the water sector is not intended as a pun. Mol and Law's (1994) formulation of the distinction between region, network and fluid space draws upon the metaphor of the body as region, the veins as network and the blood as fluid. They draw attention to the ways in which the boundaries of a fluid "come and go, allow leakage or disappear altogether" (Mol & Law, 1994: 643). The boundaries of water dynamics do indeed come and go. Times of flooding make this only too apparent, as do times of drought. The imagery of a fluid is also useful, however, for understanding the types of dynamics involved in translating sustainable water management across different contexts. It offers a way of understanding how the very specific contexts of local practices and technology introduction are enabled and reconnected into the water networks and the emergence of the regional water spaces. In this section then we are interested in how sustainable water practices are translated from the abstract strategies of regionally spaced water management into the path-dependent networks of water infrastructure to the local contexts in which changed practices take place or new technologies are introduced.

We want to illustrate our argument through the example of a small project that we consider to be an 'intermediary organization', which works inbetween the regional and network spaces by working in a more fluid space that allows adaptation and mutation across different boundaries. The organization we will call the SME Water Advice Project (SMEWAP). SMEWAP emerged from a problem faced by the environmental regulator, the Environment Agency (EA), and the constitution of SMEWAP involves the enrolment of yet more networks into the problems of water management. The problem faced by the EA was the need to promote sustainable water practices while at the same time being the enforcer of environmental standards, imposing fines for breach of environmental standards, for example. Of particular concern to the EA was the role of SMEs both in terms of water use and waste-water disposal. While the practice of SMEs might become visible to the EA when an infringement takes place - for example when a company releases waste water into a river and this is reported by the public - it did not have the resources to regularly check and monitor the activities of SMEs distributed around the region. Further still, SMEs were reluctant to approach the EA for advice because of the risk of subjecting their practices to investigation and risking high penalties or investment costs. The solution was for the Environment Agency to establish a project that would act as an advisory service for SMEs. But such a service, if it was to be acceptable to SMEs, would need to link into SME networks and to do this could not be based within the EA. A pilot project was established within a local area and was set up within an existing business advisory service. In this way, the project could work through the existing local business networks, offering free advice to business on sustainable water management issues. At first sight then we see the opening up of another regional and network space for water management. The project is established to cover a particular area geographical (a regional space) and to link into existing business networks (a network space). A look more closely at how SMEWAP works reveals the constitution of a fluid space that enables it to work. The key to this is understanding what we might call the "hidden work" (Star, 1999) of SMEWAP.

Three characteristics of the hidden work of SMEWAP are important here. First, the SMEWAP is situated within a broader set of work concerned with advising SMEs on sustainability. In approaching SMEs, water may or may not be the central concern. Water may be added on in relation to additional environmental advice or it may be the core reasons the company has sought advice. This varies and SMEWAP can adapt. Second, the ways in which SMEWAP presents itself, and the relevance of water, in that representations vary and are adaptable to different circumstances. SMEWAP might present to a company in relation to how it can avoid high fines for waste-water discharge; it may present to a company in terms of the potential costs savings of reduced water use or of reduced insurance through a sustainable drainage system (reducing flooding risk); or it may present to a company in terms of the symbolic value a company might gain by being seen to contribute to sustainability. In each of these not only does SMEWAP present a different form (for example sometimes it makes explicit its work for the EA, sometimes it presents, instead, in relation to the local business network) but it also shows how the issues of sustainable water management become transformed into different contexts: as legal practice, as commercial practice, as symbolic practice. And in doing this, through fluid space, SMEWAC is translating sustainable water practices and technologies into the localized regional space of the SME that is in turn, connected to wider networks of water supply and waste-water disposal. Through the iteration of SMEs, sustainable water practices at different sites across the region connected through infrastructure network, the emergent overall water consumption and waste-water disposal becomes reduced.

SMEWAP is one example of an intermediary activity that demonstrates the potentiality of translating sustainable water management into a particular context, in this case SMEs. Other intermediary organizations that we have identified in our work include organizations that link sustainable water management to urban regeneration, to industrial symbiosis projects, to low income households, to climate change, to schools and education, to low-flush toilets, to large scale industrial users, to river side leisure activities. Indeed, such intermediaries seem to be proliferating as the challenges of sustainable water management develop. Crucial to their work is the ability to work across different spatial scales, but also to work between different spatial forms in ways that enables the translation of sustainable water management practices and technologies into different sets of social interests.

Conclusions: Complexity and spatiality

One of the problems of developing strategies for sustainable water management is establishing an appropriate geographical scale through which such strategies can be implemented. The European Union through the Water Framework Directive has sought to introduce the 'river basin' as a the appropriate, natural, basis for managing water resources. Important to such an approach is the need to incorporate the diversity of stakeholders, who will directly or indirectly impact on the river basin level, into decision making processes. Complexity can be useful for this kind of problem, for example in providing a framework for the co-evolution of different institutional frameworks that might be relevant to such a river basin, as well as frameworks about how to create more open and creative learning environments through which stakeholders can engage in decision making. This would enable an understanding of the emergent characteristics of sustainable water management in such a regional space and to identify different forms, attractors perhaps, that this might take. Emergence will indeed be an important part of understanding the sustainability of a river basin area and the insights of complexity about nonlinearity and irreversibility will be important. However, to understand that emergence, and the ways in which nonlinearity is manifest, will require understanding the interaction of the regional and fluid spaces through which water travels, and the fluid spaces through which the concept of sustainable water management travels.

We have used this notion of travelling of the concept of 'sustainable water management' across different fluids and into the networks and regions of the water sector as an illustration of the importance of developing the conceptualization of spatiality in complexity science. More specifically our concern is with what we might call the complexity social sciences though the emphasis on complexity science, and on the hybrid nature of socio-technical systems, renders strict disciplinary division unhelpful. The opening up of the three spaces of region, network and fluid is not meant to be all encompassing. As Mol and Law first state these are just three, there may be more and recently authors have picked up upon 'fire' space to describe mutable objects that remain in fixed spaces (Law & Mol 2000). Our argument is that understanding complexity dynamics implicitly, and sometimes explicitly, involves understanding spatial dynamics. Spatiality in dominant complexity analysis is restricted to 'regional' topologies. Such a view leads to analysis of the nested nature of different regional spaces and the interactions or co-evolution between different regions or across different spaces. However, the heterogeneity of processes within those spaces, and which move across those spaces, gets lost. Such loss means the complexity of the relationships between the everyday practices and emergent dynamics becomes poorly understood. In the case of water management, drawing boundaries around a regional space does not achieve integrative practices because local practices are also embedded within other regional spaces and scales, as well as networked spaces that stretch beyond, and cut across, such a bounded area. The emergence of sustainable water management requires more work, it requires more fluid work that can translate sustainable water management across different spaces, different sets of social interests, connecting new social practices and technologies into context specific locations.

The argument we have made has sought to bring to the complexity agenda the incorporation of broader notions of spatiality than has hitherto been the case. A key characteristic of complex systems is their context sensitivity, both in terms of space and time. A complexity framework helps to understand how the localized activities of sustainable water management will require adaptability to specific sets of interests and socio-technical configurations and yet how such localized activity forms part of a large-scale emergent dynamic. Adding a spatiality understanding to this, and by proliferating the understanding of spatial topologies, we can understand the relationship between such local activity, and the emergence of sustainable water management at a larger regional scale, is not simply about a recursive dynamic of local activities leading to higher scale emergence. First, by drawing attention to the fluid dynamic of intermediaries we reveal the hidden work and translations required to enable changing patterns of practice, or the introduction of new technologies. Second, by recognizing also the constitution of network spaces we can understand how the processes of recursivity are channelled through embedded networks of infrastructures.

References

Allen, P. M. (1997). *Cities and Regions as Self-Organizing Systems: Models of Complexity*, Amsterdam: Gordon and Breach.

Ball, P. (1999). *H₂O: A Biography of Water*, London: Phoenix.

Bijker, W. E., Hughes, T P. and Pinch, T. (eds.) (1987). *The Social Construction of Technological Systems*, Cambridge Mass.: MIT Press.

Bijker, W. E. and Law, J. (eds.) (1994). *Shaping Technology: Building Society*, Cambridge, MA: MIT Press.

Chappells, H. (2003). *Reconceptualising Electricity and Water: Institutions, InfraStructures and the Constitution of Demand*, Ph.D. thesis, Department of Sociology. Lancaster, Lancaster University.

Clark, N. (2000). "Botonizing On the Asphalt? The Complex Life of Cosmopolitan Bodies," *Body and Society*, 6: 13-34.

Cohen, J. and Stewart, I. (1994). *The Collapse of Chaos: Discovering Simplicity in a Complex World*, Harmondsworth: Penguin.

European Community (2000). "Directive 2000/60/EC of the European Parliament and of the Council of 23 October 2000. Establishing a Framework for Community Action in the Field of Water Policy," *Official Journal of the European Communities*, L 327(1): 1-72.

Fonesca, J. (2002). *Complexity and Innovation in Organizations*, London: Routledge.

Giddens, A. (1984). *The Constitution of Society: Outline of the Theory of Structuration*, Cambridge: Polity Press.

Graham, S. and Marvin, S. (2001). *Splintering Urbanism: Networked Infrastructures, Technological Mobilities and the Urban Condition*, London: Routledge.

Guy, S., Moss, T. and Marvin, S. (2001). *Urban Infrastructure in Transition Networks, Buildings*, Plans, London: Earthscan.

Harvey, D. (1989). *The Condition of Postmodernity*, Oxford: Blackwell.

Hayes, E, (2002). *Mountains, Sheep and Fences: A Study of the Network of Reconciliation Within the UK Lake District National Park*, Ph.D. thesis, Centre for Science Studies. Lancaster, Lancaster University.

Illich, I. (1986). *H₂O and the Waters of Forgetfullness*, London: Marion Boyars.

Kinnersley, D. (1994). *Coming Clean*, London: Penguin.

Latour, B. (1993). *We Have Never Been Modern*, London: Prentice Hall.

Law, J. and Mol, A. (2000). *Situating Technoscience: An Inquiry into Spatialities*, Department of Sociology, Lancaster University.

Mackenzie, D. and Wajcman, J. (eds.) (1999). *The Social Shaping of Technology*, Maidenhead: Open University Press.

Mol, A. and Law, J. (1994). "Regions, Networks and Fluids: Anaemia and Social Topology," *Social Studies of Science*, 24: 641-71.

Moss, T. (2003). Solving Problems of 'Fit' At the Expense of Problems of 'Interplay'? The Spatial Reorganisation of Water Management Following the EU Water Framework Directive," in H. Briet, E. Engles, T. Moss and M. Troja (eds.), *How Institutions Change: Perspective on Social Learning in Global and Local Environmental Concerns*, Opladen: Leske and Budrich.

Perrow, C. (1999). *Normal Accidents: Living with High-Risk Technologies*, New Jersey: Princeton.

Rycroft, R. W. and Kash, D. E. (1999). *The Complexity Challenge: Technological Innovation for the 21ˢᵗ Century*, London: Pinter.

Sibley, D. (1995). *Geographies of Exclussion*, London: Routledge.

Star, S. L. (1999). "The Ethnography of Infrastructure," *American Behavioural Scientist*, 43(3): 377-91.

Swyngedouw, E. (2004). *Social Power and the Urbanization of Water: Flows of Power*, Oxford: Oxford University Press.

United Utilities (2003). *Meeting Future Requirements: Draft Water and Wastewater Services Business Plan 2005-2010*, www.unitedutilities.com.

Urry, J. (2003). *Global Complexity*, Cambridge: Polity.

White, I. and Howe, J. (2003). "Planning and the European Union Water Framework Directive," *Environment Planning and Management*, 46(4): 621-631.

CHAPTER 29

ENCOURAGING STRATEGIC CHANGE BY USING COMPLEXITY BASED PRINCIPLES: A CASE STUDY OF THE OPEN UNIVERSITY, UK

Elizabeth McMillan

This chapter tells of a major strategic organizational change intervention that took place at the Open University in the UK over a four year period. This provides a longitudinal case study which offers valuable insights into the use of ideas from complexity in a complex, traditional public sector organization. People both consciously and unconsciously used complexity based principles in order to loosen up the organization and push it towards behaving as a true complex adaptive system. The story of the program and the analysis of the research data demonstrate that complexity principles, especially self-organizing principles, can be highly effective at both operational and strategic levels in encouraging organizational change and the emergence of complex learning. A complexity based strategic change process may be encouraged by using two models: a 'Twelve Principles' model which describes how to facilitate such a process by using twelve interdependent approaches; and a 'Transition strategy' model (McMillan, 2004). These suggest ways in which to integrate traditional strategic approaches with learning organization principles in order to move towards a complexity style organization.

Managing Organizational Complexity: Philosophy, Theory, and Application
A Volume in: Managing the Complex, pages 505-519.
ISBN: 1-59311-319-6 (cloth), 1-59311-318-8 (paper)

Introduction

A number of writers on organizations and management have argued that complexity is only useful as a helpful metaphor to encourage new and enlightening insights for understanding and interpreting organizations and organizational change (see Richardson's introductory remarks to this section). This is one way in which complexity is opening up minds to fresh concepts and new approaches to management, and it is an extremely valuable one. But, in my view, that is not all that complexity offers.

Some writers contend that there is insufficient evidence to support the notion that complexity principles can be successfully used in organizations. I would argue that complexity science is a very new science and its application in non-scientific domains has only just begun. Thus there is bound to be a lack of evidence as it takes time and persistence to gather evidence on organizations.

The picture is changing, however, as understanding of complexity gains ground and evidence is emerging from the work of a number of managers who both consciously and unconsciously use ideas and approaches from complexity in their organizations. This chapter provides one such piece of evidence from my own experiences. It tells of a major strategic organizational change intervention that took place at the Open University in the UK over the four years 1993–1996. This provides a longitudinal case study which offers valuable insights into the use of complexity-based principles, especially self-organizing principles, and their application in a complex, traditional public sector organization.

The case study of this program was the subject of my doctoral research. Primary data was collected via interviews, questionnaires and workshops. Secondary data was drawn from a wide range of internal documents and papers (many of which would not have been available to an external researcher) and an external case study of the program undertaken by the Institute for Employment Studies, Sussex University. This case study used interviews, focus groups and a bipolar semantic differential questionnaire.

The Open University

The Open University was founded in 1969 and admitted its first students in 1971. By the mid 1970s it had over 50,000 undergraduates and a large number of courses of study available. At the time of writing, 2003, it is the largest university in the UK with over 200,000 students and customers. It ranks amongst the top universities for the quality of its teaching and is renowned for its research excellence. As a UK university it is unique as its programs of study are open to all regardless of qualifications. Further, its teaching is based on innovative and inventive distance learning methods whereby students study either at home or at work. This enables it to teach on an international basis too.

By the late 1980s and early 1990s the University's external environment had substantially changed. In the early days many higher education institutions had laughed at the idea of an 'open' university but now they were eagerly imitating its teaching and learning methods. Thus the University found itself facing serious competition, often from local providers. Further, new developments in multi-media teaching and the use of new technologies were challenging the more traditional aspects of distance learning delivery.

The University had developed a very complex and bureaucratic management structure. This made decision making and taking action a long and often cumbersome process. As an institution it fitted very well with Handy's (1993) model of the role culture which is typified by the image of a Greek temple. As Handy points out this kind of organization can work very well where the market for its products is stable and predictable and the product has a long life cycle. It is also particularly good where economies of scale are important, as at the University, which mass produces its courses in order to ensure their economic viability. Unfortunately, this kind of organization is usually slow to see the need for change and slow at responding, even when the need to change is recognized.

The external environment was further changed when the government altered the University's funding arrangements. It was no longer funded separately but had to compete with other UK universities for its core funding grants. These provided some 57.7% of the University's total operating budget.

Thus by 1993 changes in its environment coupled with its own structures and attitudes meant that there was a danger that the University would be left behind. Its senior management had already begun to consider this and in early 1993 it produced *Plans for Change*. This was a strategic action plan which detailed the major initiatives the University would need to take over the next five years in order to change and achieve its strategic objectives.

I had joined the Open University as a senior human resources manager in 1986. Some years later I became Head of Training and Development responsible for ensuring that some 3,500 academic and non-academic staff, drawn from a wide range of occupations were trained and developed to meet the needs of the organization and their own career aspirations. Early in 1993 I was asked by the Pro Vice Chancellor for Strategy to help design and deliver a strategic consultation process in support of *Plans for Change*. This recognized the importance of involving all employees in helping the University to achieve its strategic objectives which would be done via a process of awareness raising, management action at all levels and staff development. Changes in working practices were seen as key to this and were described in six broad 'new directions'.

It was about the same time that I first came across chaos theory and then complexity science. As a manager with over twenty years experience of organizations I had long found that much of organization and management theory did match up to, or explain, my real life experiences. Thus when I encountered chaos and complexity I became very excited by the possibilities that they offered. I followed up by reading Gleick (1993), Lewin (1993), Nonaka (1988), Prigogine and Stengers (1984), Stacey (1992, 1993) and others. I also attended seminars and lectures by Fritjof Capra, Brian Goodwin, Ralph Stacey and Gareth Morgan. These activities along with further reading of people like Capra (1996), Coveney and Highfield (1995), Kauffman (1996), Wheatley (1994), and Waldrop (1994) provided the theoretical framework that informed my actions over the next four years. I deliberately used this to influence the change process, to further develop my management competencies and to test out complexity notions in the real world of organizations.

The New Directions program

The program began as a consultation exercise designed to inform all levels of staff of the University's current challenging situation and to seek their active support in the realization of the University's new strategic objectives. The program thus set out with specific objectives which it sought to meet by a series of two-day workshops. Soon a pattern of process emerged which became the approach for all the early workshops. The Pro Vice Chancellor (PVC), Strategy would introduce *Plans for Change* and explain what it sought to do and why. The participants then worked in small groups visioning the OU of the future. These visions would be shared and key themes identified in a plenary session. The participants would then work in groups again to develop an action plan for each key theme. In a final plenary session these plans would be presented and discussed with the PVC, Strategy.

The workshops may appear at first glance to be typical of management 'away day' events, but there were significant differences. Each workshop included a wide mix of staff chosen at random from the phone book. Thus a wide range of attitudes, and views on the organization were exchanged.

"People used to working in different theoretical and bureaucratic domains encountered staff used to working with hard nosed, practical issues. It was an encounter that enriched discussions and encouraged the development of multiple perspectives." (McMillan, 2004: 114)

The workshops created an egalitarian and freeform approach to strategic action that resonated strongly with complexity principles. Each workshop had a team of facilitators from my department who worked with the small groups. I had briefed them to encourage people to let go, to experiment, to have fun and to use their intuition and imagination as well as logic and reason. We cannot accurately predict the future and we cannot control it, but we can devise new ways of thinking and acting, I told my team. Further, I explained to them the notion of sensitive dependence on initial conditions or the *Butterfly Effect*. Over time small changes can make a significant difference. This means, I suggested, that every individual can do something that may over time lead to major change. Individual action is important. This was a significant message in an organization where people were unused to making changes without authorization and where a top-down approach was the norm. The program became associated with its action approach and for the importance it attached to individual action.

The workshops generated great interest and in response to employee demand more were held in the autumn of 1993. Thus from the beginning a response dynamic arose which encouraged participation and created important feedback loops. At the same time volunteers from the workshops were invited to form a group to organize a conference for the coming year. This would enable people to update themselves, network, explore core themes and put their ideas to the Vice Chancellor and his top team.

More workshops were held in early 1994. These concentrated on some of the key themes that had emerged the previous year. Major strategic topics were explored with the senior manager responsible for their development. In doing this the program organizers recognized and acknowledged the value of the contributions made by participants in the program. It demonstrated that everyone in the organization could contribute to strategic policy-making and action.

In March a team of eight volunteers came together to form the Conference Planning Team. They had been given the task of organizing a conference on the 18th May. The rest was up to them. In just over two months they organized a highly successful one-day event. It had twenty workshops in parallel streams with a mix of internal and external speakers and an exhibition. Over 100 staff attended and there was a waiting list. The conference influenced a range of activities and initiatives across the University. These included taking a more professional and active approach to marketing which led to the setting up of a new department; and talks on a range of staffing issues, in particular, differences in terms and conditions between different groups of staff. Developments in new technologies were under consideration at the time but the conference gave a major impetus to their realization. The conference team itself went on to encourage improvements in internal communications.

The team's success was such that within days of the conference it was decided to ask volunteers from the program to organize a staff survey. For almost two years the University had talked of the need to survey staff and find out what they felt about working at the University - but nothing had been done. Conference delegates were asked to volunteer to work with the Director of Public Relations on the design and delivery of a staff survey for the autumn. Nine volunteers formed the Staff Survey Team. It selected and briefed a survey company, advised on survey design and content, organized a pilot survey and organized distribution of the questionnaire to all staff in October. There was a very good return of 65%.

Meanwhile the Conference Planning Team spontaneously decided to form a 'ginger' (action) group to follow up on the conference and further expand the program in support of *Plans for Change*. With administrative support from my department they set about organizing a range of activities. Workshops, lunchtime briefings, and a whole host of innovative activities took place such that it became known as the 'people's movement'. Thus within a year of its inception the program, now called *New Directions*, was unfolding in an unplanned, unpredictable way supported by the spontaneous activities of staff volunteers from all levels of the organization. These volunteers worked in a traditional organization imbued with mechanistic principles and practice, but they began to use complexity concepts in their everyday activities. Further, they were doing so as a result of experiential learning as well as theoretical inputs.

In January the following year several members of the 'ginger' group and the Survey Team decided of their own volition to get together and they formed the *New Directions* Action Group. They brainstormed a number of ideas which were followed up during the year. These included a range of workshops on topics such as making mistakes and improving communications. These created and used a range of innovative learning techniques. Most importantly they held workshops in different parts of the UK so that staff from regional centers could more easily participate.

The following year the Action Group organized another one-day conference and more workshops. By now however, the volunteers were losing energy. People's workloads were increasing and a difficult financial climate was affecting staff morale. Thus in January 1997 the group reluctantly decided to take a break - and it disbanded after nearly three years of volunteer activity. Thus the *New Directions* program came to an end after four years. It is estimated that some 23% of full staff were involved.

Originally it had been decided to hold six workshops in 1993 in support of the University's formal strategic planning processes. But the organizers responded to the reaction of the University's employees and continued the program. Thus a new and spontaneous response dynamic emerged which was informed and inspired by complexity principles. This emerged as a pattern of process. After the 1994 conference staff volunteers spontaneously took over the program and it ran for a total of four years. They did this on top of their existing jobs and without additional resources from their own departments. None of this had been foreseen or planned.

The workshops

By inviting employees to these workshops, regardless of status, the program ensured that discussions on strategy between all levels of staff took place directly and on equal terms. Effective feedback processes were set up which ensured that ideas were fed all around the institution. Overt strategic listening, led by the PVC, Strategy reinforced that flow. The 'themed' workshops reinforced the bottom-up process and demonstrated to all employees that they could influence University thinking. Thus fresh flows of information from staff not usually involved in strategy circulated around the institution and informed discussions at all levels. From the start the program created feedback loops with amplifying potential. Over time it became clear that these were positive feedback loops.

Out of the first few workshops an egalitarian, informal, creative, 'let's do it' spontaneous approach emerged which continued to inform the *New Directions* approach to strategic change. The program encouraged people to take action for change and in so doing sought to bridge the traditional divide between strategic planning and action.

"New Directions is all about action. The activities are designed by staff volunteers and emphasize practical results. The over-used phrase 'think globally act locally' really does fit the New Directions activities. Staff sort out where the University needs to go and then they take action to help get there." (Geoff Peters, Open House, July 1995)

Not everyone was enthusiastic about the program. Many middle and senior managers were openly hostile, concerned that their positions were being undermined. However, as the program was championed by the PVC, Strategy and other senior staff it was able to continue.

Change and learning

Many of those who participated in the program spoke of how their feelings and behaviors had changed as a result. Further, they had influenced their colleagues too. Many employees now believed that they could contribute to strategic issues and take action themselves - and many did take action. The Institute for Employment Studies report found "an organization that had become more flexible and less hierarchical, more sharing and more open with information" (Tamkin & Barber, 1998: 48). They also wrote that the University had moved "away from an organization that was resistant to change to one where there is a growing awareness of the need to change" (Tamkin & Barber, 1998: 18).

There is considerable evidence to show that double- and single-loop learning took place inspired and facilitated by the program. And learning is another word for change (Handy, 1990). People were encouraged to experiment, be creative, to have fun and to speculate. The program provided opportunities for learning and an environment which encouraged and facilitated it. It enabled individuals to innovate and evolve, developing as true complex adaptive systems in the workplace. Prior to the program such development would have been difficult given the traditional nature of the organization.

How well does the program map onto a complexity framework? First of all it demonstrates that over time small changes can make a real difference. The first few workshops led to a major program of activity that unfolded spontaneously over a four year period (see Figure 1). Ideas and insights from the workshops and the 1993 conference, in particular, either influenced or directly led to new initiatives. Entrepreneurial activities, for example, were encouraged and supported, and greater flexibility in teaching provision took place. A complex range of responses and feedback loops were created that served to disturb the organization's equilibrium and move it closer to the edge of chaos.

Self-organization

The expansion and development of the program was not pre-planned, co-ordinated or controlled in a logical, linear way. Those who organized it (the original team and then the volunteer groups) took an opportunistic approach. They built on ideas, actions and events in a spontaneous way that is essentially self-organizing (Morgan 1993). Although they may not have pre-planned things, those involved had a strong sense of what they were trying to achieve, much in the same way as Morgan's (1993) self-organizing termites. They looked for opportunities or projects which would help them move forward in pursuit of their core objective: to change the University.

Figure 1 shows the development of the program and the emergence of the volunteer groups and the activities they created. The 'ginger' group and the action group arose as a natural response to the events around them and in so doing created fresh informal networks. Their unplanned response and the way they formed into groups around issues and interests and worked to deal with them lies at the core of self-organization in organizations (Stacey, 1996).

The program encouraged the formation of informal networks and created a network of fresh shadow systems. As Stacey (1996) points out these are informal, self-organizing networks of contacts that operate outside the formal structures. The self-organizing shadow system challenged the formal systems and helped to change the University from an organization set in its ways and resistant to change, to one that was actively seeking ways to do things differently.

Spontaneity is a key attribute of self-organizing systems and was a key feature of the program. It picked up on ideas and issues as they arose and responded in an unplanned way. It had what one manager described as 'structured spontaneity'. Thus although it freewheeled along it did have a self-imposed and flexible structure shaped by its values and patterns of process. This is an example of Kauffman's (1996) *order for free* whereby self-organizing systems create their own internal patterns of order.

The two project teams that were created as part of the program were deliberately encouraged to be self-organizing. They were highly effective as project teams delivering on target and to a very high standard. They developed ways of working, communicating and making decisions that were very different to the normal mode of team working in the University. They (and the action groups) were informal, temporary, and the members decided what to do and who would do it. They empowered themselves to take action, their boundaries were influenced, but not controlled, by senior management and they were not part of the formal structures. Thus the Conference Team and the Survey Team could be described as self-organizing when compared with Stacey's (1996) definitions of self-organized and self-managed teams.

1993
Spring - Pro Vice Chancellor Strategy and Head of Training and Development organize workshops to consult on 'Plans for Change' (Planned activity)

Autumn – More workshops take place in response to demands

1994
Spring - More workshops on strategic themes employess raised in 1993 workshop

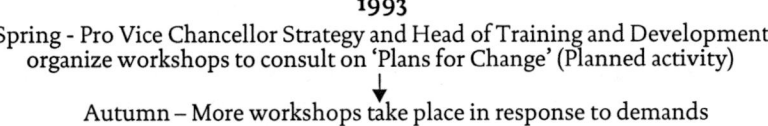

Technology Strategy ◄   ► Choosing the OU

Improving Communications ◄   ▲ Joining the OU

March – Conference Planning Team of volunteers first meet

May 18th - New Directions Conference

Themes and Issues raised ┈┈►   ┈┈► 'Plans for Change' New Version
Democratic Strategic Action Plan

May – Staff Survey Team formed by volunteers

'Ginger Group' formed that follows up on ideas from workshops and conference

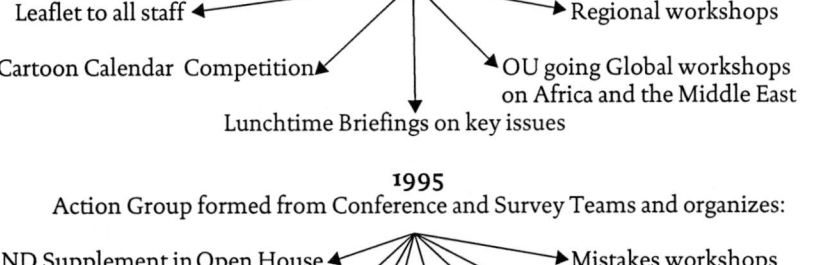

Leaflet to all staff ◄   ► Regional workshops

Cartoon Calendar Competition ◄   ▲ OU going Global workshops
on Africa and the Middle East

Lunchtime Briefings on key issues

1995
Action Group formed from Conference and Survey Teams and organizes:

ND Supplement in Open House ◄   ► Mistakes workshops

Cartoon Glendar competition ◄   ▲ Workshop for Students

Visualization workshop ►   ▲ Lunchtime Briefings

Regional workshops▼   Communications workshops

1996
Action Group organizes:
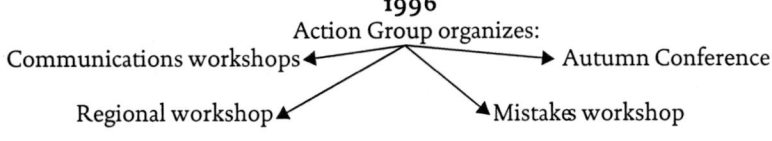
Communications workshops ◄   ► Autumn Conference

Regional workshop ◄   ▲ Mistakes workshop

Figure 1
The *New Directions* Program 1993-1996

Complexity influences

From the very beginning I deliberately injected concepts from complexity (and chaos theory) into the program. I sought to influence the workshop facilitators and key people including the PVC, Strategy. He had been a lecturer in systems so he was familiar with notions of self-organization and emergence and was very supportive. Along with myself and another 'volunteer' he attended a seminar given by Ralph Stacy on complexity. He was keen to empower individuals to take action and, in my view, his commitment to this and his willingness to let go and to support the volunteers enabled self-organizing processes to flourish for a time.

As a facilitator in the two teams and then the volunteer groups I was able to explore and discuss complexity principles and their implications for strategic change with groups of staff. People were encouraged to consider these concepts and to experiment in their own areas of influence. For many working in an organization with mechanistic overtones this required a significant change in thinking and behavior. Evidence from the case study shows that many people did introduce complexity approaches into their work. One person in particular, a key activist in the program, started to study complexity in depth. She is now working towards her doctorate and using complexity as a theoretical framework.

Complexity features

Stacey (1996) has developed a complexity based theory of organization based on nine propositions. *The New Directions* program maps onto seven of these propositions. It supports the notion of an organization as a web of nonlinear feedback loops. It helped to pull some areas of the University away from *stability* and towards the *edge of chaos*. The paradoxical nature of organizations was reflected by the program which excited some individuals and made others fearful. Unlike the formal planning processes of the University the program did not preplan but reacted spontaneously to events. It tended to pull the University away from a near to equilibrium state and its program of activities, which unfolded over a four year period could not have been predicted. The program supports Stacey's (1996) notion of long-term planning as a spontaneous self-organizing process out of which strategic directions may arise.

Nonaka (1988) describes a number of ways in which an organization can create sufficient fluctuations to transform itself. Some features of the program match his ideas. The program and especially the workshops offered strategic visions that stimulated debate and creativity. New information entered the organization and there were creative discussions and experimentation in groups. Most importantly self-organizing teams protected by senior management (the PVC, Strategy) were set up.

Facilitating a complexity based change process

Twelve interdependent principles derived from research on the program offer managers a way to facilitate a strategic change intervention using complexity. This may be the first of many steps in arriving at a complexity based organization.

1. Stimulate changes at the grass roots, encouraging people as individuals to think and behave differently. Bring in information from outside to stimulate debate. Small changes happening at this level can bring about significant changes over time.

2. Facilitate this process by setting up a *New Directions* style series of workshops. This will bring together staff from all over the organization, from all roles and all levels. This approach will:

   - alert employees to the challenges the organization faces and encourage strategic thinking at the operational level;

   - enable those employees who want to contribute to strategy development to do so;

   - encourage people to make their own changes and thus help to start small individual waves of change;

   - introduce fresh information flows around the organization;

   - help employees to develop new perspectives on their jobs; learn more about their organization; actively participate in learning experiences;

   - involve a broad range of employees in the change process and create multiple change dynamics at all levels. These will have the potential to bring about significant changes over time;

   - set up the right conditions for the development of self-organizing informal systems which will challenge the formal systems.

3. Make sure that a senior manager with strategic responsibilities participates in every workshops and feeds back into the organization the ideas and insights that arise.

4. Use 'strategic' workshops to explore the gap that exists between the future visions and current reality. This process will energize some individuals and work to introduces changes.

5. Invite employees to form self-organizing teams, as these will introduce complexity principles and encourage self organizing activities for change.

6. Provide a supportive environment for self organizing processes (see Table 1).

7. Use the *Transition Strategy* model, as such an approach blends the 'old'

with the 'new' and by so doing avoids excessive shifts of approach that both individuals and organizations often find hard to handle. Such an approach integrates spontaneous and intuitive behaviors with planned and rational ones.

8. Experienced, skilled and trusted facilitators will be needed "to ensure equality of involvement and to help with the dismantling of cultural and hierarchical barriers which could block the free flowing nature of the process and impede equality of participation" (McMillan, 2004: 163). They should also be used when setting up self-organizing groups to facilitate the development of collective experience and the emergence of group adaptation. The facilitators should understand the thinking and the principles that underpin self-organizing groups.

9. Use volunteers and employees who are energized to make changes.

10. Not only the right environment but also supportive beliefs and behaviors are needed to create the right conditions for the use of self-organization and other complexity based principles (see Table 2).

11. There should be a number of key people involved in the process who have a good understanding of the core concepts of complexity.

12. A complexity based change process may have many detractors so it will need powerful champions within the organization - as with any major change process.

Environment	Ethos and Values	Activities
Safe	Egalitarian	Fun
Stimulating	Open	Experimental
Responsive	Democratic	Challenging
Supportive	Reflect those of the orga-	Use mixed staff groups
Non-political	nization	Offer a variety of learning opportunities

Table 1
Environment, Ethos, Values and Activities
(Adapted from McMillan, 2000: 188)

The Transition Strategy model

There are powerful resonances between the views of innovative writers like Handy and Morgan, notions of the learning organization and concepts from complexity. In Morgan's (1993) view, if managers are to cope with the uncertainties of modern organizational life then they will need to help their staff to self-organize and evolve. Handy (1990) considers that organizations will need to think and act very differently in order to survive. His ideas on reframing the way we see the world and the symbiotic relationship between learning and changing resonates powerfully with many aspects of complexity. Double-loop learning (Morgan, 1993) and second order change (Dale, 1994) are essential facets of the learning organization, and are also key features of complex adaptive systems. The learning organization recognizes that these traits are necessary for survival (Pedler, et al., 1991). Complexity considers that learning and adaptation skills are vital for a species' survival. Thus socially organized insects, mammals and other species engage in complex, adaptive learning activities in order to enhance their chances of survival. Organizations too, as living systems, can use this model to improve their chances of success. The *New Directions* program demonstrated how it was possible to effectively weave together aspects of the learning organization with complexity principles. It created a range of situations and opportunities for employees to engage in experimentation and complex learning. This helped raise the level of group and individual learning in the organization and facilitated the development of adaptive skills.

Beliefs	Behaviors
One cannot predict the future	Relaxed
Expect the unexpected	Responsive
People networks and interactions create change dynamics	Listening
	Feeding back
Humor and fun can encourage changes	Communicating
Individuals can make small changes which may be very valuable and should be encouraged	Letting go
	Trusting
Experimentation goes hand in hand with innovation	Supportive
	Sharing
Energy and enthusiasm in people are a real resource	Adaptive
Change is both seen and unseen	'Walking the talk'
Change cannot be easily measured	Restraining controlling tendencies
Real change will probably feel very uncomfortable for a time but it is part of an ongoing learning and adaptation process	Resolute
	Encouraging others to let go

Table 2
Beliefs and Behaviors
(Adapted from McMillan, 2000: 188)

The *Transition Strategy* model is based on experience and analysis of the program. It is a hybrid that draws on modern approaches to organizations, traditional strategic thinking, and complexity and learning organization principles. It offers an approach which creates a bridge between old and new ways of thinking and action. It serves to integrate traditional theories of organizational change with more innovative and recent models, while moving into the complexity science domain (see Figure 2).

The 'Transition' model does not see strategy as a fixed approach but rather as a process that draws on a rich flow of theories and ideas, but with the objective of moving towards a complexity style organization. Thus as it moves in this direction it gradually breaks away from the past and the 'old' worldview. It is not as radical as some proposals, but it may prove to be more acceptable in organizations still heavily influenced by traditional ideas on change and classical scientific notions where revolutionary approaches to change would be resisted. It offers a realistic and practical way of moving an organization away from the machine model to a complex adaptive system model. The twelve principles discussed earlier should enable an organization to begin this journey.

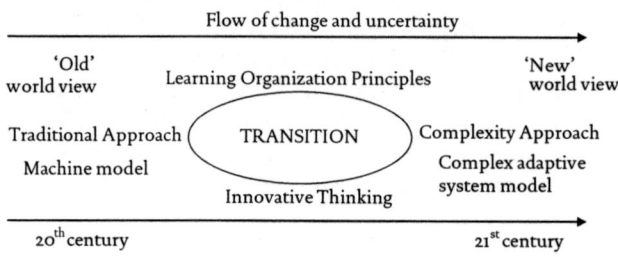

Figure 2
Transition Strategy Model
(Adapted from McMillan, 2004: 166)

Conclusion

The *New Directions* program had its origins in conventional strategic thinking and good employee consultation practice. Essentially it began as a 'deliberate' strategic intervention, but as time went on it evolved into a more 'emergent' or 'consensus' strategy (Mintzberg & Waters, 1989). This evolved through the "results of a host of individual actions" (Mintzberg & Waters, 1989: 13) which were essentially self-organizing. Complexity based principles were fed into the process from the beginning and the staff responded to the program in a way that could not, and should not, have been predicted. The two self-organizing project teams and the two self-organizing action groups arose spontaneously from the program. These demonstrated the effectiveness of using self-organizing principles in team working and in energizing and facilitating change at all levels.

People both consciously and unconsciously used complexity principles in order to loosen up the organization and push it towards behaving as a true complex adaptive system. Along with members of the teams and others involved in the program I moved from a deliberately conscious level of incompetence in my use of complexity concepts in practice, to the unconsciously competent level of learning. Thus complexity principles became interwoven into the fabric of our everyday management activities.

The story of the program and the analysis of the data demonstrate that complexity principles, especially self organizing principles, can be highly effective at both operational and strategic levels in encouraging organizational change and the emergence of complex learning. In this chapter I have presented a summary of the program and its use of complexity. For those readers who would like a more in depth review with more data, including quotes from participants and key players, I refer you to chapters 6, 7 and 8 in McMillan (2004).

References

Capra, F. (1996). *The Web of Life*, London: HarperCollins.

Coveney, P. and Highfield, R. (1995). *Frontiers of Complexity*, New York: Fawcett Columbine.

Dale, M. (1994). "Learning Organizations," in C. Mabey and P. Illes (eds.), *Managing Learning*, London: Routledge in association with Open University Press.

Gleick, J. (1993). *Chaos*, London: Abacus.

Handy, C. (1990). *The Age of Unreason*, London: Arrow.

Handy, C. (1993). *Understanding Organizations*, 3rd ed., London: Penguin Books.

Kauffman, S. (1996). *At Home in the Universe: The Search for Laws of Self-Organization and Complexity*, London: Penguin Books.

Lewin, R. (1993). *Complexity: Life on the Edge of Chaos*, London: Phoenix.

McMillan, E. (2004). *Complexity, Organizations and Change*, London: Routledge.

McMillan, E. (2000). "Using Self Organizing Principles to Create Effective Project Teams as Part of an Organizational Change Intervention: A Case Study of the Open University," in I. McCarthy and T. Rakotobe-Joel (eds.), *Complexity and Complex Systems in Industry: A Conference Proceedings*, Warwick University UK.

Mintzberg, H., and Waters, J. A. (1989). "Of Strategies, Deliberate and Emergent," in D. Asch and C. Bowman (eds.), *Readings in Strategic Management*, London: Macmillan Education Ltd.

Morgan, G. (1993). *Imaginization: The Art of Creative Management*, Newbury Park, CA: Sage.

Nonaka, I. (1988). "Creating organizational order out of chaos: self renewal in Japanese firms," *California Management Review*, Spring: 57-73.

Pedler, M., Boydell, T. and Burgoyne, J. (1991). *The Learning Company*, London: McGraw Hill.

Prigogine, I. and Stengers, I. (1984). *Order Out of Chaos*, London: Heinemann.

Stacey, R. D. (1992). *Managing the Unknowable*, San Francisco: Jossey-Bass.

Stacey, R. D. (1993). "Strategy as Order Emerging from Chaos," *Long Range Planning*, 26(1): 10-17.

Stacey, R. D. (1996). *Strategic Management and Organizational Dynamics*, London: Pitman Publishing.

Tamkin, P. and Barber, L. (1998). "Learning to Manage," Draft Report, Institute for Employment Studies, University of Sussex.

Waldrop, M. M. (1994). *Complexity*, New York: Penguin Books.

Wheatley, M. (1994). *Leadership and the New Science*, San Francisco: Berrett-Koehler.

CHAPTER 30

PROVOKING CHAORDIC CHANGE IN A DUTCH MANUFACTURING FIRM

Frans van Eijnatten and Maarten van Galen

This chapter reports on a series of 'interventions' in a Dutch capital-equipment manufacturing company that were focused at the development of the 'organizational mind'. The explicit goals of this project were to facilitate self-organization, and the creation of novelty. During a period of four and a half years, a number of change initiatives were undertaken, using a complexity framework, in which dialogue was put central as the new mode of communication in the company, in order to further develop the thinking of both individuals and groups. Although the results show improved thoughtfulness, mutual respect and trust among managers, employees, and workers, the appearance of emergent leadership and increased initiatives, the pace of change was much slower and less pronounced than originally anticipated. The project was set up as an action-research initiative, in which external consultants, company managers, and researchers collaborated. The chapter describes the steps that were undertaken by the respective parties on the basis of intensive and frequent interactions.

Managing Organizational Complexity: Philosophy, Theory, and Application
A Volume in: Managing the Complex, pages 521-556.
ISBN: 1-59311-319-6 (cloth), 1-59311-318-8 (paper)

Introduction

This chapter presents a case study in an industrial company, which we will call 'Dutch Manufacturing Firm', DMF for short. The case study describes an organization-development project that was informed by complexity thinking. Although the project is still underway, this chapter covers most of the transformation processes. Roughly, the reported study covers a period of four and a half years.

In essence, the change initiative may be described as an attempt to provoke a new organizational culture that was created and maintained by a dialogical mode of communication among its members. Although both the 'program,' project plan, and interventions were not laid out in detail in advance but rather gradually developed on the spot - 'pure randomness' might be too strong a description to typify this approach. On the contrary, although Chaordic Systems Thinking (CST)[1] as a theoretical framework (Fitzgerald & Van Eijnatten, 1998, 2002a, 2002b; Van Eijnatten, *et al.*, 2003) emerged during the project, its concepts form a coherent whole and fit well in a complexity approach to change. Nevertheless, the reader should be prepared for major theoretical diversity: Complexity, leadership, and dialogue were combined within one and the same project, in a rather eclectic way. In this chapter we will primarily focus on the application of this CST lens in the real-life setting of a manufacturing company. As researchers, managers, and consultants worked intensely together, the project could be best characterized as action research.

A Synopsis of the company's change history
General overview

The DMF in question is world-market leader in its industry. The company has been in business for over 25 years, and employs 500 people in the south of The Netherlands (750 worldwide), while 95 % of its turnover is delivered outside Dutch territory. Its market share is 60%. The company has an American subsidiary with about the same product portfolio, which employs 250 people, and is serving both the North- and South-American markets. Specialized in tailor-made complex processing systems for the food industry, the firm's product portfolio contains some 250 functions and over 2,500 variants. The company is very active in product innovation.

For many years now, DMF has played a leading role in developing and manufacturing processing equipment and systems. A market-oriented approach, quick response to change, innovative engineering, and the application of strict quality standards are the basis for this global-market leadership. The Dutch company together with its American subsidiary forms part of a Dutch concern that operates internationally and has an annual turnover of well over €1.35 billion. First and foremost, being part of this conglomerate means continuity, but also expert knowledge of many disciplines, such as product development, finance, sales support, service and production.

Due to a number of issues the company faced in the 1980s, including long throughput times, low product quality, low motivation, and low flexibility of products and volumes, in 1988 DMF initiated an organizational-renewal process based in *Socio-Technical Systems Design* with a pilot test of a self-managed team in the parts-production department. Two years later, additional self-managed teams were implemented in parts production, following a design process called *parallelization of product-order flows*. By 1992, the concept of self-management was introduced in both the assembly, stock and shipping departments. Also, planning was decentralized, while the parts production and assembly departments were fused into one new production department.

By 1993, a start was made with quality improvement by defining so-called *star roles* in production. Star roles are temporal responsibilities of selected team members to co-ordinate support tasks over teams, and communicate information about problems and improvements concerning specific aspects between teams. Next, a similar renewal project was initiated to improve office work. Self-managed teams also were introduced in the sales- and installation departments, and in the parts-and-services processes. By 1996, the design- and product-development departments fused into a newly formed systems group. As in this new department, pilot tests of two self-managed teams proved to be very successful, the company decided to set up similar 'parallel-development' teams for each new product-creation project. Parallel-development teams are multi-disciplinary product-creation teams, consisting of a small core team that stays involved during the whole project, and a peripheral group of temporary team members who come and go in the course of the project.

In 1998, four company-wide dedicated projects were carried out to improve specific performances. Also, the company started a dedicated knowledge-management project.

From structure to culture

Since 1988, the company has restructured its production processes by using the Dutch approach of *Integral Organizational Renewal* (De Sitter, *et al.* 1997). Functional departments were transformed into networks of self-managed teams. During this change process, special attention was paid to interdepartmental relationships. The implementation of the self-managed teams proved to be an intensive and time-consuming process. All employees, both the workers and professionals, were trained to execute multiple tasks and roles, requiring them to learn a variety of technical, social, and administrative skills. Ten years of experience with organizational renewal enabled the company to keep its position as a market leader, see Box 1.

However, an evaluation study carried out in 1999 revealed, that - although numerous projects had been successful both in implementing new team structures in production, sales, R&D, and service, and in increasing productivity - individual habits did not show similar developments (Van Eijnatten & Van

---

Some 'Hard' Figures

- Successful change from an 'Assemble-to-Order' to 'Make-to-Order' production regime,
- Throughput times of Production reduced by 65%,
- Costs associated with insufficient quality of products (rejects, etc.) reduced by 50%,
- Ratio of indirect / direct labor costs lowered by 30%,
- Set-up times in Production reduced by at least 20%,
- Task times reduced by 5%.

Some 'Soft' Figures

- Significantly improved market position,
- Increased controllability of business processes,
- Improved quality of quotation and order specifications,
- Equal pre- and post-calculations of orders (usually showing a difference of 2-3%),
- Very low turnover of personnel (less than 5%),
- Strong team spirit and high involvement of production personnel,
- High commitment and increase in internal flexibility.

Box 1
Performance Measures Resulting from Ten Years of Socio-Technical Redesign, Prior to the Chaordic Project Van Eijnatten and Hoen (1999: 14-15)

Galen, 1999). Workers were still somewhat reluctant to start new change efforts, as they did not yet consider change as part of their normal, daily-work routine. Although this might be partly caused by the fact that a certain percentage of the personnel was - and still is - hired from temping agencies to keep up with the actual, constantly changing, work demands, this is certainly not sufficient explanation. Here are some additional observations (Van Eijnatten & Neefs, 1999):

- Employees at DMF are not expressing their true wishes in the group about, for instance, what roles they (don't) want to play, or what expectations they have with respect to the outcomes,

- Employees at DMF feel uneasy when a manager is not taking the lead or setting the stage in a discussion,

- Employees at DMF often don't take initiatives because they feel they lack knowledge compared to managers,

- Individual managers at DMF want to make a powerful and dedicated impression in the discussions,

- Employees at DMF are afraid of taking the lead, because they lack an 'appropriate' hierarchical position.

At DMF, prior to the chaordic project another dominant pattern was that decisions had already been taken by management or other selected groups of professionals, long before a decision-making meeting took place - many issues were, so to speak, 'pre-cooked' or 'post-cooked' in bilateral contacts. Meetings then only could take the form of rituals: the outcomes were very much known in advance. Decision-makers often were pushing their arguments. In addition, even in the rare instances when there was no pre-setting of arguments by management, the employees seemed to act passively, as if that was in fact still the case. They did not speak their mind, and typically showed followers' behavior. Another dominant pattern at DMF was that in meetings, most of the time was spent on matters that were completely unrelated to the main subjects at stake. Also, during meetings both employees and managers took excessive time just to express that they were in full agreement with each other.

Usually, the general quality of discussions during meetings at DMF was low. Although this was noticed by managers, employees, and workers, it was not made the subject of any evaluation. Also, nobody was openly complaining about it. It was simply taken for granted. Consequently, the DMF meetings remained at the same low level of quality, without any improvement of the process.

The usual way to evaluate ideas and plans brought forward by employees, was to try to find - as many as possible - inconsistencies, omissions, and flaws in these ideas and plans. Such behavior demotivated the people who came with the ideas in the first place, and made it less likely that they would take the effort again to propose another suggestion in the future.

There was very little attention for non-material rewards. Openly appreciating each other's good work was not a very well developed custom. Nevertheless, the need for this kind of non-material remuneration was clearly expressed by the DMF personnel.

Here are some quotes from DMF managers and employees, made at the start of the chaordic project (Van Eijnatten & Neefs, 1999):

- "We are a company of hard-working engineers,"
- "DMF is unique, your idea is not applicable, here,"
- "We are very good in criticizing, not in praising people for their ideas,
- "You feel the need to defend your own position when somebody else is challenging it,"
- "You feel the urge to tell the other person that (s)he is wrong,"
- "In a meeting you have to be very quick to be the first to put forward a particular argument, otherwise another person defeats you,"
- "In a meeting you know that you have to score points, but the strange thing is, that the group is trying to prevent you from doing exactly that,"
- "Often, during a meeting, managers are disconnected. They read notes, memos, emails or letters. Such behavior displays their lack of interest in what is going on in the meeting,"

- "Management often tries to get its way, anyway! To reach their goals, they press their arguments, strongly. Sensitive discussions are avoided, because they take too much time,"

- "When somebody 'gets angry' during a meeting, nobody responds to him or her. Instead, this bad behavior will become the subject of a number of informal conversations (gossip) afterwards,"

- "The more people deviate from the 'dominant coalition', the more others try to stop them to express their opinions,"

- "When two or more persons strongly disagree with one another during a meeting, their personal relationship will suffer badly,"

- "If employees are invited to express their opinions in a meeting, only the most dominant persons will be able to do so. Soon, new questions are being asked that disrupt the process of inquiry, and there is nobody who is paying attention to the process,"

- "At the end of a meeting, there is no public evaluation of the process. Sometimes, this is done informally, afterwards."

In 1999, DMF management was complaining that initiative-taking by employees was running below expectation. They reported the inability of most employees to take up initiating and coordinating roles in new projects. By complaining, they often situated the problem outside themselves: presumably, they had a certain set of qualifications for their employees in mind. For instance: well-performing workers must possess a strong attitude towards taking action, a past record of successes rather than failures, and the guts to continue work whatever happens to them. In practice, management chose to allocate new responsibilities only to a very restricted group of 'high potentials.' As a consequence - in the absence of a leader or chair - any project group at DMF typically tended to be very passive, and its members hardly took any initiatives. Most of the time, people were looking at their managers for guidance.

Following the evaluation research, DMF management took some time to reflect (see Figure 1). For reasons of consolidating DMF's valuable market position in the years to come, in the course of 1999 the company started looking for both substantial and prolonged organizational transformation. This seemed only feasible when change was no longer initiated by management, but would be prompted by the employees themselves, who, after all, were enabled by management to use their intuition and tacit knowledge, whenever they choose to do so. Management, workers, researchers, and consultants collaborated to explore some possibilities on how to furnish the renewal process with new impulses. The activities they developed together to be successful in that respect are the subject of this chapter.

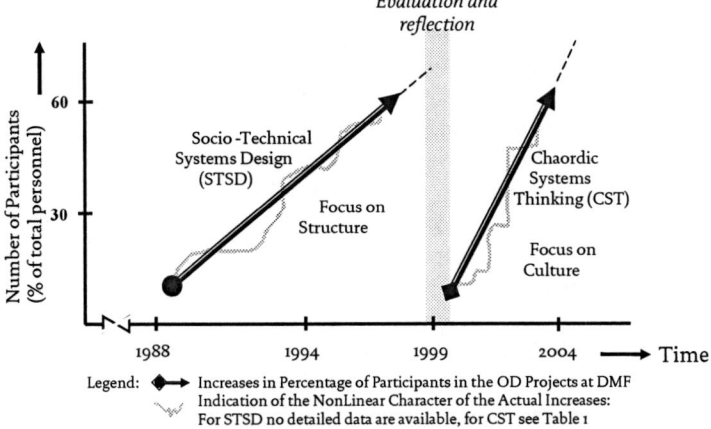

Figure 1: Time and Scope of the Organization-Development Processes at DMF

Concise description of the project

As said before, the project that is reported in this study covers a period of four and a half years, starting in September 1999 (see Figure 1). Although the project was still running at the time this chapter was submitted (June 2004), intensive monitoring was concluded in March 2003.

Although the involvement of DMF personnel / employees was considerable in both projects, the rate of entanglement of personnel in the 'chaordic' project was higher than in the socio-technical project - already after four years some 60% of DMF employees were actually participating. For quantitative details about growth in the number of people involved, see Table 1.

Period of Participation	Number of Participants	Total Number of Participants	Position / Role in the DMF Organization
First Six Months	7	7	Top Management
Second Six Months	17	24	Middle Management and Human Resource Management
Third Six Months	56	80	Middle Management and Lower Management
Fourth Six Months	25	105	Lower Management
Fifth Six Months	30	135	Employees
Sixth Six Months	130	265	Employees
Seventh Six Months	35	300	Employees (Design Network)
Eight Six Months	30	330	Employees

Table 1: Total Number of Participants in the Chaordic Project

More specific aspects of the chaordic project have been reported elsewhere, compare Van Eijnatten, *et al.* (2001, 2003); Van Eijnatten & Van Galen (2001, 2002a, 2002b). In this chapter we intend to put special emphasis on the application of a complexity framework in the actual practice of an industrial company. At DMF, *Chaordic Systems Thinking* (CST) was used as a systemic framework to describe and diagnose the history of organizational development, and consequently to provoke a process of transformational change by training the employees / participants in dialogue and emergent leadership. CST further articulated in the course of the project, and helped the stakeholders - among other things - to draw a meaningful distinction between *reformational* and *transformational* change, see Box 2.

Fundamentally, CST is a lens, a way of thinking and consequently, an approach to designing a complex organizational complete system that recognizes the firm not as a fixed structure, but as 'flow' (Van Eijnatten & Fitzgerald, 1998; Fitzgerald, 2002; Van Eijnatten, *et al.*, 2003). It brings together available concepts and methods to describe discontinuous, nonlinear processes of human development in an organizational context, and methodologies that may support organizational members in their attempts to better cope with uncontrollability, uncertainty, and complexity in their enterprise. At DMF, a minimal understanding of chaos and complexity appeared to be a prerequisite for becoming an active participant in the organization-development project. To that end, an external consultant administered a number of introductory workshops.

An important concept in CST is *attractor*. An (strange) attractor is a condition that forces a holon to repeat its typical pattern of behavior, never in exactly the same way, but each time within clear and specified boundaries. A *holon* is an entity that is simultaneously both a whole and a part of a greater whole. People - individuals or groups - can be seen as 'human holons'. Human holons inherently develop deeper levels of consciousness during their life. We call that learning. Holons are distinguished from one another by the relative degree to which they are able to tap their *holonic capacity*. Holonic capacity is the holon's ability to operate with greater mindfulness, expanded awareness, *control-ability* and *response-ability*. Control ability is the degree to which a holon is able to influence future events, and response-ability is the ability to respond in a respectful and caring way. The 'organizational mind' - the sum total of mostly tacit beliefs, assumptions, premises, values, and conclusions that members of a chaordic system hold commonly as true - is the *container* of the holonic capacity of an organization (Fitzgerald & Van Eijnatten, 1998). A holon is imprisoned in its *attractor basin*, the area within which the attractor is able to perform its magnet function. *Bifurcation* is defined as a *qualitative* change in an attractor's structure (see Box 2). The *bifurcation point* marks the moment in time at which a holon comes under the influence of multiple attractor basins: coming from a relatively stable state, the holon is entering a relatively unstable state. It will experience all kinds of dilemmas, and will face a 'window of opportunities'. By embracing the emergence of a new attractor the holon eventually may 'jump without any external help' to a higher level of complexity and coherence, while

A 'chaordic system'[1] is described as: "A complex and dynamical arrangement of connections between elements forming a unified whole the behavior of which is both unpredictable (chaotic) and patterned (orderly), at the same time" (Hock, 1995, 1999; Fitzgerald, 1996: 1). In a chaordic system it is hypothesized that a combination of chaos and order may exist (Fitzgerald & Van Eijnatten, 2002a, 2002b; Van Eijnatten 2003, 2004b, 2004c). Chaordic Systems Thinking (CST) is a complexity framework for organizational development and change that is differentiating between *Reformational Growth in Near-To-Equilibrium* conditions, and *Transformational Growth in Far-From-Equilibrium* conditions, see the sigmoid growth curve in Figure 2.

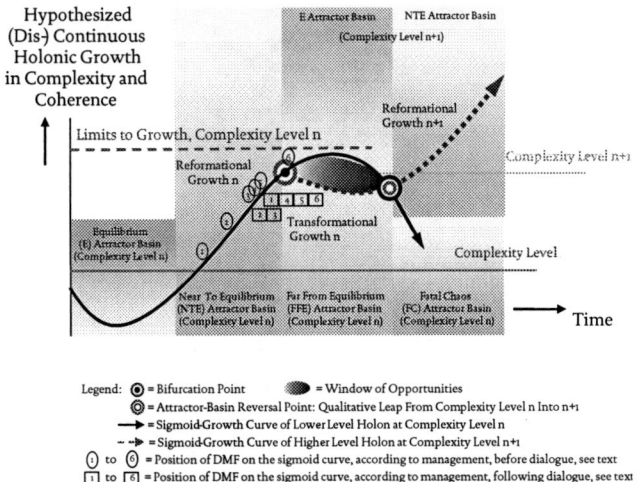

Figure 2: Reformational Versus Transformational Change
(Adapted from Fitzgerald, 1996)

At DMF, Chaordic Systems Thinking (CST) was developed and used to describe and diagnose the history of organization development, and to provoke a process of transformational instead of reformational growth.

Box 2: Chaordic Systems Thinking as Developed and Applied at DMF

sticking to the old attractor may result in fatal dissipation.

The main theoretical model of CST is the 'Sigmoid Growth Curve', or S-curve for short. The S-curve shows early exponential growth that slows down to linear growth and then decelerates until it reaches a saturation level, after which a new S-curve could develop. This broadly used model illustrates both continuous and discontinuous developments. As can be deducted from Box 2, the S-curve enables the descriptions of both linear and nonlinear changes.

The initial diagnosis at DMF, prior to the chaordic project, was inspired by Ken Wilber's concepts of 'holon' and his 'four quadrants,' see Box 3. As Wilber (1996) explains, the exterior of the individual can be described by, for instance, tasks and forms of behavior. The exterior of the collective can be seen as the noticeable structures and patterns of behavior of groups in an organization. To move to the left side of the matrix in Figure 3, the interior of the individual is

Ken Wilber (1996) states that a holon consists of both an *interior core* and an *exterior surface*, with individual and collective aspects. Applied to human organizations, the interior of a holon may be summarized as thinking and feeling ('non-observable'). The exterior of a holon may be summarized as 'doing' and its consequences, which we can perceive with our five senses ('the observable'). So, each holon is a totality of four different dimensions or holarchies - the intentional ('ME'), behavioral ('YOU'), cultural ('US') and social ('THEY'), see Figure 3.

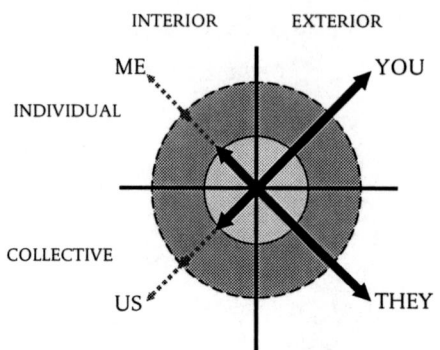

Legend: ━━━ = developed   ▪▪▪▪▪ = to be developed
ME = Intentional Holarchy; YOU = Behavioral Holarchy; US = Cultural Holarchy; THEY = Social Holarchy

Figure 3: The Holonic Development of DMF, Diagnosed Using Wilber's Quadrants

Following ten years of socio-technical redesign, DMF's organizational development has been diagnosed, using Wilber's Quadrants, see Figure 3. The individual exterior ('YOU') consists of tasks, functions, and job titles; the collective exterior ('THEY') consists of systems, processes, and individual interactions. The individual interior ('ME') consists of thoughts and includes personal intentions, values, norms, and experiences. The collective interior ('US') consists of shared intentions, values, norms, and experiences.

At DMF, the exterior was developed to a much greater extent than the interior (see the length of the bold arrows in Figure 3). This was accomplished by almost a decade of socio-technical redesign. However, the interior of DMF hardly ever had been the subject of explicit reflections and organization development. Because the holonic capacity of an organization to renew itself is thought to be dependent on equal developments in all four Wilber's quadrants, DMF's holonic capacity was evaluated as low to moderate (see the inner circle of Figure 3). This is the 'explanation' the researchers came up with: despite a prolonged period of socio-technical redesign, personal and group initiatives could not live up to the expectations of management: Also, with respect to theories of causality, the management used a 'Kantian split' in terms of Stacey, *et al.* (2000): the organization is seen as an exterior object that can be controlled like a machine, while the manager / designer sees her/himself as an intentional individual, actually making the choices that are to be imposed on the system. For both managers and employees, the 'thinking' was far less developed than the 'doing.' Therefore, it is hypothesized that further development of the interior (the 'thinking') of both individuals and groups within DMF will release the organization's holonic capacity (see outer circle in Figure 3).

Box 3: The Holonic Capacity of DMF, as Diagnosed Before the Start of the Project characterized by emotions, thoughts, and feelings, i.e., by 'individual mind.' This quadrant is about consciousness and subjectivity. When individual thoughts are exchanged and shared with other individuals, the result is a collective worldview or commonly shared belief. This is the interior of the collective, which is indicated by organizational culture or 'organizational mind.' The holonic analysis of DMF included all four Wilber quadrants, and resulted in an overall evaluation of DMF's 'holonic capacity,' see Box 3.

The diagnosis pointed towards the 'interior holarchies' - the depth of the actual thinking of individuals and groups - which appeared to be far less developed than the 'exterior holarchies' - the perfection of tasks, structures, processes, and systems. Deeper interior development was targeted as a first priority in any future organization-development project. The basic hypothesis behind this reasoning is that improving both individual and organizational minds would unleash DMF's holonic capacity to a fuller extent, which might result in a qualitative leap to a higher level of complexity and coherence, so that DMF would be able to solve its problems more efficiently and innovatively.

Another subject of the diagnostic process was DMF's position on the S-curve. The analysis was made by a group of managers working together in the change management team. As can be seen in Box 2, initially, before the dialogue process on this issue started in November 1999, there was hardly any agreement among them about the time left for DMF to reach its limits to growth. Following intensive dialogues, in which all sorts of (management) information were analyzed, consensus built in January 2000 that DMF's limits to growth most probably were to be met in about two to three years' time: so during 2003, see Box 2. This conclusion functioned as a trigger to communicate the urgency of the chaordic-change initiative to all members of the DMF organization.

Where structural approaches, like *Socio-Technical Systems Design* (STSD), may be quite helpful to develop the exterior, in CST *dialogue* can be used to both assess and develop the interior holarchies of the individual and the collective. One might think of dialogue as a stream of meaning flowing among and through a group of people, out of whom might emerge some shared meaning (Bohm, 1987; Ellinor & Gerard, 1998; Gerard & Ellinor, 1999). Dialogue moves beyond anyone's individual understanding to make explicit and build collective meaning and vision. Dialogue slows down the pace of thoughts of the following mental activities, so that we can become aware of them: reception of data, interpretations (perceptions), assumptions, and conclusions. These four stages are usually carried out in an instant. Dialogue explicitly explores the four different stages with the aim to identify our assumptions, those things that are assumed or thought to be. By learning how to identify or recognize our assumptions, we are able to identify inconsistencies.

A chaordic system may be characterized by five basic properties (Fitzgerald, 1996): 1. Consciousness; 2. Connectivity; 3. Indeterminacy; 4. Dissipation; and 5. Emergence, see Table 2. On the basis of observations and questionnaire research (Van Eijnatten, *et al.*, 2001), the researchers estimated the status of DMF on these properties prior to the chaordic project, see Table 2.

Description of Chaordic Properties	Status at DMF Prior to the Chaordic Project	Status at DMF During the Chaordic Project
Consciousness Depth of 'insight': Mind more than matter is the driving force of any further developments in an enterprise.	**Low** Interior dimensions have not been the subject of organiza-tion development, so they got under-developed both at the level of individuals and groups.	**Low to Moderate** Interior dimensions are ex-plicit OD targets in the cha-ordic project. The intentional dimension ('individual mind') is further developed than the cultural dimension ('collective mind').
Connectivity Mutual interdependence: De-partments and groups are viewed as both whole and part (holon). The parts cannot exist independently of the whole.	**Low** Holonic characteristics are hid-den, so connectivity is hardly recognized by managers and employees. Departments are perceived as psychological barriers for collaboration.	**Moderate** Explicit recognition of holonic character of the enterprise. Several attempts to engage in thinking together about inter-group- and interdepartmental collaboration. Development of coherence.
Indeterminacy Adaptability, complexity: The future is principally unknow-able in advance.	**Moderate** Long-term business planning is firmly applied; no long-term planning of any change programs.	**Moderate** Long-term business planning is firmly applied; no long-term planning of any change programs.
Dissipation Final stage of life cycle, Dis-continuous growth: Enter-prises go through cycles of creation (birth) and destruc-tion (death).	**Low** Belief in steady state. Manag-ers are trying to contol all events. They cannot let go for control. Stability is seen as the rule rather than the exception.	**Moderate** Acceptance that change is es-sential, and inevitable. Manag-ers start experimenting with letting go for control. Change is seen as the rule rather than the exception.
Emergence Appearance of higher-level behaviors caused by collective dynamics of the whole, not present in the parts.	**Low** Emergence is low because both consciousness and con-nectivity are low.	**Low to Moderate** Emergence might occur be-cause of increased conscious-ness and connectivity.

Table 2: Core Properties of Chaordic Systems and Their Status at DMF, Estimated by the Researchers, Prior to and During the Chaordic Project

1. *Consciousness*: CST assumes that holons - for instance, individuals, groups, or whole organizations - understand their world. In CST, mind is as important as matter - mental and material substance are combined; the approach is beyond the Cartesian dualism. The development of consciousness is primarily seen as a nonlinear process showing qualitative leaps, as if the holons are climbing a lad-der. Higher-level holons do have more profound understanding and show more depth of 'insight' than lower-level holons. Higher-level holons (individuals, groups, or even organizations) are able to see through their complexity more effectively. Prior to the chaordic project, the researchers estimated the degree of consciousness at DMF as being low, see Table 2.

2. *Connectivity*: CST assumes that holons - for instance, individuals, groups, or whole organizations - cannot exist independently from the whole: In complex systems everything is connected. Human interaction - the mutual relationships and the connection to the whole - actually gives meaning to events. CST verifies that the enterprise is both whole and part. No part can exist independently of the whole, nor can any whole be sustained separately from its parts. Each part is by itself a whole and this whole is part of a bigger whole. Therefore, the redesign of an enterprise should minimize boundaries and divisions. An organization is changed as a whole or it is not changed at all (Fitzgerald, 1996). Prior to the chaordic project, the researchers estimated the degree of connectivity at DMF as being low (see Table 2).

3. *Indeterminacy*: CST assumes that in a chaordic system - for instance an enterprise - every event is both cause and effect. Holons continuously develop, and each time they change they grow in complexity. The enterprise is a complex adaptive system that consists of many people who can be seen as interacting heterogeneous agents (Stacey, 2002). This complexity makes the long-term future principally unknowable in advance. The only certainty is the moment of now in which the 'past' presents itself by memory, and the 'future' exists as vision (Fitzgerald, 2002). In chaordic systems processes might evolve in an unanticipated way. Therefore, we should be careful with the detailed mapping of 'interference' in a local environment for the benefit of some future governance. We may become aware of the fundamental unknowability and unpredictability of the long-term future. So instead, we may try to grasp patterns and probabilities in the midst of complexity. Prior to the chaordic project, the researchers estimated the degree of indeterminacy at DMF as being moderate, see Table 2.

4. *Dissipation*: CST assumes that holons can be conceptualized as dissipative systems that are engaged in cycles of both destruction and creation. They may continuously 'fall apart' and then grow back together again, each time in a novel form, ungoverned by the past. Controlling processes in order to maintain a steady state in the enterprise was a popular managers' credo in the second half of the twentieth century. But times have changed drastically. Nowadays, in the turbulent environments we find ourselves in, managers can better elicit change, and might let go for control (Fitzgerald & Van Eijnatten, 1998). This implies re-directing the basic organizational renewal strategy from 'reacting' - or active adaptation - to changes in the environment, to 'initiating' or deliberately changing the own system, long before it is time to do so. Prior to the chaordic project, the researchers estimated the degree of dissipation at DMF as being low, see Table 2.

5. *Emergence*: CST assumes that holons strive toward ascending levels of coherence and complexity, made possible by their capacities for self-organization, self-reference, and self-transcendence. Jeffrey Goldstein states: "Emergent pat-

According to Chaordic Systems Thinking (CST), organizational change goes through different attractor stages (Fitzgerald, 1996, 2002): P1. 'Preparation' or development of deeper consciousness; P2. 'Practicum' or experimentation with new ideas; and P3. 'Practice' or the use of deeper consciousness, see Figure 4.

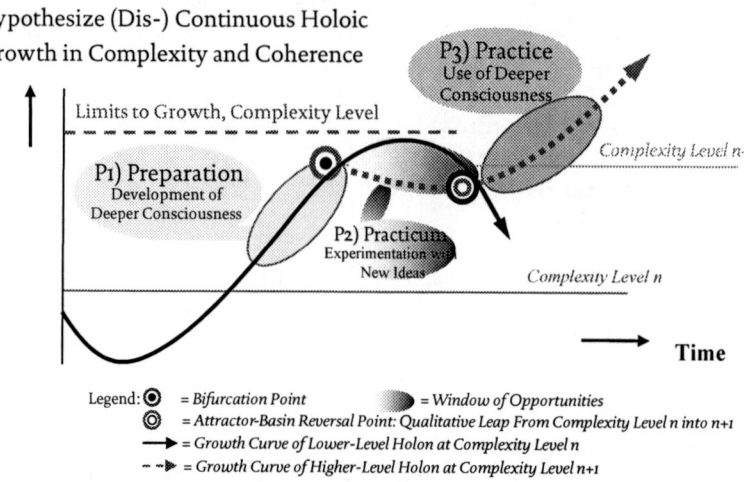

Figure 4: Three Phases in the Chaordic Process of Change
(Adapted from Fitzgerald,1996).

At DMF the first two phases, preparation and practicum, were carried out in 'social island' situations, away from the hectics of everyday business life. During these periods, reflections and experimentation took place in small project groups, while the business process was continued as usual. In order to be able to enter the third phase, a qualitative leap in behavior should take place from complexity level n to complexity level n+1, after which practising the new thinking and new doing becomes the dominant attractor.

At DMF the first two phases took much more time than expected - approximately three years for the preparation phase, and 18 months for the experimentation phase. Although a qualitative leap did occur, its magnitude was less pronounced than anticipated by the action researchers. It also could be that the weakness of the young, new patterns was the reason that the real transformation largely went unobserved, or that the researchers' attention was too much focused on exterior developments (propositional truth and functional fit) instead of interior developments (truthfulness and cultural justness), see Box 7 for more details.

Box 4: The Chaordic Process of Change at DMF

terns, structures, and properties are characterized by a radical novelty in comparison to properties and patterns of the components out of which emergence arises" (Goldstein, 2000: 7). Emergence results from self-organization, and is unpredictable (Goldstein, 1999; Bergmann Lichtenstein, 2000). Although a holon may change its form or substance, its core identity is maintained. Strong connectivity is a precondition for emergence. Therefore, foster in the core of the organizational mind a compelling and evolving collective vision that is created and shared by all, and that feeds all thought and actions (Fitzgerald, 1996). Prior to the chaordic project, the researchers estimated the degree of emergence at DMF as being low, see Table 2.

Retrospectively, the chaordic project at DMF may be analyzed as going through three different phases: *preparation, practicum,* and *practice* (Fitzgerald, 1996, 2002), see Box 4.

The respective phases will be identified and described in detail, in the next three sections.

Phase 1: Preparation or development of deeper consciousness

Following a period of reflection, DMF management hired an external consultant to start the chaordic project in September 1999. A great number of joint activities were developed over a period of four and a half years (September 1999 - February 2004). The typical approach was that the external consultant visited the company two or three times a year for a one or two-week period, in which all workshops and trainings were scheduled. In between visits, the company practised with the newly acquired skills.

All actions undertaken were highly interactive endeavors. Initially, small groups of 10 to 15 employees (both managers, staff, and production personnel) were selected to become involved in the project, starting with top and middle managers. For each consecutive group in the company, the following workshops were 'phased' as follows:

Start-up: Chaos-concepts workshop

This workshop offered an explanation of the basic assumptions of our current worldview (i.e., the empiricist assumption, the reductionist assumption, the determinist assumption, the interventionist assumption, and the conservative assumption), and presented some pathologies of classical thinking (pattern blindness, control compulsion, equilibrium obsession, addition addiction, particle bias, 'boundary-it is', aggravated egoism, and chronic certainty). Next, the five chaordic principles were presented (i.e., consciousness, connectivity, indeterminacy, dissipation, and emergence) and each principle and its new assumption was discussed in small groups. The chaos-concepts workshop functioned as a general introduction, and lasted a full day.

During the same week: Dialogue-training sessions

Per team or project group of 10 to 15 people, the principles of dialogue were explained (i.e., exterior versus interior, ladder of abstraction, postponing of judgments, indiscussibles, defensive routines, hearing versus listening, openness for error in thinking). Then the dialogue process was practiced in conversations that were about 'elephants' (indiscussibles), assumptions behind the thinking, and patterns of behavior. These dialogue-training sessions also lasted a full day, and were set up as a conversation about the past, present, and future of the change process within the company. Its main purpose was learning, or the expansion of the group's thinking.

After 2 to 4 months: Dolphin-training sessions

Per team or project group of 10 to 15 people, this training session was done in the same group composition as the dialogue-training session. The principles of emergent leadership, and the role models of carps, sharks, and dolphins were explained (Lynch & Cordis, 1988). Group members were asked to give personal examples of these role models. A considerable period of time was used to engage in a dialogue on applying these concepts in practice. The dolphin-training session lasted a full day.

After 6 months: Vision conference

The vision conference was held with several teams or project groups together in the same room, and focused on personal visions (expressed in statements and drawings), and on accomplishing that vision in the company. The conference started with a deliberation about personal visions in small groups of various compositions. Subsequently, the remaining structure was designed on the spot as an emergent, resulting in a plenary dialogue on the accomplishment of personal visions in the company. The vision conference lasted a full day.

After approximately 1 year: Deep-chaos workshop

After one year a workshop was held that reviewed the principles of chaos and confronted the participants with questions and behaviors that should fit with these principles. Essentially, the deep-chaos workshop was partly a rehearsal of the chaos-concepts workshop, and partly an exercise in using these concepts in the daily practice. It lasted a full day.

At the start of the chaordic project, a Change Management Team (CMT) was inaugurated consisting of seven managers (three members of the company's Management Team; four middle managers). The external consultant introduced them to chaos concepts, and trained them to use dialogue during several sessions in the period September - December 1999.

In February 2000, three technical problem-solving project teams were given the same kind of training, while the CMT received additional dialogue training. In May 2000, both the CMT and technical problem-solving project teams were trained in emergent leadership roles (dolphin sessions). In September 2000, all teams participated in a vision conference with the main goal to create shared vision among the participants. Individual visions were shared by using dialogue both in small and large groups. An additional vision conference was held soon afterwards, in November 2000, bringing together the same group of people, focusing on obstructions within the company to fulfill personal visions, and on possible actions to take.

In September 2000 and April 2001, five new technical support teams were introduced to chaos and dialogue, followed by more thorough dialogue and dolphin training in February 2001 and September 2001, and a vision conference in April 2001. The first deep-chaos workshop took place at the end of April 2001, and was followed by a second one in October 2001. In February 2002, the Design Network was formed, consisting of 35 employees. Six months later, another 30 employees were introduced to chaos and dialogue, resulting in a total number of 330 (60% of the personnel of DMF), see Table 1.

The external consultant facilitated all workshops and training sessions executed in the first two years. During the course of the project, the CMT, the external consultant, and the two researchers frequently interacted to discuss progress and to dialogue about next steps to take.

Because the CMT decided that everybody in the company should have the opportunity to participate in the workshops, the workshops were translated into Dutch, and were administered by a group of internal DMF employees, after training. In September 2000, a process was started to educate internal facilitators for future diffusion of chaordic concepts in the company. The need for internal facilitators was recognized, since so many new groups of employees and workers were waiting to become involved in the chaos-, dialogue-, and dolphin sessions. The company's HRM department, in collaboration with another external consultant, initiated facilitator trainings for approximately 30 people in January, March, and April 2001. Moreover, a group of three HRM staff personnel started to translate the chaos-, dialogue-, and dolphin workshops from English into Dutch in preparation for a series of sessions at shop-floor level, in January 2001. The trained facilitators started reading about chaos and dialogue up to the point they felt secure enough to teach their colleagues. Following these preparations, both employees and workers were invited to sign up for the workshops in their native language. These sessions actually did not start until October 2001, with a group of 15 workers coming from various operational departments in the company. Participation was voluntary. In the following months, additional heterogeneous groups of about ten people were formed, in order to provide a maximal mix of job functions within each workshop, so that people could meet and learn from each other. These workshops were almost similar in structure and content to the workshops provided by the external consultant. The only difference was the use of videos and some new examples. The dolphin-training workshop was shortened into half-a-day session that only focused on personal behaviors. In the end the Dutch deep-chaos workshop was not administered, because the change process went into another phase before the year was over.

Phase 2: Practicum or experimentation with new ideas

As mentioned before, the main goal of the Chaordic project was to prepare DMF for being able to make a qualitative leap to a higher level of complexity and coherence, see Box 4. Conversations about this subject already started in February 2000. In May 2000 it was recognized by the CMT that they were not the appropriate team to design a new organization, but that they primarily were in charge to enable / facilitate the process for doing that. The first activity to be set up was a search conference with the entire company to explore a new future, and to form a design team. A *design team* is a group of people whose task it is to design a whole new organization, based on the visions of the employees. However, the search conference never happened, because of the impossibility to get consensus about its content and program, the lack of experience, and the excessive preparation time needed to organize such a whole-company event. Instead of a search conference, the above-mentioned vision conference was organized and held. The dialogue on a design team started again in May 2001. In between, the topic had only been discussed informally. Until then, the design team had not 'emerged by itself,' and therefore the CMT felt the urge to help to make it happen. Eventually, in October 2001, three members from the CMT were selected to prepare for a design team. A dialogue started in the CMT on using a Network Multilogue (Van Eijnatten & Hoogerwerf, 1999) to support the design process, in July 2001. In a network multilogue different groups are exchanging ideas and adapting their positions to each other. A *multilogue* is a comprehensive, dynamic transformation event in which different processes merge, i.e., creating, learning, reification and bifurcation (Van Eijnatten & Hoogerwerf, 1999). Multilogue is based on 'Russian Open Gaming,' which was developed and applied by Andrei Zaitsev and his colleagues at the Kaluga Institute of Sociology (Zaitsev & Artemova, 1998). According to van Eijnatten and Hoogerwerf, "In a successful multilogue new ideas are created from the prolonged interaction of different stakeholders' position groups. We use the term 'position' to indicate a stakeholder's perspective, stand, or pole in a dialectic. In a fruitful multilogue, learning is taking place at an accelerated rate, due to the concentrated effort in a social island situation, the systematic practicing of active listening, and the use of both dialogue and reflections" (Van Eijnatten & Hoogerwerf, 1999: M2). Darsø (1998, 2001) speaks about 'antagonistic dialogues' that may develop in these contexts. The first network multilogue was held in October 2001. People were invited to freely sign up for this two-day session and a good mix of about 60 people actually participated. After that, the network multilogue was incorporated into the workshop cycle as the new process for the vision conference.

Although it took nearly two years of intensive dialogical / multilogical interactions within the CMT to settle upon a structure and process that would allow them to completely dissipate the old DMF, while at the same time continue to effectively manage business as usual, they finally succeeded in doing so. The CMT invited all members of the organization for several information sessions in February 2002. About 90 employees showed up. The CMT gave an overview of the process thus far, and explained the assignment that was given to the whole company to design a new organization. The people present were asked to indicate whether or not they were interested in participating. Some 35 out of 90 people, coming from all departments of the company, responded positively. They called themselves the *Design Network* (DN). During two half-day training sessions, the external consultant introduced them to the architectural dimensions of an organization. The traditional view about control, governance,

Dimension	Classical Design Choice	Chaordic Design Choice
Metaphor	Organization as a machine; an instrument of production.	Organization as a dynamical, living, thinking system, e.g., organism.
Intention	The production of profits for the benefit of stockholders.	Generation of wealth in service to all stakeholders, however 'loosely' connected.
Governance	Autocracy or more accurately, aristocracy in the form of the managerial 'ruling' class.	Self-governing, self-referencing.
Control	Externally-focused policies, rules, regulations, and procedures; implemented by supervision.	Internally-focused vision-guided local autonomy.
Measurement & Reward	Quantitative metrics.	Qualitative self-appraisal of contribution value.
Performance Stimulation	Reliance on monetary rewards (or the promise of) combined with punishments (or the threat of); 'carrots & sticks.'	Pride in ownership (may or may not be material ownership, e.g., stock).
Structure	Hierarchy, bureaucracy.	Maximally motile adhocracy.
Selection	Technical competence, combined with an impression of 'fit', i.e., willingness / ability to conform.	Alignment with core values, a willingness to challenge the status quo, commitment to lifelong learning.
Leadership	Designated by virtue of title or position.	Emergent as needed, seen as a universal obligation.
Managerial Role	Supervision, monitoring, and enforcement, i.e., 'police work'.	Stimulating, challenging, coaching.

Box 5: Core Dimensions of Chaordic-System Architecture in Comparison with and Contrast to the Classical Model. Van Eijnatten and Fitzgerald (1998: 23), adapted from Fitzgerald (1994: 42-74)

etc. were compared with the chaordic view, see Box 5.

The newly formed DN elected ten people among itself to form the 'HUB.' The HUB is a task force whose name is derived from Information and Communication Technology - whose function is to enable connections between all parts of the DMF organization. The members of the HUB were in charge of the actual organization of the design work. The other members of the DN functioned as the link to the rest of the DMF organization. After the DN and the HUB were successfully established, its members started dialogues on the way to keep the rest of the organization informed about their work, how to bring the message, and how to involve everybody in the organization in the design process. Several meetings were spent on 'solving specific issues' and 'focusing on the underlying causes'. The organization showed a great need for actual problem solving, so the DN experienced a lot of pressure to take action. Nevertheless, the focus stayed on exploring the thoughts behind this need ("Why don't we take any personal initiatives?"). All kinds of information and communication structures were built - post boxes, e-mail, info signs, and (digital) pin boards. Moreover, during a two-month period, some fancy techniques like 'brain writing' and 'mind mapping' were tried out in the network.

After two months, the DN joined for an intensive two-day training in designing a chaordic organization, see Box 5. The dimensions were further deepened. Besides, a 'company simulation' (sort of simple management game) was performed in which people could 'experience' the limitations of a traditional way of organizing. The game simulated a small company in which each DN member had a specific job (higher manager, middle manager, worker, and customer). All kinds of rules were to be obeyed (for instance, workers were only allowed to communicate with other teams of workers through their middle manager). Some six rounds were run in which the company had to find customers and had to sell and produce according to customers' demands. Afterwards, the rigidity of this functional organization was evaluated, and flaws were discussed.

Further, the DN group practiced using the *socio-political context* method. This method clarifies the use of politics to facilitate a change process. Positive, powerful people can be identified and actions can be set up to use them to convince negative, powerful people. Also, a dialogue was held about the process thus far. As things became clearer, the DN set up regular meetings and a structure to keep everybody informed. It was decided to make all information available to everybody, and minutes were distributed throughout the company. The HUB convened each week for half a day; the DN met each week for one hour. Two facilitators were added to the HUB, so that at each meeting at least one facilitator would be present. Meetings were held with the Labor Council, because problems about authority of the Labor Council versus the DN arose (both groups were to represent the whole company and might solve the same kind of issues within the company).

Extensive dialogues with both the members of the Labor Council, the employees of the organization, and the Management Team resulted in an agreement in June 2002, three months following the start-up. At this time the DN decided that the network should only focus on the design of a new organization. So, the DN did not initiate typical actions like pilot projects to solve practical issues about work - for instance, better heating or better tools. The only thing they did was discuss these issues with the people who were directly involved, and ask them why they would not take any actions, themselves. A PR flyer was developed to start a promotion campaign within DMF, in the period June-July

2002. Immediately after the summer holidays, the DN's major issues became 'how to design', and 'how to inform the organization about it'. It took almost two months for them to understand not to keep going round in circles talking about the 'how', but to just to do it. Also, meetings with middle management were held in September 2002. In an open dialogue with the DN, middle management was asked its opinions about the renewal process. Although the DN assumed a lot of coaches to be skeptical, most of them appeared to have a positive attitude towards the process. And even more importantly, the middle managers were very satisfied with this opportunity to dialogue on these issues and share experiences. In September 2002, the CEO explained the chaordic change process to all members of the organization in one of the regular information sessions that take place three times a year. He highlighted - from his own point of view - the importance of the process. Mid-September, a series of interactions started between the management, the HUB, and the external consultant. The reason for this was the rumor that the DN mostly talked with colleagues, instead of spending enough time on the design itself. The consultant held the CMT responsible for not intervening. Over a three-week period of intensive dialogues between the CMT, HUB, and the consultant, mutual agreement evolved. It was decided that the HUB should focus on the organizational design only, and the DN should concentrate on the 'building' of deeper consciousness in the DMF organization. Each week the HUB dealt with a particular organizational dimension, see Box 5. The CMT became more involved in the process and joined the HUB on several occasions. A period of relative stability began in which the HUB worked on the design and the DN organized activities like lectures. As a result, the commitment of the DN decreased, and about half of its members became rather 'passive' towards the process. The DN stepped into several organizational issues, like a new organizational structure for the service department, and the succession of a particular manager.

In October and November 2002, the HUB worked on the design and the CMT focused on facilitating the HUB in that process. In preparation of the next visit of the external consultant, the HUB spent some time on bringing the findings of the last two months together. In doing so, they created a document containing the 'Ten Pillars of the New DMF Organization', see Box 6. These values formed the foundation for the new design of DMF.

In the following months, the focus on design was even more sharpened. It was concluded that the DN had to put full efforts in finishing the design, and should not spend too much time informing and dialoguing with the rest of the company. A deadline to inform the rest of the organization about the contents of the new design was set for February 2003. Also, the support of the process by the CMT and facilitators was discussed. It was decided to focus on interaction with middle management. The HUB decided to spend two days outside the company to work on the design. Several architectural dimensions were discussed. The CMT joined the HUB for half a day. A round of intense evaluation and personal feedback was carried out. Its main reason was the discomfort of the CMT's impression that the HUB was not a real team but rather just a bunch

The Ten Pillars of the New DMF Organization

The values of the new DMF organization. The foundation on which the organizational design was built.

Trust: If you do not trust someone, you tend to control and supervise. Trust each other, trust your colleagues, and trust yourself. Compare it to your private situation; do you have trust in your family?

Freedom: This is about the way you feel yourself at ease in the DMF organization. If you have freedom, you are much more creative.

Fun: A day not laughed, is a day not lived. If you feel relaxed and have a motivational environment, you will perform at your best.

Dynamics: It is felt that the organization is rigid, slow, and tends to be bureaucratic. The dynamics of the DMF organization is the quality to adapt quickly and easily to the changing environment.

Involvement: "You are the owner of our company." Involvement is a result of the way you feel to be acknowledged for your contribution to the company. Our challenge is to solve two interpenetrated problems: Management would like to see more initiative and involvement of the lower levels, and the lower levels don't feel involved.

Knowledge: To stay world-leader in technology and services, knowledge and our joint experience are fundamental.

Equality: Each person is equal to every other person on a personal level, regardless of his or her position or function in the DMF organization. Equality does not mean that we should all be similar, but it has to do with how we treat each other.

Respect: "Respect your colleagues." You should be tough with the business, but gentle in the relationship. You do not have to agree with everybody, but that does not mean the other person is an idiot. Respect has to do with how we treat each other, also when remarks are not positive.

Openness: You should feel free to say everything to anybody. This will result in clarity and no misunderstandings.

Responsibility: Responsibility of everybody is the result of trust, involvement and respect. This brings focus to the DMF organization.

Box 6: The Ten Pillars of the New DMF Organization

of individuals. The CMT stated that it was an absolute necessity that the HUB was operating as a self-managed team.

At the end of 2002 a small questionnaire was distributed among all DMF employees. The questionnaire was about employees' appreciation of the values stated in the pillars. The response rate was 55%. Results were that freedom and fun were experienced as most satisfying in the current situation, while openness and equality were perceived as least satisfying. All ten pillars were evaluated as highly desirable.

Phase 3: Practice or the use of deeper consciousness

In January 2003 plans were developed for the *Design Day* that took place on February 25. Several teams composed of members of the DN, the HUB, and the CMT were formed to prepare for the event. Tasks were distributed as follows:

- How? - A team was created to develop the form of the presentation,
- Where? - A team was created to find a good location for the meeting,
- PR - A team was created to organize the promotion campaign, and to solve practical issues such as transportation, helpdesk, etc.,
- Coaches - A team was created to organize a meeting with middle management,
- Day After - A team was created to develop ideas about what to do the day after the meeting,
- Design - The HUB was responsible for any further development of the design.

All teams co-operated smoothly, and there were many parallel activities going on. The HUB members almost had a full-time job in dealing with the design process. There was a lot of tuning in with management. Following a full year of designing, eventually all DMF employees were invited for a plenary happening at an external location. Everybody could attend the meeting with continued payment of wages. They were all asked to wear a T-shirt with a tie and a blue-collar suit printed on it, symbolizing equality. A known Dutch comedian chaired the meeting, which started with a movie of a doom scenario for the company: 'Catastrophic Dissipation'. Two MT members rushed in to explain that such a doom scenario was only fictitious, because they were certain that DMF would grasp new goals in the near future to develop innovative products, and to penetrate new markets. Subsequently, the professional entertainer interviewed other MT members, and they expressed their commitments to the chaordic change process. In addition, the external consultant was interviewed and she explained the importance of the meeting, and invited everybody to explore the contents of the meeting in some depth, and not yet to ask the question "What is in for me?" Next, the members of the HUB introduced themselves and explained what they had learned during the design process.

In all introductions, focus was put on personal development. In a humorous sketch, two of the members of the HUB presented the 'ten pillars' to the audience, and contextually explained the process the DN had gone through. Next, the architectural dimensions were dealt with. Four short movies - scenes from professional movies as well as and home videos - were shown. Each individual member of the HUB presented one of the architectural dimensions, referring to the movie and using examples from everyday life in the company - mainly 'gossip issues'. A 'reporter' asked questions to the audience. The presentation concluded with the HUB members putting their signatures on a large plastic ball. This ball was meant to be a symbol for the survival of the company and the audience was invited to sign the ball as well. Subsequently, the large ball 'danced' and waved through the audience. The HUB members discharged themselves and resumed their place among their colleagues again. The meeting ended in an open way, with some informal drinks, and no real decisions were made.

Immediate reactions following the meeting were overwhelming. It turned out to be a unique occasion, because it had never happened in DMF's history that everyone gathered together at the same time. People stated that the design was explained briefly but firmly. The vision and direction of the whole organizational renewal process had become clearer for a large group of employees. People were impressed by the courage of the members of the HUB to stand up and share their thoughts with their colleagues, explicitly using 'gossip issues'. Since employees - working in different jobs in the company - instead of managers did the advocating, the effect was that everybody could easily and personally identify.

The following day, a red carpet and several information screens were installed in the company. A digital pin board was used to collect individual reactions about the Design Day, and several people used it to give feedback. Although the reactions were still scarce, the 'hit ratio' of the pin board (number of views) during the first days was enormous. There was also a lot of talk about the Design Day, and some small initiatives were taken. These initiatives were local, within a team or between teams, and were mostly focused on co-operation and communication. For about a month, no bigger initiatives were taken. It was around at that time, that the CMT decided to send out an open invitation to the whole organization asking for people to join them in further 'constructing' the new organization of the enterprise. The question that was asked was: "Who wants to further develop the dimensions of the new organization?" In two information sessions about 60 people showed up, including about 15 DN members. A brainstorming session was held about the most interesting dimensions to be addressed and at the end everybody was asked to sign in for these new initiatives, which most of the attendants did. The members of the CMT and the HUB decided that it would be best that each of them would be active in only one single initiative at the time. DMF workers set up six initiatives themselves, i.e., someone simply took the initiative to get the rest of the team members together. We elaborate on two of these initiatives and briefly describe the other four.

The first main initiative is called *performance stimulation*. About eight people, mainly from the technical and production departments, found each other on the basis of the question "What motivates us?" They started to organize all kinds of events in a rather unstructured way. Departing from the implicit knowledge that a number of big customer projects were not executed well, they started a dialogue on the contents of the sales process and on feedback that was received. They were convinced that this was the area in which major improvements could be made. At the time this chapter was written, the sales improvement process was carried out as a formal project. The group also started organizing visits to customers' work sites because they thought it a necessity for employees to come into contact with the customers. About 70 people of DMF were given a guided tour to a customer's workplace. Some of them had worked at DMF for more than 15 years, but never visited a customer before.

The second major initiative was about governance and decision-making. The group that was formed consisted of team leaders, production department managers, and some employees from the HRM department. The team embraced a method for decision-making that is called *Sociocracy* (Endeburg, *et al.*, 1998). This method specifies a system of government in which the interests of all organizational members are served equally. It gives both suggestions for *consent* (i.e., 'not against an idea,' instead of *consensus*, i.e., 'in favor of an idea') decision-making within groups or teams and a structure for decision-making in the organization as a whole. It focuses on structural meetings with a chair, in which only conclusions are drawn on which common consent is reached. On an organizational level, sociocracy proposes a 'linking-pin' decision-making structure.

The third initiative was about communication. The group started with providing information about DMF's performance indicators. A small questionnaire about the pillars was designed and distributed within DMF. The fourth initiative was about performance evaluation. A team focused on potential flaws in the performance-evaluation system, and set up three pilots in which new ways of approval were tested. In the past, a team coach approved all members in the team. In the pilots, the members of a team approved each other. The fifth initiative was about personal development. This group worked rather slowly, but finally organized a network multilogue including people who were viewed as being explicitly 'against' the chaordic change process. The sixth initiative focused on leadership. Ways of approving management were researched and the team started looking into more knowledge about self-management.

Evaluating the process of chaordic change

All training sessions were set up as conversations about the past, present, and future of DMF. The change process started with top and middle management. In addition, several organizational members - commonly seen as open-minded to new concepts or changes - also became involved in the first two years. Over time, all other DMF personnel were, or will be, involved in the chaordic project. For several reasons shop-floor workers were not invited to participate in the project before the start of the third year, see Table 1: 1. Most of the workshops and materials were in English, and had to be translated and reworked in order to be of any use at the shop-floor level; 2. Initially, there was skepticism about adoption of the new chaordic concepts by workers and lower management; 3. In the beginning, there were not enough people capable of playing a facilitator's role in the dialogue process.

People who have been involved in the chaordic change process thus far have positions in various DMF departments. Usually participation took place in groups. In the beginning of the project it was an explicit strategy to involve only complete, intact self-managed work teams, operational staff groups, and managerial project teams in the training. The reason was that these teams - consisting of between 10 and 15 people - frequently met professionally in between training sessions, which gave them ample opportunities to practice with the new concepts. Later in the project, the Dutch sessions consisted of maximally heterogeneous groups.

All workshops were held in a conference center outside the company, during working hours, and all participants normally were paid for it. There were no detailed plans for the sessions. Where the dialogue-training sessions focused on the training of dialogue and exploring of assumptions behind the thinking, the dolphin training sessions went into the conscious role choices one can make in complex interactions.

The chaordic project has unfolded itself at its own pace, and at the time this chapter was finished, the process was in its fifth year. No goals or paths were specified in advance. Exploring and path finding (Freebourne, 2003) were the main attitudes towards change. No pre-planned end dates were scheduled, and it is expected the chaordic project will last for several years more. Probably, it will become a continuous and ever-changing process within DMF.

Interviews

Some preliminary evaluations given to the researchers in a series of interviews administered in June / July 2000 - some six months after the start of the change project - are indicative of the kind of effects of chaordic change. Due to the dialogue training sessions, the managers have become more direct and open to others. They have apparently realized that the words actually spoken do not always represent what someone actually means, and that it therefore is good practice to search for the real meanings behind one's words. Managers involved in the chaordic change project report that they are more honest to others, and take a more vulnerable position themselves. They feel that it has become more accepted to criticize and to be criticized. At the same time managers observe that colleagues who have also finished the training behave differently than before. Also, they report that they have got to know each other better, and understand the respective work contexts in greater depth. They have gained more insights into the knowledge and competencies of others. Their patterns of behavior are different in such a way that they feel better, and are more focused on structural issues instead of operational matters. The managers have come to realize that it is impossible to control everything, so they have started to experiment with letting go, and with some coaching of their employees. Although some ineffective behavior patterns are still present, the new approach has challenged managers to reflect on their own behavior and thinking. Respondents state that it is important to work from a vision. They have started to act more on gut feeling, and may delegate responsibilities to others more easily than before. Interviewees roughly characterize the change process in the past as dominated by 'quick-and-dirty' results-oriented activities. The new change process takes far more time, is more focused on the interior - the thinking - and builds a real basis for self-organization.

In July 2000 the number of managers participating in the chaordic project was very limited, and neither employees, nor workers from the shop floor were involved. We interviewed an employee, and he confirmed that he had heard about the project. After some inquiry, he stated that - from what he noticed in the interactions with the managers - the new change process has to do with more attention for people. He experienced that managers who had been involved in the trainings actually have changed their behavior, and are listening more intensely to their employees. Also, management act differently in meetings: they accept criticism, let other people speak out, and are more patient and more open. Participants in a meeting can make a real contribution now. The interviewee stated that prior change projects focused on team performance only. They had not resulted in many improvements.

The new patterns of behavior at DMF we came to call *The Dolphin Attactor*, because managers, employees, and workers interchanged roles more easily, and leadership became increasingly emergent. However, then and now, there are potential obstructions to the chaordic change due to severe operational pressures caused by the market.

Observations

The researchers have been present at most of the workshop sessions, and have recorded and analyzed most interactions (Van Eijnatten & Van Galen, 2001, 2002a, 2002b). The workshops turned out to be successful in most cases:

The chaos-concepts workshops, as planned and facilitated by the external consultant, contained the vital elements of the new chaos lens, i.e., the assumptions of traditional scientific thinking and its pathologies, the five chaordic properties, the growth curve of discontinuous development, and some exercises to master these concepts. The goal of this workshop was to disseminate the new lens. These plenary workshops were positively evaluated by a majority of its attendants. Also shop-floor workers report that workshops in their native language helped them to master the new concepts. Most people at DMF indicate that thanks to these workshops they understand the new concepts quite well, and that they are intending to use them in their work. We conclude that there has been an effective diffusion of the new lens by both lecturing and experiential learning.

The dialogue-training sessions, as planned and facilitated by the external consultant for each respective project group separately, had differential effects. Although the necessary ingredients of dialogue were satisfactorily communicated to all groups, a deeper theoretical base for dialogue was unevenly distributed among the project groups. Three groups were studied in more detail. The group that was educated on the highest number of dialogue aspects was most positive in its evaluations; the group that received the smallest number of dialogue aspects was least positive. Secondly, although in all groups about the same amount of time was spent on exercising dialogue, individual groups showed differential effects. The maturity of the groups as project teams appeared to be the decisive factor here: the more mature, the more dialogues instead of discussions developed. Another conclusion is that developing any substantial competence in dialogue is a process that is not mastered in a few weeks: it needs months or even years of prolonged on-the-job training. Chaordic change using dialogue is a therapeutic process: personal confrontations between individuals about tacitly held assumptions frequently took place during the dialogue sessions. They were very painful and curing at the same time. At the start of the dialogue training, project groups were more action-oriented than towards the end of it. The dialogue changed the exterior orientation into an interior one: a real inquiry into the thinking. A number of issues were put on the table, including interpersonal problems and indiscussibles such as lack of trust, and management's dominance in meetings.

The dolphin-training sessions, as planned and facilitated by the external consultant for each respective project group separately, also had differential effects per group. The communication of theoretical concepts was quite equally distributed among the researched groups, but the amount of available training time deviated strongly. We conclude that, although the theoretical base was identical for all groups, training and experiencing differed for each project group. The group who had expressed the most negative attitude, turned out to be the 'minimal-session-time' group. The other project groups were positive in their evaluations.

The project group that was most positive about the dialogue-training session was most negative about the dolphin-training session. The group hardly practiced with dialogue in between training sessions. The project group that was most negative about the dialogue-training session was most positive about the dolphin-training session. This group spent several meetings in between training sessions to actually have a dialogue within the group. We conclude that practicing dialogue between sessions tends to have a positive effect on the attitudes towards taking different roles, as were shown in the dolphin-training session. For a more detailed description of the findings (see Van Eijnatten & Van Galen, 2001, 2002a, 2002b).

Questionnaire

The researchers administered a questionnaire measuring attitudes to existing and desired behaviors before and following the dialogue-training sessions. Although the results showed no differentiation between experimental and control groups with respect to attitudes towards personal initiatives, the experimental group did show increased consensus in individual attitudes concerning 'desired behaviors'. Both groups developed more dissensus in their attitudes about 'existing behaviors,' urging the researchers to conclude that the 'old' organizational mind based on distrust and control values most likely has been fading away in both the experimental and control groups, while the 'new' organizational mind based on chaordic properties and values only developed in the experimental group that had the dialogue training. For a more detailed description of the findings, see Van Eijnatten, *et al.* (2001).

Conclusions

Within DMF, the process of chaordic change has resulted in a cultural transformation. Managers, employees, and workers have gradually started to communicate more informally, and to interact on a more equal basis. Managers actually have changed their personal management styles, resulting in more instances of 'letting go of control', and more subsequent satisfaction from both sides. The 'Design Day' is a good example of an 'emergent,' and of 'emergent leadership'. In terms of CST we see an increase in holonic potential of the DMF organization, due to a further deepening of the individual and organizational consciousness and connectivity. Examples of this 'development of the interior' are increased thoughtfulness shown in the daily work, more room for and understanding of emotions, and increased mutual respect or trust between managers, employees, and workers. We conclude that - apparently - chaordic change is paying off. The 'soul' of the DMF organization has been the explicit subject of further development and growth. As a consequence, the managers, employees, and workers have started to experiment with new forms of work organization, using 'orienteering' and 'path finding' as their new search strategies. They agreed to have 'the freedom to fail'.

Looking at the Sigmoid growth curve (Box 2) we interpret the chaordic change at DMF as a qualitative leap from the old attractor basin best typified by 'one-way traffic': interaction patterns produced by 'over-active, dominant managers and passive, submissive workers who follow' into a new attractor basin characterized by 'two-way traffic': interaction patterns produced by 'reflective, supportive managers and committed workers who want to try-out new things themselves'.

Culture creation as described in this chapter is defined as a process of diffusing new ways of thinking - based on chaordic principles - throughout a company. Although changed behavior patterns might be external indicators of changed attitudes, our approach predominantly focused on transformation of individual and collective thinking. Hence, it is not a primary purpose that the involved people and groups are going to act accordingly, but rather that they are going to become like it. Basically, it is about how they internalize the new attractor. So, when looking for the results of this project, an evaluation against the same validity claims as were used in the evaluation of the socio-technical systems design project (Box 1) would be missing the point. As is illustrated in Box 7, holonic development at DMF should be evaluated against two other,

Applied to human organizations, in each of Wilber's quadrants a different type of holarchy (holonic hierarchy) is operating: The intentional ('ME'), behavioral ('YOU'), cultural ('US') and social ('THEY') holarchies. Each holarchy possesses a unique type of validity test: Truthfulness for the intentional domain ('ME'), Truth for the behavioral domain ('YOU'), Justness for the cultural domain ('WE'), and Functional Fit for the social domain ('THEY'), see Wilber (1996: 106-112) and Figure 5. Wilber states that a holon consists of both an interior core and an exterior surface, with individual and collective aspects. The interior of a holon may be summarized as thinking and feeling ('non-observable'). The exterior of a holon may be summarized as 'doing' and its consequences, which we can perceive with our five senses ('the observable'). So, each holon is a totality of four different dimensions or holarchies, see Figure 5.

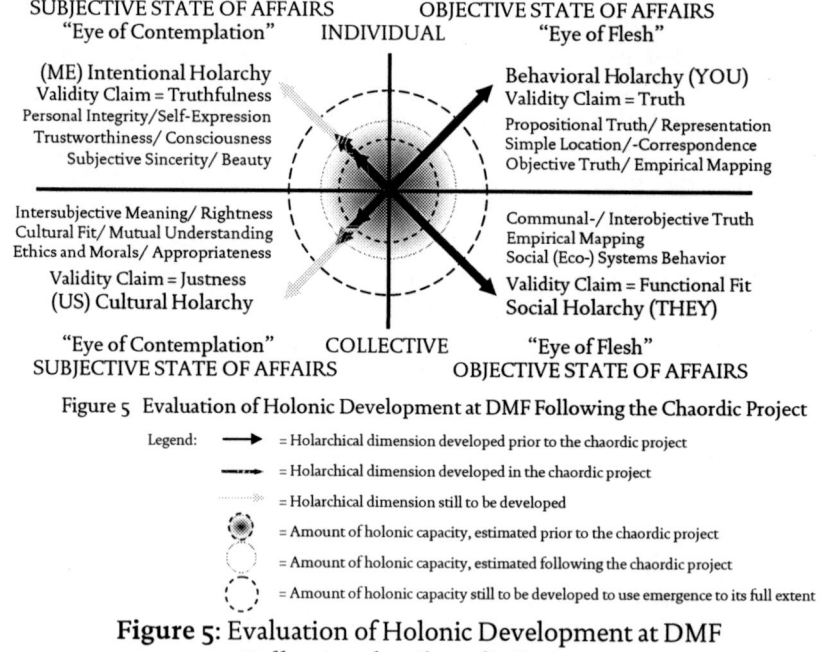

SUBJECTIVE STATE OF AFFAIRS   OBJECTIVE STATE OF AFFAIRS
    "Eye of Contemplation"   INDIVIDUAL   "Eye of Flesh"

(ME) Intentional Holarchy   Behavioral Holarchy (YOU)
Validity Claim = Truthfulness   Validity Claim = Truth
Personal Integrity/Self-Expression   Propositional Truth/ Representation
Trustworthiness/ Consciousness   Simple Location/-Correspondence
Subjective Sincerity/ Beauty   Objective Truth/ Empirical Mapping

Intersubjective Meaning/ Rightness   Communal-/ Interobjective Truth
Cultural Fit/ Mutual Understanding   Empirical Mapping
Ethics and Morals/ Appropriateness   Social (Eco-) Systems Behavior
Validity Claim = Justness   Validity Claim = Functional Fit
(US) Cultural Holarchy   Social Holarchy (THEY)

    "Eye of Contemplation"   COLLECTIVE   "Eye of Flesh"
SUBJECTIVE STATE OF AFFAIRS   OBJECTIVE STATE OF AFFAIRS

Figure 5 Evaluation of Holonic Development at DMF Following the Chaordic Project

Legend: ⟶ = Holarchical dimension developed prior to the chaordic project
           ⟶ = Holarchical dimension developed in the chaordic project
           ⟶ = Holarchical dimension still to be developed
           ◉ = Amount of holonic capacity, estimated prior to the chaordic project
           ◯ = Amount of holonic capacity, estimated following the chaordic project
           ◌ = Amount of holonic capacity still to be developed to use emergence to its full extent

Figure 5: Evaluation of Holonic Development at DMF
Following the Chaordic Project

Holonic Capacity is defined as an emergent of a holon with both exterior and interior, individual and collective dimensions. During the chaordic project the holonic capacity of DMF was increased. Although the 'thinking' remained less developed then the 'doing' (see the length of the respective arrows in Figure 5), the interior was further deepened. The intentional dimension expanded more than the cultural one: Interior, individual development was deeper than interior, collective development.

It is hypothesized that further development of the interior (the 'thinking') of both individuals and groups within DMF will release more holonic capacity resulting in more initiatives, and in improved self-organization (see outer circle in Figure 5).

Box 7: Increases in Holonic Capacity at DMF Following the Chaordic Project more appropriate validity claims: truthfulness for the intentional holarchy, and justness for the cultural holarchy.

The interior holarchies at DMF were deepened (see Box 7). DMF has shown improvements in four out of five chaordic properties (consciousness, connectivity, dissipation, and emergence), as evaluated by the researchers. These statements about interior improvements shown in Table 2 are to be considered as functional equivalents of the exterior improvements shown in Box 1.

Theoretical reflections

A first point we would like to reflect upon is the necessity and added value of the use of CST in this study. In our view, the donning of the chaos / complexity lens was a necessity and added value to this case. CST enabled us to see both the blockades and the next steps in the organizational development process at DMF. An important blockade was the extremely persistent attractor pattern of 'lack of personal initiatives', which was maintained by a dominant management and a submissive workforce. The qualitative leap was substantiated by dialogue. The 'Dolphin attractor' was a break-through, a new interaction pattern that was based of trust and mutual respect.

A second question that is open for reflection is whether a chaordic organization can be designed. The first and most formidable step in the process of shaping and making real organizational architectures capable of self-transcendence is to rise above our common ways of thinking about organizational design. It is not something one can do to an organization or - in terms of Stacey, *et al.* (2000) - can be imposed by management on the employees of a company. Researchers, managers, and consultants have to be part of the system, so they only can co-influence, not dictate or impose any changes. We must shift our own mind before we can ever hope to shift the minds of others or of the group or company as a whole.

With respect to future research, if we wish to sufficiently grasp and explain the dynamical complexity of a chaordic enterprise, tools and methodologies that allow us to simulate its evolution, as well as to model its interactions in the context of environmental turbulence must be developed. In this respect Harkema developed a CAS multi-agent modeling simulation of the interaction processes at the Dutch Sara Lee's Research & Development department (Harkema, 2003, 2004). If we are to succeed in designing chaordic companies, we must identify and learn from organizations now in existence - such as DMF - that evidence nuances of features suggested in the dimensional template presented in Box 5. While it is certain that such prototypical organizations exist, whether they grew that way by intention or not, is yet unknown. Therefore, another avenue of research could be to discover how systemic change in the direction of closer proximity to the chaordic ideal is catalyzed.

In conclusion, we believe future research should examine a number of concepts derived from the chaos-and-complexity lens that is underpinning the CST framework. This might include a focus on holons and the evolution of holarchies both intentional, behavioral, social and cultural; fractal patterns and the process of fractalization in social institutions; attractors and their basins that bound human behaviors; and, of course, the provocative notion of the *orgmind*. Only through the rigors of dedicated action research informed by CST can we advance our understanding of organizational architectures capable of driving systemic self-transcendence.

Practical reflections

The following extraordinary conditions might be considered as essential in order to adopt a CST approach such as the one that was used in DMF:

1. Organizations should be willing and able to sustain high levels of investment, trust, and patience, for a rather long period of time. This is certainly not a 'quick-fix' approach a consultant can impose on an organization. On the contrary, CST must be seen as part of a long-term organization-development process, preferably using action-research to get a good fit.

2. It might be important to have the kind of smooth labor relations as exist in The Netherlands. Unions and employers organizations predominantly negotiate on a national level, while unions and management work together constructively to experiment with new forms of work organization on a local or company level.

3. The use of an external consultant in order to keep up momentum, to provoke the organizational members to look into a mirror, to trigger decisions and activities, and to convince the respective stakeholders in the process, is essential in order to provoke change.

4. An interesting question is how many people should be involved in the dialogue in order to get a change in attractors. This question cannot be answered easily, but this study suggests that all levels in the organization should be involved, and that the cultural change only might occur following intensive training of managers, employees, and workers.

At DMF, there had never been any single master plan for long-term strategic development. Usually, the management team only was pointing into the direction where to go with the company. A major consequence of this 'ad hoc' way of working was that the path the organizational-renewal process took was far from straightforward; on the contrary, it showed all sorts of detours and strange bends and curves. This strategy is very much in accordance with CST.

References

Bergmann Lichtenstein, B. M. (2000), "Emergence as a Process of Self-Organizing: New Assumptions and Insights from the Study of Nonlinear Dynamic Systems," *Journal of Organizational Change Management*, 13 (6): 526-544.

Bohm, D. (1987). *Unfolding Meaning: A Weekend of Dialogue with David Bohm*, London: Ark Paperbacks.

Darsø, L. (1998). "The Butterfly Effect: The Difference That Makes a Difference for the Emergence of Innovation in Researcher Teams," paper presented at the *14th EGOS Colloquium*, Maastricht, The Netherlands, July 9-11.

Darsø, L. (2001), "Innovation in the Making," Frederiksberg: Samfundslitteratur, 2001, Ph.D. Thesis Copenhagen Business School., World Wide Web, 2004: http://web.cbspress.dk/FMPro?-token=12590016&-db=Products.fp3&-lay=WEB&-format=book.htm&nyISBN=8763000962&-find.

Eijnatten, F. M. van (2003), "Chaordic Systems Thinking: Chaos and Complexity to Explain Human Performance Management," in G. D. Putnik and A. Gunasekaran (eds.), *Business Excellence 1: Performance Measures, Benchmarking and Best Practices in New Economy*, Braga, Portugal: School of Engineering, University of Minho Press, pp. 3-18.

Eijnatten. F. M. van (2004a). "Chaos and Complexity: An Overview of the 'New Science' in Organization and Management," *Revue Sciences de Gestion Quarterly*, 40: 123-165.

Eijnatten. F. M. van (2004b). "Chaordic Systems Thinking: Some Suggestions for a Complexity Framework to Inform a Learning Organization," *The Learning Organization*, 11(6): 430-449.

Eijnatten, F. M. van (2004c). "A Chaordic Lens for Understanding Entrepreneurship and Intrapreneurship," in A. Fayolle, P. Kyrö and J. Ulijn. (eds.), *Entrepreneurship Research in Europe: Outcomes and Perspectives*, Cheltenham, UK: Edward Elgar Publishing, to appear.

Eijnatten, F. M. van and Fitzgerald, L. A. (1998). "Designing the Chaordic Enterprise: 21st Century Organizational Architectures That Drive Systemic Self-Transcendence," paper presented at the *14th EGOS Colloquium*, Maastricht, The Netherlands, July 9-11.

Eijnatten, F. M. van and Hoen, T. (1999). "A Decade of Organizational Renewal at DMF, The Netherlands: The Success of an Incremental Strategy for Whole-Company Transformation," paper presented at the *Sixth European Ecology of Work Conference* "New Forms of Work Organization: Innovation, Competitiveness and Employment, Bonn, Germany, Gustav-Stresemann Institute, May 17-20.

Eijnatten, F. M. van, and Hoogerwerf, E. C. (1999). "A Short Introduction to Multilogue," in T. Chase (ed.), *Readings Monterey*, 1999: Northwood, NH: The STS Roundtable, pp. M1-M9.

Eijnatten, F. M. van, and Neefs, R. (1999/2000). *Reports on the CMT Workshops at DMF, Eindhoven*, The Netherlands: Eindhoven University of Technology: Department of Technology Management, DMF Project Documentation.

Eijnatten, F. M. van, and Galen, M. C. van, (eds.) (1999). *DMF: Overzicht van 10 Jaar Sociotechniek* (DMF: Overview of 10 Years of Socio-Technical Systems Design), Eindhoven, The Netherlands: Eindhoven University of Technology, Department of Technology Management, Research Report (in Dutch).

Eijnatten, F. M. van, and Galen, M. C. van (2001). "The Dolphin Attractor: Complex

Responsive Processes Towards Chaordic Organizational Transformation," [aper [resented at the *First Meeting of the European Chaos/Complexity in Organizations Network* (ECCON), Lage Vuursche, Netherlands, October 19-20. In Proceedings ECCON, World Wide Web, 2004: http://www.chaosforum.com/nieuws/Eijnatten.html.

Eijnatten, F. M. van, and Galen, M. C. van (2002a). "The Dolphin Attractor: Dialogue for Emergent New Order in a Dutch Manufacturing Firm," *International Scientific Journal of Methods for and Models of Complexity*, 5 (1) June, http://www.fss.uu.nl/ms/cvd/isj/index02.html.

Eijnatten, F. M. van, and Galen, M. C. van (2002b). "Chaos, Dialogue and the Dolphin's Strategy," *Journal of Organizational Change Management*, 15 (4): 391-401.

Eijnatten, F. M. van, Dijkstra, L. and Galen, M. C. van (2001). "Dialogue for Emergent Order: An Empirical Study of the Development of the Organizational Mind in a Dutch Manufacturing Firm," paper presented at the *17th EGOS Colloquium*, Lyon, France, 7-8 July, http://www.chaosforum.com/nieuws/Emergent%20Dialogue.pdf.

Eijnatten, F. M. van, Galen, M. C. van, and Fitzgerald, L. A. (2003). "Learning Dialogically: The Art of Chaos-Informed Transformation," *The Learning Organization*, 10 (6): 361-367.

Ellinor, L. and Gerard, G. (1998). *Creating and Sustaining Collaborative Partnerships at Work: Dialogue, Rediscover the Transforming Power of Conversation*, New York: John Wiley.

Endenburg, G., Bowden, C. and Lindenhovius, J. (1998). *Sociocracy: The Organization of Decision-Making, Sociocratic Engineering Company*, http://www.compassion-response.net/index.htm.

Fitzgerald, L. A. (1994). *Designing Organizations for World Class Performance in the 21st Century: A Theory, Model and Process for Creating Sustainable Organizational Architectures*, Novato, CA: Columbia Pacific University, Ph.D. thesis.

Fitzgerald, L. A. (1996). *Organizations and Other Things Fractal: A Primer on Chaos for Agents of Change*, Denver, CO: The Consultancy.

Fitzgerald, L. A. (1997). *Chaordic Systems Properties Chart*, Denver, CO: The Consultancy, http://www.orgmind.com/propchart.html.

Fitzgerald, L. A. (2002). "Chaos, the Lens That Transcends," *Journal of Organizational Change Management*, 15 (4): 339-358.

Fitzgerald, L. A. and Eijnatten, F. M. van (1998). "Letting Go for Control: The Art of Managing in the Chaordic Enterprise," *International Journal of Business Transformation*, 1 (4): 261-270.

Fitzgerald, L. A. and Eijnatten, F. M. van (2002a). "Reflections: Chaos in Organizational Change," *Journal of Organizational Change Management*, 15 (4): 402-411.

Fitzgerald, L. A. and Eijnatten, F. M. van. (2002b) "Chaos Speak: A Glossary of Chaordic Terms and Phrases," *Journal of Organizational Change Management*, 15 (4): 412-423.

Freebourne, W. (2003). Pathfinder Workbook, World Wide Web, 2003: http://www.www.career-counseling.com/rep.htm.

Gerard, G. and Ellinor, L. (1999). *Dialogue: Something Old, Something New; Dialogue Contrasted with Discussion; the Building Blocks of Dialogue: A Living Technology; Behaviors that Support Dialogue*, http://www.thedialoguegrouponline.com/whatsdialogue.html.

Goldstein, Jeffry (1999), "Emergence as a Construct: History and Issues," *Emergence*, 1 (1): 49-72.

Goldstein, J. (2000). "Emergence: A Construct Amid a Ticket of Conceptual Snares," *Emergence*, 2 (1): 5-22.

Harkema, S. J. M. (2003). "A Complex Adaptive Perspective on Learning within Innovation Projects," *The Learning Organization*, 10 (6): 340-346.

Harkema, S. J. M. (2004). *Complexity and Emergent Learning in Innovation Projects*, Veenendaal, The Netherlands: Universal Press, Ph.D. Thesis Nyenrode University.

Hock, D. W. (1996). *The Chaordic Organization: Out of Control and Into Order*, 21st Century Learning Initiative. http://www.cyberspace.com/~building/ofc_21clidhock.html.

Hock, D. W. (1999). *Birth of the Chaordic Age*, San Francisco, CA: Berrett-Koehler.

Lynch, D. and Kordis, P. L. (1988). *Strategy of the Dolphin: Scoring a Win in a Chaotic World*, New York: William Morrow.

Sitter, L. U. de, Hertog, J. F. den, and Dankbaar, B. (1997). "From Complex Organizations With Simple Jobs to Simple Organizations With Complex Jobs," *Human Relations*, 50 (5): 497-534.

Stacey, R. D., Griffin, J. D., and Shaw, P. (2000). *Complexity and Management: Fad or Radical Challenge to Systems Thinking?* London: Routledge.

Stacey, R. D. (2002). "Research Perspective: Organizations as Complex Responsive Processes of Relating," *Journal of Innovative Management*, 8(2): 27-39.

The Chaordic Alliance (1998). http://www.chaordic.com.

The Chaordic Commons (2004). http://www.chaordic.com.

Wilber, K. (1996). *A Brief History of Everything*, Dublin: Newleaf.

Zaitsev, A. K. and Artemova, T. M. (1998). "Russian Open Game as a Tool for Organization Strategy Development," in T. Chase (ed.), *Readings Monterey*, 1999: Northwood, NH: The STS Roundtable, pp. M11-M17.

Notes

[1] Some Definitions:

"By Chaord, I mean any self-organizing, adaptive, nonlinear, complex organism, organization or community, whether physical, biological or social, the behavior of which harmoniously blends characteristics of both order and chaos. Briefly stated, a chaord is any chaotically ordered complex. Loosely translated to social organizations, it would mean the harmoniously blending of intellectual and experiential learning" (Hock, 1996).

Chaord: "1) Any auto catalytic, self-regulating, adaptive, nonlinear, complex organism, organization, or system, whether physical, biological or social, the behavior of which harmoniously exhibits characteristics of both order and chaos; 2) An entity whose behavior exhibits patterns and probabilities not governed or explained by the behavior of its parts; 3) The fundamental organizing principle of nature and evolution" (The Chaordic Alliance, 1998; The Chaordic Commons, 2004).

Chaordic: "1) Anything simultaneously orderly and chaotic; 2) Patterned in a way dominated neither by order nor chaos; 3) Existing in the phase between order and chaos" (The Chaordic Alliance, 1998; The Chaordic Commons, 2004).

A Chaordic System is "a complex and dynamical arrangement of connections between elements forming a unified whole the behavior of which is both unpredictable (chaotic) and patterned (orderly) ... simultaneously. Chaos then is the science of such chaotic and orderly, that is 'chaordic' entities found in abundance throughout the universe" (Fitzgerald, 1997: 1). By this definition, almost any system in the universe ranging from the complex to the simple can be considered chaordic. However, we will refer to any system designed to sustain itself (rather than natural) in an optimal dynamical balance in what millennial science refers to as Far-From-Equilibrium (Van Eijnatten & Fitzgerald, 1998).

Chaordic Systems Thinking (CST) is "a lens, a way of thinking, and subsequently an approach to designing a complex organizational system that recognizes the enterprise not as a fixed structure, but as 'flow'; a dynamical process passing from one attractor basin to the next in an incessant journey toward the 'edge of chaos' " (Van Eijnatten & Fitzgerald, 1998).

Postscript

A s a child I used to go to sleep looking up at the stars, marvelling at the sheer scale of the night sky and wondering how it all worked. Being asked to comment on complexity is a similar experience, given the sheer breadth of the subject matter and of course the complexity of it. You start to feel as if you need a touch of omniscience in order to qualify for such a job.

So where do you start with such an exercise? Alice was told to "start at the beginning... and when you come to the end, stop", but where is the beginning and how do you know where the end is. In the end I took a leaf out of an old training course on systems thinking, which stated the following rules:

- Cause and effect are not necessarily closely related in time and space;
- There are no right answers;
- The easiest way out will lead back in.

I will start with Elizabeth McMillan in chapter 29, as it fulfils all aspects of the rules stated above. Firstly, the reason it represents a way back in, is that recently the Open University started a new course on their MBA (B830: Making a difference), which has departed substantially from the normal *modus operandi* of the university. The stated intent of the course is that students *implement* something new in their organization and that they reflect on the role of theory in this process. The reason that it is the easiest way back in, is that I am an associate lecturer on this course. Secondly, at a recent gathering to discuss the course, a great deal of anxiety was expressed at the lack of guidelines and structure for the course. The response was "we do not know where this will lead, all we know is that the path will emerge as we move forward", in effect stating that there were no right answers. For me, this was music to my ears, but others struggled with the ambiguity. Thirdly, it never occurred to me, due to my lack of knowledge of the context behind the statement, that this course could have been the outcome of the changes described in chapter 29. But what is interesting is that the cause and effect are separated by quite a substantial gap in time and space.

This of course makes life much easier, as I now have a unique contribution to make to the task undertaken by this book, in that I can verify that the principles of complexity work. Everything we have been talking about for all of these years and the phenomena we have discussed and articulated have come together in this example, at this point in time. None of this was predictable in its conception and how strange that I should be writing now, at this time, and be able to show a living example of the interrelatedness and emergent proper-

Managing Organizational Complexity: Philosophy, Theory, and Application
A Volume in: Managing the Complex, pages 557-560.
ISBN: 1-59311-319-6 (cloth), 1-59311-318-8 (paper)

ties of a system.

This, I think, is articulated by Ashmos, *et al.*, (2002) in Michael Lissack's comment on page 467, "Encouraging connections through participation is essentially an exercise in complexifying everyday life in an organization, because it encourages people to enter unknown areas, unfamiliar roles, new patterns." And again in, "complexity is about the behavior of interacting entities, and the evolution of collective structure and behaviors over time." (Chapter 23, Peter Allen, Jamie Boulton, Mark Strathern and James Baldwin).

When considering what is common about complexity, we seem to agree broadly that it is about emergence, interaction and the dynamics of interaction. Where we seem to depart, or fragment, is in the discussion of how best to look at the phenomena. I have always searched for a philosophy which allows these differences to coexist peacefully, and until recently, found and participated in many of the discussions relating to the ontology in use, whether a Leibnizian approach or a Lockean approach was better or worse, whether Kant had the answer or Hegelian inquiry did, or if indeed Singer had the answer. The answer I think has come in the development of new philosophical approaches, which is logical when one considers that philosophy develops to explain the reality of the time, and in complexity we are defining a new reality or re-defining our current reality. But where is this new philosophy that we need so badly? Philosophy as a subject worldwide is in crisis, so where can we go to find that explanation and guidance? I think there are two places we can go: one exists within the body of complexity itself, with books such as this, where philosophy is developed from within, and the second exists in a new breed of philosopher such as Alain Badiou.

Philosophy, as can be seen clearly from the first five chapters, is fundamental in driving understanding. Philosophy governs choice, it articulates position and it indicates direction; it is our rudder and our start position for debate. The reason I mention Alain Badiou is simply because he has articulated a philosophical position, which not only challenges all of the traditional models, but also articulates a position I believe closely relates to that of many of the authors in this book. I believe that there is no 'right answer' philosophically, and that the truth is in differences. Badiou's *L'etre et l'evenement* is alien to almost all branches of existing philosophy. It raises the subject of "multiple multiplicities" and the concept that situations do not necessarily have mutually exclusive identities. I see this as a step towards the quantum physicists and a step towards the findings in complexity science. This is a subject discussed by Kurt Richardson in chapter 2, which I feel supports his pluralistic position.

I am constantly aware when entering into these discourses, and from the experiences of COMPLEX-M, (an email address, which I am sure many will have come across in the last few years), that almost any position you wish to take on a subject can lead to pages of dialogue. I am, therefore, not going to go any further on philosophical matters relating to complexity, other than to say that it adds substantially to the book, and looking forward might justify a literary lineage of its own in the coming years.

On the matter of how we research complexity and make our new-found knowledge accessible, I feel we have a paradox. The broad nature of complexity as a natural phenomenon allows contributions on the subject matter to be made from almost any arena of knowledge, and it is for this reason that it is so powerful; paradoxically, it is precisely for this reason we find it so difficult to apply or develop new approaches, tools, techniques, explanations etc. What is now changing as the body of knowledge and our understanding of it grows, is the change in direction, from having to prove that the phenomena exists and how it exists, to how we may actually make use of it. The development of this book from philosophy, through theory, to application, is a logical one. There are many authors on the world stage at the moment writing about complexity and offering a 'new way' of doing things. As a practitioner, I am duty bound to read these 'new ways', in case a client were to ask a question on the subject. I am, however, frequently disappointed by many of these books, as I do not see them displaying the depth of experience and research that is reflected in this book. I share Buck Lawrimore's sentiment when he states, "but I have yet to find one (book) which attempts to use Complexity to understand and manage all the key variables and challenges which confront a typical business or organizational manager" (p. 127).

The question this then poses is 'why?'. Is it that the science is still too young and developmental and there are too many unanswered questions, or is it that the science struggles to express itself? For complexity to grow and become more widely accepted as the way we view the world, two things need to happen. Firstly, people need to understand the science, and secondly, people need to be able to use the science. I feel that it is our challenge over the coming months and years, to seek methodologies and alliances that allow us to express what we are seeing and discovering, in ways that people can understand and relate to. We must not forget that it has taken forty years to persuade people that driving their car is contributing to the melting of the polar icecap and raised sea levels. Again, cause and effect are not necessarily closely related in time and space, and this makes the challenge difficult. Our search for 'solutions', as a global paradigm, prevents us from accepting that there are no right answers; right answers are invariably contextual and transient.

This book should not be regarded as just a book, but as an emergent collaboration, and as with emergent phenomenon, we cannot predict the effect that it will have; only that it will have an effect. Also, we must not allow ourselves to be constrained in our vision of what is possible; if we have learnt one thing from complexity, it is the vast range of "potential potentialities" there are.

As Kurt Richardson states in chapter 2, "If the argument that the Universe is a complex system holds then 'We must ... keep our options open and we must not restrict ourselves in advance.' (Feyerabend, 1975)."

There will be increasing pressure to compartmentalise the science and to establish commonly agreed principles. This, as they say, is 'human nature'. The 'established approach' helps to focus research, aid the education of the science and improve its adoption rate. However, it also severely constrains the adoption of new ideas, as we have then to work hard to justify why new research changes the established status quo. Much of today's scientific establishment only sponsors certain types of research, and will only accept new findings after a lengthy validation process and a substantial burden of proof. Unfortunately, as can be seen in examples such as climate change, or even my own involvement in Open University, proof is a hard commodity to find in complexity, and open-ended experiments are difficult to fund.

I feel we must choose to accept complexity as an evolving stream of consciousness, which over time will grow to explain what is inexplicable today. As with all journeys, there will always be another hill to climb once you reach the top of this one.

About the contributors

Peter Allen

Prof Peter Allen is Head of the Complex Systems Management Centre in the School of Management at Cranfield University. He teaches complexity on the MBA at Cranfield and contributes to other teaching courses in several universities. His research is directed towards the application of the new ideas concerning evolutionary complex systems to real world social, economic and management problems. He has a Ph.D. in Theoretical Physics, was a Royal Society European Research Fellow 1970-71 and a Senior Research Fellow at the Université Libre de Bruxelles from 1972-1987, where he worked on the theory of complex systems with the Nobel Laureate, Ilya Prigogine. Professor Allen has worked for 30 years on the mathematical modelling of change and innovation in urban, social, economic, financial and ecological systems, and the development of integrated systems models. He has written and edited several books and published over 200 articles in a range of fields including ecology, social science, urban and regional science, economics, systems theory, and physics. He has been a consultant to the Canadian Fishing Industry, Elf Aquitaine, the United Nations University, the European Commission and the Asian Development Bank. He has managed a number of large European and UK research contracts, including the NEXSUS Network (www.nexsus.org).

James Baldwin

James graduated from the University of Hull in 1999 with a first class honours degree in Psychology. He was subsequently awarded a Ph.D. scholarship from the University of Sheffield's Department of Mechanical Engineering to research the sustainability of complex systems, with a particular emphasis of manufacturing in South Yorkshire. This led to a Postdoctoral Fellowship (2004) awarded by the Economic and Social Research Council, UK. James joined the Management School in January 2005 as a Lecturer in Strategic Management. He has written and contributed to 25 research papers for conferences and workshops, book chapters and journal publications. His specific research interests include sustainable manufacturing and industrial ecology; uncertainty, risk and diversity in management decision-making; evolutionary systems applied to manufacturing; experimental computer modelling and simulations; manufacturing classifications, particularly cladistic classifications; practical tools for management for use during organizational change. His teaching interests include project management, risk assessment, sustainable operations management and industrial ecology. James also serves on the Editorial Board of the new international scientific referee journal *Progress in Industrial Ecology*, and has also participated in the review process on special issues for both the *Journal of Cleaner Production* and *Benchmarking: An International Journal*. James is a member of the scientific committee of the 11th Annual International Sustainable Development Research Conference with special streams on Industrial Ecology and European Environmental Policy.

Ken Baskin

Ken Baskin, an ISCE Fellow, writes, lectures, and consults on the benefits of thinking differently about the things we know best. In his book, *Corporate DNA: Learning from Life*, for example, he focused on how managers can increase innovation, productivity, and market share by thinking about their organizations as if they were living things evolving in market ecosystems. He has published articles in such journals as *E:CO, Emergence, The Manchester Review, Organizations & People, The Physician Executive*, and *Innovative Leader*. In addition, he has spoken before audiences at several ISCE and Society for Complexity in Psychology and the Life Sciences conferences, a RAND Corporation workshop on complexity in public policy, and a 1999 seminar on complexity management in Tokyo. Recently, Baskin has been exploring and writing about the integration of complexity thinking insights with those of narratology. This work arose from an ISCE-funded research project he completed in 2002, which examined the dynamics of storytelling in work group cultures at three American hospitals. His corporate experience includes work as an executive speech writer at Bell Atlantic (now Verizon), Sun Company, and the U.S. Department of Energy.

He has also run his own public relations firm, with clients including Monsanto, ITT, and Merck. Baskin earned a Ph.D. in English Literature from the University of Maryland. He now lives in Philadelphia, PA with his wife.

Jean Boulton

Jean Boulton is a Visiting Fellow with the Complex Systems Management Centre. She delivers the MBA elective 'Complexity in Management' which focuses on the implications of complex systems thinking to strategy development and organization change. Jean is also Managing Director of Claremont Management Consultants Ltd, established in 1994 and specializing in organization change and strategic organization development. Previously she was Practice Director of Organization Change for Hay Management Consultants Ltd. and prior to that she was Head of Engineering Operations for British Aerospace Regional Aircraft Ltd. Jean has a Ph.D. in theoretical physics from Cambridge University and a first degree in physics from Oxford University and a MBA from Cranfield. Her physics background combined with many years experience of organization change put her in a strong position to look at the implications of science-based theories as applied to management thinking.

Paul Cilliers

Paul Cilliers is professor in Philosophy at the University of Stellenbosch, South Africa. His research is focused on the philosophical and ethical implications of complexity. He is the author of *Complexity and Postmodernism* (Routledge, 1998) and he also has a degree in Electronic Engineering.

Patrick E. Connor

Patrick E. Connor is Professor of Organizational Analysis at the Atkinson Graduate School of Management, Willamette University, in Salem, Oregon. He received his bachelor's degree in electrical engineering from the University of Washington, a master's degree in industrial administration from Purdue University, and his Ph.D. in organization theory from the University of Washington. He also has served on the faculty of Oregon State University and visited on the faculty of the University of British Columbia. He teaches graduate courses in management, organization design, and managing organizational change. Professor Connor has published five books on management in thirteen editions, and has had some 50 articles, chapters, and book reviews published in professional journals and books. His research has appeared in the *Academy of Management Journal, Academy of Management Review, IEEE Transactions on Engineering Management, Journal of Management Inquiry*, and *Public Administration Review*, among others. His research centers on two themes, managers' personal value systems and organizational change. See http://www.willamette.edu/~pconnor/.

Eric B. Dent

Dr. Eric B. Dent is presently Dean and Professor, School of Business, University of North Carolina, Pembroke. He is committed to an interdisciplinary research agenda that has resulted in publications in behavioral science, complexity theory, systems science, education, consulting, history, communications, spirituality, organization development, and philosophy journals. Dr. Dent is a consultant to Fortune 500, government and non-profit organizations as well as an invited speaker to national audiences. He has received various awards for his scholarship, teaching, and service. Prior to joining academia, Dr. Dent worked as a computer scientist with IBM. There he worked on state-of-the-art satellite communication technology.

Frans M. van Eijnatten

Frans M. van Eijnatten, Ph.D., is Associate Professor at the Research School for Operations Management and Logistics at the Department of Technology Management, Eindhoven University of Technology, the Netherlands. His main research interest is in Socio-Technical Systems Design, an ambition he pursued for almost 20 years by initiating and coordinating Ph.D. design-oriented action research projects in R&D and information systems design. He produced several English-language reviews on the subject as well as a comprehensive bibliography of the paradigm. Currently, Dr.

Van Eijnatten is exploring the implications of Chaos and Complexity theories for Socio-Technical Systems Design and Organizational Renewal (i.e. 'Chaordic Systems Thinking' - CST). He coedited two guest issues about CST for the *Journal of Organizational Change Management* and *The Learning Organization*, and published an overview of Chaos and Complexity in Organization and Management in the *Revue Sciences de Gestion*. He is founder and coordinator of the European Chaos and Complexity Network ECCON, and convenor for the annual meetings of this network. He participated in several European-Union-funded research and development programs (4th, 5th Framework: Esprit, Brite-EuRam, IST, IMS), and is reviewer for the 6th Framework ('New and Emerging Science and Technology' – NEST, Pathfinder activity), European Commission, Brussels. He served as an invited expert to Framework 6 Integrated Project: European Collaborative Networked Organizations Leadership Initiative (ECOLEAD). Dr. Van Eijnatten chairs the NOSMO Socio-Cybernetica working group, based in The Netherlands. Recently, he spent two months as a visiting research fellow at Yokohama National University, Graduate School of Environment and Information Sciences, Eco-Technology System Laboratory, Yokohama, Japan.

James Falconer

James Falconer is president of Eagna Research and Consulting, an independent business thinking concern. He has spent nearly twenty years working in and with private-sector organizations in the high technology, financial services, and professional services sectors, as well as with public sector agencies. His role has typically been to help those organizations navigate through improvement and change, employing a holistic and highly collaborative approach that typically involves strategic realignment, process improvement, and / or information technology integration. He is also an active researcher in organizational domains, and his focus is mainly on concepts such as knowledge, strategy, culture, community, complexity, change, and form in the context of the postmodern business landscape. He has had several papers published in academic journals and has spoken at numerous conferences internationally. He holds a B.A. in philosophy from the University of Toronto, a B.E.S. in urban planning from the University of Waterloo, and an MBA from York University.

Maarten C. van Galen

Having completed an advanced degree in Industrial Engineering and Management Science at the University of Technology in Eindhoven, The Netherlands, Maarten was employed as coordinator, trainer and researcher of a change initiative focussing on the culture of a Dutch industrial company. Now he works in the field of quality management for a small coatings company in the Netherlands.

Carlos Gershenson

Carlos Gershenson is studying a Ph.D. at the Centrum Leo Apostel of the Vrije Universiteit Brussel, Belgium (2002-), on the 'Design and Control of Self-organizing Systems'. He holds a MS.c. degree in Evolutionary and Adaptive Systems, from the University of Sussex (2001-2002), and a B.Eng. degree in Computer Engineering from the Fundacion Arturo Rosenblueth in Mexico. (1996-2001). He studied five semesters of Philosophy at UNAM, Mexico (1998-2001). He has been an active researcher since 1997, working at the Chemistry Institute, UNAM, Mexico (1997-2001), and a summer at the Weizmann Institute of Science, Israel (1999). He has about thirty scientific publications in journals and conference proceedings. He has given more than thirty presentations at conferences or research group seminars. His research interests include self-organizing systems, complex systems, artificial life, cognitive sciences, philosophy of mind, artificial societies, paraconsistent logics and virtual laboratories. He is a contributing editor to *Complexity Digest* and Book Review Editor of the *Artificial Life* journal. He has taught different courses at undergraduate and graduate levels in Mexico. He has worked as a systems consultant, software and web developer. He periodically writes popular articles for scientific divulgation.

Dawn R. Gilpin

Dawn Gilpin has been working in the communication field for over ten years as an independent consultant, previously based in Italy and now in the United States. She earned her M.A. in

Journalism and Public Relations from the University of Memphis in 2002 and is currently pursuing a Ph.D. in Mass Media and Communication at Temple University. Her primary area of research interest lies in the relationships between organizations, media and public policy; other fields include public relations and organizational communication in general, organizational knowledge and learning, science communication and media representations of science, epistemology, and popular culture. She is especially interested in exploring applications of complexity, narrative, postmodern / poststructuralist, network and other nonlinear theories to the aforementioned research topics.

Jeffrey Goldstein

Jeffrey Goldstein, Ph.D., is Full Professor, School of Business, Adelphi University, Garden City, NY, as well as Associate Clinical Professor, Derner Institute for Advanced Psychological Studies also at Adelphi University. He is also Director of Research for the School of Business and directs the School's Executive-in-Residence Program. Prof. Goldstein has also taught at Rutgers University, as well as courses at Columbia University, NYU, and in 2000 was a Visiting Professor at the NATO Advanced Studies Institute on Nonlinear Dynamics held in Moscow, Russia. Prof. Goldstein is one of the pioneers in the application of complexity theory to the study of organizations and leadership. His book on that subject, *The Unshackled Organization*, was hailed by *Industry Week* as a "fascinating vision." Dr. Goldstein is the author of over 80 scholarly articles and has lectured and given workshops throughout the world at leading businesses and universities. Dr. Goldstein is currently one of the editors-in-chief of the new journal *Emergence: Complexity and Organization* and is a trustee and past- president of the Society for Chaos Theory in Psychology and the Life Sciences which publishes the internally recognized journal *Nonlinear Dynamics, Psychology, and the Life Sciences*. He is also a member of the Institute for the Study of Coherence and Emergence and in that capacity played a key role in the founding of its ground-breaking journal *Emergence*, the first such publication devoted solely to the application of the sciences of complex systems to human organizations.

Francis Heylighen

Francis Heylighen is a research professor at the Free University of Brussels (VUB), where he directs the Evolution, Complexity and Cognition (ECCO) research group. He has worked during most of his career for the Fund for Scientific Research-Flanders, first as research assistant, then Post Doc, and finally tenured Senior Research Associate. He received his M.Sc. in mathematical physics in 1982, and defended his Ph.D. in 1987, on the cognitive processes and structures underlying physical theories. He then shifted his research to the self-organization and evolution of complex, cognitive systems, which he approaches from a cybernetic perspective. He teaches an introductory course on this topic at the VUB, and has several Ph.D. students working on these subjects. Heylighen has authored some 90 scientific publications in a variety of disciplines, including a monograph and four edited books. Since 1990 he is an editor of the Principia Cybernetica Project, an international organization devoted to the computer-supported collaborative development of an interdisciplinary knowledge network. He created (and still administers) the project's website in 1993, as one of the first complex, interactive webs in the world. Since 1996 he chairs the Global Brain Group, an international discussion forum reflecting on the emerging information society. He is editor-in-chief of the *Journal of Memetics*, which he cofounded in 1996, and is a member of the editorial boards of the *Journal of Happiness Studies*, and the journals *Informatica* and *Entropy*.

Liu Hong

Liu Hong is Professor of Management and chair of Department of Business Administration of the School of Business, Nanjing University. Liu received his Ph.D. from Wuhan University of Technology and his Master's degree from Hefei University of Technology. Dr. Liu recent research focuses on managing complexity, including applying complex systems theory to organizational change management, organization design, multi-agent behaviors, and human resource management. Dr Liu has published five books, two international conference proceedings and about 100 articles including coauthorships. His two recently books are *Economic Chaos Management: Theory, Methodologies and Applications* (Bejing: Chinese Development Press, 2001, in Chinese, awarded the second prize of Excellent Social Science Achievements by Jiangshu Province Government in 2003) and *Principles and Methodologies Based Chaos Theory of Economic System Forecasting* (Bejing: Science Press, 2004, in Chinese).

James K. Horn

James Horn teaches history and philosophy of education at Monmouth University. During the late stages of a former career as a K-12 educator, he was selected to participate in one of the learning institutes that is described in his contribution to the present volume. Since the early 1990s, he has presented and written on the subject of autonomous learning and learning systems. Currently he is working on a research methodology piece that uses the metaphors and science of complexity to advance qualitative empirical research. His most recent article, "The Embodiment of Learning", will appear later this year in a special issue of the journal, *Educational Philosophy and Theory*.

Robert G. Jones

Robert G. Jones is Professor of Psychology at Southwest Missouri State University (SMSU). He received his Ph.D. (1992) in industrial / organizational (I/O) psychology from Ohio State University after a 'first' career in banking and music. During his career as an I/O psychologist, he has dealt with a broad range of research and practice questions, mostly relating to psychometrics in selection, performance assessment, and management development. His recent work centers on applications of basic research on emotive perception to measurement and management of behavior in individuals and groups. With his students, he has addressed these issues in numerous applied and scholarly settings, including assessment centers, performance management systems, service training programs, selection test development, and team and leadership development. Bob has served as Book Review Editor for *Personnel Psychology* and as Acting Department Head for the SMSU Department of Psychology. He lives in Springfield, MO with his Wife and two Sons, and currently serves on the Springfield City Council.

Tadahiko Kawai

Tadahiko Kawai is Professor of Corporate Strategy and Organization Theory at the Graduate School of Systems Management, University of Tsukuba, Tokyo, Japan. He received his B.A. and M.A. from the University of Tokyo, Japan, and Ph. D. from the University of California, Berkeley. His research interests include dynamic theories of corporate and business strategies, theories of organizational transformation and evolution, and complexity theory. He has authored several books such as *Strategic Reformation of Organizations: A Comparative Analysis of Sharp, Sony and Matsushita*; *Leadership in Complex Adaptive System: A Model of Organizational Transformation and Case Analyses*; *A Dynamic Theory of Strategy: Beyond the Positioning Theory and the Resource-based View*; and *An Analysis of Business-Government Relations in Japan: The Case of the Federation of Economic Organizations*.

Buck Lawrimore

E. W. 'Buck' Lawrimore has been president of Lawrimore Inc. in Charlotte, N.C., since 1979. His company provides marketing and strategic consulting to a wide range of business, government and nonprofit organizations. He has intensively studied the 'success secrets' of market-leading companies for over 20 years, and since the late '90s has focused on adapting Complexity science for organization development and strategic purposes. He is the author of *The Managing-Leading Edge*, an email newsletter on innovations in management and leadership, distributed to business and government leaders worldwide. He has written and published over 4,000 news and feature articles in local, state, national and international media, and has won national awards for his writing. He is a 1966 graduate of Davidson College and has conducted personally directed post-graduate studies for over 25 years in management, psychology, philosophy, business strategy, organization development, and Complexity.

Michael R. Lissack

Dr. Lissack is the director of the Institute for the Study of Coherence and Emergence (ISCE) and served for five years as the editor-in-chief of ISCE's journal, *Emergence*. His ongoing research focuses on the use of the concept of coherence to develop a complexity based theory of management. Dr. Lissack has taught economics as a lecturer at Williams, research techniques at Henley Management College (UK), business strategy at IMD (Switzerland), complexity at the London School of Economics, and business ethics at the Rotterdam School of Management, Vanderbilt, and Keele (UK), as well as run nine international conferences on the topics of complexity, management, healthcare, entanglement and ethics. His numerous books and speaking engagements have had a management and philosophy focus. In 2000, Dr. Lissack founded Knowledge Ventures Inc. an educational tools software company which publishes the Learners Library - a research tool for academics. *Worth* magazine recognized Dr. Lissack in 1999 as one of "Wall Street's 25 Smartest Players" and again in 2001 as one of the 100 Americans who have most influenced "how we think about money."

Pavel O. Luksha

Pavel Luksha is a head of a Working Group on Socio-Economic Studies at the State University - Higher School of Economics, Moscow, Russia. He received his Masters degree in Economics, and later pursued post-graduate study at the same University. Pavel has taught at the Higher School of Economics, and conducted courses in management disciplines in other institutions. He has been, and remains, involved into a number of research projects that bridge complexity science with social sciences. Pavel worked for international and domestic management consulting companies such as Accenture, Arcadis Euroconsult, ALT R&C, and also acted as an external consultant in a number of domestic and international development projects. Apart from that, he has been actively involved in economic journalism with a number of national journals and news agencies. Since 2001, Pavel works within a leading Russian automotive manufacturer, Severstal-Auto. In 2003, he held the position of the Chief Controlling Officer for the company.

Simon Marvin

Simon Marvin is Professor and lead-director of SURF. Simon is an expert on changing relations between neighborhoods, cities, regions and infrastructure networks in a period of rapid technological change, environmental concern and institutional restructuring. Simon's research has been funded by the ESRC, EPSRC, the European Commission and a number of commercial funders and public agencies. He has published widely on cities and technological change. Recent coauthored books include (2001) *Urban Infrastructure in Transition: Networks, Buildings and Plans*, Earthscan; (2001) *Splintering Urbanism: Networked Infrastructures, Technological Mobilities and the Urban Condition* Routledge, London. Recent research work has focused on the development of prospective approaches to understanding urban and regional futures. This work has been funded by the DTI Foresight programme, Treasury Placement Scheme, ODPM New Horizons programme.

Elizabeth McMillan

Elizabeth is a Senior Research Fellow at the Open University and an experienced and qualified management development consultant who worked for many years as a senior manager in both the private and public sectors. She specializes in leadership, creativity and the management of change, and is an acknowledged expert in the exploration of all the strategic and operational issues that organizational change engenders. Her book *Complexity, Organizations and Change* was published by Routledge in March 2004. She is a Fellow of the Chartered Institute of Personnel and Development, a founder member and a Director of the UK Complexity Society, and a member of the British Academy of Management.

Will P. Medd

Following a B.Sc. Hons. in Sociology and Social Policy (1992-1995) Will undertook a Ph.D. in the Department of Sociology, Lancaster University (1995-1999) exploring the applicability of models from complexity science for sociological analysis, through a case study of partnership working in social welfare. Will's post-Ph.D. research began at the University of Salford, in the Institute for

Public Health Policy and Research, working on an action-learning project to build capacity for tackling health inequalities through local strategies. In 2002, still at the University of Salford, he joined the Centre for Sustainable Urban and Regional Futures (SURF), to work on an EU funded project looking at the role of intermediary organizations in sustainable water management. Will has now returned to Lancaster as a Research Associate in the Department of Sociology and newly established Centre for Sustainable Water Management to work on developing the sociology of water while maintaining his interest in complexity science methodologies. Recent publications on complexity include: "Complexity and Social Measurement" (in Kempf-Leonard K., et al. (eds.) (2004) *Encyclopedia of Social Measurement*, San Diego: Elsevier Science), "Complexity and the social world", (in Williams, M. and T. May (eds.) (2002) *International Journal of Social Research Methodology*, 5(1): 71-81.), "What is Complexity Science? Toward an Ecology of Ignorance," (K. Richardson and P. Cilliers (eds.) (2001) *Emergence: Journal of complexity issues in organization and management*, 3(1): 45-62). He also edited a special edition on "Complexity Science and Social Policy" for the electronic journal *Social Issues* in 2001.

Mihnea Moldoveanu

Mihnea Moldoveanu is Assistant Professor of Strategic management and Director of the Marcel Desautels Centre for Integrative Thinking at the Rotman School of Management, University of Toronto. His research focuses on the conceptualization of organizational complexity and the study of complexity coping and manipulation strategies.

Ronald C. Murray

Dr. Ronald Murray's career has included organization consulting, public and private sector management, university teaching, and military service. Following seven years in the Canadian military Dr. Murray returned to university to pursue graduate studies at Queen's University at Kingston, Ontario. His doctoral studies focused on developing a humanistic approach to the use of General Systems Theory concepts in social science by interpreting them through the philosophical insights of existential phenomenology. He then applied these systems concepts to examine the evolution of international maritime relations. After obtaining his Ph.D. he taught in the School of Public Administration at Queen's for several years. Dr. Murray then spent 12 years in the Ontario Public Service in a variety of management positions with leadership responsibilities in organization development, project management, strategic planning and management, and the management of information technology and systems. Later he consulted with several organizations, designing and leading their organization development and change management projects to a successful completion. Based on his academic, management, and consulting experience Dr. Murray developed a systemic approach to organizational change management that overcomes the fragmentation that is created and exacerbated by partial and incremental change management. This comprehensive, integrated, and strategic approach to managing Large Scale Organizational Change is grounded in the philosophical insights of existential phenomenology and the organizational insights provided by complexity theory concepts.

Carole S. Napolitano

Carole Napolitano is President and founder of Synergies, a firm that provides consulting services in leadership, executive coaching, and organizational effectiveness. Skilled in designing and facilitating learning experiences for managers, leaders, and teams, Napolitano has worked with a variety of public and private sector organizations. A few of her many clients include NASA, Freddie Mac, the Federal Judicial Center, the World Bank Group, FEMA, the University of Maryland, the U.S. District Court of Nevada, the USDA Forest Service, and Xerox Corporation where she coauthored several internal publications and functioned as lead designer for the corporate first level manager program, *Navigating Planet Xerox*. For a period of eight years (1994 – 2002), Napolitano served as Executive Consultant for the Seaboard Region of State Farm Insurance Companies; she currently coaches members of the executive team at Baltimore Gas & Electric. A focus of her recent work has been the use of Appreciative Inquiry to assist individuals and systems engage new possibilities for their organizations and themselves. Napolitano holds a Masters degree in English from the University of North Carolina at Chapel Hill and has pursued advanced studies in public and organizational communication at the University of Maryland, College Park. She has been affiliated with the Center for Creative Leadership, the University of Maryland Office of Executive Programs, and the National Leadership Institute. She is coauthor of *The Leadership Odyssey: A Self-Development Guide to New Skills for New Times* published by Jossey-Bass and has recently joined the Steward Group for the Berkana Exchange, a foundation dedicated to supporting emergent leadership efforts worldwide.

Gowri Parameswaran

Gowri did her bachelors in Bombay University, India and completed her Masters and Doctoral work in Rutgers University in New Jersey. She taught in Southwest Missouri State University from 1993-2001 in the department of psychology. Currently Gowri teaches in the School of Education at the State University of New York. Her dissertation involved synthesizing the theories of Vygotsky and Piaget in the area of spatial development in girls and women. Her past research has included gender and cultural issues in development, cognitive development and developmental theory, critical literacy, multicultural issues in education and teaching issues in psychology. Gowri has recently been involved in children's development when confronted with disasters like AIDS, war and natural calamities, and has been working on a project to explore changes across generations among Indian immigrants in the United States. She has published in a number of peer-refereed journals in psychology, education and anthropology.

Julie Richardson

Julie Richardson is a writer, consultant and strategic policy advisor. She has worked for over 15 years in the broad area of sustainable development in a wide range of organizations and countries in Europe, Africa, Asia and Latin America. Previously she worked as Principal Sustainability Advisor for Forum for the Future; as a policy advisor to the Prime Minister's Strategy Unit in the UK government and as a lecturer in environmental economics at the Universities of London and Sussex. She has published widely in the field of sustainable development, corporate responsibility and new approaches to organizational change. She has recently completed a postgraduate program in holistic science at Schumacher College in Devon, England. Her thesis "Wholeness and Health in the Living Organization" investigated the links between holistic health and contemporary science applied to throw new light onto organizational dynamics. Her contact email address is Julie.richardson@blueyonder.co.uk.

Kurt A. Richardson

Kurt is currently the Associate Director of the ISCE Group, and the Director of ISCE Publishing. He has Adjunct Professorship positions at Royal Roads University, Canada (where he teaches a course on research methods) and the University of Technology, Sydney, Australia. Kurt is the Managing / Production Editor for the international journal *Emergence: Complexity and Organization*, and serves on the review boards of *Systemic Practice and Action Research*, *Systems Research and Behavioral Science*, and *Tamara: Journal of Critical Postmodern Organizational Science*. He has also reviewed papers for *Nonlinear Dynamics, Psychology and the Life Science*, and the *Journal of Artificial Societies and Social Simulation*. Kurt has a B.Sc. in Physics, a M.Sc. in Astronautics and Space Enginneering, and a Ph.D. in Physics, as well as being a Chartered Physicist and a Chartered Scientist. His current research interests are concerned with a range of issues surrounding the study of complex systems, including: the simplification of complexity, implications for policy analysis, relationship between systems theory and complexity theory, and the philosophical implications of assuming complexity. Before joining ISCE Kurt was a satellite communications consultant for the British government.

Duncan A. Robertson

Duncan Robertson is a lecturer in strategic management at Warwick Business School, UK. He has held lecturing posts at several colleges of the University of Oxford, as well as visiting posts at the Santa Fe Institute (New Mexico), Sun Yat-Sen University (Guangzhou, People's Republic of China), and The Wharton School of the University of Pennsylvania (Philadelphia). His research centers on the dynamics of competitive strategy; competition in high-velocity and turbulent environments; dynamic capabilities; agent-based modeling of inter-firm competition; and the strategic management of financial services firms. A chartered accountant and chartered physicist, he has worked for KPMG in the United Kingdom, Australia, and New Zealand. He gained his D.Phil. (Ph.D.) from the Saïd Business School, University of Oxford and his first degree in physics from Imperial College, University of London. Further details can be found at http://www.duncanrobertson.com/.

Johan Roos

Dr. Roos is the Director of Imagination Lab Foundation (www.imagilab.org), a nonprofit research institute developing and spreading actionable knowledge about imaginative, reflective, and responsible organizational practices. He is also Director of Serious Play Academy (www.spacademy.com), which offers strategy workshops, retreats and comparable engagements based on the general principle of serious play. In his research, teaching, and consulting Johan explores how people in organizations, especially in the practice of strategy, struggle to create meaning and deal with the unexpected. For five years ending in early 2000, he was Professor of Strategy and General Management at the International Institute for Management Development (IMD), Switzerland. He has generated many scholarly articles in peer-reviewed journals, books, book chapters, articles for practitioners, and research papers. A Swedish national, Dr. Roos holds a Ph.D. in International Business from the Stockholm School of Economics (1989), and an M.Sc. in Agriculture from the Swedish University of Agricultural Sciences (1985).

Stanley N. Salthe

Currently a Visiting Scientist in the Biological Sciences at Binghamton University, I'm retired from Biology at the City University of New York. My connections at Binghamton have been more with the Systems Science group of the Engineering Department. Having long standing connections to both Systems Science and Semiotics, I'm now involved in the current revival of Natural Philosophy (Philosophy of Nature), a discourse that withered away (except in Thomistic philosophy and Marxism), at the turn of the last century. Its role is systematic, not critical, aimed at constructing a contemporary mythology (sensu ethnology) based in scientific knowledge. See my WEB pages at http://www.nbi.dk/~natphil/salthe/, as well at http://www.harmeny.com/twiki/bin/view/Main/SaltheResearchOnline. Recently I've become more involved with thermodynamics as a way of grounding our mythology in the Big Bang, as in the hierarchical framework: {physical world {material world {biological world {sociocultural world }}}}. This has interested a number of ecologists in my work. As well, I have in the last decade joined Koichiro Matsuno in an inquiry into Internalism, an attempt to construct an alternative perspective on the world to that taken within classical science, which we identify as 'externalism'. My most recently authored book, *Development and Evolution: Complexity and Change in Biology* (MIT Press, 1993) presents what is still my general conceptual framework. Previous books are *Evolutionary Biology* (Holt Rinehart & Winston, 1972) and *Evolving Hierarchical Systems: Their Structure and Representation* (Columbia University Press, 1985).

Krishnankutty Sathian

K. Sathian is Associate Professor of Neurology and Rehabilitation Medicine at Emory University School of Medicine, and a faculty member of the interdisciplinary Neuroscience Program at Emory. He divides his time between clinical work in neurology and neurological rehabilitation, teaching medical students and residents, neuroscientific laboratory research and training graduate students and research fellows. His research, which is funded by the National Institutes of Health, focusses on the study of perception and its applications to neurorehabilitation. He has published extensively in these areas and frequently lectures in the USA and overseas. He received the Albert Levy Award in 2001 for the best scientific publication by a faculty member at Emory. He reviews manuscripts for numerous journals and serves on review panels for multiple granting authorities, including the National Institutes of Health. He obtained medical training from Christian Medical College, Vellore, India; a Ph.D. in neuroscience from the University of Melbourne, Australia; and did his residency in neurology at the University of Chicago.

Barbara Simpson

Barbara Simpson is a Senior Lecturer in Organization Studies at the University of Strathclyde Graduate School of Business in Glasgow. She holds a Ph.D. in Management and an Honours degree in Physics. Her current research interests are broadly located within the field of organizational learning and change, but with a special focus on dynamic processes of innovation. The generative potential of human activity and interactivity is central to her understanding of emergent novelty in social / organizational contexts. Her work in this area is informed by more than 20 years of practical experience as a scientist, science manager and consultant in innovating organizations. In addition, her early training in physics, especially modern physics, continues to weave through and shape her perspective on the world. Barbara's recent publications have focussed on the transformational change experiences of public good science organizations in New Zealand. She has also been involved in an ongoing study of innovation practices in small, knowledge-intensive enterprises.

Mark Strathern

Mark Strathern is a Research Fellow with the Complex Systems Management Centre. At present he is part of a team with the University of Sheffield undertaking a three-year project "Modelling the Evolution of the Aerospace Supply Chain" which aims to produce a framework for Evolution Management and is designed to be a core research project in the continuation of the NEXSUS Priority Network. Recently he was part of the team on the ESRC NEXSUS project to understand and model sustainability in complex socio-economic networks. He has also recently been involved with the modelling and teaching of sustainability within the EU fishing industries, and has a continuing collaboration with the Tyndall Centre working on formal and mathematical methods for use in the climate change arena. Mark has worked for over a decade at Cranfield modelling complex systems, particularly complex socio-economic systems. Amongst other projects, he has been involved in the modelling of financial trading systems, banking, the effects of climate change, Senegal, and the water quality in the Rhone valley. He also has an ongoing interest in object oriented software development for concurrent and distributed systems. Before joining Cranfield Mark worked for a number of years as a consultant in Information Systems and has held positions in accountancy and marketing. Mark has a degree in mathematics and an ongoing Ph.D. in modelling adaptability.

Andrew Tait

Andrew Tait is currently cofounder and Chief Technology Officer of Idea Sciences, a Virginia-based software and consulting firm specializing in the creative use of technology to improve organizational decision-making. Idea Sciences' mission is to 'package' powerful decision-making theories and processes in a way that makes them accessible and practical for day-to-day decision-making. In support of this mission, Andrew has designed commercial, off-the-shelf, solutions for strategic planning, performance improvement and conflict management. His work in this area has led to numerous consulting and training relationships with major commercial and government organizations. Prior to forming Idea Sciences, Andrew held various commercial (technology consulting), government (defence) and academic (management) positions. Andrew's research interests include: performance improvement, electronic voting, virtual communities; conflict management and; security and privacy in complex systems.

Shann Turnbull

Dr. Shann Turnbull is the Principal of the International Institute for Self-governance based in Sydney Australia and a Fellow of the Institute for International Corporate Governance and Accountability at the George Washington University Law School. He is an Honorary Associate of the Asia Pacific Research Institute at Macquarie University. Shann graduated in Tasmania as an Electrical Engineer in 1957, obtained a B.Sc. from the University of Melbourne in 1960, and a MBA from Harvard in 1963. He obtained a Ph.D. from Macquarie University, Sydney for developing a methodology for analyzing complex organizations. Two of his research papers at www.ssrn.com were selected for inclusion with the seminal contributions of leading scholars in the Corporate Governance volume of *The History of Management Thought* (2000). He has founded a number of enterprises with some becoming publicly traded with him as their Chairman and / or Chief Executive. He was a founding member of a vulture capitalist company that acquired over a dozen publicly traded companies. In 1975 he became a founding author of the first educational qualification in the world for company directors and wrote his first book *Democratizing the Wealth of Nations*. Google reveals that 'Shann Turnbull' is a prolific writer on socioeconomic reform. He has undertaken numerous consulting assignments for governments and the private sector. In 2002 he was commissioned by a UK 'Think Tank' to write a public policy booklet on *A New Way to Govern: Organizations and Society after Enron*. He is a shareholder activist and his research interest is self-governance.

Rajaram Veliyath

Raj Veliyath is a Professor of Management at the Coles College of Business at Kennesaw State University. Raj's Ph.D. is from the Katz Graduate School of Business at the University of Pittsburgh. He also has an MBA from the Indian Institute of Management Calcutta and a Bachelors degree in Engineering from the Indian Institute of Technology at Kharagpur. He has taught at the University of Pittsburgh's Katz Graduate School of Business, the Kellogg Graduate School of Management at Northwestern University, the University of Wisconsin at Parkside and the Pamplin College of Business at Virginia Tech, before joining Kennesaw State University in 1994. Prior to entering academia, Raj handled exports, product management and sales management functions of industrial equipment and consumer durable goods for multinational companies. He has also worked on control system design & development for military fighter jets and transport aircraft. Raj Veliyath's research and teaching interests lie in the areas of Strategic Management, International Business, Corporate Governance, Executive and Board Compensation, Planning and Control Systems, and Complexity Theory. Raj has presented and published over sixty articles and papers. His work has appeared in the *British Journal of Management*, the *Journal of Business Research*, the *Journal of Management Studies, Long Range Planning, Strategic Management Journal, Management International Review, International Business Review, Corporate Governance: An International Review* and other outlets. He is affiliated with the Academy of Management and the Academy of International Business. Raj can be reached at rveliyat@kennesaw.edu.

Andrew Wilson

Andrew Wilson is the founder of the management consulting business Futurestep Ltd., which specializes in change management implementation within organizations worldwide. Andrew has been helping organizations to change and improve for over ten years. Born in Scotland, but brought up in West and East Africa and continental Europe, Andrew learnt at an early age the interrelatedness of the planet he inhabited, and it is from this understanding and interest that his passion for complexity science developed. Andrew lectures for the Open University on its MBA program, and is currently developing with clients a number of design frameworks for use in organizational change, based on the principles of complexity. Andrew currently lives in North Devon with his wife Barbara and son Lucas.

Printed in the United States
47883LVS00001B/7